EDITOR
Lillian Herlands Hornstein
New York University

CO-EDITOR
G. D. Percy
University of Arizona

Sterling A. Brown
Howard University

Leon Edel
New York University

Horst Frenz
Indiana University

William L. Halstead
University of Miami

Robert B. Heilman
University of Washington

LITERATURE

GENERAL EDITOR
Calvin S. Brown
The University of Georgia

SIGNET CLASSICS

SIGNET CLASSICS
Published by New American Library, a division of
Penguin Group (USA) Inc., 375 Hudson Street,
New York, New York 10014, USA
Penguin Group (Canada), 90 Eglinton Avenue East, Suite 700, Toronto,
Ontario M4P 2Y3, Canada (a division of Pearson Penguin Canada Inc.)
Penguin Books Ltd., 80 Strand, London WC2R 0RL, England
Penguin Ireland, 25 St. Stephen's Green, Dublin 2,
Ireland (a division of Penguin Books Ltd.)
Penguin Group (Australia), 250 Camberwell Road, Camberwell, Victoria 3124,
Australia (a division of Pearson Australia Group Pty. Ltd.)
Penguin Books India Pvt. Ltd., 11 Community Centre, Panchsheel Park,
New Delhi - 110 017, India
Penguin Books (NZ), 67 Apollo Drive, Rosedale, North Shore 0632,
New Zealand (a division of Pearson New Zealand Ltd.)
Penguin Books (South Africa) (Pty.) Ltd., 24 Sturdee Avenue,
Rosebank, Johannesburg 2196, South Africa

Penguin Books Ltd., Registered Offices:
80 Strand, London WC2R 0RL, England

Published by Signet Classics, an imprint of New American Library, a division
of Penguin Group (USA) Inc. Published by arrangement with Henry Holt
Company, Inc. Previously published in Mentor and New American Library
editions.

First Signet Classics Printing (Second Edition), June 2002
10 9 8 7

Copyright The Dryden Press, Inc., 1956
Copyright © New American Library, a division of Penguin Group (USA)
Inc., 1973
Copyright © renewed Holt, Rinehart and Winston, 1984
All rights reserved.

 REGISTERED TRADEMARK—MARCA REGISTRADA

Printed in the United States of America

The Reader's Companion to

WORLD

Second Edition

Revised and updated by

Lillian Herlands Hornstein,
Leon Edel and Horst Frenz

An Essential
Literary Reference Book

One of the most useful and usable books ever offered to book readers, this is an alphabetically arranged encyclopedia of information about books and authors through the ages.

Edited and compiled by an editorial board of distinguished educators, this unusual volume will enhance the reading pleasure of everyone who wants to place writers in their proper historical setting, and relate them to their predecessors, contemporaries and successors. Its discussions of literary works include analysis of contents, importance, style, relationship to other writing. Subject entries cover periods, movements, and technical terms such as "comedy of humors" and "courtly love," such poetic forms as the elegy and sonnet, and many, many more.

Several years in preparation, this is an indispensable volume for all who want a reliable reference book providing the background and facts necessary for an intelligent understanding of literature, its history and dynamic development.

Preface to Second Edition

The gratifying welcome accorded the first edition of *The Reader's Companion* has prompted this new edition. Given the opportunity to reassess earlier judgments, we have incorporated some hundred revisions and new entries (e.g., *Dead Sea Scrolls,* Bertolt Brecht, Samuel Beckett, Yasunari Kawabata, Aleksander Solzhenitsyn). Readers who queried our exclusions have aided us in this re-evaluation, and we thank them for their interest and suggestions. Our hope is that this expanded revision of the book may prove even more useful to its readers.

Lillian Herlands Hornstein, Editor
Leon Edel

A Note to the Reader

When Chaucer wrote his *Troilus and Criseyde* he assumed that his readers would know the conventions of courtly love, and Shakespeare knew that the crowd who saw *As You Like It* would be familiar with the pastoral tragicomedy—just as a writer of Westerns or detective stories today counts on his audience to know the rules of the game. The work of art is always produced by a certain man in a certain time and place, and it is always related to its author's other works, his contemporaries, his sources and traditions, his intellectual, political, economic, and aesthetic climate. Background materials that can help the modern reader grasp the ideas or catch the flavor of a literary work of the past serve a valid and necessary purpose.

As teachers, we are strong in our view that a literary work can no more be read and studied in a vacuum than it can be written in one. This book is designed to fill in some measure that vacuum. Because we know that there is no substitute for the actual reading of a masterpiece, *The Companion* deliberately refrains from giving outlines of plots for major works. Rather, it gives material designed to orient and deepen that reading, and this material may include summaries of works which the nonspecialist is not likely to read. The general scheme called for the inclusion of those entries which would be most useful, and these naturally fell into several different categories. Some, such as the major authors and works in world literature, are obvious. There are also writers like Spenser and Alfieri who are centrally important in their own national literatures. Historical importance is considered as well as abstract "greatness," and this leads to the inclusion of some figures like Tasso and Howells (strange bedfellows) who are not currently popular, but whom we must at least know if we are to understand a literary tradition. To select the entries we examined the various "great books" lists, the syllabi of the courses in over fifty colleges, and the authors represented in the major anthologies. Then we added brief notes on a number of other writers—Hölderlin, Leopardi, Swinburne—whom the reader was likely to find mentioned and to want identified. Finally, though we were planning a reference book on literature rather than the history of ideas, we included a few men who are not literary figures, but whose ideas have profoundly influenced literature—men like St. Thomas Aquinas in the Middle Ages and Marx, Darwin, and Freud in our own era. It was natural to stress Occidental literature more than Oriental, but this is genuinely a handbook of world literature in that the greatest writers and works of the East are included.

To make *The Companion* as easy to use as possible, everything is arranged in a single alphabetical listing, which thus includes authors, works, literary types and terms, mythological figures, and literary periods and movements. (A brief history of Occidental literature can be obtained, however, by reading successively the articles on Classical Antiquity, Middle Ages, Renaissance, Neo-Classicism, Romantic Movement, and the various articles cited at the end of the one last named.) The listing under the name of a major author gives a brief biography and an account of his minor works, with cross references to separate articles on major works. (Cross references are indicated by an asterisk placed at the beginning of the word under which an entry is alphabetized: thus Thomas *De Quincey will be found under *D*, but Alfred de *Musset under *M*.) The length of the critical discussion is determined partly by the importance of a work and partly by the difficulty it presents to the average reader. No brief essay can tell anyone what he will get out of a book, but comment can clear away difficulties, set him on the right path, and show him where to look for greatness. In general the essays try to suggest why a work is both historically and intrinsically worthy of study.

Those of us listed on the title page (and Professors William M. Gibson of New York University, S. F. Johnson of Columbia University, and the late Napoleon J.

Tremblay of the University of Arizona) have all contributed materials for the entries. To Professors Hornstein, Percy, and Brown has fallen the task of making a unified whole of these contributions. But there has been no attempt to make all the entries conform to exactly the same pattern or point of view, and this is true not only because different works call for different treatment, but also because we feel that it is good for the reader to be made to realize that there is no single "right" technique, no set formula, for the study of a work of art.

We express our appreciation to the following for their suggestions and criticism: Professors Wallace K. Ferguson (The University of Western Ontario), George D. Hornstein (New York University), Walter MacKellar (New York University), Mary Gaither (Indiana University). To Mrs. Helen Beards we are indebted for expert secretarial assistance. The General Editor also wishes to express his thanks to his colleagues at The University of Georgia for reading and checking some of the more difficult entries and to Dimmes McDowell of The Dryden Press for the sound scholarship and critical judgment which she contributed to the final stages of the undertaking.

Abelard, Peter: theologian, poet, and teacher (1079–1142). Abelard has retained a twofold fame as a philosopher and as the lover of Heloise. As a philosopher he wished to shift theological argument from reliance on authority to analysis by logic. To challenge the theologians and make them seek logical reconciliations, he prepared a treatise, *Yes and No (Sic et non)*, which compared passages in the most authoritative writings of the Church and exposed their contradictions. He took a middle position in another controversy of scholastic philosophy, the relation of universals and abstract ideas to the world of individual things (Idealism versus Nominalism). In his writing and his teaching he gave a tremendous impetus to learning by his dedicated search for truth and by his exposition of a critical method. But, attacked as a heretic by St. Bernard and condemned by a Church council, Abelard was forced to withdraw from the schools, finally settling at the monastery of Cluny, where he died.

Abelard's remains were sent for burial to Heloise, a nun, and in this gesture we see symbolized the other aspect of his fame. At 37, he had become involved in a passionate love affair with Heloise, a beautiful and brilliant girl of 17 whom he was tutoring. After a child had been born to them and they had married, her uncle, a fellow canon of Abelard at the Cathedral School of Notre Dame of Paris, forced their separation and hired thugs to waylay Abelard and emasculate him. Abelard described the relationship in a brief autobiography, *History of My Calamity (Historia calamitatum)*. A group of remarkable love letters survive, tender and passionate, which Heloise wrote to Abelard after she had become a nun. Heloise and Abelard are a fascinating and tragic couple, inseparably linked in the galaxy of lovers such as *Romeo and Juliet, *Tristan and Isolt.

absurd: Such phrases as theater or novel of the "absurd" describe for modern literature a mood, a tone toward life where man's existence is an ironic dilemma of pointless activity (cf. *Sisyphus). The anti-hero of this literature is alienated to the extreme, even from any relation to the biosphere itself and not just (as are the *existentialists), from society and government. The notion of Providence (and anthropopathism) totally disappears; in a universe without purpose, intention, or interest in him, man exists in isolation. Rejecting the pathetic fallacy of a meaningful relation to nature, man breaks away from the Kantian notion of a designed universe. This sense of unrelatedness to the world and of the purposelessness of experience leaves man aimless and absurd. (see *Beckett, *Camus, *Pinter, *Pirandello, Alain Robbe-Grillet, *Sartre, *Ionesco).

Achilles: the son of Peleus and Thetis and the hero of the *Iliad*.

Adams, Henry Brooks: grandson of John Quincy Adams, sixth president of the U.S., and son of Charles Francis Adams, the American minister to England during the Civil War (1838–1918). He seemed destined for public life, like his distinguished ancestors, and served as his father's secretary abroad during the latter's ambassadorship. But scholarly and literary interests and an inward-turned, dilettantish mind kept him from self-assertion. He spent his life as a figure behind the political scenes in Washington, "a stable companion," as he ruefully put it, "to statesmen." His sense of family and his talent for imaginative organization made him a fine historian, so that his monumental history of America during the *Jefferson and Madison administrations, published in nine volumes (1889–91), remains a landmark in historical writing. Otherwise Adams's writings show a constant leaning toward the life of art and a certain amateurism.

He wrote two anonymous novels—a political novel, *Democracy* (1880), and *Esther* (1884), a study of New York society. He combined his sense of history and his aestheticism, in a remarkable study of the cult of the Virgin in the *Middle Ages, *Mont St. Michel and Chartres* (1904). After the suicide of his wife, he traveled in the South Seas with his friend John La Farge and wrote the memoirs of the last queen of Tahiti (1893). In addition he wrote lives of Albert Gallatin (1879), John Randolph (1882), and George Cabot Lodge (1911). His letters are fascinating in their pictures of people and places and in their cultivated pessimism. His best-known work was his autobiography, *The Education of Henry Adams* (1907), a brilliant and cynical self-portrait of himself as an anachronism in a world that had created the dynamo; yet the volume contains many shrewd prophecies, not the least his grasp of the future of Russia in the modern world.

Addison, Joseph: the leading British prose stylist of the early 18th century and one of the distinguished essayists in English (1672–1719). His life and art reflect good manners, a calm moderation after the excesses of Puritanism and the Restoration, a golden mean of moral refinement and witty morality, and a capacity to popularize culture. His ideals were those of the middle class whom he so well represented and for whom he wrote. Although he is now remembered chiefly for his prose, one of his poems and one drama caught the public at the right moment and greatly added to his contemporary fame. The mediocre poem, *The Campaign* (1704), is a eulogy in *heroic couplets of Marlborough's spectacular victory at Blenheim. And the stodgy tragedy, *Cato* (1713), written in strict conformance to the *unities, became an enormous success, again because of the political meanings read into its subject. It was to be extremely popular in America also with George Washington and other worthies of the American Revolution. His writings led to a career in government and brought him the high office of Secretary of State (1717).

Addison's real genius, however, lay in the essay. In

collaboration with his lifelong friend, Richard Steele (1672–1729), he tried his wings on mildly ironic and gossipy flights in *The Tatler* (1709–11), a triweekly periodical of news and essays. Then the two collaborated on a far more ambitious periodical, *The Spectator* (1711–12). Appearing every day but Sunday, *The Spectator* was a single sheet chiefly filled by the leading essay. These essays formed a sequence something like the modern serial, a running commentary on the customs and follies of the times, its morals, philosophy, and literature. The mythical Spectator, a mellow philosopher, and four other members of his club were types representative of various walks of life. One of them, "the first of our society," was the country squire, Sir Roger de Coverley. (The series which deals with this group is often called "Roger de Coverley papers.") The wit and literary art, the irony and satire which had often been licentiously used by the Restoration courtiers were, in the *Spectator*, enlisted on the side of morality and humanitarianism. This was in itself notable. The humanitarianism and urbanity were widely influential. Benjamin* Franklin, for example, learned from them matter and style.

Learned and genial Addison, under the influence of Steele's warmth and sentiment, found "the model of a middle style between pedantry and garrulity," "exact without apparent elaboration, always easy." Dr. Samuel Johnson advised: "Whoever wishes to attain an English style, familiar but not coarse, and elegant but not ostentatious, must give his days and nights to the volumes of Addison." Posterity has confirmed this judgment.

Adonis: a beautiful youth beloved by the Greek goddess *Aphrodite. His early death symbolized the decay of plant life and the harvesting of the crops.

Aeneid: the great Roman national epic. It was written by *Vergil in the last decade of his life and published two years after his death by his executors in accordance with the wishes of the Emperor Augustus. Vergil lived in that period of Roman history which witnessed the collapse of the Republic and the foundation of the Empire. It was a time of great violence. For half a century revolution and civil war harassed the people and ruined Italy and the provinces. And when peace came it brought with it a new form of government that concentrated all power in the hands of Augustus, although Augustus was careful to preserve the outward semblance of the old Republican institutions which his rule had in reality replaced.

Vergil began the poem in 29 B.C., two years after the battle of Actium brought this period of civil war to an end. He had long been preparing for the task. His purpose was national: he desired to glorify the Roman people by his theme and to exalt the Emperor in the person of his hero. But he did not wish to write a historical epic. For his material he went back to the heroic age, to the legend that the Roman nation was founded by Trojans who survived the war at Troy, and that the family of Augustus was established by their leader Aeneas.

Although the legend of Aeneas has no basis in history, it had been popularized by the Greeks of southern Italy and Sicily, and it was accepted at Rome as fact. In outline form it is as follows. Aeneas, the son of Anchises and Venus, was a prince of the royal house of Troy, destined by the divine will to rule over the people. He fought through the Trojan War; and, when the city was taken, though he lost his wife Creusa, he brought his father and his son Iulus to the safety of the nearby hills. Here other Trojans joined him. He built a fleet and the following summer set sail to establish a home for his people in Italy beyond the seas. The voyage was long and filled with peril; for seven years the Trojans wandered, driven by fate from land to land. After they reached Sicily, Anchises died. Saddened by his loss, but hopeful that their journey was almost over, they put to sea again. But a storm was sent against them by the malignity of Juno, and their fleet was wrecked on the coast of Africa. Here Dido, an exile from Tyre, was founding the city of Carthage, the great enemy of Rome in time to come. She welcomed the Trojans at a feast, promising to aid them to continue on their way if they desired. But Dido was consumed by an uncontrollable passion for Aeneas. She neglected her duty as queen and abandoned her reputation as a woman; and when Aeneas left Carthage by divine command, she was swept by a frenzy of emotion and died of a self-inflicted wound.

The Trojans sailed northward from Carthage and landed near Cumae on the west coast of Italy. Here Aeneas sought out the Sibyl, an ancient prophetess who lived in a cave nearby. With her to guide him, he descended to *Hades, where he found his father among the spirits of the blessed. Anchises taught Aeneas the glorious destiny of his people, showed him the souls of the great Romans yet to be, and, through the Stoic doctrine of the World Soul and the Pythagorean concept of reincarnation, introduced him to the meaning of life and death.

From Cumae the Trojans followed the coast of Italy to Latium and cast anchor at the Tiber's mouth. Latinus, the king of that country, had an only daughter, Lavinia, who, an oracle had predicted, would marry a foreign prince. Recognizing Aeneas as the fated stranger, Latinus prepared to give his daughter to him. But Juno aroused Turnus, king of the Rutulians and Lavinia's former suitor, to call the people to arms against Aeneas. Each side sought allies: Turnus in Mezentius, the Etruscan king, and Aeneas in a band of Greek colonists who were living under their leader Evander on the hills destined to be the site of Rome. The war was long and bitter. Only after Aeneas slew Turnus could he establish his people in Italy and build his city, named Lavinium in honor of his wife. Here he ruled three years and then was taken up into heaven. In the next generation Iulus or Ascanius, as he is also called, moved the people to Alba Longa where Romulus and Remus, the founders of Rome, were born. But these last events are only foreshadowed in the *Aeneid*; the poem itself ends with the death of Turnus, which removes the last barrier to the fulfillment of Rome's destiny.

The *Aeneid* does not proceed throughout in chronological order. It begins at the point of greatest interest in Aeneas' fortunes, with the storm that drives him to Carthage and the feast (Book I) at which he tells Dido the story of Troy's fall (II) and his own wanderings (III).

Vergil thus plunges at once into the midst of things and later gives the reader by retrospective exposition the details he needs to know of previous events. This technique (sometimes called *cutback* or *flashback*) Vergil borrowed from the *Odyssey* (see **Iliad*), in which Odysseus tells his adventures to King Alcinous in the tenth year after he set out from Troy (*Od.* IX–XII). Other Homeric techniques used in the *Aeneid* are the invocation to the Muse, the expanded simile, the conventional or repeated epithet, and the use of the supernatural to influence events. Vergil is much indebted to Homer for material also. Aeneas' wanderings are modeled on the *Odyssey* and his wars on the *Iliad*; and many specific episodes, such as the descent into the Underworld (based on *Odyssey XI*), go back to one or other of the two Greek epics. But Vergil borrowed creatively; and his poem is an integrated whole in which each incident, no matter what its source, has its bearing on the poet's theme, the destined establishment of Roman power in Italy.

In the *Aeneid* fate unfolds its master plan for a Roman Empire without limit either of time or of place. Individuals like Dido or Turnus who oppose the destiny of Rome are doomed. Hostile nations like the Greeks, triumphant over Troy, will pass beneath the yoke. Even the goddess Juno must learn to cherish "the Romans, the masters of the world, the race clad in the toga." Over this empire Augustus will rule by divine right as the direct descendant of Aeneas. Under him there will be peace. And when he has completed his life on earth, he will be received into heaven and worshiped as a god. The note of imperial destiny sounds like a trumpet call through the *Aeneid*. It is the central thought of the whole poem. And it indicates that Vergil was attempting a new type of epic, in which the most vital issue of his time, the substitution of the rule of Augustus for the old rule of the Republic, is presented in a heroic setting modeled on the *Iliad* and the *Odyssey*.

This new concept of epic places a heavy burden on the hero. Aeneas bears on his shoulders the weight of the future Roman Empire. He must fulfil his duty to his people, soon to be Romans; to his family, from which the Roman Emperor will come; and to the gods, who

7

minister to Roman fate. Hence he is never free to choose; his every action is foreordained or dictated by divine command. Vergil gives him the devotion, the submission and self-sacrifice, the courage needed for such a role, and, above all, the power of patient endurance. Aeneas is the type of leader Stoicism provided the Roman Empire. But despite his virtues, he fails to satisfy the reader: he lacks human warmth and charm. This fact is especially evident in his treatment of Dido. It can be said in his defense that he left her because of a repeated command from the gods—but he does so without a struggle. The gods sent him to her court, forced her to fall in love with him, and made him leave her, but his manner toward her was his own choice, and it offends the reader.

Moreover, Vergil lavishes all his art, understanding, and sympathy on Dido, going far beyond his model (Medea, in *Apollonius of Rhodes). She has in full measure—perhaps even to excess—the impulsiveness which Aeneas lacks. We must remember, of course, that the Roman reader would see her as the Queen of Carthage, the archenemy of Rome. He would be horrified when, in her agony, she prays for the Punic War and conjures up from her ashes the Carthaginian general Hannibal, who almost destroyed the Roman state forever. Nevertheless, Vergil makes of her a truly universal and tragic figure. She is a fine example of his ability both to glorify the Roman Empire and to sympathize with the victims of its destiny.

When Vergil died the *Aeneid* was not finished, and it is unequal in its parts. Excellent passages can be found in all the books; but the fame of the poem depends on II, the fall of Troy; IV, the tragedy of Dido; and VI, Aeneas' journey into the Underworld. These are the books Vergil chose to read to Augustus, and with them he was presumably most nearly satisfied. In each he deals with the pathetic, a mood in which he works with consummate skill.

It is in Book VI that Vergil sets forth what appears to be his own philosophy of life. While Aeneas stands spellbound watching the long line of Roman souls waiting to enter bodies here on earth, Anchises explains the meaning of life and death to him. There is a Spirit, he says, that pervades the universe and gives life to all things. Though divine, its tranquility is disturbed when it is united with the matter out of which the body is composed. Emotions and passions arise within it; it loses its original purity, and it must be cleansed by punishment after death. When its punishment is completed, it is sent to the Elysian Fields, the abode of the Blessed; but only a few souls remain permanently there. Almost all must undergo a second trial; and these drink the waters of forgetfulness that flow in the river Lethe before they return to the earth. In this doctrine the influence of Stoic pantheism, Platonic mysticism, and the Pythagorean concept of reincarnation can be seen.

The *Aeneid* does not possess either the freshness or the simplicity of the Homeric epics. It was written in an age of cultivation, and it is adorned with literary and historical allusion and pervaded by philosophic thought. Its pace is slower than that of the *Iliad* and the *Odyssey*. It is less successful as a representation of life, although it shows deep insight into human character and much concern for its perfection. It blends human and divine action, as Homer does; but the crushing power of Fate reduces the stature of the gods and turns the human actors into puppets. It is emotional. Vergil does not accept suffering and death without question; he inquires into their meaning, and his poem is filled with an intense pity for human sorrow. The *Aeneid* is national and patriotic, and it is greatest where it is most national. It shows dramatic skill of a high order and endless powers of description. It is most carefully organized, and its finished parts are polished with exquisite taste. It is the first of the great literary epics of Europe, the direct inspiration of *Dante, and possibly the most influential book ever composed in Latin.

Aeolus: the ruler of the winds in Greek and Roman mythology.

Aeschylus: Greek tragedian (525–456 B.C.). The life of the first important writer of Greek drama is largely hid-

9

den in obscurity or confused by legend, but his epitaph suggests at least one aspect of his career: "Beneath this stone lies Aeschylus, son of Euphorion, the Athenian, who perished in the wheat-bearing land of Gela; of his noble prowess the grave of Marathon can speak or the long-haired Persian who knows it well." Aeschylus took part in the history-making wars between Greece and Persia and saw Athens rise as the center of Hellenic civilization. His play *The Persians* (472 B.C.) reflects in particular what all his drama shows in general: experience in an epic period. If Aeschylus' characters are of heroic stature, it may well be because he himself was the product of a heroic age. The struggle and crisis of his own days are the raw material of drama; the stage is a fit medium for a man vitally concerned with the moral conflicts between men and between man and god in an evolving world.

The contemporary theater was, however, very limited, both physically and artistically. Greek drama had originated with choral celebrations in honor of the god Dionysus, and even by Aeschylus' time the program was still primarily a religious pageant, with one priest-actor and with dialogue merely an interlude in the choric dance. To Aeschylus justly belongs the title of father of Greek drama, since he introduced the second actor and thus extended greatly the possible scope of action and narration; he reduced the size of the chorus from 50 to 15 members and made it function actively in the dramatic episode; he developed costuming and staging, designing the high padded shoes and painted masks (also serving as megaphones) which the large Greek theaters made necessary; and, above all, he wrote the first memorable tragedies of Greek literature.

Greek drama was written to be produced in the annual spring festival and dramatic contest known as the City Dionysia, though some plays were presented in midwinter at the Lenaea festival. Playwrights submitted a series of three dramas—the characteristic trilogy—and a "satyr" play. From the competitions only a few works of Aeschylus,* Sophocles, and *Euripides have survived. Of the ninety-odd plays which Aeschylus is credited with writing, only seven are extant, but these include the sole remaining Greek historical drama, *The Persians*, and the only complete trilogy we have, the famous **Oresteia*. Moreover, these seven plays give scholars a good opportunity to study the development of his art. The earliest, *The Suppliants* (*c.* 490 B.C.), is a predominantly choral play (with the old chorus of 50) treating the question of the right of sanctuary. Dramatic characterization begins to take form in the Queen-Mother of *The Persians* (472 B.C.). In *Seven Against Thebes* (467 B.C.) the theme of the family curse appears for the first time, as does the "tragic hero," in the person of Eteocles. This type of hero is raised to superhuman stature and presented against a background of eternity in *Prometheus Bound* (465? B.C.). Finally, the family curse reappears as the driving force in Aeschylus' masterpiece and last prize-winner, the *Oresteia* (458 B.C.), a trilogy consisting of *Agamemnon*, *The Choephori*, and *The Eumenides*.

Aeschylus and Euripides, as characters in **Aristophanes'* **Frogs*, debate which is the greater tragedian. It is one of Euripides' arguments that he puts on the stage "things that come from daily life and business." The genius of Aeschylus lies in quite the opposite direction: his concern is with the affairs of gods and the godlike. Prometheus, Agamemnon, and Clytemnestra are magnificent creations, larger than human size. A **Titan* rebelling against tyrannic deity, an aristocratic house destroying itself under a hereditary curse, a blood feud giving way to divinely established justice, the capriciousness of a god evolving toward benevolent omnipotence—these are the subjects which occupied Aeschylus and which gave rise to a verse that was equally lofty.

Aesop: Greek writer of fables (6th century B.C.). So little is known of Aesop that some scholars deny his existence altogether. They consider him an invention of the later Greeks, intended to provide an author for the fables current among the people long after their origin as folk literature was forgotten. But, although this theory finds support in the mass of incredible anecdote which gathered around Aesop's name in antiquity and the Middle Ages, it disregards the evidence of **Herodotus*, the first

Greek historian. He states that Aesop was the slave of a certain Iadmon, who lived on the island of Samos in the 6th century B.C., and that he met a violent death at Delphi, where, according to tradition, he was sent on a mission by Croesus, king of Lydia, presumably after Iadmon set him free. Whatever the truth may be, the Greeks of the classical period attributed almost all the fables they knew to Aesop, believing that he initiated this literary type.

It would seem that Aesop's fables were cast originally as prose tales and that they were transmitted by word of mouth for many generations. *Plato represents *Socrates as turning them into verse, and *Aristophanes speaks of them as told at banquets. The oldest written collection of which we know was made in the 4th century B.C. by Demetrius of Phalerum. It was apparently in prose, but it has perished. The ancient versions now extant are those of poets, Phaedrus and Avianus in Latin, and Babrius in Greek. These were the bases for the editions of the Middle Ages (the most important is that of Maximus Planudes), which in turn inspired the work of *La Fontaine and others in the modern period.

A fable of Aesop, as we know it, is a brief anecdote in prose or verse describing a single incident and designed to teach some rule for the wise conduct of life. The characters are typically, though not necessarily, animals endowed with speech and clothed in the virtues and vices of human beings, although the particular qualities attributed to them are in each case those universally regarded as predominant in their own animal nature. The ass, for example, is stupid, the fox cunning, the lamb helpless and innocent of wrongdoing. As these characteristics remain constant in all the stories, the animals become easily recognized symbols of various types of individuals. The point of the fable is the moral, which is invariably drawn from the common experience of mankind and is therefore easy to understand. The language used in telling the tale is simple, direct, and free of rhetorical ornament. Although the fable is suited to the instruction of the young, it was not, in antiquity, considered children's literature, being composed from an adult point of view as a recognized type of satire, often turned to political use. Thus Aesop is said to have told the Athenians the story *The Frogs Who Chose a King* when they expressed dissatisfaction with their ruler Peisistratus.

Modern editions of Aesop often contain fables of oriental origin, such as are gathered together in the great Hindu storybook, the *Panchatantra*. Some of these, we know, entered Europe during the Middle Ages. But it is a vexed question whether oriental influence was present in Greek fable from the beginning, although foreign sources are mentioned by Greek writers from time to time in connection with individual tales.

Agnon, S. Y.: penname of Shmuel Yosef Czaczkes, Israeli poet and novelist, winner of the 1966 Nobel prize (1888–1970). His stories preserve the life style of the *shtetl*, the tiny East European village now extinct. Although the setting, the folklore, the characters, look back to Agnon's childhood, the mood (dislocation and otherworldly ambiguity) and the style (witty, allusive, symbolic) are in the modern temper. His major works are *Ha-Khnassat Kallah* (*The Bridal Canopy*, 1931), *Oreah Nata la-Lun* (*A Guest for the Night*, 1937), and a six-volume collection of short stories.

Aias: see *Ajax.

Ajax: the Roman name for Aias, the son of Telamon, one of the greatest of the Greek warriors at Troy, or for Aias, the son of Oileus, who also fought there. When spoken of together, these two are called the Aiantes.

À *la Recherche du temps Perdu:* see *Proust.

Albee, Edward: American dramatist (1928–). Abandoned in infancy by his parents, Edward Albee was adopted by a wealthy family whose name he took for his own. His early rejection, however, influenced his dramatic work. The abandoned or adopted infant and the solitary vagabond occupy a predominant place in many of his plays. After a brief attendance at Trinity College

13

in Hartford, Connecticut, he went to Greenwich Village where he wrote novels and poems which were never published. In 1953 Thornton *Wilder advised him to turn his talent to the writing of plays.

His two earliest plays, *The Zoo Story* (1958) and *The Death of Bessie Smith* (1959), were first presented in Germany. They, like his later plays, show the influence of *Ionesco, *Beckett, *Strindberg, Jean Genet, and possibly *Brecht. In addition to the themes of solitude and alienation, Albee is concerned with people living in a world of illusions. His characters, out of touch with reality, build a world of dreams making communication with others almost impossible. Albee's third major theme is that of sexual obsession. In the constant war between the sexes it is usually the woman who exerts the more destructive force.

In *The Sandbox* (1959) and *The American Dream* (1959–60) Albee satirizes American life: its emptiness, its conformity, its search for status, its pseudo-culture. *Who's Afraid of Virginia Woolf?* (1962), Albee's first play to be presented on Broadway, is also a play of denunciation—a criticism of the lie, the dreamworld, the life of illusions. *Tiny Alice* (1965) adds the problem of a man in search of God and illustrates the betrayal of purity on all levels of society.

Albee's purpose in his plays is not to teach but to point out, satirically or ironically, the sham and deceit of the contemporary world. He succeeds because of his imagination, his sensitivity for language and dialogue, and his sense of construction and dramatic progression.

Alcaeus: Greek lyric poet (*fl. c.* 600 B.C.). Alcaeus wrote hymns, political songs, and drinking songs in a large variety of meters, one of which is named for him (see *Alcaic). Much of his poetry is lost, including most of the love songs which *Horace says that he wrote. Alcaeus uses a spare style, with little in the way of adjectives or ornamentation of any kind.

Alcaic: a Greek lyrical meter written according to the pattern of some of the poems of *Alcaeus. An Alcaic is

14

a stanza containing four lines, each with four stresses in a fixed and complicated pattern. The form was adopted into Latin with great skill by *Horace and used in English in *Tennyson's *Milton*.

Alcestis: (438 B.C.). Although from an artistic point of view *Alcestis* is not one of *Euripides' finest dramas, its theme has been a popular one, both in literature and in opera. The play contains a mixture of tragic and comic elements not entirely fused. In ancient Greece *Alcestis* seems to have been regarded primarily as a comic play, for it concluded a tetralogy, taking the place of the customary satyr-farce which was intended to give to the three preceding tragedies a gay and happy ending. Indeed the tragic element—Alcestis' decision to die in place of her husband Admetus and her actual death—is counteracted by the happy outcome. Alcestis is brought back by the "jovial demi-god" *Heracles, who has snatched her out of the arms of Death.

Only one heroic figure —Alcestis—exists in this play, and her character creates the tragic and heroically uplifting element. The noblest member of the royal family, she has offered her life not only for the sake of her husband and her children but, most important of all, for the sake of the continuation of the royal line. The weight of this last factor must not be underestimated, for Admetus' father is too old to rule and his children are still too young; if Admetus were to die now, the throne would go to strangers. For this reason, a sacrifice is vital. Yet, although Alcestis is the initiator of the heroic-tragic element, Admetus, not she, is the central character of the drama. The knowledge that his wife has been pledged to the Fates by his own consent and that the decision, once made, can be revoked by no power on earth gives Admetus a tragic role to play, at least up to the moment when Alcestis is miraculously restored to him.

A strange encounter between *Apollo and Thanatos (Death) follows. Since neither is omnipotent, and since they belong to entirely different realms of the supernatural world, neither can influence the other, and there can be no real communication between them. Euripides now brings Heracles onto the scene, and in order to motivate the demigod's later rescue of Alcestis, Heracles is made to drop by on his way to another place and to be entirely unaware of the preceding events. Admetus invites him to stay without telling him about his wife's death. Once the truth is known, Heracles' gratitude to Admetus for having offered hospitality in face of his grief prompts him to bring Alcestis back to life.

At this point the tragic element tapers off. Alcestis is brought back veiled. Sensing the similarity to his deceased wife, Admetus is tempted to fall in love but manages to keep himself in check by recalling his last promise to Alcestis that he would never marry again. When she finally drops her veil and allows the audience to enjoy Admetus' astonishment, the initial tragic conflict has been forgotten; what prevails is only the magic accomplishment of Heracles and the happy ending which he has wrought.

Alexandrine: a line of verse consisting, in English and French prosody, of six iambs (iambic hexameter), totaling 12 syllables, with a caesura after the sixth; there is no enjambment (no run-over line in thought or sentence structure). The *Spenserian stanza ends with an Alexandrine: *e.g.*, "So dark are earthly things compared to things divine." A French Alexandrine frequently adds a thirteenth syllable and (in the absence of syllabic stress in French) is likely to be phrased with four main stresses. The name of the line is derived from a 12th-century romance about Alexander the Great (356–323 B.C.), written in this form. It became the standard line of French epic and dramatic poetry after being revived by *Ronsard and the *Pléiade, and it remains the preferred form of serious French poetry.

Alfieri, Vittorio: Italian dramatist and poet (1749–1803). After a period of schooling in Turin ("eight years of uneducation, an ass among asses under an ass"), extensive travel, and a number of love affairs, Alfieri found his proper form of expression in tragedy. His plays are clas-

16

sical in form, scrupulously observing the *unities, but their spirit is a romantic nationalism. The guiding principle of Alfieri's life was a hatred of tyranny—a concept which, not being much of a political thinker, he conceived in rather melodramatic terms. His plays are a vehicle for this sentiment, presented with considerable effectiveness and vigor. To this end, he deliberately used a rough, often harsh *blank verse strikingly different from the polished smoothness of his predecessors. *Saul* (1782) is usually considered his best tragedy. His last one, *Brutus the Second* (*Bruto secondo*, posthumously published), was dedicated in 1789 "to the future Italian people." In addition to his tragedies he wrote two political treatises (one of them *On Tyranny*, 1777), a series of verse satires (1793–97, including a devastating one on education), and an *Autobiography* (*Vita*, 1803). His works exerted a great influence on subsequent Italian writers and nationalists.

allegory (Greek: "to speak in other terms"): a form of art which sustains simultaneously both literal and abstract levels of meaning. Any object may be used as the metaphor or symbol of an idea or act (as an orchid given by Swann to Odette early in *Proust's Remembrance of Things Past* represents their sexual relationship); and a symbol can often stir the imagination more than the bare fact. Allegory is often thought of as expanded or integrated combinations of metaphors, symbols, personifications, in which two levels of meaning are sustained with characters, actions, or ideas functioning not only in a literal surface meaning but on another level of implied meanings (moral or abstract teaching) not expressly stated. It is an effective way of making a moral lesson palatable or of writing a satire. An obvious method of indicating the allegory is to give identifying tag names to concrete characters who personify abstract ideas. For example, in Bunyan's *Pilgrim's Progress*, Lord Hategood is the judge, and Envy is a witness, and the jurors' names are No-good, Live-loose, Lyar, Hate-light; in *Piers Plowman*, when Lady Meed personifies bribery, her companions are Liar, Wrong, Simony, and Guile, but

17

when she represents "honest reward," her companions are Theology and Conscience. Other conspicuous examples of sustained allegory occur in such literary types as parables, which are briefer, less systematic allegories (*Plato's parable of the cave in *The *Republic*); morality plays (*Everyman*); *beast epics (fables); and in such works as *Romance of the Rose*, *Dante's *Divine Comedy*, *Spenser's *Faerie Queene*, *Swift's *Tale of a Tub*.

Amazons: a race of warrior women famed in Greek mythology. They fought against the Greeks in the Trojan War.

Ambassadors, The: a novel by Henry *James written during 1900–1901 but not published until 1903. Certain critics regard it as the first "modern" novel in its use of scenic narrative and "montage" as in cinema, its adherence to "point of view," and its general formal inventions. Told in twelve sections, with the climax in the fifth and eleventh parts, it has a classical symmetry within its modernity. James considered it "quite the best, 'all round,' of my productions." Most critics have agreed. He went on to use similar devices in his two other major works which followed this one, *The Wings of the Dove* (1902) and *The Golden Bowl* (1904).

The Ambassadors is a "philosophical" novel, with a middle-aged hero. Lambert Strether goes to Paris to bring back to Woollet, Massachusetts, the wayward son of a rich lady, but finds himself converted to the idea that the young man should remain abroad because of the superior sensuous and intellectual experience available to provincials in Europe. The novel thus uses James's old "international" theme, but it contains also a philosophy of life, reflecting James's belief in determinism. Strether argues that man lives by his illusions—that is, by his imagination. In this novel James seems also to say to his fellow countrymen—or at least to New Englanders—that they take life too hard; that life is too complex to be enfolded in provincial rigidities. "Live all you can" is the cry at the center of this novel, and by "live" James means observe and feel.

Written in a vein of ironic comedy, the book presents a varied group of characters, largely expatriate Americans, and one of James's most successful—and pathetic—Frenchwomen, Marie de Vionnet. A portentous character is Mrs. Newsome of Woollet, Massachusetts, whose presence is felt throughout, although she remains in America and we see only her successive ambassadors carrying out her directives.

James's method is to allow information to be supplied to the reader piecemeal by the characters. Scenes, as in a play, are staged in regular alternation with long passages in which we are brought close to the consciousness of Lambert Strether. He is a rare character in fiction, one who at middle age shows himself capable of undergoing a considerable evolution in feeling and experience. But his Puritan roots hold. In the end he returns to Mrs. Newsome and to Massachusetts. The sense of duty, the New England conscience, prevails. He has had his "adventure," and morally he must get nothing out of it for himself, save his impressions and his nostalgia. Strether returns to America having "lived," therefore knowing now how to live.

ambrosia: the food of the Greek gods, usually mentioned with nectar, their drink.

Anacreon: Greek lyric poet (*c.* 572–*c.* 488 B.C.). Anacreon was born at Teos on the eastern coast of the Aegean Sea but migrated to Thrace about 545 B.C., when the Persians began to attack the Asiatic Greek cities. He spent much of his life as the guest, first of Polycrates, tyrant of Samos, then of Hipparchus, tyrant of Athens. Anacreon lived to an advanced age, but nothing certain is known about him after 514 B.C., the year of Hipparchus' death. The available evidence suggests, however, that he visited Thessaly and then returned to Teos, where apparently he died. The Athenians erected a statue in his honor, and the Teans put his portrait on their coins.

Anacreon's poems are *monodies*, that is, songs for a single voice, and for the most part they celebrate love and wine. In form and matter, therefore, they resemble the work of the great poets of Lesbos, *Sappho and *Alcaeus. But their spirit is different. They were written to please the gay society of the courts Anacreon frequented; and although characterized by wit and fancy and flawless in construction, they show little emotional depth.

Anacreon's poems are extant only in fragments, but they inspired a host of imitative love and drinking songs, some of which have survived under the name *Anacreontics*. The *Anacreontics* are short and easy pieces varying greatly in merit; but the best—*Love's Night Walk*, *Love and the Bee*, *The Grasshopper*, and others—are marked by lightness, grace, and charm. The *Anacreontics* were very popular in Europe and widely imitated during the 17th and 18th centuries, and they have been well translated into English.

Andersen, Hans Christian: Danish poet, novelist, and dramatist (1805–75). Andersen's *Fairy Tales* appeared intermittently from 1835 to 1872, making him a worldwide reputation and an international household name. Some of his stories were translated into English as early as 1846. In his artistic retellings of folk tales and in the original details that he added, Andersen emphasized moral, symbolic, and often tragic meanings. His best-known stories are *The Ugly Duckling* and *The Emperor's New Clothes*.

Andromache: a tragedy by *Racine (*Andromaque*, 1667). Although *Andromache* appeared only three years after the production of Racine's first extant play, it contains all that is characteristic of his mature genius: brilliant feminine characterizations, carefully achieved dramatic tension, and a powerful exposition of *amour-passion*, all framed in lines that are at the same time polished and emotionally charged.

In *Andromache* there is a climactic maelstrom of love and hate in the interlinked relationships of the four leading characters—Orestes, who loves Hermione, who loves Pyrrhus, who loves Andromache, who is loyal to the memory of her slaughtered husband. Upon this complex board, Racine plays his pawns, the action pivoting on Andromache, who alone is not driven by irrational passion and who alone survives, serene and steadfast.

Hers is an excellent characterization, but a greater favorite among tragic actresses has been the role of Hermione. Adoring Pyrrhus, the proud princess is forced to taste repeated humiliation as the king's attitude toward her fluctuates in accordance with his success or failure in winning Andromache. Finally, when Andromache agrees to marry Pyrrhus in order to save her son (whom the Greeks wish destroyed because he is the child of the great Trojan hero Hector), the forsaken Hermione orders devoted Orestes to kill the man who has insulted her. On Orestes' return to announce that the Greeks have already anticipated him in the deed, there occurs one of the most powerful scenes in the theater. Hermione, half insane with love and jealousy, turns on her hapless lover and denounces him. And the final touch of irony is her frenzied demand, "Who bade you do it?" She rushes off to kill herself over the corpse of Pyrrhus, and Orestes is left to go mad.

Andromache is more than just an important achievement in Racine's career; it is also an influential work in the history of tragedy. The playwright has turned from a Corneillian (see *Corneille) concept of the supremacy of will and reason to what is in many respects the modern world of emotion, with all its weaknesses and their tragic consequences. "I blindly yield myself to Passion's sway," cries Orestes, pointing up the psychological mood of the play and heralding its inevitable, tragic conclusion.

Anna Karenina: a novel by *Tolstoi (1877). This work, written after *War and Peace*, invites comparison with it. *Anna* does not approach *War and Peace* in scope, development of secondary characters, or climactic progression. Whereas *War and Peace* was an integrated work ending with domestic peace, *Anna Karenina* reflects a conflict in purpose and explores the destructive power of love.

The main plot deals with Anna and Vronsky, who first

covertly and then openly defy the established code of marriage. Tragedy follows because neither of the lovers is strong enough to withstand the steady retaliation of society. In our time of relatively easy divorce, Anna's marital and extramarital situation has intensity only in so far as the reader is able emotionally to accept the mores of the society depicted. The personalities of the main figures come from social convention; and, when they are overwhelmed by love, they have no principles to guide them. In the beginning, Anna is magnificent, capable of heroic tragedy, but under pressure of social disapproval she disintegrates and finally commits suicide. Vronsky is more solidly built; but he too makes a melo-dramatic departure.

Tolstoi's favorite character was Levin, whose spiritual gropings reflect Tolstoi's own dilemmas when writing the novel. Levin's efforts to find himself through useful work parallel Tolstoi's life on his own estate, and Levin's spiritual regeneration is akin to Tolstoi's.

The multitude of secondary figures who weave in and out of the story lend verisimilitude to the pattern. This ability to create a whole living society is perhaps the special mark of Tolstoi's genius. He did it in *War and Peace* and again in *Anna Karenina*.

The world of Anna Karenina, as Tolstoi creates it, is a slice of 19th-century Russia. Her tragedy is never quite raised from the limited social plane to a more symbolic or universal one. *War and Peace*, avowedly a historical novel, is still modern. *Anna Karenina*, at one time a "modern" novel, has become historical.

Annunzio, Gabriele d': see *d'Annunzio.

Anouilh, Jean: French dramatist (1910–87). Anouilh was born in Bordeaux but grew up in Paris, where his family had settled. He planned to be a lawyer and attended the Sorbonne for a while, but lack of money forced him to give up his studies.

Anouilh has divided his plays into two main groups: "rose plays" and "black plays." This distinction merely attempts to describe the dominant mood of each play, for the contrast between comedy and tragedy is not always clearly marked. The "rose plays" include *Thieves' Carnival* (*Le Bal des voleurs*, 1938), a *comédie-ballet* which explores the interaction of truth and deception, reality and play-acting, and *Ring Around the Moon* (*L'Invitation au château*, 1947), the story of a poor girl introduced into a world of luxury. Among the "black plays," *Traveller Without Luggage* (*Le Voyageur sans bagage*, 1936), Anouilh's first success, based on the theme of the amnesic soldier, shows the greed and hypocrisy of bourgeois society, while *Antigone* (1942) contrasts the heroine's intransigent attitude with the political expediency of her uncle Creon.

In the following plays, which deal with similar themes, Anouilh tends to repeat himself. One of his most cynical plays, *The Waltz of the Toreadors* (*La Valse des toréadors*, 1952), is a biting satire of marriage. Only in his historical plays, *The Lark* (*L'Alouette*, 1953), the story of Joan of Arc, and *Becket ou l'honneur de Dieu* (1959), does Anouilh find a new source for his inspiration.

Anouilh, the most prolific among contemporary French playwrights, is also the most brilliant craftsman. In spite of his comic verve he is deeply pessimistic. His work appears as the embodiment of revolt against whatever may sully the purity of human beings, more particularly the revolt of youth against the power of money, the rules imposed by families, and empty social conventions. His young people yearn for an unattainable purity and an ideal love, rebel against the vulgarity of life and the selfishness of their elders, and refuse all compromise. Anouilh's tone is a mixture of fantasy and harsh satire.

Antigone: a tragedy by *Sophocles (*c.* 441 B.C.). The story of Antigone is part of the Oedipus legend. The curse on the house of Labdacus not only brought about the double fratricide of Eteocles and Polynices but also involved their two sisters Ismene and Antigone. Antigone, the heroic daughter of King Oedipus, insisted upon giving her brother Polynices (who had been named a traitor to the city of Thebes) the last human right, the rite of burial. By this deed Antigone knowingly risked her life, for she was violating the ancient custom of denying burial to enemies and traitors, as well as the decree of Creon, her uncle, who had just succeeded to the throne.

Sophocles was, apparently, the first to create a drama out of this legendary material, which he used to express his belief in the spiritual capacity of man. The poet endowed his heroine, Antigone, with the highest qualities of character, setting her up as a kind of ideal for all mankind. Possessing a strong sense of the duty based on close family ties, Antigone remains firm to the end and permits no doubts or hesitations to undermine her decision. Conflict springs from contact with outside forces rather than from doubts within herself. It reveals her idealized strength of character and steadfastness of purpose, as, for example, in her discussion with Ismene of their brother's burial. Her sister, representing the typical, average young girl with a conventional point of view, may realize in her heart that Antigone's cause is right, but her primary concern is that of any ordinary young person: to live. Because of her desire for life and her reluctance to disobey the law, she lacks the courage to support her sister's cause. Antigone's strength of character, however, is able to resist not only these calls of youth but also the call of love (love for Haemon, Creon's son) and the fulfillment of her womanhood.

The climax of the tragedy (and the scene of greatest contrast) is the encounter between Creon and Antigone. Here the incompatibility between the world of physical power and the world of spiritual, idealistic strength comes to a breaking point. Antigone remains firm, and the rage of Creon's hurt vanity aroused by the stubborn disobedience of a mere madwoman (as he sees it) cannot bend or break her. Creon, made to recognize his error, must yield; he decides to reverse his earlier stand because he will not "fight with destiny." But this decision comes too late.

Finally, the feeling of contrast is heightened by the chorus. Representing the loyal people of Thebes, it expresses the logic of the plebeian everyday world. Again and again these people challenge Antigone by their reproaches: "In the battle with might which you have taken upon yourself you have had to lose. . . . It was your own self-determining will which has brought on your ruin." The chorus thus represents the opinion of the external world of average life and civil law, as interpreted by "the man in the street." It can have a human sympathy for Antigone until she offends its prejudices, but it is afraid of its rulers. It also tends to be on the side of whoever has spoken most recently. Little do these simple people know that Antigone has long since reconciled herself to her death, that she has consciously let her own free will direct her actions, and that she is, in spite of her great loneliness in which even the gods seem to have deserted her, ready to die, without regret, for her conviction and ideals.

The denouement of the tragedy shows which side Sophocles himself favors: that the gods have taken Antigone's side is symbolic of the victory of the individual whose cause is idealistic, just, and humane and supported by a strong will. The power of the spirit conquers the power of physical might: even Creon must succumb to the decision of the gods and receive his punishment, which is the result of a stubborn action, rectified too late. The *Nemesis descends upon him, taking his whole family from him and leaving the once so mighty ruler a broken man. Haemon, his son, the beloved of Antigone, threatens his own father's life before he is found—dead by his own hand—clasping Antigone, who has killed herself. Crushed by her son's death Haemon's mother commits suicide and dies cursing her husband.

Sophocles added this powerful ending to the old legend, for, according to his philosophy, the gods cannot watch quietly while the violation of the integrity and human dignity of man remains unpunished. The spiritual weight of the tragedy lies in this conclusion, which is more uplifting than hopelessly tragic. Sophocles has given this message to his own people as well as to those of succeeding ages: it is a hundred times better to die as Antigone than to go on living as Creon.

Yet Antigone is not to be understood as a perfect character. Her tragic flaw lies in an uncalled-for insolence toward civil authority, her determination not merely to do her duty by her brother, but also to be unjustly put to

25

death for it. Her manner toward Creon when he questions her clearly shows this "martyr complex," but her insolence in the right cause is, of course, preferred to Creon's equally opinionated defense of the wrong; and the revolt of the individual conscience against the edicts of an evil civil authority is fully justified.

It is because of its respect for the freedom and individuality of man that the ancient tragedy of *Antigone* has meaning and significance in the modern age. Only rarely has this magnificent portrayal of man's potentiality as a free spiritual being been equaled in the literature of the western world.

Aphrodite: the love goddess of the Greeks, identified by the Romans with Venus. The meaning of her name is uncertain, though the Greeks derived it from *aphros*, "foam," and said she was born of the sea.

Apollinaire, Guillaume: French poet, short-story writer, and art critic of Italian-Polish origin (pseudonym of William Apollinaris de Kostrowitsky; 1880–1918). Apollinaire opened many new paths of modernism—cubism, dadaism, and *surrealism. A friend of Picasso and Braque, Apollinaire wrote *The Cubist Painters* (1913) to explain cubism and its aims: to portray the "ubiquitous and simultaneous" and thus avoid the conventional techniques of perspective. Although he is the author of novels and a drama, most important are his two volumes of poems, often written without punctuation. By original versification and imagery, in which are juxtaposed new and traditional images with puns and plays on words, Apollinaire tried to show how modern life fuses the classical and contemporary (*Alcoöls*) or imposes order on the haphazard (*À Nîmes in Calligrammes*). He has been a potent literary influence on the modern generation of French poets. His *L'Esprit Nouveau et les poètes* is considered the manifesto of modernism; he is also credited with inventing the word *surrealism*.

Apollo: one of the most complex divinities of the Greek pantheon, the son of Leto and *Zeus. He is often called Phoebus and in some myths is identified with the sun. His chief provinces were archery, medicine, music, poetry, and prophecy, his shrine at Delphi in central Greece being famous for its oracles. The Greeks attributed pestilence and sudden death to him and to his sister *Artemis.

Apollonius of Rhodes: Greek epic poet, born in Egypt near the beginning of the 3rd century B.C. He was the pupil and friend of Callimachus, one of the most influential poets and scholars of the Hellenistic Age and an official in the library maintained by the Ptolemies at Alexandria. About 260 B.C., Apollonius became librarian, thus outranking Callimachus, who was making the first catalogue. A dispute arose between the two men, traced by modern scholars to difficulties they presume existed in the library, but attributed by tradition to a difference of opinion concerning the possibility of writing epic poetry with success in that age. Whatever the controversy, Apollonius was defeated, resigned his librarianship, and retired to the island of Rhodes. The circumstances under which he composed his own epic, the *Argonautica* or *Story of the Argonauts*, and its relation to his dispute with Callimachus are, however, subjects of disagreement among scholars.

The *Argonautica* is based on one of the most romantic of the Greek legends. It tells how Pelias, the king of Iolcos, induced his nephew Jason to sail to the Black Sea in quest of the Golden Fleece, which hung on a sacred oak in the barbarous land of Colchis. Jason gathered some fifty of the bravest heroes of Greece and set out with them in the *Argo*, the ship that gave them their name, Argonauts or *Argosailors*. They passed through the Clashing Rocks into the Black Sea, skirted its southern shore, and arrived safely in Colchis, where they sought out Aeëtes, the king. Aeëtes promised to give Jason the fleece if he would plough the field of the war-god Ares with the king's fire-breathing bulls, sow dragons' teeth in the furrows, and slay the giants who would spring up from the seed. Jason could never have accomplished the task had not Aeëtes' daughter Medea, a sorceress, fallen in love with him. She used her magic power to enable him to complete the labor; and, when her father plotted to kill him, she helped him steal the fleece and set out with him for Greece. The return was long and difficult. Pursued by the Colchians, the Argonauts fled from the Black Sea up the Danube River and, crossing by its headwaters to the Adriatic Sea, endured many perils in the west before they reached their homes again.

The legend of the Argonauts is rich in character and incident and worthy of heroic verse, but Apollonius failed to turn it into a great epic. He could compose short sections, sometimes very skillfully, but he could not weld them into a long poem; and his *Argonautica*, lacking all structural unity, remains a series of disjointed passages. The work is, moreover, very unequal in its parts; much of it is tedious and dry and burdened with learning, and its permanent value rests on a few strikingly effective scenes.

Among these the passage in Book III describing Medea's love for Jason is famous. Few writers have portrayed the first awakening of love and the emotional upheaval that follows with the psychological insight and literary charm Apollonius reveals in this episode. His Medea is not the cruel and wicked sorceress whose middle age *Euripides describes in his play *Medea*. Though endowed with magic power—for the myth requires it—she is a young and innocent girl, overwhelmed by a passion she does not understand. And she yields to the hero who has fascinated her only when the conflict between her desire and her ideals of modesty and filial devotion has driven her to the verge of suicide.

But, although Apollonius is without an equal among the epic poets of antiquity in the portrayal of romantic love, he is less successful when he presents the traditional material of heroic verse. Unlike *Homer and *Vergil, he has no way of life to lay before his reader. His gods, depicted as middle-class Greeks in domestic surroundings, have lost their essential majesty. His heroes are not of epic proportions; Jason is weak and colorless, and lacking both in energy and resource.

In composing his epic Apollonius imitated the verse form and vocabulary of Homer, though he avoided the repetitious expressions characteristic of the *Iliad* and the *Odyssey*. His *Argonautica* was not without admirers among the Greeks of the Hellenistic Age, and at Rome it influenced Vergil, who based the story of Dido in Book IV of the *Aeneid* on Apollonius' description of Medea's love.

Apology: *Plato's version of the speech which *Socrates delivered in his own defense when he was tried for his life on the charge of corrupting the youth of Athens and believing, not in the gods of the city, but in gods of his own (4th century B.C.). There is no way of determining how far the *Apology* preserves the actual words spoken by Socrates at his trial. It seems to idealize him, but it was published not long after his execution, when many who had heard him were still living, and its tone is exactly that which *Xenophon tells us characterized his address.

The *Apology* is divided into three parts. In the first, Socrates tries to refute the charges leveled against him by describing the origin and conduct of his mission and the nature and operation of the divine sign which guided his actions. Because he knew that, if the jury found him guilty, they would do so largely because they resented his whole way of life, Socrates attempted to explain why he did not participate in civic activities, why he was surrounded by young oligarchs, why those who heard him thought he was wise, and other matters of this nature. And he struggled to convince the jury that he was neither a physicist nor a sophist, though often confused with both. But he refused to seek an acquittal by promising to end his mission, or by bringing his wife and children to wail for him in court.

When Socrates concluded, the jury found him guilty and the prosecution demanded that he be put to death. Socrates now spoke a second time, to suggest an alternative punishment, in accordance with the law. At the urging of his friends, but with great reluctance, he proposed a fine of 30 *minae*, which they agreed to pay. He himself had no money, and, in any case, he felt he should not be punished as a criminal but rewarded as a benefactor to the state. The jury, choosing between the two penalties, voted to condemn Socrates to death; and, in the third part of his speech, he bade his supporters farewell.

The *Apology* is one of the great masterpieces of European literature, and its high moral tone and rich biographical detail give it universal appeal. The cross-examination of Meletus illustrates Socrates' method of question and answer, his remarks on Evenus contain something of his accustomed irony, and his famous comparison of himself to a gadfly makes use of the homely type of expression so characteristic of him.

Apuleius, Lucius: Roman rhetorician, Platonic philosopher, and novelist, born in northern Africa *c.* A.D. 125, and educated at Carthage and Athens. After traveling widely in Greece and Asia Minor and practicing for some years as an advocate at Rome, he returned to his native land, where he made an extraordinary reputation as a writer and lecturer. There survives a collection of purple passages, known as the *Florida*, or *Garland*, gathered from his speeches, as well as three or four philosophical treatises, of which *On the God of Socrates* is perhaps the best.

Apuleius married a wealthy widow some years older than himself, and her relatives brought him into court on the charge of using magic to win her. He was, of course, found not guilty, but it was true he was interested in magic, a fact his prosecutors may have hoped would lend some color of truth to their case. Apuleius published his *Apology*, or *Defense*, in an expanded form after the trial.

Apuleius' rhetorical and philosophical writings are all but forgotten now, and his reputation depends on his novel, *The Metamorphoses*, or *The Golden Ass*. In it, he tells the story of Lucius, a young man who sets out on a journey to Thessaly, a district of northern Greece traditionally associated with witches. Here he plunges into a career of licentious conduct with a servant girl named Fotis, from whom he obtains a magic ointment that, she informs him, will change him at will into a bird. When he applies it, however, he becomes an ass instead, and, in this form and speechless, but possessing human understanding, he is stolen by a band of robbers. With them he begins the series of adventures that form the main theme of the novel. At the same time he overhears a number of stories—for people speak freely before him, thinking him but an ass—and these are woven into the narrative, which they serve to adorn and diversify. The most famous among them, and the best-known part of the whole book, is the story of the love of Cupid and Psyche, an ancient folktale found nowhere else in Greek or Latin literature. Apuleius tells it with extraordinary charm and touches it with *allegory, suggesting that Psyche is really the human soul.

Through all his adventures, Lucius seeks in vain for roses, the one food that can restore his human form. As the book ends, he finds them with the help of the goddess Isis, who appears to him in a vision of great beauty and power. She directs him to attend her festival and there to approach her priest, who will expect him, and to eat the rose wreath from his head. As he does so in trembling obedience, the miracle occurs. His bestial form falls away, and, restored to human shape, he adores the goddess and in due time is initiated into her rites and those of her brother, the god Osiris. The book thus ends on a strong autobiographical note, for Apuleius was a devotee of the Eastern mystery cults and seems to have spent much of his life in their service. The symbolism is clear also: man serving his lusts is little better than the brute.

Although indecent in some of its details, *The Golden Ass* quickly became one of the favorite works in Latin and a model for later storytellers. *Boccaccio borrowed freely from it, and *Cervantes attributed at least one of Lucius' exploits to Don Quixote. William Adlington's English version (1566) is a classic in its own right, and there is a new translation by Robert Graves. The story exists in brief form in Greek under the title *Lucius, or the Ass*.

Aquinas, Thomas: see Saint *Thomas Aquinas.

Arabian Nights, The (also called *The Thousand and One Nights*): a collection of tales in Arabic, built up during the *Middle Ages. As early as the 10th century some of its 264 tales were transmitted orally by story-tellers among the Mohammedan peoples of the Near East (some of them even reached Europe during the Middle Ages). As time went on, the Arabs increased the collection by the addition of tales from other sources and cycles and organized it, in the Oriental manner, within a framework supplied by a *frame-tale of Persian origin. By about 1450 the work had assumed its present form.

The frame-tale recounts how the jealous Sultan Shahriar, persuaded of the faithlessness of women, married a new wife each evening and put her to death the following morning, until his bride Shaharazad won a reprieve by commencing a story on her wedding night and artfully sustaining Shahriar's curiosity about the outcome of her tales within tales. For a thousand and one nights, he kept reprieving her (during which time she produced three male heirs): then he abandoned his original plan.

The first European translation was a French one by Antoine Galland, 1704–17. Since then Ali Baba, Open Sesame, Aladdin and his Magic Lamp, Sinbad the Sailor, the Magic Horse have become familiar references. The stories inspired the Russian Rimsky-Korsakoff to compose a symphonic suite entitled *Scheherazade.*

Even in the expurgated version of most English translations, the tales convey the spirit of the Eastern and Mohammedan life, its exotic setting and customs and its sensuality. Although there is no specific moral purpose, there is a moral core beneath the fantasy. The astounding narratives cover an amazingly wide range of fact and fiction. Camel trains, desert riders, the insistent calls to prayers—the solid ground of reality—form the tissue of the scenes. The adventures are fabulous and supernatural, or aristocratic and romantic, bawdy and satiric. As it figures in these tales, the fabulous, mysterious East with its spirit of adventure, its black magic, its seductive scents, its ecstatic lovers, its enchanting blossoms and enchanted princes, produces an effect unique and unforgettable.

32

Arcadian: applied to art, an adjective which exhibits idealized rustic beauty, simplicity, and innocent pastoral bliss. The term derives from Arcadia, a district in ancient Greece celebrated as the home of musical and pious shepherds (and of their God, *Pan). Though they were in fact also poor and primitive, *Vergil imagined them enjoying a harmonious, idyllic, pastoral life, uncontaminated by the miseries and constraints of civilization, saddened only by frustrated love and death. Thence the co-mixture of idealized rural happiness and melancholy—an Arcadian myth of a nonhistorical Golden Age—entered the West, to develop into a major tradition in literature (delightfully satirized in Gilbert and Sullivan's *Iolanthe*) and representational art. Giovanni Guercino's painting (c. 1623) shows two shepherds come upon a decayed human skull as it lies atop a slab of masonry on which is incised the now-familiar phrase *Et in Arcadia ego,* "Even in Arcadia [there am] I" (i.e., Death). This first use, a *memento mori* "reminder of death," was transformed in meaning and tone by Nicholas Poussin (1594–1665) in his famous painting *Shepherds in Arcadia*; the tombstone epigraph now appears to be spoken by the dead shepherd and to mean "I too [have dwelt] in Arcadia."

Areopagitica: see *Milton.

Ares: the Greek god of war, identified with Mars by the Romans.

Argonautica: see *Apollonius of Rhodes.

Argonauts: see *Apollonius of Rhodes.

Argus: a creature covered with eyes, which *Hera set to watch Io, one of the illicit loves of her husband *Zeus. *Hermes killed him, thereby earning the title *Slayer of Argus.*

Ariosto, Ludovico: Italian poet and dramatist (1474–1533). After spending his youth at the elegant court of Ferrara, Ariosto, at his father's insistence, studied law for five years, and, like *Boccaccio, considered the time wasted. Only when he was past twenty was he allowed to follow his own interests, studying classical literature and writing Latin elegies, epigrams, and odes in imitation of *Catullus and *Horace. But his father died in 1500, and Ariosto was forced to give up "Homer for records of household expenses." As confidential secretary to Cardinal d'Este, he traveled throughout Italy on delicate political missions. In 1518 he entered the service of the Cardinal's brother, the Duke of Ferrara, and eventually became his director of entertainment. Under Ariosto's supervision, the court enjoyed an endless series of pageants and dramatic productions. He himself designed the theater and scenery and wrote a number of the plays. Most important were his comedies, the first in Italian modeled on *Plautus and *Terence. One, translated by George Gascoigne as *The Supposes* (the Italian title means "the dissemblers"), was popular on the 16th-century English stage.

As early as 1505, Ariosto had begun his masterpiece, *Orlando Furioso*, one of the most influential poems of the *Renaissance. He continued to revise it for nearly thirty years, bringing out the first edition in 1516 and the last in 1532, only a year before his death.

Orlando Furioso ("Roland in a Mad Fury") is a "romantic epic" of "Loves and Ladies, Knights and Arms. . . . Of Curtesies, and many a Daring Feat." The romantic element is supplied by the subject matter—medieval chivalric war, knightly adventures and loves. The epic elements are many: Ariosto depended heavily on the Graeco-Roman tradition of *Homer, *Vergil, and *Statius, borrowing incidents, character types, and such rhetorical devices as the catalogue of troops and the extended simile. And the *Orlando Furioso* is a poem of epic proportions—46 cantos, totaling over 1,200 pages in a standard modern edition. Its style is polished and graceful, its stanza a melodious and adroit *ottava rima. Like the *Aeneid*, the poem was designed for a sophisticated and urbane audience, and, to suit their taste, Ariosto added the new sensuousness of the Italian Renaissance. The work is thus a synthesis of the classical, the medieval, and the Renaissance.

The plot continues the narrative of an earlier Italian poem, *Orlando Innamorato* ("Roland in Love," 1495), by Matteo Boiardo (1434–94). The background of both poems is a pseudohistorical war, the invading pagans attacking the Christian Charlemagne and besieging Paris. Boiardo had added to the traditional Charlemagne material the chivalric love and magical adventures characteristic of the Arthurian romances. Orlando falls a victim to Angelica, a heathen princess, whose purpose it is to disrupt and divide the Christian army by inducing its leading knights to fall in love with her. The dilemmas of war and love in this half-conscious parody of chivalric romance were never resolved, for Boiardo did not complete his poem.

To this narrative Ariosto added the new theme of his title—Orlando gone mad, fittingly punished for falling in love with a pagan. Passion, rage, and jealousy overcome him, and his wits are taken away and deposited on the moon. For three months he rages. Then a sorcerer brings them back—in a bottle; Orlando inhales them and is restored to sanity; and the Christians are able to defeat the pagans and drive them into Africa.

A second plot (which Ariosto took over from Boiardo) concerns the knight Ruggiero, a descendant of King Priam of Troy, and his beloved, the lady warrior Bradimante. Their story is quite as important as Orlando's, for, after many misadventures, they marry and become the ancestors of Ariosto's patrons, the House of Este.

Orlando Furioso is a medley of supernatural, allegorical, and romantic adventure, magic rings and wells and swords, sudden disappearances, a trip to the moon, allegorical incidents that preach modesty and chastity—the kind of potpourri that fascinated the 16th century and disconcerts the 21st. The characters are static and shallow. Ariosto makes no attempt to delve deeply into human emotions or important issues. Except for an indulgent, gentle irony, his attitude is objective and implies no serious values or goals.

35

Ariosto's claim to fame (apart from his profound influence on such English and French Renaissance poets as *Spenser, *Milton, and the *Pléiade) rests on a combination of qualities. His poem is vigorous and brilliant, with ironic and humorous contrasts. The dream-world of escape contrasts with the ironic humor of real life. References to contemporary persons and events shift the mood from fantasy to realism, adding meaning to both. The juxtaposition of scenes and phrases from the romances with others from the classics demands the active participation of the reader. Individual incidents and scenes are worked out with meticulous care; each plot is carried to a climax, then dropped while another is developed, until finally all the loose threads are tied and all the stories completed. *Orlando Furioso* served the Renaissance as a model of the large-scale narrative poem written with the technical facility, smooth versification, and gracefulness of the classics.

Aristophanes: Greek comic poet (*c.* 450–*c.* 385 B.C.). Aristophanes was born during the great era of Athenian history that followed the defeat of the Persians at Marathon and Salamis, wrote most of his plays during the Peloponnesian War (431–404 B.C.) that brought this period to an end, and lived on into the postwar years when Athens was stripped of power and freedom by the victorious Spartans. Aristophanes was opposed to the Peloponnesian War and the decadent Athenian democracy whose policies he considered largely responsible for it. He was also opposed to the new ideas current at Athens in the fields of religion, education, and literature, and to those who taught them.

In his comedies, therefore, Aristophanes attacks the democratic institutions of the Athenian people, ridicules their political and intellectual leaders, and advocates peace, aristocratic government, and traditional morality. His earliest extant play, *The Acharnians*, produced in 425 B.C., is a direct attack on the war party at Athens. So also are *The Peace* (421 B.C.), in which the hero, a farmer named Trygaeus, fattens an enormous beetle on which he flies to heaven to seek an end to hostilities, and the *Lysistrata* (411 B.C.), in which the women of Greece unite in the determination to abstain from sexual relations with their husbands until they bring the war to an end. *The Knights* (424 B.C.) is a bitter personal assault on the demagogue Cleon, who succeeded Pericles as the leader of the Athenian democracy. *The *Clouds* (423 B.C.) lampoons Socrates and, through him, the new movement in education led by the sophists. *The *Frogs* (405 B.C.) abuses *Euripides for lowering the moral tone of tragedy, a charge made earlier in the *Thesmophoria-zusae* (*Women at the Festival of Demeter,* 411 B.C.), in which the women of Athens try the tragic poet for slandering their sex in his plays. *The Wasps* (422 B.C.) makes fun of the Athenian passion for hearing lawsuits, and its best scene is that in which the dog Labes, on trial for his life, brings his pups into the courtroom to whine for him. The *Ecclesiazusae* (*Women in the Assembly,* 392 B.C.) mocks such utopian schemes for human betterment as the community of wives later advocated by *Plato in *The *Republic. The *Birds* (414 B.C.), sometimes considered an allusion to contemporary events, is more probably pure fantasy. In the last extant play, the *Plutus* (388 B.C.), the blind god of Wealth is healed of his blindness with the amazing result of enriching the good and condemning the bad to poverty.

Except for the *Ecclesiazusae* and the *Plutus,* Aristophanes' dramas are classified as Old Comedy. There is much variation in the pattern of events from play to play; but all are constructed of the same elements, the most important of which is a fantastic idea conceived by the leading character to solve a difficulty or further some amazing enterprise. The idea and the background of trouble that gave rise to it are presented by the actors in the *prologue* or first scene of the play. Then the chorus appears singing the *parode* or entrance song. After this is finished, an *agon* or debate is held between those who favor and those who oppose the idea. When all opposition has been crushed, the actors retire and the chorus comes forward for the *parabasis,* a song in which the playwright addresses the audience directly on a topic of interest, not necessarily connected with the subject of the play. After the *parabasis* is over, the actors return

37

to show the audience in a number of brief *episodes* how the idea works in actual practice. When the episodes are completed, the chorus sings the *exode*, or final song, and retires with the actors, sometimes in a scene of wild revelry.

Though the origin of Old Comedy is obscure, the part played by the chorus is thought to have come from the performance of the Athenian *comus*, a band of revelers who danced and sang and amused the crowd with obscene buffoonery and personal satire at what seems to have been a fertility rite, connected probably from the beginning with the worship of *Dionysus. One type of *comus* wore animal disguises, the apparent inspiration of such choruses as those of *The Birds*, *The Frogs*, and *The Wasps*. The actors' share in Old Comedy is believed to have originated in the Doric farce. The farce, unlike the performance of the revelers (which was extemporized), had a prepared plot. It presented amusing situations in short scenes with stock characters of a generalized type. The performances were indecent, for the farce was connected with phallic rites; but personal satire seems to have been avoided. There was no chorus. It is not known under what circumstances the farce was combined with the revel to form the basis of Old Comedy, or what elements may have been added from other sources or invented by the early poets. As *Aristotle explains, we cannot trace the history of comedy because it was not taken seriously in its early stages.

When Aristophanes wrote, six comedies were presented annually in the theater of Dionysus at Athens, one being given each afternoon during the two great festivals, the Lenaea in January and the City Dionysia in March. The comedies were written by poets competing for a prize and each was presented by three actors and a chorus of twenty-four provided by the state. The actors wore masks imitating the features of those they were lampooning and were dressed in grotesquely and obscenely padded clothes. The chorus was divided into two semi-choruses, each under a leader. Sometimes there was a second subordinate chorus, as in *The Frogs*. All the parts in a comedy were played by men or boys, and few women attended the performances.

No type of modern play is closely equivalent to Greek Old Comedy. It is frequently compared to light opera, and it does resemble this form in its songs, its elaborate costumes, and its fondness for the fantastic. But unlike such opera it was not intended merely to entertain. Aristophanes was a teacher as well as a comic poet. His merciless satire of political and intellectual movements and their leaders was clearly designed to persuade the Athenian people to modify their public policies and correct certain tendencies in their cultural life. Almost all the plays are, therefore, built around local problems and persons. There is, moreover, much indecency, although in some comedies it is less obtrusive than in others, and in all except the *Lysistrata* it is incidental. There is evidence tending to show that Aristophanes attempted to minimize it.

Aristophanes is the greatest of the comic poets of antiquity. Imagination runs riot in his plays. The ideas on which he bases them are so ridiculous, fantastic, and contrary to experience, that the whole comedy becomes one great joke. In *The Birds* the hero Peisthetaerus founds an empire in the air, intercepts the sacrifices as the smoke ascends, and starves the gods into submission. In *The Frogs* the cowardly divinity Dionysus faces the terrors of the Underworld to bring—of all people—Euripides back to the earth. In the *Acharnians* an honest Athenian farmer abandons Athens to its folly and makes a private peace of his own with the Spartans; then he goes back to the farm to stuff and swill and revel while the Athenians and their enemies alike sink deeper into the miseries of war.

In transforming his basic ideas into plays Aristophanes makes use of every device known for moving men to laughter. He excels in parody, burlesque, and farce; he is a master of word play; he knows the comic value of the apt quotation and the unexpected turn. A great many of his jokes are not told at all, but acted. In *The Peace*, war appears as a character who throws the cities of Greece (represented by garlic, leeks, cheese, etc.) into a huge mortar and grinds them up. In *The Frogs*, huge scales are brought in, and Euripides' plays are weighed and found wanting. In *The Clouds* Socrates' influence on

the young becomes all too clear when his pupil Pheidippides not only thrashes his father but proves by sophistic
argument that the old man deserved the beating. And
embedded in all this nonsense the choral songs are
found, so spontaneous and beautiful and clever that they
put Aristophanes in the front rank of Greek lyric poets.

In Aristophanic comedy, scene is added to scene with
a minimum of plot. Invented characters are not fully
developed, and those taken from life, like Socrates, are
wildly burlesqued. No attempt is made to be fair. Aristophanes knew as well as we do that Socrates did not
pretend to be a meteorologist. But he was lampooning
the whole sophistic movement in the person of one man,
he was taking advantage of the license granted the comic
poet, and he was trying to win the first prize. Moreover,
Aristophanes was prejudiced. He came of a landowning
family, and his point of view was consistently conservative. But he was right in his estimate of the Peloponnesian War.

The last two comedies, the *Ecclesiazusae* and the *Plutus*,
written after the fall of Athens in 404 B.C., are somewhat
different from the others and may be taken as marking
the transition from Old to Middle Comedy. In this form
the part of the chorus was reduced to a series of musical
interludes, while the episodes increased in importance.
Political satire disappeared, the obscene element was discarded, and personal abuse gave way to the milder satire
of domestic types. Middle Comedy continued to be written
until about 320 B.C., when it was supplanted by the New
Comedy of Diphilus and *Menander.

Some 40 plays were attributed by the ancients to Aristophanes. Of the eleven that have survived, the three
most commonly read are *The Birds*, the poet's acknowledged masterpiece, and *The Frogs* and *The Clouds*,
which take on added interest because of their leading
characters.

Aristotle: Greek philosopher (384–322 B.C.). Aristotle
was born at Stagira in Chalcidice but perhaps spent part
of his childhood at Pella, the Macedonian capital, where
his father was court physician. When he was about sev-

40

enteen years of age Aristotle came to Athens to study philosophy with *Plato, and he remained a member of the Academy until Plato died in 347 B.C. Aristotle then went to the Troad, where a group of philosophers had gathered at the invitation of a local tyrant, and three years later to the island of Lesbos, where he did considerable scientific work, particularly in zoology. In 342 B.C. he was invited to Pella by Philip of Macedon, who wished him to act as tutor to his son Alexander the Great, then a boy of thirteen. Shortly after Alexander became king in 336 B.C., Aristotle settled at Athens, where he established a school called the *Lyceum*, his disciples being known as *Peripatetics*, from the covered walk, or *peripatos*, which was a feature of the place. Here Aristotle continued teaching, writing, and conducting research until the death of Alexander in 323 B.C. led to outbreaks of hostility against the Macedonians and their friends at Athens. A charge of impiety was leveled at him, as it had been leveled at *Socrates earlier, and, believing that his life was in danger, he retired to Chalcis on the island of Euboea, where he died the following year.

During the early part of his life, Aristotle wrote many popular works in dialogue form, but they have perished, and what we now have from his pen are his lecture notes, or perhaps in a few cases the lecture notes of his students, pieced together to form treatises. These writings are dry, abrupt, and elliptical in style; often muddled in arrangement, and characteristically uneven in their presentation of subject matter. And yet, in spite of their lack of finish, they are far more valuable than the works which we have lost, for they represent Aristotle's mature views and they are sufficiently complete to permit the recovery of his basic doctrines and the general direction of his thought.

Aristotle's treatises may be divided into four large groups. The first, called the *Organon* or *Instrument*, consists of studies in logic, a science which he invented and which remained much as he left it until recent times. Aristotle codified the rules of valid thinking, analyzing the deductive syllogism in particular so effectively that he left little scope for later scholars. In this field he made what is probably on the whole his greatest contribution to knowledge. The second group of Aristotle's works is composed of essays on *biology*, in which close observation and acute reasoning easily place him first among the ancients, and on *physics*, in which he did not succeed as well. He was not equally master of all the sciences he investigated, and his failure to realize the importance of mathematics sometimes led him to assumptions which, in the absence of exact measurement, seemed probable but were actually untrue. The third group of Aristotle's writing contains his studies in *metaphysics*, in which he inquires into the true nature of reality. For the time came when he could no longer assert with Plato the separate existence of Forms or Ideas, holding instead that they are present, not in another world apart from material things, but in this world inside material things, a view which makes the universe *a universe of form and matter in whose union reality is found*. Things about which we learn through the senses are not, therefore, mere Imitations of Ideas hidden in the heavens, as Plato said, but rather the beginning of truth and part of the structure of reality. The fourth group of Aristotle's treatises deals with *practical philosophy* and *literature* and is best represented by the **Nicomachean Ethics*, perhaps the finest introduction to the study of conduct ever written; the **Politics*, one of the most widely read books on government in modern as in ancient times; and the **Poetics*, now a fragment, but still the greatest piece of literary criticism in existence.

Throughout his writings Aristotle is more scientific than Plato and drawn less to the ideal. His temperament was different, he saw the world through different eyes, and, although there is no evidence to support the ancient belief in a break between him and Plato, his writings show him gradually modifying Plato's position until he evolved a new system of his own. This development is apparent in the *Metaphysics*, where, instead of seeking refuge from this changing and imperfect world, he accepts and tries to explain it. He pictures it as arranged in a hierarchy of existence, a Ladder of Nature, proceeding from all but formless matter at the bottom to pure form, which is the Unmoved Mover, at the top. And he describes the Unmoved Mover as energizing the massive Whole, so that, as each thing strives to attain its complete or perfect form, the universe is constantly moving and changing. Change is therefore merely our name for this struggle and can best be understood through the doctrine of the four causes, the material cause, the formal cause, the efficient cause, and the final cause, which operate throughout nature and in man's handiwork as well. Thus, for example, in making a statue, the material cause is the wood or whatever from which it is fashioned; the formal cause, the shape that it assumes; the efficient cause, the sculptor or workman who carves it; and the final cause, the purpose to which it will be put.

Not long after Aristotle died, the manuscripts of those of his works that we possess were lost; and, although they were recovered and published in the first century B.C., they seem to have been little read until the time of *Neo-Platonism. They were preserved through the *Dark Ages by the Byzantines and from Byzantium were passed on to the Moslem peoples of the East, who gave them in turn to the nations of Western Europe, where in the 13th century they were accepted by the Church. It was then that Aristotle became for the *Middle Ages what *Dante calls him, "the Master of those who know."

Arnold, Matthew: English poet and critic (1822–88). After an excellent education at Rugby (where his father was headmaster) and Oxford, Arnold taught classics for two years, served for a while as private secretary to a liberal statesman, and then was appointed inspector of schools—a position that he held for 35 years. Though this job entailed a great amount of drudgery, he managed to publish five volumes of poetry between 1849 and 1858. In 1857 he was made the Oxford Professor of Poetry, and he held this appointment for two five-year terms, declining a third. During this period he began to write literary, theological, and educational criticism, and his poetic writing almost ceased. The new direction is shown by two books published in 1861: a series of lectures delivered at Oxford, *On Translating Homer*, and a report of his Educational Commission, *The Popular*

Education of France. A record of Arnold's principal publications tells much of the interests of his remaining years: his first *Essays in Criticism* (1865), *New Poems* (1867) and the first collected edition of his poems (1869); two books on Celtic literature (1867–68); *Culture and Anarchy* (1869) and *Friendship's Garland* (1871) on social criticism; *Literature and Dogma* (1873) and *God and the Bible* (1875) on theology; *Mixed Essays* (1879); *Irish Essays and Others* (1882); *Essays in Criticism, Second Series* (1888); and two records of an American lecture tour, *Discourses in America* (1885) and *Civilisation in the United States* (1889).

Arnold's first two volumes of poetry, *The Strayed Reveller and Other Poems* (1849) and *Empedocles on Etna and Other Poems* (1852), were signed only by "A." Their questioning and melancholy surprised friends who knew Arnold as a debonair lover of hoaxes at Oxford. In spite of their felicities, Arnold himself withdrew these books from circulation, and in the preface to his *Poems* (1853), he gave his reasons for omitting several works, especially *Empedocles on Etna,* from the first volume of poetry bearing his name. He condemns the inevitable morbidity of writing about situations "in which there is everything to be endured, nothing to be done." The eternal objects of poetry, he states, are human actions that most powerfully appeal to the primary affections. Expression should be subordinated to what it is designed to express; the power of execution which creates and forms is more important than single thoughts, rich imagery, or abundant illustration. "Clearness of arrangement, rigour of development, simplicity of style"—these virtues, found pre-eminently in the ancients, he cherishes. He favors the objective—the dramatic and the epic—over the subjective.

This preface is significant in Arnold's critical thought, and much of it was needed to prune the romantic excesses of his age. Yet Arnold's poetics and his poetry did not mesh together well. His ambitious imitations of the ancients were comparative failures; his epic episode, *Sohrab and Rustum,* succeeds better in passages than in totality, as does *Tristram and Iseult.* Arnold was not a skillful portrayer of character in action. His best poetry is self-analytic, and the self is divided. A real love for laughter and friendship he restrained or renounced. Admiring *Byron for his force, he nevertheless rejected Byron's type of emotionalism and continued instead *Wordsworth's tradition of meditative lyricism. The "Marguerite Poems," dealing with a real or imaginary romance of the poet in Switzerland, probably express most directly an actual experience.

More and more Arnold came to a position of ethical earnestness without certainty; many of his memorable poems are a search for serenity. But no easy solutions are acceptable; we are "Wandering between two worlds, one dead,/ The other powerless to be born." In *Dover Beach* Arnold speaks of faith as a sea which was once at high tide, but now he can hear only its "melancholy, long, withdrawing roar." The poet sees only the solace of lovers' being true to one another. Elsewhere he urges uncomplaining endurance, "to think clear, feel deep, bear fruit well." In *Rugby Chapel* he praises his father, who would not be saved alone but beckoned to the trembling and gave the weary his hand. Here and elsewhere, Arnold seeks whatever hope can be found. Nevertheless, in spite of the unconquerable hope, Arnold's philosophic poetry, with its religious doubt, regret for the loss of man's earlier harmony, disdain of the "comfortable moles" blinded by materialism, and insecurity about the future, is a poetry of austere melancholy.

Arnold's poetry is seen at its best in his elegies, especially *The Scholar Gypsy* and *Thyrsis*. The former is a pastoral with echoes of *Theocritus, beautifully portraying the countryside around Oxford, which Arnold had always loved. *Thyrsis*, written to commemorate Arnold's friend, the poet Arthur Hugh Clough, is a companionpiece using the same stanzaic form, the same pastoral conventions, and the same scenery, but closing on a note of hope.

These two poems contain Arnold's most musical verse. He disliked *Tennyson's overelaborated music and sometimes in his willful roughness moves close to *Browning. But poems like *The Forsaken Merman* and *Dover Beach* have distinctive melody. He experimented with many stanzaic forms and meters, often rhyming irregularly, often not at all, and sometimes doing without both rhyme and meter in a kind of *free verse. But if his form is various, the manner—verbal style, cadence, tone, and structure—and the content of his poetry are individually his own. Recognizing that Tennyson had more sentiment and Browning more intellectual vigor, he was nevertheless correct in believing that his poetry represents "the main movement of mind of the last quarter of a century."

Arnold's important poetry was written before he was 45 years old. But what his age considered his best poetry did not meet his own critical ideals, and he abandoned the self-analytic verse of his early manhood for the vigorous prose of social criticism. His inspectorship had sharpened his awareness of flaws in England's educational, political, and social structure. The aristocracy (or Barbarians, to Arnold), though possessing lands, revenue, and leisure, is impervious to ideas; the middle class (or Philistines) is marked by vulgarity and unintelligence; and the lower class (the populace) cares for little save "beer, gin, and fun." Arnold had some hope for the middle class and set about reforming its Philistinism, not with the Jeremiads and solemn preachments of *Carlyle and *Ruskin, but with a bantering persuasiveness. Respecting its energy and moral fiber (its Hebraism), Arnold deplored its provincialism and urged it to develop openness and flexibility of mind (or Hellenism), and to pursue Culture—"the knowledge of the best that has been thought and said in the world." He also urged "disinterestedness," "the effort to see the object as in itself it really is," and "sweetness and light," by which words, taken from *Swift, he meant "reason and the will of God." Though in education he favored the classics over the natural sciences, he respected the achievements of modern science and he believed that religion must abandon the supernatural; but the Hebrew and the Christian mythology, though repudiated as fact, are to be retained as poetry.

In his social and theological writings, Arnold was pre-eminently a literary critic; conversely his literary criticism is seriously concerned with life. To him the health of a society was indicated by the quality of its literature.

As a humanist, Arnold stood for restraint, lucidity, and balance, and he praised the ancients most highly for their "intense significance, noble simplicity, calm pathos and profoundness of moral impression." Poetry was paramount in literature, with its "power of forming, sustaining, and delighting us, as nothing else can." In judging poetry he warned against the personal fallacy, by which our affinities lead us to overrate, and the historical, by which the groundwork is laid so elaborately that the real quality is ignored. From the best poetry Arnold demanded the "grand style," "high seriousness," "criticism of life," "the application of ideas to life." In his search for these qualities he used as "touchstones" lines from the greatest poets. Most poets he finds wanting, or only fitfully successful. His criticism has endured more because of its general principles than its estimates of individual authors.

He remains, however, a critic of the first order. Though he perhaps overused catch-phrases for purposes of compression and propaganda, many of his terms are of critical service today. He is the master of a clear, precise prose, without purple passages, but with its own warmth, insinuating grace, and effective irony. Its seeming ease is the fruit of study as scholar and craftsman. In a grasping, acquisitive age Arnold persuasively set forth anew the great claims of literature. He wrote of Marcus *Aurelius and *Emerson that they were "friends and aiders of those who would live in the spirit," and in that fine company Matthew Arnold himself belongs.

Artemis: a virgin goddess of the Greeks, called Diana by the Romans, the daughter of Leto and *Zeus and the twin sister of *Apollo. She was often identified with Selene, the goddess of the moon, and with Hecate, the goddess of witches.

Arthur: a legendary king of Britain. The story of King Arthur, which developed early in the *Middle Ages and became one of the chief subjects of *medieval romance, tells of a pseudohistorical 6th-century Welsh chieftain whose parents were brought together at Tintagel Castle in Cornwall by the magic of Merlin. Arthur grew up to become the defender of the Celts against the Saxon invaders of Britain and something of a world conqueror, and, in later literary works, develops into the noble and generous king of the Knights of the Round Table, almost all of whom are supreme examples of medieval courtesy and chivalry. Gradually, however, the moral tone was lowered, and either the treachery of Arthur's nephew Mordred or the illicit love affair of his wife Guinevere with his knight Lancelot spelled the ruin of king and court. Arthur was mortally wounded at the battle of Camlam and carried away by fairy queens to be healed at Avalon, whence, the story goes, he will return when his country needs him.

Fragmentary and shadowy allusions to a great fighter first appeared in the Latin chronicles of Gildas (6th century) and Nennius (9th century). Geoffrey of Monmouth's Latin *History of the Kings of Britain* (1136) treats Arthur as a historical personage and adds details of his parentage and career. During the 12th century, the romantic element was heightened—in a French version (by Wace) of Geoffrey's history, in the French poetic romances of *Chrétien de Troyes, and later in the English *Brut* of Layamon and the German romances of Hartmann von Aue. Thus around a supposedly British king there grew up a vast literature reflecting Celtic folklore and mythological tradition, with the settings and language of French courtly romance. Arthurian literature (and films) continue to be produced with considerable success, both artistically and commercially. (See *Malory.)

assonance (sometimes called "slant rime" or "oblique rime"): the identity of accented vowel sounds in syllables without the identity of the following consonant sounds. *Take—fate* and *wise—high* are examples of assonance. In Old French (*e.g.*, in the *Song of Roland*) and in Old Spanish, assonance was used in line endings as later poetry used rime. It has also been employed within the line to enrich its music. In modern poetry like that of *Whitman or *Hopkins it becomes a major pattern of sound. A similar technique, notable in the poetry of Wilfred Owen (1893–1918), is "dissonance" (off-rime or para-rime, close but not exact rime), where the riming words have the same consonants but dissimilar vowels: *mystery—mastery*; *spoiled—spilled*. *Auden has made considerable use of para-rime.

Athene (or Athena): a virgin goddess of the Greeks, called *Minerva by the Romans. She was the daughter of *Zeus, from whose forehead she sprang fully grown and fully armed. At first a goddess of war, she later became a goddess of wisdom and women's handiwork. The Parthenon was built in her honor.

Atlas: the *Titan who carried the weight of the sky on his shoulder.

Atreus: the father of Agamemnon, who fed his brother Thyestes the flesh of his own children at a banquet.

Attic: an adjective derived from Attica, whose capital city was Athens, describes both the dialect (which became standard Greek) and the qualities that characterized Athenian art: simplicity, polish, delicacy of suggestion, grace, intelligence, and wit. The term has broadened to describe any literature, particularly prose, which displays these qualities. The essays of Joseph *Addison, for example, exhibit the qualities of "Attic" prose.

Aucassin and Nicolete: a 13th-century French tale in alternating prose and verse. This charming and delicate story is the "polished jewel" of medieval French narrative art. It tells of the love of the French Aucassin for the captive Nicolete (bought from Saracen pirates, but in fact daughter of the King of Carthage); their difficulties with Aucassin's ambitious father who wished a loftier match for his son; the flight of the couple and their separation by pirates; and their final reunion, achieved by Nicolete disguised as a **jongleur*.

The episodes of the plot appear in dozens of medieval romances; the author's originality and appeal lie in his style and treatment, his concentration on the characters, his realism and humor, and his faith in the power of love and the beauty of life. This story is the only one extant from medieval France in the form of alternating prose and verse (7-syllable, assonant lines), a style called *chantefable*, which the unknown author might have found in Old Irish or in Arabian romances. He uses the lyric interludes purposefully, to heighten the romantic tone of the tale and then to bring about the denouement. He is, moreover, an understanding observer of people and passions, and realistic details of the labors and sufferings of the lower classes contrast with the romantic adventures of the young lovers. The real world of poverty and illness and such details as Nicolete's picking up her skirts to protect them from the damp night grass heighten the otherwise naive and idyllic nature of the love story. The author smiles wryly at his own exaggerations as he burlesques chivalric battles and other stereotyped incidents from the chivalric romances. But Aucassin and Nicolete themselves are an irresistible pair, full of beauty and charm, "gracious and well-bred and compact of all good qualities."

Auden, Wystan Hugh: English poet (1907–73). Auden was educated at Oxford, where he acquired or deepened a wide range of literary interests. Chief among these were Greek literature, Old English poetry, and the Icelandic *sagas, all of which influenced his own writing. In 1936 he went to Spain in support of the Loyalist (left-wing) cause; and in 1939 he left England to become a resident and then a citizen of the United States, where he taught in several universities. He returned to Oxford as professor of poetry, 1956–61, then, ten years later, left the U.S. to return to Oxford. His early poetry was marked by a considerable emphasis on social and personal problems, but he seems to have become disillusioned about *Marx and *Freud, his earlier guides, and his later work was essentially skeptical, satiric, and ironic, though occasionally taking on a semireligious tone.

Auden is one of the most versatile and witty of modern writers. In addition to such hack work as anthologies and the text of a documentary film, he wrote plays, social criticism, travel books, war reports, and both satirical and lyric poetry. His real importance lies in his poetry, which is of the school of T. S. *Eliot, though it has its own individual note. Here, too, he is remarkably versatile. His forms range from free verse through strict stanzas of *rime royal to a free adaptation of the alliterative verse of Old English poetry. His tone can be sober, bitter, ecstatic, or flippant, and one of his most effective devices is a sudden, shocking shift of tone. Technically, he is an astonishing virtuoso—and both the praise and the reservations implied by this description are appropriate.

Among Auden's more important works are his *Poems* (1930), *The Orators* (1932), *For the Time Being* (1945), *The Age of Anxiety* (1947), and *A Baroque Eclogue* (1948), an ironic idyll on man's isolated condition when without tradition or belief, which won the Pulitzer Prize. In *Epistle to a Godson and Other Poems* (1972), the fiery innovation has been supplanted by a gentle, mannered civility. He also published a collection of his criticism, *The Dyer's Hand* (1963), and *A Certain World: A Commonplace Book* (1970), an "annotated personal anthology," with commentary, a "map of his mindscape."

Augustan: an adjective derived from Augustus, emperor of Rome from 27 B.C. to A.D. 14. The term connotes literature or a literary period notable for its learning and consciously polished style. The Roman Augustan Age was the most fruitful era of Latin literature, when *Vergil, *Horace, and *Ovid flourished. The Augustan Age of English literature is the early 18th century, when *Addison, Steele, *Swift, and *Pope were writing. The Augustan Age of France refers to the Age of Louis XIV, or sometimes to the entire period of *Neo-Classicism (1610–1740). The term is applied to early 19th-century German literature and to the 15th and 16th centuries in Portugal, which produced the famous writers Montemayor (1520–61, who influenced *Shakespeare) and *Camoëns.

Augustine, Saint: Christian theologian and philosopher (A.D. 354–430). Aurelius Augustinus, the greatest of the Fathers of the Western Church, was born at Tagaste, a small town in northern Africa. His mother Monica was a devout Catholic, whose chief concern in life was the spiritual welfare of her son, but his father Patricius was a pagan. Though indifferent to religion, Patricius was interested in education, and in spite of his poverty he contrived to send Augustine to a neighboring city for more advanced training than his own town could provide. How long Augustine attended school there is not known, but he was forced by lack of funds to remain at home during his 16th year, at the end of which time a wealthy friend named Romanianus undertook to support him while he finished his education at Carthage. Here his attention was centered on *Cicero and *Vergil, studies which confirmed his natural bent for literature, and when he was 20 years of age he returned home as a teacher of rhetoric. While in Carthage, however, he had taken a mistress who bore him a son Adeodatus, and he had espoused the cause of the Manichees, a sect professing a dualistic concept of the universe, which views life as a conflict between the independent powers of light and darkness. This period in Augustine's development was, therefore, a source of great distress to his mother, who longed to see him a Christian. It was at this time also that his father died, a Christian on his deathbed.

Augustine taught for some years at Tagaste and Carthage, but he was troubled by the lack of discipline in the African schools, and in A.D. 383 he set out for Italy. He went first to Rome, then to Milan, where his mother Monica joined him, and where he came strongly under the influence of St. Ambrose, the city's learned and eloquent bishop. He was converted in July, A.D. 386, and baptized Easter week of the following year. Augustine was now a Christian, his mother's fondest hopes were realized, and together they prepared to set out for Tagaste. But St. Monica (as she now is called) fell ill at Ostia, the port of Rome, where she died while waiting to embark, and Augustine was left to complete the journey alone later. He spent some time at Tagaste, immersed in theological studies, then moved to Hippo, a city on the coast about 40 miles to the north, where he was ordained a priest, A.D. 391. He was consecrated bishop A.D. 395, and he remained at Hippo until his death, which occurred while the city was undergoing siege by the Vandals.

St. Augustine is a voluminous writer, and, besides sermons and Biblical exegeses, his works contain letters, philosophical and rhetorical essays, polemical treatises directed against various types of heresy, and doctrinal compositions connected with Church teaching and administration. Some of these writings are, of course, highly technical, but others contain much of interest to the general reader. Among them all, however, two stand out as supremely great: the *Confessions*, Augustine's spiritual autobiography, and the *City of God*, his long and incredibly learned philosophy of history. Augustine wrote the *City of God* as a direct result of the sack of Rome by the Goths, A.D. 410, a disaster which spread consternation throughout the world and revived the age-old pagan lamentation that nothing had gone well since the Christians came. In the first 10 of its 22 books he upholds the thesis that the gods are of no avail either in this life or in any other. In the last 12 he develops the concept that every man owes allegiance to one or the other of two cities, the city of God or the city of this world; he describes the origin, progress, and destiny of these two cities; and in so doing, he finds an adequate means of explaining the whole spiritual experience of mankind.

Augustine is the last of the great Roman writers, as he is the first of the great medieval ones. He stands between two worlds. Trained in the literature and philosophy of the ancients, he owed much to Cicero's *Hortensius* and the *Neo-Platonism of Plotinus and Porphyry. But he also knew the name of Jesus from his boyhood days in Tagaste, and in the end he surrendered his will to the Church. In its service he found full scope for his talents; and he labored with so much diligence that, more than any other Father, he left his mark on the whole subsequent tradition of Western Christianity. This he accomplished by his theological publications. In the *Confessions* he composed one of the few truly great classics in the history of literature, a book simple, direct, sincere, and calculated to appeal to every human heart.

Aurelius, Marcus: Roman emperor and philosopher (A.D. 121–180). In the midst of the almost constant wars which occupied the later years of his reign, Marcus Aurelius Antoninus found time to compose a brief work of ethical and religious devotion known traditionally in English as the *Meditations.* Its basis is *Stoicism, particularly as found in *Epictetus, with some modifications derived from the philosophies of *Plato and *Aristotle. But it does not set forth any doctrine in an orderly fashion, being intended not to instruct others but to aid the writer in his own daily struggle with the trials and sorrows of life. The *Meditations* is an exhortation to right thought and right action addressed by a man to himself without reference to possible future publication. Its tone is detached, with few personal allusions except at the beginning. Its style is abrupt and marked by repetition; for the most part, it is written in the form of memoranda or jottings. But, though it has little literary merit, it has brought comfort to many thousands and is one of the precious documents of humanity.

Austen, Jane: English novelist (1775–1817). Between the surface of Jane Austen's novels and the surface of her life there is a remarkable parallel: both are without any striking eventfulness. Both novels and life give us primarily a view of middle-class people in the daily rounds of family life in provincial towns—a life in which there is good breeding, and wit, and sufficient hope of a reasonably satisfactory outcome of whatever difficulties may intrude. In the novels we come occasionally upon disappointments in love and the threat or actuality of seduction, but these seem less significant than the constant routine of family and neighborhood conversations and entertainments. Yet this quiet mode of life does not mean that in her characters Jane Austen does not explore human experience with all the thoroughness possible to the comic mode she has chosen. She does not require spectacular events to deal with important problems.

The evidence does not permit much speculation about intensities that may have lain beneath the placid exterior of her own life. The seventh of eight children, she spent her first 25 years in the village of Steventon, Hampshire, of which her father was rector. The family was congenial and gifted in self-entertainment—by games, charades, reading (particularly in 18th-century literature), and the practice of an ironic criticalness by which they punctured literary vogues. At one time or another Jane lived in several small towns, where her provincial life was quiet to the point of being static. She at no time participated in a literary society or had a literary correspondent.

Living in the high years of the major English Romantics, she in effect rejected the Romantic cult of personality, just as she was largely indifferent to Romantic literature. She derived from a neoclassical tradition of the *comedy of manners; in harking back to an 18th-century tradition, she rejected those parts of it which anticipated Romanticism. Her juvenilia, *Love and Freindship* [sic] and *Volume the First* (written in the early 1780's, but published respectively in 1922 and 1933), are for the most part clever parodies of the sentimental and romantic clichés of popular fiction. *Lady Susan*, a fragment perhaps written in the mid-1790's and published in 1871, is in the 18th-century letter form. The history of *Sense and Sensibility* is typical of Jane Austen's early literary disappointments. It was written before 1796, rewritten in 1797–98, rejected by a publisher, revised in 1809–10, and published in 1811. (All dates given below refer to publication.) As the title indicates, *Sense and Sensibility* juxtaposes an ideal which might have been set forth in the *Spectator* (see *Addison) with the emotional self-indulgence of later 18th-century sentimentalism; yet here the author avoids the effect of allegory by making Elinor (Sense) neither priggish nor unemotional, and Marianne (Sensibility) essentially intelligent and generous. *Northanger Abbey* (1818) makes fun of a current literary fad by telling of the imaginary thrills and dangers experienced by Catherine Morland, an indiscriminate reader of *Gothic novels. Of the novels written before the century's end, only *Pride and Prejudice* (1813) has no apparent basis in topical or literary satire but has an independent life at her mature level of work—an ironic, unillusioned, and yet sympathetic view of human nature and its flair for comic incongruity.

Whatever influences initiated Jane Austen's second period of writing, successful publication was unquestionably an important stimulus to continuing creative work. Novels begun after 1810 include *Emma* (1815), *Persuasion* (1818), and *Mansfield Park* (1819). Some fragmentary work was not published until the 20th century.

Emma represents a culmination of the manner which Jane was developing in her early novels; it is the ultimate achievement of the artist viewing her heroine with detachment. Jane's detachment takes the special form of an awareness of the heroine's capacity for self-deception. Emma Woodhouse is the very embodiment of self-deception: she misreads evidence, misleads others, and discovers her own inner feelings only by accident. In Fanny Price of *Mansfield Park* and Anne Elliott of *Persuasion*, Miss Austen paints more gentle and self-effacing heroines in the tradition of Jane Bennett of *Pride and Prejudice*; there is a little more awareness of theme and a little less comic gaiety. But there is still all the wide social perspective, the sense of frailty, and the awareness of complication of motive by which Jane Austen, who had had scarcely a tenth of the worldly experience of her model, Fanny Burney, far surpassed her model and set a permanent standard for comedy of manners.

Avesta: see *Zoroaster.

Bacchae: female worshipers of the god *Dionysus, also called Maenads.

Bacchus: see *Dionysus.

Bacon, Sir Francis: philosopher, scientist, essayist and jurist (1561–1626). With his versatility, ambitions, and materialistic bent, Bacon is a fine illustration of the disquieting paradoxes of the *Renaissance. The English poet *Pope described him as "the wisest, brightest, meanest of mankind." He came of a family interested in state affairs, his father being Lord Keeper of the Seal and his uncle Elizabeth's principal minister. Bacon attended Cambridge, studied law, and was elected to Parliament and appointed Queen's Counsel (1598). Under James his fortunes rose still higher, until he finally became Lord High Chancellor (1618), the highest judicial post in the country. He was knighted, created Baron Verulam and Viscount St. Albans. Then, when he was at the height of the wheel of fortune, he suddenly tumbled down. He was charged with and admitted accepting bribes from litigants. He was imprisoned briefly, banished from court, and removed from public office. After five years of retirement he contracted a fatal chill while stuffing a chicken with snow in an effort to test the preservative effects of refrigeration.

Bacon's place in the history of thought rests on his pioneer exposition of the modern inductive method and his attempt at a logical systematization of scientific procedures. His attitude he described as a "passion for research, a power of suspending judgment with patience, of meditating with pleasure, of assenting with caution . . . of arranging my thought with scrupulous pains . . . and with no blind admiration for antiquity." With the titanic aspirations typical of the Renaissance, he boasted, "I have taken all knowledge to be my province."

In *The Advancement of Learning* (1605), a sketch in English of his key ideas, he explained his wish to review all the sciences of his own time, all methods of acquiring truth, and to work out a system of classifying the various branches of knowledge. He reserved fuller exposition of his thought for works in Latin, which was still the standard language for scientific treatises. In the *Novum Organum* (*New Instrument*, 1620), he championed the inductive method of reasoning, the method of proceeding from the particular to the general. Famous is his description of the "idols," his word for bad habits of mind that cause men to fall into error and prevent them from seeing the truth. He hoped to eliminate the superstitions and quibbling which during the *Middle Ages had confused science and philosophy. These two volumes and several other treatises were parts of a projected *Instaurato Magna* (*Great Renewal* of science), which Bacon never completed.

The New Atlantis (unfinished and published in 1627 after Bacon's death) is a Utopian sketch, like Sir Thomas More's *Utopia*, of an ideal commonwealth of scholars. The emphasis is not on governmental or social institutions, but on scientific achievement. The plan calls for the creation of a research institute of scientific workers, a "Solomon's House" producing "great and marvelous works for the benefit of man."

It is the *Essays* (1597, 1612, 1625) which have given Bacon his fame in world literature. "Dispersed meditations," impersonal, almost curt, these 58 essays are a tissue of maxims quite unlike the subjective, conversational essays of *Montaigne. And their purpose is quite different. Their subtitle, *Counsels Civil and Moral*, is indicative of their point of view, a concentrated worldly wisdom designed, it has been remarked, as "guides to commonplace living," or, if one prefers, as a handbook for success. They are realistic, epigrammatic dissertations based on Bacon's own observations even when he adduces support for his conclusions by quoting the classics. A circle of aphorisms, each essay touches its subject from various points without making any logical or structural progress. Their greatness lies in their closely packed thoughts, so loaded with insight and practical wisdom as to have become current proverbs: "Some books are to be tasted, others to be swallowed, and some few to be chewed and digested. . . . Reading maketh a full man; conference a ready man; and writing an exact man" (*Of Studies*). "He

58

that hath wife and children hath given hostages to fortune" (*Of Marriage and Single Life*).

Both in his life and in his writings, Bacon always showed the practical bias. "We are concerned," he said, "not with pure skill in speculation, but with real utility and the fortunes of the human race." He completely accepted the Renaissance idea that it is life on earth which is important and that all studies should be directed to improving that life. In his political attitude, which was almost Machiavellian, he separated his legal decisions from morality and ethical ideals; in his scientific writing he aimed to give mankind mastery over nature by discoveries and inventions; in his *Essays* he hoped to teach man mastery over the world in social and civil life. He himself achieved success in a legal career (although it ended disastrously); in his scientific works, which make him one of the most important figures in the philosophy of science; and in his *Essays*, whose compact wisdom has never been duplicated in English.

ballad: a short narrative song-poem, simple in plot and usually relating a single, dramatic incident, in a form suitable for singing or rhythmical chanting. The commonest ballad stanza in English has four lines, the unrimed first and third lines having eight syllables, the riming second and fourth having six. Ballads have conventionally been classified as "folk" (also called "popular" or "traditional")—those whose authors are unknown—or "literary"—those written by modern authors. The latter are relatively less important, for these conscious attempts to capture the qualities of the folk ballad have never been completely successful. Yet this dichotomy is of dubious accuracy since our only texts of old English ballads are necessarily preserved in written sources—the earliest from the 15th century.

Folk ballads, with their traditional melodies, were transmitted orally, and most were constantly modified in the process. They are striking for their great compression, abrupt transitions, and dramatic contrasts. Cumulative effect is achieved by incremental repetition (of phrases or whole lines) and by refrains, either a line repeated at the end of each stanza or a separate stanza. Frequently the ballad is a dialogue with the "he said" omitted. The form often relies on conventional figures of speech and descriptive clichés, but the best ballads are vivid and concrete. Although they deal with strong passions, ballads are usually objective and impersonal and devote little attention to character analysis, setting, or moralizing. Their subjects are almost infinitely varied: "domestic episodes" *(Blow the Candles Out)*, dying for love *(Barbara Allen)*, murder *(Edward)*, loyalty *(The Three Ravens)*, riddles *(Riddles Wisely Expounded)*, outlawry *(Robin Hood)*, loss at sea *(Sir Patrick Spens)*, war *(Hunting of the Cheviot)*, humor *(The Farmer's Curst Wife)*, fairy enchantment *(Thomas Rymer)*, the demon lover *(Aage and Else)*, supernatural visitations *(The Wife of Usher's Well)*.

Ballads (Spanish *romance*, Russian *bylina*) appear to have sprung up about the 12th century, and many that are still sung can be traced back to the *Middle Ages. But they have been written and sung ever since and cannot be confined to any one period. Modern literary enthusiasm for ballads was stimulated in the 18th century by the antiquarian interest of the *Romantic Movement. The Romantics also hailed the ballad form as the literature of the "folk" before they were spoiled by civilization; and, as most ballads had survived only orally, *Burns, *Scott, *Herder, Grimm, and Grundtvig began to collect them. Bishop Percy's *Reliques of Ancient English Poetry* (1765) was the first noteworthy collection of texts. The largest collection of English and Scottish ballads is that of F. J. Child (1882–98).

ballade: a verse-form developed and extensively written in France during the 14th and 15th centuries. There are several variants of the form, but they differ only in the number of lines and the rime-scheme of the stanza, and agree in all other features. The commonest form has an eight-line stanza riming ababbcbc and a four-line *envoi* riming bcbc. A ballade has three stanzas and an *envoi* but uses only one set of rime-sounds for the entire poem, so that any line rimes not only with other lines of its own stanza, but with the corresponding lines of any stanza. The same line is used as a refrain to end each stanza and the *envoi*. The *envoi* ("sendoff") is a direct address to someone and frequently begins with the word "Prince," that having been the title of the judge in medieval French literary competitions. During the *Middle Ages, Guillaume de Machaut, Charles d'Orléans, Francois *Villon, and *Chaucer were among the writers of ballades. During the 19th century the form was revived by French and English poets, including *Swinburne, *Rossetti, Andrew Lang, and Austin Dobson. The ballade is now used almost exclusively for light verse.

Balzac, Honoré de: French novelist (1799–1850). The pattern of Balzac's life and novels reflects his revolt against the well-to-do, middle-class family into which he was born. The "de" he added to his name was a mere pretense of noble origins. His overweening ambition to earn huge sums of money and spend them extravagantly was, in large measure, fostered by his hatred of his avaricious mother. The theme of money pervades his novels, and his chief characters are often, like their creator, in search of wealth and social position.

Although trained in law at the University of Paris, Balzac decided to make a career in writing. When in 1819 the family consented to let him try, he shut himself in the conventional dingy attic and went to work with indomitable will and a fury that became habitual. Volumes of thriller fiction flowed from his pen, quantity making up for low pay per item, but, aware that he was prostituting his talent, Balzac never allowed his name to appear on these novels.

In 1824 he launched the first of several ambitious, large-scale, but unsuccessful business enterprises. When this printing business soon went bankrupt, his family and other investors were heavy losers, and a life-long pattern was initiated: Balzac in debt, writing (like *Scott and *Dostoevski) to pay his creditors. He could earn huge sums—often receiving them from publishers in advance before a word was written—and he could write convinc-

61

ingly about business, but he could never manage his own finances. He was improvident, a spendthrift, and his bills were always greater than his income.

In 1829 Balzac published under his own name *The Last Chouan (Le Dernier Chouan)*, beginning the series that formed the famous *Comédie humaine* (*The Human Comedy*, in contradistinction to *Dante's *Divine Comedy*). The novels of this series combine Balzac's verve, energy, and exaggeration with a realistic study of contemporary life new in French literature. Their detailed settings, minute descriptions, and analyses of such dominating passions as social climbing and money-making mark the beginnings of French *realism. In nearly 100 novels and short stories, the *Comédie humaine* realistically studies every social class and touches on most fields of knowledge.

Of the early novels, *Eugénie Grandet* (1833) and *Father Goriot* have real literary merit. *Eugénie Grandet* deals with a tenderhearted heroine who suffers from the cruel miserliness of an inhuman father and from misplaced love for an elegant, worthless cousin. A multitude of details gives an air of realism, but the exaggerated portrayal of Grandet as a sharp, avaricious schemer makes him into a monster and the unhappy love affair is overdrawn, oversentimentalized. Such excesses, strong passions, individualistic social climbers, and agonizing scenes remained typical of Balzac's works.

Balzac's flamboyant life—his mistresses with money and titles, his constant search for a rich widow, his disastrous business enterprises, his ridiculous indulgences in ornate dress and expensive bric-a-brac, his attempts to mix in "society," his long pursuit of the wealthy Madame Hanska, until she became first his mistress and then his wife—shows the same traits of his character as his fiction. Both are grandiose, exaggerated, boldly ambitious, and careless in workmanship; and above all both give an impression of tremendous verve, exuberance, and energy. Characteristically, Balzac died of apoplexy when he had just turned 50, and the *Comédie humaine* remained unfinished. Even so, he had fulfilled his intention of being the "secretary of society." In the process his power and expansiveness transformed fiction

and made the modern novel a compreh░░
type.

baroque: a term used to designate a style and period in music and the visual arts. The style is essentially one of large-scale, dramatic tendencies, with elaborate and profuse ornamentation; and the period is the 17th and early 18th centuries. The term is being increasingly used, especially by European critics, for some aspects of literature as well, though the literary tendencies do not correlate very well with those of music and the visual arts during this period. *Milton's *Paradise Lost* might be considered as a literary example of the baroque style.

Baudelaire, Pierre Charles: French poet and critic (1821–67). The pattern of Baudelaire's short life was apparent very early. He was a high-strung boy, respondent, as he said, to both the horror and ecstasy of life and "destined to eternal solitude." Resenting military school at Lyons, he strove to be as unlike his provincial schoolmates as possible. His recklessness caused his family to send him on a voyage to Calcutta, but he left the ship and spent three weeks on the Isle of Mauritius in the Indian Ocean, fascinated by the tropical life, storing up sensory impressions.

In Paris, in the Bohemian freedom of the Latin Quarter, he swiftly ran through his inheritance. His liaison with a quadroon, Jeanne Duval, lasted for over 20 years. Associated with artists and writers, he dedicated himself to the two cults of Dandyism and Art. Dandyism was the cult of the ego, a ceremonial with severe laws: to be original, to be emotionally restrained, to be independent of every social tie to family, friends, or nation, to despise the bourgeois rabble. More sincere was Baudelaire's passion for Art. "Literature," he wrote, "must come before everything else, before my hunger, before my pleasure, before my mother." Accusing himself of sloth, with some justice, he drove himself to continual work.

His early art criticism was distinguished for its sensibility. Around 1846 his discovery of a few fragments of

...ed him and started him on a 17-
...on of Poe's *Tales* that is in itself a
... Poe, who is a nobody in America,
... man in France." In 1857 appeared his
... poetry, *Les Fleurs du mal* (*The Flowers*
... followed by *Petits Poèmes en prose* and
... *rtificiels* (*Artificial Paradises*—part of which
w... ...ated from Thomas *De Quincey). With an apparent drive to self-destruction, he lived dissolutely, drank excessively, experimented with opium and hashish, and was physically broken at 40. Impoverished, diseased, fearing insanity, and at times contemplating suicide, he spent his last years in torment. After an unsuccessful lecture tour, he remained a few years in Belgium. Then he returned to Paris, where, a helpless paralytic, unable to remember his name or recognize his face in a mirror, he died in 1867.

Many of Baudelaire's literary projects were left unfinished. He was a perfectionist, preferring to labor long hours correcting a poem rather than begin a new one. It is chiefly to *Les Fleurs du mal*, announced in 1850, published in 1857, and corrected and enlarged in 1861, that he owes his fame. Baudelaire was a counterromantic, disliking the vagueness, exuberance, emotionality, and carelessness of the romanticists (see *Romantic Movement). From *Gautier, to whom he dedicated his book, he learned the discipline of form, but although he admired Gautier's objectivity, Baudelaire was intensely subjective. He had a horror of the commonplace and of nature, both external and human. Landscapes bored him, though some of his finest analogies come from nature; the new "religion of nature" shocked him, and as for the nature of man: "We do evil without effort, naturally; good is always the product of art." Virtue and beauty are always "artificial," that is, contrived by art. Poetry should be free of preachment, whether ethical, metaphysical, political, or economic.

Poet of the "religious intoxication of the great cities," he found poetry in subjects unused before: in streetwalkers, beggars, drunkards, and the wretched poor. From their ill fortune, squalor, and evil, he wanted to extract beauty—not idealization, for he revealed ugliness as ugliness, but truthful rendition in perfect phrasing and form. He recognized the paradox of the existence of good and evil in man, and in a period of expansive optimism he emphasized original sin. Although his book was condemned and several of its poems banned, Baudelaire felt that it inspired "only fear and horror of evil." In the prefatory poem *To the Reader*, Baudelaire denies any peculiarity in his attraction to evil and salutes his hypocritical reader as a likeness and a brother. In the "infamous menagerie of our vices"—Satanic pride, lust, perverted love, prostitution, drunkenness, drug addiction, murder—Baudelaire finds the worst to be "ennui," or spiritual torpor. Death is omnipresent in the poems; such a poem as *A Carcass (Une Charogne)* carries the physical horror of dissolution farther than even Poe and *Gothic novels. Love is often treated as vampirish lust; debauchery and death are likened to two companionable women of the streets. Occasionally expressing pity for the aged and the poor, Baudelaire most often speaks his fear and disgust at the nightmare of life; all is abyss: action, desire, dream, and speech. In *Le Voyage*, the last poem in the original *Les Fleurs du mal*, he expresses his wish "to plunge into the gulf, no matter whether hell or heaven, to find, at the bottom of the unknown, something *different*."

In *Poems in Prose* are the same splenetic melancholy, portraits of characters torn with conflicts, and brief narratives in which the paradoxes of the poems turn into surprise endings. Likening life to a hospital, a typical prose poem concludes: "Anywhere, anywhere, as long as it be out of this world."

Baudelaire's posthumous *Intimate Journals (Journaux intimes)*, consisting of two parts, *Squibs (Fusées)* and *My Heart Laid Bare (Mon Coeur mis à nu)*, is fragmentary, but it shows his development from Dandyism to the religious humility which is implicit (though often disguised) in most of his work.

As the first of the decadents, Baudelaire influenced such English poets as Algernon Charles *Swinburne and Ernest Dowson, but his influence is too important to be limited to a single school. He has been called "the starting-point for subsequent French poetry and for English poetry from *Pound and *Yeats onward." T. S. *Eliot calls his verse and language "the nearest thing to a complete renovation that we have experienced." He strove, not to make poetic statements, but to actualize experience in metaphors and symbols. Using the imagery of common life about observable experiences, he lifted this imagery by making it represent something much more than itself. He attained precision and startling, often paradoxical metaphors that came to be recognized as true analogies. Wishing to give sensation as exact experience, he made much use of associations and of correspondences between sensory reactions, and between the external and internal worlds. His images, though clear, were also aimed at "suggestive magic." Fashioning a type of poetry to express the complex sensibility of modern intellectuals, he was one of the precursors of French *symbolism. His influence was, of course, more than that of a technician. He looked into himself without pretense and flinching; he did not deny his own degradation nor dull his suffering; he studied both and strenuously attempted to understand and express them. Farthest from didacticism, his poems still serve as allegories, as "object-lessons" of the misery, despair, and corruption of a complex civilization; of the duality in man of good and evil; of the folly of explaining man as a purely physical organism; of the necessity for the consciousness of sin, damnation, and redemption. By recording with such honesty and intensity what happened to him, Baudelaire also recorded something that was happening to human nature as a whole.

beast epic: a series of allegorical stories in which the characters are animals with human qualities whose conduct satirizes the foibles of contemporary life, manners, and social classes. In the beast epics of the *Middle Ages, the central character of each story is the sly and ingenious rogue Reynard the Fox (in Oriental versions, the jackal), who triumphs except over the cock and crow. The most famous episodes are the funeral of the fox who was not dead after all; the fox's advising the sick lion that he will be healed by wrapping himself in a wolf's skin; the fox's rape of the wife of Ysengrim the Wolf and the tricky way in which he escapes punishment.

The genre derives from *Aesop's *Fables in general, and especially from his tale about the fox and the sick lion. This fable occupies a central position in the first medieval beast epic, Ecbasis captivi ("the prisoner's escape"), written in riming Latin verse about the year 930. By the time of the Latin Ysengrimus (c. 1150), the characteristic names were established—Noble the Lion, Ysengrim the Wolf, Reynard the Fox, Chanticler the Cock, etc.—and the distinctive traits of each animal were fixed. These animal fables were originally separate stories, like *Chaucer's Nun's Priest's Tale in the *Canterbury Tales, although the Ecbasis captivi, which is a fable within a fable, already contained the germ of a more elaborate organization. In France and Germany, however, these separate tales coalesced into a complete cycle, now called the Beast Epic, satirizing specific social groups. Thus, Reynard is said to represent the Church, Ysengrim the barons, Noble the king. (The lion was already the king in Aesop.) Perhaps in reaction against chivalry, the tales made fun of pilgrimages and *courtly love and always let cleverness win over brute strength. The French version, Le Roman de Renard (1130–1250), a poem of 30,000 lines, is the longest and most famous. The German Reinhart Fuchs (1180) had originally only 2,000 lines, but it was expanded in the 14th century. A Flemish version became influential in English when it was translated and published by Caxton (1481), and in German when *Goethe rewrote the story (Reineke Fuchs, 1793) to satirize the vices of the people and leaders of the French Revolution. *Spenser's Mother Hubberd's Tale illustrates the type in the *Renaissance. In America, the Brer Rabbit stories of Joel Chandler Harris are in the same genre.

Beaumarchais, Pierre-Augustin Caron de: French adventurer, speculator, and dramatist (1732–99). Beaumarchais is remembered for two plays which combine hilarious comedy with a good deal of sharp criticism of the privileges and insolence of the hereditary aristocracy: *The Barber of Seville* (1775) and *The Marriage of Figaro* (written 1778; performance not permitted until 1784). Though the plays are excellent in their own right and are still performed in France, they hold the stage today primarily in the operatic versions by Rossini and Mozart respectively.

Beckett, Samuel: Irish novelist, poet, dramatist, critic (*Proust*, 1931) (1906–89). Beckett was born in Dublin, attended Trinity College, and went as exchange lecturer to the École Normale Supérieure in Paris (1928–30). There he met and became a friend of James *Joyce. In 1931 Beckett returned to Trinity as a lecturer in French; in 1938 he settled permanently in Paris.

Beckett's first works—written in English—include poems, essays, stories, and two novels, *Murphy* (1938) and *Watt* (1953). In these novels as in Beckett's later ones, the protagonists are compulsive searchers for an elusive external reality. They find only an *absurd world, resistant to description or interpretation. Equally at home in French, Beckett for many years wrote exclusively in that language, notably a series of novels (with later English versions by the author himself)—*Molloy* (1951), *Malone Dies* (*Malone meurt*, 1952), and *The Unnamable* (*L'innommable*, 1953)—solopsistic stream-of-consciousness monologues dealing with man's quest for his identity in the midst of loneliness, decay, and death.

Beckett's first play, *Waiting for Godot* (*En attendant Godot*, 1952), brought him renown and assured him a prominent place among the exponents of "the theater of the absurd." It displays his characteristic idiom in persona and stage: the characters are clown/tramp figures linked in a double-act (in other plays the relation may be master-slave, executioner-victim); the set is stark, bare, and unlocalized; there is hardly any action, and the dialogue is repetitive and contradictory—language, like everything else, being incapable of giving meaning to an absurd world. The central theme of the play appears to be simply "waiting," but what the two bums wait for is not certain, in spite of the numerous critical exegeses provoked by the play. Although Beckett himself showed a marked reluctance to offer any explanation which might elucidate the meaning of his works, he did say that "Godot is life—aimless, but always with an element of hope."

Endgame (*Fin de partie*, 1957), an allusion to the last moves in a chess game, stages characters in a closed-in space, who wile away the time by playing games and telling stories. The same "search for meaning and achieving meaninglessness," a sense of the vanity of life, its triviality and frustration, appears in *Act Without Words* (*Acte sans paroles*, 1957). In *How It is* (*Comment c'est*, 1961), Bom and Pim "crawl naked in the darkness and mud of existence." In Beckett's later plays (written in English), *Krapp's Last Tape* (1958) consists of a dialogue between the protagonist and an earlier recording of his voice; *Happy Days* (1961) presents the isolation of an elderly couple, the wife, buried in sand, carrying on a "dialogue" with her almost completely silent husband. A later Beckett—a two-page text—is simply titled *Suns* (*Without*, 1970). *Beginning to End* (1970) is an anthology of Beckett's works, edited as a one-man play. *Not I* (1972) is "a magnificent cry of anguish of a woman in conflict with herself who relives the past," while another character comments on her monologue.

Beckett's grim exposition of the tragicomic plight of man, lonely, moving aimlessly or immobilized by paralysis, listening endlessly to his own compulsive voice, is to a certain extent lightened by humor—for the most part a painfully hilarious "black humor" of grotesque and tragic force. These perceptions of the human condition would not be possible were human values altogether denied. It is the combination of the "exotic imagination of the surrealist poets, the inner compulsiveness and significance of *Kafka or *Camus," and a rich verbal substance which have proved a seminal influence on modern drama, e.g., on Edward *Albee and Harold *Pinter. Beckett was awarded the Nobel prize in 1969.

belles-lettres ("fine letters"): literature intended to be enjoyed for its own sake (for its imaginative and artistic qualities) rather than to convey information or serve some immediate practical purpose. Although all literature must have purposes outside itself unless we subscribe to a pure "art for art's sake" theory, and although the border line may be rather fuzzy in individual cases, the general distinction is clear enough. Most poetry, fiction, drama, and personal essays fall in the category of belles-lettres, while textbooks, reference works, technical treatises, newspapers, and all the other manifold uses of language do not. The habit of writing novels and plays on social, political, and economic issues does not invalidate the distinction but rather underlines it: the novel is written to reach and impress a public which reads novels for their own sake but may not read or react favorably to treatises or works of political or social controversy. *De Quincey distinguished between "literature of knowledge" (e.g., a cookbook—to inform or explain) and "literature of power" (e.g., a poem, essay, novel—to affect). The latter would be *belletristic*, the adjective formed from *belles-lettres*. The term is now sometimes used pejoratively for flowing writing thin in content.

belletristic: see *belles-lettres.

Beowulf: an Old English epic, composed *c.* A.D. 725. The earliest extant poem in a modern European language, *Beowulf* is deservedly the most celebrated survival from Old English literature. Yet its author is unknown; and the manuscript, which dates from the late 10th century, was not studied until the 18th century. Although individual episodes, the echoes of old legends, may at one time have circulated separately and orally, *Beowulf*, as we know it, is an artistically finished and unified whole.

Its 3,182 lines are in the unrimed alliterative verse which was common to the early Germanic peoples. Each line is divided into halves by a caesural pause, and the half lines, each with two accented and a varying number of unaccented syllables, are linked by alliteration ("Grim and greedy the gruesome monster"). A distinctive and picturesque stylistic effect is achieved by the use of two-term metaphors instead of similes. The *kennings are drawn from nature, customs, and beliefs (*e.g., whale-path* for sea; *ring-bestower* for king; *battle-flash* for sword; *treasure-hoarder* for dragon).

These and other stylistic aspects of the poem, the historical elements, the natural scene, and the deeds of the folk-tale hero are paralleled in the literature of the Germanic continental tradition and of pagan Scandinavia. The hero Beowulf is identified as a Geat (probably from southern Sweden), and there are references to an actual raid down the Rhine, *c.* A.D. 521, by the king of the Geats, Beowulf's uncle, Hygelac. England is never mentioned. Yet the poem was written in England, where the original pagan and continental elements of history and folklore were modified by the poet's civilized, Christian view of society. The scenes in Hrothgar's court reflect, not the crude barbaric civilization of the Baltic, but the cultivated Christian aristocracy of an 8th-century Anglo-Saxon court. Vestiges of belief in magic runic symbols, of heathen cremation ceremonies, and of the pagan power of Wyrd (Fate) remain side by side with faith in God's power over man, in the existence of Heaven and Hell, in the significance of Biblical story from the sinfulness of Cain to the sacrifice of Christ. A complete reconciliation is never achieved; Wyrd, for example, is both Fate and God's plan for the world. But the poem is tempered throughout by the Christian spirit.

It is probable also that the sophisticated poet knew such Latin classics as *Vergil's *Aeneid.* His craftsmanslike use of certain rhetorical devices of language and structure, contrast and climax, boast and understatement seems to reflect the classical epic tradition, as does the use of "flashbacks."

The main narrative of the poem is, however, made up of three folk stories, to which the historically accurate raids and savage feuds between Danes, Geats, Swedes, and Frisians are only incidental. In the first of these episodes, Beowulf, a mighty swimmer and wrestler, frees the mead-hall (Heorot) of the Danish king Hrothgar by wrenching out the clawlike arm of the male monster Grendel, who has decimated Hrothgar's band by his ravenous nocturnal visits. In the second, the hero slays

Grendel's dam, a hideous water-hag, in her cave beneath a mysterious mere. These two episodes are closely related, and the second brings the poem to a dramatic climax. The third, however, is quite different in tone, for Beowulf is no longer merely fighting for youthful glory. Now a wise and aged king who has ruled the Geats for 50 peaceful and prosperous years, he fights and dies to save his people from a fire-breathing dragon who has laid waste their countryside.

The lamentations over Beowulf's funeral pyre extol not only his striving for honor and fame, his valor and loyalty—typical characteristics of primitive Germanic heroes—but also his kindness, mildness, and gentleness—the Christian virtues.

This elegiac mood and ethical spirit, as well as the literary artistry, provide unity between the various sections of the poem and elevate it from a fairy tale of a monster-fighting folk hero to a mature and complex work of art.

Béranger, Jean-Pierre de: song-writer (1780–1857). The most famous composer of French popular songs *(chansons)*, Béranger was the son of middle-class working people. A staunch republican, he was in and out of prison with each change in government. His closeness to the people, however, helped him to capture and crystallize popular reactions. His themes are widely varied— gay and bacchanalian, political and patriotic, sentimental and nostalgic. Although he helped popularize the legend and cult of Napoleon I, his best-known poem, the *King of Yvetot*, is a gentle rebuke to Napoleon's undemocratic government.

Because the songs were intended for popular singing, Béranger used various tricks of style and published in newspapers to gain immediate and widespread attention. The songs have simplicity and directness, pronounced rhythms, memorable refrains, and wit. This combination of qualities gave them their charm and vogue; but critics who place more value on subtle and profound poetry scoff at Béranger's stilted diction and his emotional and rhythmic poverty.

Bergson, Henri: French philosopher and psychologist, primary exponent of "psychological" time, which is subjective, as against clock-time, which (like calendar-time) represents arbitrary measurements of duration in the interest of conformity (1859–1941). Bergson's discussion of "duration" in *Time and Free Will* (1889) exerted a profound influence and is said to have provided the impulse for *Proust's "quest for lost time." Bergson followed this work with *Matter and Memory* (1896), which influenced Proust in his insistence on man's ability to store within himself the totality of his experience. His final work, *Creative Evolution* (1911), defined the mind and its *élan vital*—that vital energy which provides intuition and enables man to be endlessly creative. These works of high originality (though hints are to be found in the *Neo-Platonism of Plotinus, in *Rousseau, in *Schopenhauer) profoundly influenced the modern movement in literature. Bergson also wrote a study of the phenomenon of laughter and, in a late work, discussed "duration and simultaneity." The *stream-of-consciousness novel, in its attention to mental flux and association, had its philosophical foundations laid by Bergson. His lectures at the Collège de France drew multitudes; he was a brilliant explicator of ideas, finding the metaphors and verbal plasticity to give them body and form. Bergson won the Nobel prize in 1927; he had been elected to the French Academy in 1914 and was named by the League of Nations as the first chairman of the International Committee on Intellectual Cooperation.

bestiary: a work which describes the alleged habits of various beasts (hence the name), following each account with an interpretation giving its moral or theological significance. Bestiaries were widely written in the *Middle Ages, both in Latin and in the vernacular languages, and are an outgrowth of the concept that the physical world is merely a symbol of the moral and religious one. For example, a Middle English bestiary says that the whale has a sweet breath with which he lures little fish to him; then he sucks them in. But he cannot eat the big fish. Also, sailors sometimes land on a floating whale, mistaking him for an island; they build a fire on him, and he sounds, carrying them to their death. The whale represents the devil. His allurements bring those small in faith into his reach and he devours them, but the great in faith are immune. Whoever establishes his hope on the devil will sink with him.

Bhagavat Gita: see *Mahabharata*.

Bible, The: a collection of books held sacred by Jews and Christians. The Bible is divided into two parts: The Old Testament, identical (except as noted below) with the Law, the Prophets, and the Writings that make up the Jewish Scriptures; and the New Testament, comprising the earliest documents extant on the life and teaching of Jesus and the establishment of the Christian Church.

The Old Testament is longer and richer in literary types than the New, presenting, besides the tremendous sweep of its histories, the minute detail of its law codes, and the high ethical doctrines of its prophetic books, the lyric poetry of Psalms and the Song of Solomon, the wisdom literature of Proverbs and Ecclesiastes, the dramatic dialogue of Job, the apocalyptic vision of Daniel, and the tale or short story, nowhere developed more perfectly than in Ruth.

The first books of the Old Testament are Genesis, Exodus, Leviticus, Numbers, and Deuteronomy, which together are called The Pentateuch. They are narratives describing Creation and the primeval history of the world, and then turning specifically to the Children of Israel, whose fortunes they relate from the call of Abraham to the death of Moses on the wilderness journey that followed the flight out of Egypt. The Pentateuch contains some of the most famous of stories, including ancient traditions such as the building of the tower of Babel, didactic legends such as the destruction of the Cities of the Plain, literary masterpieces such as the tale of Joseph and his Brethren, and narratives of great religious importance such as the giving of the Ten Commandments on Mt. Sinai. Indeed, the whole Mosaic code is set forth in these books, which are called in the Jewish tradition the Torah, or Law.

The Pentateuch represents the highest point ever attained by Hebrew prose, but Joshua, Judges, Samuel, and Kings, the four books that follow, are almost as great. Their subject is the conquest of Canaan by Joshua and the victories of the *judges* or chieftains against the tribes round about; the establishment of the kingdom by Saul and David and its division after the death of Solomon; and the history of Judah and Israel as far as the destruction of Jerusalem by Nebuchadnezzar and the deportation of the people to Babylon in 586 B.C. The most heroic figure in these books is David, but many others are of note also, among them the strong man Samson deceived by his mistress Delilah, the child Samuel presented to the Lord in the temple, and the prophet Elijah, that great figure of the decline, standing alone and succeeding against all the priests of Baal.

In the Hebrew Bible, Joshua, Judges, Samuel, and Kings are known as the Former Prophets in contrast to the Latter Prophets, Isaiah, Jeremiah, Ezekiel, Hosea, Joel, Amos, Obadiah, Jonah, Micah, Nahum, Habakkuk, Zephaniah, Haggai, Zechariah, and Malachi—books devoted to men who ministered from the 8th through the 5th century B.C. These men taught the people directly in the name of God, expressing their thought in some of the most exalted poetry ever written, and using striking symbols to emphasize it. They were highly individualistic, and they spoke with specific situations in mind; but they can be considered together, as their basic theme is always the necessity for righteousness. "What does the Lord require of thee," Micah asks, "but to do justly, and to love mercy, and to walk humbly with thy God?" Amos, Hosea, Micah, Jeremiah, and others among the prophets are famous; but Isaiah is probably the best known, in part because of the great Messianic passages in his volume, traditionally regarded by Christians as fulfilled in the birth of Christ.

The remaining books of the Old Testament, classified in the Hebrew Scriptures as the Writings, are miscellaneous in nature. Some are histories like Chronicles, Ezra, and Nehemiah; others are short stories like Esther, the dramatic account of a Jewish queen who risked her life to save her people, and Ruth, a pastoral romance in which the heroine, although a Moabite girl, won a place in the lineage of David. These works are in prose. Ecclesiastes, a book of wisdom literature composed in deep pessimism, is partly in prose and partly in verse, as is Daniel, whose narrative is famous for the episodes of the Fiery Furnace and the Lions' Den. Job has a prologue and an epilogue in prose but is otherwise in verse. In it, the ancient story of a perfect and upright man who lost all that he had is made the occasion for a philosophical examination of the problem of evil. The other books of the Writings are wholly in verse. They are The Song of Solomon, a poem of love; Lamentations, a series of dirges; Proverbs, a collection of wise sayings; and the Psalms, an anthology of sacred poetry, more familiar and better loved throughout the world than any other part of the Old Testament.

The books named thus far are found in all versions of the Old Testament, though the texts vary, particularly in Esther and Daniel. In addition, the Catholic Bible includes certain works not contained in the Jewish Scriptures and no longer commonly printed by Protestants. They are Tobit (or Tobias), a story of piety and its reward; Judith, a tale of heroism in time of war; Baruch, a composite book made up of prayers, hymns, and other forms including a letter; Wisdom and Ecclesiasticus, both of the same type as Proverbs; and the histories called I and II Maccabees. These writings, often referred to as the Apocrypha, were found in the Septuagint, a Greek translation of the Old Testament in use at the time of Christ; they passed into the Vulgate, as St. *Jerome's great Latin translation of the Bible is called; and they were pronounced deuterocanonical at the Council of Trent, A.D. 1546.

The New Testament possesses neither the length nor the variety of the Old, being written almost entirely in prose and in comparatively few forms. Beginning with the Gospels attributed to Matthew, Mark, Luke, and John, which describe the life and teaching of Jesus, it continues with the Acts of the Apostles. This history of the missionary labors of Peter and Paul, ascribed traditionally to Luke, was intended as a sequel to his Gospel, though it serves equally well as an introduction to the Epistles that follow it in the text. A few of these were written by James, Peter, John, and Jude, but the majority are the work of Paul, whose Epistle to the Romans heads the great series of his messages to the Churches, the others being addressed to the Corinthians, Galatians, Ephesians, Philippians, Colossians, and Thessalonians. There are also four short personal letters bearing Paul's name, two to Timothy and one each to Titus and Philemon; and one beautiful letter called Hebrews, which bears no superscription but is traditionally considered Paul's. At the end of the Epistles, the New Testament closes appropriately with the Revelation of John, a work filled with splendid apocalyptic visions resembling those of Daniel.

Such then is the Bible, not a book, but a collection of books, or rather almost the whole religious literature of a people as it developed for more than 1,200 years. Vast though it is, its difficulties arise largely not from its scope but from its anonymity, for much of it is of unknown authorship and uncertain date. Much, too, that is named and dated has undergone revision and accretion, sometimes for centuries. Nothing, therefore, in the whole history of literature presents so many difficulties as the critical study of the Bible, and nothing has led to so many extreme and conflicting points of view. But in spite of its diverse origin, the Bible presents an unmistakable harmony from Genesis to Revelation.

The Old Testament was first written in Hebrew except for certain Aramaic passages in the books of Ezra and Daniel, but the Apocrypha were composed apparently for the most part in Greek, which was the original language of the New Testament also, so far as is known. When Christian communities arose in the western provinces of the Roman Empire, the Bible was rendered into Latin for their use, the older versions finally giving way to the *Vulgate, begun by St. *Jerome, A.D. 382. This version became the official Scripture of the Roman Catholic Church and the basis for such Catholic translations into the modern languages as the Douay Bible in English. The great Protestant versions arose, of course, with the Reformation. *Luther completed his translation of the Bible into German in 1534, and the committee of English scholars commissioned by King James to render the Scripture anew finished their work in 1611. Their translation, known as the King James or Authorized Version, soon came to be recognized as one of the glories of the English tongue and a model for much of the prose written subsequently in that language. Because of its great beaúty, it is commonly used in courses in which the Bible is studied chiefly as literature. Based on the Hebrew and Greek originals as they were then known, it also drew largely on earlier English translations, particularly that of William Tyndale. The King James Version is the basis of the American Revised Standard Version completed in 1952.

Bion: Greek pastoral poet (*fl. c.* 100 B.C.). Bion was born near Smyrna in Asia Minor but apparently spent much of his life in Sicily. He is remembered as the author of the *Lament for Adonis*, a poem bewailing the death of a beautiful youth beloved by the goddess *Aphrodite. Though called *Adonis by the Greeks, this youth is probably identical with the Babylonian divinity Tammuz, whose death and resurrection symbolized the annual withering and renewal of the crops. The festival of Adonis was celebrated all over the eastern Mediterranean area every year, and the *Lament* with its tearful refrain—*Woe for Cytherea! The beautiful Adonis is dead!*—is probably modeled on the lamentations actually uttered at these rites. Hence, the poem should be compared with *Theocritus' poem *The Women at the Adonis Festival*, based on another part of the ceremony. Bion's *Lament* provided the inspiration for *Shelley's *Adonais*, on the death of *Keats, and has been translated into English by Elizabeth Barrett *Browning.

Birds, The: a comedy of *Aristophanes produced in the theater of Dionysus at Athens during the festival of the City Dionysia in March, 414 B.C. In June, 415 B.C., in the midst of the Peloponnesian War, the finest military force ever to leave the shores of Greece set sail

78

from the Piraeus to conquer the city of Syracuse and reduce all Sicily to the status of an Athenian province. In the months that followed, when Aristophanes was writing *The Birds*, the people of Athens were prey to the wildest rumors and the most exaggerated expectations concerning the vast new empire their armies were about to create in the west. As Aristophanes' plays normally deal with the immediate situation in Athens, some scholars have interpreted *The Birds* as satire on the high-flown schemes fostered in the city by the Sicilian Expedition. But the evidence for this view seems faint and uncertain; and it may be that *The Birds* is simply a play of escape, reflecting perhaps the excited atmosphere of the time, but with no serious comment on the great undertaking that ended in disaster the following year.

The plot is carefully constructed. Two old Athenians, Peisthetaerus and Euelpides, disillusioned with life in Athens, set out to find a peaceful city in which to spend their declining years. Guided by a crow and a jackdaw, they make their way to the home of Tereus, who was once a man, but is now a Hoopoe and king of the birds. They believe he can direct them to the kind of place they have in mind. But the Hoopoe's suggestions are unacceptable—there seems to be trouble everywhere— and the talk turns to the better life lived among the birds.

At this point Peisthetaerus conceives the idea on which the play is based. Why should the birds not build a mighty city in the air? Then they could rule the nations as they rule the bugs and force the gods to do their will by intercepting the sacrifices—their food supply. The Hoopoe is overjoyed at Peisthetaerus' scheme; and, along with his wife, the Nightingale, he calls the birds to consider it. When they hop into the orchestra as the chorus of the play, they catch sight of the two old men and are filled with rage, for men are their natural enemies. But in the debate that follows, Peisthetaerus wins their confidence; and, when he has finished speaking, they are wild with enthusiasm for the plan. The building of *Nephelococcugia*, or Cloudcuckootown, begins, and Peisthetaerus and Euelpides retire to the Hoopoe's dwelling to receive their wings.

News of the enterprise spreads quickly. The ramparts have scarcely been finished when a messenger comes from the earth to report that men everywhere welcome the revolution and are flocking to the city in droves. The advance guard—a comic array of miscellaneous nuisances—are, in fact, there already. Meanwhile, the rainbow goddess Iris is arrested for crossing the border without a visa. She had been sent to earth to ask why the sacrifices had ceased. Prometheus, *Zeus's age-old enemy, sneaks in beneath an enormous umbrella. He crows in delight that the starving gods are in all but open rebellion. In a few minutes, *Poseidon, *Heracles, and a barbarian deity who cannot speak Greek arrive to arrange terms of peace. The rule of the world is granted the birds; a young lady called *Basileia*, or Sovereignty, symbolizing the power of Zeus, is promised in marriage to Peisthetaerus; and the play ends appropriately with their wedding hymn.

The Birds is famous for the brilliance of its wit and imagination. It contains more true fun, perhaps, than any other Aristophanic comedy. Its lyrics are among the finest in the Greek language; the Hoopoe's serenade to his mate is one of the great songs of literature. The construction of the play is excellent, the character of Peisthetaerus unusually attractive. The scenery used is simple—a sheer rock with a door opening into the Hoopoe's nest, and a single tree—but the bird costumes were both beautiful and striking. Yet, for some reason we do not know, *The Birds* won only the second prize. Modern critics, however, usually consider it Aristophanes' masterpiece; and for the modern reader it has the advantage of not requiring a detailed knowledge of Athenian politics. It can be read, without loss, as pure fantasy.

"black literature" in America: is a tentative title for different genres in which black Americans write about the experience of being black. Booker T. Washington (1856–1915; *Up From Slavery*, 1901) and his followers believed blacks could find a good place in American society by being proficient. For other writers, there came, with the "awareness" of their color, a feeling of being handicapped partners, unequal participants in the American dream. Disillusioned with "accommodation," "poised on the edge of despair," they urged racial pride and institutional changes. W. E. B. Du Bois (1868–1963; *The Souls of Black Folk*, 1903) was the most humanistic, eloquent, and thoughtful voice of his generation. The decade following the civil rights legislation of the 1950's and the civil rights movement led by Martin Luther King, Jr. (1929–1968, awarded Nobel Peace Prize 1964), saw the emergence of strong ethnic feelings among American blacks, glorying in their separate and distinct culture, life style, speech. Distinguished black writers have hewed to literary tradition while celebrating the cultural heritage of the blacks and expressing with high individuality and art their deepest problems. These include Jean Toomer (1894–1967; *Cane*, 1923), Countee Cullen (1903–1946), Langston Hughes (1902–1967), Claude McKay (1890–1948), Sterling A. Brown (1901–89; "the dean of American Negro poets"), Richard Wright (1908–1960; *Native Son*, 1940; *Black Boy*, 1945), Ralph Ellison (1914–94; *Invisible Man*, 1952), James Baldwin (1924–87; *Go Tell It on the Mountain*, 1953), Lorraine Hansberry (1931–1965; *A Raisin in the Sun*, Drama Critics' Circle Award, 1959).

The psychological and moral dehumanization of slavery, its brutality and corruption, have found a counterpart in and infected a black revolutionary literature where the "black aesthetic" becomes a violent rage against all things Western and white. The revolutionary writers include "Malcolm X" (Malcolm Little, 1925–1965, *Autobiography*) and LeRoi *Jones (Arabic adopted name Imamu Amiri Baraka, 1934–   ). Much black literature is flawed by polemics, specious ideological arguments, and stereotyped situations and characters. But black writers have produced work of great passion and considerable art. This brief entry has named only a few of the most influential.

Blake, William: English poet, painter, and engraver (1757–1827). Although unworldly and always poor, Blake enjoyed the good fortune of living a happy life.

As a shopkeeper's son, he was largely self-educated, but his talent was recognized early and he was apprenticed to an engraver. The most famous of the engravings by which he earned his living were his book illustrations, especially those for Blair's *The Grave*, *Dante's *Divine Comedy*, and the *Book of Job*.

Blake abhorred the rationalism and materialism of his times. What he saw and painted were human beings beset with evil, yet striving for the divine within them: "For Mercy has a human heart,/Pity a human face,/ And Love, the human form divine." He saw and painted the Godhead peering in at his window and angels sitting beside him in the garden, gathered in the shadows of trees, resting in leaves and flowers.

Blake's poetry was published in a manner most unusual in literary and art history; he personally manufactured every copy. The verses were not typeset but were, with the engravings that illustrated them, cut into copper plates. The pages themselves he illuminated in water colors. Little valued by his contemporaries, Blake's illustrations have become prized collectors' items.

Both in his engravings and in his poems, the purpose of Blake's art was primarily moral. By showing men his vision of the possibility of true freedom of the spirit, he hoped to free them from the shackles of convention and tradition, to help them realize their potentialities by trusting their intuition ("The tigers of wrath are wiser than the horses of instruction"). His vision was also social and political. He believed in man's dignity and natural right to liberty ("A tyrant is the worst disease, and the cause of all others"). But the mystical tone and the symbols, the revolutionary attitudes in theme and imagery, the impatience with codified ethics, the completely new kind of art which sought not outward but inner reality, all went to convince his own generation that he was a lunatic. Blake, who was far more revolutionary in subject matter, diction, and technique than *Burns or *Wordsworth, was not appreciated until the mid-19th century. Indeed the mystic rhapsodies of his later *Prophetic Books* are so much a secret language that the poems are still bewildering despite a century of commentators.

The most familiar of Blake's lyrics appeared in *Songs*

of Innocence (1789) and *Songs of Experience* (1794). In such poems as *The Lamb* and *The Little Black Boy* from the first, and *The Tiger* and *The Chimney-Sweeper* from the second, adult wisdom and poetic intuition are brilliantly intensified by being voiced with the charming artlessness of a child. Unlike the later poems, these are vivid and direct, their symbolism readily understood. These two volumes, together with *Poetical Sketches* (1783) and *The Marriage of Heaven and Hell* (1790), show Blake at his lyric best.

Blake is especially important to world literature for his historical position: he defied reason in an age of rational philosophers and glorified intuition and imagination in an age of scientific skepticism. His revolt is of additional significance because of his genuine greatness as a poet—his capacity to concentrate and thereby intensify a complex emotion in a single image and thus to project that emotion with dramatic force and moving harmony.

blank verse: unrimed iambic pentameter, a form first developed by the Italians (*versi sciolti*—"verses loosed" from rime). The use of blank verse was encouraged by the *Renaissance humanists because, in its lack of rime, it resembled classical poetry. Introduced into English literature by the Earl of Surrey (1517?–47) in his translation of part of *Vergil's *Aeneid, first used in English drama in Sackville and Norton's *Gorboduc* (1565), blank verse first manifested its potentialities of range and flexibility in *Marlowe's "mighty line." It became the standard form of *Shakespeare in drama and *Milton in epic. Although blank verse has no stanza divisions in the conventional sense, the use of run-on lines and other devices permits the grouping of thoughts into blocks or "verse paragraphs," a technique notable in Milton's *Paradise Lost. The form is established in English as the line for dignified and stately verse, but it has been used for every type of poetry. During the 18th century it became the standard meter of poetic drama in German and Italian.

Bloomsbury group: not a formal group, but a name applied to certain Cambridge graduates and certain of their friends who lived in Bloomsbury in London and met frequently, often at the home in Gordon Square of the daughters of Sir Leslie Stephen, the Victorian writer. These daughters were Virginia, who became Virginia *Woolf, the novelist, and Vanessa, who married Clive Bell, the art critic, and was herself an artist. By their subsequent achievements in their various fields the members of this group exercised a considerable influence on art and thought in England in the first half of the 20th century. The novelists of the group were Mrs. Woolf and E. M. *Forster; the artists were Vanessa Bell, Duncan Grant, and Roger Fry. Also members of the group were John Maynard Keynes, the economist; Leonard Woolf, the journalist and social critic; Desmond McCarthy, the literary critic; Lytton Strachey, the biographer. Later the novelist David Garnett also became identified with the group through his marriage to Vanessa Bell's daughter Angelica. The group remained, said Leonard Woolf, "a group of friends" whose roots were in Cambridge. All the men had been more or less contemporaries at Trinity and King's. Between the wars "Bloomsbury" was used as a term of abuse, and the group was often accused of "snobbism" and criticized for its unconventionalities. But it was always innovative and brilliant. In art it was largely responsible for the interpretation and popularizing of the post-impressionists. In fiction it was experimental and subjective. In biography, Lytton Strachey achieved a high originality of style and method, while the economic theories of Maynard Keynes profoundly influenced the modern world, particularly his conception of deficit spending as a means of thwarting depressions. Leonard Woolf was one of the "brain trust" of British socialism in the early years of the Labour Party.

Boccaccio, Giovanni: Italian storyteller and poet (1313–75). Boccaccio is distinguished in world literature for the brilliant storytelling of *The *Decameron*. But he has more than one legitimate claim to fame. The first biographer of *Dante and the intimate friend of *Petrarch, Boccaccio is worthy of his place in this triumvirate of 14th-century Italian geniuses. He was an ardent

84

love poet, a masterly narrative poet, a writer whose rich and harmonious prose popularized the Tuscan dialect and helped make it the literary language of Italy; he was one of the earliest to represent in literature the antiascetic point of view of the rising middle class and a pioneer in the revival of classical learning which was to mark the *Renaissance.

His place of birth is unknown (early tradition held that he was born in Paris, the illegitimate son of a French mother and a Florentine banker). The young Giovanni was brought up near Florence and lived a life even more interesting and dramatic than his writings. Despite his own preference for classical studies, he was trained for commerce. "If only my father had been indulgent to my wishes," lamented Giovanni, ironically unaware of his future place in world literature, "I might have been one of the world's famous poets." When he was still in his teens the boy was sent to Naples to engage in business related to the famous Bardi Bank. Later he probably studied canon law. In Naples he remained during his most impressionable years, from 1328 to 1341; and, although he often referred to these years of business and the law as wasted, and he never lost his bitterness over them, he found many opportunities for social and literary pleasure in the gay and magnificent city.

In Naples, too, early in the 1330's, he fell desperately in love with one Maria d'Aquino, whom he calls "Fiametta," or "Flamelet." She soon became his mistress, and a short period of happiness was followed by jealousies, suspicion, and her final desertion of him—apparently because she merely tired of him. There has been endless debate and conjecture about the actual history of this affair, largely because we know of it only from Boccaccio's works, in which it is so overlaid with allegory, symbolism, and poetic ornamentation that biographers can hardly dig out the actual facts. Modern critics have tended to suspect that there are not many facts to find— that Boccaccio may have elaborated some slight and casual affairs into a great literary passion which he treated according to the conventions of *courtly love. The important thing about Maria is that, whether real or imaginary, she made a poet out of Boccaccio and supplied him with the inspiration and (often indirectly) the material for a distinguished group of romances written in the late 1330's and early 1340's. These works are highly original productions, most of which are "firsts" of one sort or another in Italian literature.

The *Filocolo* ("Labor of Love," 1338) is a prose retelling of the medieval romance of Florio and Biancofiore. The *Filostrato* ("Laid Low by Love," 1336–38) marks the first appearance of *ottava rima, a stanza which Boccaccio invented and which has been widely used in many languages since his time. It tells the love story of Troilus and Cressida and is of especial interest in that *Chaucer based his *Troilus and Criseyde* on it and actually translated more than half of it in the course of his own poem. Though the tale of these lovers had gradually developed in the medieval stories about the siege of Troy, Boccaccio was the first writer to give it an independent life by devoting an entire work to it. The *Ameto*, in prose and verse, is a group of pastoral tales with allegorical intent. The *Teseide* is a long narrative poem (same number of lines as the *Aeneid*) telling a story (apparently invented by Boccaccio) about rivalry in love—a story which Chaucer took from him for the tale told by the Knight in the *Canterbury Tales*. The *Amorosa Visione* is an allegory in *terza rima. And *Fiametta*, a psychological love story in prose, is one of the numerous candidates for the title of "the first modern novel."

Then, in 1341, Boccaccio was recalled to Florence because of his father's financial downfall. The next decade held much sorrow—continuing animosity between Giovanni and his father, increasingly serious financial difficulties, and the ravaging plague known as Black Death (1348), which took the lives of three-fifths the population of Florence, including Boccaccio's father and Maria. Boccaccio's youth was gone. But with its passing came a new plenitude of powers, and for a brief time he gave free play to his highest capacities.

The Decameron is the product of these years (1348–53). No longer engrossed in his own amorous passion, he became the sardonic and disinterested observer, recording with incomparable artistry and sense of comedy the follies of his and every age. Unlike Dante, who at the same age faced a similar emotional crisis and emerged into a mystic vision of eternity in *The *Divine Comedy*, Boccaccio remained in Florence with the completely profane and earthy *Decameron*.

In the years that followed, Boccaccio achieved fame as a man of learning and a public servant, although he continued to complain constantly of poverty. Sent on numerous missions for his city (including visits to the German Emperor and to the Pope at Avignon), he came to know the great and near great of his age. But the most important single influence on the second half of his life (as Maria had been on the first), was Petrarch, whom Boccaccio first met in Florence in 1350, whose classical scholarship he revered, and whose counsel he determined should guide the future course of his studies and writing. Under Petrarch's urging, Boccaccio agreed "to direct the mind toward eternal things, leaving aside the delights of the temporal." He abandoned composition in the vernacular to follow Petrarch's guidance and write exclusively works of high seriousness in Latin. He undertook the study of Greek (perhaps the first western European of modern times to do so) and the translation of Homer. He turned more and more to a life of pious austerity, to scholarly research into old manuscripts, to the writing of scholarly works in Latin.

The four learned treatises which resulted from this inspiration were enormously popular and became the textbooks of the Renaissance. *The Genealogy of the Gentile Gods (De genealogia deorum gentilium)* is a handbook of classical mythology which includes a famous defense of poetic art. The compendious *Downfalls of Illustrious Men (De casibus virorum illustrium)* begins with Adam and illustrates the vanity of human success. *Of Famous Women (De claris mulieribus)* begins with the life of Eve. The fourth *(De montibus, sylvis, . . .)* is an alphabetical dictionary of geography.

Boccaccio's last public act was a labor of veneration. He had for many years admired Dante's writings, had collected as many first-hand biographical details as he could from contemporaries, had written the earliest *Life of Dante* (1353), and had copied out the whole of the *Divine Comedy* and sent the manuscript to Petrarch. Now, in 1373, Boccaccio was asked by Florence to deliver the first public lectures ever to be given on *The Divine Comedy*. He began but never completed the series because of ill health, and only a rough draft of his lecture notes survives. He died at Certaldo and was buried there, as he had requested.

In many ways Boccaccio may be regarded as the first modern man. The classical-humanistic aspects of the Renaissance are recognizable in his study of Greek, his endless search for manuscripts, his scholarly productivity. The passionate energy, individualism, and love of life so characteristic of the Renaissance are exemplified by his originality in the series of early romances. The Renaissance rejection of medieval austerity, allegory, and otherworldliness and its affirmation of joy in the natural world are best illustrated by *The Decameron*, in which Boccaccio faced the facts of middle-class life with humor and happiness. And all his life he venerated poetry—wrote it, studied it, compiled handbooks for poets and students of poetry. In keeping with the classical-Renaissance tradition that the poet, in the broadest sense of the term, is the noblest leader of men, Boccaccio asked that the epitaph on his tomb be *studium fuit alma poesis*—"his study was gracious poetry."

Boethius: Roman philosopher (*c.* A.D. 480–524). Anicius Manlius Severinus Boethius was a member of the highest Roman nobility and for many years a favorite of Theodoric, King of the Ostrogoths and ruler of Italy, A.D. 493–526. Toward the close of Theodoric's reign, however, Boethius became involved in a charge of treason and was put to death without a trial. While in prison awaiting execution, he wrote his best-known work, *The Consolation of Philosophy*, a dialogue in alternate prose and verse, in which Philosophy appears with the comforting reflection that happiness cannot be found in such transitory externals as the power and wealth Boethius has lost, but only in goodness, that is to say, in God. For God and true blessedness are one and the same. Boethius' *Consolation* was widely read throughout the *Middle Ages, it influenced *Dante profoundly, and it was translated into English by King Alfred (*c.* 800, Old English), by *Chaucer, and by Queen Elizabeth I. The other works of Boethius include translations from *Aristotle and commentaries on his works, and treatises on logic, geometry, and music.

Boiardo: see *Aristotle.

Boileau, Nicolas (called Despréaux): French poet and critic (1636–1711). The Golden Age of French classical literature (1660–85), also called the Age of Louis XIV, is generally associated with the splendor of Versailles and the names of *Molière, *Racine, and *La Fontaine— three friends of Boileau. It was an age characterized by rigid etiquette in society and a marked formalism in literary expression; and Boileau, the "Legislator of Parnassus," was the self-appointed codifier of its literary rules and practices. His wide reading, his own literary achievements, and his relationships with the principal poets of the period admirably equipped him for this task, and he carried it out in such a way as to raise the general literary taste of his age.

Before Boileau's time, the practice of French *Neo-Classicism had been largely worked out and its theory had been widely discussed, but all in a haphazard and fragmentary way. Boileau took it upon himself to define true, artistic literature in unequivocal terms; he established a hierarchy among authors and literary subjects; and he accomplished his purpose with an almost infallible discernment, with fearless courage, and in a style which no one since has dared to challenge.

Boileau's cult of common sense and of the sovereignty of reason in matters of taste endows his doctrine with an element of durability in time and space. It is this trait chiefly which he shares with the other great writers of his age. One might say that it is Descartes' rationalism applied to poetry. But it is also court etiquette. A stickler for order and regularity, Boileau disciplined poetry just as Louis XIV did society; he made class distinctions among literary works; he insisted that literary style be elegant. This stress on refinement at any cost makes

Boileau's doctrine more exact than tolerant, more discerning than profound. His limitations are obvious: he valued nature only when it wore the decorous garb of the formal garden; he clung stubbornly to classical mythology as the only proper theological system for poetry; he scorned as crude and barbarous all the literature, art, and civilization of the *Middle Ages; and he insisted that the Latin and Greek classics were the unique and eternal models for all literary endeavor. Yet in all these opinions he was merely reflecting the convictions of his age, with perhaps the added dogmatism that usually comes from flatly stating what has been hitherto tacitly assumed.

Boileau's literary life reached its climax with the publication of *The Art of Poetry* (*L'Art poétique*, 1674), and this poem on literary creation is a fine illustration of its own principles. He skillfully follows a Latin model, the *Ars poetica* of *Horace (and is himself later combined with Horace in the *Essay on Criticism* of Alexander *Pope). His earlier *Satires* had given him a high degree of technical competence, and in *L'Art poétique* he demonstrates the common sense, wit, and polish which he demands of the finest poetry.

Boileau wrote, in addition to the works already mentioned, a mock epic, *Le Lutrin* (1674–83), and various other works in verse and prose, but he remains essentially the poet of *L'Art poétique*, a work which put the official capstone on its age with such neatness that many of its judgments have remained as proverbial sayings for later ages.

Book of the Dead, The: an Egyptian religious work (*c.* 4250–*c.* 2000 B.C.). The book (a papyrus roll 90 feet long), whose exact title is *The Coming Forth by Day*, was intended to guide souls on their Journey to the Land of the Dead. A complete copy was placed in the tomb, or excerpts were inscribed on the mummy case. Magic incantations, prayers, and poems provide ethical instruction in right living. The soul is to exonerate itself by such statements as "I have not caused the slave to be ill-treated"; "I did not kill"; "I did not commit adultery"; "I did not steal." (There are many such parallels to the Ten Commandments and the Proverbs.) A persistent feature is lyric exultation in the experience of eternity ("my Form is Everlastingness"). The most famous section is the song of fervid praise to the Sun God, the *Hymn to Ra*.

Boswell, James: English biographer and diarist (1740–95). For a long time Boswell was remembered almost entirely as the writer of one of the world's greatest biographies, *The Life of Samuel Johnson, LL.D.* (1791), and a related travel sketch of a tour to the Hebrides with Johnson. In the last few years, however, a vast quantity of Boswell's personal papers have come to light, and their publication is revealing Boswell as an extraordinarily lively, entertaining, and penetrating diarist. These include Boswell's *London Journal* (1950), *Boswell in Holland* (1952), and *Boswell on the Grand Tour* (1955).

Brecht, Bertolt: German dramatist (1898–1956). The son of a factory manager, Brecht studied natural science and medicine at the University of Munich until he was drafted into the army in 1918. Experiencing the horrendous effects of war while serving as a medical orderly caused him to become a pacifist. In his two early plays, *Baal* (1922) and *Drums in the Night* (*Trommeln in der Nacht*, 1922), he adopted a nihilistic philosophy which he combined with a demand for radical change. In collaboration with Kurt Weill, Brecht modernized John Gay's 1728 comedy, *The Beggar's Opera*, to produce *The Threepenny Opera* (*Die Dreigroschenoper*, 1928), an exposé of the hypocrisy of society interested in money and power.

Because his Marxist beliefs were becoming more and more evident in his plays, Brecht was forced into exile when the Nazis came into power. From 1933 to 1948 he lived in the Scandinavian countries and in the United States. It was during this time that his most significant works were written. Continuing to rail against the evils of society, he condemned religious intolerance in *Galileo* (*Leben des Galilei*, 1939), capitalism in *Herr Puntila and*

His Servant Matti (*Herr Puntila und sein Knecht Matti*, 1941), and the miseries and stupidities perpetrated by war in *Mother Courage and Her Children* (*Mutter Courage und ihre Kinder*, 1939).

Brecht's "epic theater," through the use of unusual stage effects and lighting, sought to keep the audience from identifying with the characters and to appeal to reason rather than to the emotions. Even in his later plays, Brecht continued to experiment. He called *The Good Woman of Setzuan* (*Der gute Mensch von Sezuan*, 1940) a parable, but leaves it to the audience to discover the solution. His last major play, *The Caucasian Chalk Circle* (*Der kaukasische Kreidekreis*, 1945), a confrontation between good and evil, is based upon an old Chinese legend. After the war Brecht returned to Germany and directed the Berliner Ensemble in East Berlin.

Breton, André (1896–1966): see *surrealism.

Brontë, Charlotte: see Emily *Brontë.

Brontë, Emily (Jane): English novelist (1818–48). Brought up by an eccentric father and an old servant in a village on the Yorkshire moors, Emily Brontë and her two sisters and brother were early thrown on their own resources for entertainment. They read everything from the best English literature to dreary religious tracts; they took long walks on the moors (Emily was especially fond of this pastime); and they invented mythical lands which were the setting for many homemade volumes of manuscript tales.

Except for brief schooling and service as a governess, less than a year in study at a " 'smart' school for young misses" in Brussels where the 24-year-old Emily was unhappy and lonely, and an occasional trip after her books were published, Emily stayed close to her beloved moorland. She was proud and secretive; only by accident did Charlotte discover in 1845 that Emily had been writing poetry, even as she and Anne had been doing unknown to each other. Emily resented the invasion of her privacy but was persuaded to allow her poems to be published, together with her sisters', under pseudonyms, as *The Poems of Currer* [Charlotte], *Ellis* [Emily], and *Acton* [Anne] *Bell* [Brontë]. Only two copies were sold, and critical attention was scarce; Charlotte Brontë wrote frankly that only Emily's poems merited publication.

The neglect of their poetry did not destroy the young women's passion for writing. Each set about completing an already started novel. After numerous rejections by publishers, Charlotte's *Jane Eyre*, Emily's *Wuthering Heights*, and Anne's *Agnes Grey* all appeared in 1847. *Wuthering Heights*, attributed by one critic to a "man of uncommon talents, but dogged, brutal, and morose," shocked the Victorians, but it made its way slowly into critical favor. Charlotte staunchly defended her sister's book, "hewn in a wild workshop, with simple tools, out of homely materials." Though she and Anne continued writing novels, Emily wrote little more in the single year left her.

A Victorian critic attributed *Wuthering Heights* to a morbid or diseased mind; but *Swinburne ecstatically compared it to *King Lear*, and Lord David Cecil considers it the greatest Victorian novel. It is not without blemishes: the casual boxed-in narratives, sometimes boxes in boxes, and the implausible point of view, where the chief narrator, Nelly Dean, uses many prose styles, now talking like a peasant and now like Emily in her "literary" moments. But the narrative sweeps over structural flaws and gains immediacy. Superficially related to the *Gothic novel, it has little real violence. The supernatural is only an evanescent flavor in this story of doomed passions set against the gloomy background of the moors. Here, where people live hard, fierce lives, the marred, willful, tempestuous children—Heathcliff the foundling, and Catherine Earnshaw—grow up together, the loneliness heightening their need for each other. Heathcliff's vengeance over Edgar Linton who married Catherine, over Hindley Earnshaw who brutally tyrannized over him as a boy, and over Linton, his son by his abused, unloved wife Isabella Linton, make him one of the diabolic heroes of romantic fiction. But Emily Brontë understands him and does not leave him as a villain. His dying scenes, when his vengeance has been achieved and found empty and he still conjures up vainly the ghost of Cathy and then is buried in a grave next to hers, have real romantic power.

As in *Hardy's novels, the moors are there as background, sometimes, in Catherine's words, described with love, but generally somber and gloomy. From the very opening, when the mystery of the ill-kept house startles a visitor, down to the very close, when the questions have all been answered, *Wuthering Heights* exerts a hypnotic power. It is a wonder that a young woman of such meager experience could create such an individual masterpiece. For though Yorkshire speech and ways are accurately portrayed, Emily Brontë was not gregarious and mingled less with the folk than did Charlotte. But she was obviously one of those rare talents on whom, as Henry *James said, "nothing is lost."

Emily Brontë's sparse poetry has been highly praised, but like much romantic poetry, it is better in random lines and stanzas than in totals. Much of it deals with parting, loneliness, and death.

Brothers Karamazov, The: a novel by *Dostoevski. *The Brothers Karamazov*, completed a few months before its author's death in 1881, is regarded generally as Dostoevski's most penetrating and most *achieved* novel, although critics hold in higher regard his other masterpieces, notably *Crime and Punishment*, *The Idiot*, and *The Possessed*. Like so many of Dostoevski's books, this novel is the story of a crime. Some say its substance may go back to the death of his own father, who was murdered on his small estate by a group of serfs. The murder in *The Brothers Karamazov* is, however, of quite another order: here it is a question of parricide.

Threaded through the novel is a main plot filled with as much suspense as the cleverest of modern thrillers; and this is surrounded by a wealth of incident and a series of subplots of great intricacy. But central to the work, as to all of Dostoevski's novels, are the questions of good and evil and of the necessity for suffering and avowal as the ultimate road to redemption. Indeed, one of the key episodes is Ivan Karamazov's account of the poem he would write called "The Legend of the Grand Inquisitor": The godless Spanish inquisitor is an individual who mistrusts his fellow men and seeks to keep the truth from them. Opposed to him is the figure of Christ, who trusts the soul of man and is prepared to give him the gift of freedom even if this means suffering and destruction.

Old Karamazov is one of Dostoevski's characteristically salty characters, a greedy, sensual Falstaff of a man, twice married, first to a girl who ran away from him, then to a meek young orphan. Dmitry, the oldest son, is a typical Dostoevskian mixture of good and bad; undisciplined, lustful, he has an awareness of his own low qualities and rises above them at times to heights of religiosity and pity. Ivan, the second brother, has some of the qualities of Dostoevski's murderer-hero of *Crime and Punishment*: he is intelligent rather than feeling and he is caught up in the twisted labyrinth of his own mind. In Dostoevski's novels, such characters are always lost souls who must redeem themselves.

The third brother, Alyosha, is at the local monastery, dedicated to the life of the spirit. But the Karamazov strain militates against such a life, and he is as worldly as his brothers. The fourth son, Smerdyakov, is illegitimate, begotten on a half-wit in a fit of drunkenness. He is logical, calculating, monstrous in his evil nature, a kind of composite caricature of the other brothers. All the sons are involved with characteristic Dostoevskian women.

When Smerdyakov murders his father, all the circumstantial evidence points to Dmitry. And Ivan, who realizes that he has unintentionally provided the intellectual background for the murder, implicates himself as the inciter of the crime. His ultimate need for confession corresponds to Raskolnikov's. Before confessing he has had his debate with the "devil," who offers a long and subtle argument on behalf of the need for evil as a counterpoise to good. It is once again a Dostoevskian split personality confronting itself.

The novel has a rich background against which the study of the brothers and their lurid crime is carried out: peasants, merchants, a monastery, judges, lawyers—all are here, all sketched with the mature powers of the novelist. It is as though in his last novel Dostoevski was pulling together in a final endeavor the fundamentals of his belief: man can achieve salvation only through suffering and through Christ; life cannot be worked out by rule of intellect but only through feeling and love.

Browning, Elizabeth Barrett: see Robert *Browning.

Browning, Robert: English poet (1812–89). Robert and his wife, Elizabeth Barrett (1806–61), are among the most celebrated of literary lovers. When they eloped in 1846, her poetry was, in fact, better known than his; and for many years (especially after the publication of their famous letters) his reputation rested more on his rescuing her from her father's house in Wimpole Street than on his writing. She was already admired for two volumes of verse (1838, 1844). But her best work, *Sonnets from the Portuguese*, appeared in 1850 and recorded her love for her husband. It avoids her usual faults of diffuseness, sentimentality, and didacticism by the genuine passion of inspiration and the necessarily compressed form of the sonnet. On the other hand, *Aurora Leigh* (1857), a long blank-verse romance, suffers from many of these faults and from an excess of social comment produced by Mrs. Browning's conviction that literature should provide moral guidance. She is, nevertheless, usually considered the best English woman poet.

In his marriage, as in everything else, good fortune attended Robert Browning, and this fact may explain his robust optimism and his blindness to the tragedy of aspiration without fruition. Since his family was well-to-do and indulgent, he was given an excellent education in music and art as well as literature, encouraged to search for the ideal, and allowed to devote himself to writing.

Browning's greatness and his modernity lie in his ability to convey passionate intensity and psychological truth in his analyses of character. He focuses on the fortunes of a single mind as it reveals itself against the background of social life, especially the Italian *Renaissance, with which he was particularly well acquainted. This type of short character sketch presented through a dramatic speech, called a *dramatic monologue, was largely evolved by Browning and is the form used in his best-known poems: *My Last Duchess*, *The Bishop Orders His Tomb*, *Andrea del Sarto*, *Fra Lippo Lippi*, and *The Ring and the Book* (1868–69). This last poem is made up of a dozen dramatic monologues woven together to interpret the same events from the differing points of view of the actors, judges, and spectators in an Italian murder. The bare facts of the story, which was an actual court case and can be told in five minutes, became, with Browning's examination of motives and impressions, one of the longest poems in the language; but Browning's special technique created memorable characters and re-created the epoch.

Browning rebelled against Victorian "moral" didactic verse and against imagery used only for decoration and elaboration. He treated even his presumably "bad" characters, like Fra Lippo Lippi, without moral condemnation, with ironic sympathy. Like *Donne, Browning in his own day was not understood and was considered obscure; and, like Donne, he is now recognized as far more original in spirit and technique than his contemporaries. Part of Browning's reputed obscurity comes from the range of his allusions; part comes from his originality in the use of condensed phrasing, elliptical syntax, sudden jumps from thought to thought. These are not, however, eccentricities but a conscious technique calculated to show subtle associations, to secure psychological reality in depth and passionate intensity. This technique and its fruition are his significant contributions to poetry.

Bruno, Giordano: Italian Dominican friar (1548–1600). Bruno intuitively formulated certain ideas about the universe which have been scientifically confirmed by modern astrophysics. His treatise *Of the Infinite Universe and Worlds* (*De l'infinito universo e mondi*, 1584) suggests an infinite universe of interrelated forces which can be expressed only by mathematics. Bruno accepted that part of Copernicus' hypothesis which held that the sun, rather than the earth, is the center of our world. But Bruno argued further that the stars were themselves the suns of innumerable worlds extending into infinity. His religious philosophy was a mystical pantheism in which he concluded that God was a single unifying spirit manifest in numberless suns. For these theories he was excommunicated, imprisoned, and finally burned at the stake by the Inquisition. His philosophy influenced Edmund *Spenser's *Four Hymns*. Bruno is the "Nolan" alluded to throughout James *Joyce's *Finnegans Wake.*

Buddha: "The Enlightened One" (Sanskrit *budh*, "to know"), founder of Buddhism, one of the three great religions of the Orient (563–483 B.C.). Wholly devoted to the basic spiritual and ethical teachings of Hinduism, Buddha unintentionally founded a rival religion. Born Prince Siddhartha Gautama, he nevertheless speculated about the causes of poverty, disease, death, and renounced his luxurious life to become an ascetic. After six years of solitary meditation, he received the "enlightenment." This experience did not mark a complete break in his thinking. He continued to believe with the Hindus in an ultimate blessed state and the transmigration of souls, in reincarnations based on a cosmic law of retribution for past deeds. To Buddha, however, the blessed state was serenity of soul, a sense of re-absorption in universal life which he called Nirvana. This state was reached not through priests and rites, but through conduct. Men must avoid all extremes, rid themselves of futile desires for material prosperity and transitory pleasures. They must lead upright lives following the "Noble Eightfold Path" of righteousness in belief, aspiration, speech, action, life, effort, thought, and meditation.

Buddha, who was a humanitarian, disapproved of divisions into castes: "In whom there is truth and righteousness, he is blessed, he is a Brahman." He preached to all: "My doctrine makes no distinction between high and low, rich and poor; it is like the sky; it has room for all." Many of his moral ideals are like those of the Western world: Do not kill; do not steal; speak the truth; be not covetous; "give up lust, ill-will, delusion, wrath, pride, spite, . . . let a man overcome anger by love, evil by good, the greedy by liberality, the liar by truth."

Buddha left no manuscripts, his teachings being at first transmitted orally. About 250 B.C., King Asoka had them written down in Pali, a dialect of northern India. These scriptures are the *Tripitaka* ("Three Baskets") of wisdom: rules, teachings, elucidations of abstruse points. Buddha, who rejected the concept of a God requiring prayer, was ironically deified by his followers as an incarnation of the God Vishnu; statues of him have become shrines before which men pray, and his teachings formalized into a cult with the elaborate ritual which he decried. Today 140 million Buddhists live in the Far East.

Bunyan, John: see **Pilgrim's Progress*.

burlesque: a term applied to comic art, especially literary and dramatic, in which an attitude, style, or subject matter is made to appear ridiculous by ludicrous exaggeration or grotesque parody (from Italian *burla*, "mockery"). The work may ridicule the style and manner of other works by distorted imitation (mock-epic). Or it may treat trivial, frivolous material with mock dignity or treat lofty, serious subjects in a vulgar, slap-stick manner. In this sense, the essential characteristic of burlesque is the disparity between theme and treatment, and it is this disparity which is amusing. The reader's pleasure results from the recognition of the subject that is being ridiculed. Striking examples of the form are to be found in *Chaucer's *Sir Thopas* (*medieval romance), *Cervantes' *Don Quixote* (medieval romance), Paul Scarron's *Yirgile travesti* (contemporary French epics), Butler's *Hudibras* (1663–78, self-seeking hypocrisy of Presbyterians and Puritans), *The Rehearsal* (1672, heroic tragedy), *Pope's *The Rape of the Lock* (classical epic), John Gay's *The Beggar's Opera* (drama and conventional morality), Jane *Austen's *Northanger Abbey* (*Gothic novel), Gilbert and Sullivan, *Patience* (1881, burlesque of the attitudes of aestheticism).

Burns, Robert: Scottish poet (1759–96). A poor farmer who spent most of his life, as he himself said, in "an uphill gallop from the cradle to the grave," Burns for some years earned a meager living by combining with farming a post as government exciseman, but he was always in desperate poverty. A wide reader and brilliant conversationalist, he learned from his friends and the earlier Scottish poets hundreds of traditional ballads and songs. These he rewrote, transforming them by his energy, passion, and metrical skill into a new lyric art. And for tunes without suitable words he composed original lyrics. When he published his first collection of poems (1786), he became a literary sensation. "Rab the rhymer was now Caledonia's bard." He remains the most beloved poet of the Scots and the symbol of their national spirit.

His themes were necessarily limited by the meagerness of his experience and schooling (although he knew the English poets as well as the Scottish). Hence, he dealt, as he said, with the "sentiments and manners he felt and saw in himself and his rustic compeers around him." But this was not a disadvantage. It produced poetry which springs straight from life, "humanity caught in the act," with Burns in the center of it. Burns's "sentiments" are convivial and jovial, tender or satiric—and always intense, vivid, honest, and singable. The music of the words sticks in the memory. They are based on the elemental emotions and ideas—humanitarian equality and patriotism (*A Man's a Man for a' That*; *Scots Wha Hae*), friendship (*Auld Lang Syne*), the dignity of old age (*John Anderson, My Jo*), nature (*To a Mountain Daisy*), fantasy and humor (*Tam o' Shanter, To a Louse*), the grotesquely sordid (*The Jolly Beggars*), satire of hypocrisy (*Holy Willie's Prayer*)—and are especially about love, in the incomparably tender lyrics inspired by the many lasses with whom Burns was successively and genuinely smitten (*My Love Is Like a Red Red Rose, Ae Fond Kiss*).

Although he grew up in an age of *Neo-Classicism, Burns is one of the first great Romantics. His interest in folklore, his passion for freedom and respect for the dignity of the common man, his feeling for the world of

100

nature, and above all his faith in emotion as a higher guide than reason mark a new spirit.

In general, he used his own idiom of Lowland Scots, in which he wrote with great verve and abandon; but occasionally (as in *Flow Gently, Sweet Afton*) he used standard literary English.

In his employment of dialect he points the way to Thomas Moore and Walter *Scott. The artistry which conceals the art of these lyrics makes them seem indeed a "spark o' nature's fire."

Byron, George Noel Gordon, Lord: English poet (1788–1824). Byron has exerted the widest influence outside England of any English poet except *Shakespeare. This esteem was stimulated, especially in his own day, as much by his life as by his art. His "sable curls in wild profusion" swept back from a high brow above dark, liquid, brooding eyes; he was strikingly handsome in his loose open collar. Although he walked with a limp, he swam the Dardanelles (Hellespont), later composing witty verses about this and other exploits. Beautiful and aristocratic women pursued this aristocratic and artistic rebel. He had inherited a title and a seat in the House of Lords. His maiden speech was on behalf of factory workers. Proud and arrogant, with a low opinion of most men, he loved mankind, abhorred injustice, and died fighting the Turks to help the Greeks secure freedom. Byron was cynical and scornful of convention, yet capable of passion and remorse. Young, intrepid, moody— "man of loneliness and mystery . . . that dazzles, leads, yet chills the vulgar heart"—he became the hero of his own poems. The combination of man, myth, and poetic hero infected and affected a whole generation. The poetry, which reflects this personality, is sometimes tawdry, but more frequently powerful, brilliant, metrically superb.

The Byronic type, equally capable of rapture or cynicism, first appeared in *Childe Harold's Pilgrimage*, written (in *Spenserian stanzas) during a trip to Albania, Greece, and the Near East. The first two cantos of the poem appeared in 1812. "I awoke one morning," said Byron, "and found myself famous." He was the "curled darling" of society. A series of exotic, oriental romances (1813–14)—*The Giaour, The Bride of Abydos, The Corsair*, and *Lara*—took London by storm and drove out Sir Walter *Scott from the field of narrative verse. In the later cantos of *Childe Harold* (published in 1816 and 1818, after the scandal of Byron's separation from his wife had made him a social outcast in England), another trait of the Byronic hero came into prominence—a cosmic despair engendered by contempt for mankind. As in the first two cantos, the hero still meditates over the decaying monuments of human glory, but now he turns more and more to the companionship of nature, to forest, mountain, and sea. What Byron had said of *Rousseau was applicable to himself: "He who threw/ Enchantment over passion, and from woe/ Wrung overwhelming eloquence." For better or for worse, Byron made embittered disillusionment (or the pretence of it) and defiance of convention fashionable. He also wrote some exquisite lyrics (*Hebrew Melodies*, 1815) and two powerful dramas (*Manfred*, 1817, and *Cain*, 1822).

Popular and famous as he became for his narrative and travel poems, his real genius lay in verse satire, the type in which he had first seriously entered the lists. Byron's earliest book, *Hours of Idleness* (1807), had been severely castigated. The review, says Byron, "knocked me down but I got up again. Instead of bursting a blood vessel, I drank three bottles of claret and began an answer." The answer, the best verse satire since *Pope, was a brash and brilliant poem, *English Bards and Scotch Reviewers* (in *heroic couplets, 1809). Byron returned to this vein in *Beppo* (1817) and *The Vision of Judgment* (1822).

Byron's masterpiece is *Don Juan* (1818–21), an unfinished verse satire in *ottava rima. A *picaresque novel in verse, it is a potpourri of matters and styles, all things for all moods. "August conception of man and contemptuous of men." The hero is a libertine, who in Spanish legend ended by being dragged off, like *Marlowe's Dr. Faustus, to Hell. (Mozart's opera *Don Giovanni*, 1787, is a famous musical treatment of the theme.) Byron's Don Juan is not satanic, however, but is a victim of social corruption and embodies Byron's most serious

102

criticism of life. His character and adventures allow the poet much latitude—sharp satire and witty mockery, lyrical descriptions of love, hope, and pathos, the grandly heroic, the realistic and ironic. Burlesque imitations of classic myths and of ordinary conversations are used for comic effect with the greatest cunning. Time has confirmed *Goethe's opinion that the poem is a "work of boundless genius."

Byron has an assured place in world literature both as a personality and as a poet. He was one of the great emancipatory forces in 19th-century Europe. Cosmopolitan (not insular), critical of specific social abuses (not a visionary idealist like *Shelley), capable of bitter indignation and oratorical invective, he was the symbol of political and intellectual liberalism. If the myth was greater than the man, the poetry was worthy of the myth. It shows an amazing versatility and virtuosity—a combination of lyricism and passion, of narrative energy and speed, of love of beauty and biting irony. Byron was a superb metrist, with a genius for deft and comical rimes running into rimed polysyllables ("But—Oh! ye lords of ladies intellectual,/ Inform us truly, have they not henpecked you all?"). Melody, wit, and the most ingenious surprises move with the utmost ease through complicated stanzaic patterns. In a passage in his *Faust*, Goethe summed up Byron's contribution—"a sharp and penetrating view of the world . . . and a song entirely his own."

caduceus: a staff carried by the god *Hermes, or Mercury, having two serpents coiled about it and two wings near the top.

Caesar, Gaius Julius: Roman soldier and statesman (100–44 B.C.). Caesar was a member of one of the noblest families in ancient Rome. He entered public life at an early age on the side of the popular party and, after serving as quaestor, aedile, and praetor, was elected consul for 59 B.C. The next year he took office as governor of Gaul, to which Illyricum was added. From 58 B.C. to 50 B.C. Caesar conducted the series of campaigns described in the *Gallic War*, but although he thoroughly conquered the tribes living to the north of his province and invaded Germany and Britain, his policy was bitterly attacked in the senate, which was under the control of the aristocratic party. His growing military reputation also alienated Pompey, who repudiated his former friendship for Caesar and came forward as the military leader of the senatorial oligarchy. In 49 B.C. Caesar was ordered to lay down his command and return to Rome as a private citizen. To do so meant political suicide; he refused and led his armies into Italy. In the civil war that followed, Pompey lost his life, the power of the senate was broken, and Caesar became master of the Roman state. He undertook to reform its political and economic structure, but his efforts were cut short by assassination at the hands of Brutus, Cassius, and others on March 15, 44 B.C.

Caesar's orations and all but a few of his letters have perished, and his reputation as a writer depends chiefly on the *Gallic War (Commentarii de bello gallico)*, the most widely studied military handbook in literature and a model of clear, straightforward composition. His other extant work, the *Civil War*, was published posthumously in an unfinished state.

Calderón: Spanish dramatist (Pedro Calderón de la Barca, 1600–81). It has been said that Lope de *Vega epitomizes the genius of a nation and Calderón the genius of an age. As the literary successor to the prodigious Lope, Calderón resembled his master in producing a large body of material, achieving with it an eminence and popularity almost equal to that of the other great playwright.

Unlike Lope, Calderón had a relatively tranquil life. He too was soldier and priest as well as author, but in none of these activities does he display the exuberance that marked the other's career. Born in Madrid and educated at the Jesuit college there, he is reputed also to have studied law at Salamanca. His first poetic efforts were his entries (one of which won a third prize) in the literary competitions celebrating the beatification (1620) and canonization (1622) of St. Isadore the Laborer, the patron saint of Madrid. After the death of Lope, Calderón's reputation was such as to make him the foremost dramatist of the day. He enjoyed court patronage as well as popular approval: Philip IV made him first a knight of the order of Santiago and later honorary chaplain to the king. He had a happy, productive life, and in 1681—just 30 years after being ordained a priest—he died, "still singing," a contemporary recorded, "as they say of the swan."

From Lope, Calderón inherited the three-act *comedia* (not to be confused with the English "comedy," but a more loosely defined, purely Spanish type) and, from earlier dramatists, short religious plays called *autos*. On this inheritance he built his own drama, extending, refining, and endowing it with personal and contemporary characteristics. More philosophic and religious than his predecessor, Calderón wrote accordingly, and, if he is inferior in characterization to Lope, he is much more lyrical. (Calderón was "rediscovered" by the German romantics and was very much admired by *Shelley.) As products of their age, his plays—a great body of comedies, tragedies, and allegories—reflect 17th-century Spain in their sentiments of loyalty to king and church, in a chivalric concept of honor, and in a growing artificiality of style.

In his own day Calderón was especially renowned for his *autos*, dramatic representations of the mystery of the Eucharist. To modern readers he is best known for two secular plays, *Life Is a Dream* (*La vida es sueño*, 1635) and *The Prodigious Magician* (*El mágico prodigioso*, 1637). The second of these is based on the Faust theme: a philosopher is so tempted by desire for a beautiful Christian that he signs away his soul to gain her; but by her virtue he is converted, and they seek martyrdom together. *Life Is a Dream*, although it does not have many religious implications, has a characteristic serious or philosophic intent. It is the story of a prince who, because of a prophecy that he will subjugate his father and perform other evil deeds, has been kept a prisoner all his life, unaware of his real identity. To judge the validity of the warning and test his son's character, the king has him drugged and brought to court, where he awakens and behaves so wildly that he is returned to prison and persuaded that the interlude was merely a dream. When he is subsequently released by an uprising, he is confused about what is real, but he has learned through the earlier experience to control his passions, thus conquering himself rather than his father, who cedes him the crown. Underlying all, of course, is the theme that life itself may be a dream and death the awakening. An ingenious play, with interesting lyric passages, it is typical of its thoughtful, pious author.

Calvin, John: French Protestant theologian (1509–64), second only to *Luther in his influence as a religious reformer in the *Renaissance. Educated at the University of Paris and the law schools of Orléans and Bourges, Calvin was thoroughly trained in logic, law, and, in keeping with the *humanism of his time, Latin, Greek, and Hebrew. The logical form and legal cast of his thinking, the respect for Biblical text, and the Latin quality of his prose continued throughout his life to reflect this Renaissance education. The citation of almost 200 Latin and Greek authorities in his first published book (a commentary on *Cicero's *De clementia*) reveals the scholar-humanist.

By 1533 Calvin had come to accept many of Luther's ideas and was forced to flee from Paris. Two years later he fled from France to Basle, Switzerland. Here, in 1536, he published the *Institutes of Christian Religion (Institution de la religion chrétienne)*. Written originally in Latin, then expanded, and translated into French by Calvin (1541), the *Institutes* embodies the essence of Calvin's thought. In trenchant language, he attacks the Catholic clergy and defends the "reformers." This book, more than any other, was responsible for the spread of Protestantism to non-Lutheran countries; its remorseless logic was more persuasive than Luther's mystical fervor.

When, in 1541, Calvin was invited to Geneva to head the "reformed" Church, he was the acknowledged leader of the Protestant world. And, during a 20-year rule, he set the character of Swiss Protestantism—a rigorous, austere theology which subscribed even to the burning of heretics at the stake.

Although the essential ideas of Calvinism are derived from Luther, the emphasis shifts from man's faith to God's grace. Adam's fall resulted in Original Sin; man is totally depraved and can be saved only by the grace of God, not by faith or good works alone. And God has predestined those to be saved, the Elect. Clearly, however, God would choose neither a faithless man nor an immoral one. Thus, although an upright, believing life is no guarantee of salvation, its absence is a certain sign of damnation. Calvin believed that religion should enter into society as well as into individuals, that governments and social institutions are religiously responsible—in short, that politics and religion must mix. Calvinism insists on the Bible as the veritable word of God and the only authority in matters of belief and observance. A strict, literal interpretation of Biblical texts is the only guarantee of truth.

As a theologian, Calvin shaped the ideas of the Huguenots in France, the Puritans in England, and through them the early culture of America. His influence is particularly notable in *Milton, John Bunyan, and Jonathan *Edwards. In literature Calvin is important for having produced the first theological treatise in French prose (the *Institutes*) and for his mastery of French composition. The style is clear and precise, and, although the ideas are reinforced by numerous quotations, the form is compact. His prose aims for and achieves the forcefulness of oratory.

Calypso: a nymph who kept Odysseus a prisoner for eight years on her island, as he was returning from Troy to Ithaca. (See *Iliad* and *Odyssey*.)

Camoëns, Luís vaz de: Portuguese poet (Portuguese: Camões, 1524?–80). Most famous of Portuguese poets,

Camoëns is celebrated for his national epic, *The Lusiads* (*Os Lusíadas*, 1572). His life was peculiarly bound up with the subject of his poem, the Portuguese voyages to India, and his own experiences brought home to him how much the imperial glory of a nation depends on the devotion and heroism of individuals. But, except for his art, his life was apparently one continuous failure.

Few actual details of his life are known. He may have been born in Lisbon, probably in the year of the death of Vasco da Gama, his kinsman and the hero of his epic. He may have attended the University of Coimbra—it is certain that he knew both the Latin classics and such Italian *Renaissance poets as *Petrarch, Boiardo, and *Ariosto, and he seems to have been something of a poet in courtly circles. It may have been involvement in a love affair which sent him into the army, thence to Africa, where he was wounded and lost his right eye. He had been back again in Lisbon only a few years when, as a result of a street brawl, he was imprisoned; his sentence was commuted upon his agreeing to serve in the army in India (1553). "I set out," he wrote, "like one leaving this world for the next," for the trip to India was known to be fraught with peril. Of a fleet of four which set sail, only the ship bearing Luís arrived, and it too was wrecked on the return voyage. Finally, after 17 troubled years in India, Camoëns returned to Lisbon with the poem which traced the life of his nation through the life of a national hero from his own family. The poem was published in 1572 and won him a small pension from the king, but otherwise almost no recognition.

The Lusiads is the story of the sons of Lusus, mythical first settler in Portugal (Lusitania): "This is the story of heroes, who leaving their native Portugal behind them, opened a way to Ceylon." Although the title, opening lines, construction, and many devices were suggested by *Vergil's *Aeneid, Camoëns wished to exalt not one man but a nation of heroic men: "my theme is the daring and renown of the Portuguese." The narrative thread is the voyage to India (1497–98) of Vasco da Gama, the first man to reach India by way of the Cape of Good Hope. The story plunges *in medias res with the storm-tossed mariner da Gama already past the Cape on his voyage

108

up the east coast of Africa into the unknown to found a new empire. By flashbacks, prophecies, and a final worldview from a high mountain, where da Gama has been taken by his goddess-mistress, the history of Portugal at home and abroad is recorded. This conquest of the East represented to Camoëns more than a national victory; it meant the triumph, in addition, of the spiritual values of Europe and Christianity. By this interrelation of national history with geographic discoveries and the spread of religion, the story became epic in scope, greater in time and space than the life of one man.

Camoëns' greatness lies in his epic conception, which surveys life and God's design for the world, and in his fused attitudes—as a European, a Christian, a thinker, and a poet. To Camoëns the merchant adventurers were also crusaders, and he tried to probe the deeper meaning of their heroism and their faith. Discoveries had enlarged the frame in which man moved. The challenge to explain man's position in it was pressing. The Portuguese discoveries, as Camoëns saw them, were proof of God's design that the world should be united in one faith. Camoëns urged Europeans to enhance their spiritual strength by unity.

The greatness of *The Lusiads* thus lies in the development of the idea on many levels of meaning and also in the careful interrelations and the structure of the plot, in which the charming interludes and lyrics serve both to give variety and to reinforce the theme. The plot is enriched by four interludes carefully spaced in the ten cantos into which the poem is divided. The central one deals with the Cape of Good Hope (Canto 5): the giant Adamastor, the "Unconquerable," relates his punishment for his love of Thetis, his metamorphosis into the huge headland rock which symbolizes the stormy spirit of the Cape. The other three interludes tell of the tragic murder of Ines de Castro (Canto 3), the chivalric romance of the Twelve of England (Canto 6), and finally the Island of Love, a sensuous paradise where the mariners are mated with sea-nymphs, symbolizing Portuguese mastery over the ocean (Canto 9). There are also exquisite lyrical passages on courage, poetry, government, and the power of woman's beauty. These derive their music from the verse form, the eleven-syllable lines in *ottava rima. The story, moreover, for all its *baroque mixture of Olympian deities, medieval enchanters, and Christian saints, for all its unrealities, is based on the realities of voyaging which Camoëns had himself experienced. These elements are fused by his poetic vision, his realistic psychology of character and conduct, and by his sense of an ever-expanding "brave new world." (In addition to his epic, Camoëns' extant works include three plays and a large body of distinguished lyric poetry.)

Camus, Albert: French novelist, associated with *existentialism and the *absurd (1913–60). His career was brief, for he was killed in an "absurd" automobile accident in 1960 just two years after he received the Nobel prize. He first attracted attention with his novel *The Stranger* (*L'Étranger*, 1942), published when Camus was in the underground, editing a paper called *Combat*. His editorials, after the war, attracted attention and won him wide recognition. *The Stranger* remains his best-known work, although *The Plague* (*La Peste*, 1947) is also widely admired, as is his monologue-novel, *The Fall* (*La Chute*), of 1956. He was a brilliant polemicist, a skilled playwright known for his adaptation of *Dostoevski's *The Possessed* (1959) and *Faulkner's *Requiem for a Nun* (1957). His own plays include the dramas *Caligula* and *Cross Purpose*, both of 1944. His book *The Myth of Sisyphus* (*Le Mythe de Sisyphe*, 1942) illustrates man's existential state and argues the "absurdity" of an existence in which an individual never knows when the life he seeks to endow with meaning will be terminated. In denying the consolation and belief of religion, Camus, with other French writers of the war period, accepted life as wholly irrational; and *The Stranger* was written by him to prove the grim irony that a man might be executed for not crying at his mother's funeral. In reality his protagonist is condemned in the novel for shooting an Arab: but the jury sends him to the guillotine not for this so much as for the testimony of his unemotional state at his parent's funeral. Two earlier works, collections of essays published just before the war, dealt with Camus's experience of North Africa, where he was born and grew up. Camus was deeply influenced by the Nazi occupation of France during which Frenchmen were wholly subject to the arbitrary whims of the army of occupation, a highly "existential" situation. While his philosophical position continues to be debated, no one questions his art. His works—brief, tightly written, dramatic—show profound insight into the human problems of his subjects.

Candide: a philosophical tale by *Voltaire (1759). One month after *Candide, or Optimism* (*Candide, ou l'optimisme*) was published in Geneva, it was condemned by the City Council; shortly after, copies of the book were being read in Paris and in other European cities. When an accusing finger was pointed in the direction of Voltaire he mischievously defended himself by asserting that he had absolutely nothing to do with this "schoolboy trifling." The book saw 40 editions during the author's lifetime; it has since been translated into all the important languages of the world and has been called the greatest of short stories.

One of Voltaire's purposes is to parody the romances of adventure and the so-called philosophical novels which were in vogue at the time. To this end, he takes as his main hero the young man Candide, who, as his name indicates, gazes upon the world with eyes that are astonished, naïve, and shortsighted. His manners are polite, his judgment good, but he is very unsophisticated. Candide is raised in Germany in the castle of Thunder-ten-tronckh (the name is Voltaire's invention) in Westphalia, with Cunégonde, the baron's daughter. Because Candide was brought up under the tutelage of master Pangloss, a believer in the Leibnitzian philosophy that all is for the best in the best of all possible worlds, it would seem that the pupil's optimistic point of view should prepare him for a rather happy life. But Providence rules otherwise. Candide, because of an indiscretion with Cunégonde, whom he loves, is kicked out of the castle and compelled to enlist in the Bulgarian army. He deserts, flees to Holland, finds Pangloss in a deplorable state, and learns from him that all the inmates of the former best of all possible castles in Westphalia have been scattered to the four winds.

A Dutch Anabaptist takes Pangloss and Candide into his service and brings them to Lisbon, where they arrive in time to witness the famous earthquake and to be condemned by the tribunal of the Inquisition. Pangloss is hanged, but Candide is rescued by Cunégonde, who happens to be in Lisbon, too. He leaves with her for Buenos Aires, but only after killing a Jew and the Great Inquisitor, both of whom have tried to take Cunégonde away from him.

Arriving at his destination, Candide learns that the Inquisition is hot in pursuit. He then leaves Cunégonde and takes refuge among the Jesuits of Paraguay, who are waging war on Spain and Portugal. He kills a colonel-priest—none other than Cunégonde's brother—and escapes to the country of the man-eating Oreillons. Later he spends some time in the ideal kingdom of Eldorado, which he leaves only after acquiring great treasures.

Candide is ever on the move; we find him next in France, where he is threatened with imprisonment; in England, where he witnesses the shooting of Admiral Byng; then in Venice, a free state, where many dethroned kings have come together for the carnival. Finally Candide's wanderings take him to Constantinople; here he discovers to his great amazement Cunégonde (who has grown repulsively old and ugly), Pangloss (from whose neck the noose had slipped), and Cunégonde's brother (whom Candide had wounded but not killed). The long-lost friends settle down on a farm. Pangloss is still the inveterate optimist; but, after the old tutor has tried to prove rationally that all events are linked in his best of all possible worlds, Candide sums it all up in his famous words of advice: " 'Tis well said, but we must cultivate our garden."

Candide is, above all, a rollicking and caustic satire which deals a strong blow at the blissful optimism of the inveterate followers of Leibnitz. Voltaire had for a time leaned towards philosophical optimism, but his own experience at the hands of men and circumstances brought him to consider at close range the problem of evil in the world. Moreover, the concentrated reading that he had been doing in preparation for his exhaustive *Essay on Man-*

ners, as well as his personal observations, had provided him with a multitude of examples of the tyranny, fanaticism, and ignorance of man.

Voltaire believes that mere chance governs the world, except during rare epochs when a few great men impose their enlightened wills and cause civilization to flourish. What stupidity to call upon Providence at random, and to proclaim that "all is for the best," assuming that every effect has its adequate cause! Facts themselves and contemporary events provided Voltaire with fearful weapons. The Lisbon earthquake of 1755, for instance, was a hard fact that bitter-end optimists found difficult to reconcile with their theological pronouncements about a loving God. Questions such as the following remained unanswered: Why then must we suffer if God is just? What am I? Where am I? Whither am I going? How to explain my origin?

Since the earthquake there had occurred other events which grieved Voltaire and seemed to justify his conviction that everything in the world was amiss: the war was still going on; the French had been defeated at Rosbach; the British Admiral, Sir John Byng, was unjustly shot to satisfy public opinion; an attempt was made on the king's life; the *Encyclopedia* was suppressed; the Government, backed by the Church, intensified its campaign against the *philosophes*. Voltaire, disgusted with human stupidity and cruelty, had in mind one single objective: to make fun of man's aberrations and heap sarcasm on them.

Voltaire's peculiar type of pessimism requires some elucidation. He does not claim to be personally unhappy, nor does he accuse Providence of having been unkind to him. One must observe also that, if his judgment on the march of the universe is disillusioned, it is far from hopeless. It is true that he no longer believes in a beneficial Providence, yet he still has faith in true progress. Indeed, his opponents who proclaim that "all is for the best" are precisely those who would like to maintain humanity in the lamentable situation in which it is at the present, and always by invoking the most sacred causes. They are the enemies of philosophy, and this "all is for the best" is their only recourse.

Candide is the violent and impatient reaction of a philosopher who believed that progress was possible and immediately realizable, and who observed with bitter disillusion that the good cause was still far from being victorious. *Candide* is the ill-humored outburst of an Alceste (see *The *Misanthrope*) who has aged and who has taken the measure of the innate perverseness of men and yet not lost faith in the perfectibility of the human species.

The only positive advice in *Candide* is contained in the famous "but we must cultivate our garden." Voltaire has been criticized for not explaining the lesson of his diatribe at greater length; he has been accused of excessive sarcasm without the redeeming counterbalance of adequate moral teaching. Yet he might have ended on a completely hopeless note, instead of holding out, as he does, the possibility of remedying human stupidity by energetic action and hard work. Mental weariness, despair, and melancholy are romantic reactions which Voltaire never experienced himself, nor could he understand them in others. Inaction seemed absurd to him. When Voltaire gave *Candide* to the reading public, he was 65; from that time until his death in 1778 he strove with youthful ardor and disinterestedness to act, to work, to struggle against ignorance and tyranny, to build, to sow, to defend the cause of the oppressed and underprivileged.

Canterbury Tales, The: a group of stories, mostly in verse, written by *Chaucer in the closing years of the 14th century. This *frame-tale is Chaucer's most comprehensive and absorbing work, the product of his later years and fullest genius. The framework is established in the General Prologue: Chaucer meets some 29 or 30 folk at the Tabard Inn and joins them to make a pilgrimage to the popular shrine of Thomas à Becket in Canterbury Cathedral. At the suggestion of the innkeeper, the Host, who has made himself master of ceremonies, each pilgrim agrees to tell four stories, two on the way to Canterbury, two on the way home. The Host is to decide which is the best tale, and the travelers are to reward the winner with a banquet. Thus, Chaucer's scheme calls for 120 or 124 tales, but the plan was never carried out. Only 23 pilgrims have their turns; and all that survive are 20 complete tales, two incomplete (Squire's and Cook's), and two others deliberately left unfinished (Sir Thopas' and Monk's) when the narrators are silenced by the group. It is quite clear, furthermore, that Chaucer did not arrange or link the tales in any final order. Incomplete as it is, *The Canterbury Tales* is a splendid example of originality and poetic craftsmanship. Its greatness lies in Chaucer's ability to make his pilgrims creatures of flesh and blood; in the technical skill with which he integrated framework, characters, and tales (which are themselves masterly examples of versification and narrative art); in the scope of the materials; and in the genial humor and humanity that set the tone and make the poem a universal human comedy.

In the General Prologue, Chaucer first describes each pilgrim, later adding further details and characterization as the frame-tale develops. From the outset, Chaucer's originality and genius are apparent. A few graphic details and a pilgrim is created: the belligerent Miller, who can butt down a door and who has a wart on his nose from which grows a tuft of red hairs; the Cook, who suffers from an inflamed ulcer on his shin; the wispy-haired, thin-voiced Pardoner, who never had and never will have a beard; the Squire, whose locks "curled as if they had been set in a press"; the Clerk of Oxford, who would own 20 books of Aristotle rather than rich robes "and gladly would he learn and gladly teach"; the Wife of Bath, gap-toothed and big-hipped, an excellent weaver. So vivid and so lifelike are these people that their parallels in medieval *allegory (and there are many) seem inadequate to account for them. The Knight is more than Courtesy, the Pardoner more than Hypocrisy, despite the common details of their descriptions. Indeed, Chaucer's pilgrims are so real as to have sent scholars in search of 14th-century prototypes. There was, for example, a Tabard Inn in Southwark on the Thames opposite London, and a convent of Stratford-at-Bow, and a notorious Shipman whose vessel was the *Madeleine*.

Individual and universal as these pilgrims are, they are also representative in a social sense. And herein lies another facet of Chaucer's greatness. The device of the pilgrimage permitted Chaucer to bring together, without the limitations of ordinary rules of etiquette and precedence, representatives of the professional and social groups, all linked in a common purpose. So there appears before us a panorama rarely equalled, presenting in one way or another the whole range of intellectual and social interest of the age. The mind and manners of the courtly and worldly society are represented by the feudal knight; his son the Squire, who is a typical courtly lover; the Prioress, who tried to adopt the manner of the court. The religious world is represented by a nun, monk, friar, pardoner, parson, priests, and a scholarly clerk. The learned professions of law and medicine are here, as are the folk of the manor—its officials (Franklin and Reeve), its miller, and a peasant farmer. From the urban classes come a manciple, merchant, shipman, and guild craftsmen who have brought along their own cook. And along the road the company is unexpectedly overtaken by an alchemist and his assistant. Never before in English had so broad a canvas been attempted.

As their journey proceeds and we get to know them better, the pilgrims more than their tales engross us. For Chaucer uses the frame-tale in a new way. No longer merely introductory, formal, and mechanical, it keeps the pilgrims in continuous interaction and emotional tension. They engage in quick interchanges of repartee; they get drunk and insist on being heard (Cook and Miller); they quarrel and wish to confound a fellow traveler to whom they have taken a dislike (Friar and Summoner); they interrupt one another (Knight and Monk); they comment on one another's character (Reeve and Miller); they tell tales designed to bear a direct or oblique relation to another tale (the Clerk's tale is a reply to the militant feminism of the Wife of Bath); they recognize among the pilgrims, as the Pardoner thought he did, potential customers. This dynamic relationship provides a much tighter frame for the tales than would a merely formal plan. In the realism and irony of these links which precede, follow, and connect the tales and which are artistically integrated with them, in unwitting exhibitionism and self-revelation (Host, Wife of Bath, Pardoner, Canon's Yeoman), lies not only a further development of character but also an undeniable element of greatness and a major charm of the work.

The carefully devised framework, the role of the Host as master of ceremonies, and the position of Chaucer as observer and narrator are necessary to hold together the wide divergence of the tales themselves. For the range of the stories is as miscellaneous as the range of their tellers: chivalric romance (Knight's Tale) and a parody showing the decadence of the type (Sir Thopas); *lai (Franklin's); mock-heroic beast-fable (Nun's Priest's); *fabliau (Miller's, Reeve's, Shipman's); saint's life (Second Nun's), miracle of the Virgin (Prioress'), literary folk tale (Clerk's), sermon (Parson's), and *exemplum (Pardoner's). Each is an unsurpassed example of its type.

Although analogues, actual sources, and tales similar to Chaucer's have in some instances been found, Chaucer has in every case heightened the dramatic effects, deepened the philosophic and intellectual import, made the protagonists more complex and real, so that the imprint of his personality and style completely transforms even a well-known sequence of incidents. The subtle integration of teller and narrative enhances tale as well as character. And the tales, moreover, follow recurrent themes and motifs, one suggesting or provoking another. The famous Marriage Group (Wife of Bath's Tale, Clerk's, Franklin's, Manciple's, Merchant's) discusses the proper relationship between husband and wife. Within larger groups, smaller sections are unified by juxtaposition of tales and personalities. The Miller's fabliau suggests to both the Reeve and the Cook that they tell the same sort of story. The unsentimental Shipman's bawdy narrative of a shrewd, lewd monk is followed by the sentimental Prioress' pious account of the martyrdom and miracle of an innocent child. The candor and earthiness of the sexy Wife of Bath arouse some wishful thinking and hypocritical boasting from the effeminate Pardoner (described in the General Prologue as a "gelding or a mare"); and his companion, the unattractive pimply Summoner, quite as we might expect, irritates and repels the Friar.

The nature and relationships of the characters are pointed up by a masterly handling of all the devices of literary style. Not only are the tales suited to their tellers, but each moves in its own world, and everything—vocabulary, point of view, figures of speech, and general tone—is consistently handled in such a way as to create the illusion of that particular world. Thus Emily is the only important female character in the Knight's Tale, and Alison is the only one in the Miller's Tale, which immediately follows it. But the Knight's story is a romance of chivalry set in a legendary time, and the Miller's is a bawdy yarn about a contemporary Oxford carpenter and his wife. The descriptions of the two women help to establish this contrast. Emily is presented in vaguely standard poetic terms, but Alison is portrayed by concrete details and everyday comparisons which are appropriate both in the mouth of the Miller and in the world of his tale. Emily is fairer than the lily and fresher than May, and she sings "like an angel, heavenly"; but Alison is like a pear tree in bloom, her face is bright as a new-minted coin, and she sings "like a swallow sitting on a barn." She is also softer than the wool of a wether. There is no comparable statement about Emily, for the Knight will not allow his hearers to think of handling his heroine, but the Miller will not let them think of anything else. These few illustrations are enough to characterize the entire descriptions: Emily is a poetically idealized abstraction of womanhood in the tradition of the *medieval romance of chivalry, but Alison is a highly provocative physical object typical of the fabliau. The difference is that between a fair damsel and a likely wench.

Sometimes Chaucer complicates the simple and consistent presentation of his characters by adding levels of irony above it. In the Knight's Tale, for example, the absurdities of lovers in the tradition of the romance is pointed out at the same time that the tradition is followed. Chaucer manages all his skill of characterization and complexity of tone with a relaxed ease which lends the whole performance an air of unforced naturalness. His virtuosity extends to the mechanics of his verse, for he uses a variety of forms (some of which he introduced into English poetry) with the same casual skill. Even a technical stunt like the epilogue to the Clerk's Tale is so easily handled that many readers never realize what a difficult task of riming he has set for himself.

The strength of *The Canterbury Tales* rests on the power of this total artistic performance. Chaucer's social understanding and psychological realism should not make us read his work as a treatise on sociology or psychiatry. But his total meaning is part of his greatness, and his wit, humor, and tolerant humanity are a pervasive element of his originality. "The laughter [of the Canterbury Pilgrims] comes never to an end, and their talk goes on with the stars" (E. B. Browning). Chaucer's comic realism seems to imply that laughter is the best way to meet the irrational vices, the ridiculous follies of men. But he also strikes a more serious note: man's dignity and integrity are to be valued above all else. The Franklin's solution to the problems of marriage, for example, lies in mutual respect, love, and honesty, for truth is the highest thing a man can keep. Chaucer never forgets how fickle is the wheel of fortune, which may at any moment hurl a man down; and the Clerk points to the true import of his tale—man in the hand of God must learn to bear adversity like a man, with understanding and courage. The Nun's Priest's Tale, though on the surface merely a story of a cock and a fox, raises problems which agitated the 14th century and still concern us —free will and fate and man's personal responsibilities. On the corrupt and the corrupting, who yet have the wits to know better, Chaucer pours his deepest scorn; and the moral indignation which men should feel against the Pardoner and the Summoner Chaucer emphasizes by making these two hypocrites unmanly. The Knight, Parson, Ploughman (the three pilgrims whom Chaucer treats without even the remotest hints of satire) are the three self-disciplined and honorable characters who are consistently aware of their roles in the social good, who think in terms of their contribution to the "common profit." And from the old crone in the Wife of Bath's tale we hear Chaucer's eloquent statement of life's true standards: "Whoever in public or private strives always to do those virtuous deeds which he can, take him for the greatest gentleman. True gentility does not go with wealth or heritage. One is not a gentleman just because he is duke or earl; the villein's sinful deeds are what make him a churl. Gentle is he that does a gentle deed."

Carducci, Giosuè: Italian poet and critic (1835–1907). Carducci represents a classical reaction against decadent romanticism in literature and an anticlerical rationalism in general thought. As a professor of literature at the University of Bologna (1860–1904), he exemplified the historical method of criticism (as opposed to the aesthetic), stressing factual information rather than impressionistic interpretation. Yet he was a poet through and through, a poet who saw the Italian landscape not as "nature" in the romantic sense, but as a reminder and symbol of the past and future of Italy. After two volumes of tentative poetry, he published his notorious *Hymn to Satan* (*Inno a Satana*, 1865), in which, taking the extreme religionists at their word, he accepts progress, reason, and the joys of the world and the flesh as things of the Devil—and thanks their creator for them. He continues to demand a return to a pagan frankness and joy of life, a rejection of Christian mysticism and abnegation. These ideas are especially clear in his *Barbarous Odes* (*Odi barbari*, Vol. I, 1887), a collection inspired by "a vain desire for ancient beauty." These poems discard rime for the ancient classical meters, reproduced in modern Italian. His last volume of verse, *Rimes and Rhythms* (*Rime e ritmi*, 1899), includes other notable poems and experiments. Though Carducci's poetry was constantly under attack during his lifetime, practically all the attacks were directed at its content by people who held different political or religious views. Even his enemies admitted its excellence and power as poetry, and he is now generally considered the voice of Italy during the late 19th century.

Carlyle, Thomas: British historian and social critic (1795–1881). Carlyle was the scourging conscience of 19th-century England. A dour Scot, he lashed out at the foundations of British daily life—its materialism, profit motive, and competitiveness, its increasing mass rule through Parliament, its lack of appreciation of real heroes, its mechanization at the expense of the best in human nature, its formalism in religion. All were castigated by the "Sage of Chelsea." At the same time he insisted on the moral value of work and the importance of duty, on the need for a spiritual rebirth, not a mere tinkering with the machinery of government.

Carlyle attended the University of Edinburgh but soon concluded that a career in the Church was impossible for one with his individualistic religious views. A trial at teaching mathematics convinced him that he could not endure teaching. Then followed a period of writing hack articles. After he became familiar with the work of the German romantic and transcendental philosophers (Kant, Fichte, *Goethe) his mature thought began to take form. From 1826 to 1834, Carlyle wrote essays for the *Edinburgh Review*, including the famous *Essay on Burns* (1828). His masterpiece of this period was *Sartor Resartus* ("the tailor with a new suit of clothes," 1833). The book purports to be the autobiography (edited by Carlyle) of a philosopher whose German name means Godborn Devildung, Professor of Things in General at Don't Know Where University. Its style is at first baffling, and the suddenly varying moods of satire and preachment confusing. Carlyle could not believe in the world of the Deists—a "dead, steam-engine" universe— and "The Everlasting No" of the first part of *Sartor* is the spirit of negation which denies spiritual values to the universe and makes it wholly materialistic. "The Everlasting Yea" of the second part is the spiritual transcendentalism which Carlyle had found in the German philosophers. The American *Emerson, sympathetic to this view of the mystery of existence and the mystery beneath the facts of physical science and greatly impressed by the author, brought the work home and persuaded an American firm to publish it.

In 1834 the Carlyles moved to the Chelsea district of London. Here Carlyle found a coterie of admirers, including John Stuart Mill; and a change in fortune and reputation came with the publication of *The French Revolution* (1837).

Henceforth, history and biography were his major interests. He delivered and subsequently published a series of lectures *On Heroes and Hero-Worship* (1838–41), a collection of biographies ranging from Odin and *Mohammed to Napoleon. *Past and Present* (1843) includes a glorification of the simple life of a medieval monastery, by which Carlyle hoped to give the ideals of the past a new form and suggested that a natural aristocracy should govern the country. This attack on *laissez-faire* and parliamentary government offended economists, industrialists, politicians, and, in fact, all the middle-class English who were weeping over the poverty-stricken characters in *Dickens' novels. Then Carlyle published a fusion of history, biography, and political theory in *The Letters and Speeches of Oliver Cromwell* (1845), in the life of a hero of his own making, his disciple John Sterling (1851), and in a monumental six-volume *History of Frederick the Great* (1858–65).

For Carlyle the hero was a revelation of the infinite, literally an inspired seer able to perceive intuitively what God wants. In this philosophy, Christ himself becomes "the greatest of Heroes." In his chapter *The Hero as a Man of Letters*, Carlyle expresses the Victorian idea that the writer should provide the moral guidance formerly given by the priesthood. This belief in his prophetic role explains Carlyle's style, which was intended to persuade by its passionate exhortation and imperatives, not by analysis or logical argument. If the Hero as Writer succeeds by intuition, then he will not try to persuade by rational argument but by positive statements (even about highly debatable matters), statements charged with the "shock" images and the quick shifts of idiomatic speech.

carpe diem (Latin: "seize the day"): a phrase made memorable in *Horace's *Ode* I, xi, 8: "seize today; trust as little as possible to the future." To those who did not anticipate a life after death, the import of this phrase was that life in the present world should be made the most of and not wasted. The expression came to exemplify not only a serious idea but also a witty, amorous one—the spirit of "eat, drink, and be merry, for tomorrow we die." The theme was common in classical Latin

(*Ovid), in the *Goliardic verse of the *Middle Ages, in medieval Persian poetry (*Omar Khayyam), in French *Renaissance lyrics (*Ronsard). In English love poetry, especially of the 16th and 17th centuries, the beloved was urged to enjoy love while she still had youth and beauty. A variant is *carpe rosam*, "gather the rose," exemplified in Herrick's "Gather ye rosebuds while ye may,/Old Time is still a-flying."

Castiglione, Baldassare: Italian diplomat and courtier (1478–1529). Castiglione demonstrated in his own person that the ideal *Renaissance humanist-courtier whom he portrayed in *The Book of the Courtier* (*Il Libro del cortegiano*, 1528) could be a reality. Reared at the court of Duke Sforza of Milan, Castiglione studied the Greek, Latin, and Italian poets, music and painting, as well as horsemanship. His good looks and intelligence are memorialized in the painting by his friend Raphael which hangs in the Louvre. In 1504, Castiglione entered the service of the Duke of Urbino, whose palace, with its famous library, was the rendezvous of European scholars and artists. As a diplomat, he visited England, became advisor of Pope Leo X, and Papal Nuncio (1525) of Pope Clement VII to the court of the Holy Roman Emperor Charles V. When the Emperor's troops sacked Rome (1527), Castiglione was the subject of unfounded rumors of treason. He died shortly thereafter "I tell you," the Emperor declared to his courtiers, "that one of the finest gentlemen in the world is dead."

Although Castiglione wrote some insignificant Latin elegies, Italian sonnets, and a pastoral eclogue, his important work is *The Book of the Courtier*, the outgrowth of four magnificent years with the Urbinos—years of stirring associations with the humanists (see *humanism) who figure as speakers in the book. The manuscript, commenced in 1508, was circulating by 1516; but it was not printed until 1528 because of Castiglione's repeated revisions. Written in the style of *Cicero's *Orator*, the treatise is a prose dialogue. The discussions, which were widely imitated in 17th-century salons, are represented as having taken place in the Urbino palace in 1507 on four successive evenings (whence the division into four books). The speakers are actual, well-known humanists who conduct themselves in the give-and-take of conversation with characteristic sophistication and graciousness. Their discussions cover every aspect of the life of an ideal aristocratic gentleman—his appearance (handsome and graceful), his bearing (modest and urbane, avoiding affectation and ostentation), his pastimes (warfare and sports), his conversational and literary style (forceful, clear, and not pedantic), his intellectual attainments (classical and contemporary learning), his ethics (courage, honor, and tact, avoidance of the vices of ignorance and egotism), his culture (music, poetry, painting, and architecture). Nobility of birth is not essential in the courtier, for the "highest gifts of nature are found among the most obscure." The courtier's intelligence should be used in the service of the state, as soldier and political advisor to a prince who should know that "there cannot be a greater praise . . . than to call him a good governor." The courtier's instincts should be further inspired and refined by association with a lady of similar qualities.

Interpolated are discussions of other intellectual interests of the age: the problem of a pure Italian language, the nature of jests, the character of women (beasts or angels?), and finally an exposition by Cardinal Bembo of Platonic love. His peroration is so eloquent that at the conclusion he himself is in a trance. When roused by the reminder that such thoughts may make his "soul also to forsake the body," the Cardinal answers: "Madam, it should not be the first miracle that love has wrought in me."

The popularity of this "manual of gracious living" was immediate. In the 16th century alone there were 50 Italian editions, as well as translations into the principal languages of Europe, including Latin. The Italian text and an English translation (1561, by Sir Thomas Hoby) had a wide influence on Elizabethan England, and on Sir Philip Sidney, *Spenser, *Shakespeare, and *Milton.

The unique character of *The Book of the Courtier* lies in the realistic manner in which the conversations are manipulated and the differences of opinion introduced; in the skill with which monotony is avoided by anecdote and witty repartee; in the urbanity and pleasant dignity of the speakers, who exemplify the intelligence and taste of their ideal courtier. Above all, the standards of the *Courtier* voice the humanist's ultimate ideals—men and women of intellectual refinement, cultural grace, moral stability, spiritual insight, and social consciousness. It was the ideal of an aristocratic Renaissance society. Yet the principles set forth are for the most part still the standards of good behavior, and our quite different society would wholeheartedly agree with Castiglione that true worth is determined "by character and intellect rather than by birth."

Castor and Pollux: twin brothers worshiped by the Greeks and the Romans as the Dioscuri or Sons of *Zeus. They were regarded as patron divinities of sailors. Pollux' Greek name was Polydeuces. The pair is also known as Gemini, or the Twins.

catharsis: the purification and "purgation" of emotions by art. As used by *Aristotle in his *Poetics*, it connoted the emotional experience of a spectator of Greek tragedy, who, having his "pity and fear" aroused by the play, finally experienced a "catharsis," which purged him of these debilitating emotions and enabled him to face the real world with strength and courage.

Cather, Willa: American writer of fiction (1873–1947). Willa Cather's best-known novels catch and mirror the pioneer spirit of the frontier. In *O Pioneers!* (1913) and *My Antonia* (1918) she extols the heroic qualities of the men and women—first-generation Bohemians, Poles, Germans, Swedes, Russians—who broke the ground in Nebraska and had the vision to see the future of the new land. *One of Ours* (1922) and *A Lost Lady* (1923) mirror the way in which the second generation betrayed the hopes of the first and nostalgically mourn the passing of the earlier vigorous era. In *The Song of the Lark* (1915) and *The Professor's House* (1925), Willa Cather again extols the qualities of strength and endurance in the struggle with nature or in the effort to carve a successful career in contemporary midwestern and south-western America. In her later years she turned to the past to write of the French missionaries in the Southwest (*Death Comes for the Archbishop*, 1927) and the French in Quebec (*Shadows on the Rock*, 1931), again celebrating the pioneer spirit.

Although not a major novelist in scope and design, she had an artist's vision of the life she portrayed and was particularly successful in the shorter forms, such as the tales included in *Youth and the Bright Medusa* (1920) and the three novelettes of prairie life that make up *Obscure Destinies* (1932).

Her style is elegiac, her manner retrospective. Late in her career she elaborated a theory of the "unfurnished" novel, by which she sought to return her fiction to simple storytelling in revolt against the overloaded novels of British and American *naturalism. This was largely an effort to justify her own attempt to convey in her fiction a poetic mood, a nostalgic emotion, rather than to paint a social scene.

Catullus, Gaius Valerius: Roman lyric poet (*c.* 84–*c.* 54 B.C.). Catullus, the greatest of the Latin lyric poets, was born into a wealthy and distinguished family residing at Verona in northern Italy. Like many promising young men from the outlying areas, he was attracted by the excitement and glitter of the capital and came to Rome in his early twenties. Family friends introduced him to the most fashionable circles of society, and in that sophisticated atmosphere he met Clodia(called Lesbia in his poems), the wife of the consul Quintus Metellus Celer.

Clodia was an aristocrat, beautiful and intelligent, and Catullus fell overwhelmingly in love with her. But she had no real affection for him. She regarded their liaison merely as an amusing interlude, and, although intrigued by his adulation and flattered by his poetry, she was in no sense inclined to bestow herself on him alone. As Catullus began to suspect her infidelities, the rapture he expressed in his early poems became increasingly clouded with doubt; but, even after he knew her for what she really was, he still remained vacillating between love and hatred, unable for a long time to make the final, complete renunciation. Catullus traced the whole tragic story of this misplaced love in the *Poems to Lesbia*, a series of verses unsurpassed in literature for the expression of direct personal emotion. They are his best work and alone would assure him immortality.

But Catullus composed much else of the highest merit. Two poems connected with a year he spent in Asia on the staff of the governor of Bithynia are especially famous: the *Farewell*, addressed to his brother, whose grave near Troy he visited, and the *Sirmio*, written on returning to his villa in northern Italy. Catullus is noted for his wedding songs, his satires against *Caesar and others, and the long, scholarly compositions in which he imitated the Hellenistic Greeks. But all his work is excellent. Deep and true in his feelings, and strong in his expression of them, he ranks with *Sappho and *Shelley among the greatest lyric poets of the world.

Cellini, Benvenuto: Florentine goldsmith and sculptor (1500–71). Unrivaled for his miniature human figures, Cellini is equally celebrated as the author of an autobiography, "the nearest approach there is to a great Italian novel of life and character." Whereas Cellini's contemporary *Castiglione saw the *Renaissance from Olympian heights of aristocratic breeding and humanistic ideals and *Machiavelli moved closer behind the scenes of practical government, Cellini views aristocrats from the *atélier* of the artist working for them. And, because he traveled widely and met most of the famous people of his age (Michelangelo was his teacher), the autobiography gives remarkable insight into the manners of the times. It exposes the paradoxical character of the Renaissance by placing in unwitting juxtaposition tempestuous lawbreakers who were also sensitive artists and their distinguished patrons who shared their characteristics.

Cellini's life was a lurid series of brawls, plots, pardons, murders, accusations, escapes. By the time he was 15, he had been banished from Florence for his part in a duel. On a subsequent visit to the city he killed the murderer of his brother; nor was this the only murder he committed. Such turbulence would seem the very antithesis of the discipline and concentration needed for artistic creation; yet it was the miracle of the Renaissance—a miracle in which Cellini shared—that the vitality that led to such violence also led to great art.

A perennial vagabond, Cellini practiced his varied crafts in many cities, especially in Rome, Paris, and Florence. A beautiful vase which he made in Rome attracted the attention of Pope Clement VII, who gave him a boost on his way to success. He made a gold and enamel saltcellar for King Francis I of France, and designed a statue of *Perseus to stand in front of the ducal palace of Florence—and both are great achievements of Renaissance art. His description of the casting of the *Perseus* is one of the most dramatic episodes in his book, and it is still our best guide to the Renaissance techniques of casting bronze.

Characteristically, this technical chapter is imbedded in tales of ambition, quarrels, and chicanery, exaggerated by Cellini's unbounded conceit. Although his work was very highly regarded, he was always jealous of rival artists and, as he saw it, was ever the victim of envy. He was always seeking "revenge"—one of his favorite words. Cellini is always the hero, whether he is defending a great city (Sienna) by his engineering skill, or making a thrilling escape from a castle, or denying that he stole the Pope's jewels, or dragging a mistress by her hair, or fighting over a woman with a rival while "there was a glorious heaven of stars which shed good light to see by," or setting up his world-famous *Perseus*.

Perhaps what seem to be bragging lies are only inaccurate reminiscences, for Cellini turned 60 while he was dictating his biography to a young apprentice (1558–62), but his recollections are narrated with characteristic gusto. The vitality of his book was sufficiently appealing to lead to a translation by *Goethe and an opera by Berlioz.

Cellini, with his tremendous imagination, tremendous ambition, and tremendous energy, was arrogantly aware of his daring and of his ability. Yet he has left a uniformly interesting picture of his age. More than that, he revealed with all its paradoxes and all its strength a type of new Renaissance individualist.

Celtic Renaissance: see *Irish Literary Revival.

centaurs: a race of monsters prominent in Greek mythology, usually described as being half horses and half men.

Cerberus: a monstrous three-headed dog guarding the entrance to *Hades.

Ceres: see *Demeter.

Cervantes Saavedra, Miguel de: Spanish novelist, dramatist, and poet (1547–1616). As the son of a poor apothecary-surgeon, Cervantes spent his childhood here and there in Spain. After visiting Italy and service in a cardinal's household, he saw service in 1571 with the Spanish-Venetian-Papal fleet in one of history's decisive battles. At the Gulf of Lepanto, this fleet defeated the Ottoman Turks, who had hoped to destroy Christian power in the Mediterranean. Cervantes received three musket wounds, one of which made his left hand useless for life. On his way home after four more years of soldiering, he was captured by Turkish pirates and held in Algiers for ransom. His nearly successful escapes only sent him back to his cell in chains. When he was ransomed in 1580, Spain had all but forgotten the heroes of Lepanto. Through it all, luckless Cervantes was writing poetry. He believed that "two roads lead to wealth and glory, that of letters and that of arms." But at 33 he was no nearer to either goal than he had been at 22. While an illegitimate daughter, his wife, his mother, two sisters, and later a niece, all of whom he supported, waited hopefully, he settled down to a literary career. His verse was uninspired, his plays unsuccessful, and his pastoral romance *La Galatea* (1585) little more than another artificial pastoral romance. Burdened by debts, he took a job as commissary for the Invincible Spanish Armada (defeated the next year, 1588, off the coast of England). Cervantes ran into more trouble. A banker to whom he had entrusted government funds went bankrupt, and when deficits were found in Cervantes' accounts, he was jailed. Out at last, by 1603 he was writing *Don Quixote de la Mancha (El ingenioso hidalgo Don Quijote de la Mancha).* He was again briefly detained by the police in 1605, the year in which he published Part I of this work.

Before the appearance of Part II in 1615, Cervantes issued several minor works. The *Exemplary Novels (Novelas ejemplares,* 1613) are 12 short tales of romantic adventure set against a realistic background and offering various "examples" of behavior to avoid. The *Journey to Parnassus (Viaje del Parnaso,* 1614) is a satirical review of contemporary poets in *terza rima. Eight Plays and Eight New Interludes Never Acted* (1615) formed an undistinguished collection, although the *Interludes* are fast moving and realistic.

Although Cervantes passed his life during Spain's Golden Age, when its argosies were rich, its language spoken by the cultivated, and its literature known throughout Europe, he himself never knew prosperity. He died on April 23, 1616 (*Shakespeare had died ten days earlier). Of *Don Quixote,* Cervantes himself had said: "Children handle it, youngsters read it, grown men understand it, and old people applaud it. In short, it is universally so thumbed, so gleaned, so studied, and so known that if people but see a lean horse, they presently cry, 'there goes Rocinante!' " Although he died impoverished, Cervantes tasted the fame for which he thirsted.

chanson de geste: "song of (heroic) deeds," a French type of medieval narrative poem, intended to be sung or chanted and purporting to have some basis in French history. Similar to stories of *Arthur and his knights of the Table Round, the *chansons* describe a series of fabulous exploits, usually involving Charlemagne and his paladins, the Twelve Peers. The most famous *chanson de geste* is the *Song of Roland.* The poems vary in length from 1,800 to 18,000 lines, arranged in verse paragraphs called strophes or *laisses*, with *assonance of the final stressed vowel and only occasional rime. The lines themselves contain ten syllables, with a çaesural pause after the fourth syllable. The *chansons de geste*, of which some 80 are extant, were for the most part composed in the 12th century.

The historical events which the *chansons* purport to immortalize are treated with little regard for the facts; but the poems are unintentionally revelatory of the customs, manners, and attitudes of their day—the crusades and the infidel, feudal relationships and feudal loyalties. On the basis of these attitudes and other stylistic characteristics, the *chansons* may be conveniently divided into three groups. The earliest are stark and terse in style and deal in grim terms with the treacheries of the "paynim" (pagan) Saracen and with his conversion after many heroic battles, much bloodshed, and, often, the death of the hero. The heroes of this first group of *chansons* accept the feudal concatenation of society and quite unabashedly seek land and plunder in Palestine as avidly as the Holy Sepulcher. The second group of *chansons*, later, longer narratives, monotonously repetitious in plot, are concerned with civil war and with violent deeds of disloyalty and revenge among Charlemagne's retainers. These tales reflect the growing incompatibilities of the feudal system and the dissatisfaction of the knights with the increasing royal power. Embodying the special point of view of the barons, many of these poems represent Charlemagne as harsh, unreasonable, and splenetic. Into still later *chansons*, which may be said to constitute the third group, were introduced romantic elements such as foundling princes, giants, and fairies. These last longwinded and fantastic tales include a mass of adventures which bears no organic relation to the plot and are punctuated by outbursts of frenzied hate and equally passionate love between the protagonists—easily converted Saracen princesses and handsome, crusading Christian knights. It was these tales in the still more distended Spanish versions which *Cervantes had read; in *Don Quixote* he laughed them out of existence.

Chanson de Roland: see *Song of Roland*.

Charites: the Graces, three beautiful daughters of *Zeus, originally symbolizing the springtime, but later personifying loveliness and charm, and thought of as conferring grace and joy upon human beings: they were named Aglaia, "splendor," "bright"; Euphrosyne, "mirth"; Thalia, "the blooming one," "abundance."

Charybdis: a whirlpool in which no ship could survive, imagined to lie in a narrow channel opposite a monster called Scylla, who seized and destroyed sailors. *To pass between Scylla and Charybdis* therefore became a proverb. The water they infested was eventually identified with the Straits of Messina, which separate Italy and Sicily. A dangerous whirlpool is still active there.

Chateaubriand, François-René de: French writer (1768–1848). Chateaubriand spent his boyhood in the Breton peninsula in an environment permeated with Celtic myth and folklore. Then, during 1791–92, he traveled to America in hope of finding the elusive Northwest Passage. He returned with a ludicrous knowledge of American geography and an exaggerated tenderness for the American Indian.

Two romances, *Atala* (1801) and *René* (1805), in the tradition of *Rousseau's "Noble Savage," were the first published products of this trip. They are amusing to the modern reader for their extravagantly emotional style and the European drawing-room concept of the American wilderness and "noble red Indian." The Indian princess, Atala, is endowed with the sensitivities of the typical 18th-century heroine and, for good measure, with the fervor of an early Christian martyr. Yet the characters and the love passages in the forest have charm, and the story moves in the sweep of eternal passions and tremendous expanses. René, the hero of the next volume, suffers from the cultivation of insatiable desires; the natural scene is described with great color and echoes the passions of the hero. The third in this series, *The Natchez*, was published in 1826.

The Genius of Christianity (*Le Génie du christianisme, ou beautés de la religion chrétienne*, 1802), published just

132

as Napoleon was restoring Catholicism to France as the state religion, was a brilliant success. As a reward, Chateaubriand was appointed to the French legation at Rome. Later (1815) he won the gratitude of Louis XVIII by a defense of the Bourbon line and was rewarded by being named Minister of the Interior and, for short intervals, Ambassador to Rome, Berlin, London.

During the last of his life he dominated the *salons* as literary and social oracle. He also translated *Milton's *Paradise Lost* and prepared his autobiography, *Memoirs from Beyond the Tomb* (*Mémoires d'outre-tombe*, 1848–50), a work which makes better reading than his fiction. The volumes dwell on Chateaubriand's formative years, the dreams of adolescence, vivid sketches of important political and literary figures.

Chateaubriand owes his place in world literature to his influence on the romantic writers rather than to any literary masterpiece of his own. He led the *Romantic Movement toward Medievalism, the revival of Catholicism, sympathy with exotic nature, and a passionate preoccupation with the melancholy and melodramatic ego of a sentimental and intense hero. *Lamartine, *Hugo, and even *Flaubert were, in their earlier work, much influenced by this writer who poured out his melancholy soul on every beauty of nature.

Chatterton, Thomas: British poet (1752–70). Chatterton attributed his own poems to a nonexistent 15th-century poet-priest, Thomas Rowley. Although a product of genius, only one of the poems, *Elinoure and Juga* (1769), was published in Chatterton's lifetime. In poverty and despair, he committed suicide before reaching eighteen, having composed within some six years a witty satire (*Apostate's Will*, 1764), a history of painting in England, a burlesque drama (*The Revenge*, 1770—a London theatrical success), and a small body of fine poetry which he purported to have "discovered." The fraud was exposed by the celebrated Chaucer-Shakespeare scholar Thomas Tyrwhitt in 1777–78, who along with Horace Walpole had originally accepted the authenticity of the "Rowley" attribution.

Chaucer, Geoffrey: English poet (*c.* 1340–1400). Though *The *Canterbury Tales* and **Troilus and Criseyde* are the most widely known of Chaucer's poems, he also wrote four ambitious *dream-allegories (two of which were left unfinished), a considerable body of lyric poetry, translations of *Boethius and at least a part of the **Romance of the Rose*, and a technical scientific treatise on the use of the astrolabe in astronomical observations and computations. The volume and variety of his literary production are all the more remarkable when we remember that, though his poetry won royal favor and thus aided his career as a civil servant, it was never his primary occupation. His life was crowded with public business ranging all the way from soldiering in France and carrying out diplomatic missions in Italy to serving as a member of Parliament from Kent, as Controller of Customs of the Port of London, and as Clerk of the King's Works, in charge of docks, walls, bridges, sewers, etc., on the lower Thames.

The England in which Chaucer played his many roles was in transition between the *Middle Ages and the modern world. The feudal system still existed, but it was becoming increasingly easy for serfs to run away from the estates where they belonged and find employment in the cities, or, with the seller's market in labor created by the Black Death, to hire out as independent agricultural laborers. The king still exerted tremendous power, but the rise of the cities and of large-scale manufacturing and trade had created a wealthy and influential middle class of merchants and artisans who governed London. The royal court was not only a source of power and pageantry, but it was still an artistic and intellectual stimulus to the courtiers. And a number of complex causes, including the Hundred Years' War with France, were producing a national consciousness quite different from the earlier regional and personal loyalties. England was becoming a nation, and her citizens were proud of her.

Chaucer's father was one of the rising middle class, a prosperous wine merchant with modest connections at court. We know nothing of the poet's formal studies (if any), but we do know that at some time during the course of his life he acquired a good deal of knowledge of bookkeeping, civil law, philosophy, and astronomy, and learned to handle French, Italian, and Latin competently. In his teens he served as a page in the household of King Edward III's second son. Later he rose to the rank of Esquire in the royal household and received a stipend for life from the royal exchequer.

It is customary to divide Chaucer's literary production into three periods, according to the dominant influence under which he was writing: a French period (to 1372), an Italian period (1373–85), and an English period (1386–1400). This division is useful and essentially true if we remember that the periods are not so much successive as cumulative. *The Canterbury Tales*, for example, belongs to the English period and is dominated by the contemporary English scene, but it still owes a great deal to both French and Italian models.

Chaucer began his literary career under the influence of a medieval French literature which included satires, romances, *fabliaux, and such contemporary poets as Deschamps, Machaut, and Froissart. Under French influence he began his translation of the *Romance of the Rose*, and, more important, produced his first ambitious original poem, *The Book of the Duchess* (1369). This is an elegy on the death of Blanche, the wife of Chaucer's patron John of Gaunt, written in the form and manner of contemporary French poets, and with considerable borrowing from them. But already in this poem, as in the other dream-allegories that followed, there are distinctive marks of Chaucer's individual genius—the use of the setting to intensify the dreamlike mood of the poem, the sense of immediacy in the portrait of the bereaved knight, and the characteristic flashes of psychological insight. With remarkable originality and tact, Chaucer made himself merely a well-meaning but obtuse listener and put the praise of Blanche into the mouth of her husband.

In 1372–73 Chaucer went to Italy (probably for the first time) to arrange a commercial treaty with the Genoese. This journey, reinforced by another visit to Italy in 1378, had a tremendous effect on Chaucer. *Dante, dead for half a century, was already a classic, and *Petrarch and *Boccaccio were nearing the end of their literary careers. Not only did Chaucer draw heavily on the works of these men for the rest of his life, but they taught him to understand the importance of narrative structure and technique, to individualize his characters and give them dramatic intensity, and to seek the rhythms and idioms of popular speech. Thus the poems of Chaucer's Italian period show progress in his mastery of rhetoric, technique, style, and meter. *The House of Fame* (*c.* 1374–80), *The Parliament of Fowls* (*c.* 1377–86), and *The Legend of Good Women* (1380–86) are still dream-allegories containing many of the old familiar features of this French literary type, but Chaucer breaks with the conventional patterns by his broader range of ideas, his greater subtlety of characterization, and his attitude of humorous detachment. In *The House of Fame* the poet is carried by an eagle to the House of Fame, where he is to hear important tidings of love. The poem breaks off just as these tidings are about to be announced, but the ostensible purpose of the poem could hardly have been as rewarding as the comic characterization of the learned, vivacious, and somewhat pedantic eagle. *The Parliament of Fowls* tells how the birds assemble on St. Valentine's day to choose their mates, and the courtly and chivalrous eagles, platitudinous goose, common-sense duck, romantic dove, and jibing cuckoo are masterpieces of comic satire. *The Legend of Good Women* ("Legend of Cupid's Saints") has a remarkably fresh and original prologue telling how Chaucer came to write a set of accounts of women who—whatever their other failings—were faithful in love even unto death. Chaucer left it unfinished, and it is not hard to see why. It calls for too much repetition of what is essentially the same story, and the poet admits at one point that he is fed up with writing about these melancholy jilted females. The great masterpiece of Chaucer's Italian period, however, is *Troilus and Criseyde*, an amazingly rich and original work in spite of the fact that it is based on a narrative poem by Boccaccio and follows the well-worn conventions of *courtly love.

The great work of the English period is *The Canterbury Tales*, with its realistic setting in contemporary England. Here we immediately notice a difference from the other periods: the English influence is not a literary one, like the French and Italian, but is simply the influence of the breadth, scope, and zest of Chaucer's own land and age. The specific literary influences are still French, Italian, and Latin, but the setting is no longer in dreamworlds or in ancient Troy: it is on the road between London and Canterbury. Into this setting Chaucer could pour the whole wealth of his reading, his knowledge, his wide experience of men, and his humorous tolerance.

Even when following earlier writers, Chaucer was always an innovator. He introduced Italian literature to England. He was the first to use many of the meters and stanza forms which have become standard in English poetry. He was the first English poet to deal extensively with the contemporary scene, to draw sharply individualized portraits, to analyze his characters psychologically, to impress his readers as a personality in his own right. It is a tribute to him that since his death each age has admired him, but for different reasons ranging all the way from his satire on religious corruption to his humanism and his realism. Even at his funeral he made an innovation which established a new tradition, for he was buried in what has come to be "The Poets' Corner" of Westminster Abbey.

Chekhov, Anton Pavlovich: Russian dramatist and short-story writer (1860–1904). One of the most important writers to grow out of the conditions of prerevolutionary Russia was Anton Pavlovich Chekhov. His was a Russia of stagnant atmosphere where the poor suffered from severe want, the rich from idleness and boredom. Intellect and initiative were diverted into unproductive or, at best, official channels. Highly impressionable, Chekhov often complained of the stultifying effect of Russian life: "It is very monotonous and boring; one day is very much like another," he wrote at 44, shortly before his death. Perhaps his long and severe illness contributed to this general feeling of frustration. The tragedy of a life either not yet lived or already outlived emanates from Chekhov's plays and stories.

His ancestors having been serfs, Chekhov always felt

a sincere sympathy for the poor and oppressed, a feeling which was deepened by his contacts as a physician. He aimed at their betterment in his study of peasant life in the censuses he helped conduct and the projects he planned for them (*i.e.*, a people's palace in Moscow). To oppose oppression and to lead the way out of drabness into a more purposeful future was his main concern.

The writer Chekhov was most at home in short forms: the play and the stort story. The subtle power of his descriptions of prerevolutionary Russia is equalled only by *Dostoevski. Too human to perceive only one side of life, Chekhov never failed to see a bit of sunlight and delicate beauty in a tragic situation. Yet it is his simplicity in all its different manifestations which is most outstanding in Chekhov's art. Constantin Stanislavsky, director of the Art Theatre in Moscow, wrote of Chekhov's plays (in *My Life in Art*): "They are plays written on the simplest themes which in themselves are not interesting. But they are permeated by the eternal and he who feels this quality in them perceives that they are written for all eternity."

For his conciseness as a storyteller Chekhov has been compared to *Maupassant. Like the French story writer, he excels in brevity and emphasizes the small detail. The life depicted in his stories is insignificant as such; the general tone is drabness. Their humor is that of satire, their tragedy is one of failure. In their brilliantly drawn contours and their poignancy, Chekhov's stories perhaps outshine his plays.

The realism in Chekhov's plays has had the effect of simplifying plot to stress characterization, environment, and underlying social philosophy. Chekhov's plays thus mark the de-theatricalization of the stage through elevation of atmosphere above plot and transformation of the inner, seemingly passive battle with life into vital dramatic material. The language of these plays gives the flavor of real conversation through incoherence, desultoriness, and digression. This is again made possible by keeping the plot to a minimum.

By paying little attention to the development, climax, and denouement of the play, Chekhov achieved his famous "technique of understatement." He avoided the "big scene" and ignored the "heroic hero." In *The *Cherry Orchard* (1904), for instance, the scene in which Lopakhin buys the estate must be considered the climax, but his statement of the fact seems so incidental and is received so quietly that its effect is quite different from the usual climactic scene. The figure of the "unheroic hero" (who has many counterparts in modern world literature) first emerged in Chekhov's play *Ivanoff* (1889), in which man is portrayed as being oppressed—like the author himself—by the dullness and the commonplace qualities of life.

The best-known plays of Chekhov, besides *The Cherry Orchard*, are *The Sea-Gull* (1896), *Three Sisters* (1899), and *Uncle Vanya* (1902). They give the reader or spectator a glimpse of life, but there is no definite beginning or end to the action; it is veiled and unveiled suddenly, quietly, and undramatically, offering no judgment and no moral. The fleeting moment with its delicate interplay of light and shadow, the laughter that ends in a groan, the smile on the verge of tears—these are the emotional undercurrents that permeate his plays. Chekhov also reflects the social undercurrents of prerevolutionary Russia. In an atmosphere of hopelessness, he portrays an idle aristocratic class craving to lose itself in pleasure and work. Vershinin, in *Three Sisters*, who has never worked in his life, prophesies that "within another twenty-four or thirty years, everyone will work! Everyone!"

Although Chekhov's dramas are realistically concerned with the problems of society, criticizing it and pointing to its future, they are first and foremost artistic portrayals of life. His ability to create atmosphere and to delineate characters, and his realization of aspects of life seemingly insignificant but psychologically important, have made Chekhov the forerunner of modern playwrights like *O'Neill, William Saroyan, and Tennessee *Williams.

Cherry Orchard, The: a play by *Chekhov (1904). It was Chekhov's innermost conviction that "to judge between good and bad, between successful and unsuccessful, would need the eye of God." This statement explains why he did not portray his characters as they *should* be but as they really *are*. He did not judge them; he sympathized with them. In this great, yet subtle sympathy for his characters lies Chekhov's strength as a dramatist.

In the simple image of the cherry orchard, Chekhov found a symbol of a complicated problem—the social, economic, and general cultural change which Russia was beginning to undergo, the decay of one epoch and the rise of a new. This orchard undergoes the same fate as Russia: to the feudal landowning class of the old tradition, represented by Madame Ranevsky, the estates meant Russia—a land of private property, ruled and enjoyed only by its owners. Under this system the oppressed suffered—the serfs, the "owned souls" who seemed to look at Trophimof from every tree trunk in the cherry orchard. But the time had now come for Russia to throw off its yoke of partitioned ownership and to become an all-embracing, whole, and unified country. Peter Trophimof, the young intellectual idealist, tries to convince one of Madame Ranevsky's daughters that not just the cherry orchard but "all of Russia is our garden." The coming of such a change is exemplified in the action of the bourgeois Lopakhin, who takes the cherry orchard away from the parasitic landowning class to transform it into a piece of real estate, an act perhaps symbolic for all the estates. Madame Ranevsky and her household are just as reluctant and unhappy to hand over the cherry orchard to Lopakhin as the whole feudal class is unwilling to surrender its Russia to a new generation of which the self-made Lopakhin is in many respects typical.

In *The Cherry Orchard*, as in his short stories, Chekhov knit together the tragic and comic elements of life. For the representatives of the old tradition it is tragic to watch their once flourishing heritage disintegrate, whereas, to the members of the rising generation who can joyfully and idealistically look forward to a prosperous future, this stubborn clinging to ancient and worn-out ways seems somewhat ludicrous. A true note of tragedy is struck when the lonely, forgotten old serf, Firs, whose whole life had been dependent on his master and his

140

cherry orchard, lies down to die—the only thing left for him to do.

Chimaera: a fire-breathing monster, part lion, part goat, and part serpent, slain by the hero Bellerophon.

Chrétien de Troyes: French narrative poet (*fl. c.* 1170). Practically nothing is known of the life of Chrétien beyond the names of two of his patrons. Even without this information, his combination of the Arthurian legends with the *courtly-love tradition, his play with subtleties of feeling, and his general sophistication would mark him as a court poet. His known works were a *Tristan* (which has not survived); *Erec*; *Cligès*; *Lancelot, or The Knight of the Cart*; *Yvain, or The Knight of the Lion*; and an unfinished *Perceval, or the Grail*. Chrétien was primarily a skillful entertainer with no particular aptitude for the mystical elements of Arthurian legend. As one French critic comments, "Nothing troubles him: he explains everything, understands nothing, and makes the whole incomprehensible." Nevertheless, he had a tremendous reputation in his own time and was one of the direct sources of most later Arthurian writers—who were able to supply more than enough of the mysticism which Chrétien lacked.

Cicero, Marcus Tullius: Roman orator and statesman (106–43 B.C.). Cicero was born at Arpinum, a small town in the Volscan hills about 60 miles southeast of Rome. As a child he showed unusual promise; and his parents, who were middle-class people, took a house in the city so that he and his brother Quintus might receive the best education obtainable in Italy. After a long and difficult course in literature, philosophy, public speaking, and law, Cicero began to plead about 81 B.C., and although he interrupted his practice for advanced study in Greece, within little more than a decade he was considered the ablest Roman advocate, particularly when acting as counsel for the defense. Meanwhile he married a woman of noble birth named Terentia, who bore him two children, a daughter Tullia, to whom he was devoted, and a son Marcus, whose indolent and extravagant habits caused him much concern.

When he was 30 years of age, Cicero set out on a political career in which, after holding several offices with distinction, he was elected consul for 63 B.C. That year an aristocrat named Lucius Sergius Catilina, who had twice been defeated for the consulship, formed a conspiracy to overthrow the government by force. Cicero's good fortune in discovering the plot, and the energetic measures he took to suppress it, saved the Republic from civil war. But he erred in executing five of the conspirators without a trial before the people. Such a trial was the legal right of every Roman citizen, and Cicero's disregard of it was resented by a large section of the population.

In 60 B.C. Caesar, Pompey, and a wealthy banker named Crassus formed a coalition known as the First Triumvirate. They invited Cicero to join them, but their purpose was to destroy the power of the Senate, and his loyalty to that body made it impossible for him to accept. His refusal, however, exposed him to the malice of his enemies, who succeeded in having him exiled in 58 B.C., on the charge that he had put Roman citizens to death without a trial. Cicero was recalled the next year, acted as governor of Cilicia in 51 B.C., and, when civil war broke out between Caesar and Pompey two years later, joined Pompey's forces, although with misgivings. But this whole period in Cicero's life was marked by great frustration. Government as he knew it was breaking down, and he was beset with personal sorrow also. In 46 B.C. he divorced his wife Terentia, and the following year he lost his beloved Tullia.

Pompey was murdered in 48 B.C., and Caesar in 44 B.C. Cicero now hoped the Senate would regain its old supremacy. But it failed to reassert itself, and the Roman world was left divided between Antony, Caesar's colleague in his last consulship, and Octavian, afterward the Emperor Augustus, Caesar's adopted son and heir. While Antony and Octavian were still enemies, Cicero attacked Antony in a series of speeches called the *Philippics*, and this rashness cost him his life. For when Antony and Octavian composed their differences and joined Lepidus to form the Second Triumvirate in 43 B.C., Octavian, in return for certain concessions, sacrificed Cicero to Antony's hate. Cicero was killed by Antony's troops, and his head and right hand were nailed to the Rostra, or public platform, where he had been accustomed to speak against Antony.

If Cicero was unsuccessful as a statesman, he had few rivals as a man of letters. His extant speeches give ample proof of his supremacy in oratory. The *Catilinarian Orations* are probably the best, but others are almost as famous: the *Archias* for its praise of literature, the *Milo* for its perfection of form, the *Caelius* for the picture it gives of social corruption among the upper classes, and many more. The *Fourth Verrine* is a masterpiece in Cicero's early manner, and the *Second Philippic* is an excellent example of his later style. Cicero's treatises on rhetoric, among which the *De oratore (On the Orator)* is one of the most important, present a detailed account of the history and practice of public speaking at Rome. His philosophical essays reproduce much of the best Greek thought on ethics and politics in Latin. They are eclectic but lean toward *Stoicism, though Cicero professed himself a follower of the New Academy. The most frequently read are probably the *De amicitia (On Friendship)*, the *De senectute (On Old Age)*, and the famous *Somnium Scipionis (Dream of Scipio)*, preserved from the *Republic*, which exists only as a fragment. But the *De officiis (On Moral Duties)*, the *Tusculanae quaestiones (Tusculan Disputations)*, and the *De natura deorum (On the Nature of the Gods)* have and deserve a high reputation. Cicero's private letters are of immense historical and literary interest. They provide an intimate picture of men and events at one of the great crises in human history. They are composed in a free and easy style that became a model for all later letter writing. They are completely natural, revealing the writer in all his activities and moods, for it seems never to have occurred to him that they might be published. Cicero's letters are preserved in four collections, of which the most important are the *Ad Atticum*, edited by his closest friend Atticus, and the *Ad familiares*, probably edited by his secretary Tiro. The *Ad familiares (To Friends)* contains a number of letters addressed to Cicero by various correspondents. If these are counted—there are about 90 of them—the total number of letters is something over 900.

Cid, the: Spanish hero (*c.* 1040–99) whose legend has been widely treated in literature. Rodrigo (or Ruy) Díaz de Vivar was a daring figure who at one time or another fought on both sides in the wars between Christianity and Islam. "Cid" is a corruption of an Arabic word for "lord," and with the addition of a Spanish epithet meaning "fighter" Ruy Díaz soon became a hero under the name of El Cid Campeador. He is the subject of the best of the Spanish *chansons de geste, the Poema de mío Cid*, a poem of 3,730 lines written about 1140. An extensive ballad literature on the subject also developed, and the original unprincipled adventurer gradually became, in legend, not only a man of tremendous courage and daring, but a great champion of Christianity, a model of chivalry, and the very soul of honor. The *Cantar de Rodrigo* (*c.* 1400) is already decadent; it is a romance dealing with the Cid's marriage and has practically no historical basis or literary interest. The extensive ballads on the Cid were taken over, quoted, adapted, and put on the stage by the dramatists during the Spanish Golden Age. Lope de *Vega Carpio's *Las almenas de Toro* (*c.* 1612) deals with him, and Guillén de Castro's *Las mocedades del Cid* (*The Youthful Adventures of the Cid, c.* 1612) served as the immediate source of *Corneille's *Le Cid* (1636). Since Corneille's play, the hero has been known to all Europe and has become common literary property.

Circe: an enchantress who changed Odysseus' sailors into swine.

classical antiquity: the period of European history completely dominated by Greece and Rome. It extends from about 1000 B.C., when the history of Europe (as

144

distinguished from mere archaeological deductions) may be said to begin, to around A.D. 500, a convenient date falling almost exactly between the end of the Roman Empire in the West (A.D. 476) and the Emperor Justinian's suppression of the pagan schools of philosophy in the Eastern Empire (A.D. 529). By this reckoning, classical antiquity includes the first half of Occidental civilization.

A period including 1500 years and two different civilizations will obviously not be uniform or static. The Greece of Homer is not that of *Socrates, and the Greece of Socrates is not that of St. Paul. And none of these bears any close resemblance to the Rome of the legendary kings or the early Republic, or to the Roman Empire's early solidity and later deliquescence. In spite of this variety, however, the treatment of classical antiquity as a single unit is justified, especially from a literary point of view, for the literatures of both Greece and Rome during this period, varied though they are, tend strongly toward the characteristics and point of view known as *classicism.

Shortly before 2000 B.C. the Greeks came down from the north in two streams, one of which occupied the mainland of Greece and became fused with the people and civilization already there, while the other crossed the Dardanelles and settled on the shores of Asia Minor, probably as members of the Hittite Empire. The Trojan War (see *Troy Tale), during the 12th century B.C., was a conflict between these two branches of the same stock. At about the time that it was being fought, another wave of Greeks from the north arrived and settled in the southern part of Greece, largely in the Peloponnesus. Later developments aggravated the differences in values and character between these new invaders and the earlier groups, and the war between Athens and Sparta in the 5th century B.C. was the final result.

Greek literature (and consequently European literature) begins with the Homeric poems, the *Iliad and Odyssey, but only because they are the earliest works which have survived. All metrical, linguistic, and structural evidence indicates that these works have behind them a long tradition of epic and lyric poetry. Even if we had no other evidence, the fact that the minstrels

145

described in the *Odyssey* are all professionals would be conclusive on this point. Furthermore, we know the titles and subjects of a number of other epics composed at about the same time (*c.* 850 B.C.) which have not survived. The first period of Greek literature, then, is an epic period. If we had more detailed information, we would doubtless draw dividing lines between Homer and *Hesiod, whose work is essentially didactic rather than epic, and between Hesiod and the lyric poets Tyrtaeus, Archilochus, *Alcaeus, and *Sappho, for they clearly belong to different states of social and intellectual development, as do the early philosophers, who also wrote in verse. In the absence of such exact knowledge, however, it is customary to consider all these diverse writings as belonging to a first period of Greek literature extending from Homer to the defeat of the attempted Persian conquest of Greece in 480 B.C. During this period all forms of Greek poetry except *pastoral had their beginnings, and some reached their highest development. Though the Greek lyric continued on a high level for a thousand years more (see *Greek Anthology*), Sappho was never surpassed. After Homer, the epic ceased to be composed for some five centuries, though Homer's works continued to be recited and revered; and when epics were again written during the Alexandrian period (see *Apollonius of Rhodes) they were inferior to Homer and dependent on him. Tragedy and comedy were developed into established literary types well before the Persian War: tragedy became a regular part of the Athenian festival of *Dionysus in 534 B.C., and comedy was added in 486 B.C. Thus the early period laid the foundations on which the great achievements of later times were built.

During this first period the political organization of Greece had developed from the small kingdoms of the Homeric poems to the system of city-states. Each city, with its surrounding territory, was an independent unit— as long as it could keep its independence. The situation was approximately what one would find in one of the United States if each county were an independent power with its county seat for a capital and its own alliances, wars, conquests, and colonies. The city-states had various forms of government, ranging from democracy and direct (not representational) self-government, through various types of aristocracy and oligarchy to rule by a "tyrant"—an absolute ruler who might or might not be a tyrant in the modern sense of the word. A series of these rulers in the 6th century B.C. made a point of encouraging the artistic and intellectual activities of the citizens of Athens, and eventually an essentially democratic government evolved there. During the same century a sudden revolution made Sparta into a military police-state. Thereafter, Athens and Sparta gradually became not only the leaders of two different factions in Greece, but the prime representatives of two totally different philosophies of life.

Ironically enough, it was not the military state but the democracy which led the resistance to the Persian Empire's efforts to overrun Greece and which bore the brunt of the fighting at the decisive battles of Marathon and Salamis, though the Spartans did win undying glory in the heroic delaying action at Thermopylae. Athens' part in the Persian War put her in a strong position in Greece, and she was quick to take advantage of it by organizing a league for mutual defence with herself at its head. The next and greatest period of Greek literature, extending from the end of the Persian War in 480 B.C. to the death of Alexander the Great in 323 B.C., is so dominated by Athens that Greek literature and Athenian literature mean almost the same thing. During the early part of this period Athens rises in both power and brilliance and becomes the unquestioned intellectual and artistic capital of Greece. The high point of Greek civilization—and one of the climaxes of all civilization—was reached in Athens during the second half of the 5th century B.C. *Aeschylus was already dead by this time, but *Sophocles, *Euripides, and *Aristophanes were active in drama; Socrates was pursuing his philosophic mission; *Herodotus, *Thucydides, and *Xenophon were establishing both the discipline of history and the literary medium of artistic prose; and the great public buildings of Athens were setting new standards in architecture, sculpture, and painting. This great flowering of Athenian genius is frequently known as the Age of Pericles, from the man who, as chief general and chairman of the popular

147

assembly, was more or less the ruler of Athens from 461 to 429 B.C. The last years of the 5th century were clouded by the Peloponnesian War between Athens and Sparta which extended (with one period of uneasy truce) from 431 B.C. to the surrender of Athens in 404 B.C. But Sparta's triumph was of short duration. She lost to Thebes, and soon a general state of chaos followed—a state which made it both necessary and possible for an outsider, Philip of Macedon, to unify Greece under his power and pass it on to his son, Alexander the Great. In the absence of any rival, Athens kept the intellectual leadership during this period of decline and produced some outstanding figures, including the philosophers *Plato and *Aristotle and the orator *Demosthenes.

Alexander the Great had built up a great empire, and at his death it was divided among his generals. Ptolemy Soter acquired Egypt and established his capital at Alexandria, by the mouths of the Nile. He not only dominated the trade of the Mediterranean, but set out to dominate its culture as well. He invited all the outstanding scholars, writers, and philosophers of the age to his court, and he also founded the great Alexandrian library, which eventually grew to nearly three quarters of a million volumes. The Alexandrian Age is well named: because of the policy of Ptolemy Soter and his successors (plus the decline of the city-states of Greece following their inclusion in an empire), Alexandria was the center of Greek learning and literature until the sack of Corinth began the period of Roman domination in 146 B.C.

At the very beginning of this period Athens still had enough vitality to produce the comedies of *Menander, the philosophy of *Epicurus, and the *Stoicism of *Zeno, but these works were hardly more than an afterglow. The work written in Alexandria is a good illustration of what can and what cannot be produced by deliberate planning, grants-in-aid, excellent facilities—all the things that an ancient king or a modern foundation can do to encourage the arts. The scholars of Alexandria produced a quantity of scholarship, biographical research, textual criticism, and antiquarian studies. Not only is a great deal of our knowledge and understanding of earlier Greek literature due to their labors, but much

148

of the literature itself was preserved by their efforts, as in the case of poems and passages quoted in their critical works. Alexandria also encouraged creative work and can claim the credit for some fine minor talents like *Theocritus, *Theophrastus, and Apollonius of Rhodes. In general, however, poetry became an abstruse and learned game, and the scholars wrote their poetry for each other rather than for a general and interested public. There was plenty of creditable literary activity, but genius is not to be had for the asking, and the Alexandrian Age did not produce, in its nearly two centuries of effort, a single writer who can take his place with the half dozen or so outstanding ones produced during the 32 years of Periclean Athens.

The Roman period of Greek history extends from the sack of Corinth in 146 B.C. to the founding of Constantinople, A.D. 330. It continues many of the tendencies of the Alexandrian period, especially the dominance of scholarship over imaginative literature. Here we find the historians *Polybius and *Josephus, the geographers Strabo and Pausanius, the literary critic known as *Longinus, the philosophers Plotinus and Porphyry and the general movement of *Neo-Platonism which they founded. In imaginative literature we have the satirist *Lucian and, toward the end of the period, the striking development of the prose romance—an early forerunner of the novel (see *Longus). Over all these works of specialized or minor interest rise two productions in Greek which have, in different ways, exerted a great influence on subsequent civilization—the *New Testament* (see *Bible) and *Plutarch's *Parallel Lives*. These are the really enduring achievements of the Roman period.

With the founding of Constantinople, Greek became the official organ of one branch of Christianity. For a time the ancient faiths existed uneasily alongside the newcomer, and Julian the Apostate even abandoned Christianity and made a brief effort to restore paganism. But the vitality of the pagan world was gone, though its interest remained, and when Justinian closed the pagan schools of philosophy in A.D. 529 the act was more pointless than tyrannical. This act marks the complete extinction of classical antiquity, but it had really passed away some time before, and after the founding of Constantinople there is nothing of general interest in ancient Greek literature. The Byzantine period, which followed, lasted until the fall of Constantinople to the Turks in 1453, and we owe it a great debt for its preservation of classical Greek works and learning (see *Greek Anthology*), but it was an essentially different civilization and one which means far less to the Western World than that of classical Greece.

As we turn to Latin literature, we shall find that, in spite of some differences due to tone and national character, it bears a strong resemblance to the literature of Greece. This is no accident, but is a result of the simple fact that Latin literature was borrowed and imitated from the Greeks. The earliest Latin verse had its own system of meters based (like those of English) on accent, or syllabic stress, and this system survived in popular poetry at least until the time of Julius *Caesar, whose troops sang obscene songs in accentual meters. But all classical Latin poetry is in quantitative meters (based on long and short syllables) borrowed from the Greeks. The first work of Latin literature is a translation of the *Odyssey* made about 240 B.C. by a Greek slave. Epic, comedy, tragedy, lyric—all literary types written by the Romans, with the possible exception of satire, were modeled on Greek types and often on specific examples of these types. It is one of the paradoxes of literary history that the Romans were able to reach such a high standard of creation in what was essentially an alien medium.

Perhaps the greatest distinction between Greek and Roman literature is a difference of their audiences, and this difference seems to be a result of the Roman adoption of a foreign literary tradition. Before the Alexandrian Age, Greek literature was composed for the general public and was genuinely popular. The audience at an Athenian dramatic competition was much like that at a modern football game, and the man in the street could not only appreciate Sophocles and Euripides, but he knew them so well that he could be counted on to recognize quotations from their works and to appreciate satirical literary criticism when it was applied to them in Aristophanes' The *Frogs*. Roman literature, on the other hand, was always written by and for a small intellectual elite and seems to have excited little interest or esteem among the masses. As a result of this separation, literature was cut off from daily speech and tended to develop a different vocabulary and structure. This difference, slight at first, constantly widened until, in the *Middle Ages, classical literary Latin had developed, with only slight changes, into medieval Latin, but the everyday, or vulgar, Latin had become Old Italian, Old French, Provençal, etc., according to the particular local changes of speech.

The people of Italy represent a fusion of three principal stocks, with various minor ingredients. The earliest inhabitants of whom we have any direct knowledge were the Etruscans, and the early kings of Rome were Etruscan kings. Nothing is known of the ultimate source of the Etruscans, but their language was not a member of the great Indo-European family to which Sanskrit, Greek, Latin, German, Russian, Irish, and English belong, and their civilization showed considerable differences from that of the Latins and contributed largely to it. To the Etruscans were added the Latins and other related groups in central Italy, and Greeks from very early Greek settlements in Sicily and southern Italy. The legendary date for the founding of Rome, 753 B.C., agrees well enough with the archaeological and other evidence, but the date is about the only thing in the standard legend which is even approximately right. All educated Romans, including Vergil, were doubtless aware that the widespread legend, perpetuated in The *Aeneid, which derived Italian civilization from fugitive Trojans was merely a poetic fiction. Rome was at first ruled by a series of kings, but the last of these was expelled in 510 B.C., and a republic was set up. The history of the next few centuries is largely a matter of two developments: externally, Rome began to extend her power over Italy and beyond; and internally the embattled aristocracy gradually lost power to the plebeian masses. The span of Roman history from the beginnings up to 240 B.C. is often referred to as the preliterary period, for though there were a few rituals, folk songs, and chronicles (of which some fragments survive), they were crude efforts of no literary interest.

The period of early Latin literature is usually defined as from 240 B.C. to 70 B.C. It was during this time that literature began to be produced as a deliberate undertaking, that Greek influence became dominant (in Greece, literature was already far past its zenith), and that the split between literary and spoken language began. Of the various surviving plays and versified chronicles from this period, only the comedies of *Plautus and *Terence are of general interest today.

The Golden Age of Latin literature (70 B.C.–A.D. 14) falls into two clear and almost equal subdivisions. Before the accession of Augustus to power in 27 B.C., the preeminent figures were the philosophical poet *Lucretius, the lyric poet *Catullus, the orator and statesman *Cicero, and the military historian Julius Caesar, whose assassination in 44 B.C. is sometimes taken as the dividing line between the Ciceronian and *Augustan periods of Roman literature. The Augustan Age of Rome corresponds in a way with the Periclean Age of Athens as a brief period when, after an arduous climb, a civilization stood on a high peak before beginning a long descent. The Augustan writers Vergil, *Horace, *Ovid, and *Livy are not only pre-eminent literary artists but have exerted a continuous influence on human thought from their own time to the present. Other poets of the period include the elegiac poets Propertius and Tibullus, who continued the earlier lyric tradition of Catullus.

The period from the death of Augustus to about A.D. 180 is frequently called the Silver Age of Latin literature—a good description in that it implies a high standard of value, but not so high a standard as the preceding age. Here are found the philosopher and tragedian *Seneca, the novelists *Petronius and *Apuleius, the epic poets *Lucan and *Statius, the two *Plinys, the historian *Tacitus, and the satirists *Martial and *Juvenal. Excellent as much of the writing of the Silver Age is, the decline is already visible in that the writers have begun to lose their sense of equilibrium. Instead of achieving a perfect balance, they tend to exaggerate. Seneca's tragedies try too hard: they are too rhetorical, too sententious, and sometimes too clever to be impressive. The satirists can be devastating, but they are too violently and too constantly indignant, so that the reader sometimes turns against them, and they thus defeat their own purpose. They have lost the urbanity of Horace's satire. In much the same way, the epic poets are too rhetorical and too descriptive. Tacitus idealizes his barbarians to shame his Roman readers into better conduct: the end is perhaps admirable, but the means is again exaggeration.

The final stage of classical Latin literature extends approximately to the so-called fall of the Western Roman Empire, in A.D. 476. It is a period of decline in political organization, in territorial holdings and administration, and in power and prestige, as well as in intellectual achievement. The Empire crumbled away. The Roman legions were recalled from England. Barbarian hordes— Franks, Huns, Goths, Vandals—slashed off chunks of Roman territory and even invaded Rome itself. The last of the pagan Roman poets, Claudian (author of an interesting epic of *Pluto's rape of *Persephone), died about the year 408. What vitality literature had in these later days was largely due to the one new and living force in a dying civilization—Christianity. This manifested itself in two ways. Philosophers and theologians like *Boethius, Saint *Jerome, and Saint *Augustine, writing for purely philosophical and religious instruction, produced works of such power and sincerity that they became literary classics almost by accident. And a group of such Christian poets as Ausonius, Prudentius, and Sedulius began to use the traditions of classical poetry to celebrate Christian themes. It is significant, however, that we usually think of these groups as forerunners of medieval philosophy and hymnody rather than as the last representatives of classical antiquity.

It should be emphasized that the end of classical antiquity did not mean the end of literature in either Greek or Latin. Greek has an unbroken literary tradition from Homer to the present day, and the language has not changed nearly so much in 3000 years as English has in 1000. Latin was extensively used for both scholarly and literary works throughout the *Middle Ages and by men

153

like More (see *Utopia*) and *Erasmus during the *Renaissance. Thereafter its literary use became more of an elegant accomplishment than a serious pursuit, but as a language of learning it was used in Swiss and German universities within the last century.

classicism: a general literary style and point of view. The term originated with the application of the word *classical* to the literature of ancient Greece and Rome (see *classical antiquity) but soon extended its meaning to include any similar literary style or point of view whether in literature or art, philosophy or criticism. Thus we speak not only of the *Neo-Classicism of the 17th and 18th centuries, but of the classicism of A. E. *Housman's lyrics or of some of *Byron's early satire.

Classicism is usually opposed to romanticism (see *Romantic Movement) which is both a specific literary movement and a general manner of thinking and writing. The opposition and fluctuation between classicism and romanticism is found in music, painting, sculpture, architecture, and the dance, as well as in literature. In fact, one scholar goes so far as to summarize the entire history of all the arts—including women's fashions—as a regular swing of the pendulum between classicism and romanticism (Curt Sachs, *The Commonwealth of Art*); it is important to remember that characteristics overlap and are not mutually exclusive.

Since neither classicism nor romanticism is found in an absolutely pure state, any discussion of their characteristics will necessarily involve a certain amount of schematic oversimplification. With this warning, it can be said that classicism is social, formal, intellectual, logically organized, and static, whereas romanticism is individual, informal, emotional, and dynamic. (This description will lead most readers to consider romanticism much the more attractive of the two, simply because the last two centuries have been dominated by romanticism. Only a man who automatically prefers action to contemplation— who prefers running in circles to standing even in a good position—will automatically make *static* a term of condemnation and *dynamic* an expression of approval.)

154

Classicism is social in that its emphasis is on the qualities that men have in common rather than on their individual differences. Its characters are likely to be basic human types rather than unique eccentrics. *Addison's Sir Roger de Coverley could be found in every county of England, but *Dickens' Mr. Pickwick could exist only once—if at all. In the same way, the classical emphasis is on conformity to established social norms and subordination to the general good, whereas the typical romantic hero—as popularized by Byron, for example—is the rebel.

Conformity leads naturally to a certain amount of formality, to the acceptance of predetermined standards and patterns of conduct. In the arts this tendency is reflected in the careful workmanship, the polish, the accepted conventions of classical art, as opposed to the negligence of detail, the fragmentary state, and the constant experimentation of a good deal of romantic work. Classicism will accept conventions like the *unities in the theater, and the triumph of romantic drama is marked by the overthrow of these conventions. Similarly, English Neo-Classical poetry perfects and uses almost exclusively the *heroic couplet, but English romantic poetry has a bewildering variety of forms. Yet the innovative temper in form and subject matter must not be equated with artistic shoddiness; such "Romantic" poets, to take but three examples, as Byron, *Keats, and *Shelley, were meticulous craftsmen.

Whenever craftsmanship is valued, the workman must be fully conscious of every detail of his task and in complete control of it. It is this type of control which is meant by the intellectualism of classical art. Emotion is present and is valued, but it is always consciously controlled and kept subordinate to the writer's general purpose. With the romantic writer, the display of emotion may become the primary purpose, and the assumption may be that emotion which is uncontrolled must *consequently* be very strong and hence admirable. As far as the relationship between intellect and emotion is concerned, the danger of the classicist is that he may produce a piece of dead workmanship totally devoid of any genuine feeling or inspiration. The danger of the romanticist is that he may be led to mistake an uncontrolled fit of hysterics for a work of art. The famous *Wordsworth definition, "emotion recollected in tranquility," combines these two aspects.

The opposition between the static and the dynamic is most clearly seen in the visual arts. Classical Greek sculpture, for example, even when dealing with an action like the throwing of a discus, chooses a position which is balanced and can be maintained, thus producing an effect of repose even within action. The flowing lines of hanging draperies produce a similar effect. The romantic (including the newspaper sport-photographer) tries to catch a fleeting and necessarily impermanent instant—a discus-thrower just releasing the discus, or a hurdler in mid-air. Similarly, the classical writer is likely to be concerned with the permanent aspects of things, while the romantic tries to catch the transient aspect or mood. The *stream-of-consciousness technique, with its attempt to catch the fleeting impressions and half-formulated thoughts of an individual's mind, would have seemed a fantastically misplaced effort to a man like *Milton, who was bent on stating nothing less than *eternal* truths. In *Paradise Lost* Milton shows a magnificent organization and control of romantic elements.

The oversimplification in this contrast between classicism and romanticism lies in the fact that the qualities of both are necessarily present in every work of art, and the contrasts which have been stated as matters of choice are actually matters of emphasis. To take only one example, a character who is entirely a type, with no individual characteristics whatsoever, is incapable of arousing the slightest interest or sympathy, and hence the characters of Addison (who do arouse interest and sympathy) must have *some* individual traits. On the other hand, if Mr. Pickwick bore no resemblance to anyone the reader had ever known, he would not even be recognizable as a human being, much less a lovable and entertaining one. Nevertheless, the fact remains that the classical character is *primarily* a type and the romantic character is *primarily* an individual. In popular speech, *classic* describes a work which by common consent is recognized to be of

superior excellence; so, one may refer to *Melville's
Moby-Dick as a classic of American literature.

Clemens, Samuel L.: see *Mark Twain.

Clouds, The: a comedy of *Aristophanes produced in
the theater of Dionysus at Athens during the festival of
the City Dionysia in 423 B.C. Though popular with modern readers, *The Clouds* won only the third or lowest
prize, much to the annoyance of Aristophanes, who rewrote the drama in the version we possess.

A farmer named Strepsiades (or Twister), forced by
the Peloponnesian War to leave his farm and live in
Athens, is tormented into insomnia by the debts with
which his son Pheidippides has saddled him. As he lies
tossing on his bed, waiting for the dawn to come, a great
idea strikes him. He will prepare Pheidippides to de-
fraud his creditors, by sending him as a student to *Socrates' Thinking Shop. Socrates will train him so thoroughly
in argument that he will win every case he takes into the
courts, especially when justice is on the other side, for
it is Socrates' forte to teach his students how "to talk
unjustly—and prevail."

Filled with his new idea, Strepsiades wakes Pheidippides, but the boy stubbornly refuses to become one of
Socrates' students. He despises the philosopher and the
starvelings by whom he is surrounded, and, besides, he
is interested only in horse racing. His old father, therefore, is forced to go himself to the Thinking Shop, where
he finds the Master and his disciples investigating "things
beneath the earth" and "things in the heavens." After
a comic initiation into these scientific pursuits, Strepsiades is accepted as a student by the chorus of Clouds,
who, together with the Air, are the gods worshiped by
the philosopher and his dupes.

At this point the actors retire, and the chorus comes
forward to sing the *parabasis*, or address to the audience,
in which Aristophanes takes the judges to task for their
failure to appreciate the play at its first presentation.
When the song is finished and the actors return, Socrates
is ready to expel Strepsiades from the Thinking Shop.

In all his years of teaching, he has never seen a student so inept. Not only is the old man stupid and forgetful; he is willing to learn only "how one may speak and conquer, right or wrong," and he wishes to proceed at once to this rather advanced study without attention to prerequisites. As it is obvious that he will never learn anything, the chorus suggests that he send Pheidippides to school instead; and this time, somewhat contemptuously, Pheidippides consents.

The situation now undergoes a complete change. Pheidippides is an excellent student, and in an incredibly short time he is turned into an accomplished Sophist. But he shows one unexpected quirk of character—he will not use his learning to rout his father's creditors. Instead he quarrels with his father, whips him, and then proves to him by specious logic that he deserved the beating. When he proposes to beat his mother also, the old farmer recovers his common sense; he gathers his slaves around him and burns the Thinking Shop.

The most difficult problem in the interpretation of *The Clouds* is caused by the marked difference between *Plato's description of Socrates and Aristophanes' caricature. The discrepancy is generally explained by assuming that Aristophanes has attributed the physical speculations of certain other Greek philosophers to Socrates and that he has, at the same time, identified him with the Sophists, or professional teachers of the day, by giving him a school in which he offers instruction in public speaking for a fee. In this view, the comic Socrates is a composite figure. Like Anaxagoras, he is interested in natural phenomena. Like Protagoras, he makes the worse appear the better reason. Like Diogenes of Apollonia, he insists on the supremacy of Air and is therefore surrounded, in the play, with clouds. But he keeps his grotesque personal appearance and those eccentricities of conduct that made him a perfect butt for ridicule. He goes barefoot, he needs a haircut, and he lives in utter poverty.

The Clouds, then, may be understood as an attack, not on Socrates alone, but on the whole movement in Athenian education known as the New Learning. As the most eminent philosopher of the time, Socrates is cast in the leading role. But the caricature is not true to life, and Socrates repudiates it in the *Apology* of Plato. In defending himself before the jury, he assures them that he is neither a Sophist nor a physicist, though popular prejudice has long identified him with both, "as you have seen yourselves in the comedy of Aristophanes."

The plot of *The Clouds* is well developed, but the characters are mere puppets, and the chorus does little except to mark the passage of time. The tendency to minimize low comedy shows a distinct advance over the earlier plays, but at times the dialogue seems too intellectual, although the opening scenes in particular are brilliantly conceived. The effect of tragedy on the structure of *The Clouds* is interesting: the hero Strepsiades undergoes a mock tragic fall, with reversal and recognition, during the course of the action.

Cocytus: a river of *Hades.

Coleridge, Samuel Taylor: English poet and critic (1772–1834). In spite of Coleridge's substantial achievements and his important place in the English *Romantic Movement, his life can be viewed only as tragic in the light of his potentialities. A victim of lifelong neuralgia and of the opium prescribed to relieve his pain, he nevertheless spawned ideas like a herring, but rarely completed the "stately pleasure domes" which his imagination decreed. When in his early twenties he became friendly with the poet Robert Southey, Coleridge hit on a fantastic scheme for a utopia on the banks of the Susquehanna; their "Pantisocracy" ("all-equal rule"), as they called it, was a kind of Rousseauistic dream to "combine the innocence of the patriarchal age with the knowledge and genuine refinements of European culture." Since each member would require a wife, Coleridge suddenly found himself married to one of Southey's sisters-in-law—and a most unhappy marriage it proved to be. "Pantisocracy" was abandoned. To earn a living, Coleridge tried lecturing, writing articles, preaching as a Unitarian minister. He was a brilliant conversationalist *(Table Talk)*.

Then came the decisive meeting with *Wordsworth.

The two years of their close association led to the best work of both poets, and to this general period belong Coleridge's *France, an Ode, Kubla Khan*, and *The Ancient Mariner* (first printed in *Lyrical Ballads*, 1798). But by the end of 1798 Coleridge had composed nearly all the poetry on which his reputation rests. Then a long visit to Germany familiarized him with German idealism and he became the principal conduit through which this philosophy came to England.

Coleridge's life after he was 30 was an anti-climax, as he grew more and more dependent on opium and drink, although he was still able to produce a few fine poems *(Youth and Age)*. He was "an archangel," as *Lamb said, "a little damaged," still able to engross visitors, such as the Americans *Emerson and *Cooper, who made the pilgrimage to hear him. To a younger contemporary, *Shelley, "Coleridge is a cloud-circled meteor of the air, a hooded eagle among blinking owls."

As a philosopher, Coleridge tried to reconcile science, religion, and politics, anticipating a modern need, still unsolved. As a literary critic, he anticipated modern psychological criticism by stressing the concept of organic unity. His remarks on *Shakespeare, stressing the unity of his dramatic art, are still important. Coleridge presented his philosophy of poetry and a critique of Romantic ideals in life and art in what he acknowledged as an "immethodical miscellany," a literary autobiography *(Biographia Literaria*, 1817). Coleridge explains that, in his poetry dealing with the supernatural, he sought to give "a semblance of truth sufficient to procure for these shadows of imagination that willing suspension of disbelief for the moment which constitutes poetic faith." His greatness lies in his ability to do so.

Coleridge is best known for three poems, *The Ancient Mariner, Kubla Khan*, and *Christabel*. All three are in a field uniquely Coleridge's, a dream-territory arising out of the subconscious. All three evoke a mood magical and mysterious, in which the subtleties of rhythm and rime and the sophistication of symbolism create unforgettable poetic impact: "And close your eyes with holy dread, /For he on honey-dew hath fed/ And drunk the milk of Paradise."

The Ancient Mariner, the only long poem which Coleridge completed, is written in an adaptation of the ballad stanza and is memorable for its skillful unity, vivid phrases ("painted ship upon a painted ocean"), and "shadows of imagination" made real. For innumerable readers the emotional experience is so mysterious that they carry through life the dread of killing an albatross. *Kubla Khan* (1797; published 1816) emerged, as Coleridge himself tells us, from a vision seen in an opium dream. Subconsciously it fuses images and ideas from Coleridge's wide reading; his eye as he fell asleep had been on a passage in a travel book: "In Xamdu did Cublai Can build a stately Palace. . . ." All that Coleridge could remember of his dream vision (after he had been interrupted by "a person on business") was 54 lines about "A savage place! as holy and enchanted/As e'er beneath a waning moon was haunted/By woman wailing for her demon-lover!" *Christabel* (1797–1800; published 1816) is likewise a fragment of murky story and vague characters, but one which creates a unique effect of medieval atmosphere through suggestion, penetrating beyond the plane of appearance and sense to suggest the terror of a vague menace. The demoniac lamia Geraldine weaves her spell on victim and reader through hints, images, and the swing of an unusual meter (four accented and a variety of unaccented syllables in strongly alliterative verse, reminiscent of the Old English and medieval types).

comedy: a type of drama which aims primarily to amuse and which ends happily. The play presents the incongruous aspects of human speech, character, and conduct as they are displayed in social life. Comedy deals with the "ways of the world" and does not often come to grips with or provide solutions for profound moral issues; it is not primarily concerned with the basic problem of good and evil. Concerned with man's relation to society, it is willing to seek a solution in compromise and the best judgment of society rather than in immutable truths or one's own conscience.

To the Greeks, comedy meant drama that interspersed

beautiful lyrics with obscenity, slang, and broad verbal humor. As seen in *Aristophanes, comedy is also penetrating social satire. Hence, *Aristotle pointed out that psychologically there is only a very fine line of distinction between great comedy and great tragedy (*Molière's comedies, for example, verge on tragedy and do deal with basic social and ethical problems—religious hypocrisy and avarice).

To the Romans, comedy (exemplified by *Plautus and *Terence) meant a presentation of social types in a stylized intrigue of stratagems and conspiracy which ended happily.

In medieval times the word "comedy" was applied not only to plays but also to nondramatic literary compositions which had a happy ending and were written in the vernacular language. Hence, *Dante called his poem a *Comedy*.

*Renaissance European comedy often imitated Plautus and Terence, who had been revived by *Ariosto. For the Elizabethans, a play was a comedy if it ended happily for the chief characters, even though other elements might tend to be tragic. The Renaissance *comedy of humors, such as *Jonson's *Volpone*, stressed the idiosyncracies of characters who were for the most part unpleasant, whereas the native English tradition (exemplified by *Shakespeare's *As You Like It* and *The *Tempest*) was gayer, more romantic, less satiric. Yet great comedy always makes a serious point.

Molière's plays exerted a major influence on Restoration comedy and resemble the *comedy of manners in their accurate depiction of the social scene—a page from real life. Comedy of manners (as it appeared in *Congreve) and sentimental comedy flourished in England in the late 17th and 18th century.

In modern times, notable writers of comedy have been Oscar *Wilde, George Bernard *Shaw, and Sean *O'Casey. Philosophers have tried to explain the comic: Aristophanes (ugliness not great enough to cause pain); *Hobbes (observer's self-delight in not being in an inferior position); *Freud (release of suppressed sexual or aggressive impulses).

162

comedy of humors: a type of play based upon the "humor," or dominant trait, of the individual. In old theories of physiology, the humors were four liquids in the human system on which physical and mental health depended. If these liquids were not in proper proportion and any one was in excess, bodily health, moral character, and temperament were correspondingly affected. So excess of *blood* was thought to produce a *sanguine*, joyful, amorous disposition. Excess of *phlegm* created a *phlegmatic* disposition, dull, pale, cowardly. *Bile* (yellow bile or choler) made one *bilious* and irritable, impatient and obstinate. *Melancholy* (black bile) led one to be meditative and unenterprising (*Shakespeare's *Hamlet suffers from this "humour"). The term *humor* was gradually vulgarized to refer to any oddity of dress or manner, to any amusing eccentricity, or to any dominant trait (avarice, trickiness, jealousy, hatred of vice, etc.). This method of character analysis tends toward oversimplification and freakish or farcical characters. Because exaggeration is an element in the comic, characters suffering from an excess of one or another "humour" tended to appear comical; then the word "humour" itself came to mean "the comic." "Humorous" characters were popular on the Elizabethan stage (*e.g.*, Jacques in Shakespeare's *As You Like It*). The comedy of humors was best developed in the plays of Ben *Jonson.

comedy of manners: a type of play which satirizes the extremes of fashion and manners—the acquired follies—of a highly sophisticated society. Ridicule is directed at those who lack the polished urbanity admired by such an elegant society, and especially at those who vainly strive for it—the jealous husbands, the would-be wits or dandies or lovers. In this form of comedy, the plot (unrealistic, but clever and complex) is less important than the characters (who are seldom highly individualized); and both plot and characters are less important than the air of refined cynicism and the witty, scintillating dialogue. Men and women are on a par intellectually and socially and are equally unrestrained and sparkling in their repartee. Often, as in the comedy of the English Restoration, the characters are licentious and immoral, but this characteristic is not a necessary part of the comedy of manners. It merely occurs because society not infrequently combines a high sense of etiquette and decorum with a rather uninhibited moral code.

The essential attributes of the comedy of manners—intelligent and witty female characters, brilliant conversation, and perceptive social satire—are well exemplified in the comedies of *Molière, *Congreve, Sheridan, and *Wilde.

commedia dell' arte: a type of comedy developed in 16th-century Italy, whence it spread to the rest of Europe. None of the theories as to its origin is entirely satisfactory. The essential characteristic of the type is that it was based on a plot *(scenario)* outlined in advance, but the dialogue was improvised during performance. For this reason the emphasis was on complicated and absurd intrigues, and the characters were merely a group of stock types: the silly old man, the braggart soldier, the pedant, the lover, the various types of cunning servants, etc. It seems likely that each actor in a troupe regularly played the same character in all the different plots. The actors wore appropriate masks, and thus the audience immediately placed each character in his proper type.

Since a play is a literary work by virtue of its text and the *commedia dell' arte* had no fixed text, it is not, strictly speaking, a literary form. It did, however, exert a good deal of influence on literary comedy, especially in 17th-century France. ·

Confessions: the most widely read of St. *Augustine's works, usually described as his spiritual autobiography, composed some years after his conversion to the Catholic faith, perhaps between A.D. 397 and A.D. 401. The *Confessions* is addressed to God, being cast in the form of a prayer, in which Augustine praises God for the action of divine grace within him during the years of his spiritual wandering, while at the same time he laments the sins and follies that disfigured his life. Thus he not only acknowledges or *confesses* the greatness of God and His infinite goodness, but, by recalling the abyss from which he had been rescued, he edifies the reader and encourages him to seek his own redemption. Augustine first narrates his life from infancy to baptism, or rather to the death of his mother, St. Monica, and then describes himself as he was at the time of writing; after which he proceeds to comment on the opening chapters of Genesis. As he constructs the *Confessions* in this manner, it falls naturally into two parts, the autobiographical section consisting of Books I–X, and the section detailing the story of Creation which occupies Books XI–XIII. The two parts find essential unity, however, in the fact that both are devoted primarily to the praise of God.

The *Confessions* is one of the greatest books ever composed in Latin, famous not only for its deep religious fervor and its tumultuous emotions, but for its psychological insight and its vast descriptive powers. It contains some of the best-known scenes in literature: the scene in the garden at Milan, for example, when Augustine was converted, and the scene at Ostia on the Tiber, when he talked with his mother for the last time on earth. And some of its characters are familiar to people everywhere: Augustine himself, of course, and St. Monica, but Patricius also, Adeodatus and his mother, Alypius, Ambrose, and the African official Ponticianus, who told the story of the *Life of St. Anthony.*

Confucius (Latinized form of K'ung fu-tzü, "The Master K'ung"): Chinese philosopher and religious teacher (551–479 B.C.). Confucius was the author of the *Analects* and collector-editor of the six classics of Chinese literature: the *Books of History, Poetry, Music, Spring and Autumn Annals* (local history), *Changes* (a mystical system used for divination), and *Rites* (ritualistic teachings designed to inculcate filial piety and sanctify ancient traditions). Although Confucius achieved the office of chief magistrate and was worshiped after his death, he was and remains important as a teacher who felt, like *Socrates, that it was his mission to rescue the world from its misfortunes. During his lifetime his pupils numbered some three thousand.

Confucius' social philosophy affected Chinese ideals and government more deeply than that of any other man. Much concerned with social relationships, he held that "it is impossible to withdraw from the world and associate with birds and beasts that have no affinity with us." He taught that human society depends upon sincerity and piety in private and political conduct. Man's benevolence, intelligence, and justice must show in the five relationships of life: "parent and child, brother and brother, husband and wife, friend and friend, ruler and subject." He wished by his teaching and example to produce noble persons and devoted public men, who would inspire others and so produce the noble government whose only function, as he saw it, was to bring about the well-being of the people. He himself sought out willing rulers, just as *Plato went to Dionysus.

After his death his pupils honored his memory by collecting his aphorisms in the *Analects* ("collected fragments"). Originally entitled *Discourses and Dialogues*, the book is a disconnected compilation of the philosopher's conversations and pithy maxims. They emphasize rational thinking rather than dogma, regard men as essentially equal irrespective of rank, and stress the virtue of altruism. The volume has remained basic reading for Chinese scholars and has won devotees among such diverse Europeans as Leibnitz, Oliver Goldsmith, and *Voltaire. Confucius regarded himself as a transmitter of the best in Chinese culture, not as a prophet. He believed he was merely reviving the moral precepts of the ancient Chinese religion. Like *Buddha, however, he was elevated to a position where his sayings are revered as the dogma of a full-fledged religious system. Confucius has been canonized as the "co-assessor with the deities of Heaven and Earth," and regular sacrifices are made to his spirit.

Congreve, William: English dramatist (1670–1729). Congreve was the outstanding writer of Restoration comedy (1660–1700). His first play, *The Old Bachelor*

(1693), had an extraordinary success; and *The Double Dealer* (1693) and *Love for Love* (1695) established Congreve as a leading comic dramatist. Oddly enough, his greatest financial and popular success proved to be a stilted tragedy, *The Mourning Bride* (1697). Everyone has heard its opening line, "Music hath charms to soothe the savage breast," and another passage, "Heaven has no rage like love to hatred turned, / Nor Hell a fury like a woman scorned."

The next year Congreve was violently attacked by Jeremy Collier in *A Short View of the Immorality and Profaneness of the English Stage.* Unfortunately, Congreve's finest play, *The Way of the World*, appeared at just this time, and, whether Collier's denunciations or the growing taste for sentimentality worked against its success, it was unappreciated by the public. Congreve left the theater, virtually retiring from literary work at the age of 30.

With the income from three government sinecures, Congreve seems thereafter to have been content to play the role of a man of society. He was a friend of *Swift, *Pope, Gay, and Steele, a devotee of the celebrated actress Anne Bracegirdle, and the lover of Henrietta, Duchess of Marlborough. The tablet she erected to his memory in Westminster Abbey praises his "virtue, candor, and wit." His plays memorialize the same qualities.

The Way of the World is a brilliant example of the *comedy of manners. The central issue is the way of the world in matters of sex relationships. A series of heightened variations and parallels on the theme of love illustrate the problem—how real love can flourish in the sophisticated and shallow world of idle gallants and fashionable society ladies. The answer does not lie in an illicit affair (Mrs. Marwood and Fainall), or in a conventional marriage undertaken for money (Fainall) or to cover up a mistake (Mrs. Fainall). Congreve parodies both lust (Lady Wishfort) and romantic, sentimental courtship (Waitwell and Lady Wishfort). But from the first appearance of Millamant, "with her fan spread and streamers out" (Act II) to her famous bargaining scene with Mirabel (Act IV), Congreve shows that the dignity of personality, the poetry of love, and disciplined reasonableness can coexist. Although they keep their eyes on

Millamant's fortune, they do not let it distort their values. In struggling with themselves, each other, and the world, they rise above the ways of the world.

As the society here depicted is shrewd and scheming, the plot is a tangle of complex interrelationships. The conversations are, for the most part, like the plot and the characters, brilliant and artificial. The tensions of these people, expressed in witty repartee, show that they know the ways of the world and want the others to know that they know. The genuine values of Mirabel and Millamant add special piquancy to talk which otherwise would be purely glitter. Revealing both the ways of the world and of real love, the succession of rapid-fire retorts and sparkling epigrams constitutes the charm of the play.

Conrad, Joseph: novelist and short-story writer (born Teodor Jozef Konrad Korzeniowski; 1857–1924). Born of Polish parents in the Russian Ukraine, Conrad shipped aboard a French vessel in 1874 and thus began 20 years of seafaring life. Within the next dozen years, he learned English (in which he wrote all his literary works), won his certificate as a master seaman, and became a British citizen, sailing as the master of a ship in 1884. Ten years later he retired, and the next year (1895) published his first novel, *Almayer's Folly.* Then followed a long list of narratives, including *The Outcast of the Islands* (1896), *The Nigger of the "Narcissus"* (1898), *Lord Jim* (1900), *Youth* (1902), *Typhoon* (1903), *The Secret Agent* (1907), *Chance* (1913), *Victory* (1915), *The Arrow of Gold* (1919), and *The Rover* (1923), as well as various volumes of short stories and an autobiography (1912), published in England as *Some Reminiscences* and in America as *A Personal Record.*

Insofar as Conrad's stories reflect his melodramatic experiences at sea and his journeys in strange, out-of-the-way places, he appears romantic. Essentially his greatest skill lies in his capacity to evoke an atmosphere, whether of a typhoon at sea or of the sultry mystery of the jungle. And this he does by a treatment as careful and detailed as that of the realists.

Conrad's method of putting together materials from

the points of view of several persons gives a feeling of discontinuity, as does his use of story within story—the interminable digression. But this method, used to convey his sense of the inexplicable inner character of life and of the shifting quality of the mind, is akin to Impressionism in painting. The material is presented not by direct analysis but as it appears in momentary impressions. The artist's mood may be one of strangeness or apprehension and all the events are seen through this mood as his moment of vision reveals one facet of the real truth. A persistent part of that truth is man's inescapable loneliness. All Conrad's characters suffer from a sense of isolation, and their greatest need is for fellowship. Ironically, the understanding or opportunity comes too late.

Cooper, James Fenimore: American novelist (1789–1851). Cooper grew up in the new American republic, a young gentleman landowner, with every expectation of making a career in the navy or in a profession. Apparently by the merest chance, he turned instead to writing novels. He soon shared with Washington Irving the reputation of a major author both at home and in Europe, where in seven years of residence and travel (1826–33) he came to know Lafayette and many of the literary great of England and France. In spite of a long-continuing quarrel with his countrymen provoked by his social novels, which criticized coonskin democrats for their bad manners and equalitarian bumptiousness, Cooper achieved tremendous popularity with his best work—tales of the sea and forest frontiers, often set in Revolutionary times. His dialogue may be impossibly stilted and the logic of his action imperfect at times, as *Mark Twain charged. But in *The Last of the Mohicans* (1826), *The Prairie* (1827), and *The Deerslayer* (1841), to name the three best of the five Leatherstocking Tales, action is piled on action, suspense cumulates, and the frontiersman, Leatherstocking himself, in his role of scout, hunter, and trapper, moves the imagination deeply. Natty Bumppo or La Longue Carabine shares the virtues of Indians and whites, hates the ax and the settlements, fears God, and is pre-eminently self-reliant.

He is an almost mythical American figure, no more to be forgotten, as *Lowell concluded, than *Fielding's Parson Adams.

Corneille, Pierre: French writer of tragedies (1606–84). When 1636 brought to the stage Corneille's *The Cid*, it also ushered in the great Neo-Classical period of French drama, an age in French theater comparable in importance to the Elizabethan in English (see *Neo-Classicism). The 17th century in France was characterized in general by a veneration of order and restraint that had its political expression in the absolutism of Louis XIV's reign. In the theater this attitude was reflected in obedience to the rules of classical drama, with careful adherence to the three *unities. It was Corneille who helped re-establish this restriction and who emphasized the study of psychological crisis with its conflict of human values, thus becoming the first "modern" French playwright.

Corneille was a bourgeois lawyer from Rouen who had already gained a considerable reputation as a writer of comedies before he achieved the beginning of his real fame with the first of his tragedies, *The Cid*. Based on Spanish dramas about a national hero (see the *Cid), this is a typical Corneille play, with the theme of conflict between honor and love. Don Gomès, the father of the heroine, Chimène, has insulted and struck the father of her lover Rodrigue; and, as a point of honor, Rodrigue must vindicate his father even though this will mean the end of the romance. Don Gomès is killed and Rodrigue, no longer interested in life, leads a fighting group against the Moors and becomes a hero. Even so, Chimène, who still loves him, feels that her father's blood must be avenged; so Rodrigue fights a duel with her champion, Don Sanche, the victor to win the girl. The play ends happily with Rodrigue's triumph and the understanding that the two will be married after a suitable period of mourning.

The play was so enthusiastically received by its audience ("beautiful like *The Cid*" became a catchword) that jealous rivals sought to discredit it as "irregular" in terms

170

of classical rules. And it is true that, although Corneille was careful to have all the numerous events take place within the prescribed day, the vigor of the action negates the spirit of restriction. As he did his most significant writing in the first half of the century, before regulation became rigorous, Corneille's plays do bear traces of an earlier independence as well as the new classical spirit which he was to defend staunchly in his critical essays. But *The Cid* is still a powerful play—perhaps because of its transitional nature—and academic attacks did not discourage the public in its approval. Moreover, in spite of the controversy over it, the tragedy is, in many respects, very much a product of its age; its theme, that a principle like honor is superior to any personal emotion, is one that the century thoroughly endorsed.

After *The Cid*, Corneille's plays tend to conform more and more to the patterns which were being established. There is *Horace* (1640), presenting the problem of divided loyalties in time of war; *Cinna* (1640), treating self-conquest as the greatest and most difficult conquest that an emperor can achieve; *Polyeucte* (1643), dealing with the theme of Christian martyrdom; and *Le Menteur* (1644?), a comedy of Spanish source involving the predicaments of a young liar. Any one of these would serve to illustrate the Corneillean concept of life and drama: the concept of a life governed by a knowledge of what is right and a faith in free will; a dramatic theory that sought psychological truth, relying on historical subjects for authenticity and for a type of classical hero that approximated the 17th-century French noble. And all of these dramas, especially *The Cid*, provide numerous examples of a powerful dramatic verse, eloquent but precise.

Although Corneille was not to die until 1684, 40 years after *Le Menteur*, that play marks the end of his important production. For a period he withdrew to compose religious verse; when he again took up dramatic writing he found that another generation had come into power, an age which no longer found his plays to its taste but was acclaiming the polished work of *Racine. Impoverished and unhappy, he had outlived his early triumph.

courtly love: a code of love-making which flourished during the *Middle Ages in the literature of aristocratic, chivalric society and presumably reflects actual social conditions at the great feudal courts like those of Eleanor of Aquitaine and her daughter Marie de Champagne. The system derived ultimately from three principal sources: from the socio-economic environment of feudalism; from a literary tradition influenced by *Ovid, Arabic poetry in Spain, and the lyrics of Provençal *troubadours; and from Christianity, particularly the veneration of the Virgin Mary. As developed by the French poets of the 12th century (*e.g.*, in *Chrétien de Troyes' *The Knight of the Cart*, the love story of Lancelot and Guenevere), the chief tenets of courtly love were the devotion of the lover to the ideal of womanhood and his abject humility, complete loyalty, and veneration of his beloved. As Sir Kenneth Clarke has said: "Where there was marriage without love, it is not surprising to find love without marriage." The code required that the lovers must not be married to one another and therefore that the relationship must be secret. Their love was sensual, illicit, and adulterous. Yet it inspired the lover to selfless and noble deeds requiring the greatest courage and strength. (Nothing is said about its having a corresponding ennobling effect on the woman.) The rules were codified and explained by Andreas Capellanus in his *Art of Courtly Love* (1170). They are exemplified in the Arthurian romances, the lyrics of the troubadours and *minnesingers, in the *Romance of the Rose*, in *Chaucer's *Troilus and Criseyde.* When the concept of courtly love reached Italy, it was given spiritual and Platonic overtones (with adultery eliminated) by the school of *Dante writing in the "sweet new style." Through *Petrarch it reached the Elizabethans and the French writers of the *Pléiade. In this idealized form it remained an important literary conception of love well into the 19th century.

Crane, Stephen: American novelist, reporter, and short-story writer (1871–1900). Although he died at 29, Crane achieved perhaps the widest success of any of the early American *naturalists by his stark portrayal of the working of the environment on character. He won fame by writing *The Red Badge of Courage* (1895), a tale of the Civil War, although he had never seen a war, and was inspired mainly by his reading of history and of *Tolstoi. An earlier book, *Maggie: A Girl of the Streets* (1893), had not found a regular publisher because of its subject: it was privately printed by him, but rode into print again on the strength of his war novel. The war book had powerful appeal in its truthful picture of a young soldier who overcomes fear when faced with the terrors of battle, after an initial phase of cowardice. Having written the book without personal experience of battle, Crane found himself in demand as a war correspondent and was the first of the line of journalists involved in foreign wars, from Richard Harding Davis to *Hemingway, who made both newspaper copy and literature out of their adventures. He was in Cuba in 1896, and the sinking of a ship on which he sailed gave him the material for one of his great tales, "The Open Boat." He returned to Cuba for the Spanish-American War, and these sketches appeared posthumously as *Wounds in the Rain* (1900). He also went to the war between the Turks and the Greeks, with the woman with whom he lived thereafter in a common-law marriage, Cora Taylor. Crane returned from the wars exhausted and tubercular. Unable to live his unconventional life in the U.S., he went with Cora to England, where they took up residence in an Elizabethan manor house. Here Crane became the friend of such eminent writers as Henry *James and Joseph *Conrad and the young H. G. *Wells. He did not survive long. Cora rushed him to Germany for a cure, but it was too late, and he died there in 1900. His works were collected in 12 volumes in 1925.

Crime and Punishment: a novel by *Dostoevski (1866). In this psychological novel Dostoevski's interest in the multiple personality, the obscure and confused motivations of human action, is combined with his other chief theme—moral redemption through suffering.

The principal character, Raskolnikov, is a solitary, intellectual, and morose student who early in the story murders an old woman, a blood-sucking moneylender whose death is certainly no loss to society. He has already written a brilliant article contending that superior persons are above ordinary laws and moral standards, and he has convinced—or is trying to convince—himself that he is such a superior person. At the same time, he wants money for his education and argues that he will do society good with his victim's ill-gotten wealth. Furthermore, complications revealed in letters from home urge him to make himself independent of his family. The murder itself is as confused as its motives. Though it has been very carefully planned, it has been planned as a sort of daydream which Raskolnikov himself hardly believes in, and the plan is finally carried through on impulse, and almost mechanically, with a mixture of devious cunning and neurotic blundering. For example, he forgets to shut the door while he is searching the apartment, and his search is so panicky that he misses most of the money. The money and jewelry that he does get, he later hides without even counting or examining them. His character drives him to play a sort of game with the police, to excite their suspicions and then try to make fools of them; but eventually he runs into Porfiry, who looks for the solution in the evident psychology of the criminal rather than in the mechanical details associated with the crime; and Porfiry plays his own cat-and-mouse game of suspicions and hints confident that he has found the murderer and (since he has no proof that will stand up in court) that he can drive him sooner or later to confess or to overplay his hand and give himself away completely. On one level, then, the novel is a fascinating detective story which gains a great deal in tension and excitement by being told from the criminal's point of view, for the criminal always has more at stake than the detective.

Almost from the beginning, though, and long before Raskolnikov has any idea of what is taking place, the story is one of moral regeneration. It is only long after his confession that he is able to admit, as an intellectual proposition, the wrongness of his crime. The sources of his surrender lie far deeper than his logic, and are almost as confused as the motives of his crime. He is both disgusted with a life of perpetual lying, fear, and alertness, and exhausted by the effort of leading such a life. Before he is able to renounce his theory about superior men and common morality, it backfires on him with his realization that the very fact of his ineptness and worry prove that he himself is not such a superior person, for if crime really were trivial to a man of his stature, he would be able to regard it as trivial. Finally, the saintly prostitute Sonia, who knowingly leads an evil life in a desperate and genuine attempt to help others and who, by admitting its wrongness, does evil in a spirit of self-sacrifice rather than self-promotion, is an example who makes him realize the falsity of his pretensions at the same time that she gives him the human pity which he is too proud to accept from others. In fact, it is her faith in him that steels him for the final confession when he has almost abandoned his intention of making a clean breast of his crime.

Woven into the story of Raskolnikov and his crime are a number of other characters and threads of action. Raskolnikov's family and his friend Razumihin, Sonia's pathetic family, several members of the police force, the would-be seducer of Raskolnikov's sister, and her utterly offensive fiancé—all these make the novel a broad picture of low- and middle-class Russian life in the late 19th century. But this is incidental. Their real function is to provide a setting for Raskolnikov, both to show him in other roles than that of murderer and to show how his crime—both before and after he commits it—is intertwined with many lives and destinies.

The most remarkable single characteristic of this novel is the way it forces the reader to think seriously about the many problems which it treats. Primarily, it does this by not permitting any of the standard oversimplifications which we normally substitute for thought. Take, for example, our frequent confusion of morality with respectability. The only perfectly good character in the book is the prostitute Sonia, who is the most openly disreputable. The only one who is utterly evil is Raskolnikov's sister's fiancé, who is far and away the most respectable character in the book. Though we do not think of it in just that form, the novel forces us to see that morality depends on what a person is, and respectability on the sort of front he puts up, and that there is no necessary relation between the two. In fact, we are not even allowed to assume that they are opposites, for that would be merely a reversal of the original oversimplification. In a similar way, we are forced to think about money, about social position, about sanity and insanity, and above all about crime and punishment, and the issues are presented so grippingly and convincingly that we cannot escape them and we cannot explain them away with trite formulas.

Crito: a dialogue by *Plato continuing the story of the trial and death of *Socrates from the point reached at the end of the *Apology (4th century B.C.). The scene of the *Crito* is the prison at Athens two days before Socrates' death. The sacred ship, which had sailed for Delos at the time of the trial, has almost completed the return voyage across the Aegean and will soon enter the harbor of the Piraeus, bringing to an end the festival that has delayed Socrates' execution. Alarmed by this fact, Socrates' aged friend Crito comes to the prison early in the morning in a last attempt to persuade him to make use of a plan devised for his escape to Thessaly, where he can live in safety and educate his sons, as is his duty. For Socrates should not have begotten children if he is willing to die when he need not and leave them orphans. Nor should he permit his friends to be disgraced, as he will surely do if he makes no attempt to avoid "the crowning absurdity" of execution. For people will say they could have saved him, had they been willing to spend the money necessary to bribe the jailers to let him go. And no one will ever believe that it was ready and he refused it.

Socrates answers Crito by reminding him that we must not render evil for evil, a principle applying to our relations with our country even more than to those with individuals. He then demonstrates that, if he runs away, this is exactly what he will be doing. In his resentment at the injustice he has suffered, he will injure the laws

176

and destroy them, at least insofar as it is possible for him to do so, and thus render evil to his country and make himself guilty of the charges brought against him, whereas now he is innocent. And he concludes that he must examine what he does to make certain it is just, without regard to the reputation of friends or the education of children, while Crito must either accept his words or realize that he is himself one of the multitude for whom the rule is to requite wrong with wrong.

Although one of the shortest and simplest of Plato's dialogues, the *Crito* is a masterpiece of construction from the opening scene in which Crito waits with anxious solicitude beside the sleeping Socrates to the closing words, which leave him in baffled silence "not knowing what to say." The purpose of the piece is to answer those who said Socrates was not a good citizen, by demonstrating that of all the Athenians he was the only one willing to die out of simple respect for the law. But it is impossible to determine the historicity of the incident on which the dialogue is based.

Cuchulainn: central hero of the Ulster Cycle (collection of traditional tales of eastern Ireland's remote past, first century B.C.–A.D. eighth century, preserved in medieval manuscripts), and hero of five plays by *Yeats. Cuchulainn's father was, in some versions, Lug, prince of the Tuatha De Danann ("the Tribes of the Goddess Danu"—fairy folk); his mother was Dechtire, sister of King Conchubar of Ulster. *The Cattle Raid of Cooley (Tain Bo Cualnge)*, from *The Book of the Dun Cow (Lebor na Huidre*, 12th century), narrates the destruction of the famous hound of the smithy Culann by Setanta, aged seven; the victor was thereupon renamed Cuchulainn—"the hound of Culann." One of the purple passages of Irish literature is Cuchulainn's lament after he has killed Ferdiad, his sworn brother. Equally moving is *The Tragic Death of Cannla* (from *The Yellow Book of Lecan*, 14th century), a parallel to the Sohrab-Rustum story, where Cuchulainn, unaware of the relationship, kills his son Connla. See *Deirdre.

Cupid: see *Eros.

Cyclopes (plural of Cyclops): giants of enormous size, each with one great eye in the middle of his forehead. Sometimes they are represented as pasturing flocks and herds, at other times as forging the thunderbolts of *Zeus.

dadaism: see *surrealism.

Daedalus: a mythical artist, craftsman, and inventor, who constructed the labyrinth for King Minos of Crete. Stephen Daedalus is the name given to the semi-autobiographical hero of *Joyce's *Portrait of the Artist as a Young Man*, who prays to "the old father, old artificer."

D'Annunzio, Gabriele: Italian poet, novelist, and dramatist (1863–1938). After publishing his first volume of verse at the age of 16, D'Annunzio went on to a career in poetry, in fiction (largely 1886–1900), and in drama (1897–1912). His later years were given to nationalistic and fascist propaganda. His seizure of Fiume (1919) as a self-appointed patriot, in order to hold it for Italy in defiance of the Treaty of Versailles, and his later championing of Mussolini and his fascist state led to a great inflation of his reputation in his own land and time— and to an exaggerated depreciation of his talent elsewhere and later. D'Annunzio's work presents a strange mixture of aesthetic sensibility and almost perverse cruelty and violence. What really gives it life is a marvelous vitality and exuberance of language, and therefore it suffers especially in translation. In addition to some of his lyrics, his best works are the two novels *The Triumph of Death* (*Trionfo della morte*, 1894) and *The Flame of Life* (*Il Fuoco*, 1900, a description of his love affair with

Eleonora Duse), and the play *Jorio's Daughter* (*La Figlia di Iorio*, 1904).

Dante Alighieri: Italian poet (1265–1321). Dante, best remembered as the author of *The *Divine Comedy*, was a man of varied talents and interests—a soldier, a politician, an idealistic lover, a man of affairs, a lyric poet, and a philosopher. He was reared in the stimulating artistic society of Florence, studied the usual classical and medieval texts of rhetoric and theology, and early tried his hand at both poetry and painting. Tradition has it that in 1289 he fought in a local Florentine war "vigorously on horseback in the front rank."

The last decade of the century was a critical period for Dante. It marked his real self-education, his first large literary work, and his entry into politics. His education took the form of a serious study of Latin poetry and of ancient and scholastic philosophy. The results of this activity are visible both in the thoroughness and in the range of learning exhibited in his mature works.

To understand Dante's first important literary work, we must turn back to his youth. At the age of nine he had first seen Beatrice Portinari, who was of the same age. She had made a lasting impression on him and affected him in a way somewhat baffling to the modern mind. Dante saw her only a few times, and he and she were both married (to others) before her death in 1290, at the age of 24. Yet she became his ideal, the inspiration of his life, and (as *The Divine Comedy* makes plain) the direct agent of his salvation. By the age of 20 he was writing poems to her in the manner of the *troubadours. Between 1292 and 1294 he put together *La Vita nuova (The New Life)*, an account of his devotion to her made up of a slight autobiographical framework connecting 31 of the symbolic poems which she had inspired, each accompanied by a prose commentary. Here his earthly passion (if such it ever was) is already sublimated to philosophy, and Beatrice (Latin *beata*, "blessed") is identified with Christian salvation. The *Vita nuova* looks forward toward *The Divine Comedy*, for it closes with

Dante's hope eventually "to say of her what has never been said of any other woman."

The political stage on which Dante made his entrance during this decade was a turbulent one. For half a century Italy had been torn by civil wars between the Guelphs (nominally supporters of the Papacy) and the Ghibellines (nominally supporters of the authority of a German emperor over Italy). After the Guelphs gained control of Florence, the party splintered into the Blacks and the Whites, and to the latter faction Dante's family belonged. This group, representing the urban nobility and the wealthy commercial classes of relatively humble birth, wanted Florence to be a strong republic free of pope and emperor. The poor but aristocratic Blacks were willing to compromise with the pope if they could thereby crush the upstart democracy. In such stirring times Dante could not be a hermit, "for sitting on down or under coverlet, men come not unto fame" (*Inferno*, XXIV, 47–8). About 1295, he joined one of the powerful Florentine guilds, and by 1300 he had been elected one of the six guild representatives to govern the city. The feud between Blacks and Whites broke out anew. Dante and his cogovernors refused aid for the papal armies. Pope Boniface threatened reprisals, and, in 1301, Dante was sent to Rome to seek peace. He never saw Florence again. During his absence, a coup d'état put the Blacks into power; and in January, 1302, Dante was fined, exiled, and sentenced to be burned alive should he ever return to Florence. Forced "to abandon everything beloved most dearly" and "almost a beggar," Dante became an exiled intellectual, a wandering Jeremiah. For a brief while he made common cause with other banished Whites, but soon, finding that their aims were little better than those of their enemies, he "made a party for himself." For the rest of his life he moved about Italy in wanderings that cannot be clearly reconstructed. Temporary asylums granted by patrons could not save him from learning "how salt doth taste another's bread, and how hard the path to descend and mount upon another's stair" (*Paradiso*, XVII, 58–60).

Bitter though his exile was, it gave Dante time to continue his studies and his writing. During the first few years he began two important treatises, both of which were left unfinished. *The Banquet (Il Convivio)* explains some of Dante's later lyrics both literally and allegorically and contains important statements of his literary views. *The Illustrious Vernacular (De vulgari eloquentia)* defends (in Latin) the use of Italian as a serious literary language and discusses many of the linguistic problems confronting an Italian poet in a time of rapid linguistic change and diverse dialects.

As these two treatises prepared for *The Divine Comedy* by explaining its allegorical method and defending its use of the vernacular tongue, so a third treatise, *On Monarchy (De monarchia)*, thought out and justified the poem's political views. This work, written in Latin about 1312–15 (after the *Comedy* had been begun), is essentially an exposition of Dante's demand for separation of church and state, for a strong emperor as well as a strong pope. Ever since the Church took on civil powers under Constantine, the struggle between spiritual and temporal rulers has been disastrous, and the only solution lies in destroying the rivalry by effecting a clear separation of powers. Only when this separation has been achieved will pope and emperor be able to act with mutual good will for the general good. This point of view explains why, in the nethermost pit of hell in *The Divine Comedy*, Satan condemns not only Judas, traitor to the Church, but also Brutus and Cassius, traitors to the Empire.

We cannot be certain when Dante began *The Divine Comedy* (estimates range all the way from 1307 to 1313), but we do know that it was the chief occupation of his last years. Its fame began to spread, and he worked on in exile, hoping to the last that "the sacred poem to which both heaven and earth have set hand" would win for him an honorable return to his native city (*Paradiso*, XXV, 1–10). (He had already refused an offer to return under dishonorable conditions.) But this hope was in vain. After his death in Ravenna, the last cantos of the *Paradiso*—apparently recently finished—were found in his study. He was buried in Ravenna where, in spite of centuries of efforts by the Florentines to bring his body home, he still lies.

Daphnis and Chloe: see *Longus.

Dark Ages: a term sometimes used to designate the first half of the medieval period, approximately A.D. 500–1000. See *Middle Ages.

Darwin, Charles (Robert): English scientist (1809–82). After a medical education and a good deal of independent study of zoology, Darwin spent five years as naturalist on the ship *Beagle*, which was primarily engaged in a survey of South America. The specimens and notes collected on this voyage provided the basis for most of his later work. He retired to a village in Kent soon after publishing *Zoology of the Voyage of the Beagle* (1840) and followed it by works on coral reefs and the geology of volcanic islands and of South America. All this time he was gradually working out an evolutionary theory. In 1848 Alfred Russel Wallace sent him a manuscript setting out a theory very similar to Darwin's own. This situation could have led to a lifelong struggle over claims of priority, but with remarkable forbearance and good sense the two men presented their theories jointly before the Linnaean Society. Darwin's *The Origin of Species* (1859) presented evolutionary theory to the general public with such plausibility and such an overwhelming mass of evidence that, in spite of religious objections, the victory was never really in doubt. He went on to publish a long list of distinguished books and papers on subjects ranging from earthworms to orchids, from movement in plants to the expression of emotion in animals. The most important of these later works was *The Descent of Man, and Selection in Relation to Sex* (1871). Darwin had prodigious energy (in spite of ill health) and a penetrating mind, though he said that the only talent he had was "an unusual power of noticing things which easily escape attention, and of observing them carefully." His works are masterpieces of scientific exposition, written in a clear, logical, and eminently readable prose. His ideas not only touched off controversies which reverberated through almost all literature of the later 19th century;

they became a part of the basic thought of man and his way of experiencing his universe.

Daudet, Alphonse: French novelist (1840–97). Daudet is significant for his combination of excellent storytelling, the realistic technique, and a personal, happy tone. This tone reflects his own kindliness and good humor (*Zola called him a "charmer"), for his life and art were singularly one. The stories are in part autobiographical or based on the lives of people he knew: "to invent for him was to remember." His novels divide into those set in Provence and those in Paris. Those of the first group, drawing on the southern France of Daudet's birth, are characterized by a humorous, joyous approach to life (*Tartarin of Tarascon*, 1872; *Tartarin on the Alps*, 1885). The second group depicts admirably the atmosphere and the social classes of Paris: the humble (*Froment Junior and Risler Senior*, 1874), the wealthy (*The Nabob*, 1877), the evil power of a courtesan (*Sapho*, 1884).

Unlike his friends, the naturalists *Zola and *Flaubert, Daudet is not objective or severe, but tender and sympathetic with the misfortunes of humble people. Like *Dickens, with whom he has frequently been compared, he combines with great effectiveness details of a whole environment and background of manners, humor and pathos. He "struck a note comparatively new, laughter and tears, and moral beauty."

Dead Sea Scrolls: the popular term for Old Testament (*Bible) and other religious and secular manuscript scrolls, the first group of which was found in 1947 in caves near the Wady Qumran (then Jordan), an area about a mile and a half inland from the northwest corner of the Dead Sea. The antiquity of the manuscripts (a fragment of Exodus dates from the mid-third century B.C.) and their extensive and continuous texts make them of incalculable importance for the study of the evolution of the Biblical text, for our knowledge of daily life in pre-Christian Palestine of an ancient Jewish desert community, and for the history of Judaism and Palestine from the fourth century B.C. to A.D. 135. Here is a considerable literature (occasionally similar in language and thought—e.g., rite of baptism—to that of the New Testament) produced by a sect of Jews, possibly the Essenes, "during the time while the Temple was standing and before the authoritative norms for Jewish life were codified in the Talmudic period."

Scrolls of sheepskin inscribed in Hebrew and Aramaic were the initial finds, presumably come upon accidentally by a Bedouin goatherd while chasing a goat which had wandered into the cave. Apparently preserved for two thousand years in pottery jars, a few manuscripts were still wrapped in their ancient linen cloth. By 1965, after extensive excavations radiating for eleven miles and up to an area north of Jerico, discoveries also comprised copper scrolls, parchment manuscripts, and papyri (one can be dated March 18, 335 B.C.)—more than five thousand manuscripts preserving over a hundred different works including every book of the Old Testament and also Gospels of Mark and John in Greek; there are nonreligious legal collections and even some contracts written in Greek.

The early and still major discoveries are eleven scrolls in which are represented six distinct compositions: (1) the largest of the scrolls (one foot by twenty-four feet long when unrolled) contains the whole of the Old Testament Book of Isaiah, dating from 125–100 B.C., one of the earliest known manuscripts of any book of the Bible. It is of vital significance for the study of Hebrew orthography, language, script, early bookmaking, the Septuagint; but even more important is the fact that it is in virtual agreement with the Masoretic text and thus supports the fidelity of that tradition. (2) Two scrolls, in Hebrew, dating from not much later than 100 B.C., are successive portions of what had once been a single manuscript which had come apart. They have been given the single name *Serek ha-Yahad*—"the order of the Community" or "Manual of Discipline"; although ending with a devotional thanksgiving poem, the text is a manual or scrapbook of liturgical directions and rules of personal conduct; these are more ascetic than the beliefs and practices of the "normative Judaism" of the Masoretic texts. (3) Another Hebrew scroll, dating from about 25 B.C. (measuring five and a half inches by five feet

184

when unrolled), is a commentary on the Old Testament book of Habakkuk. Of all of the Dead Sea Scrolls, this appears to be the richest in historical allusions, which unfortunately are today too vague or mysterious to permit identification. (4) A fourth scroll, in Aramaic, dating from early in the first century A.D., is badly decomposed, but has been tentatively deciphered as the lost book of Lamech, hitherto known only by name. (5) A fifth manuscript (six inches wide, nine feet long when unrolled) describes a war of the "sons [children] of light" against the "sons of darkness." The "war" is tentatively interpreted to be a Messianic speculation or an apocalyptic vision, "referring not to any war but to the final struggle of the Messiah with God." This apocalyptic tradition, largely repudiated in Rabbinic (non-mystic) Judaism, survived in some liturgical practices of the primitive Christian community. (6) A sixth scroll contains twenty "Thanksgiving Hymns" (*Hodayot*) in a Hebrew closely resembling that of the Old Testament.

The preceding summary records informed current opinion. But the scholarly world is far from unanimous in these conclusions. Controversy still rages over the origins of the scrolls, dates of composition, dates of the extant manuscripts, and reasons for and dates of their deposit in the caves. Some scholars have argued, for example, that the caves were used as a storehouse for the scrolls, not because highly valued but because they were defective; under Jewish law, writings containing the name of God cannot be destroyed. But whatever the differences of opinion, all scholars agree that the Dead Sea Scrolls reveal for the last two centuries before the fall of the Temple in A.D. 70 a Judaism far richer and more variegated than had ever been suspected.

Dead Souls: a novel by *Gogol (*Mërlvye dushi*, 1842). This minutely detailed narrative is a humorous, satirical account of a great hoax. Yet one cannot be sure whether Gogol saw his creation as basically comic or tragic. (He wrote an entirely serious continuation, or second part, of the novel but destroyed the manuscript; and what is sometimes printed as the second part is merely some early draft material which happened to survive. In discussions of *Dead Souls* they are usually ignored, as they are in this account.)

The chief character, Tchitchikov, moves about the country buying up serfs who have died since the last census, but who must be carried on the tax lists until the next. Mystified owners are willing to part with the useless tax burdens for virtually nothing. Tchitchikov's motive is to raise money by mortgaging his ghostly holdings as living property. At first Tchitchikov appears shrewdly consistent in purpose. Later, as his scheme seems to be succeeding, he vacillates between carrying out his original swindle and trying to secure a legitimate estate and respectability. His arrest, trial, and release give Gogol an opportunity to satirize officials and legal procedures (as he had done in his stage triumph, *The Inspector General*).

Dead Souls ends without conclusion; it remains a torso. But the travels of Tchitchikov develop a variety of situations and a number of personalities, and the confusions in Tchitchikov's own personality and aims show Gogol's skill in developing a real, complex character. The book's value lies in the humor, the characterizations, and the insight into Russian life. *Dead Souls* was the first novel from which the world began to form its ideas of 19th-century Russia.

Decameron, The: a collection of short stories by *Boccaccio (*Il Decamerone*, 1348–53). *The Decameron* is one of the most celebrated collections of short stories in the world. Throughout the early *Renaissance, Boccaccio's fame was based on his Latin treatises. His continuing reputation depends, ironically, on *The Decameron*, a volume which he regretted having written and would willingly have destroyed. Boccaccio wrote *The Decameron*, as he says in a half-whimsical, half-serious preface, only to provide relaxation and escape.

The *frame-tale opens in the plague-ridden city of Florence. Ten young people (seven women, three men), "discreet, of noble blood, fair of favor, and well-mannered," decide to withdraw to their country estates in the healthier climate of the suburbs. To help time pass, each agrees to tell a story on each of ten days (hence the title, which is a portmanteau word from the Greek meaning "ten days"). A different person presides each day, appointing his successor and prescribing the theme of the next day's tales. Within this simple unifying frame, Boccaccio tried to achieve reality and avoid monotony by a variety of means: a brilliantly vivid opening which describes Florence during the plague; detailed references to country scenes and houses as the group journeys from one villa to another; conversational links between the tales; servants' quarrels; daily dancing and song; a considerable variety of stories.

Little effort is made, however, to individualize the cultured aristocrats who are the narrators, and the tales do not consistently reflect what personalities they have. Boccaccio never achieved the integration of narrator and story that is the glory of *Chaucer's art. Nor does he achieve any particular intensification of effect by his framework. The plan automatically groups the tales into blocks of ten at a time, all on the same general theme. The contrast between these themes on successive days and the differences between individual tales afford some variety, but it must be admitted that the framework is really just that—an essential but not particularly interesting part of the structure.

Boccaccio was above all a teller of tales, and all his art and attention are lavished on the individual stories. This art is simple and direct. The stories are generally short and unified. Although manners and customs are minutely described, the tales move straight to their conclusions without rhetorical descriptions or tangential displays of erudition. Whatever intricacies there are come from plot, not from philosophy or learning or character; and the plot moves swiftly, whether the teller relishes the "dulcet kisses" of sexual intrigue or laments the pathetic suffering of a tortured wife. The flavor is achieved by continuous blending of good humor and irony, by the unexpected ending; frequently, indeed, the conclusion is a double disclosure, one surprising denouement leading to a second even more ironic and unexpected. Often the plot depends on an ironic point made by a clever phrase or turn of speech. The dialogue, written for everyday people in limpid and vivid prose, responds to every mood, now racy and colloquial, now elevated and eloquent.

Boccaccio's interest is in the actual world. Gone is the medieval otherworldliness of his predecessors; ignored are saints' lives and allegories. The tragedies and joys are the tragedies and joys of this world, not the next. And Boccaccio never fails to find this world good. He is the intelligent, tolerant, and amused spectator of eccentricities and vice, of ignorance, knavery, and hypocrisy; but he sees also nobility, generosity, and the joys of life.

Boccaccio's treatment of love and sex is distinctly modern, even when he retains some features of the system of *courtly love. Love is a praiseworthy human relationship which has no need of being symbolically interpreted or haughtily unrequited or deviously concealed. It is good in and for itself and for the virtues of altruism and consideration which it involves. Like any other human relationship, it can exist on various levels, depending on the persons and the circumstances. Love and sex go together, and the highest love does not lead to renunciation or Platonism, but to happy marriage. The lowest, which is almost entirely sexual, may lead to an amusing affair and a good jest for the disinterested spectator—if only he is not a prude. It is interesting to note that the victims of trickery in the lower love affairs are usually people whose avarice or jealousy makes them incapable of any form of love whatsoever, so that there is frequently a sort of unintentional moral justice involved in an immoral escapade. For all this, the ribaldry of *The Decameron* has been exaggerated, and the reader who goes to it for bawdiness will have to read about three innocent stories for every scandalous one that he finds.

The essential thing, though, is that all four will be good stories. They will not have original plots, for Boccaccio took the tales from all sorts of sources—just as writers like Chaucer, *Shakespeare, *Lessing, *Swift, and *Keats have taken them, directly or indirectly, from Boccaccio. But they will be always entertaining, often amusing, and occasionally edifying. And the reader who knows Boccaccio only by his general undergraduate reputation will be surprised to find him quick to sympathize with misery, to admire virtue, and to praise generosity, kindliness, and courtesy.

Defoe, Daniel: English novelist and journalist (*c.* 1660–1731). Before Defoe turned to writing the fiction that made him famous, he was a businessman and journalist. Apparently always interested in politics, he defended the accession of William of Orange after the deposition of James II in *The True Born Englishman* (1701), a poem satirizing those who objected to the King's foreign birth. In 1702, *The Shortest Way with Dissenters* attacked the Church of England. Defoe was pilloried, fined, and imprisoned; but, after his release, he became a secret agent for the government. Thereafter, he did undercover jobs for a number of persons and groups, and there are indications that he sometimes worked for both sides simultaneously.

From 1704 to 1711, Defoe published *The Review*, forerunner of the periodicals of *Addison and Steele. He did not begin writing fiction until he was almost 60; *Robinson Crusoe* appeared in 1719. This narrative, inspired by the actual experience of Alexander Selkirk on the island of Juan Fernandez from 1704 to 1709 and written with the admirable straightforwardness of good reporting, had a tremendous sale. Other novels followed rapidly. *Captain Singleton*, a story of adventurous piracy, appearing in 1720. *Moll Flanders* came two years later with its easily seduced, picaresque heroine, whose fortunes rise and fall on her amorous experiences until she reaches old age only slightly pricked by conscience for a wicked life. In 1722 appeared also the famous *Journal of the Plague Year*, often considered Defoe's best work, for this fictitious account makes more vivid the terrible London plague of 1665 than does an eyewitness account like Samuel Pepys'. *Roxana, or the Fortunate Mistress* (1724) returns to the pattern established by Moll Flanders, and the occasional half-denunciations by the heroine do not detract from the rollicking account of her rising fortunes by the use of sex-appeal and bold methods of seduction.

Although Defoe always states conscientiously the moral of his immoral examples, his tolerance for the disreputable characters is apparent. The prostitute heroines and male adventurers usually make a matter-of-fact statement of regret for dissolute lives, and this satisfied a reading public which avowedly sought moral instruction by devouring the details of the lives of criminals, pirates, and debauched prostitutes. Defoe wrote of and for the middle and lower classes, and they were pleased by his racy realism, sentimentalism, and pious exhortation. His stories usually had a foundation in fact and, in addition, his choice of realistic detail within loosely spun plots gave his work an air of verisimilitude. Even more, he achieved his effects by his "easy, plain, and familiar language." And, despite an output of some 250 works, Defoe's narrative pace never slackened.

Deirdre: a heroine of Irish legend, fated from birth to bring calamity to those she loves and death to many men. Like Helen of Troy, she surpassed all the women of her time, for "she had the six gifts most desired in a woman—beauty, voice, speech, needlework, wisdom, chastity." Like Cassandra, she expounded an ominous foreknowledge which was not credited. Although deeply in love, Deirdre and the man of her choice are not secure from disaster. Reared to become King Conchubar's wife, she can love only the man who has "the color of the raven on his hair, the color of the calf's blood on his cheeks, and the color of the snow in his skin." It is unfortunately not the elderly king, but Naisi, his young kinsman, who meets these amatory specifications. The young couple elope but are lured back, while Deirdre's foreboding dreams and her sound counsel go unheeded. Naisi and his two brothers, the "Three Lights of Valor," are then treacherously murdered (the death of the sons of Usnach). Deirdre cannot survive their loss. (She dies in various ways in different versions of the tale.) And so despite their charm, their sensibility, and their passion, "for love of each other they die."

The central theme of the tale gives some clue to the obscure origins of Arthurian romance, for *Deirdre* is the earliest version of a celebrated type of love motif—the girl's passion for the handsome vigorous nephew, her elopement with this hero who is at first somewhat unwilling and "slow to do so," their idyllic life in primitive surroundings. The theme was to achieve its most celebrated treatment in the story of *Tristan and Isolt; the latter also an Irish aristocrat.

The Deirdre story, this "most sorrowful of storytelling," is the best-known section of the old Irish cycle centered around the Ulster hero *Cuchulainn, who here appears only at the very end in an unimportant role. Extant in many versions and still told in country districts in Ireland and Scotland, the tale was known as early as the 9th century; but the oldest extant manuscript, in the *Book of Leinster*, is of the 12th century. From the influence of Lady Gregory's 19th-century English version (based on an Irish version from about the 15th century), the story has entered upon a second literary life in the plays and poems of *Yeats, *Synge, and other writers of the *Irish Literary Revival.

Delphic oracle: the famous oracle in the temple of *Apollo located at Delphi, Greece, believed by the ancient Greeks to be the center of the world. It was a national sanctuary and religious shrine for all Greece. The priestess, first inhaling the vapors which arose from a natural chasm in the center of the temple, went into a state of frenzy induced by means no longer ascertainable and then pronounced the words which were believed to be revelations of Apollo. These utterances were transcribed into verse by the temple priests and thus reported to the suppliants. The oracle played an important role in Greek culture, well illustrated in the history of *Oedipus the King* and in the life of *Socrates. The riddlelike character of the oracle is illustrated in the story of Croesus, who undertook an expedition against the Persians because the oracle foretold that "When Croesus has the Halys crossed / A mighty kingdom will be lost"; not until after the event did it appear that the oracle had meant *his* empire, not that of the Persians. Because of such answers, the phrase "Delphic oracle" is often applied to any ambiguous statement.

Demeter: the Greek goddess of the grainfields, identified by the Romans with Ceres.

Demosthenes: Greek orator (384–322 B.C.). The Athenian statesman Demosthenes is justly famous, not only for his mastery of the art of public speaking, but for the political insight which enabled him, alone of his contemporaries, to foresee the danger to Greece inherent in the rise of Macedonia under King Philip II, father of Alexander the Great. This danger Demosthenes pointed out to the Athenian people in a series of brilliant addresses known as the *Philippics* and the *Olynthiacs*, but his warnings went unheeded until Philip seized the Greek city of Elatea in 339 B.C. In the crisis that followed, Demosthenes persuaded the Athenians to unite with the Thebans against their common enemy, but the allies were overwhelmed at Chaeronea and Philip established Macedonian hegemony over Greece. Eight years later (330 B.C.), a certain Ctesiphon proposed that a crown of gold be voted Demosthenes for his services to the Athenian state. When Demosthenes' enemy, the orator Aeschines, attacked the proposal, Demosthenes was called upon to defend his whole political career, a task he accomplished in the finest of his speeches, *On the Crown.* The details of Demosthenes' life from the time he delivered this oration to the death of Alexander in 323 B.C. are obscure, but when Alexander died, hopes of Greek freedom revived and Demosthenes came into prominence once more. He sponsored a revolt against the Macedonian general Antipater, but it was crushed; and, rather than fall into the hands of his enemies, he took poison and died in 322 B.C.

De Quincey, Thomas: English prose writer (1785–1859). After an unhappy and oversensitive childhood and an irregular education interrupted by periods of vagabondage in Wales and London, De Quincey first took opium on a visit to London during 1804 and thereafter became gradually enslaved by it. He was an excellent classical scholar and student of German philosophy, but his own literary career began relatively late, with *Confessions of*

an English Opium-Eater (1812). After this he contributed a long series of articles to the reviews, many of no
permanent interest, but a few still remembered. One of
these is the essay *On Murder Considered as One of the
Fine Arts* (1827), in which he first makes a flippant inquiry (based on *Aristotle's *Poetics*) into the essential
characteristics of an aesthetically good murder, and then
proceeds to give soberly horrifying accounts of two famous murders by way of illustration. During his later
years he produced two more works which can take their
place beside the *Confessions*: *Suspiria de Profundis*
(1845) is a series of essays often approaching the quality
of poems in prose. *The English Mail Coach* (1849) is
another fine example of his rhetorical prose, especially
in its two final sections, *The Vision of Sudden Death* and
Dream-Fugue.

De Quincey is one of the great deliberate stylists of
English literature. He developed an intricate, sonorous,
ornate prose which owes a good deal to *Milton's poetry
and to such earlier prose writers as Robert Burton and
Sir Thomas Browne. This style can be, and sometimes is,
mechanically written; but at its best it is an incomparable
instrument for conveying the rich, tumultuous, and terrifying dreams which it was designed to reproduce.

De Quincey's influence was greater in France than in
England. Both *Musset and *Baudelaire translated from
him, and from the time of Baudelaire on he was the
common property of a great many of the symbolistic and
fin-de-siècle writers.

deus ex machina ("God out of a machine"): a term
applied to any artificial trick or unexpected, improbable
intervention by some external force to bring about development or resolution of a plot. The term was used
by *Aristotle and by *Horace to describe a technique in
Greek drama dependent on a mechanical device that
lowered a god onto the stage, so that he might extricate
the characters from a difficult situation that could not
be resolved by logical motivations of plot or character.
Deus ex machina thus refers to a saving agency appearing without proper cause, reason, or justification.

The king's intervention at the end of *Molière's *Tartuffe* is a good example.

Diana: see *Artemis.

Dickens, Charles: the most popular English novelist of the 19th century (1812–70). The son of an impoverished government clerk, Dickens had little formal education and at 15 went to work as an office boy for a lawyer. In a few years he taught himself shorthand and became competent enough to be a parliamentary reporter. Soon he was doing creative writing as well. His first literary efforts, vivid sketches of London types, were published as *Sketches by Boz* (1836). The exuberantly comic *Posthumous Papers of the Pickwick Club* (1836–37) was originally proposed by the publisher as an illustrated sporting serial, a type much in vogue at the time. Because Dickens knew practically nothing about sports, he changed the plan and dealt with a group of amiable eccentrics instead of sportsmen. Although the suicide of the original illustrator necessitated some changes, Dickens carried the plan through with another artist. *The Pickwick Papers* is lacking in plot and design, for it grew as it was written: the famous Sam Weller, for example, was added to the original cast of characters in the course of the writing. Nevertheless, it was a continuously amusing and sentimental narrative which immediately caught the popular fancy and made Dickens famous.

Dickens never forgot the poverty of his early years, and he felt strongly that his fiction should give an impetus to much-needed social reforms. *Oliver Twist* (1837–39), exciting and humorous but also pathetic, is an indictment of orphanages and of the London slums where victimized paupers were bred in crime-schools; and the satirical *Nicholas Nickleby* (1838–39) describes the brutal country schools. *The Old Curiosity Shop* (1840–41) exploits sentimental pathos, especially in the death scene of Little Nell.

With these successes behind him, Dickens turned to historical fiction. The central event of *Barnaby Rudge* (1841) concerns the anti-Catholic riots of 1780. For thousands of readers the fictionized account *in A Tale of Two Cities* (1859) *was* the French Revolution and Sidney Carton was more real than Robespierre or Danton.

In 1842 Dickens lectured with great success on his first American tour. But his *American Notes* and his satirical treatment of the frontier in *Martin Chuzzlewit* (1843–44) aroused a storm of disapproval from Americans. He turned to sentimental Christmas stories: *A Christmas Carol* (1843), *The Chimes* (1844), and *The Cricket on the Hearth* (1845). In an equally sentimental vein was *Dombey and Son* (1846–48).

Dickens' skill as a novelist reached its height in *David Copperfield* (1849–50). With its strong autobiographical element, it is the most varied in characterization and the best proportioned of the novels. Among other themes, it expresses Dickens' hatred of debtors' prisons: his father, the prototype of Micawber, had been in them more than once. Other social problems play a part in most of Dickens' later novels: *Bleak House* (1852–53), *Hard Times* (1854), *Little Dorrit* (1855–57), *Great Expectations* (1860–61), *Our Mutual Friend* (1864–65), and the unfinished mystery story, *Edwin Drood* (1870).

Dickens always fancied himself an actor, and many of his lectures were, in fact, readings from his own novels. His dramatic sense is everywhere in evidence: much of the story is carried by dialogue—realistic, comic, eloquent, and always lively. And the intense melodrama and emotion of individual scenes, the rapid variation and range of moods and situations and the exaggerated characters are often positively theatrical. Dickens did not penetrate deeply into personality and motivations, but his characters are nonetheless vivid. The underlying theme—the uselessness of reason and the value of cheerfulness and kindliness as an antidote to the cruelties of the time—was and is appealing to the general reader. If his novels are full of episodic plots, strained coincidences, exaggerations, and repetitions, his readers have not particularly objected during the past hundred years.

Dickinson, Emily: American poetess (1830–86). Born in Amherst, Massachusetts, where her father was a prominent lawyer and later treasurer of Amherst College, Emily Dickinson spent almost all her life in the same house and yard. The exceptions were a few months' schooling away from home at Mount Holyoke and visits to Washington and Philadelphia while her father was in Congress. In Philadelphia she met Charles Wadsworth, a preacher; and biographers have guessed that she fell in love with him but renounced him because he was married. For this, or some other mysterious cause, her shyness and withdrawal from the world increased; and for the last 25 years of her life she was a recluse, hardly ever leaving her home and grounds in Amherst.

She had always been an eccentric and an extreme individualist, with a quick mind and an elfin sense of humor. Answering a request for a picture of herself, she sent a verbal one: "small, like the wren; and my hair is bold, like the chestnut burr; and my eyes, like the sherry in the glass that the guest leaves." She had various minor peculiarities, like wearing only white and avoiding visitors, but her two great passions were her garden and her poetry, both being cultivated for her own pleasure and not for public display. The poems, carefully reworked, and often with alternate readings, were scribbled on the backs of envelopes and odd scraps of paper and stored in bundles in her room. One of her small group of old, tried friends—"The soul selects her own society/Then shuts the door"—persuaded her to send four of them to T. W. Higginson, a respected writer of the time. He was startled by their enigmatic quality but advised her to "delay to publish." She took the advice: only five of her poems appeared during her lifetime. Higginson and Emily thereafter carried on a long and interesting correspondence in which he gave her poetic advice and she signed herself his scholar. He was one of the few outsiders at her funeral.

After Emily's death, her sister Lavinia found the unexpected manuscript hoard and arranged for some of the poems to be edited (the editing was necessary because of the difficult handwriting and the many variant readings) and published in two volumes (1890, 1891). Publication of poems and letters has continued intermittently even up to the present, more than 600 of the poems appearing for the first time in *Bolts of Melody* (1945).

Higginson and others tried at first to explain poetic traditions and conventions to Emily but soon saw that her greatest strength lay in her freshness and unconventionality. Her poetry is like her life, strange and different, sometimes affectedly whimsical, but at its best it has a quality all its own. This poetry is Emily Dickinson's "letter to the world," which, she said, never wrote to her. It is not the verse of a lonely, self-pitying recluse, absorbed in private grief. "To live is so startling," she wrote, "it leaves but little room for other occupations." A walk in her garden, a sunset, the death of a friend, a theological riddle, a rushing locomotive—all went into the alembic of her revery and thought. The resultant distillate was unlike any other. In looking at nature, her microscopic eye catches new images: a snake becomes "a whip-lash unbraiding in the sun," and the jay is "a prompt, executive bird." But nature is not her chief concern: "I thought that nature was enough / Till human nature came." Though she saw little of people, she saw through them steadily. She was sharp on a pompous churchman who "preached upon breadth till it argued him narrow," and on the "dreary somebodies," who, froglike, "told their name the livelong day / To an admiring bog." She took her stand against trade, pillars of society, and public officials, and for the dignity of the unregimented individual: "I took my power in my hand / And went against the world." Most of her poetry, however, is devoted to her own mind and thoughts, although she warned against her subjectivity's being taken too literally. "When I state myself, as the representative of the verse, it does not mean me, but a supposed person."

Her poetry is full of startling figures of speech, familiar words in unfamiliar uses, learned expressions (Noah Webster's *Dictionary* was one of her favorite books), sudden shifts of tone, metrical irregularities, deliberately imperfect rhymes, and grammatical difficulties. She was quite literally ahead of her time, and she has exerted a considerable influence on American poets of the present century, who have been attracted by her technical restraint, her bold imagery, her experimentation with words and concern for ideas, her cryptic brevity, and her revolt against sentimentality and poetic diction. Her

197

fame has continually increased, and the little New England spinster, confined in her lifetime to a single house and garden, is now recognized as one of the world's few great women poets.

Diderot, Denis: French philosopher and writer (1713–84). Diderot is one of the most brilliant, stimulating, and contradictory writers in world literature. He was educated by the Jesuits, who were the best pedagogues of the age. After an unsuccessful marriage, he became the life-long friend of Sophie Volland. The many letters which he wrote her give us the most vivid account of the daily lives of the "philosophers," as the French rationalists of the time called themselves. His earlier works include *Les Bijoux indiscrets* (1748), a collection of stories which he later disavowed; *Pensées philosophiques* (1746), a treatise on the adequacy of natural religion; and *Lettre sur les aveugles* (1749), in which Diderot attempts to prove that man's spiritual and moral concepts depend on his senses. Following through on his basic premise, Diderot, far in advance of his time, envisioned the possibility of teaching the blind to read through the sense of touch. Yet, the philosophical implications of the *Lettre* were too bold to be accepted by the authorities, and Diderot was imprisoned in the dungeon of Vincennes for three months.

When he emerged from prison, he devoted all his energies for 20 years (1752–72) to the great work of which he was the inspiration, and to which his name is inseparably attached, the *Encyclopédie*. More than a century earlier, Descartes had championed the exclusive rights of reason in the solution of all problems, and his ideas had come to be accepted by the advanced thinkers of the 18th century. Indeed, the period was later to be called "The Age of Reason" because of its critical reexamination and restatement of formerly accepted religious, political, and other doctrines. Diderot seized upon this passion for renewal and reform and brought together, in a common effort, all the outstanding writers and thinkers of the age. His aim was to collect in one huge work the summary of all human knowledge, to judge the past from the point of view of modern science, to bind together, by a unity of purpose, the most brilliant and diverse talents, and to make of this imposing array a formidable instrument, against which all the opposition of antiquated opinions would dash themselves to pieces. This was the thought which inspired the *Encyclopédie*, the great organ for the diffusion of ideas during the "age of enlightenment."

Diderot's industry, shrewdness and enthusiasm made the *Encyclopédie* what it was: a publication that assumed that religious tolerance and speculative freedom should hold sway, and that drove home the doctrine that it is the common people whose condition ought to be the main concern of the French governing classes, whose spirit at the time was absolutist, religious, and militaristic.

In 1759 the *Encyclopédie* was officially suppressed and Diderot, almost unaided, carried on his work clandestinely. He worked like a slave, writing several hundred articles, living in constant dread of the spies of the authorities.

The *Encyclopédie* is Diderot's monumental work. Although the individual articles are by various hands and the arrangement is alphabetical, the massive work is unified by its general spirit, which is that of the 18th century itself: hatred or scorn of the past; a gradual breaking away from traditional religion; a marked preference for ideas derived from experience and the senses; and the glorification of the arts, the sciences, and industry.

Though most of Diderot's efforts went into the *Encyclopédie*, his other writings are extensive and various. In his plays and critical essays he broke away from the convention of Neo-Classical drama to establish the bourgeois drama, a serious treatment of the lives and problems of contemporary middle-class people. He thought the drama should preach the domestic virtues and benevolence. He wrote a series of novels dealing with philosophical and religious problems, and his *Salons* (1759–79), critical accounts of annual art exhibitions, can serve as models of this type of criticism. Diderot has been excellently summed up as "a philosopher in whom all the contradictions of the time struggle with one another."

Dionysus: a Greek god of vegetation, particularly of the vineyards, and therefore a god of wine, also called Bacchus. Tragedy and comedy grew out of his worship.

Dis: see *Hades.

dissonance: see *assonance.

Divine Comedy, The: a poem by *Dante, completed shortly before his death in 1321. Dante called his poem simply *The Comedy (La Commedia)*, and the adjective was added to the title by later generations, in reference both to the subject of the poem and to its excellence. It is not a comedy in the modern sense of the word; the title was used because the poem depicts a progress from grief to joy (damnation to heavenly bliss) and is written in the vernacular tongue. It is often called an epic, but in its usual sense this term is as much a misnomer as comedy. The difficulty of assigning the poem to a type arises from the fact that both its structure and its consistently simultaneous levels of meaning make it actually unique.

The framework of the poem is a perfectly straightforward narrative. Dante, lost in a forest, is met by *Vergil, who, through the intercession of Beatrice in heaven, has been sent to guide him through the world after death, for he has strayed so far that only this spectacle can lead him to salvation. First Vergil leads him through Hell, an inverted cone descending by terraces at various levels to its apex at the center of the earth, where Satan himself is confined. From here a subterranean channel leads them to the base of Purgatory, a mountain on the opposite side of the earth from Hell and corresponding to it in a general way, being an extrusion caused by the opposite depression. On the terraces of Purgatory the sins of those who are ultimately to be saved are cleansed away, and at its top is the Garden of Eden, from which the elect ascend into Heaven. Here Vergil (who is not permitted beyond this point) leaves Dante, and he is led to Beatrice. Under her guidance, he ascends through the concentric spheres of the various planets, including the moon and the sun (for the earth is the center of Dante's universe), and on through the fixed stars and the *primum mobile* to the ultimate heaven, the Empyrean. Here Beatrice passes him on to St. Bernard of Clairvaux, whose prayers gain for Dante a final magnificence—a vision in which, for an instant, he sees the Trinity itself and the whole universe, down to its last detail, as one vast and coherent whole. With this moment of illumination the journey and the poem end.

Physically, the poem is organized about this journey, but structurally the work—like the afterworld—is organized on the basis of an elaborate use of the symbolical numbers 3, 7, 9, and 10. *Terza rima (a poetic form invented by Dante for this poem) is a chain of interlocking triple rimes, and the poem has the three divisions of Hell, Purgatory, and Heaven. (Many translations use the terms *Inferno* and *Paradise*, for the first and third of these.) If the first canto be considered as a general introduction, then each of the three sections has 33 cantos: the entire poem has 100. The sevens are most clearly visible in the seven deadly sins which create the main subdivisions of Hell and Purgatory. Actually, each of the three departments of the afterlife consists of seven parallel divisions, plus two not exactly parallel to these (making nine), plus one of a totally different sort (making ten). The topography and architecture of Dante's world are worked out in such consistent symbolic detail that scholars have sometimes succumbed to the temptation to add further details of their own, and some of the charts and diagrams which are often printed with the poem contain things which cannot be found in the text.

In its meanings and symbolism, as in its structure, the *Comedy* presents a mass of complex details organized about a few clear levels and concepts. In a letter to his patron Can Grande della Scala, Dante points out that the poem has one literal meaning (the account of the journey itself) and multiple allegorical meanings. For example, in the opening lines Dante comes to himself in "a dark wood." Literally, we have a picture of a man lost in a forest; but there are also three different allegorical meanings: theologically, the dark wood is a state of spiritual separation from God; politically, it is the anarchy of Dante's Italy; and morally, it is an unworthy or evil way of life. Dante explains that the literal subject of the poem is "the state of souls after death," but the description of this state is not its ultimate purpose. "It may be briefly said that the end of the entire work . . . is to remove those living in this life from a state of misery and to lead them to a state of happiness."

This emphasis on present happiness is important, for Dante is often misread as an otherworldly theologian or fanatic. His own explanation of his levels of meaning makes it nonsensical to inquire whether he meant us to take his Hell literally or figuratively. The sinners with whom he speaks are all relevant to our own present state—in fact, the damned are incapable of repentance, and their tormented existence in Hell is a mere continuation of their lives on earth. So close is the relationship that some whose bodies still move among us already have their souls in Hell. And Dante's attitude toward them is not the sadistic one sometimes attributed to him but is predominantly one of pity both for their individual fates and for the loss of their potentialities. The emphasis is placed more on their common humanity than on their individual failings, and many of them—Francesca da Rimini, Ugolino, Ulysses—are admirable. Even the great rebels whose pride cannot be broken—Farinata degli Uberti, holding his head high "as if he had a great contempt for Hell," or the defiant Capaneus, "who held, and still seems to hold, God in disdain"—excite a certain respect at the same time that, as Vergil points out, their pride is really their punishment.

Dante's arrangement of Hell depends on a classification which is almost equally theological and moral and is based as much on *Aristotle's *Nicomachaean Ethics as on Christian doctrine. It is always reasonable and intelligible, though sometimes startling to those of puritanical background. The illicit lovers, for example, are far above the forgers because their sin is a misapplication of love, which is in itself good, whereas forgery is a form of fraud, which is entirely evil. With our emphasis on order and against violence, we are likely to condemn the bank robber more than the absconding cashier, but

Dante's system reminds us that a sneaking breach of trust is morally worse than taking by open force from those who have no reason to trust us. The whole arrangement of Hell is based in part on the seven deadly sins and their subdivisions, and the punishments of sinners have a symbolic appropriateness, as is clearly seen in the hypocrites who stagger under the terrific burden of cloaks of gilded lead.

Each of the ascending terraces of Purgatory is devoted to the expiation of a particular sin, and thus the organization parallels, in general, that of Hell, but the tone of this section is entirely different. All who enter Hell must leave hope behind, for damnation is eternal. But those in Purgatory are destined for salvation; they are "contented in the fire" and, being penitent, gladly accept their penance. As the burden of one sin is removed, the soul easily rises to the next terrace, and on each terrace the length of the expiation is determined by the burden of the sin which is cleansed there. The completely purified soul reaches the Garden of Eden, whence it ascends to its proper sphere in Heaven.

Each sphere of Heaven has its own planet and rank of angels, its particular virtue and branch of knowledge (for to Dante there is a direct connection between virtue and knowledge), and its own group of the redeemed. But we are told that the redeemed are only *manifested* in different spheres, for they actually *are* all together with God. And when Dante asks one of them whether she ever wishes for a more exalted rank, she joyously explains that such a wish would be impossible for anyone in Heaven, since it would be contrary to God's will, and "His will is our peace." As Dante and Beatrice ascend through the heavens, they stop, as Dante had done in Hell and Purgatory, to talk with those that they meet along the way. It has been pointed out that the conversations in Heaven are less human and more abstract, philosophical, and theological than those in the lower worlds. This difference is intentional. The souls in Hell are unchanged, sinful human beings, and those in Purgatory are in the process of casting off their human imperfections. The redeemed, however, having found God, being at one with Him, and being incapable of further change, are essentially different from earthly creatures—more admirable, but necessarily less "colorful." Here there are no accidents, no events, no progress or retrogression, but only a perfect and eternal equilibrium. It would be a sign of failure on Dante's part if he had represented the redeemed as essentially like the damned or pictured Heaven as differing from Hell only in its superior physical comfort. If the reader feels somewhat out of place in Heaven, that is entirely as it should be. Dante's imagination has soared beyond the normal human range, so that he can remember the illumination and the feeling of his final vision but cannot retain or express its details. It is a stroke of genius that he leaves his reader on this exalted plane at the end of the poem, rather than bring him back to earth.

The organic unity of this world of Dante's creation is an amazing feat. Everything from the topography to the philosophical, moral, and theological concepts fits together with perfect consistency and with the inevitability of natural law. Furthermore, the result is not only logical, but immediate and credible. Dante's angels, devils, and monsters are more convincing than the everyday people in a good many contemporary novels.

This credibility results from the style as much as from the organization. Some elements of Dante's art, such as the sheer beauty of sound, are inevitably lost in a translation, but the essential quality of his style will remain if the translator is competent. This style is a plain, straightforward one, neither ornate nor flashy. It is full of colloquial words, homely expressions, earthy comparisons, and it makes no attempt at specifically poetic diction. Above all, it is a stripped-down style without a trace of padding. Dante never inserts a word merely to fill out a line or lets a rime tell him what to say or uses words loosely to produce something that merely sounds good. He always means something and knows precisely what he means. He sometimes confronts the reader with a riddle, but the riddle always has an answer. No other writer demands from his reader such strict and unflagging concentration, and no other writer deserves it.

Doctor Faustus, The Tragical History of: a play by *Marlowe (c. 1589–92). The legend of Faust, the man who sold his soul for knowledge and power, developed in Germany and was brought to England by a translation of a German chapbook on the subject. This translation appeared shortly before Marlowe's play and appears to be its immediate source. Marlowe's is the first of many dramatic treatments of the story.

The essential plot is simple enough. Faust, tired of his own limitations and the pettiness of human knowledge, turns to magic. He makes a contract with Mephistophilis (a minor devil, who has to get it ratified by Lucifer); Mephistophilis is to be Faust's slave for 24 years; at the end of that time, the situation is to be reversed for all eternity. For 24 years Faust has magic powers which he uses for everything from calling back Helen of Troy to playing practical jokes. Then, on the last night, he waits in agony and terror until Mephistophilis comes and carries him off to hell.

Marlowe's best play shares at least one characteristic with many other literary works of the *Renaissance: it is a product both of its own day and of the *Middle Ages, which still had a great deal of influence in the 16th century. Marlowe's medieval plot shares with *Dante's The *Divine Comedy the fundamental premise that the present life has meaning because it determines what eternal life will be. From medieval tradition, also, come the allegorical presentation of the seven deadly sins, the use of the good angel and the evil angel (the medieval *morality play was based on the struggle between the vices and virtues for the soul of man), and the presentation of the action in an unbroken text (the customary scene divisions have been made by modern editors) instead of in the acts and scenes which under classical influence became general in the 16th century.

From the spirit of his own day Marlowe draws the passion for knowledge—for absolutely uncircumscribed learning—which is the source of the superabundant vitality in his hero. Faustus embodies the Renaissance zest for knowing which surmounted old barriers both by studying anew the literature of Greece and Rome and by laying the foundation for the modern inductive study of the physical world. But if Faustus is a devotee of "science," his science has not yet become a vast, cooperative, almost impersonal thing: rather his unlocking of the secrets of the universe is a private, intensely personal quest, the very expression of sharp individuality. He is the man of the Renaissance; his is the robust, expansive personality, the acme of all that has come to be admired in the modern cult of the individual.

The Renaissance return to the classics appears in the drama in lesser ways: in the numerous classical allusions (Musaeus, *Delphic oracle, *Elysium, Homer, etc.), in the conjuring up of such figures as Alexander and Helen, and even in the fragmentary use of the Chorus. And in using *blank verse Marlowe not only adopted a verse form which was created in the 16th century but used this form so successfully that it became the regular poetic medium for the drama of *Shakespeare and all his contemporaries. *Jonson's phrase, "Marlowe's mighty line," described its influence as well as its powerful rhythms.

This synthesis of medieval and Renaissance is of a special kind—not a mere bland eclectic combination, but a tense yoking of forces which Marlowe must have felt as irreconcilable. For he draws the main tension of his play from the clash between Dr. Faustus' Renaissance desire for unlimited knowledge and power and the medieval dogma of the retribution which awaits one who uses the means necessary to gain such ends. Not that Marlowe had to look backward to another age to find a suitable nemesis for his hero: rather he lived at a time which made it possible for him to feel equally the force of different values competing with each other. Faustus is caught between the medieval and the modern world and destroyed in the clash between their different sets of values. And it is worth noting that it is such fundamental human clashes which are at the heart of tragedy. In the *Oresteia of *Aeschylus, the *Antigone of *Sophocles, and the *Lear of Shakespeare, for instance, we see such clashes set forth.

What is it in *Dr. Faustus*, then, which is more than historical, more than a quaint record of the early Renaissance, which is long past, and of medieval habits of mind which belong to a still more distant past? What is the general human significance of the story of the man who sold his soul to the devil, a story which in one form or another is even older than the Middle Ages? In Marlowe's interpretation of the legend, the emphasis is upon the conflict between human expansiveness and human limitations. In Faustus, expansiveness takes the form, not so much of a desire for infinite knowledge, but rather of a desire for infinite knowledge-for-power. The play is less a study of the intellectual, of the student with an infinite capacity for study and contemplation, than it is of the lust for power that may be got through special learning (rather than through military force, political control, economic pressure, or other such agencies). What the play says is that man uses power badly and that he goes so far in this self-indulgence that he is finally unable to make a moral recovery. In the Christian terms which Marlowe uses, Faustus is unable to ask for or to submit himself to grace, however much he wants to or thinks he wants to; perhaps we might say that he has infinite regret but falls short of repentance. In secular terms he has undergone a hardening which finally destroys him; he has persisted in his desperate course in defiance of the moral values of his society, and they eventually catch up with him.

To say this is not to say that Faustus is a villain. Indeed, he is far from being the evil character whom the spectators of a melodrama may hate. He is instead the "tragic hero" with whom the spectator or reader of tragedy must identify himself. This identification is made necessary first of all by the structure of the play, of which the hero has such exclusive possession that we can be seriously concerned only with him, and secondly—and more importantly—by the characterization of him. For Faustus is not a willful seeker of evil; rather he is a kind of *Everyman* in whom we can recognize various representative human traits: he seeks power to satisfy all his longings, he is sure that he can "beat the game" and be immune to consequences, he has qualms of conscience but cannot resist temptation, and at the end he is caught in a mad storm of terror, self-reproach, and fantastic schemes to escape retribution. He is neither cruel nor criminal; he is well-meaning but full of pride and self-deception.

The comic scenes in mid-play, thought to be later substitutions by Thomas Nash, are usually considered too farcical in manner. Although in tone they are out of harmony with the rest of the play, their author at least did know what the play was doing and how these scenes should function. For they show Faustus using his power and using it trivially, and thus they give dramatic substance to Faustus' bitter phrase in the final scene, "vain pleasure of twenty-four years." Faustus was dissatisfied even with a brilliant career. He played for something more spectacular, but he succeeded only in frittering away his life and losing his soul. Here is the irony which is almost inevitable in tragedy.

It is the powerful poetic language of the play which gives extraordinary reality to the character of Faustus. Except perhaps for those of Shakespeare, Marlowe's images are the finest in 16th-century drama. In the first scene the images which Faustus uses to express his vision of personal omnipotence give a magnificent picture of a fantastically irresponsible egoism in operation. Near the end, after Faustus summons up and kisses Helen, he hits upon images which vividly set forth his ecstasy and yet, with their strong note of conflagration and destruction, suggest at the same time the spiritual downfall which he is now completing: "Was this the face that launch'd a thousand ships,/And burnt the topless towers of Ilium?" And probably nowhere else in dramatic poetry is terrified anguish more wonderfully imaged than in the final scene. Yet the poetry does more than endow individual scenes with vibrant life: it binds scenes together thematically. The recurrence of *heaven* and *heavens* in Faustus' speeches is more than idle repetition, for in this word pattern we see subtly suggested Faustus' inability ever to break loose from the realities which at the start he must deny. He cannot escape from a world order and from responsibility; nor can he escape from a dream of unfettered domination. That is his tragedy.

Dodgson, Charles Lutwidge: author of *Alice's Adventures in Wonderland* (1865) and *Through the Looking Glass* (1872), known to the world by his pseudonym of Lewis Carroll (1832–98). Although written for children, these works have been popular adult reading for more than a century. Their wit, inexorable logic, and absurdity have had wide appeal in the English-speaking world. Dodgson was lecturer in mathematics at Oxford for a quarter of a century and also an early practitioner of photography. *The Hunting of the Snark* (1876) is another of his well-known works; he also wrote *Sylvie and Bruno* (1889) and several mathematical works.

Doll's House, A: a play by *Ibsen (1879). Although, after its first appearance, *A Doll's House* was celebrated most for its social theme—the emancipation of women—Ibsen and its modern audiences consider its importance to lie in its concern for the true basis of wider human relationships. Whether Nora Helmer has the right as a woman to leave her husband is of secondary importance to the significance of her leaving him as an assertion of herself as a seriously thinking, individual human being. *A Doll's House* shows the development of a woman who awakens to her responsibility as an individual and, as a result, throws off the yoke of subjugation imposed on her by her selfish, egotistical, and shallow husband.

Ibsen shows quite clearly here that it is degrading for a man and woman to live together when one refuses to accept the other as a socially responsible individual with independent ideas. Torvald Helmer was unwilling to believe that Nora could have any serious thoughts, and, even when it was pointed out to him that she was capable of assuming responsibility through independent actions, he was still unwilling to concede that such action was becoming or desirable in a wife. For eight years Nora had been a doll-wife, living in a doll's house, playing with her doll-children. But suddenly when the "wonderful thing" did not happen—when her husband failed to support her in a crisis and turned against her as an unscrupulous, irresponsible woman—she realized that her whole life with her father and her husband had been a doll-life in which her own personality had been subjugated and her worth as an individual ignored. The revelation "that before all else I am a reasonable human being" required a decisive step. So Nora left her hus-

209

band and her children in order to learn for herself the conditions of the world, to see "who is right, the world or I."

The drama ends with Nora's departure. Whether she succeeds in finding the answers to her questions and becoming the individual she feels she is meant to be the audience is not told. Ibsen said at one time, "A dramatist's business is not to answer questions, but merely to ask them." *A Doll's House* is one of his best examples of question-asking. Does a person have the right and freedom to do what Nora Helmer did? Are duties to husband and children more sacred than duties to oneself? The answers must come from the audience as it considers the situation and characters which the dramatist has presented.

The action of *A Doll's House* is tight and fast moving and, despite the relatively small span of action within the play itself, tense and exciting. Both a fine sense of action and a careful character development are combined in this drama to make it one of the most popular of all Ibsen's plays.

Donne, John: English poet and preacher (1573–1631). In his youth, Donne was "a great visitor of ladies, a great frequenter of plays, a great writer of conceited verses," for which he is chiefly known today. But, seemingly, in his later life, he preferred to gloss over these early years. Always concerned with religious matters, born a Catholic, converted to Anglicanism, he took holy orders in 1615 and became famous for his eloquent preaching. Most of his writings, both prose and poetry, were published posthumously (1633–51).

Donne's prose, as great in its way as his poetry, includes *Essays in Divinity*, *Devotions upon Emergent Occasions*, *Letters*, and over 160 sermons. (It came to popular attention after *Hemingway used a phrase from the *Devotions* as the title *For Whom the Bell Tolls*.) The sermons are distinguished by their harmonious prose, their complex evolution of ideas, and their dramatic and bold juxtaposition of opposites, a technique that Donne had already developed in his poetry.

Certain of the early poems, *Of the Progress of the Soul, Satires*, and *Divine Poems*, manifest the concern with theology that eventually led Donne into the church. But the poems of the secular *Satires, Sonnets, Songs*, and *Elegies* have quite a different tone. They are erudite, witty, tender, and cynical and reveal a profound insight of human motives. Many are love poems and, in reaction against Petrarchan idealization, Donne stressed love's dualism of body and soul, flesh and spirit, its subtle passions, its cynical bitterness (he willfully praises inconstancy in love). In the best poems, intellect and passion intensify each other by startling and ingenious juxtaposition.

Donne also protested shopworn poetic images. For him the image was not a superficial decoration but an integral part of the poetic structure, the theme frequently being developed by an extended and elaborated metaphor. Because he found the play of intellect a passionate experience, he drew striking images from his erudition—"the recesses of learning not very much frequented by readers of poetry." This sort of verse is called "*metaphysical poetry" because the surprising, ingenious comparisons often played with details taken from philosophical, psychological, or theological thought. Thus, metaphysical poetry is poetry which expresses a complex thought or emotion through an image (conceit) which at first seems far-fetched or paradoxical. (For example, Donne forbids his mistress to kill the flea which has sucked his blood and hers because it is their "bridal bed," the "temple of their wedding.") Donne knew that he was playing with the image, but in all Donne's poems there is the ironic paradox that the play is serious. When humor was added to emotion and analysis, critics called the combination *wit*; and recognizing Donne's originality, they hailed him as "a king that ruled as he thought fit/the universal monarchy of wit."

Donne's attitude toward rhythm was equally revolutionary. Objecting to the metrical exactness of Elizabethan lyrics, he freed accent and rhythm from conventional metrics. He wished to secure a dramatic accent, to capture the intonation and rhythm of everyday speech, although he was content with more regularity than is found, for example, in modern *free verse.

Donne's influence on his own age was threefold. Certain of the love poets learned thoughtfulness and deeper passion. Some religious poets applied the metaphysical technique to their verse. The satirists who stemmed from Donne later reached their culmination in *Dryden and *Pope. His influence on *Coleridge, *Browning, *Hopkins, and on the modern poets has been pervasive and profound. They are attracted by Donne's content—his recognition of the tensions and disparities between the physical experience and its real meaning—and by his flouting of conventional poetic language and attitudes. In matters of technique, modern poets have learned from Donne's use of language and rhythms drawn from everyday speech, his dramatic emphasis on metaphor or image, his method of anticlimactic understatement, and his devices of irony and psychological probing. In Donne they see one who, like themselves, cherishes the intellect, yet feels the need for a spiritual center.

Don Quixote: a novel by *Cervantes (*El ingenioso hidalgo Don Quijote de la Mancha*, Part I, 1605; Part II, 1615). *Don Quixote* began as a burlesque of the already exaggerated deeds of chivalric heroes. As Quixote says, "I know I am capable of being . . . all the Twelve Peers of France and all the *Nine Worthies as well, for my exploits will be far greater than all the deeds they have done, all together and each by himself." The book is concerned with his attempts to make good this boast. Alonso Quixado (*Quijana*, "Lantern-Jaws") is a hidalgo (one of the lower nobility), tall and lean, bordering on 50, "with cheeks that appeared to be kissing each other on the inside of his mouth [and a] neck half a yard long." Having gone out of his mind from reading books of chivalry, with their enchantments, battles, challenges, wooings, agonies, he fancied that he should make himself a knight-errant and roam the world in full armor, righting every kind of wrong and exposing himself to peril; thus he would reap eternal renown as the undoer of injustice, the protector of damsels, the terror of giants, and the winner of battles.

Having changed his name to Don Quixote de la Mancha and invented the necessary chivalric ladylove, Dulcinea del Toboso (in his saner moments, a sturdy farm lass to whom he has never uttered a word), the hero sets out on his bony nag, renamed Rocinante ("formerly a hack"). After his first sally alone, he always takes with him, as his squire, Sancho Panza, a neighboring farmer of big belly and short body, "an honest man, if indeed that title can be given to him who is poor." One of their earliest adventures is a fight against a giant who turns out to be a windmill (originating the familiar expression "to tilt at windmills"). Then follows a battle with a hostile army—a flock of sheep. "This is the work of a magician!" cries Don Quixote. He is almost stoned to death by the enraged shepherds. Finally, misadventure following misadventures, Don Quixote is persuaded that he has been enchanted; he is placed in a cage and brought home. So ends Part I.

In the decade intervening between the publication of Parts I and II, Cervantes became absolute master of his man and matter, and the comic quest developed into a serious search for the real behind the appearance. "This world is nothing but schemes and plots, all working at cross-purposes," mournfully comments the mighty Knight of the Lions, as Quixote now calls himself. A second series of mishaps is more than Quixote can endure. Admitting that he has been mad, he takes to his bed and dies of a broken spirit.

Though *Don Quixote* grew during the many years of its writing and was never planned as a whole, it emerges as a unified work. Even the inserted stories (a standard feature of the fiction of the time) can be weakly defended as providing a romantic world by way of contrast to the chivalric and realistic worlds which contend in the main episodes. These episodes, which are strung together to form the main part of the book, are all variations on one fundamental theme, the relationship between an ideal and a workaday existence. The book was begun as a burlesque on the absurdities of the romances of chivalry, to amuse the reader by showing what a fool a man would be to take them seriously; but it soon grew beyond this intention. Before the end of Part I we admire Don Quixote even in his folly and respect him more than we do the down-to-earth realists who constantly frustrate his idealistic efforts. Here the absence of deliberate planning was an advantage, for the shift which took place naturally as the characters grew in Cervantes' own mind is far more convincing than any deliberately devised transition could have been. In Part II there is profounder delineation of character, more consideration of general problems of morality, government, and society, and a tighter structure. The backgrounds are filled with the color and costume of busy seaport and pastoral countryside—chamber scenes, hunting, garden fetes, a wedding feast, until Cervantes has created a variegated spectacle of Spanish life.

The humor implicit in the theme of a medieval knight in a modern world is enhanced by the verbal byplay— the mock-heroic parody of the redundant eloquence of the romances; the puns, malapropisms, colloquialisms, and homely proverbs unsuitable to chivalric dignity; the use of abrupt and unexpected turns ("Who killed him?" queries Quixote, ready to avenge a death; the answer: "God, by means of a fever").

The adventures achieve their humor partly from the attitude of the hero, partly from the incongruous team which Don Quixote and Sancho form. The ironic paradox is that Quixote, the idealistic dreamer, is the doer, and Sancho, materialistic touchstone of reality, is the talker. But Quixote's inner vision limits the world he sees and acts in; Sancho is the practical, corrective lens. At first Sancho judges every experience as a possible advance toward the goal of his aspirations: the promised governorship of an island. Gradually, as Quixote reveals the virtues of a self-determined reform movement, Sancho's comprehension is broadened; he becomes less intolerant of the Quixotic visions, comes eventually, indeed, to respect them. Association with Quixote adds to Sancho's native wit a philosophic eloquence. ("You are growing less simple and more shrewd every day, Sancho." "Yes," said Sancho, "it must be that some of your worship's discretion sticks to me.") Sancho recognizes that those considered wise are often foolish and morally inferior, and that the man who wishes only to do right is set down as mad. The eternal conflicts between dream and experience, between noble ideal and ignoble reality, between the purity of the goal and the disturbing results of impractical conduct are pointed up by the Quixotic delusion that virtue is easy to define and will automatically triumph. Yet in the conflict, the only touchstone by which to evaluate the deluded universe is the ideal. When Sancho comes to this realization, the world of the comic shifts to tragicomedy.

Although interpretations of *Don Quixote* have varied with the centuries, its influence has continued to affect all European literatures, until Cervantes' name has become one of the best known in literature, and his novel has been translated into more languages than any other book except the Bible. Its admiring imitators have pillaged it for incidents and tried to capture its spirit of kindly irony, its satire without bitterness, and its depth.

Dostoevski, Feodor: Russian novelist (1821–81). Dostoevski, one of the greatest of 19th-century Russian novelists, was born and bred in Moscow. While Feodor was at school, his father was brutally murdered by his own serfs. Although Dostoevski was early interested in literature, he did brilliantly at the College of Military Engineering in St. Petersburg and postponed his writing until he had completed the obligatory two years in the army. Then he became an immediate success with a short first novel, *Poor Folk* (1846).

Dostoevski associated himself with a group of utopian schemers and political revolutionaries. (Exactly what his motives were, how far he was really a plotter and how far merely interested in new ideas, how serious the plots of the group were, and how this episode squares with Dostoevski's later conservatism have been endlessly debated.) When the group was rounded up, he was tried and sentenced to death along with the rest. A reprieve—apparently planned all along by the Czar, who was having his little joke with the plotters—arrived when the prisoners were already in front of the firing squad. But

Dostoevski was deported to Siberia, kept at hard labor for five years, and then forced back into the army. Not until 1859 was he finally pardoned. This sequence of harrowing experiences aggravated his congenital epilepsy and made him bitter. Paradoxically, however, he accepted his imprisonment as an opportunity to expiate sin. His conviction about man's need for penitence, about salvation through suffering, was almost an obsession—one which was to dominate his novels.

The Siberian experiences were reflected in *The Manor of Stepanchikovo* (1859); and *The House of the Dead* (1862). These helped him regain his public, and his improved finances enabled him to travel in western Europe. Like *Tolstoi, he disliked what he saw and henceforth was antagonistic toward the "westernizing" movement in Russia. He became a Slavophile, obsessed with the idea that the Russian people and their Orthodox Christianity would be the salvation of mankind.

During the next decade he suffered from real poverty. The review *Time*, which he edited and in which he first printed *The Insulted and Injured* (1861), and *The House of the Dead*, was suppressed in 1863. When the periodical *Epoch* failed in 1864, Dostoevski was left heavily in debt. His next novels—*Notes from the Underground* (1866), *Crime and Punishment* (1866), *The Gambler* (1867)—were written at top speed (like some of those of *Scott and *Balzac) in an effort to earn enough to pay his creditors. *The Gambler* was based on his own almost insane passion for gambling, *Crime and Punishment* on the inner life of a murderer, the psychological aspect of a crime. But the novels did not pay the creditors and Dostoevski spent four more years in western Europe (1867–71). During this period of unmitigated misery, of gambling, poverty, and illness, he nevertheless managed to write *The Idiot* (1869) and *The Possessed* (1871).

After his return to Russia, he was ranked with *Turgenev and Tolstoi. He edited a conservative magazine, *The Citizen*, to which he contributed a column, later published as *A Writer's Diary*, and he wrote *A Raw Youth* (1875). His political conservatism brought favor even from the Czar. His personality, however, was still marred by the consciousness of his own dual personality and an inner struggle of good and evil which had been foreshadowed as early as *The Double* (1846). This conflict is brilliantly dramatized in his two greatest novels, *Crime and Punishment* and his last, *The *Brothers Karamazov* (1880). This work, while not so tense in atmosphere as *Crime and Punishment*, offers like it a galaxy of fascinating characters and considerable action highlighted by a typical Dostoevskian murder with its multiple and uncertain human motivation. The strengths of these two novels—the probing of the depths of the mind and the revelations of the startling contradictions in men's souls and personalities— are the hallmarks of Dostoevski's genius.

drama: a literary work written in dialogue and intended for presentation by actors. The essence of drama is the make-believe by which an actor impersonates a character of the play. Wherever drama has evolved—in ancient Greece, medieval Europe, India, China, Japan— its basic origin is the same; it arises from religious ritual, in the exchange of speech or song between leader and chorus, or between antiphonal choirs. Once the germ of the idea appears, even in a four-line form (see *trope), it rapidly expands until complete plays are developed, and it may become entirely secularized—and even be condemned by the religion from whose rites it rose.

The element of make-believe in drama is much greater than the average playgoer realizes. When we see *Shakespeare's *Julius Caesar* we not only have to assume that a living person is Caesar. We have to assume further that it is now 44 B.C., that Caesar and the other Romans spoke a slightly archaic form of English, that New York or London or Podunk is Rome to begin with, but can become Greece instead at a moment's notice. In the modern theater we must regard it as entirely natural that rooms, houses, and even the Roman Senate chamber have one wall missing. The playgoer becomes conscious of the conventions of drama only when he encounters a play using a different set from his own.

Many of the conventions arise from the physical ar-

217

rangements of the theater for which a play was written. A Greek drama did not have scenes taking place in different cities because there was no curtain and the action was continuous from start to finish. Elizabethan drama contained fine descriptive speeches because there was little scenery on the stage; it was written into the play instead. Thus anyone who approaches dramatists not in his own tradition needs to make a deliberate attempt to understand the arrangement of their theater and to learn the conventions which their audience accepted.

Drama is usually subdivided into *tragedy and *comedy, though at times these basic types have been mixed. During the 18th century there arose a type which was neither of these, but merely a drama (French *drame*) of middle-class life and problems. This tended to become a "problem play," and many plays of *Ibsen, *Shaw, and the contemporary theater really fall into this category, though they may be loosely called tragedies or comedies. Within the general framework of the drama a bewildering number of special types and subtypes have been developed— things as various as the Greek *satyr-play, the Spanish religious play known as an *auto* ("act"), the *Renaissance pastoral play and *commedia dell' arte*, the Elizabethan revenge play, tragicomedy, *comedy of humors, and *masque, the 18th-century bourgeois tragedy, the proletarian play, the *comedy of manners, the farce. The "closet drama" requires special comment because it violates a part of the definition given above. It is written in dramatic form but is a poem intended for private reading rather than performance on the stage. *Milton's *Samson Agonistes* is a fine example.

In spite of a great growth of urban centers, the number of professional theaters has declined sharply during the last century. On the other hand, there has been a great increase in the number of college and amateur performances, so that the "legitimate" drama is still holding its own. Furthermore, drama is the literary form most viable with the modern mass media, and film, radio, and television are producing a vast quantity of it, ranging all the way from "soap opera," Westerns, and farce (a staple of the television comedians) to serious new works and fine productions of old ones. Most of this material is ephemeral and worthless but we must remember that the theater, as an agency of entertainment, has always had a high proportion of ephemeral and worthless plays. The film has already produced some masterpieces in its own right, and the broadcasters may similarly rise to the level of occasional greatness.

dramatic monologue: a poem in which one character speaks throughout, but the presence, actions, and even words of other characters are implied. Caught at a dramatic moment or crisis in his life, plunged, so to speak, *in medias res*, the speaker unconsciously, often ironically, reveals his innermost character, his "soul in action," and tells much of his history, social position, and relationship to other persons present. Some of Robert *Browning's poems *(My Last Duchess, Andrea Del Sarto, The Bishop Orders His Tomb)* are the most famous examples of the type. *Shakespeare's soliloquies and many of *Donne's poems provided Browning with models of realistic studies, idiomatic in diction, psychological in focus, emotionally intense. The form was used also by *Tennyson (*Ulysses*) and by the American poets *Frost, *Lowell, Robinson, and Sandburg. T. S. *Eliot's *The Love Song of J. Alfred Prufrock* may also be considered a dramatic monologue.

dream-allegory: a standard type of medieval poem. The dream-allegory goes back ultimately to a passage in *Cicero's *Republic* known as *The Dream of Scipio*, in which a man is taken into the sky in a dream and shown a vision of the world and the life after death. The first example of the medieval type, and the model for all the rest, is the *Romance of the Rose*. The dream-allegory rapidly became a highly conventionalized poetic form, typically running as follows: The poet, unable to sleep, finally takes a book to read and falls asleep over it. He dreams that he is in a beautiful garden in the spring. Some animal usually guides him into the garden, or to some specific part of it. In the garden, or starting from it, he experiences a series of events involving characters who have some allegorical significance and usually allegorical names. This dream is the major part of the poem, both in importance and in length, and the poem concludes briefly with the poet's awakening. Often the reader is called on to interpret the dream.

*Chaucer wrote four dream-allegories: *The Book of the Duchess*, *The House of Fame*, *The Parliament of Fowls*, and the *frame-tale (Prologue) of *The Legend of Good Women*. His contemporary William Langland also used the form, in an entirely different vein, as a vehicle of sharp social criticism in his *Piers Plowman*.

Dreiser, Theodore: American novelist, one of the foremost exponents of Zolaesque *naturalism in the United States (1871–1945). His best-known works, *Sister Carrie* (1900) and *An American Tragedy* (1925), argue the force of heredity and environment; his characters are treated as pawns of circumstance. In spite of his awkward style and crudity of expression, Dreiser's works carried in them the power of his belief in the involuntary "chemistry" of humans. His trilogy, *The Financier* (1912), *The Titan* (1914), and *The Stoic* (1948), is a study of financial power and the worship of success and materialism. The sense of the irrational brute energy of human endeavor and the fateful predicament of man in the modern world animates all his work. In his novels he thus made a claim for the dilemma of mediocrity, insisting that such figures are "tragic" and transcend mere pathos. He embraced socialism in his later years and wrote widely both as journalist, traveler, and theater critic. His works are massive, detailed, and sincere in their overall "social consciousness"; but the want of style and form has militated against their reputation in recent years. *Sister Carrie* continues to be a favorite, however, as a story of a working girl who transcends her subservience to the man whose mistress she is, to acquire an identity of her own.

Dryden, John: English dramatist, satirical poet, and literary critic (1631–1700). Dryden was the foremost man of letters in England during the last quarter of the 17th century. He received a good education at Cambridge, and the intellectual interests of his later life are attested by his study of Descartes and *Hobbes and his membership in the Royal Society. The important events in his life are reflected in his writings, which mark his shifts in politics and religion. In an early poem he praised the Puritan Cromwell (*Heroic Stanzas*, 1658); but with the Restoration he celebrated the Stuart King Charles II (*Astraea Redux*, "Justice Restored," 1660). He defended the Church of England (*Religio Laici*, "A Layman's Religion," 1683), and later becoming Catholic, praised James II and the Roman Catholic Church (*The Hind and the Panther*, 1687). For the courtly Restoration audience he wrote comedies (*The Rival Ladies*, 1663; *Marriage à la Mode*, 1672); such poems as *Annus Mirabilis* (1666, the "year of wonders"—the Plague, London Fire, Dutch War); satires directed against political and religious opponents (*Absalom and Achitophel*, 1681); and numerous heroic tragedies. These last were bombastic plays filled with great deeds and greater dilemmas of love and honor, composed in *heroic couplets (*The Indian Queen*, 1664; *Aureng Zebe*, 1675). His best tragedy, *All for Love* (1677), was, however, written in blank verse in the Elizabethan manner. Although modeling his play on *Antony and Cleopatra*, Dryden observed the *unities as *Shakespeare did not. Dryden also wrote excellent lyrics (*Ode for St. Cecilia's Day*, *Alexander's Feast*) and translations of *Vergil (1697) and a miscellany of *Fables* (*i.e.*, narrative poems, 1700).

Dryden's greatest contribution lies in two fields, satire and criticism. He was a brilliant and merciless satirist, *Mac Flecknoe* (1682) being one of the most famous personal satires in literature. In the history of English verse satire, his only rivals are *Pope and *Byron. In addition, Dryden by his practice established the rimed couplet as the principal English meter for satire and terse epigrammatic statement. As a literary critic he was forceful, lucid, and perceptive—the inaugurator of an "age of prose and reason," as Matthew *Arnold said. His numerous essays (*e.g., Essay of Dramatic Poesy*, 1668) and prefaces are intellectually acute and carefully arranged. Models in their prose style as well as ideas, they won him the title of "father of English prose." These pieces are, moreover, the first considerable body of literary crit-

221

icism in English. In an age which valued craftsmanship and vigorous, sensible thinking, Dryden well earned his position as leader. The example of his poetry formed Pope, as his prose formed *Addison and the 18th century.

Dumas, Alexandre: a father and son, both French novelists and dramatists (1802–70 and 1824–95). Dumas *père* ("father"), son of a distinguished part-Negro general of the French Army under Napoleon, is notable for historical novels and plays. A man of boundless energy and limitless conceptions, he wrote with fantastic productivity, lived riotously, earned tremendous sums, and was frequently penniless. Characteristic is his building of a castle which he called "Monte Cristo" and soon had to sell to pay his debts.

In his plays (*Henry III and His Court*, 1829; *Napoleon*; *Antony*, 1831) and the dramatizations of his novels, he introduced to the French stage a combination of sweeping historical tableaux and flamboyant romantic emotions (see *Romantic Movement). The dramas are well-plotted but violent and sensational. Whether purely fictional or based on historical subjects (Dumas preferred the latter), they are always extravagant in their passions.

Inspired by Sir Walter *Scott and with the assistance of a "factory" of collaborators, Dumas turned out over 300 lengthy cloak-and-dagger tales. *The Three Musketeers* (1844) and *The Count of Monte Cristo* (1844–45) are the most famous of these swashbuckling pseudohistorical novels. As in the plays, the characters are oversimplified and the plots suffer from excessive brutalities and coincidences. Although individual details are realistic, the whole is completely improbable. Yet the stories maintain interest by their vigor and their intensely melodramatic scenes. The novels were designed for mass consumption, and, although they lack distinction in style or character, they have long enjoyed great popular success.

Dumas' illegitimate son, Alexandre Dumas *fils* ("son") was also a dramatist and novelist; but unlike his father he had no taste for dissipation or melodrama. He preferred the realistic technique and social-problem themes (see *realism). His plays deal with deviations from morality by the higher social classes. Most famous of these is *Camille* (*La Dame aux camélias*, 1852), a sentimental story of a prostitute who gives up the man she loves so as not to ruin his career and is herself purified by her act of renunciation. (This play is the source of Verdi's opera *La Traviata*.) In addition to their brilliant technical construction and realistic dialogue, the plays of Dumas *fils* have the historical importance of being the earliest of the modern "problem plays."

eclogue: a Greek term originally applied (like its exact English equivalent, "selection") to almost any moderately short poem, or to a passage from a longer one. Since its application to *Vergil's *Bucolics*, the term has been restricted to mean a *pastoral poem in which shepherds are the speakers. The eclogue may be a song of courtship, a lament about disappointment in love, a dirge for the death of a fellow shepherd. It may be a monologue in the first person, a poetic dialogue, or a singing contest; and it may conceal an *allegory of political, artistic, or religious ideas or developments. Vergil was the first writer to give any prominence to allegory in pastoral poetry. During the *Renaissance the Latin eclogues of Baptista Mantuanus were extremely influential on the Spanish eclogues of V. G. de la Vega, the French ones of *Ronsard, and the English *Shepherd's Calendar* of *Spenser.

Edda: a name of unknown meaning given to two different compilations in Old Icelandic, the *Poetic* (or Elder) *Edda*, composed *c.* 900–*c.* 1050, and surviving in a manuscript of the 13th century; and the *Prose* (or Younger) *Edda*, written by Snorri Sturluson (1178–1241).

The *Poetic Edda* is a treasure house of Scandinavian mythological and heroic poetry. Yet it is only a haphazard collection of 34 fragmentary, nonsequential poems by unknown authors. They vary in length from 14 to 165 four-line stanzas, each line of verse sharply divided by a caesural pause into two half lines and linked by initial and internal alliterations.

One group of poems conveys a lively impression of titanic giants and humanized gods. The gods have ideals of courage and loyalty, but they are activated by love of wisdom, women, and wandering. Odin, the All-father of the gods, has achieved his wisdom at the cost of an eye and a persistent mysterious pain. The *Lay of Thrym*, a swift-moving ballad of broad humor and sharp characterization, describes the delightfully comic disguise by which Thor pretends to be the goddess Freya in a mock marriage.

The lays about the heroes deal with climactic moments in the history of the Volsungs (tales later embodied in the *Volsung Saga* and *Nibelungenlied*). These poems are terse in style and rapid in action and at the same time profound in the delineation of character. Sigurd the Volsung is a folk hero of remarkable strength, nobility, and wisdom. He can understand the language of birds; he wins great treasure, rescues a supernatural warrior-maiden, is impervious to poison—only to meet his death by treachery at the hands of his own kinsmen. All the characters move toward their doom with compulsive persistence, accepting as inevitable the sufferings and tragedy of human life: "Ever with grief and all too long are men and women born in the world." The graphic scenes which record this turbulent action and the emotional conflicts of extraordinary passion are created not by straight, consistent narratives but by dramatic dialogues and laments, of which the best known are *The Death of Fafnir*, *The Long Lay of Sigurd*, *Brynhild's Hel-Ride*, *The Lay of Gudrun*. Discrepancies between the separate ballads are due to the fact that they are based on different versions of the legend.

The *Prose Edda*, a compilation prepared as a textbook for apprentice poets, contains prose paraphrases of many of the verses in the *Poetic Edda*, together with a number of quotations from it and a summary of Old Norse mythology. For a complete and more coherent version of the fate of the Volsungs one must turn to the *Volsung Saga*, which drew heavily on the *Poetic Edda*.

Edwards, Jonathan: a rigidly Calvinistic American preacher and theologian (1703–58). In his own time Edwards was best known as a master of the hell-fire sermon, of which the best example is his *Sinners in the Hands of an Angry God* (1741): "The God that holds you over the pit of hell, much as one holds a spider or some loathsome insect over the fire, abhors you, and is dreadfully provoked." More valuable and ingratiating are his autobiography, *Personal Narrative* (written about 1740–42), and his theological and psychological studies on the freedom of the will, the problem of evil, and the nature of religious experience, the most important of these being *A Careful and Strict Enquiry . . . of That Freedom of the Will . . .* (1754).

Eichendorff, Joseph Freiherr von: German poet (1788–1857). Eichendorff was a master of the romantic lyric, in which he achieved a perfect balance of feeling and expression, of form and content. His lyrics have been extensively set to music by the greatest masters of the German art-song. Of his numerous prose tales, only one really survives as living literature, *The Happy-Go-Lucky (Aus dem Leben eines Taugenichts,* 1826).

Electra: a tragedy by *Euripides (413 B.C.). Electra, the daughter of Agamemnon, urged her brother Orestes on to kill their mother, Clytemnestra, in order to avenge the latter's murder of their father. The legend is also treated in the second play of the *Oresteia* of *Aeschylus and in the *Electra* of *Sophocles. In Aeschylus' version the light has been focused on the action, the characters appearing only as shadows or reflections thereof. The *Electra* of Sophocles and that of Euripides, however, are the products of a more individualized age that demanded emphasis on character. Action becomes important only as it portrays character and not as an end in itself.

In the character of Electra, Euripides has caught the

most immediate reflection of the horror arising from the hereditary curse on her family, for the tragedy mirrors itself more sharply in her life than in that of her brother Orestes, who, having been cast out as a child, has spent his life in exile. Euripides, adding a new concept to Greek tragedy, regards the forces of human emotional life as a power comparable to a deity. Thus in *Electra* revenge requires no supernatural inciting or manipulation but has its origin and justification in the souls of those most directly concerned, Orestes and Electra.

Many critics contend that Euripides wrote his *Electra* out of a desire to awaken his fellow Athenians from their blind and superstitious acceptance of the deity, to arouse them to independence and criticism, to develop their sense of values. He intended to point out that a god who commands a man to murder his mother cannot be regarded as a moral example for any human being. Hearers were to weigh the justification for such a demand; rather than look beyond the clouds for a supreme judgment, they were to concentrate on the basic nature and qualities of his hero and heroine.

No matter how gruesome the deeds that Electra contemplates and Orestes commits, both characters are above all intensely human. Orestes may be able, without hesitation, to murder Aegisthus, the rude intruder into his father's palace and his mother's bed; yet, at the sight of his mother he pales and trembles, and it is Electra (whose jealous hatred of her mother has grown violent during the course of the years) who must goad him on to the actual killing. The conflict between a natural love for his mother and the terrible knowledge of her guilt gradually tears Orestes' soul apart. (The results of this conflict are powerfully described in Euripides' later tragedy *Orestes*, 408 B.C.). Equally human is the portrayal of Electra. The primary concern of her grief is not the murder of her father by her mother, but her own humiliation, her degradation to extreme poverty and a marriage beneath her station, and her frustrated womanhood. For all these things she has her mother to blame (even though Clytemnestra did have maternal feeling enough to save her daughter from death). The most violent hatred in Electra's soul arises when she is confronted by women (here her mother and later, in *Orestes*, Helen of Troy) who have everything: beauty, marriage, and riches. Electra takes an almost masochistic delight in contemplating her degradation while she keeps recalling to herself: "I was born Agamemnon's daughter."

Euripides' amazing psychological insight is perhaps best revealed in the speech in which Electra is portrayed as a woman whose desire for revenge has unbalanced her mind. Her utter loneliness and prolonged virginity have obscured the true cause for her revenge; her own misery and her envy of her mother's luxurious life have overshadowed the original cause, her mother's part in the murder of her father.

The hero and heroine are saved from death in the end. Their suffering unites them and intensifies their love for each other. But their guilt must be atoned for: their exile from Argos separates them.

A comparison between Euripides' *Electra* and his *Medea* is almost inevitable. The heroines of both plays are driven by a passion for revenge, a revenge which Medea directs primarily against her husband, Electra against her mother; and the strength of both women lies in their relentless pursuit of their object. Their lust for revenge eventually grows so great that it fills their lives completely, becomes the sole content and purpose of their existence, and grows greater than themselves. Revenge makes them bestial and inhuman.

elegiac couplet: a pair of unrimed lines of poetry, the first being a regular dactylic hexameter and the second a hexameter with only the first syllable present in the third and sixth feet. Strangely enough, it can be perfectly illustrated from Walt *Whitman: "Sing from the swamps, the recesses, pour your chant from the bushes, / Limitless out of the dust, out of the cedars and pines."

The form goes back to the 7th century B.C. in Greece and was extensively used by the Latin elegiac writers, especially *Catullus. In an accentual form it has been used in various modern languages.

elegy: in ancient Greece, a poem written in *elegiac couplets, sung to the accompaniment of the flute. Its

227

themes included martial and convivial subjects, laments, and epitaphs in which the dead spoke in the first person. In modern usage, there is no prescribed metrical form, but the themes have become more rigidly restricted. The Elizabethans, like *Ovid before them, called a love "plaint" (complaint or lament) an elegy. But they also used the word in the sense it most often has today: a mournful lyric whose theme is either death in general or the death of a specific person. The most famous English example of an elegy inspired by musings on death is Thomas *Gray's *Elegy Written in a Country Churchyard* (1751). The most famous American elegy, Walt *Whitman's *When Lilacs Last in the Dooryard Bloom'd*, was inspired by the assassination of *Lincoln.

The combination of elegiac and *pastoral traditions produced the pastoral elegy, in which the imagery is rural and the mourners and the dead appear in the guise of shepherds. English examples of this special form are *Spenser's November eclogue in the *Shepherd's Calendar*, *Milton's *Lycidas*, *Shelley's *Adonais*, *Arnold's *Thyrsis*.

Eliot, George: pseudonym of Mary Ann Evans, English novelist (1819–80). Born in rural England and reared in a strict Methodist family, Mary Evans lost her orthodox religious zeal in her twenties and became one of the first of her time to accept the scientific attitudes demanding sound reason and objectivity in religious questions. But, as her works show, she never lost a deeply rooted moral sense that preached resignation to duty and recognition of the doctrine of retribution.

Her literary efforts began with a translation of David Strauss's *Life of Jesus* (1846). In 1851 she became assistant editor of the *Westminster Review*. Soon thereafter she went to live with the critic George Henry Lewes, who was unable to obtain a divorce from his wife. He diverted her from philosophy to fiction, and her first three tales appeared as *Scenes from Clerical Life* (1858). Her next three stories, set against the background of the rural life she knew so well—*Adam Bede* (1859), *The Mill on the Floss* (1860), and *Silas Marner* (1861)—established her as a novelist of warm sympathy for the humble and disgraced. Although she went to Italy to acquire at first hand the setting for *Romola* (1863), this historical novel of Renaissance Florence never comes to life. The Reform Movement of 1832 furnished the background for her one venture into the political novel, *Felix Holt, the Radical* (1866). In both *Middlemarch* (1872) and *Daniel Deronda* (1876), two main plots are skillfully interwoven. Her skill in portraying a whole community in *Middlemarch*, her best novel, invites comparison with *Balzac, and her picture of village life has been compared to that in *Flaubert's *Madame Bovary*.

George Eliot's contribution to the development of the novel came from her conscious attempt at *realism, especially in probing character and social situations of provincial life. She had the ability to analyze the interdependence of people in a restricted community, to assess their motivations, and to treat the intricate effects of the social climate on personality. It is true that her tendency to write as though she were giving a lesson in ethics or psychology slowed up the story. Nevertheless, she must be placed among the first significant writers of the psychological-sociological novel.

Eliot, T(homas) S(tearns): American-born British poet, dramatist, and critic (1888–1965). Eliot became a British subject in 1927 and spent the greater part of his life in England. An exponent of tradition in literature, politics, and religion, he was anything but traditional in his technical innovations and experiments with language and form in his poetry. The frame of his thought is conservative; the picture within the frame can be said to come close, sometimes, to the art experiments of painters as different as Dali and Picasso. Indeed, there are paintings by Dali of timeless bent clock faces against waste desert spaces that remind one of Eliot's principal symbols— time that merges past and present in a world that is a waste land that must be reborn.

Eliot, however, considered himself a "classicist in literature" and this he was to the extent that he was a 20th-century rational man whose intellect presided over his emotions. Moreover, his inner world was policed by a New England heritage, retransplanted to Old England, where Eliot developed a firm belief in an aristocratic order of society and in Anglo-Catholicism. Behind these seeming paradoxes was a man who renovated poetry and redirected criticism to fundamentals, notably to a close and searching reading of the text. Eliot was deeply influenced by French *symbolism, by James *Joyce's *Ulysses*, and by his friend Ezra *Pound. His most celebrated poem, *The *Waste Land*, which marked a veritable revolution in modern English poetry, derives much from the Joycean experiments in rendering consciousness—particularly in the way in which the mind latches on to seemingly unrelated observations and unifies them.

Eliot's poetry is generally considered "difficult" in its use of sequences of images and symbols that the reader must himself bring into relationship in his own mind. It is, moreover, filled with borrowings of lines and phrases from poets and prose writers past and present. In his use of language he sought always to arrive at a sense of speech and the verbal uses of our time.

To understand Eliot's poetry two fundamental concepts must be grasped: the first is that his poetry is a kind of continuous and complex stream of thought, a composite of memories in which what we have experienced in the past is constantly merging with our experience of the moment. Once we have read any poet, some of his lines may become part of our personal experience. We often quote him to ourselves; we derive a repeated emotion or series of emotions from the sequence of words he has set down. And so Eliot quotes writers to himself in his poetry, mulls over their images and phrases, like so many possessions in the jewel box—or some will say the attic—of his mind.

This leads to the second concept: we must grasp Eliot's obsession with the problem of time, which characterizes the work of so many contemporary writers, among them Joyce, *Proust, *Mann and Eliot's younger contemporary *Faulkner. "Time present and time past/ Are both perhaps present in time future/And time future contained in time past." The essence of this thought, expressed by Eliot in one of his *Four Quartets*, is that if our past can determine our present, then our present determines our future; and also that memory can dredge up incidents and feelings of long ago and render them actual, so that they once again become part of the present. Thus when Eliot evokes the Thames in a poem, it is the river that runs through London now. But it is also the river on which the royalty of England rode in their barges centuries before, and the very name Thames is redolent with memories historic and personal not only to Londoners but to those in far-off places who have never been to London. It is also the Thames celebrated by *Spenser, whose line "Sweet Themmes! runne softly, till I end my Song," he remembers.

Eliot himself explained this once in a lecture on *Ulysses*, saying: "In some minds certain memories, both from reading and from life, become charged with emotional significance. All these are used, so that intensity is gained at the expense of clarity." This concept Eliot expanded into what he called the "objective correlative"— "a set of objects, a chain of events" which become the formula for a particular emotion. In this much used formulation, Eliot tried to convey the simple idea that language in a poem is the objective form of the poet's preverbalized subjective world.

In criticism, Eliot provided for the present generation a reinterpretation of certain classical writers. He made critical readjustments which are inevitable in the light of our world, the peculiar bent of his own mind, and the special formation of his own taste. He rendered homage to *Dryden and examined *Baudelaire and the French Symbolists; he attacked *Milton and exalted *Donne; he brought about a rereading of *Dante. And in the theater he reasserted the force of poetry on the stage. During three decades he wrote some 500 pieces of criticism— essays, reviews, broadcasts, lectures. Central to his criticism was an attempt to discuss the *experience* of reading a given writer, and the sharpening of critical perceptions upon this experience.

Eliot, though of New England descent, was born at St. Louis, Missouri, and studied at Harvard, the University of Paris, and Oxford. He settled in England in 1914, when he was 26. He taught, worked in a bank, and ultimately joined the publishing firm of Faber & Faber. *Prufrock* appeared in 1917 and was followed by *Poems* in 1920, a volume that was enlarged during the years to include later work. The body of his poetry is small, and the early works were strong in their pessimism and disillusion. *The Waste Land* (1922) pictured the world as dry and hopeless, and *The Hollow Men* (1925) was no less despairing. Editor from 1917 to 1919 of the *Egoist*, Eliot founded in 1922 and edited until 1939 *The Criterion*. His first collection of essays, *The Sacred Wood*, appeared in 1920.

Publication in 1928 of *For Lancelot Andrewes*, containing *Essays on Style and Order*, set forth Eliot's fundamental tory beliefs in the form of critiques of *Machiavelli, Lancelot Andrewes, Baudelaire, Middleton, and Crashaw. The book also contained a discussion of the humanism of Irving Babbitt, which inaugurated a controversy that raged for a long time in the literary journals. A strong vein of religiosity subsequently marked his writings, as in *Ash Wednesday* (1930), *Four Quartets* (1943), and his first important drama, *Murder in the Cathedral* (1935). This play was followed by *Family Reunion* (1939), the highly successful *The Cocktail Party* (1950), and *The Confidential Clerk* (1955). Eliot's theory of poetic drama was that the play must be a "musical pattern" which intensifies the action and the resultant emotion. He warned against allowing "bursts of poetry" to be a substitute for action.

Eliot's critical volumes also include *Elizabethan Essays* (1934), *Essays Ancient and Modern* (1936), *The Use of Poetry and the Use of Criticism* and *After Strange Gods* (both of 1933), *The Idea of a Christian Society* (1939), and *Notes Toward the Definition of Culture* (1949). He received the Nobel prize in 1948.

Elysian Fields: the abode of the blessed dead in *Hades.

Elysium: the *Elysian Fields.

Emerson, Ralph Waldo: American essayist, lecturer, and poet (1803–82). Emerson, the descendant of a New

England ministerial family, was brought up in poverty, graduated from Harvard, and tried teaching for four years before deciding to preach. Six years after becoming a Unitarian preacher, he resigned (1832) because of his unwillingness to administer communion. He was not actively hostile to the rite: "that is the end of my opposition, that I am not interested in it." But he could not administer a religion to which he did not fully respond. Depressed by the death of his wife, his break with his past, and his ill health, he made a trip of nearly a year to Europe, where he met *Coleridge, *Wordsworth, and, most important to him, *Carlyle, with whom he began a life-long friendship. He returned to America stimulated and recuperated, settled in Concord with a new wife, and spent most of the rest of his life there in literary pursuits and civic activities.

Nature (his first book, 1836), *The American Scholar* (an address delivered before the Harvard Phi Beta Kappa Society, 1837), and his *Divinity School Address* (delivered at Harvard, 1838) mark a decisive turn in his life and contain most of his basic ideas. *Nature* went practically unnoticed, but *The American Scholar* sold well, and, although the *Divinity School Address* alarmed Harvard by its religious radicalism, his audience was increasing and he soon became a full-fledged lyceum lecturer. As a "lay preacher" he traveled over America by wagon, stagecoach, sleigh, canal boat, steamboat, and train. The tours were physical ordeals —several times he had to walk across the Mississippi on the ice, his stagecoach turned over, he escaped from a burning hotel— but, in spite of the "squalor and obstructions of travel," he enjoyed his direct contact with American places and people. He did not talk down to his audiences or indulge in spread-eagle oratory; he respected them, and they him. Some of his mystical transcendentalism may have been beyond them, but his individualism, couched in homely metaphor, was a credo they could grasp. For more than 30 years the lecture platform was the support of his abstemious life. Concord continued to be his base of operations, and there he knew *Hawthorne and *Thoreau. For a brief period he edited *The Dial*, a magazine of advanced thought. He continued to produce books regularly: *Essays, First Series* (1841), *Essays, Second Series* (1844), *Poems* (1847), *Nature, Addresses and Lectures* (1849), *Representative Men* (1850), *English Traits* (the long-ripened fruit of an earlier year of lecturing in England, 1856), and *The Conduct of Life* (1860). Although not generally a joiner, he took considerable part in the antislavery agitation of the abolitionists. During his last years his activities gradually slowed down and his memory failed him: at *Longfellow's funeral, looking at his dead friend's face, he said, "I cannot remember his name, but he was a good man."

Although Emerson admitted his lack of systematic philosophy, he claimed that his teaching was unified, setting forth "the infinitude of the private man." This doctrine was cardinal in New England Transcendentalism, of which Emerson was the greatest exponent. It is an eclectic doctrine combining elements from the idealistic German philosophers as interpreted by Coleridge and Carlyle, from *Plato and *Neo-Platonism, from Oriental religions and mysticism, and from Emanuel *Swedenborg. It holds that man has faculties that "transcend" the senses, that give him ideas and intuitions that "transcend" sensational experience. It does not conceive God in terms of man or as a Trinity, but, like Unitarianism, conceives God as one and Christ as not divine but the highest realization on earth of man's potentialities. For Emerson, God is immanent in man, is the omnipresent and benevolent Over-Soul, a source of spiritual energy from which knowledge comes to man by intuition. No intermediary—no church, preacher, or sacred book—is essential. As early as the *Divinity School Address*, Emerson attacked formalized, historical Christianity. The part of God in a man is his *self;* every man relying on himself is trusting to the God in him. "Trust thyself; every heart vibrates to that iron string." "Nothing is at last sacred but the integrity of your own mind." Since every man has equal right to this self-reliance, it cannot involve either an egotistic attitude or a predatory line of conduct.

Though he read widely, Emerson opposed the use of books as a substitute for thought. Great figures of the past, "representative men," are only exhibitions of human possibilities. In *The American Scholar* (sometimes called America's Intellectual Declaration of Independence) Emerson spoke out strongly against the subservience of American writers to Europe and for a contemporary democratic literature. But democracy is no substitute for thought either: Emerson denounced "the hypocritical prating about the masses," whose lives "are not worth preserving." And he was well aware of many of the flaws of American democratic society, of commercial corruption and political hypocrisy. He clearly distinguished between "law for man and law for thing" and found that "Things are in the saddle / And ride mankind."

Emerson's style is terse and concise rather than ornate. He favored the oldest, simplest English words, the strong language of the streets and of daily talk, words which "if cut, would bleed." He is one of the most quotable of authors, more remembered for epigrams than for consistent, total essays. This is a distinction that he would approve, for he loved literature chiefly for its sententiousness and had little respect for prose fiction and drama. His poetry shows the same epigrammatic terseness, although it is often marred by a contempt for technique and craftsmanship. At its best, however, its very directness and unconventionality give it its characteristic tone and strength. Typically, his poems are short and pithy, and his freedom of vision and expression influenced poets as divergent as Walt *Whitman and Emily *Dickinson.

Emile, or a Treatise on Education: a book by *Rousseau (1762), giving a carefully worked out plan for the upbringing of male children from infancy through adolescence. The guiding principle Rousseau set for himself was his basic theory that "natural man" is good and that giving free rein to nature must result in a good education. He thus began by urging that children be suckled by their own mothers; that they be kept free of swaddling clothes so that the body's natural movement not be hampered; that they be given love and devotion.

Aware that fathers cannot carry out their paternal duties because of the demands made by society on men, Rousseau would substitute a tutor, and he lays down proper rules for his fitness. Doctors must be called in as little as possible. Man has not allowed himself to discover just how far nature itself will take care and heal. Let Emile's mind develop through conversation, experiments arranged by the teacher, indeed everything that will help him to use his eyes and his senses and his imagination. Punishment must not be used. The child must learn that his own destructiveness can only contribute to his own discomfort.

Teach Emile to be self-reliant. If he tumbles or bumps his head—no fussing. The child must learn to suffer the accidents and pains of life. Give the child free rein in sports. Let him commune with nature. Let him experience *feeling*. Let him do a certain amount of manual labor. Let him learn its dignity. He must not have big words foisted upon him or be made to memorize and repeat lessons. Let the child run around barefoot: but also see to it that his path is not strewn with glass.

The first book Rousseau prescribes for Emile is *Defoe's Robinson Crusoe*, because that book is the story of a man brought face to face with nature and a record of steadfastness and self-reliance. This is to be read at 12, when it can be understood. And now geography, and elements of science, must be taught, and the wonders of existence made known to the developing mind.

As for faith, the child must believe in God and see Him in all life. Rousseau would have no books, no church, no priests, no rites, where religion is concerned. He would substitute Deism for the dogmas of the Church.

At the end—it seemed almost an afterthought—Rousseau made some suggestions for the education of women. But he saw women as the mere servants and handmaidens of men. For them he provided the role Thérèse Le Vasseur had played in his life: a role confining them to the limits of what he deemed to be their competence.

In his psychological understanding of childhood, Rousseau laid the foundations for modern child care. Some of the ideas—then so revolutionary—long ago were applied with success. In *Emile*, as in his other writings, Rousseau struck a forceful blow for a more healthy man. And the people of that time recognized the sanity of the book. It remains one of the world's great works on education, and even today, when Rousseau's other works seem somewhat tamed by time, *Emile* is a thoughtful and highly readable study.

Enemy of the People, An: a play by *Ibsen (1882). This play was the answer to the critics and the "compact majority" who had objected to Ibsen's preceding play, *Ghosts*. Here he brought out the spiritual laziness, backwardness, and dishonesty of a community whose water supply was poisoned. Dr. Thomas Stockmann, the chief character of the play, comes to see only the one great basic evil: "I have said that I would speak of the great discovery I have made within the last few days—the discovery that all our sources of spiritual life are poisoned and that our whole society rests upon a pestilential basis of falsehood." Often the question has been raised how far Ibsen is to be identified with his idealistic hero. Although there are many parallels between the character and his creator, Ibsen did not want to identify himself with Dr. Stockmann. "The Doctor and I get on very well together," wrote Ibsen to his publisher; "we agree on many subjects. But the Doctor is more muddleheaded than I am." Dr. Stockmann is basically a simple and somewhat crudely gay and optimistic human being. His enthusiasm is wilder, more thoughtless, his disregard of bourgeois possession and responsibility more Bohemian than Ibsen's could ever have been. These are matters of temperament, however, and one important trait they share is their stubbornness. On the basic issues—the ideological ones—Ibsen and Dr. Stockmann are in agreement. Nothing could ever prevent Ibsen from expressing what he felt to be the truth. Opposition spurred rather than hindered him. Experience had taught him that a singular and independent mind stays approximately ten years ahead of the dull majority which lives by the dead slogans of the past. "In ten years the majority will, possibly, occupy the point which Dr. Stockmann held at the public meeting. But during these ten years the doctor will not have been standing still. He will still be at least ten years ahead of the majority."

Like many of the leading thinkers of his time, Ibsen thought that the "compact majority" must be led and spiritually uplifted by the few select individuals who believe in progress. Again Dr. Stockmann is his spokesman as he attacks "the confounded, compact, liberal majority."

The problem of a society whose life is "rooted in a lie" is extended to include the conflict between might and right, a problem which has grown acute in our modern civilization. The mayor is used to illustrate the alliance between moral or ethical dishonesty and social bureaucracy or political dictatorship. Peter Stockmann is really only a *petit* bourgeois, wearing a mask of public importance. He will do anything for the sake of his reputation: he will hush up the truth and have the town continue to use the poisoned water rather than reveal the misfortune which might endanger his position. His belief that "the public has no need for new ideas," that it "gets on best with the good old recognized ideas it has already" makes the mayor a spiritual relative of Pastor Manders in *Ghosts*.

Seeing the social morass into which the townspeople have followed their smug leader, Dr. Stockmann decides that "the strongest man in the world is he who stands most alone." This, his last discovery, gives him the courage to stay in the community which has ostracized him and branded him "Enemy of the People," and he realizes that he can be the greatest "servant of the people" by being the doctor and teacher of its poor. In Dr. Stockmann, Ibsen has created a true and persevering, although stubborn and at times unreasonable, idealist who remains faithful to his ideal despite rebuffs and calumnies. But in spite of the seriousness of the play's issues, it is essentially not a tragedy, or even a "problem play," but a comedy. The attack on social corruption is delivered with a light heart and a sense of humor—"you should never wear your best trousers when you go out to fight for freedom and truth."

ephebic oath: the oath taken by an Athenian youth (Greek: *ephebe*) entering his training for military service and citizenship. Since this was a pledge of loyalty and civic responsibility, the term is sometimes extended to apply to any similar oath.

epic (Greek: "tale"): a long narrative poem in which the characters and the action are of heroic proportions. The greatest classical epics are by *Homer (*Iliad* and *Odyssey*) and *Vergil (*Aeneid*); until the 18th century the latter was better known and more admired in Western Europe. From the example of Homer and Vergil certain characteristics became established in the West as standard attributes of the epic: the underlying *theme* concerns basic and eternal human problems; the *narrative* is a complex synthesis of experiences from a whole epoch of man's history or civilization; the *hero* embodies national, cultural, or religious ideals; the *style* is earnest and dignified; the poet plunges into a low point in the middle of the action (*in medias res*). Not all of the following poems, called epics, conform to all these conventions, although they agree in each instance with most of them: *Mahabharata*, *Beowulf*, *Song of Roland*, *Nibelungenlied*, *Divine Comedy* (*Dante), *Lusiads* (*Camoëns), *Faerie Queene* (*Spenser), *Paradise Lost* (*Milton).

Epictetus: a Stoic philosopher (*c.* A.D. 50–*c.* 120). Epictetus was born a slave in Asia Minor but came while still young to Rome, where he somehow obtained an education and eventually won his freedom. How old he was at the time is not known, but he spent his remaining years teaching, first in Rome and later at Nicopolis, across the Adriatic Sea from Brundisium. Epictetus was lame during the greater part of his life, supposedly as a result of brutal treatment received in childhood.

Like *Socrates, whom he admired, Epictetus wrote nothing, the *Discourses* that bear his name being notes taken from his discussions of Stoic texts of conversations with students by his disciple Arrian, who also compiled the famous *Enchiridion*, or *Handbook*, as a digest of the philosopher's views. Epictetus' doctrine is representative of the popular *Stoicism of the period, being confined almost entirely to ethics presented from a practical point of view and based on a firm religious faith. Its central point is the necessity of accepting with contentment whatever life may bring or fail to bring, realizing that all is determined by the will of God, who chooses for men better than they could choose for themselves. Epictetus was a powerful lecturer, and his personality shines through his *Discourses*, although almost excluded from the *Handbook* because of its brevity. For this reason the *Handbook* may appear dry and harsh.

Epicurus: Greek philosopher (342–271 B.C.). Epicurus was the son of Athenian parents who migrated as colonists to the island of Samos. He became interested in philosophy at an early age and, after studying and teaching for some years in Asia Minor, went in 306 B.C. to Athens, where he established a school known as *The Garden.* His philosophy was a materialistic hedonism. He took his metaphysics from Democritus' theory of the atomic structure of the universe, but to preserve free will he rejected the determinism taught by Democritus in favor of a theory whereby there resides in the atoms themselves a tendency to swerve. He based his epistemology on the infallibility of sense perception, a concept that serves as a test for truth throughout his whole system. In ethics he taught that pleasure is the chief end of life, the elements desired being largely painlessness of body and tranquillity of mind and soul. Epicurus' philosophy is not atheistic, although it teaches that the gods do not interfere in the life of man and that the soul, being composed of atoms, is mortal. It is highly individualistic in its ethics, but it was not intended to justify excess. Epicurus himself was known for the simplicity of his life.

Epicurus was a very voluminous writer, but his chief works have perished. We depend for our knowledge of his system largely on *Lucretius' poem *On the Nature of Things.* This poem, though faithful to Epicurean doctrine, does not discuss it completely. There is therefore doubt concerning some details.

epigram: a concise, witty composition of not more than a few lines or a sentence or two. The word means, literally, "inscription" and was at first used by the Greeks in this sense. Many of the poems of the *Greek Anthology* are inscriptions. But, since such a poem calls for concentration and brevity, the word was extended to include other works showing the same qualities. In Latin literature, the epigrams of *Martial (which served for centuries as models) were not designed as inscriptions. In modern times an epigram may be in verse or prose: the prose epigrams of *La Rochefoucauld and Oscar *Wilde are famous. Even when it is primarily a lyric expressing feeling, it must still have some wit in its form of statement.

epithalamium (Greek: "nuptial song"): a poem to celebrate a wedding. *Pindar, *Sappho, *Theocritus, *Catullus, *Ronsard, and *Spenser wrote poems of this type. Spenser's *Epithalamion*, commemorating his own marriage, is the best example in English.

Erasmus, Desiderius: Dutch scholar and humanist (1466?–1536). Friend and correspondent of every notable figure of the day, a scholar par excellence, Erasmus was a seminal force in the *Renaissance. Always seeking the relation between knowledge and piety, the rational basis of Christianity, the truth both pagan and Christian, he found no conflict between secular and religious truth; and, by meeting the problems of his day with sound learning, he hoped to free men from entrenched traditions.

Erasmus was born in Rotterdam of parents who never married. (Their love story is the central theme of Charles Reade's *The Cloister and the Hearth*, 1861.) Educated at the universities of Paris, Turin, and Bologna, Erasmus was ordained a priest and became Bachelor and Doctor of Theology.

In 1499 he made the first of six trips to England. The Englishmen who became his friends—Sir Thomas More (see *Utopia*), Colet, Fisher, Linacre, Grocyn—were a distinguished nucleus of teachers of Greek, Latin, and

Biblical texts, scholars who were integrating classical and Biblical learning. Their influence on Erasmus was of lasting significance; they encouraged his study of the Scriptures in their historical context and his belief that the true worship of Christ lies not in ceremonies but in imitation of His life. During Erasmus' third trip to England (1509–14), he taught Greek at Cambridge, completed his edition of the Greek text of the New Testament and, in a single week, at the home of Sir Thomas More, wrote *The Praise of Folly*. Erasmus also traveled widely on the Continent, at home wherever there were artists, libraries, and men of letters. Holbein painted him, and Albrecht Dürer did an engraving of him.

In the violence of the Reformation, Erasmus sought a nonviolent, nonrevolutionary, nondogmatic solution, actually hoping that the conflict between Luther and the Catholic Church could be settled by a committee of arbitrators. Believing that moderate rationality would resolve the controversy, he saw no need to take sides; neither group welcomed this point of view.

Erasmus' fame in world literature rests on three quite different types of work: an extremely popular collection of adages, a scholarly text of the Greek New Testament, and the satirical monologue, *The Praise of Folly*. The *Adages, Familiar Quotations from the Classics* (1500) contains over 3,000 apothegms with explanations which show an appreciation of classical rhetoric. It made a handy compendium, and the satirical comments on women, monks, lawyers, and anti-humanist forces helped to send the volume into 120 editions before 1570.

Erasmus' Greek New Testament (1516) was the first printed edition of the Greek text. Equally significant is the fact that, based as it was on intensive study of early manuscripts, it exposed inaccuracies in the *Vulgate and shook the foundation on which Christian theological discussions had relied for a thousand years. It created a sensation when it was published and may be said to have initiated Biblical textual criticism. Erasmus also translated the New Testament into Latin.

The Praise of Folly (*Moriae encomium*, 1511), written in Latin and dedicated to Thomas More, is a speech of self-praise in which Folly proclaims her superiority over wisdom. The ironic praise of stupidity and corruption exalts the Christian-Humanist way of life and the freedom of mind that avoids what Folly (or the fool) values. Erasmus was familiar with Sebastian Brant's *Ship of Fools*, one of the better-known medieval literary treatments of folly, but his work makes the symbol far more complex and witty.

The book is divided into four sections: Folly's self-introduction, her powers and pleasures, her followers, the Christian Fool. Folly is, in a broad sense, misdirected effort, whether in human nature, worldly activities, scholarship, or religion. Her followers come from every trade and every profession; they are the devotees of drunkenness, empty pleasure, self-love, ignorance, everything the humanists held in contempt. Folly praises the life of instinct, and her very praise implies the superiority of a disciplined and reasoned existence. She delivers formal orations which are themselves parodies of formal orations and of the irresponsible citations of authority by lawyers and theologians. The attacks on the ascetics and the ignorant, on the violent and greedy, point up the values of Christian humanism. Folly concludes cynically that, as all life is folly, it is folly to be wise. Erasmus' argument is that it is folly not to see things as they really are; scholars should not abandon ideals just because they cannot be fully realized but should apply their learning and reason as best they can to daily living. Erasmus in his person and by his writings supplied the model of the Christian-scholar-humanist. His influence can be traced in a host of Renaissance figures including *Luther, *Rabelais, and *Montaigne.

Erinyes: *Eumenides.

Eris: the Greek goddess of strife.

Eros: the Greek god of love, identified by the Romans with Cupid.

essay (French: "attempt"): a short piece of expository prose which "attempts" to shed some light on a restricted subject of discussion. Beyond this brief definition, it is impossible to limit or classify essays. A convenient division, however, groups essays according to content and mood as "familiar" (also called "informal" or "personal") and "formal."

The familiar essay was more or less created by *Montaigne (who gave the essay its name). It plays up the personality of the author, draws openly on his prejudices, recognizes that its conclusions are incomplete and tentative, develops the ideas in a loose structure, has a sprightly conversational style which uses description, narration, and humor to make its point. It is often, however, highly informative, full of ripe wisdom and insight into universal human ideals and motivations. *Lamb, *Hazlitt, *De Quincey, Robert Louis Stevenson, Oliver Wendell Holmes (*Autocrat of the Breakfast Table*, 1857), and our contemporary E. B. White are notable for this style.

"Formal" essays were introduced in England by *Bacon, who adopted Montaigne's term. Here the style is objective, compressed, aphoristic, wholly serious. During the 18th century, in the mild-mannered social criticism of the periodical essays of *Addison and Steele, Samuel *Johnson, and Goldsmith, a compromise was achieved between the whimsical personal essay and the hard, compact formal type. In modern times, the formal essay has become more diversified in subject matter, style, and length until it is better known by such names as article, dissertation, or thesis, and factual presentation rather than style or literary effect has become the basic aim.

Ethics, Aristotle's: *Nicomachean Ethics*.

Eumenides: in classical mythology, primeval spirits who avenged crime, especially crime against kindred. For this reason, they play a prominent role in the story of *Aeschylus' *Oresteia*. *Eumenides* is a propitiatory name meaning "kindly, well disposed." The Greeks also knew them as the *Semnai* ("holy ones") and the *Erinyes*, a name of unknown origin. In Roman mythology they were called the *Furiae*, or Furies, and are pictured with their hair wreathed in serpents and with blood dripping from their eyes. They are named Alecto, Megaera, and Tisiphone.

euphuism: a style of writing which takes its name from the prose romances by John Lyly, *Euphues: The Anatomy of Wit* (1578) and *Euphues and his England* (1580). Letters, conversations, and dialogues, which develop a thin plot, are couched in a style characterized by balance and antithesis, heightened by heavy alliteration both simple and cross-linked, puns and word play; classical allusions and anecdotes from history and mythology; and "unnatural" natural history, i.e., comparisons drawn from the reputed habits of beasts, fowl, and fish, and from the presumed magical attributes of herbs and stones. Elements of this style appear in Greek and Latin rhetoricians, but the immediate stimulus probably came from a Spanish writer, Guevara (d. 1545). A more subtle, sophisticated, and famous development of the style is seen in the poetry of Luis de Gongora (1561–1627). In his *Defense of Poesie* (1585), Sidney condemned the excesses of euphuism for its "courtesan-like painted affectation"; *Shakespeare parodied it in *Henry IV, Part 1.

Eurlpides: Greek writer of tragedy (*c.* 480–407 B.C.). Euripides did not share with *Aeschylus and *Sophocles the classical vision of life with its absolute values and its optimism. Whereas Sophocles had possessed outward ease, charm, and elegance—qualities which perhaps caused and certainly furthered his popularity—Euripides lived a life of intense and introverted individualism which by its very nature lessened the possibility of great popular success. Misunderstood and unappreciated, Euripides devoted his life exclusively to his art. His own personal individualism was responsible for his deep perception of the tragedy of the individual: the conflict between man's intellect and his soul. The more this great poet gave to the people of Athens, both of aesthetic and ethical values, the more deeply he was disappointed by their rejection. Compared to Aeschylus and Sophocles, he achieved few dramatic victories, for during his whole life he won first prize only four times. Except among small groups of young admirers, Euripides' greatness was not recognized until after his lonely death far away from his native Athens. Then, as a final tribute to the tragedies he had left behind, his people, aware of what they had lost, gave him the prize for the fifth time.

Of about 90 dramas only 19 have survived. *Alcestis* (438 B.C.), his earliest drama, has as its theme rewarded loyalty. It is a tragedy with comic elements, a combination which exemplifies the extent of Euripides' ability to portray actual life. Although *Medea* (431 B.C.) is today regarded as his greatest tragedy and one of the most moving dramas of all time, it received only third prize at its first performance. Both *Medea* and *Electra* (c. 413 B.C.) show tragedy arising from strong, deep-seated loyalties, and present conflicts and struggles in terms of psychological motivations that strike one as being amazingly modern. It is because of Euripides' insight into the workings of human nature that these dramas, along with *Hippolytus* (428 B.C.), *Andromache* (c. 426 B.C.), *Iphigenia in Tauris* (c. 414–412 B.C.), and the unfinished *Iphigenia in Aulis* (c. 405 B.C.), have remained alive; they have been a rich source for dramatists of all ages. Euripides' insight into the misery and brutality of war is clearly seen in *The Suppliants* (421 B.C.) and the powerfully tragic *Trojan Women* (415 B.C.). His original and distinctive treatment of traditional material is found in *Ion* (417 B.C.), *Helen* (412 B.C.), and the *Phoenissae* (c. 409 B.C.), the latter a compact portrayal of the fate of the house of Oedipus. One of Euripides' last plays, *The Bacchae* (c. 405 B.C.), which has as its source and inspiration the god of the theater himself, illustrates his poetic artistry and sense of the dramatic. Presumably it is the drama for which the first prize was posthumously awarded.

Euripides' tragedies center on great human individuals who no longer struggle with fate but, finding the cause of tragedy within themselves, fight with the demon of their own souls. The well-known figures of ancient legends and myths were re-created into new beings whom the author drew directly from real life; each familiar character was given new, individual treatment. Perhaps Euripides' independent and modern treatment of old material was responsible for his contemporaries' resentment toward his works and indifference to him.

Yet Euripides was not altogether a revolutionary. In many respects he kept close to the old tradition of tragedy. Even if his conception of deity was far wider and more encompassing than the traditional one, Euripides kept the concept of the divine order as an integral part of the drama, as a framework within which all his characters moved. To Euripides the concept *theos* (Greek, "god") did not always imply a full degree of personification, and he often used this term to designate an eternal impersonal power which is greater than man. Thus, "theos" includes such forces within man as struggle, reverence, sorrow, hope, and ambition—even evil and destructive qualities, for Euripides recognized that both good and bad forces make up life. He frequently portrayed the gods as amoral and destructive, for to him the eternal, beautiful, and terrifying struggle between all the opposing forces, in men and divinities alike, makes up the content of life and thus also of drama.

Everyman: the best of the English *morality plays (late 15th century). *Everyman* so strongly resembles the Dutch morality *Elckerlijk*, which was printed earlier, that it has been assumed to be a free translation from the Dutch. Actually, however, the theme was common enough, the plays cannot be exactly dated, and it is quite possible that they both go back to a common source.

Everyman tells, in slightly less than a thousand lines of good verse, how Everyman is summoned by Death; how Fellowship, Cousin, Kindred, and Goods refuse to accompany him on his journey; how Knowledge and Confession prepare him and strengthen Good Deeds to accompany him; how Beauty, Strength, Discretion, and Five Wits desert him one by one as he approaches the grave; and how Good Deeds alone accompanies him on the journey. The vitality of the play is remarkable: it was repeatedly performed in the 20th century, not merely in esoteric "revivals," but for long and successful "runs" in the competitive commercial theater. It has been translated into many languages, and the Austrian poet Hugo von Hofmannstahl made an excellent German adaptation of it (*Jedermann*, 1911), which has also been widely translated and performed.

exemplum: a short tale or anecdote told to teach a lesson or illustrate a point (plural: *exempla*). Such "examples" or illustrations were typically used in the *Middle Ages by preachers to reinforce the lesson and point up the moral of a Biblical phrase or theological doctrine. Collections of *exempla* (humorous as well as serious), made for the use of preachers, drew stories from history, legend, and folklore. These concrete narratives, full of human interest, were adapted by laymen and had a great influence on literature. The story of how Death overtook the three rioters in *Chaucer's *Pardoner's Tale* is an *exemplum* on the text "The love of money is the root of all evil."

existentialism: a philosophical doctrine which has recently become the basis for a literary school. Its fundamental tenet is an insistence on the actual *existence* of the individual as the basic and important fact, instead of a reliance on theories and abstractions. Though the idea is ancient, the modern restatement by *Kierkegaard is the basis for its present development. Such philosophers as Jaspers, Heidegger, and Unamuno worked with this idea, and it is reflected in the writings of *Dostoevski and especially *Kafka. Its real literary impact, however, came in the 1940's with the writings of Jean-Paul *Sartre, Simone de Beauvoir, and their followers, in their periodical *Les Temps modernes*. Their literary productions were able to attract the followers and interest which a philosophical theory alone could hardly have attained. Some other well-known writers, especially André Malraux and Albert *Camus, have been influenced by existentialism, though they have never considered themselves a part of the movement.

The central doctrine is that man is what he makes of himself: he is not predestined by a God, or by society, or by biology. He has a free will, and the responsibility which goes with it. If he refuses to choose or lets outside forces determine him, he is contemptible. Hence the literary works of existentialism insist on actions—including acts of will—as the determining things. (*Aristotle said in his *Poetics* that character is revealed wherever a choice has to be made.) The existentialists stress the basic elements in man, including the irrationality of the unconscious and subconscious act. They consider life as dynamic, in a constant state of flux—a human life is not an abstraction, but a series of consecutive moments. And they always insist on the concrete instead of the abstract, on existence itself rather than the idea of existence. Since existentialism is a point of view about life rather than about literature, it has no particular style or literary form associated with it; hence it is really a philosophical school which has conditioned some highly effective literary works rather than a literary school.

There is also a Christian existentialism, led by Gabriel Marcel. It agrees with Sartre's premises up to the point of demanding a positive act of the will *(engagement)*, but it holds that this act is a matter of religious choice and must ultimately lead to God. Christian existentialism also has its literary expressions (including a number of plays by Marcel), but so far they have not been especially distinguished.

expressionism: a movement in literature and painting, centering in Germany in the first quarter of the 20th century. It attempted to *express* the basic reality of its subjects rather than to reproduce the mere appearance or surface—hence the name. In this respect it was a revolt not only against current art, but against current civilization, which was considered to be superficially prosperous and attractive, but rotten at the core. *Strindberg and *Dostoevski influenced the literary aspects of expressionism, as did the philosopher *Bergson and the psychologist *Freud. An expressionistic work relies heavily on distortion of salient features; it is exclaimatory and dynamic, and sometimes so cryptic as to be baffling. The most widely known expressionists are *Kafka and Franz Werfel; other adherents of the movement include the dramatists Fritz von Unruh and Georg Kaiser and the Austrian poet Georg Trakl. The influence of expressionism is visible in a good deal of the work of James *Joyce and T. S. *Eliot.

fable: a short allegorical tale conveying a moral or a principle of behavior; the characters are usually animals talking like human beings, but keeping their animal traits. Often the moral is appended in the form of a proverb; the fable itself might be called an acted-out proverb.

The earliest fables explain some feature of an animal (*e.g.*, why crows are black) and establish certain animal characteristics (the fox as sly, the lion as dignified). Later fables, the product of a more sophisticated culture, use animals to teach a moral lesson or to satirize human beings. In style they are compressed, epigrammatic, and dramatic. The earliest extant fables come from Greece and India, the oldest Western examples being the fables of *Aesop, and the oldest Oriental collection the *Panchatantra*. Some famous fables are about the Country Mouse and the City Mouse; the Fox and the Grapes (which has given rise to our expression "sour grapes"); Chanticleer and the Fox (see *Chaucer's *Canterbury Tales*). The *Fables* of *La Fontaine, the best-known collection since Aesop, are distinguished for sophisticated wit and brilliant poetic technique. Other collections were made by John Gay (England), *Lessing (Germany), who also wrote a critical history of the fable, and Ivan Krylov (Russia). See *beast epic.

In earlier use the term *fable* often means merely "narrative" or "plot."

fabliau: a short amusing tale, often bawdy or obscene, cynically and slyly satirical, directed usually against women, the clergy, and marriage (plural: fabliaux). The humor arises from the plot, an intrigue or practical joke told in a rapid succession of events that form a single episode. Among the standard characters are the jealous, stupid, or miserly husband, the clever rogue, the braggart, the unfaithful wife, the lecherous monk. Although description and character analysis are kept to a minimum, the setting is realistic and contemporary, and the ultimate effectiveness of the story depends on conduct deeply rooted in typical, easily recognized human nature. Some measure of poetic justice is achieved by having the hypocrite found out and the would-be trickster tricked. This type of story is found in pre-Christian Oriental literature and in Latin. In the *Middle Ages, especially in France, fabliaux, narrated in eight-syllable, riming couplets, were extremely popular. *Chaucer's *Canterbury Tales* (Miller's, Reeve's) and *Boccaccio's *Decameron* contain brilliant illustrations of the type in its elaborated literary form.

Faerie Queene, The: an allegorical epic by Edmund *Spenser (1590, 1596). Although left unfinished, *The Faerie Queene* is one of the outstanding poems in English. Turning from the "oaten reeds" of his earlier *pastoral poetry to the "trumpets sterne" of chivalric romance, Spenser planned a long chivalric *allegory of philosophical and moral import, a national *epic to glorify England and Queen Elizabeth. He proposed to set forth, in twelve books, the twelve moral virtues represented by twelve knights of Arthur's court (actually one is a woman). Spenser's artistic ambition was to rival *Ariosto and *Tasso, perhaps even *Vergil.

Like *Ariosto's *Orlando Furioso*, the English poem was conceived on a grand scale, as a romance with "a continued allegory." Its superiority over Ariosto, thought Spenser, would be its consistency and integrity of purpose and its idealistic hero, "fashioned a gentleman of noble person in virtuous and gentle discipline." Only six of the proposed twelve books were completed; and within the six the allegory is not apparently consistent; certainly scholars dispute its tangled and complex meanings. The narrative leaps *in medias res*, as an epic should. The hero is Prince Arthur, representing Magnanimity (or, in Spenser's word, Magnificence); he was to play the unifying role, appearing at some point in each book. The champions are the Red Cross Knight (representing Holiness, Book I), Sir Guyon (Temperance, II), Britomart (the female warrior, Chastity, III), Triamond and Cambell (Friendship, IV), Artegall (Justice, V), and Calidore (Courtesy, VI). Each is engaged in a single, separate adventure, but en route they all accept innumerable challenges, and some kill giants and dragons, are misled by magicians, rescue ladies, and fight off the enemies Error, Pride, Envy, Despair, Guile, Avarice, and so on, before their main objectives are achieved.

The equation of each knight with one of the moral virtues is made very clear, but Spenser was not satisfied with simple allegory. In addition to expounding the system of Christian ethics, he wished to incorporate *Aristotle's scheme of virtues and vices and *Plato's ideal world. And to this already complicated moral, theological, philosophical allegory he added contemporary persons, events, politics, religion, ethics, and education. Thus, one allegorical figure may mean many things. And, conversely, one "real" person may appear in several allegorical guises. Elizabeth, for example, is Glorianna, the Faerie Queene from whose court the adventures start; and she is also Una (Truth, who is also the True Anglican Church), Britomart (Chastity, who is also the True Defender of Britain and Platonic Idealism), and Belphoebe (again Chastity).

Spenser's greatness lies not in narrative organization but in the lyrical and picturesque. In consequence the story lags, and the effect is not so much of action as of slowly developed vignettes, representing spiritual conditions. It is the great pictorial scenes which are memorable. The poem has, in fact, been called "one of the world's most magnificent picture-books."

Spenser's effect is achieved by the sensuous richness of his descriptions combined with an exquisite verse technique and the creation of a highly effective form, the *Spenserian stanza. Onomatopoeia is common, as well as other types of sound effects—rich vowel sequences and all the devices of alliteration, *assonance, and rime. The stanza can be full of sensual warmth and color, as in Guyon's visit to the Bower of Bliss, or can convey by chiaroscuro a shadowy horror, as it does in the Cave of Mammon, or can paint in verse the grotesqueness of Falsehood (Duessa) and the horribleness of Error. The poetic unit is closed by the final *Alexandrine of the stanza, a "linked sweetness long drawn out," which slows down the narrative while it rounds out the picture and the rhythm and brings them both to a gentle close in a rare union of musical and pictorial elements. It often sums up the theme or reinforces it by a bit of aphoristic wisdom. The unified lyric tone and the fairyland setting serve an additional function by bringing the endless digressions into a single harmony: "For all that pleasing is to living eare,/Was there consorted in one harmonee,/Birdes, voyces, instruments, windes, waters, all agree." The archaic-looking spellings and words (often historically inaccurate) led Ben *Jonson to his famous complaint that Spenser "writ no language," but they do have a certain poetic effect, "making beautiful old rime/ In praise of ladies dead and lovely knights."

fairy tale: a short story in which there occurs some supernatural or magical event. The origin and the history of the diffusion of fairy tales are still matters of debate. The characters, who are neither individualized nor localized, are often not even given names, being called merely "a king," "a queen," or "a princess," or "a poor farmer." One character, however, may be a supernatural spirit or a fairy who appears in a human form but has magic powers. There are over five hundred distinct types of fairy-tale plots. Utilizing many folklore motifs and commonplace expressions, typical themes develop from such stock characters as the cruel king, cruel stepmother, haughty sister, substitute bride, and are developed by magic talismans, magic changes of shape and restorations, supernatural marriages and births (*e.g.*, *Cinderella*, *Snow White*, *Apuleius'* story of *Cupid and Psyche*). Despite the setting in a never-never land where any sort of supernatural event may occur, the story has an inner consistency, and, once the strange element in the situation is accepted, the other aspects of the tale have reality. The fairy tale always has a happy ending: virtue is rewarded. The most famous collections of fairy tales are those by Hans Christian *Andersen (Danish), Basile (Italian), the Grimm brothers (German), Keightley and Croker (English), Perrault (French). For lack of a more adequate English term, "fairy tale" is frequently extended to describe other types of nursery tales *(The Ugly Duckling, Goldilocks and the Three Bears)* that have nothing to do with fairies or supernatural beings.

Fates (also called the Destinies, the Weird Sisters—Anglo-Saxon *weird*-"fate"): three mythological goddesses (Greek *Morai*, Roman *Parcae*), in some versions daughters of Zeus and Themis (herself the personification of justice or of order established by law) were named Clotho (Greek "spinster," i.e., spinner of the thread of destiny), Lachesis (Greek "disposer of lots"), and Atropos (Greek "inexorable," "inflexible"). Clotho with her spindle spun the thread, Lachesis with her rod measured it, and Atropos cut it. No mortal can escape the Fates' decree, nor any god force them to alter it. Even if we do not subscribe to Greek myths, the imagery of the Fates has entered our vocabulary, e.g., "implacable fate," "the thread of life," and probably affected *Shakespeare's conception of the three witches in *Macbeth*.

Father Goriot: a novel by *Balzac (*Le Père Goriot*, 1835). Father Goriot is representative of Balzac's genius. It has intense stimulation, rapid change of pace, realistic detail, and a central monolithic character who meets his death by his own fault (here a mania of parental love). Although the parallel to *King Lear* is at first striking, the similarity remains superficial. In both, a generous father is deserted by two daughters. But there is nothing in Goriot comparable to Lear's pride, mistakes of judgment, mental breakdown, and gradual regeneration. Lear is tragic. Goriot, with his excessive parental devotion, is merely pathetic. Like Grandet's miserliness in

Eugénie Grandet, Goriot's sacrifices for his daughters have reached the proportion of a mania.

None of the other characters remains admirable. Rastignac appears originally to be a man of integrity; yet he too succumbs to the feverish ambition for money and social success, obtainable by extramarital love affairs and other corruptions. Only the master criminal Vautrin is really strong, but ironically he is betrayed by two otherwise despicable weaklings.

Apart from the lack of subtlety in treating the passions, the novel has many virtues. With incomparable energy, Balzac has individualized each article of furniture and each character; given us the "social center" and the spirit of the age. The total effect is a panorama of early 19th-century Parisian life. Penny-pinching, retired, and lonely boarders in Mme. Vauquer's lodging house (seven very different people brought together by poverty), the grand salons of the old decadent aristocracy and of the new social climbers, marriages of convenience, passionate love, financial manipulations ranging from pawnbroker bickering to international banking, the master criminal, gambling, law, and medicine are so interlaced as to provide a cross section of all Paris. The speed and speculation, the vicious passions, and the fierce inhumanities of man to man grow from the carefully worked out environment. This close attention to material circumstances, to the social and financial history of the characters and the ways in which they made or inherited their money, was Balzac's innovation in the art of the novel. *Father Goriot* is more than a study of a father; it is the case history of what Balzac described as a "monstrously sad" society.

Fathers and Sons: a novel by *Turgenev (*Ottsy i deti*, 1861). Turgenev's masterpiece is a realistic novel set in contemporary Russia. The characters are drawn from the professional and intellectual classes, and the ideas which are discussed throughout the book include scientific materialism, the problem of serfdom, social reform, and the radical philosophy of nihilism. But the book is not, as some critics have mistakenly thought, about these things.

As the title indicates, it is about the age-old conflict between parents and their children, between different generations with different points of view; and the issues discussed in this novel are simply those on which sons happened to be at odds with their fathers in Russia just before the liberation of the serfs.

The problem is generalized by using two sons with their different families and circumstances. Bazarov, with his uncompromising scientific utilitarianism, his contempt for conventions, manners, and human feelings, his ruthless self-criticism, is a remarkable creation and is made all the more credible in that he cannot live up to his own stern principles—he falls in love with an aristocrat. His young friend Arkady is essentially his disciple, a follower rather than a leader, but still far above the silly parlor liberals who are mercilessly caricatured. We are shown much more of Arkady's family than of Bazarov's because the obedient son who forsakes his father to follow a leader of his own generation causes far more bewilderment and heartache than does the child who has always been an independent individual. These two main characters, and the crowd of minor ones, are portrayed in a forceful but indirect way. They are seldom explained or analyzed but are shown in action, and they affect the reader by their effect on other characters.

Most of the aspects of this novel which have been attacked become comprehensible once we accept the fact that it is really about personal relationships rather than social issues. There is no closely knit plot leading to a climax, but rather a succession of plausibly linked scenes and episodes, each of which shows another facet of the general theme. Turgenev does not take sides but views both generations with a somewhat ironical sympathy. Finally, Bazarov dies of typhus (contracted in his scientific studies), not because Turgenev wants to imply that science destroys its creators, not because he wants to indicate that the reform movements will die without issue, not because he means to show the idealist destroyed by the careless stupidity of the traditionalist—but because the son-father relationship has been explored and has about come to an end. Whatever Bazarov might have done or become as a mature man would have been another story, not a part of the one Turgenev set out to tell.

Faulkner, William Cuthbert: American novelist and short-story writer (1897–1962). Faulkner said in his Stockholm speech accepting the Nobel prize (1949) that the subject of the literary artist is "the human heart in conflict with itself." In his work, which extended to more than 20 novels and carried characters through different phases of life in the imaginary Southern "Yoknapatawpha County," he showed how the heart in conflict with itself could bring about violence, guilt, and bigotry and disrupt the life of entire communities. Saturated with Southern legend and ancestral stories of the Civil War, Faulkner pictured the American South as in a condition of stasis, unaware of changed time, feeding on old memories and atrophied by old hurts.

He was born in Mississippi. His great-grandfather had served in two wars and built a railroad, dying a violent death after being elected to the legislature. His grandfather ran the railroad; his father worked on it and had a livery stable in Oxford, Mississippi, where Faulkner's empathy for horses and horsemanship, reflected in his work, originated. His first book of poems appeared in 1924. Calling the book *The Marble Faun*, he signed it Faulkner, inserting the "u" although his family name was Falkner—very much as *Hawthorne had changed his from Hathorne. After holding various jobs, seeking an education at the University of Mississippi, living in New Orleans, traveling abroad, mainly in Paris, and working in a bookshop in New York, Faulkner wrote two novels, *Soldier's Pay* (1926) and *Mosquitos*, and was encouraged by Sherwood Anderson. The latter urged Faulkner to stay in his work with "that little patch up there in Mississippi," and probably with *Balzac's *Comédie Humaine* in mind, he wrote the first of his Yoknapatawpha series, *Sartoris*; he found in the modern experimenters, and particularly *Joyce, the forms and techniques needed to express the Southern myth; and in 1929 wrote his most difficult and most admired novel, *The Sound and the Fury*, which put his readers into the *stream of consciousness of two brothers but also attempted to render the sensory world of a third brother, who was a mental defective. This bold extrapolation of the inner world of an idiot remains one of Faulkner's most poetic creations; through the inner worlds of the three brothers we meet the other members of the Compson family and are given a symbolic picture of Southern decay. Writing in the same inspired vein he produced his short novel *As I Lay Dying*, which is composed of a series of subjective monologues. He had attracted wide attention to himself in 1928 by writing a deliberate shocker called *Sanctuary* and in the early 1930's he succeeded in selling a number of short stories. Continuing during his first and finest period, he produced *Light in August* in 1932, a powerful realistic novel of the confused state of mind of a man uncertain of his racial identity but regarded as a black, and in 1936 brought out *Absalom, Absalom!* Established as a writer, though far from a popular one, he purchased a pre-Civil War mansion in Oxford and in the ensuing years built up his saga of Yoknapatawpha with such works as *The Unvanquished* (1938), *Go Down, Moses* (1942), and *Intruder in the Dust* (1948). The theme of the Balzacian Snopeses in the saga shows Faulkner's sardonic qualities. The Snopes stories are embodied in the trilogy *The Hamlet* (1940), *The Town* (1957), and *The Mansion* (1959). In his storytelling, both in the shorter and longer works, he showed himself capable of fluent narrative and acute observation; but his style, as he grew older, became highly rhetorical and orotund.

He seems to have been an intuitive artist, who instinctively latched on to the technical devices of his time and in some instances enlarged and perfected them. He had a genius for giving voice to the inarticulate, and did not hesitate to use the poetry of language to express their poetic feelings which they themselves would be incapable of expressing. Thus his is the voice that speaks for the idiot Benjy, who cannot speak. Faulkner's methods of narration include a tendency to envelop rather than develop his story; often he began a story at the end and then told it against chronological time—that is, he moved from present to past. Some critics have seen in these devices the influence of the cinema. He often told two or more stories, seemingly unconnected and going back many years, at the same time. In his stream-of-consciousness portions he utilized italics to convey different phases of thought. He often prefers to let the reader deduce certain events rather than to relate them. And, as in the cinema, Faulkner likes to "shoot" certain of his scenes from unfamiliar angles.

This wedding of a formidable technique to the rich elemental material from which he drew his subjects constitutes the great power of Faulkner. It won him a place as perhaps America's most serious and most highly integrated artist of the first half of the 20th century.

Faunus: *Pan.

Faust: a poetic drama in two parts by *Goethe (1808, 1832). The theme at the heart of Goethe's dramatic poem *Faust* is an old one. Man's desire to transcend his physical limitations, his search for answers to the eternal questions of the meaning of life and the universe is not peculiar to the modern period or to the great German poet. However, the breadth of vision and the grandeur of poetic expression as Goethe concerns himself with this universal problem are peculiar to him and are, in the main, the measure of his greatness.

The modern Faust story has its origin in the legends and chapbooks of the 15th and 16th centuries which grew up around a real person, one Doctor Johann or Georg Faust who gained a reputation as a notorious magician and worker in black magic and was said to have sold his soul to the Devil in exchange for knowledge. It is this same legend that was the basis for Christopher *Marlowe's *The Tragical History of *Doctor Faustus* (1588) in England.

Faust was in the making over a longer period than the dates of publication would indicate, for Goethe worked with the idea for the greater part of his life, from 1771, when he finished the manuscript of the *Urfaust*, until 1831, when he ceremoniously sealed the completed *Faust II*. The growth and development of *Faust* correspond to the intellectual growth of its creator, reflecting a mind as it grasps and develops ideas, matures in its poetic concepts, and expresses the profound wisdom and considered philosophy of a creative genius. Many critics have made studies of Goethe's own life and the progress of *Faust* to show how closely parallel they run, and to what extent *Faust* may be considered autobiographical.

The basic premise upon which Goethe bases his entire concept of Faust and the searching Faustian spirit is contained in the introductory *Prologue in Heaven*, in which we see God, the creative, divine force, and Mephistopheles, the nihilistic destructive force, debating over the soul of man. Goaded by Mephistopheles' taunts that man's misery has almost stopped Mephistopheles' desire to plague him and that it would be easy to lead him from his "confused service" to God and train him in the way of the Devil, God assures him that man will err as long as he strives. As a divine creation, though tempted and beguiled, he cannot be forever misled because he still has an "instinct of the one true way." On this concept of his creation of man, God rests his case with Mephistopheles and allows him to attempt to lead man in the way of the Devil. That Mephistopheles is a servant of God in the whole scheme of creation this "waggish knave" does not realize—it is beyond his comprehension. Goethe himself wrote, in 1815, "Nature is a grand organ on which our Lord God plays and the Devil blows the bellows." That Mephistopheles will never succeed in winning man's soul so long as man strives is further indicated in the condition of the pact between Faust and Mephistopheles. If Mephistopheles can satisfy Faust's desires and ambitions to the point that Faust can say to the moment of fulfillment, "Linger awhile—thou art so fair," then Mephistopheles will have won the wager both with Faust and with God and will win Faust's soul. But the *Prologue in Heaven* and the striving nature of Faust both point to eventual salvation. Goethe's emphasis is on that aspect of man that makes him never content— it is man's nature never to be satisfied but to feel a compulsion to strive on and on. It is worth noting that the pact is really superfluous: any man is lost at the point when he becomes entirely satisfied. Furthermore, Faust makes it clear that he is not seeking mere pleasure or abstract knowledge, but the full range of possible human experience, of which these are only small parts. At the end of the poem, as the angels bear Faust's body off to Heaven, they sing of the noble soul redeemed from the Evil One: "Whoso with fervent will strives on/We angels can deliver."

It is a long and tortuous way from the beginning, when God and Mephistopheles debate the nature of man, to the end, when Faust is redeemed through his own striving and accomplishment; and Faust is permitted to avoid no single step in the long climb. The turning point of his struggle is the Gretchen tragedy. Caught in a snare devised by Mephistopheles, Faust, by his love for Gretchen, satisfies the sensual in his nature. As the sensual desire is heightened by the orgy of the Walpurgis Night, it is, at the same time, abashed by the reminder of the sweet love and sacrificing nature of Gretchen. Faust has deserted her for the temptations offered by Mephistopheles, in whose scheme the redeeming love of Gretchen has no place. Faust's innate goodness and sense of guilt require him to go to Gretchen's aid—but too late. As Gretchen suffers the agony of her sin and punishment, Faust recognizes his role in her fate and his anguished "O had I ne'er been born!" reveals his full realization of his guilt. From now on the relation between Faust and Mephistopheles assumes the nature of a struggle in which Mephistopheles, bound to execute the wishes of Faust, fights a losing battle. Mephistopheles finds it harder and harder to tempt Faust; Faust is impervious to Mephistopheles' taunts and scoffs. The sensual and material temptations, unsatisfying as they were, no longer hold any attraction for Faust.

In Part II the demands and desires of Faust are beyond the comprehension of Mephistopheles, who, always earth-bound, a denier and a destroyer, cannot comprehend Faust's desire for the intellectual and the beautiful. As the Gretchen tragedy is the high point of Part I, so the Helena drama is the high point of Part II, though with a decidedly different emphasis. Helena is a symbol of classical, ideal beauty and her union with Faust, the representative of the romantic medieval spirit, produces

261

Euphorion, the symbol of Modern Poetry, the offspring of the union of the classic and the romantic. (This episode was based on the life and character of *Byron.) The Helena drama serves to acquaint Faust with the whole stream of man's history and culture from the Greeks to his present, but he still remains unsatisfied. His dissatisfaction, however, is the source of his continued striving for a higher ideal. At the age of 100, though hindered by Worry and blinded by Care, he finally reaches a state in which he has power—controls lands and peoples—and has for the first time the opportunity to see himself as a man of action. Having made great progress on a vast land reclamation project that will provide homes and sources of livelihood for millions, he looks forward to the point when he may be able to say "Linger awhile, thou art so fair" after this work has been completed. But he does not say it. He dies of natural causes, and Mephistopheles is disappointed. Faust's never-ceasing striving and endeavor have saved him, God's angels are sent to snatch his immortal part from the legion of devils, and he is borne off to Heaven.

In this great poetic drama, with its large lyrical element and its great variety and richness of verse forms, Goethe has allowed character rather than action to be the unifying force. Simply as a drama, large portions of *Faust* are unwieldy and unactable—but as a history of man's cultural, intellectual, and spiritual development as he strives to burst the bonds of physical limitations, *Faust* is without peer. Faust stands for every man who is inspired to action by dreams of power—both physical and intellectual—and who is prevented from becoming a victim of his desires by the very nature of his activity: He who strives is never lost—that is Goethe's central message in this monumental work which represents the best thought of sixty years of his life.

Faustus, Doctor: see *Doctor Faustus.*

Fielding, Henry: English novelist (1707–54). Probably no other contemporary man of letters had a career which marked so clearly as Fielding's two of the major literary developments of the 18th century: the decline of the drama and the rise of the novel. Fielding's success in fiction tends to make us forget the fact that he had an equally long and more concentrated career in the theater. When he was a novelist he had various other interests, but in his London theater days—1728 to 1737—he devoted all his time to the stage, as playwright and manager. Working close to the popular theater, and intent upon making a living, Fielding in the main fell in with the habits of current drama, which was declining, on the serious side, toward the sentimental and didactic, and on the comic side, toward the topical and farcical. Yet he did one comedy of more than passing interest, *The Miser* (1737, based on *Molière) and one satire of permanent appeal, *The Tragedy of Tragedies, or the Life and Death of Tom Thumb the Great* (1730), in which, in burlesquing heroic drama, he exhibited the sharp eye for bathos and rant that later appeared in his novels. Two plays of political satire (*Pasquin*, 1736, and *The Historical Register for 1736*, 1737) were a principal cause of the Licensing Act of 1737, which, by imposing a stifling censorship, ended Fielding's theatrical career.

Fielding was now a well-educated, happily married, able man of 30, with his occupation cut out from under him. He entered the Middle Temple to resume the study of law, and in 1740 he was called to the bar; his observations of law and lawyers led to many satirical passages in his novels. From 1739 to 1741 he got out three issues a week of *The Champion*, a periodical in the tradition of the *Spectator* essays. From 1741 until his death, he devoted himself to the practice and the enforcement of the law (as a justice of the peace) and to the writing of political journalism, essays, and fiction.

At the age of 21 Fielding had turned to the theater as a trade; at the age of 34 he turned to fiction for fun. No longer a literary mechanic in search of bread and butter, older, long practiced in the observation of men upon which his genius fed, he discovered in the novel a form which gave full scope to his great creative power. What set him off was Samuel Richardson's *Pamela* (1740), in which the author, intending to idealize chastity, had instead succeeded in emphasizing the material rewards which accrue for the stubbornly chaste young woman. The author of the pamphlet *Shamela* (1741), generally thought to be Fielding, parodies *Pamela* by making its latent meaning overt: by discreet temptation Shamela consciously maneuvers her would-be seducer toward matrimonial captivity. In the next year (1742) came Fielding's first full-size novel, *Joseph Andrews*, which also begins as a parody of *Pamela*—her self-conscious "virtue" is here transposed to her brother Joseph—but gradually expands into a broad comic narrative with genuine characters. In the last part of the book Fielding again picks up the burlesque of Richardson and integrates this literary satire with his own story; yet in its satirical aspect *Joseph Andrews* moves beyond *Pamela* to bigger game—the hypocrisy of "high life," clergyman, doctors, lawyers, and innkeepers. But standing out above the satire is the sheer humor of Parson Adams, who, with his idealism, his inconsistency, and his proneness to fall into ridiculous situations, is one of the first memorable characters in English fiction. In developing, in *Joseph Andrews*, what he called the "comic prose epic," Fielding was influenced by both the *Odyssey* (see *Iliad* and *Odyssey*) and *Don Quixote*. His next work, *Jonathan Wild* (1743), purported to glorify a famous criminal by ironically showing that the "greatness" we admire in distinguished characters of history is not substantially very different from the moral quality of successful criminals. In *Tom Jones* (1749), however, Fielding neither aimed at literary satire nor modeled the story to a theme, but let himself go with a freedom that produced his most elaborate and yet most unified story, his widest range of humor and social satire, and his most fully developed and carefully distinguished cast of characters, and at the same time canvassed a number of different principles of moral conduct. His last novel, *Amelia* (1751), was his most ambitious. Dealing with the tribulations of married life instead of the trials of lovers, it essayed a full and serious picture of corruptions in society and various institutions. But the structure is not so good as that of *Tom Jones*, and the sentimental and didactic make numerous intrusions.

Three years later, in search of health, Fielding took a

Mediterranean trip on which he died. He wrote almost until the end; in his *Journal of a Voyage to Lisbon*, published posthumously, he wrote interestedly and good-humoredly about the world he saw. Here he continues as the man of the world which, in the best sense, he was in his novels. As such he is an especially appropriate representative of the new literary genre, the novel, which, unlike the serious drama and narrative poetry of preceding periods, found its materials not in the grander spiritual and metaphysical problems, not in the nature and destiny of man, but in daily relationships at home and abroad, in the adjustment of individuals to groups, in the mechanics of unspectacular life, in the achievement of average expectancies—in short, in society and the world.

Finnegans Wake: an experimental fiction by James *Joyce published in 1939. All Joyce's innovative tendencies are carried to their logical conclusion in his last work, 17 years in the writing. When it came out in serial form in the Parisian magazine *transition*, it was known merely as *Work in Progress*. As the successive parts appeared, the work seemed to be a meaningless surrealist jumble of words, a stew of many languages, a book of elaborate puns in which Joyce mocked his readers. Gradually it became clear that the writer was creating another large-scale labyrinth like *Ulysses*. After *Work in Progress* was officially baptized *Finnegans Wake* and published as a book, it was possible to discern the imaginative qualities and the remarkable resources of the writer. Joyce himself made a recording of a portion, showing, with an extraordinary display of his fine voice and capacity for mimicry, how the work should be read, and the importance of treating it as an aural as well as a visual creation. The book deals with an Irish pub keeper, H. C. Earwicker, his wife and two sons, all of whom are asleep throughout the entire story, but whose relations as a family are developed in their night-thoughts and dreams. They are also shown to us as human beings who, while asleep, are surrounded by all of history, a timeless blur of past and present, of myth and legend, expressed in language that blends and blurs words into musical expression of experience. Thus for the line "Wait till the rising of the moon, love," which Joyce first wrote, he substituted "Wait till the honeying of the lune love," adding to the original image the idea of honeymoon and the honey-colored moon, and by changing the word *moon* to the French *lune*, he obtained liquid alliteration. In another place he coins the word *bluddlefilth* to suggest the word *battlefield* and grafts into it the words *blood* and *filth*. The influence of such "portmanteau" coinages and collapsed meanings has filtered into the work of other writers and even into the popular magazines. What commends this strange book to certain of its scholarly readers is the verbal humor, the manner in which Joyce fondles words and invokes a kind of sentimental—and extremely Irish—tenderness in projecting the cycles of birth and death, marriage and propagation. The work also conceals many venomous barbs leveled by choice at those Joyce deemed his betrayers.

Finnish literature: see *Kalevala*.

Firdausi, Abu'l Qasim: Persian epic poet (*c.* 940–1020). The name by which the poet is known (transcribed also as Firdawsi, Firdowsi, Firdusi) is actually a descriptive term meaning "the heavenly one." Firdausi devoted a lifetime to his *Shah-Nameh (Book of Kings)*, a poetic history of Persian rulers from about 3600 B.C. to A.D. 651. The poem, which runs to some 60,000 couplets, had no Persian predecessor or successor of comparable merit and is regarded as the supreme expression of Persian genius in the epic. Firdausi's episode of Sohrab and Rustum is the most famous version of the tale in which a father and son, their relationship unknown to each other, engage in mortal combat, and the son is killed. Since the *Shah-Nameh* inspired gifted miniaturists, many manuscripts of the poem are masterpieces of the illustrator's art.

Fitzgerald, Edward: see *Omar Khayyam.

Fitzgerald, F. Scott: American novelist who wrote the novels of the Jazz Age and lived them (1896–1940). Possessed of an excellent prose style, he captured his public by his novel of the 1920's *This Side of Paradise*. With his wife, Zelda, who early had shown signs of mental illness, he lived extravagantly and had to keep writing to maintain his position in the fast set of his time. His best novel is considered to be *The Great Gatsby*, a picture of the prohibition era and the success and failure of his third-rate protagonist. Other works include *Tales of the Jazz Age* (1922), *The Beautiful and Damned* (1922), *All the Sad Young Men* (1926), and his late novel *Tender Is the Night*, which incorporates the vampire-nature of his marriage to his unstable and mentally ill wife. A posthumous novel, *The Last Tycoon*, deals with Hollywood, where he was working when he died. *The Crack-Up* (1945) contains unpublished letters, and essays by those who knew him.

Flaubert, Gustave: French novelist (1821–80). Flaubert was born in Rouen, France. Both his father and brother were physicians and this medical-clinical environment left its mark on Flaubert's work. He himself went to Paris to study law, but liked neither the city nor the profession. Then a nervous illness sent him traveling in search of relief and finally brought him to a quiet and retiring life. He returned to the family home to become "a galley-slave of letters" giving all his time to his writing.

With meticulous attention to securing the absolutely right word *(le mot juste)* in the right place, he developed a brilliant prose style which seems on the surface disarmingly simple and direct. As assiduous as *Balzac, but unlike him a perfectionist who lived entirely for his art, Flaubert spent years on each of the few but excellent books that he finally published.

He labored for over five years on *Madame Bovary* (1857), his first published work. It was greeted by a government prosecution of author and publisher for "outrage of public morals and religion." Flaubert was acquitted and found himself famous. This first novel was realistic, controlled in form, and disillusioned in spirit; but Flaubert also had an opposite tendency toward romantic exoticism and formlessness. He was fascinated, like the romantics whom he read—*Chateaubriand, *Byron, *Hugo—by remote antiquity and the exotic. He traveled extensively through the Near East and undertook a trip to Carthage (1858) to gather documentation for *Salammbô* (1862), a historical novel set in the third century B.C. The story and setting are romantic in their emotions and opulence, but the method is completely objective. The *Éducation sentimentale* (1869) is an ironic novel about a sort of male Emma Bovary, set in the revolutionary epoch of 1848, with careful documentation that required years of preparation. More romantic, lyrical, and philosophical is *The Temptation of St. Anthony* (*La Tentation de Saint Antoine*, 1848–49, published complete 1874), the outgrowth of Flaubert's intense interest in religious creeds.

A volume of short stories, *Three Tales* (*Trois Contes*, 1877), contained *A Simple Heart, The Legend of St. Julian the Hospitaller*, and *Hérodias* (which is the source of Oscar *Wilde's Salomé*). These established Flaubert among the notable short-story writers. The realistic *Simple Heart* shows closeness of observation, detachment in style, and, at the same time, real human sympathy in the description of the faithful servant, who is a symbol of all those whose frustrated lives turn them from humanity to another object of affection—here a parrot. At his death, Flaubert left a fragment, *Bouvard et Pecucher* (1881), a satire on the futility of human knowledge and on middle-class mediocrity.

An inspiration to many realistic writers, among them *Maupassant and *Zola, Flaubert is often called the first French realist. He, however, had no intention of reproducing a "slice of life," and he was certainly aiming at more than mere photographic duplication. His method illustrates many characteristics usually associated with classical literature. He has the classic economy of expression, the restraint of emotion, the concreteness of detail, the detached and objective point of view, and the highly developed sense of form. Moreover, he concentrates every detail to secure unity of tone. Whether a passage be narrative, descriptive or figurative, it is obviously written to contribute to the totality of effect. Notable are the agricultural fair in *Bovary* and the scene when Emma waits vainly in the cold garden for the note from Rodolphe, the sunrise scene in *Salammbô*, the rich rhetoric of the final scenes of the *Temptation*. Each is designed by its precision of diction and rhythms to intensify a unified artistic effect. This superb technique, this concern with the novel only as a work of art, made Flaubert a model not only to French authors but to Americans and Russians as well, notably Henry *James and *Turgenev.

flyting: Like *stichomythia, or the dialogue of shepherds in the *Pastoral, flyting is a verbal duel of mutual abuse between speakers who alternate and echo half-lines, lines, or even longer speeches. The device, often a sardonic interchange between contenders striving to outdo one another, is not uncommon in *Shakespeare, e.g., Don Pedro-Hero in *Much Ado About Nothing*; Anne-Gloucester, Elizabeth-Richard in *Richard III*; Lysander-Hermia in *A Midsummer Night's Dream*.

folklore: the traditions, customs, and beliefs of the people as they appear in nonliterary tales, songs, and sayings. The basic requirement of living folklore is that it be traditional, widely current, and transmitted primarily through memory and practice rather than by the printed page. This requirement relates folklore to the materials of ethnology and anthropology and also implies the existence of an artistic or sophisticated literature different and separate from that of the folk. In actual experience, however, folklore and the literary tradition cannot be separated in airtight compartments; they are mutually influential, and the distinction between "folk literature" and "art literature" becomes one of degree.

Folklore literature is, then, a traditional literature that has developed independently of the written word. It may take the form of *fairy tale, *ballad, proverb, *beast epic, jingle, incantation, riddle. The most inclusive type is the folk tale, a story which consists of one or a combination of many folklore themes (motifs). Folk tales easily pass from language to language and spread all over the world; hence they are sometimes called "migratory tales." Art literature often appropriates themes from folklore, usually modifying them to suit their new social environment. (This process is amply illustrated in such courtly medieval romances as *Sir *Gawain and the Green Knight*.) Most of the world's greatest writers have incorporated some themes from folklore into their work. The most important and widely known study of folklore and anthropology is Sir James Frazer's monumental *The Golden Bough* (1890–1915).

Forster, E(dward) M(organ): English novelist (1879–1970). Forster wrote few novels yet occupies a distinguished place in the history of 20th-century fiction. A member of the original *Bloomsbury group, he was, with Virginia *Woolf, one of its most creative spirits. His first four novels were written during the Edwardian era. They were *Where Angels Fear to Tread* (1905), *The Longest Journey* (1907), *A Room with a View* (1908), and *Howards End* (1910). Fourteen years later he brought out his most famous work, *A Passage to India* (1924). An individualist, he had an alert and playful mind, and in his essays and fiction, as well as later in life in his broadcasts, he revealed a profound humanity and a belief that barriers between humans and races can be overcome through a fundamental breaking of social differences. "Only connect" are the words in *Howards End* which have caught the public imagination. His nonfiction includes *Aspects of the Novel* (1927), a series of Cambridge lectures; *Abinger Harvest* (1936); and *Two Cheers for Democracy* (1951). Forster believed in personal relations; he was hostile to rigidity and dogmatism. He collected his short stories in a volume called *The Celestial Omnibus* in 1911. He also wrote a book on Alexandria (1922) and a biographical volume, *Marianne Thornton* (1956). Other writings, not published during his lifetime, e.g., *Arctic Summer* (written in 1912–14) and *Maurice* (written in 1913–15), were found among his papers after his death.

frame-tale: the narrative frame of a series of tales: a tale from which other stories develop or which contains other stories within it. The frame-tale itself can be high art. It was popular in classical literature (*Ovid, *Metamorphoses*), in the *Middle Ages (*Chaucer, *Canterbury Tales*; *Boccaccio, *Decameron*), and in the Orient (*Arabian Nights*). Examples from modern times include Washington Irving's *Tales of a Traveller*, *Longfellow's *Tales of a Wayside Inn*, William Morris' *The Earthly Paradise*.

France, Anatole: pseudonym of Jacques-Anatole Thibault, French satirist, novelist, and critic (1844–1924). A 20th-century *Voltaire, Anatole France was the most piercing satirist of his generation. He was also a classical scholar, a religious skeptic in the tradition of *Renan, and a social reformer. Although the critical method which he praised was impressionistic ("the good critic is he who relates the adventures of his soul among masterpieces"), his own literary criticism (*Literary Life*, 1888–92) was guided by classical and humanistic standards.

The subject matter of his mordant satire was principally early Christianity and modern society. His skeptical studies of the inner drives of the early Christian saints and martyrs (*e.g., Thaïs*, 1890) have been called "Bibles of modern unbelief." Delicately ironic and striking is the short story about Pontius Pilate, *The Governor of Judea* (*Le Procurateur de Judée*, 1892).

France's satires of modern life can take the form of biting allegory (*Penguin Island*, 1908, a satire of French politics, religion, and art); or a bitter exposé of social groups (*Contemporary History,* a series of four novels, 1897–1901); or a disarming philosophical fantasy in which angels and devils change places (*The Revolt of the Angels*, 1914). The nature of his attack is seen in his oft-quoted sentence: "The State, with its majestic sense of justice and equality, forbids the rich man as well as the poor one to sleep in the streets." Yet beneath the raillery and mockery there is a romantic fervor and love of the beauty of the world, as in the description of Thais, and a feeling that men wish to do good, clearly shown in *The Crime of Sylvester Bonnard* (1881). France's skeptical irony, paradoxes, and wit are tempered by tenderness and pity for humanity.

Francis of Assisi, Saint: Italian mystic (1182–1226). The Little Poor Man of Assisi exerted a great influence on his own and subsequent ages through his emphasis on simple love, kindness, and compassion. He founded the Franciscan Friars, a mendicant order dedicated to the ideal of personal poverty and help to the failing. He himself was famed for his gentleness of spirit and his love of all living things, for he regarded men and beasts alike as the sacred mirrors of God's spirit. His *Hymn to the Sun (Cantico di frate sole)* shows a new awareness of nature's beauty as one of the gifts of God: "Praised be my Lord God . . . ; and especially our brother the sun . . . : O Lord, he signifies to us Thee!" The *Sermon to the Birds* is a touching illustration of his simple faith as he goes with "wondrous fervor of spirit" among his "brother and sister" birds, making the sign of the cross over them. (The scene has been immortalized in a fresco by the painter Giotto.) Other writings include a few letters, parts of a monastic rule, etc. In the 13th century disciples recorded his sayings and doings, revering his humility, acceptance of poverty, and loving kindness. A collection of these brief narratives in Italian prose is known as the *Little Flowers of St. Francis.*

Frankenstein: see *Gothic novel.

Franklin, Benjamin: American diplomat, scientist, publisher, inventor, etc., who did a good deal of distinguished writing (1706–90). During the 84 years of Franklin's busy life (only the first 50 of which are described in his *Autobiography*), he was so active in politics and diplomacy, in both theoretical science and practical invention (he proved the identity of lightning and electricity and invented the Franklin stove and bifocal glasses), in organizing new projects and institutions (he founded the first subscription library in America and an academy which developed into the University of Pennsylvania), and in a host of other activities, that his literary work seems almost accidental. It extends over the whole of his life, however, and is basic both as a means of organizing his other interests and as a reflection of them.

Beginning in his youth with imitations of *Addison and *Pope, he soon moved on to *Poor Richard's Almanac*, which started in 1733 and ran for 25 years. This work, appealing to the average American of its time, fathered the long line of cracker-box philosophers down to Josh Billings and Will Rogers. Poor Richard's sayings both drew on the proverbs of the past and contributed some new ones to the common stock, the best being collected in *The Way to Wealth* (1758). Utilitarian ethics and "getting ahead" are also central in Franklin's *Autobiography*, which he began in 1771 for the instruction of his illegitimate son. For what it sets out to do, it is a masterpiece of simplicity and candor. It recounts a self-made man's rise in a land of opportunity, with frank admission of the errors. Further valuable autobiographical material is contained incidentally in a number of Franklin's other works and in his voluminous correspondence.

Franklin was also remarkably active and effective as a satirical pamphleteer on a number of subjects. *Rules by Which a Great Empire May Be Reduced to a Small One* (1773) attacks the unwisdom of British policy and is uncannily prophetic of the steps leading to the American Revolution. *Remarks Concerning the Savages of North America* (1784) is sympathetic to the Indians in their distrust of the white man's education, manners, and religion; and various other works attack the injustices done to the Indians. *On the Slave Trade* (1790) neatly turns proslavery arguments topsy-turvy: a wise man of Algiers defends the enslavement of Christian Europeans by North Africans, using the same arguments as those advanced by the Christian nations for the enslavement of Africans, and pointing out that emancipation of the Christians would create an insoluble problem. Franklin wrote a large number of effective satirical pamphlets like these. In France (where he succeeded in his mission of cementing friendship between France and America) he played the expected role of a backwoods philosopher but associated on equal terms with a sophisticated and brilliant society and composed a number of bagatelles in a playful, humorously allegorical vein. Some of the best of these are *The Whistle* (1779), *The Ephemera* (1778), and *Dialogue Between Franklin and the Gout* (1780).

In matters of religion, Franklin was a rather skeptical Deist. Revelation had no weight with him, and he disregarded theological sanctions of morality. He rebelled against the wrathful God of the Calvinists in favor of a benevolent Deity whose goodness is expressed in the harmony of Creation, but who, as Franklin uncomfortably confessed, pays scant attention to "our particular little affairs." Believing that the soul of man is immortal and that "the most acceptable service to God is doing good to his other children," he was tolerant of all faiths and opposed to dogmatic theology.

In Franklin's makeup there was little spirituality and little poetry. (He practiced verse writing in his youth in order to improve his prose, and he later respected poetry primarily as a means of instruction.) If he is a true child of his century in these respects, he is also its true child in his balanced, humorous common sense, which often rises to wisdom, in his genius for practicality, in his generous feeling for mankind, and in his industrious efforts to build a better world.

free verse: a type of poetry in which the line is based on the natural cadence of the voice, following the phrasing of the language, rather than a repeating metrical pattern. The rhythm of a free-verse line is marked by the grammatical and rhetorical patterns of normal speech and by the "sequence of musical phrase" (Ezra *Pound). A single line of free verse will normally contain varied types of feet, and a single poem will contain lines with varying numbers of feet. Hence the poem is unconfined, "free" of the traditional repeated metrical patterns of foot and line. Free verse is never so free as prose, never really free in the sense of being formless or unrhythmical. Rather its rhythms follow a pattern more varied than that of traditional verse, moving away from and returning to certain rhythmical norms and regularities. Although most people associate free verse with modern poetry, the type is found throughout literature from Hebrew poetry (Psalms and Song of Songs) through *Goethe (who used it extensively in such poems as *Prometheus* and *Harzreise im Winter*, in the 1770's) and *Hölderlin (*c.* 1800) to *Heine, Matthew *Arnold, Walt *Whitman. In contemporary poetry it developed along with the French *symbolist movement at the end of the 19th century and with the later American *Imagists (Ezra Pound, Amy Lowell). T. S. *Eliot's The *Waste Land, which has been called the greatest poem of the 20th century, is written in free verse.

Freud, Sigmund: Austrian founder of *psychoanalysis (1856–1939). One of the towering figures of modern times, Freud was the first to develop through what he called psychoanalysis the probing of man's "unconscious" in the study of human behavior. To do this he explored the world of dreams. His seminal work, *The Interpretation of Dreams* (*Die Traumdeutung*, 1900), has had a profound influence both in clinical and meta-psychology. Psychoanalysis must be understood therefore as a technique which belongs to psychology and psychiatry, but as Freud showed, its discoveries about man's ways of dreaming and using symbols have literary applications as well. Literary psychology has no relation to "therapy"; it is concerned with using in literary studies the insights of Freud and the modifications of Freudian theory developed by subsequent workers, notably Kris, Hartmann, and Lowenstein. They expanded Freudian theory into ego-psychology, which Erik Erikson has popularized.

Freud's ideas significantly influenced 20th-century literature, and even some of the popular misunderstandings of his ideas led to further explorations on the level of the creative imagination. There are three distinct aspects to Freud's impact on literature. First, literary *surrealism has been based on the idea of breaking man's psychological defenses and giving uncensored expression to the irrational symbolic modes of the unconscious. Second, biographers and critics have tended to "psychoanalyze" writers and explain literary productions through their "conditioning," a reductive procedure much confused by those who used it with concepts of "therapy." However, a later school, seeking the symbolic statement and modes of expression in the works themselves, has tended to show that one may recover some part of the history of a creative imagination by its characteristic modes of expression; in this way the psychoanalytic approach may be made more fruitful and nonreductive. Third, writers, especially novelists and dramatists, have tended increasingly to conceive and present their characters in psychoanalytical terms. This is true in more recent works of the *stream-of-consciousness school where the character's inner monologue imposes upon the reader the task of deducing the personage from the data of his personal experience.

As a consequence of this large influence of Freud and his followers, especially in the areas of symbolic statements, some elementary knowledge of psychology has become a part of the necessary equipment of the modern reader and of literary criticism.

Frogs, The: a comedy of *Aristophanes (405 B.C.). *Dionysus, the patron god of the drama, finding life empty without *Euripides, decides to go to the Underworld and bring him back. He obtains a club and a lion's skin, the traditional costume of *Heracles, who had made the journey before him, and sets out for the kingdom of the dead with his slave Xanthias and a donkey. After a series of fantastic adventures, including a crossing of the Styx through a chorus of frogs, they are arrested and taken before the king.

Meanwhile the audience learns the cause of a tumult raging among the dead. Hades maintains a Chair of Honor for the greatest master of every art, and *Aeschylus had held the chair for tragedy unchallenged for 50 years. But after Euripides died, he laid claim to Aeschylus' place and created such an uproar that he forced Hades to hold a contest to decide the issue. Since the contest is about to begin and Dionysus is an expert in the drama, Hades appoints him as judge. In return for his services, he may have whichever poet he chooses to take back to the earth.

Aeschylus and Euripides now appear and attack one another in a long debate, after which scales are brought in, and they quote from their tragedies into the pans. But though Aeschylus wins with his weightier verses, Dionysus is still in doubt which poet to choose, until—quite unexpectedly—he decides to take the one who gives the best advice on public policy and begins to ask questions about affairs in Athens. Euripides now reminds Dionysus that he had come for him and had sworn by the gods to take him; but Dionysus replies with one of Euripides' own lines, "It was my tongue that swore it [not my heart]," and chooses Aeschylus. As Aeschylus prepares to leave, he asks that Sophocles be installed in the Chair of Honor during his absence and that Euripides be excluded from it forever.

The Frogs was produced the year before Athens was defeated in the Peloponnesian War. The worst elements were in control of the city—as in the play they are in control of the Underworld—while many of the best citizens were disfranchised or in exile and the demagogues misruled Athens and prevented the making of peace. Such was the tragic background against which Aristophanes wrote *The Frogs;* and its setting in the Underworld and the preoccupation with literary criticism are tied directly to comments on the immediate situation. The *parabasis*, or address of the chorus, urges the audience directly to save their city by recalling the political exiles and placing the direction of affairs in the hands of the older and worthier families. The noble patriotism of the *parabasis* was so much admired by the Athenians that *The Frogs* not only won first prize, but the performance was repeated and Aristophanes was crowned with Athena's sacred olive.

In modern times, attention has centered chiefly on the contrast pointed in the play between Euripides' poetry and the older poetry of Aeschylus. But it should not be forgotten that even in its literary scenes *The Frogs* is a comedy and its criticism not all serious. Aristophanes knew that Euripides' tragedies would survive, but what joke could be better than Aeschylus' complaint that it was not fair to hold the contest in the Underworld? "For my dramas live on earth above, but his died with him and are here as witnesses."

The criticism of the two playwrights is concentrated in the *agon* and the scenes that follow. Against Euripides it is urged that his style is prosaic, his prologues monotonous, the innovations in his lyrics trivial or debasing, and the whole effect of his drama both immoral and unpatriotic, for his themes are psychological studies of love, and the sophistry of his dialogue proves him the "teacher" of the base demagogues ruining Athens. Aeschylus' plays, like those of Euripides, show some stylistic defects. His choral odes are interminable, his characters maintain long silences, and when they do speak, they baffle the audience with great words no one can understand. But Aeschylus' tragedies improve the morals of those who see them, they avoid themes that involve passion, and they are filled with the loftiest patriotism. It was, in fact, Aeschylus' verses that inspired the men of Marathon and Salamis.

There is much truth in Aristophanes' criticism of the style of both poets, although even here his dislike of Euripides is evident. He chooses his quotations so as to do most harm to Euripides and most good to Aeschylus. He allows Aeschylus the defense that the great men who appear in his plays must speak with dignity and grandeur, but he does not permit Euripides the counterplea that realistic writing requires less elevated language as well as kings clothed sometimes "in tatters." But when Aristophanes goes beyond questions of style to represent Euripides' themes as immoral, he is in fact maintaining the thesis that certain areas of human experience should be forbidden to the drama, a point of view that can easily be challenged. And when he credits Aeschylus with the former glory of Athens and makes Euripides responsible for the city's decadence, he is doing no more than state his own prejudice. It should be noted, however, that by equating Euripides with the corrupt politicians of the day, Aristophanes is able to connect the literary theme of *The Frogs* with its serious political purpose.

In some translations of *The Frogs* Latin names are used for the characters. When this is done, Dionysus is called Bacchus; Heracles, Hercules; and Hades, Pluto. The other names are unchanged.

Frost, Robert (Lee): American poet (1874–1963). At the age of ten, Robert Frost was brought from San Francisco, his birthplace, to New England, where eight generations of his family had been rooted. After that New England was his home, and he became its best poetic interpreter. After high school in Lawrence, Massachusetts, Frost attended Dartmouth briefly and then worked as bobbin-boy in a cotton mill, as cobbler, schoolteacher, and journalist. In 1895 he married; two years later he entered Harvard. A good student in the classics, he gave up college after two years for a New Hampshire farm, purchased by his grandfather. Eleven years of unorthodox farming were followed by seven years of teaching. In 1912 he settled in England with his wife and four children, determined to "write poetry without further scandal to friends or family."

At 19, Frost asked his skeptical grandfather for a 20-year apprenticeship to poetry. He was a canny prophet; in that time he published less than 20 poems and earned little from them. In England, however, he found ready and perceptive appreciation among the Georgian poets and from a publisher who issued *A Boy's Will* (1913) and *North of Boston* (1914). The praise of English reviewers opened American eyes; returning to America at the age of 40, Frost was hailed by Ezra *Pound and other sponsors of the "New Poetry," by editors, and by publishers. From then on, his steady but unhurried production received its deserved recognition.

He was professor and poet in residence at the University of Michigan and at Amherst. He was awarded the Pulitzer Prize four times and numerous honorary degrees from American universities and Oxford and Cambridge. Two other unusual distinctions are also noteworthy: a unanimous resolution honoring him by the United States Senate on March 24, 1950; his participation—reading his poem "The Gift Outright"—in the 1961 inauguration ceremonies for President John F. Kennedy. Following the first two volumes, his most important books are

Mountain Interval (1916); *New Hampshire* (1923); *West-Running Brook* (1928); *Collected Poems* (1930 and 1939); *A Further Range* (1936); *A Witness Tree* (1942); *A Masque of Reason* (1945); *A Steeple Bush* (1947); *A Masque of Mercy* (1947); and *Complete Poems* (1949).

Much of Frost's poetry is a new kind of *pastoral. Versed in country things, with senses alert to the object, he builds slowly from observation to symbolic meaning. *Birches*, starting with a lonely boy's diversion, tells of the charm of escapism and the needed return to earth; *Mending Wall* tells of tradition-bound exclusiveness; *Stopping by Woods on a Snowy Evening* sets absorption in the dark loveliness of the woods against the promises that man must keep. *The Cow in Apple Time*, *The Runaway*, and *Mowing* are other examples of precise sense impressions built up to revelations of man. But Frost is not a mystic; nature, however suggestive, is always separate from man.

He is a regionalist in the best sense: his loving care for the local leads to the universal. His *dramatic monologues and dialogues round off a picture of the barren farms and tough-grained people north of Boston: the loneliness in *Home Burial*; the bleakness in *The Housekeeper* and *Snow*; the eccentricity in *The Witch of Coös*; the neighborliness in *The Death of the Hired Man*; the self-respect in *The Code*; the pawky humor and grit in *Brown's Descent*. Here are living people, rooted in New England, but realized so deeply that their lives have meaning for the world. Their language is not dialect; Frost aimed at recording "tones of voice," the translation of living speech into poetry. His more subjective poems keep to this low-keyed conversational level.

From the start Frost was a lyrical as well as a dramatic poet. The personality that he reveals opposes romantic self-pity, scoffs at "literary tears," is that of a ruminative, quizzical stoic, an individualist kin to *Thoreau. Aware of the evil of the world, he still will take his chance; "As long as the Declaration guards/My right to be equal in number of cards." A liberal, who "never dared to be radical when young for fear it would make [him] conservative when old," he was no joiner, satirizing the doctrinaire and the departmentalized. He disliked industrialization but decried futile rage against it; he was a lonely striker, a

"West-Running Brook" in contrast to the many running eastward. In his later books his interest in self-portraiture and didacticism increased. But the latter is not underscored; it is that of a Yankee *Socrates rather than of a Jonathan *Edwards. An increased love for riddling is seen. Frost's philosophical concerns occupy *A Masque of Reason* and *A Masque of Mercy*, which re-examine the age-old problem of God's treatment of Job and of man and the connection man cannot reason out "Between his just deserts and what he gets." A brooder from the long, long thoughts of *A Boy's Will* to his last speculations, Frost recognizes how out of joint the times are, how science and religion agree that we are "the belittled human race." He often expressed his wry disillusionment. "We all are doomed to broken-off careers," he wrote; "I take my incompleteness with the rest." But the epitaph he wished for was: "I had a lover's quarrel with the world."

Furies: *Eumenides.

Galilei, Galileo: Italian scientist (1564–1642). Galileo (as he is usually called) is credited with the invention of the geometrical compass, the thermometer, the pendulum (as a means of measuring time), and the telescope. With this last invention he observed and recorded for the first time sunspots, the craters of the moon, the phases of Venus and Mars, and the satellites of Jupiter. He thus provided some new facts to bolster the Copernican theory, which made the sun rather than the earth the center of our astronomical system; and his discovery of the fact that the Milky Way is composed of an almost infinite number of stars gave a further jolt to those who believed that man was the center and purpose of the universe. Galileo had been highly honored and had taught mathematics at various universities, but in 1616 he was summoned before the Inquisition as a heretic and was forbidden by Pope Paul V to teach that the earth moves. He promised to comply, and was left alone until he published his *Dialogue on the Two Greatest Systems* (*Dialogo sopra i due massimi sistemi*, 1632), a study of the Ptolemaic and Copernican systems. Thereupon he was again summoned to Rome, was forced to abjure the theory of the earth's motion, and was subject to several years of rather indulgent imprisonment.

Galileo is important in the history of literature on two counts. His writings are models of expository prose and helped to set a literary standard for the newly developing natural sciences—a standard which, in spite of occasional gifted writers like *Darwin, they have largely lost. Furthermore, his discoveries soon entered into almost every branch of thought, so that they became an essential background in many literary works.

In addition to the great dialogue mentioned above, Galileo's works include *The Sidereal Messenger* (*Sidereus nuncius*, 1610), in which he reported his astronomical observations, and *Dialogues on the New Sciences* (*Dialoghi delle nuove scienze*, 1638).

Galsworthy, John: British novelist, playwright, essayist (1867–1933). Galsworthy made his early reputation with plays about problems of striking laborers and the injustices of a money-hungry culture (*Strife*, 1909; *Justice*, 1910). It is now recognized that his more substantial contribution comes from his fastidious, cumulative insight into three generations of the well-bred, well-to-do British upper middle class as it appears in the dozen novels which make up *The Forsyte Saga* (1906–29). Although he has imaginative sympathy and a certain fondness for the varied personalities of the Forsyte family, Galsworthy through them explores the class prejudices and the acquisitive possessiveness of the propertied classes, as in *The Man of Property* (1906). *The Forsyte Saga* was adapted into a popular series of hour-long vignettes for television. Galsworthy received the Nobel prize in 1932.

García Lorca, Federico: Spanish poet and dramatist (1899–1936). While still a university student in Spain,

Lorca showed his artistic versatility by producing poems, musical compositions, and paintings. After winning acclaim for his early volumes of verse, *Book of Poems* (*Libro de poemas*, 1921) and *Songs* (*Canciones*, 1927), he published some of his finest poetry in *First Gypsy Ballads* (*Primer romancero gitano*, 1928). In 1929–30 he traveled and studied in the United States and came strongly under the influence of Dali and *surrealism— an experience recorded in the posthumously published *Poet in New York* (*Poeta in Nueva York*, 1940). Because both the manner and the content of these poems lie outside his own proper sphere, they are not among his best efforts. Andalusian folk poetry and music, the Spanish romance, and the gypsy ballad are his primary domain and inspiration and lie behind his best work. His finest single poem is a funeral ode dedicated to the memory of a friend of his, a famous bullfighter, *Llanto por Ignazio Sánchez Mejías* (1935).

Upon his return from the United States, Lorca became codirector of an academic theater group which toured Spain, performing both Lorca's plays and those of Spain's Golden Age. In 1933, the troupe was enthusiastically received in South America. Returning to Spain, Lorca settled in Madrid and devoted himself primarily to drama, but tensions were mounting toward the breaking point of the Civil War. In August 1936, the poet was captured in Granada and shot by members of the Fascist Falange. His death seems to have been a private murder perpetrated under cover of the Civil War.

Lorca's early plays are comedy-fantasies in a light, impressionistic manner, steeped in the tradition of the puppet-theater and somewhat related to the *commedia dell' arte*. One of the best of these is *The Shoemaker's Marvelous Wife (La zapatera prodigiosa)*. Much weightier is the substance of three tragedies uniformly concerned with the theme of frustrated love: *Blood Wedding* (*Bodas de sangre*, 1933), *Yerma* (the title is a proper name, 1934), and *The House of Bernarda Alba* (*La Casa de Bernarda Alba*, 1935). *Blood Wedding* is a poetic drama of passion with lyrical interludes, while the other two show the gradual fusion of Lorca's poetry with dramatic realism.

Lorca's art is true to its origins in that it is essentially oral: many of his poems were spread by word of mouth and were widely known even before publication. He secures a marvelous fusion of the divergent elements of Spanish literary tradition, all the way from the folk ballad to the self-consciously difficult style of Gongora and his school. In such devices as the use of bold and unexpected metaphors his poetry recalls that of the English metaphysical poets, though it is far more sensuous. The passion and somberness resulting from the poet's preoccupation with love and death are enhanced by his insistence on showing their ceremonial, and thus dramatic, consummation in the ritual of birth, marriage, and funeral.

Although rooted in and derived from indigenous sources, Lorca's poetry transcends the individual and the national. It achieves universality not by the superficial cosmopolitanism that avoids local references, but by probing deeply enough into human life to strike its foundations.

Gargantua and Pantagruel: a fantastic satire by *Rabelais (published 1532–64). This work is a higgledy-piggledy tale of education and adventure, a humanist's dream, a burlesque (like *Don Quixote*) of chivalric romances, a satire of contemporary life, and one of the wildest, gayest, and earthiest books ever written. It was published intermittently during three decades, with the last part appearing posthumously; and, although it was condemned by the Faculty of Theology of the University of Paris, it was nevertheless a best-seller in its own day. It has continued for 400 years to delight readers with its ebullient humor, to swamp them in the floods of its erudition, to shock and bewilder them by its rush of witticism, puns, and pranks.

The ribald irreverence and the gargantuan accumulation of ideas in *Gargantua and Pantagruel*, the classical learning and up-to-date scientific thought tickled the sophisticated humanists of Rabelais' day, but the volumes were anathema to the conservative clerics. His work was officially condemned, book by book, as it came out, and

284

it seems that he himself was several times in grave personal danger and was saved only by his powerful patrons or by actual flight.

Rabelais' merry dedication to drinkers encouraged the opinion that he was merely an erudite buffoon and led even *Voltaire at one time to call him a "drunken philosopher" and describe his book as "prodigal of erudition, ordures, boredom." Although Rabelais continues to live as a humorist, he cautioned his readers that "following the dog's example, you will have to be wise in sniffing, smelling, and estimating these fine and meaty books; . . . by careful reading and frequent meditation, you should break the bone and suck the substantial marrow of my meaning." Rabelais was teasing his readers as usual—yet as usual the truth lay hidden beneath the trappings of his exaggeration. Rabelais further compares himself to *Socrates, implying thereby that the outside ugliness is a deliberately ironic disguise to point up the merit of the inner meaning. In another paradox he compares his book to an onion, where, as layer after layer of meaning is peeled off, there is finally nothing inside; in short, the outside and inside of life are equally interesting and important. This elusive many-sidedness and Rabelais' brashness have at times almost hidden his real stature, but his greatness is now generally recognized.

The sources of *Gargantua and Pantagruel*, like everything else about the volumes, were extravagantly copious, ranging from prose writers of classical and scientific treatises such as Hippocrates, Galen, and *Pliny to the poetry of *Villon and the *Adages* of *Erasmus, from *Plato, *Vergil, *Cicero, *Plutarch, the satirist *Lucian, and the Church Fathers, to the Italian humanists, *Arthurian romances, *fairy tales, *picaresque narratives, *mystery plays, *folklore anecdotes, *ballads, and *fabliaux. During the summer of 1532 an anonymous volume called *The Grand and Inestimable Chronicles of the Great and Enormous Giant Gargantua* had appeared. For this crude chapbook, which Rabelais tells us sold more copies in two months "than there will be Bibles in nine years," he decided to provide a sequel. This sequel was *Pantagruel*, now the second book of Rabelais' completed work. It appeared in November 1532, under a pseudonym. When Rabelais realized the popularity of his own *Pantagruel*, he apparently felt that it ought to have a more worthy beginning than the anonymous *Chronicles;* hence he wrote *Gargantua* (1534), now the first book.

Gargantua and Pantagruel is the history of two stupendous, genial, and gigantic kings. Both Gargantua (the father) and Pantagruel (his son) were popular medieval names for giants. Their origins, birth, appareling, education, and adventures form the narrative frame, but these are vitalized by the chief currents of *Renaissance experience—its insatiable appetites and energy, its intellectual curiosity and classical scholarship, its ideal of the whole man sound in body and mind, its love of art, freedom, and pleasure. Interspersed are numerous references to the burning literary, scientific, social, and political issues of the day; and the entire narrative shows the most amazing erudition on every subject from medicine to music, from architecture to astronomy, from natural functions to navigation.

Book I has three major themes. The first is Gargantua's initiation into the new learning by his tutor Ponocrates, and a contrasting of medieval and Renaissance education. The second and central episode is the war between Grandgousier and Picrochole, satirizing the frivolous causes which lead men to fight and the lamentable methods, like gunpowder, which they use. These chapters are brilliantly ironic, insinuating their seriousness under the guise of ridiculous buffoonery. Book I concludes with the famous section on the Abbey of Thélème, a monastery open to both sexes, without "rule," to which the members may come and go at their pleasure, whose motto is "Do as you will," and whose plan of activities is a model of the best Renaissance thought in reaction against the absolutism of the *Middle Ages. Book II (the one actually written first) is in much the same vein. Pantagruel, by name, is the symbol for thirst. But he becomes far more than the folklore pixy who keeps drunkards forever parched. He makes one drunk with curiosity, with the dignity and pleasures of the human body, with the capacity for work and study, with the joyfulness of life even in the face of adversity. When

Pantagruel grows up, he goes to Paris. There he meets Panurge, the witty and knavish vagabond whom Pantagruel loves all his life and "who cut a very gallant figure though he was a trifle lewd by nature."

These first two books introduced a group of inimitable characters and gave shape to the humanists' ideals of liberty, government, and education. The theories illustrate both Rabelais' faith in the natural goodness of man and his encyclopedic appetite for all technical excellences, all truth, all history, all languages, all philosophy, all the sciences, all the great books, all poetry and arts. The sloth, slovenliness, and aridity of scholastic education are ridiculed (I, 7, 14; II, 11), and a theory of education announced which will cater to man's moral, intellectual, physical, and social needs (I, 21–24; II, 8). The methods by which this knowledge is to be acquired are startlingly modern, not to say "progressive." The child's interest is to be cultivated by an education informal and happy; he is to debate and test new ideas, absorbing them not by memory but by understanding. Sports, games, even card tricks, physical exercise, personal hygiene are to be a part of the curriculum and are the methods by which even arithmetic and biology, for example, can be taught. Experience is to be a further solvent of this education, with field trips to the hills for an examination of plants, visits to the apothecaries' shops for the study of chemicals, attendance at the courthouses for the understanding of law and politics. And the purpose of this education is equally modern, to develop personality, to create a whole man generous and well-adjusted, able to apply his skills in the world about him, and to fulfill his duties with courage, competence, and courtesy. "I build," said Rabelais, "with the live stone that is man."

In Book III, Panurge, who becomes the central figure, has a flea in his ear which keeps suggesting that he marry. Thus does Rabelais introduce the current quarrel over "the woman question," and he devotes almost the whole book to a parade of learning, satire, science, vulgar jokes, and fabliaux, ostensibly to resolve Panurge's perplexity as to whether he should marry, whether a wife will prove faithful. The obscenities, however, do not humiliate human nature but are merely a part of a frank, full, and joyous acceptance of life. A conspicuous element in this book is the satire on all the fraudulent seers and fortunetellers who pretend to be able to predict the future.

In Book IV, Pantagruel, Panurge, and the monk Friar John set out on a search for the Northwest passage to India, in order there to consult the oracle of the Holy Bottle, which will give Panurge an answer. En route they visit a number of extraordinary lands which, like Gulliver's, are symbolic representations of human grotesqueness or depravity. Finally, in Book V (posthumously published and in all likelihood chiefly an expansion from Rabelais' notes), the Bottle's answer to Panurge's question is *Trink*, which the priestess interprets to mean *Drink*.

The greatness of Rabelais' book rests on the brilliant narrative technique, the ironic humor, and the eloquence which serve as catalysts for his erudition, realism, and forward-looking ideas. Rabelais can tell a story with incomparable directness and verve. The book is filled with memorable vignettes—Gargantua stealing the bells of Notre Dame of Paris, Friar John entering upon the Picrocholine War, Panurge setting the dogs upon the Parisian lady, the terrifying storm at sea where the nauseous coward Panurge announced that he was afraid of nothing—but danger, Epistemon's one-sentence summary of the popular tale about the man who married a dumb wife. One whole chapter (I, 11) is devoted to a parody on proverbs and conventional clichés, hundreds of them, which Gargantua systematically reversed or disobeyed: he struck while the iron was cold, put the cart before the horse, bit off more than he could chew, beat the dog for the lion, looked a gift horse in the mouth, and so on and on and on.

The burlesque Picrocholine War involving bakers is elevated to comic epic grandeur—when suddenly the mock-heroic tone shifts to a biting satire on the stupidity of the ambitions which motivate militarism. Delightful Rabelaisian paradoxes occur on every page. Judge Bridlegoose's tremendous legal learning and his punctilious observance of juridical procedure are doubly ironic; Bridlegoose is to be relieved momentarily of his judgeship for handing down an unpopular decision. Yet for four decades he has never been reversed although he based all his decisions not on the appalling string of citations which he viewed and reviewed, weighed, thumbed, studied, and pondered, and gave as authority, but on the throw of the dice. His only explanation for his present plight is that with old age and weaker eyes he misread the dice. Teeming with the life of his time, Rabelais makes uproarious fun not only of lawyers but of monks, pedants, and scholastics, who spend considerable time debating, as they imbibe, "which came first, thirst or drinking?"

The unique quality of Rabelais' technique is the humor and power achieved from the sheer mass. He names not dozens but hundreds of books, games, fishes, wines, celebrated authors, musicians, cooks, proverbs, epithets, plants, animals, serpents, even 61 verbs to describe Diogenes rolling his tub. This ingenious play upon words, synonyms, euphemisms, puns, enigmas, riddles, and neologisms (he introduced almost 600 new words into the French language) reflect not only his humor but a delight in the plastic language like his delight in life.

Rabelais hoped that his "merry writings" would give pleasure and that from the gargantuan laughter of his tales would come ever new joys and fresh consolations. The basis of this laughter is a respect for the dignity of human fecundity, a profound delight in man and nature, in the beautifully organized interdependent human body and universe. "This world, Panurge insisted, was based on mutual help and succor. . . . O Happy World inhabited by happy, thrice-happy, fourfold happy people!"

Gautier, Théophile: French poet, novelist, and journalist (1811–72). After youthful training as a painter—a training which may have influenced the strong descriptive element in his writing—Gautier began his literary career with two volumes of poetry in the violent romantic manner made popular by the international vogue of *Byron. These works (published in 1830 and 1832) are of no permanent interest, but Gautier's early novel, *Ma-*

demoiselle de Maupin (1835), is still read—partly because of its notoriety as a book that explores almost every phase of sexual sensuality. The preface to this work—a blast at the ignorance of journalists and at the neo-classical artistic and middle-class moral standards of critics—has become something of a classic in its own right.

Gautier had to support himself and his perpetually increasing family by journalism, and for most of his life as editor, critic of art and drama, and writer of travel sketches he turned out an appalling amount of hack work. He estimated that his writing would fill 300 volumes. Some of the better parts of this journalistic work were published as books, especially the descriptive sketches of travel in Spain (1840), Italy (1852), the Near East (1854), and Russia (1866).

Gautier's real literary importance, however, depends on his later poetry, written as pure art and kept scrupulously separate from his journalism. Most of it appears in a single small volume, *Enamels and Cameos* (*Emaux et camées*, 1852). In this volume the cult of art for art's sake, implied in the preface to *Mlle. de Maupin*, is put into practice. There is little concern with either ideas or emotions, but instead a meticulous craftsmanship which aims at perfection from the general form to the most minute detail—at a brilliant reproduction of the surface of things. Here also we find characteristic attempts to reproduce the effects of one art in another, or to combine those of several arts into one, as in the famous *Symphony in White Major (Symphonie en blanc majeur)*. In a poem entitled *Art*, Gautier sums up his poetic creed. The artist does his best work when struggling with rebellious forms and intractable materials (the poem illustrates this principle by the apparent ease with which it moves in a difficult stanza form). And art is not only its own justification; it is the most enduring of human productions: "The bust outlasts the city. . . . The gods themselves die, but supreme poetry remains more durable than brass." "All passes. Art alone stays." Both the precepts and the practice of Gautier's verse have helped to shape the tendencies of poetry during the past century and particularly affected *Baudelaire.

Gawain and the Green Knight, Sir: a Middle English Arthurian romance (*c.* 1370). Attempts to identify the author of *Gawain* have been unsuccessful, but he is known as the Pearl Poet because an English manuscript beginning with another poem, the *Pearl*, is the only one in which the romance is found. Layman or cleric, he was a creative genius who, with subtle charm, was able to unite themes from Latin, French, and Celtic literature.

The greatness of the poem lies pre-eminently in its beautifully integrated structure, in a unity that provides real dramatic suspense. Two central incidents, well known in folklore—the Challenge of the "beheading game" and the Temptation with exchange of promises—are here combined and made mutually dependent. Gawain's steadfastness is tested by both adventures, the first time openly, and the second without his knowledge.

Gawain accepts the challenge to exchange blows with a mysterious Green Knight who appears on New Year's Day at King Arthur's Court and offers to be beheaded if Gawain will submit to the same ordeal a year later. On Christmas Eve of the following year Gawain stops at a splendid castle close by the chapel of the Green Knight. Gawain and his host promise that each shall give to the other what he receives during three days. The host honorably turns over to Gawain the results of three days' successful hunting. Gawain in return gives the host the kisses bestowed on him by the host's wife, who has been unsuccessfully tempting Gawain to make love to her. Gawain does not reveal, however, that on the third day he has also been given a magic girdle—a sash to save his life in his forthcoming encounter with the Green Knight. In this encounter, Gawain's honesty in having "given up" the kisses saves his life; his failure to reveal the girdle is punished by a slight nick on the neck. The challenges, the temptations, the gifts, and the blows are adroitly built up, by numerous parallel incidents, scenes, symbols, and meanings, to the climactic denouement in which it is revealed that the host of the castle and the Green Knight are one. The three days spent at the castle, at first seemingly unrelated to the main adventure, are thus revealed as an integral part of it.

The charm of this skilfully contrived plot is increased by the dramatic and significant conjunction of civilized life and primitive natural surroundings. Gawain himself combines the primal virtues of courage and endurance with the feudal and Christian virtues of loyalty, honesty, and good faith. The colorful indoor scenes of luxurious, sophisticated gaiety contrast with the stark winter outdoors, where on bare, icy boughs the "birds pipe piteously." The vigorous hunt through the woods, with its excitement and details of physical movement, contrasts with the quiet and subtly humorous bedroom scenes where Gawain and his beautiful hostess spar verbally in sophisticated chitchat.

Even the versification reveals a similar subtlety of harmony through contrast. The poem is narrated in stanzas of varying lengths: Each of the long, highly alliterative lines is developed on the Anglo-Saxon verse principle of two strong accents and an unlimited number of unaccented syllables to each half line, and, under the influence of French versification, each stanza ends with five short riming (ababa) lines. The manuscript closes with the motto of the Order of the Garter: "Honi soit qui mal y pense" (Evil to him who evil thinks"), but whether the poem bears any relation to the Order is not known. *Sir Gawain and the Green Knight* is generally acknowledged as the best of the Middle English metrical romances.

Gemini: see *Castor and Pollux.

Genji, The Tale of: a Japanese novel *(Genji monogatari)* written between 1001 and 1015 by "Lady Shikibu Murasaki," whose real name is unknown. The work is a novel in the full modern sense of the term and is, in the words of a German critic, "probably the finest narrative work ever created by a woman." It is the story of the early life and loves of Prince Genji, told in a quiet, subtle, sensitive style, with a complicated plot and a restrainedly realistic approach. Strangely enough, *The Tale of Genji* strikes a present-day Occidental reader as more "modern" than most later Oriental literature. The standard English translation is *The Tale of Genji*, by Arthur Waley, first published 1925–33. Lady Murasaki's diary for the years 1007–10 *(Murasaki Shikibu nikki)* confirms and rounds out the picture given in the novel both of the author and of Japanese court life of the period.

Germinal: a novel by *Zola (1885). *Germinal* is an account of the struggles and tribulations of the workers in a coal-mining district of northern France. Few novels offer its scope of scene, wealth of detail, exact information about a community and the workings of a huge industry, or make so vivid the personalities and lives of so many individuals. Well-integrated with the story and theme, the expository elements contribute to the total artistic effect.

Germinal may be compared with *Tolstoi's *War and Peace*, for the artistic problems are similar and the resolutions equally successful. In fact, *Germinal* is more tightly knit; the progression is more straightforward; the characters are more individualized; the life depicted is more emotionally affecting. The problem or theme is felt emotionally as well as intellectually.

In keeping with his usual practice, Zola, in planning *Germinal*, immersed himself in the relevant documentation, here industrial and labor problems. Then he spent weeks studying a great strike that was in progress—acting as secretary to a radical leader so that he would be accepted by the miners and taken into their confidence. But, once the writing was begun, Zola integrated the facts from his books and observations imaginatively, and, as a result, a whole community came to life and grew on his pages—a mining community with its hard work and simple pleasures, its exploitation and misery, its strikes and industrial strife, its sabotage and mine disasters, its laboring people at a particular moment in the evolution of French society and industry. The impression on the reader is profound, as the human element triumphs over documentation and the thesis.

The problem in *Germinal* is the survival of the miners in the face of the rise of impersonal corporate ownership and the introduction of machinery that displaces hand labor. The situation is similar to that in *Hauptmann's *The Weavers*, and, like that play, *Germinal* has value as social history. Its artistic quality, however, lies in the individual, family, and community tragedies. The complexities of human personality transcend classes and social theory. Goodness, meanness; heroism, cowardice; faithfulness, adultery; sacrifice, selfishness; love, hate— these are individual, not class, characteristics.

Zola, at heart a reformer, was partisan in his attitude toward social problems, sympathetic to the oppressed and the unfortunate. But in *Germinal* he was much more the artist than the crusader. His principal characters are miners, and he lets them present their own case both by their actions and in their own words; he does not intrude himself into his story. The situation has the inevitability of great tragedy. Fate, ironically taking the form of change and progress, is the villain. And the evil persons who appear among the laborers and management are only flotsam in the inevitable currents of change. Their wickedness makes for particular misery, the individual instances reinforcing the general tragedy.

Like most great tragedies and epics, *Germinal* ends on a note of optimism. As Etienne (the leader of the strike which has just been broken) looks back upon the stricken community which he is leaving, he thinks of the miners at work far below him as seeds—Germinal ("seed-time") was a spring month in the calendar of the French Revolution—ready to sprout and burst the earth asunder.

Ghosts: a play by *Ibsen (1881). Ibsen stated the purpose of this play admirably when he wrote to a friend: "It seemed to me that the time had come for moving some boundary posts." The play achieved this purpose by extending the boundaries both of what may be said on the stage by way of criticism of society's sacred principles and of what may be presented there as the theme of a drama. Ibsen's conquest was not for himself alone, for other dramatists—notably *Hauptmann in Germany—were encouraged to show similar daring.

In *Ghosts*, Ibsen emerges as a hater of the society of his time. He reveals it as a hollow framework, so rotten at its foundations that it is ready to collapse at any moment. It is based on falsehood, hypocrisy and lies; it loves only good appearances and scorns the revelations of truth. It is a society afraid of itself, for it dreads scandals—dreads sincerity, simplicity, and the naked truth. It is a society haunted by the "ghosts" of tradition and custom, too weak to break away from the past and unable to carry the weight of new ideas.

The ghosts of inherited physical characteristics as well as of old, worn-out ideas haunt the lives of the characters in everything they think and do. "And then we are all, one and all, so pitifully afraid of the light," says Mrs. Alving, who is constantly fighting against these ghosts. But even she lacks the courage to act. "I am too timid and faint-hearted because of the ghosts that hang about me, and that I can never quite shake off." Her own and her son's lives are already ruined when she finally gathers strength to reveal to her son, Oswald, who had been sent away to Paris under the illusion that his father was a virtuous and moral person, that the late Mr. Alving had actually led a loose and lascivious life. Suffering from inherited syphilis, Oswald pays for the sins of his father. He yearns for light, sunshine, and the "joy of life" and dreads the dark and gloomy atmosphere of home. When the final curtain falls, he is insane.

Ibsen reveals Mrs. Alving's liberal point of view (which she is too weak to live by), contrasting her with Pastor Manders. In their long conversations, Ibsen presents two different ethical concepts. With raised finger, Manders proclaims his shallow doctrines. His very existence is a hypocritical sham. He refuses to insure the orphanage for fear public opinion will criticize him for not trusting Divine Providence, and, when it burns, the worst thing for Manders is not its loss, but "all the malignant attacks and imputations"—what people and newspapers will say. Then, too, he has robbed himself and Mrs. Alving of the beauty of life by making her go back to her husband. He calls this "a victory over my life," but Mrs. Alving rightly terms it "a crime against both of us." All Manders' theories are made up of "oughts" and "plain duties" whose falsities Mrs. Alving describes thus: "I began to look into the seams of your doctrines. I wanted to pick only at a single knot; but when I had got that undone, the whole thing ravelled out. And then I understood that it was all machine sewn."

Particularly interesting is Ibsen's use of the analytic technique. When the curtain opens, the action of the plot is almost completed. The play itself is concerned with the fatal results of previous happenings, which are revealed through the long conversations between Manders and Mrs. Alving. (The parallel with the *Oedipus* of *Sophocles is striking.) Through this unraveling of her past history, Mrs. Alving becomes the central figure of the play, the one who is fatefully and tragically responsible for all the misery. Some other features of the play are "dated": for instance, it is no longer considered possible for a child to *inherit* a venereal disease from his father. Basically, *Ghosts* is valuable for its frank criticism of the misconceived values by which people attempt to live.

Gide, André Paul Guillaume: French writer (1869–1951). Gide's poems, plays, novels, journals, letters, and critiques represent a continuous, self-absorbed self-examination, during which he preached a doctrine of the liberation of feeling and of finding the good life in the actual experience of living. His avowed homosexuality created a storm in the French literary world. An admirable stylist, he was awarded the Nobel prize in 1947. Gide's writings were originally influenced by the *symbolists. A visit to Algeria in 1893 liberated him from his narrow Protestant upbringing and resulted in his interest in *Nietzsche and *Dostoevski; in this period he wrote *The Fruits of the Earth* (*Les Nourritures terrestres*, 1897), *The Immoralist* (*L'Immoralist*, 1902), and the work that brought him his first popular success, *Strait Is the Gate* (*La Porte étroite*, 1909), followed by *Lafcadio's Adventures* (*Les Caves du Vatican*, 1914). After the First World War Gide obtained a following for his searching and rational self-expression, and in this period were written *La Symphonie pastorale* (1919), *L'Ecole des femmes*

(1929), and the novel *The Counterfeiters* (*Les Faux-Monnayeurs*, 1926), which symbolized the life between the wars—the counterfeit being the lives led by individuals pretending to abide by society's codes. Gide regarded this as his only novel, his other works being described by him as *récits*, or narratives. There is a mirrorlike quality in *The Counterfeiters*, since the novelist in the novel is writing a novel about counterfeiters, and he keeps a journal about it. This parallels the journal Gide kept while writing the novel. In its discontinuities and playfulness, Gide seems to mock and question the mechanics of the very form he is practicing, but the book is a discerning study of the ethical ambiguities faced by the young in French society. Perhaps the most illuminating of Gide's works is his autobiography, *If It Die* (*Si le grain ne meurt*, 1920). His journals, covering the years 1889–1949, have been translated in four volumes by Justin O'Brien.

Gilgamesh: a Babylonian *epic poem (*c.* 2000 B.C.). From ancient records it is known that this poem was once more than twice as long as what has survived from it. In its present form it is pieced together from nearly 30,000 tablets or fragments in three languages. The poem tells the adventures of Gilgamesh, who begins as a harsh ruler, has a terrific battle with a primitive figure and then becomes his staunch friend, loses this friend, tries vainly to regain him, and finally confers with his shade in the land of the dead. The poem, like most primitive epics, is probably pieced together from a good many stories originally independent. One of the most interesting sections is the Babylonian tale of the Flood (Tablet XI), which is a remarkable parallel to the story of Noah's Flood in Genesis. The final section, which describes the world after death, is a literal translation from a Sumerian poem.

Giraudoux, Jean: French novelist and dramatist (1882–1944). Born in the little town of Bellac, Giraudoux attended the École Normale Supérieure in Paris, where he specialized in Germanic studies. Active in the diplomatic service, he started writing relatively late in life. He first turned his attention to fiction, writing slight but subtle poetic novels. Out of one of these, *Siegfried et le Limoúsin* (1922), came his first play, *Siegfried* (1928), the drama of an amnesic soldier in which Giraudoux analyzes the opposition between the French and the German temperaments. From then on, he devoted himself mostly to the stage, successful in comedy as well as in tragedy.

His comedies are subtle pieces, combining a dreamlike quality with an acute intelligence. The best known are: *Amphitryon 38* (1929), in which Giraudoux renews the ancient myth by putting Jupiter in a less than exalted position, thereby proclaiming the prevalence of the human over the divine; *The Enchanted* (*Intermezzo*, 1933), in which the supernatural and the fantastic triumph briefly over established conventions; *Ondine* (1939), which dramatizes the conflict between ordinary humanity and the mysterious forces of nature; *The Apollo of Bellac* (*L'Apollon de Bellac*, 1942), which in a good-natured way satirizes men's vanity and gullibility; *The Madwoman of Chaillot* (*La Folle de Chaillot*, 1945), which, under the mask of comedy, condemns the various types of greed which prevail in contemporary society.

Giraudoux also revived classical tragedy, using Greek themes to treat the problems of our time. *Tiger at the Gates* (*La Guerre de Troie n'aura pas lieu*, 1935) deals with the problem of war, which was becoming increasingly pressing at that time in Europe; *Electra* (*Électre*, 1937) dramatizes the conflict between justice and the state.

Giraudoux instilled a new life into the French theater, chiefly through the virtuosity of his style. Language—elegant, brilliant, witty—plays an important part in his plays. It underscores his love of paradox, fantasy, and digression. But under this dazzling surface lies a serious purpose. Giraudoux was essentially a moral writer, and for him the theater constituted a form of education. The broad themes he deals with—love, friendship, faithfulness, war, death—are meant to arouse the spectator's reflections.

gnomic verse: poetry composed of "wise sayings"—brief maxims or aphorisms corresponding to the modern proverb. This style was characteristic of a school of Greek poets in the 6th century B.C. The term is applied also to certain portions of the *Poetic *Edda* and to two sets of verses in Old English which express moral or religious truths and popular beliefs, *e.g.,* "Woden created false gods, but the All-ruler the gloriously wide heavens."

Goethe, Johann Wolfgang von: German poet, dramatist, critic, novelist, and scientist (1749–1832). Goethe comes as close to deserving the title of a universal genius as any man who has ever lived. Though he will be considered here as a man of letters, it is important to remember that he had an intelligent grasp of all the arts, that he successfully carried burdensome responsibilities as a public administrator, and that his scientific interests led him to make significant contributions to mineralogy, optics, comparative anatomy, and plant morphology.

As the son of prosperous middle-class parents with artistic and intellectual interests, Goethe had excellent early teaching and encouragement. The French occupation of Frankfurt-am-Main, his home, brought with it a French theater in which young Goethe became so much at home that his earliest dramatic attempts were in the style of French *Neo-Classicism. At the age of 16 he began a three-year study of law (and of other subjects that interested him more) at the University of Leipzig. A serious illness brought him home for a year and a half as a semi-invalid, during which time he studied alchemy and chemistry and went through a phase of the sentimental religious pietism which was currently in vogue. He then finished his legal studies at the University of Strassburg (1770–71), but his real education there came from *Herder, who was leading a revolt against the "artificial" literature of Neo-Classicism by opposing to it the strong "natural" voices of Homer (see *Iliad* and *Odyssey*), *Shakespeare, the *Ossianic Poems, and the folk song.

During the next five years Goethe engaged in a desultory practice of law at his home, but his real activity was the building of a literary reputation. He had already published some unimportant works and written some fine poetry—especially love poetry, for Goethe was always in love and inspired by it. He had already begun to work on *Faust*, but publication was far in the future. In 1773 he burst on the literary horizon with *Götz von Berlichingen*, a play named for its principal character, a noble of the late *Middle Ages who sided with the peasants in an abortive revolt. In its vigor, its rejection of standard dramatic form, and its wild devotion to the ideal of freedom, this play was the most powerful work of the *Sturm und Drang* period. Goethe immediately followed it with a totally different and equally successful work, *The Sorrows of Young Werther* (*Die Leiden des jungen Werther*, 1774). This epistolary novelette about a young man who brooded over a hopeless love until he finally blew his brains out plunged all Europe into tears. But though its sentimentality is out of fashion now, it remains a remarkable work both for its effective presentation and for its psychological penetration. (It may be noted that it had some basis in Goethe's own feelings and experience at this time—he once remarked that all his works were "fragments of a great confession.")

Interested in Goethe's literary works, the young Duke of Weimar invited him to his court in 1775. Though Weimar was only a small duchy with a population of about 100,000, and though the inhabitants of the isolated little town itself numbered only some 9,000, Duke Karl August managed to make it the intellectual capital of Germany by surrounding himself with such men as Wieland, Goethe, and later, Herder and *Schiller. Goethe's invitation was promptly made permanent, and he was saddled with various heavy administrative tasks which, while giving him greater breadth and objectivity, slowed down his literary production. Some ten years later, feeling restive and confined in Weimar, Goethe made a long-dreamed-of trip to Italy (1786–88). This visit, which he recorded in *The Italian Journey* (*Die italienische Reise*, 1816–17), completed his development away from the earlier influence of Herder and towards a form of *classicism. The change was reflected in a group of plays written at about this time. *Egmont* (1788), a drama in prose dealing with a hero of the Netherlands in their revolt against Spain, is transitional. *Iphigenia in Tauris (Iphigenie auf Tauris)*, written earlier in prose, was revised in 1787 to make a classical play in verse. *Torquato Tasso* (1790) was another outstanding play of this same type, this time with an Italian subject, the poet *Tasso. In 1790 Goethe also published the first version of his life work as *Faust, a Fragment*, but the completed *Faust* was published later, Part I in 1808 and Part II in 1832.

After Goethe's return from Italy his life in Weimar was uneventful. He was relieved of most of his official duties, though he did direct the court theater for more than a quarter of a century. A close and fruitful friendship with Schiller, begun in 1794, was cut off by the latter's death in 1805. Goethe's marriage to Christiane Vulpius in 1816 merely legalized a situation of some 17 years' standing. During Goethe's latter years he was an isolated and somewhat lonely figure, universally known, widely admired and reverenced, but without the true friendship which can exist only between equals. He had none, and more and more his contemporaries considered him as an "Olympian," looking down from his own unattainable height on our little affairs with an indulgent but detached approval.

The real events of his last 40 years were creative. A novel showing the theater as an educational force, *Wilhelm Meister's Apprenticeship (Wilhelm Meister Lehrjahre, 1795–96)* was continued in *Wilhelm Meister's Journeyman Years (Wilhelm Meister Wanderjahre, 1821–29)*. In 1798 appeared *Hermann und Dorothea*, a narrative poem telling (in hexameters on the classical model) a charming story of village life and love. During his last 20 years Goethe was occupied with installments of an autobiography whose title is usually rather ineptly translated as *Poetry and Truth from My Life (Aus meinem Leben, Dichtung und Wahrheit, 1811–33)*. In 1819 appeared a series of lyrics inspired in part by a study of Persian poetry, *West-Eastern Divan (Westöstlicher Divan)*. The vein of song which made Goethe one of the greatest lyric poets had flowed intermittently since his youth, and it continued until the end, for some of the finest sections of Part II of *Faust*, completed a few months before Goethe's death, are lyrical.

Long before his death, Goethe was recognized both in Germany and abroad as one of the great figures of world literature. (Appropriately enough, he invented the term *world literature*.) He was translated by men like *Scott, *Carlyle, and Gérard de Nerval and widely read all over the civilized world. He is now generally admitted to be the most recent writer who can confidently be placed in the class of the supremely great—the class of *Homer, *Dante, and *Shakespeare.

Gogol, Nikolay Vasilevich: Russian novelist and dramatist (1809–52). After failing as an actor and a poet, Gogol turned to writing short stories. His first volume, *Evenings on a Farm near Dikanka* (1831), conjuring up the manners and folklore of his native Ukraine, was a striking success. Only in 1834, however, after he had failed dismally as professor of history at the University of St. Petersburg, did he decide that his real career lay in literature. He scored another success with a farcical comedy, *The Inspector General* (1836), a satire on rapacious and irresponsible petty officialdom. The play pleased the sophisticates and won Gogol the approval of the Czar himself, although it enraged the bureaucrats at whom it was aimed. During the next dozen years Gogol lived in western Europe and visited Russia only occasionally. Meanwhile he worked at his masterpiece *Dead Souls* (*Mërtvye dushi*, 1842). This novel met with acclaim, for the public saw it as an attack on the institution of serfdom. Gogol hoped to carry the novel further, to make the second part a picture of all Russia, and to effect the country's spiritual rebirth.

While working on this continuation he began to show signs of religious obsession. In 1848, after a pilgrimage to the Holy Land, he felt confirmed in his belief that he was eternally damned. Convinced of the sinfulness of his creative work, he destroyed the manuscripts of the second part of *Dead Souls*. What remains is only a disjointed fragment.

Gogol's real forte was humorous satire, and he used

it to make the Russians aware of the decadence of their institutions. When Gogol began to write, romanticism was dominant, and *Pushkin and Lermontov were giving Russia transplanted Byronism. Gogol introduced a realistic literary movement that led directly to the masterpieces of *Turgenev, *Tolstoi, and *Dostoevski.

Golden Legend, The *(Legenda aurea):* a collection of saints' lives by Jacobus de Voragine (*c.* 1230–98), who at the time of his death was Archbishop of Genoa. His saints' lives were written between 1255 and 1256 as a popular work. They are of no historical value, being merely a collection of the popular tales about the saints that had gradually developed—the folklore of Christian heroes. The work soon became standard and was widely translated and read—many a medieval child was brought up on it. The title as we now have it is not the author's. *Legend* means simply "a saint's life," and *Golden* is a tribute of later ages. The work is frequently referred to by its French title as *La Légende dorée*, and the author is called also Jacques de Voragine and Jacobus Januensis.

Goldoni, Carlo: Italian dramatist (1707–93). Goldoni gradually forsook his profession of law to become a writer of comedy and the reformer of the Italian theater. In his early years he wrote plots for the *commedia dell' arte*, tragedies, tragicomedies, and throughout his life operatic libretti, but he is remembered as a writer of comedy. In this capacity, he substituted a swift, natural comedy of character with ethical implications for a formalized, incredible comedy of intrigue. The two mechanical changes necessary were the writing out of the dialogue instead of leaving it to be improvised, and the abandonment of the masks which the players traditionally wore. In a time when the Italian theater was highly stylized, Goldoni's irreverence towards classical authority was fruitful. Speaking of the unity of place (see *unities), he said that he would never sacrifice a comedy which might be good to a prejudice which might make it bad. *Molière was his model for the spirit and purpose of comedy but was not a model to be mechanically or slavishly followed. The precedent of Molière's pure literary French, for example, did not keep Goldoni from abandoning literary Italian in some of his plays and achieving greater realism by using the Venetian dialect.

In 1762 Goldoni left Venice and began a new career in France, where he directed an Italian theater and became tutor in Italian to the royal household. Here he wrote comedies in French, which was also the language of his *Mémoires*, a highly interesting account of his life and work. The French Revolution cut off his royal pension, and he died in poverty in 1793.

Goldoni wrote approximately 250 theatrical pieces (he produced 16 in one season!). *The Mistress of the Inn* (*La Locandiera*, 1753) is probably his most famous play and is an excellent example of his art at its best.

Goliardic verse: Latin lyrics traditionally ascribed to the Goliards, wandering scholar-poets of the 12th and 13th centuries who had had clerical training. Golias (the name has been variously and unsatisfactorily explained) became the legendary head of a legendary order of Goliards, disreputable tramp-scholars who lived by their wits and their poetry. Although wanderers of this general type existed, they were not an organized order and they were probably incapable of composing the verse attributed to them, with its technical virtuosity, its thorough scholarship in both classical and medieval Latin literature, and its familiarity with learned and popular vernacular poetry. The satirists about whom we have some information—Hugh Primas, "The Archpoet," Walter of Châtillon—bore only a superficial resemblance to the typical Goliard.

Goliardic poetry assumes an attitude of debauchery and carefree gaiety and contains many satires directed at derelict churchmen. It even parodies parts of the Church services. In contrast to the Church's contempt for the world, it praises a *carpe diem philosophy and glories in a vagabond existence, singing the beauties of the natural world and the pleasures of wine, women, song, and dice. *The Archpoet's Confession* describes the wandering student, with his promiscuous love-making, his passion for gambling, and the vinous inspiration of his poetry. Probably the most familiar example of the Goliardic type today is *Gaudeamus igitur*, a German student song written in Latin in the Goliardic tradition during the 18th century.

Gongorism: see *euphuism.

Gorky, Maxim: pseudonym of Aleksei Peshkov, Russian writer of fiction and drama (1868–1936). A study of the life and works of Gorky is at the same time a study of the social and political affairs of Russia as she threw off the Czarist rule and became a Communist nation. Gorky came from a provincial proletarian family and early learned how brutal life can be. Orphaned at 7 and self-supporting at 9, he ran away from unkind relatives when he was about 12. In his wanderings over the whole of Russia, his many jobs in many environments, he encountered all kinds of people and situations that became both the basis for his social feeling and the subjects for his stories and plays. He soon began to participate in radical agitation (he once said, "I have come into the world—to disagree"), and his activity in the abortive revolution of 1905 necessitated his flight to western Europe, where he remained until 1913. His sympathy with the successful revolution of 1917 and with Communism won him a prominent literary place in Soviet Russia which (in spite of another long period of residence in western Europe) he enjoyed until his death.

Gorky's writings fall into three general periods. Before he was 30, he had attracted notice with some short stories based on his early vagabondage about Russia. He shows a deep sympathy for the masses of Russia in their misery and poverty, for he sees beneath their squalor a certain dignity and worth and regard for humanity that may one day be their salvation (*Chelkash*, 1894; *One Autumn Night*, 1894; *Old Woman Izergil*, 1898). In the second period he produced plays and novels dealing with the degradation, ugliness, and immorality of the Russian masses. These works are somber, bitterly realistic, and full of philosophizing in which the characters, often cast loose from their moorings, attempt to get at the "meaning of life." While sympathizing with these people, as in *The Lower Depths* (1902), he also ridicules and satirizes them (*Smug Citizens*, 1902; *Summer Folk*, 1905). Critics feel that Gorky did his best, most tempered work in his last period. His autobiographical writings and recollections of writers reveal a maturity of thought and a perspective that are lacking in his earlier writing and establish him as a writer devoted to his country and to a humanity that will, if intelligently guided, triumph over its own stupidity and slavery (*Childhood*, 1913; *Reminiscences of Tolstoy*, 1919; *Reminiscences from My Youth*, 1923; *Recollections*, 1925). Throughout all his work there is this dual theme of contempt for what man is and reverence for what he might be.

Gorky's play *The Lower Depths*, probably his best-known work outside Russia, is representative of both his writing and his ideas. First produced by the Moscow Art Theatre, it makes great demands on its audience, for there is little action and no character development. Gorky gathers the very dregs of society in a tenement basement where they witness death, sordid brawling, the effects of alcoholic psychosis, a prostitute's wishful dreaming for a "fatal love," and human treachery—to them, all a part of normal routine. To this miserable scene comes a man who with soft words and persuasive talk, sometimes telling the truth, sometimes telling lies when it is easier and more effective, tries to bring some happiness and awareness into the lives of these people. He leaves as mysteriously as he came, but those "at the bottom" are not unaware of what he has done, though they can see through his subterfuge. His presence was enough to give them some hope, so that one of the most bitter and sardonic can say, "Everybody lives for something better to come." The strength with which Gorky projects his ideas and the power of his belief in the eventual worth of man make *The Lower Depths* a notable play.

Gothic novel: a novel of horror based on the supernatural. One of the first signs of the weakening of 18th-century rationalism was a revival of interest in the supernatural. In poetry this development was a part of the revival of medievalism and the *ballad; in fiction it took the form of the Gothic novel. The original work which set the type once and for all was Horace Walpole's *The Castle of Otranto* (1764). Haunted castles, strange noises, and an acceptance of the supernatural with all its trappings mark this work, and the style has not changed except that later examples sometimes enjoy their ghosts and then cravenly explain them. Other outstanding specimens of the type were Ann Radcliffe's *The Mysteries of Udolpho* (1794); M. G. ("Monk") Lewis' *The Monk* (1796), which terrified a generation; Mary Shelley's *Frankenstein* (1818), which introduced scientific horror; and Wilkie Collins' *The Woman in White* (1860). It is an essential element of the Gothic novel that the horror should be its primary purpose, a cultivation of the *frisson*, the shudder of terror evoked by the inexplicable and mysterious—"primitive" medieval ruins, decaying castles, crumbling churches, and graveyards. Though Henry *James' *The Turn of the Screw* (1898) has all the regular properties, including apparitions on the staircase in the moonlight, it is not a Gothic novel because the interest is psychological and analytical rather than melodramatic. The type still flourishes, however. Perhaps the purest and best-known recent specimen is Bram Stoker's *Dracula* (1897). There are at present a number of pulp magazines entirely devoted to the Gothic novel, though they never use the term. On the Continent the type did not establish itself in a pure form, but its elements entered into a great deal of the writing of French and German romanticism and *fin-de-siècle* decadence.

Gottfried von Strassburg: see *Tristan and Isolt.

Graces: see *Charites.

Grail: see *Holy Grail.

Gray, Thomas: English poet (1716–71). Gray is an interesting transitional figure between English *Neo-Classicism and the *Romantic Movement. His earlier poetry is essentially in the classical tradition. Even *An Elegy Wrote in a Country Churchyard* (as it was entitled when first published in 1751)—perhaps the most famous single poem in the language—impresses by its perfection of statement rather than anything novel or striking in the sentiments expressed. It belongs to the "graveyard school" of reflective poetry but rises above its surroundings. During this period Gray also wrote some excellent light verse, such as his *Ode on the Death of a Favorite Cat Drowned in a Tub of Gold Fishes* (1748). In his later poetry he fell in with the interest in medieval subjects and folk literature which preceded the triumph of romanticism. His important poems on early Celtic and Norse themes included *The Bard* (1757), *The Fatal Sisters* (1761), and *The Descent of Odin* (1761).

Greek Anthology: an extensive collection of Greek poetry made by Constantinus Cephalas about A.D. 925. The unique manuscript of this collection was discovered in the Palatine Library at Heidelberg in the 17th century, and for this reason the collection is frequently known as the *Palatine Anthology.* In modern editions the collection of Cephalas is usually augmented somewhat from other sources. It contains more than 6,000 poems written by 320 authors over a period of 17 centuries, from the 7th century B.C. to Cephalas' own time. The poems are classified according to type and subject, into epitaphs, inscriptions, rhetorical exercises, love poems, etc. Most of them are short, and the general standard is remarkably high.

Grillparzer, Franz: Austrian dramatist (1791–1872). Grillparzer led a long and frustrating life in the Austrian civil service, finally rising to be head of the department of archives. All his life he was tormented by a feeling of inadequacy and by general misgivings; he described his habitual state of mind as "distraction alternating with confused brooding." The fact that his superiors disapproved of his plays did nothing to assure him. He was engaged for years but never brought himself to the point of marrying. And in the prime of his life, discouraged by the reception of his comedy *Woe to the Liar* (*Weh' dem, der Lügt*, 1838), he ceased to publish his works. Three of his best plays were found in his papers after his death, along with his lyrics and epigrams. In one of these epigrams, written a few years before his death, he summed himself up neatly: "Cleverly thought and stupidly done—/That's how the course of my life has run."

The central idea of his plays is that an individual's salvation depends on his being able to remain aloof— that involvement spells disaster. Something of the struggle implied by this idea is seen in the handling of his plays, except that here he achieves a perfect balance rather than a struggle. It is interesting, however, to note that he typically presents romantic themes and attitudes with classical polish and detachment. He began with a "fate play" of a sort in vogue at the time, *The Ancestress* (*Die Ahnfrau*, 1817), but soon found his own style, themes, and smooth *blank verse. His more notable plays include the problem of the conflict between art and life in *Sappho* (1818); a trilogy on the legend of the Argonauts and Medea, *The Golden Fleece* (*Das goldene Vliess*, 1822); a patriotic historical play, *King Ottokar's Fortune and Fate* (*König Ottokars Glück und Ende*, 1825); a dramatic version of the story of Hero and Leander, *The Waves of the Sea and of Love* (*Des Meeres und der Liebe Wellen*, 1831); and his last play, *Libussa*, which reflects social problems while treating the myth of the founding of Prague.

Grillparzer also wrote two distinguished prose tales, *The Monastery at Sendomir* (*Das Kloster bei Sendomir*, 1828) and *The Poor Minstrel* (*Der arme Spielmann*, 1848).

Guillaume de Lorris: see *Romance of the Rose*.

Gulliver's Travels: a satire by *Swift (1726). *Gulliver's Travels* is perhaps the sole major work in all English literature that has continuously led a double life: it has been at once one of the most glamorous of children's adventure stories and one of the most pungent critiques of humanity addressed to the mature imagination. This almost incredible marriage of opposites is possible because in the main the disturbing satire for adults lurks inconspicuously behind the pleasantly exciting façade of the explorer's tale; the child can rarely see behind the façade, and the adult can never cease seeing behind it or trying to pierce through it. Further, there are times when Swift is entirely concerned with the façade—with the elaboration of the details of the story for its own sake (for instance, in the military drill in Book I, Chap. 3, and the description of the Floating Island, Book III, Chap. 3), and the presence of such passages assists the young reader—or the unperceptive reader generally—to take the whole story at the simplest level of meaning. Throughout Books I and II there is the immediate fascination of the change of perspective, just as in Book III the superficial charm is that of the "wonders of science." Swift's obvious enjoyment of playing the game—of unusual sizes, mysterious phenomena, and strangely shaped creatures—gives zest to his narrative without in any way impeding him when he chooses to make the game philosophical.

Not any story of the marvelous is good for over two centuries of vigorous life, and Swift's success is due to a very careful management of materials. First of all, he does not condescend to his materials; rather he treats them with utmost seriousness. He makes the narrator, Gulliver, an earnest, solid, trustworthy traveler who is scrupulously careful in reporting exactly what happened; he is as far away as can be from the flippancy or the wink or the self-consciousness of one who is engaged in an elaborate hoax. Swift takes great pains to invent a multitude of such concrete facts as a conscientious voyager would set down in his log (drawing, of course, upon the extensive literature of travel of his own day). His technique is that of circumstantial realism; all techniques communicate in themselves, and the use of this technique is a way of asserting the entire reliability—and importance—of what is conveyed. Second, Swift is extremely diligent in establishing the inner consistency of

310

the strange worlds which Gulliver discovers; all aspects of life in Lilliput, Brobdingnag, and Houyhnhnm-land are punctiliously worked out according to scale or pattern (Lilliputians are six inches tall, Brobdingnagians sixty feet tall). This is more than "realism." It is giving order to something that lies outside our usual sense of order; it is combining the rational and fantastic in a wonderful amalgam that both astonishes and convinces. Finally, the narrative manner tones down the marvelous rather than plays it up. Gulliver eschews all hectic, open-mouthed amazement and weds himself to a stubborn, moderate factuality; the ironic discrepancy between his calm plainness of style—his simple vocabulary and orderly, unpretentious sentences—and the richness of the secondary levels of meaning is one of the special sources of pleasure in the work.

Yet the style is at once simple and not simple; it is ambivalent whenever the Gulliver-Swift ratio is present, that is, whenever the work is both a tale for children and a symbolic narrative for whoever can so read it. Gulliver's simplicity is Swift's deadpan subtlety; Gulliver's plain style is Swift's ambiguity and irony. Gulliver writes about the royal edict that Lilliputians cannot approach him "without license from court; whereby the secretaries of state got considerable fees." Coming from Gulliver, these words say simply that he was a very popular sideshow; coming from Swift, they take on the dimension of ambiguity and actually invite us to speculate on the various ways in which the secretaries of state acquired their profits. Gulliver records that the giant farmer's wife, on seeing him, "screamed and ran back, as women in England do at the sight of a toad or spider." From Gulliver, this is a simple image supplied by his memory; from Swift, it is an ironic comment on the status of Gulliver (and hence of humanity generally) and on the amusing timidity of women generally. Gulliver honestly admires the destructiveness of modern weapons of warfare; the expression of his common man's pride is Swift's ironic comment on the achievements of civilization. The effectiveness of this indirection is so great that the reader regrets the occasional passages in which Swift, forgetting his own role as Olympian outsider and Gulliver's as as ordinary Englishman, uses for both of them a single voice railing not only directly but violently against the state of affairs in Europe. The work is least successful at those moments—they occur most frequently in Book III—at which Swift fails to keep Gulliver in character as a mild, factual, patriotic, middle-class Englishman.

Familiarity blunts our sense of the imaginative daring of Swift in creating his midgets, giants, and remarkable horses. Here is the heart of both adventure story and symbolic narrative. As a critic of society rather than as an entertaining fabulist, Swift has been found to be hitting off a number of contemporary characters and events: Lilliput is England, Blefuscu is France, Flimnap is Sir Robert Walpole, and so on. But a historical allegory is the least of his achievements. Rather he has used the method of fantasy for a profound comment on human nature as it may be observed in all times and places. The littleness of the Lilliputians symbolizes the moral and spiritual pettiness of which humanity is capable—its jealousy, malice, infidelity, ingratitude, its lust for power, and, above all, its hatred of greatness. The hugeness of the Brobdingnagians is a symbol of large-mindedness, so that from their point of view Gulliver's self-satisfied normal humanity seems, in both size and character, to be something verminous. In Book III, the least coherent of the four parts, various symbolic devices are used to suggest the unsocial behavior, unimaginativeness, and pedantry of various scientists and scholars, and—in the brilliant final section—the fundamental error of human beings who want to live forever. But what goes on in the early books is by no means as simple as this. In fact, it needs to be strongly emphasized that Swift is neither a mere cynic nor a mere debunker, for he is as well aware of moral potentiality as of failure. His central theme, indeed, is the dual nature of man— man's capacity for both good and evil. In Book I, even the ordinary Englishman Gulliver, in contrast with the Lilliputians, comes to embody the best of human endowments; and in Chapter 6 Swift paints a utopian picture of certain aspects of Lilliputian life. The Brobdingnagians are both idealized and given human defects, so that they become a complex picture of what some men are, *i.e.*, sadistic, shameless, inhumanly bent on profits, and of what excellence men may achieve. A still further complication in Books I and II is that, side by side with his unwavering moral insight, Swift introduces a striking optical relativism, whereby identical physical characteristics become, when reduced in scale, either invisible or even beautiful, but when enlarged, positively monstrous. Thus Swift utilizes new scientific knowledge of his day without permitting it to unsettle his moral vision.

Swift's uncompromising sense of man's potentiality for evil, a theme somewhat neglected after the decline of tragedy, has had the effect of making readers overemphasize this part of his worldview. This unbalanced reading has been especially true of Book IV, one of the most misunderstood of all symbolic writings. Swift simply is not saying, as has often been thought, that mankind is only a tribe of Yahoos, that is, bestial anthropoids; rather, in creating Yahoos and Houyhnhnms, he is splitting man into certain component elements—the animal and the rational. The animality of the Yahoos is unmistakable; the Houyhnhnms are admirably reasonable, of course, but their rationality is schematic, arid, devitalized—the product of eliminating the emotional foundation of life. In discovering that he is akin to Yahoos as well as Houyhnhnms, Gulliver is so shocked that he falls into a neurotically distorted view of life. To get as far away as possible from the subhuman element, he wants to live exclusively in terms of Houyhnhnm rationality, which is inhuman in its own way, as is dramatically suggested both by equine grotesqueness and by the limitedness of equine life. Gulliver's wrong-headed attachment to Houyhnhnm life as a sole good is not Swift's; in the very important last two chapters Swift makes Gulliver return to Europe, find not only that not all Europeans are Yahoos but that the Portuguese sea captain has more humanity than he, fresh from the Houyhnhnm altitudes, and begin the hard readjustment to a full human life. Swift does not preach; he makes the narrative conclusion itself point the meaning of his most brilliant travelogue.

Gulliver's Travels draws upon at least five traditions of world literature, some of them active from classical times to the present: the literal travel account, realistic fiction, utopian fiction, *symbolism, and the fantastic voyage. Interestingly, the use of fantasy for serious statement, virtually eliminated by two centuries of emphasis upon *realism, is reappearing in our own day.

Hades: the Greek god of the Underworld, also called Pluto, and by the Romans Dis. Also, the Underworld itself.

Hafiz, Shams-ud-din Muhammad: Persian poet (1320–89). Hafiz is so appreciated among his own people that his tomb at Shiraz is a shrine for pilgrims. His reputation rests on the *Divan (Odes)*, a collection of poems in Persian which, like *Omar Khayyam's, tell of the joys of wine and women, flowers and nightingales, and bemoan the instability of all things human. Some poems celebrate his love in the intense, adoring manner to be found in the English Elizabethan poets and some, with the frank realism of the later cavaliers: "Thy rosy limbs, unless I may embrace, / Lose for my longing eyes full half their grace, / Nor does the scarlet mouth with honey drip / Unless I taste its honey lip to lip."

These poems have often been given allegorical and mystical interpretations, much like the double construction attributed to the Song of Songs in the *Bible. The earthly mistress of Hafiz thus becomes a symbol of the Nameless Divine, and the adoration of the lover is read as the indefinable yearning of the soul for God. Such an interpretation has much to recommend it, for Hafiz's poetic imagery is drawn from Sufism, a form of medieval Persian mysticism. Some of the poems, however, are clearly erotic, with no allegorical intent.

To *Emerson, who translated some of Hafiz's poems (from a German version), he "is the prince of Persian poets, and in his extraordinary gifts adds to some of the attributes of *Pindar, *Anacreon, *Horace, and *Burns the insight of a mystic."

Hafiz (literally, "preserver, rememberer") is not a name, but a title of honor applied to one who has memorized the entire *Koran* (see *Mohammed).

Hamlet: a tragedy by *Shakespeare (1600–01). *Hamlet* is the world's most quoted play and its hero the most discussed character in dramatic literature. Shakespeare is responsible for the temperament of Hamlet, the passion and vitality joined with brooding intellect and lyric sensitivity. But the plot of a son avenging the murder of a father was not original. Even the fratricide, usurpation of the throne, feigned madness, forged letter, the characters of Ophelia and Horatio, the duel of wits between uncle and nephew go back ultimately to a tale in a Latin *History of the Danes* by a Danish cleric, Saxo Grammaticus (*c.* 1200). It was revived in a French collection, *Tragic Histories* (1582) by Belleforest, and dramatized on the English stage (*c.* 1589) in a play no longer extant (referred to as the *Ur-Hamlet*, "Source-*Hamlet*").

To the main plot Shakespeare gave tragic intensity both by the character of his hero and by a series of parallel situations and characters, with ironic duplications and contrasts. "Frailty, thy name is woman" can be said of both Gertrude and Ophelia, and both are victimized by plotting males; but more affecting is the contrast between the quick remarriage of middle-aged Gertrude and the suicide in the madness of spurned love of young Ophelia. There is a striking parallel of three sons—Hamlet, Laertes, and Fortinbras—each seeking to avenge a murdered father. Hamlet and Fortinbras (who have both been deprived of their thrones by uncles) are the inheritors of a blood-feud. Fortinbras' father was killed by the elder Hamlet, and Laertes' father by Hamlet himself. A fight between Hamlet and Laertes is inevitable; and both die by the same poisoned foil. Hamlet had recognized the essential similarities of their positions: "by the image of my cause, I see the portraiture of his." Fortinbras, though "of unimproved mettle hot and full," is not weakened like Laertes by silly impetuosity, nor like Hamlet by passionate introspective intellectuality. The paradox is that Laertes' hot-headed devotion to his family's honor and Hamlet's cautious hesitations lead equally to tragedy. Only Fortinbras goes into action with cold shrewdness. He is not so attractive as Hamlet, but he will survive to reassert the moral law and carry on the kingdom.

Plunged into misery by his father's death and into a tragic disillusionment by his mother's overhasty second marriage, Hamlet moves about silent and despondent in "inky cloak and customary suit of solemn black." His normal world has been shattered, and the duty of revenge forces him to play a role essentially foreign to his own nature. Ironically, he is undone by his need to be certain of his victim's guilt—a need which is both a genuine, honorable scruple and an excuse for procrastination. To confirm his suspicions Hamlet puts on an "antic disposition" (feigned madness); and it is this "madness" which first arouses the suspicions of the king. Similarly with Hamlet's next test "the play's the thing wherein I'll catch the conscience of the king"—the king's behavior confirms Hamlet's suspicions, but the play also confirms Claudius' conviction that he has been found out. Hamlet then rejects the opportunity to kill the king at prayer, because to do so would send him to Heaven. In this chain of moves and countermoves, the decision to spare the king releases him to plot further against Hamlet.

This is Hamlet's problem, but he sees in it a symbol of the deeper mystery of life. "The times are out of joint" and "something is rotten in the state of Denmark." Avenging his father is only one facet of the struggle of good against evil. "There are more things in heaven and earth," he tells Horatio, "than are dreamt of in your philosophy." Throughout the play, his speeches are packed with these more-than-private meanings; and his dialogue, under the guise of madness, bristles with irony and paradox. Desirous of revenge, he yet must weigh the impulses which keep him from it, wonder whether man is the author of his woe or there is a "divinity that shapes our ends." He feels responsibility for the "safety and health" of the state, recognizes that he is heaven's "scourge and minister," and reluctantly accepts his destined mission.

Despite the sensational details of a revenge-tragedy, Hamlet's character remains central. He is, it is true, in part an idealized *Renaissance prince, whose "courtier's, soldier's, scholar's eye, tongue, sword," conform to *Castiglione's dream of the courtier. He is also another conventional Elizabethan dramatic type; a victim of the *humor of melancholy. Yet he is more than these. He is complex and subtle, sensitive to the imponderable ironies of life and the mysteries of human destiny. Even as he moves from passion to rational control and to determination, neither we nor he can pluck out the heart of his mystery. Only when, at the moment of his own death, he has rid the state of the source of its disease by killing Claudius is moral order reasserted so that the world of the play, impoverished as it is, returns to normal.

Hardy, Thomas: English novelist and poet (1840–1928). Hardy brought to the English novel a sense of tragic pessimism expressed with stoical restraint. Nothing in the external circumstances of his life explains this point of view. He was brought up in Dorsetshire (the Wessex of his literary work), and his closeness to simple rural life probably helped him to penetrate to the central motives of existence. After a local apprenticeship and a stint with a London architectural firm, Hardy returned to Dorsetshire, preferring to try his hand at writing, even though he had won two architectural prizes.

His first novels were not great successes either artistically or commercially, but *Far from the Madding Crowd* (1874) established his reputation. His next story, a "somewhat frivolous narrative" (as he said), was followed by his most famous and in many ways his best novel, *The *Return of the Native* (1878). In this work he achieves a perfect balance between the realistic and the romantic elements in his world, between man and nature (the heath being felt as the most powerfully drawn character in the book), and between human responsibility and the workings of blind chance. In subsequent novels his world became increasingly one of grim determinism—"crass casualty" equally devoid of divine intent and of materialistic logic. Chance, accident, coincidence—Hap, as he calls it—determine the outcome of human effort. The traits and actions of an individual play only a small role in his tragedy. Though the inner conflicts of characters like Henchard and Jude are not negligible, their idealism and will to good are really frustrated by random combinations of circumstances. A man's destiny depends on the fall of the dice, and the dice are loaded against him. *The Return of the Native* showed enough of this philosophy to disturb the reading public and outrage the Victorian critics, and the uneasiness and indignation mounted with the stronger medicine of the best of the novels that followed it—*The Mayor of Casterbridge* (1886), *Tess of the D'Urbervilles* (1891), and Hardy's final novel, *Jude the Obscure* (1896). *Jude* provoked such a general outcry that Hardy abandoned the novel and wrote only poetry for the last 30 years of his life.

The shift from fiction to poetry, however, involved no essential change. Both are bare, unadorned, often deliberately harsh in their diction. Both frequently use rustic dialect and local or archaic words. Above all, the poetry in no way retracts the somber view of existence which had led to the condemnation of the novels. It too finds man's only faint hope in pity and loving kindness, which may at least palliate the evils beyond our cure. Hardy's lyric poetry has had a profound influence on later writers. Much of it exists in isolated poems, and some of the finest is included in *The Dynasts* (1903–08), a vast poetic drama about the Napoleonic Wars and their impact on England. It, too, closes with Hardy's perpetually unanswered question about the universe: "To what tune danceth the Immense?"

Harpies: mythical winged creatures, originally winds, which carry away persons and things. *Vergil describes them as filthy creatures having the bodies of birds and the faces of women.

Hauptmann, Gerhart: German dramatist (1862–1946). Hauptmann's influence on German life and letters stretched over a period of almost 50 years and was felt not only by the intelligentsia, but by German people of all ranks and classes. Like *Lessing and *Goethe before him, Gerhart Hauptmann became a symbol to the German people. Yet unlike these classical poets Hauptmann reached the heart of everyone—even the simple farmers, miners, and weavers—for it was their joy and their suffering that offered him his richest material. Emphasizing the motivation of action rather than the action itself, Hauptmann took his cue from the turmoil, doubt, and conflict of everyday life and created a new drama that deals with modern man in a modern world.

After trying his hand at various vocations (including sculpture), Hauptmann wrote his first successful play in 1889. Because it frankly and naturalistically shows environment and heredity controlling the fate of man, *Before Dawn (Vor Sonnenaufgang)* created a furor in the theater. Hauptmann's name became known to everyone almost overnight. Officially banned, this play became the center of many controversies; with its scientific and sociological interest it soon took Berlin and other German audiences by storm.

Whereas *Before Dawn* revolved around the specific types of farmer and socialist, *Lonely Lives (Einsame Menschen*, 1891) presented the emotional-psychological problem facing a whole generation of young intellectuals. Here Hauptmann shows that the idealism of his contemporaries must yield to the disillusionment and drabness of the everyday world. The emptiness in the lives of his sensitive and basically weak characters isolates them, making them spiritually lonely.

Even more revolutionary than *Before Dawn* was *The Weavers* (*Die Weber*, 1892), today his best-known work. It presents an incident in the struggle of the Silesian weavers in the 1840's and draws on accounts which Hauptmann had heard from his grandfather, a former weaver. The play uses more than 40 characters to present a powerful account of the exploitation of the weavers in which the whole group, rather than any individual, is the real hero.

In the next year Hauptmann wrote *The Beaver Coat* (*Der Biberpelz*, 1893), a sharply satirical and profoundly human comedy. Realistically and humorously it tells the story of a thieving washerwoman who outwits the law and its discreditable representatives.

In *The Assumption of Hannele* (*Hanneles Himmelfahrt*, 1893), he used a style in which he felt as much at home as in naturalism. Realizing that allegory, symbolism, the domain of the supernatural and the dream are as much a part of nature as "real life" situations, Hauptmann wrote this "dream poem," as he called it. Although this play has many naturalistic characteristics, its heavenly visions and its use of verse depict the world of fantasy and the realm of the spiritual. The interest in the symbolic continues in *The Sunken Bell* (*Die versunkene Glocke*, 1896), a play which presents the problem of the artist, torn between the symbolic and the everyday worlds.

Most of Hauptmann's dramatic work was produced between 1889 and the first World War, but his great dramas came between 1891 and 1903. Depicting the people and places he knew best, he gained fame throughout Europe with his impressive and successfully experimental dramas. His treatment of subjects and themes which had been taboo on the stage, as well as his real concern for dramaturgy in all its aspects—insistence on realistic settings, natural and unaffected movements on the stage, simple but expressive speech—all contributed to the growth of the art of the modern theater.

Hauptmann's international fame—he was awarded the Nobel Prize for Literature in 1912—rests almost solely on his great dramas of the late '90's; and his prose and poetry, an integral and important part of his work, have been less known outside Germany. As he reached artistic maturity he turned to the recreation of great figures and themes of world culture and literature: Christ in the novel *The Fool in Christ, Emmanuel Quint* (1910), the German folk hero in the narrative poem *Till Eulenspiegel* (1928), Hamlet in the drama *Hamlet in Wittenberg* (1936), and the ancient legend of the house of Agamemnon (see *Oresteia*) in the *Atreus* tetralogy. Many of his mature works reflect a certain duality of his nature, a tension between the antique and the modern, paganism and Christianity, nature and civilization. This tension is clearly seen in such works as the novelette *The Heretic of Soana* (*Der Ketzer von Soana*, 1918) and the novel *The Isle of the Great Mother* (*Die Insel der grossen Mutter*, 1924). The play *Before Sunset* (*Vor Sonnenuntergang*, 1932) is symbolically a counterpart to *Before Dawn*. Hauptmann considered the poem *The Great Dream* (*Der grosse Traum*, begun during World War I, published 1942) as perhaps his most profound personal revelation. It is a symbolic work modeled on *Dante's *Divine Comedy* and relating the author's own life to the life of his age.

Although Hauptmann was a versatile and prolific writer, his dramatic work is his most significant contribution to world literature. The social awareness that distinguishes Hauptmann's drama, making him Germany's foremost social poet, underscores his deep feeling for humanity—a quality which may be traced throughout all phases of his life and work.

Hawthorne, Nathaniel: American novelist and short-story writer (1804–64). For 12 years after his college days, Hawthorne struggled with his writing, and this self-disciplined apprenticeship made him the best craftsman among the New England writers. From this period came his short stories, published in *Twice-Told Tales* (1837). Then, after a year in the Boston Custom House (1839), Hawthorne went to Brook Farm (an experiment in communistic living). Realizing the impracticability of its arrangements—and finding manual labor not so edifying as he had expected—he withdrew, married, and settled in the Old Manse at Concord (*Mosses from an Old Manse*, 1846). A three-year political appointment in the Salem Custom House preceded *The Scarlet Letter* (1850), Hawthorne's masterpiece. Its success was a surprise to both author and publisher, and it was promptly followed by *The House of the Seven Gables* (1851) and *The Blithedale Romance* (1852, a book giving Hawthorne's impressions of Brook Farm). When President Pierce, a friend of Hawthorne from their Bowdoin College days, appointed him Consul at Liverpool (1853), he had his first opportunity to travel and to meet European celebrities.

One novel, *The Marble Faun* (1860), was composed during his European stay.

Hawthorne was like his contemporary *Poe in being strongly influenced by the current vogue of the *Gothic novel of terror and in being an American romantic without being a Transcendentalist.

He is utterly different, however, in his fascination with the Calvinistic idea of the damnation of man, with its attendant consciousness of sin and sin's impact on the human soul. This concern with the Puritan conscience led him to consider moral themes, and to deal with neuroses, fixations, and the influence of environment—concepts which seem strangely modern.

The moral significance of these concepts is presented by means of *symbolism and *allegory, in settings which sometimes have a haunting atmosphere of the supernatural. The meaning of the symbols is often complex. The scarlet letter *A* which Hester Prynne wears is not only a public sign of her adultery and a token of her humility as a confessed sinner; it is also her badge of pride in her naturalness and in her defiance of her neighbors' bigotry. *The House of the Seven Gables* and *The Marble Faun* are similarly concerned with the effects of sin on the characters, and here too the theme is prefigured by symbols. In Hawthorne's notebooks the first jotting of the idea for a story frequently contains a direct statement of what it is to symbolize, but in the story itself the statement is replaced by implication. This technique (which influenced Henry *James) brings to fiction all the suggestiveness of the poetic imagination.

Hazlitt, William: English critic and essayist (1778–1830). As a critic, Hazlitt played an important role in the rediscovery of *Shakespeare for what he was rather than what the 18th century had made him, and in a revival of interest in the Elizabethan drama in general. As a familiar essayist he had an infectious verve and gusto, a knack of finding enjoyment in things and sharing his enjoyment with a reader. Some of his best essays are *Of Persons One Would Wish to Have Seen*, *On Going a Journey*, *On Disagreeable People*, *On Reading Old*

Books, *The Fight*, *On the Feeling of Immortality in Youth*, and *On the Pleasures of Hating*.

Hebbel, (Christian) Friedrich: German dramatist, poet, and critic (1813–63). The son of a poor stonemason, Hebbel grew up in dire poverty and managed to educate himself only by a heroic struggle against adverse circumstances. He attracted the attention of the king of Denmark, who gave him a small scholarship that enabled him to spend some time in Paris and Italy (1843–45). Then he settled in Vienna, where he married a successful actress and spent the rest of his life in moderately comfortable circumstances. His early hardships are reflected in the bitterness of his early plays; his later works, though remaining tragic, are more serene.

Hebbel drew his subjects from ancient and modern history and from contemporary life, from heroic legend and bourgeois self-righteousness. *Judith* (1840) is a powerful, almost brutal, treatment of the patriotic murderess in the Apocrypha. *Maria Magdalena* (1844) is a middle-class "problem play" pointing the way to *Ibsen later in the century. *Herodes and Mariamne* (1850) returns to the ancient Jewish world for a barbarous plot which is handled with great psychological finesse. *Agnes Bernauer* (1852), based on medieval German history, shows a beautiful and lovable woman coldly sacrificed to political expediency. *Gyges and His Ring* is a psychological treatment of a tragic anecdote from *Herodotus. *Die Nibelungen*, Hebbel's most ambitious work, is a trilogy of plays dramatizing the medieval narrative of the *Nibelungenlied*. In all these works Hebbel distinguishes himself by his subtlety in dealing with the complex motivations of his characters (especially his women) and by a tragic sympathy with individuals who cling to an old order and go down in defeat before a new one which they cannot accept or even comprehend. As he himself once commented, "The first or last representative of a movement is likely to be either tragic or comic." In some of the earlier plays he used a terse prose. The later ones are in distinguished *blank verse.

Hebbel also wrote a considerable body of poetry, including lyrics marked by solidity and power rather than grace or elegance. His letters and diaries, with their extensive discussions of his struggles with the problems of his art, have become classics in their own right, not only personally interesting, but important in the history and theory of literary criticism.

Hedda Gabler: a play by *Ibsen (1890). When describing his intention in writing *Hedda Gabler*, Ibsen said that he wanted, above all, "to depict human beings, human emotions, and human destinies, upon a groundwork of certain social conditions and principles of the present day."

Hedda Gabler, whom Ibsen calls by her maiden name, since he considers her more the daughter of her father than the wife of her husband, is the product of her time and her environment. Brought up in the traditions of the typical military class and expected to conform to a conventional pattern of marriage for wealth and position, she lacks the strength and courage to face life. Unable to feel anything—unable to give herself entirely to something or someone—she is endlessly frustrated and bored. To her there is no beauty, and love is nothing but an empty word. For a person like Hedda suicide becomes the only heroic and beautiful, the only truly great, moment. This act offers freedom and represents a deed of "deliberate courage and spontaneous beauty."

Hedda Gabler is a study of a frustrated, isolated personality striving to assert herself. The circumstances are unfavorable: outwardly she is assured, subtle, and clever; inside she is as hollow as a rotten tree, without support, ready to collapse at any instant. Married to a pedantic scholar for whom she has no affection, and living in a small, slow, backward Norwegian town of the 1860's, Hedda devises schemes for subtly asserting her power over the people who come into her life. Her former lover, Lövborg, becomes her chief victim. She ruins the noble intentions of Thea Elvsted, who sincerely loves Lövborg and wants to free him from bad influences. Hedda makes him the victim of her love and hate: she burns his manuscript—his life's work—and expects him to use her revolver to end his life "beautifully." Hedda seems to have succeeded in her design to dominate and control a human destiny until she learns that Judge Brack's knowledge of the facts behind the suicide gives him power over her. She cannot prevent the trick that fate plays upon her: not only does Mrs. Elvsted find Lövborg's original notes, but her own husband comes to consider it his life work to reconstruct, with the help of Mrs. Elvsted, the lost manuscript. Realizing that she has been unsuccessful in her desire "to mould a human destiny," she takes her own life.

The supporting characters of the play are all built around Hedda and make her stand out vividly. The only strong person among them is Mrs. Elvsted, who is contrasted to Hedda and has the strength to live a life independent of moral and social conventions. *Hedda Gabler* is Ibsen's most interesting and most revealing study of a woman character.

Heine, Heinrich: German poet and critic (1797–1856). Heine was born of intelligent Jewish parents of moderate means, and his literary bent was marked by an early love of reading, *Don Quixote* and *Gulliver's Travels* being among his favorites. His rejection by a proud and beautiful cousin, who prudently preferred a wealthier match, left permanent scars on his character. A wealthy uncle (who continued to aid him throughout his life) enabled him to study at the Universities of Bonn, Göttingen, and Berlin—and to pay more attention to literature and to Jewish history and problems than to law. In 1825 he was baptized into the Lutheran Church—a step necessary for his advancement in the law, and one of which he was afterwards ashamed. He had already published lyric poetry and an unsuccessful tragedy when he took a walking tour through the Harz Mountains (1824) and described it with great success in *Die Harzreise*. His *Book of Songs* (*Buch der Lieder*, 1827) established his pre-eminence as a lyric poet. The success of his travel sketch led him to travel extensively in England, Holland, and Italy and to write six volumes of *Travel Pictures* (*Reisebilder*, 1826–31).

Under official censure because of his enthusiasm for freedom, and believing the French to be "the chosen people of this new religion," he settled in Paris in 1831. Here he soon came to know all the leading French literary figures and became a sort of unofficial interpreter of the French and the Germans to each other. Germany was still central in his thinking, and the ambivalence of his feeling toward his native land is clearly shown in the satirical *Atta Troll* (1841–42) and *Germany: A Winter's Tale* (*Deutschland: Ein Wintermärchen*, 1844). Always sickly, with progressively failing sight, he was confined to his bed with almost total paralysis from 1848 until his death, but from his "mattress grave" he issued some of his best poetry in *Romancero* (1851) and *Last Poems* (*Letzte Gedichte*, 1853–56), as well as some of his best *bon mots*. On the last day of his life he jested, "God will pardon me—that's His profession." During these last years he was attended by a *grisette* who knew no German and had never read his poetry, and whom he had lived with and finally married, and by a mysterious girl whom he called "The Fly" (La Mouche), who took dictation, read proof on his books, and read to him.

Heine once wrote: "I have never set great store by poetic glory, and whether my songs are praised or blamed matters little to me. But lay a sword on my bier, for I have been a good soldier in the wars of human liberation." Certainly he was a significant fighter in the war against bigotry and oppression, but it is as a poet that he will be remembered. Romanticism and the folk song are the two dominant influences on his poetry (*Die Lorelei* illustrates both), but it is a sophisticated folk song and a tongue-in-cheek romanticism. When he is being most sentimental, Heine is always aware of—and a bit amused by—his sentimentality; and the wry comment or sudden epigrammatic twist may come at any moment. It is this balance between sentiment and irony which gives the lyrics of Heine their bittersweet taste. As a satirist, in *Atta Troll* and *Germany*, he is more topical, direct, and brutal. He also wrote some very fine literary ballads, especially in *Romancero*—for example, *Schachtfeld bei Hastings*, which tells how Edith Swanthroat, the cast-off mistress of King Harold of England, was taken to the battlefield of Hastings and succeeded in finding her former lover's body among the slain, after others had failed.

Heine's personality and gifts made him a clear mirror of the ironic complexity of modern life, its contrasts between the ugly and the beautiful, the real and the ideal. His poems have attained world-wide fame, both alone and in the fine settings of such composers as Schubert, Schumann, and Brahms. Hitler and his cohorts, with all the apparatus of their anti-Semitism and secret police, found it impossible to suppress *Die Lorelei*—the best they could do was to ascribe it to an unknown author. It would be hard to find a clearer proof of real popularity.

Hemingway, Ernest: American novelist and short-story writer (1898–1961). The chances are that posterity will regard the novels of Hemingway as less important than his influence as a craftsman. Hemingway, in a certain sense, erased the dividing line between journalism and literature: and it is his style and manner, his terse representation of simple acts, his sparse dialogue, and his understatement of emotion, which created an easily imitable combination. The imitators have been numerous and, as usual, inferior to their model. In theme, his subjects have emphasized the sensual, rather than the life of the spirit: his men are overassertive in their masculinity and his women usually tend to be wax figures created for the delectation of the men.

Placed beside the major novels of the past, Hemingway's works are slight: cynical, disillusioned, his characters spend their time drinking, fishing, fighting, wenching. These activities are, of course, time-honored diversions of epic and fictional heroes. But in Hemingway they cease to be diversions and become not only goals of existence, but a sort of mystical masculine moral obligation of a "lost generation" (as Gertrude *Stein called it), "tough," courageous, and honest, but broken physically and emotionally by the brutality of war and disillusioned by the insensitivity and hollowness of civilized society. This feeling led Hemingway to suicide.

It is difficult to build anything very solid on such a negative philosophical foundation. Probably Hemingway's best attempt is his novelette *The Old Man and the Sea* (1952), in which the fishing is a grinding necessity rather than a sport, and the real subject is a quality of epic endurance. The same theme invests his semiautobiographical novel, *Islands in the Stream*, posthumously published, 1970. Hemingway's first work of importance, *The Sun Also Rises* (1926), pictures American expatriates in Europe. *A Farewell to Arms* (1929), with its deserter-hero, is a study in disillusionment. Hemingway's most ambitious effort, *For Whom the Bell Tolls* (1940), places his characteristic hero in the setting of the Spanish Civil War, mixing up a sense of duty with his usual romantic love situation; but the title (*Donne: "Ask not for whom the bell tolls; it tolls for thee") implies that loss of liberty anywhere means loss everywhere. Some of his books are not fiction, but direct glorification of such primitive sports as bullfighting (*Death in the Afternoon*, 1932) and hunting (*The Green Hills of Africa*, 1935), and memories of the Paris of the expatriates, 1921–26, especially of Ezra *Pound and Gertrude Stein (*A Moveable Feast*, 1964), posthumously published.

Hemingway's indirect way of narration is at its best in his short stories, in which he has often, within small compass, successfully evoked a sense of the tragic through the overtones of his prose. There is an impersonal quality in his tales, and a sustained picture, which he cannot maintain in his longer works. One is led to the conclusion that the substance of most of Hemingway's work is shallow and made brilliant only by a studied lucidity that constitutes the most important side of his achievement in contemporary American literature. He was awarded the Nobel prize in 1954.

Henry IV, Part 1: a history-play by *Shakespeare (1597). This is one of a group of four plays, beginning with *Richard II* and ending with *Henry V*, that deal with material from English political history at about the beginning of the 15th century (*i.e.*, about 200 years before the peak of Shakespeare's career). Shakespeare does not attempt to reconstruct the historical conditions of this era; rather he imposes Tudor political theory on the events of the plays and sets the Falstaff scenes in a reasonable facsimile of an Elizabethan London inn.

Part 1 of *Henry IV* integrates actions that suggest comedy and tragedy as well as history—the historic in Henry IV and his political problems, the tragic in the Hotspur action, and the comic in the Falstaff action—although its true hero, Prince Hal, belongs to the historic vision of the national state. But the historic view is dominant and requires the ridicule of Hotspur, who threatens to be a tragic scapegoat-hero, and the unequivocal rejection of Falstaff (in Part 2), who threatens to dissolve the historical seriousness into comedy. Only by such harsh treatment of Falstaff and Hotspur (tag names both, though the latter is historical) can the historic vision emerge triumphant when Prince Hal becomes Henry V.

Henry IV, in the first of the group of four plays, had usurped the throne of Richard II, the rightful king. He is not, therefore, according to Tudor political attitudes, a proper example for his son and heir to follow. Prince Hal, the true hero of the last three plays of the group, stands in the middle of a triangle of forces which he must transcend. The defining points of the triangle are his father, Henry IV, at the apex; Hotspur, whom Henry IV sees as better crown-prince material than his own madcap son; and Falstaff, who tries vainly to play the role of father-substitute to Hal. All three of them are "rebels" against the good order of the state in one way or another: Henry IV as a usurper, Hotspur as a rebel against Henry IV (his duly constituted king whether a usurper or not), and Falstaff as a participant in highway robbery and other violations of the king's laws. Moreover, just as Falstaff and Hotspur are equated as rebels against their lawful king, so Falstaff and Henry IV are equated in the resort to "counterfeiting" in the battle scenes of Act V.

At the beginning of the play, Prince Hal seems to have accepted Falstaff as a model to imitate, although the very first speeches of the two point out a significant difference between their attitudes toward the use of time, and Hal's soliloquy at the end of Act I, scene ii, makes it clear to the audience that he has not permitted his association with Falstaff's group to blind him to his historical mission. Actually, Hal is educating himself—despite Henry IV's despair and Hotspur's scorn—by getting to know his society from top to bottom; he sounds the very bass-string of humility and earns the title "king of courtesy." When the time for serious action arrives, he proves himself by killing Hotspur and "usurping" his title, "king of honour." Later, when he has become Henry V, he rejects Falstaff just as he had rejected his other mentors. In *Henry V*, he is presented as the best of all possible kings, if not as one of Shakespeare's ideal heroic figures, for he exists in the relative political world of national history, not in the ideal worlds of tragedy or comedy.

In reading this play (or for that matter the group of four plays), it is profitable to observe the recurrences of the word "redeem," in both its theological and commercial senses, and the contrast between leanness and fatness, usually associated with states of health and corruption. In this play particularly, discussions of time and honor furnish valuable clues for appraising Hal and the triangle of forces that surrounds him. These discussions serve to define the uses of time and the possibilities of honor in the historic (not ideal) world of the play. They are most easily seen in the contrasting attitudes of Falstaff and Hotspur, but they are to be found also in the calculating attitude of Henry IV and the more human, if also calculating, attitude of Prince Hal, who fulfils his resolution (I. ii. 240) to redeem time when men least think he will.

Hephaestus: the blacksmith god of the Greeks, called Vulcan or Mulciber by the Romans.

Hera: the sister and wife of *Zeus, identified by the Romans with Juno.

Heracles: a great Greek hero, the son of *Zeus and Alcmene called Hercules by the Romans.

Hercules: *Heracles.

330

Herder, Johann Gottfried: German folklorist, literary critic, translator (1744–1803). Herder was by vocation a Lutheran preacher and teacher; but his avocation was the study of literature. While still at college he became interested in primitive literature, in the return-to-nature movement that *Rousseau was popularizing, and in a new mystical philosophy of antirationalism which suggested that Nature expresses herself through the senses and "feelings," not through reason.

His interest in the "primitive" led him to an enthusiasm for folk literature and a glorification of Macpherson's sentimental *Ossianic Poems. He went about collecting and translating folk ballads and songs from "all nations and peoples" to show that folk literature expresses the "innermost soul" of a nation (*Folksongs*, 1778, called in later editions *Voices of Nations in Songs*). His best poem, *The Cid* (published posthumously, 1805), is an adaptation of Spanish folk traditions and ballads about Rodrigo Diaz de Vivar, an 11th-century Christian hero fighting against the Moors (see *Cid). In his essay *Shakespeare* (1773), the same preoccupation with the natural appears—for he extols the Englishman as a "natural" Titan writing plays by the laws of his own genius. Herder's *Ideas on the Philosophy of History of Mankind* (1784–91) developed the theory that societies (and literary types) grow like individual human beings from birth to decay, but each cycle marks a step forward; and in this ever-onward march the poet is the prophet, the product and spokesman of the people whom he is leading.

Herder's importance lies more in his influence than in the value of his actual works, many of which are fragmentary. He did, however, originate or put into circulation a number of fruitful ideas. In addition to his evolutionary conception of history, he helped to popularize "feeling" as against "reason"—natural spontaneity and freedom as against literary rules and precepts. His influence freed German literature from rigid adherence to French *Neo-Classical rules and directed the young writers to the wellsprings of their own native traditions. He thus exercised an incalculable influence on *Goethe and other German rebels of the *Sturm und Drang* movement.

331

Hermes: the Greek messenger god, called Mercury by the Romans. See *Caduceus.

Hero and Leander: tragic lovers of ancient Greek mythology. Leander, a youth of Abydos (on the Asian side of the Hellespont, modern Dardenelles), swam the strait each night guided by a torch held by his beloved Hero, a priestess of the temple of Aphrodite at Sestos (on the European side of the strait). When Leander was drowned, Hero committed suicide (versions differ: by drowning or by throwing herself from a tower). In *Ovid's *Heroides*, the oldest surviving version, Leander and then Hero tell of their passionate relationship as they lament social obstacles and the heavy seas which keep them apart. A short dignified version (343 lines) by the Greek Musaeus (A.D. fifth century?), was the one which stirred the *Renaissance imagination, e.g., it was translated into Latin by *Tasso, into French by Marot, paraphrased (rather than translated) and transformed by *Marlowe into, as Douglas Bush said, "the most beautiful narrative poem of the age." In the Marlovian version theme and poetry become one. The poem, glowing and sensuous (as in the rich opulent paintings of his contemporary Titian), exalts physical nature, the unrestrained sexual play of the lovers, half-animal, half-gods. Drunk with their own voluptuous eroticism, they feel "all sensuality is beautiful, all beauty sensual." "Whoever loved who loved not at first sight?" the poet asks. The instantaneous ardor of these passionate young lovers sparkles their assent. Marlowe's poem (1593?), 800 lines of end-stopped couplets, was unfinished. It was completed and published in 1598 by Chapman, who divided it into Sestiads (Chapman's term for a canto or division, from Sestos, by analogy with the *Iliad*). Chapman himself added four Sestiads. "Love is a golden bubble full of dreams," for Chapman, and lawless, unconstrained love must end in tragedy. The poem was referred to and imitated even before it was printed, and indeed set the fashion for erotic poems on mythological subjects (cf. *Shakespeare, *Venus and Adonis*).

Herodotus: Greek historian (*c.* 484–*c.* 428 B.C.). Herodotus was born in Asia Minor, but while he was still young, political strife drove him into exile. He set out on his travels through Greece and the Black Sea region and all those lands to the south and east which formed a part of the Persian Empire. In Asia he crossed the desert to visit Babylon, and in Africa he sailed up the Nile as far as the first cataract. Such journeys were longer than any undertaken by a Greek before, and they were supplemented by the study of sites and the questioning of natives, for their purpose was to gather firsthand information for the great *History of the Persian Wars*, which was already beginning to take form in Herodotus' mind.

The *History* of Herodotus, as we have it, is divided into nine books, the first six describing the expansion of Persia under Cyrus, Cambyses, and Darius, the last three the campaign against Greece conducted by Darius' successor, King Xerxes. The early books are subordinate to the later, and the subject matter they contain on the conquest of Lydia, Assyria, and Egypt, the invasion of Cyrene, Scythia, and Thrace, the revolt of the Asiatic Greek cities, and the landing of the Persians at Marathon, is introductory to the description of the attack and repulse of Xerxes' forces, which forms the main theme of the *History.* As Herodotus informs us, his object in composing the work was to preserve the memory of this campaign, so that the causes of the conflict might be reported accurately and the exploits of the Greeks and the Barbarians might be transmitted to future generations. By making all he wrote contribute to this purpose, Herodotus was able to unify large masses of matter, create the first great prose work of Europe, and become, in *Cicero's phrase, the "Father of History."

Not that Herodotus' volume is history in the modern sense. It is history, geography, ethnography, and folklore. And not that it is unified closely. It is filled with digressions of every type. It was intended for oral presentation, and its content was selected to please an audience, a fact which explains the stress laid everywhere on stories, the prominence given to strange countries and peoples, and the frequent inclusion of marvels—sometimes accompanied by the warning, "They say, but I do not believe." For Herodotus is more critical than is generally supposed, and mistaken less often than one might think. His main source of information was necessarily tradition, but he had mastered the writings of his predecessors, and although he knew no language except Greek, he used inscriptions and other documents, when possible, to verify what he was told. If he did not submit all he wrote to the investigation of reason, as his successor *Thucydides did, the fault lies largely, at least in serious matters, with his interpretation of history as *human action subject to the law of divine retribution.* Herodotus believed that events demonstrate the truth of the saying "Pride goeth before a fall." He found in Croesus, Cyrus, Polycrates, and Xerxes examples of men who were prosperous, but who in their prosperity became insolent and were destroyed by the gods, for the gods abase all who exalt themselves and allow none to be haughty.

The *History* of Herodotus is one of the most fascinating books of literature, abounding in famous passages that range in tone from the amusing anecdote of Hippoclides, who danced away his marriage, to the legend of Solon and Croesus, with its solemn warning, "Look ever to the end." But the high point of the narrative is reached only in the great battle scenes of the last four books, particularly in the descriptions of Marathon, Thermopylae, and Salamis.

The circumstances under which Herodotus composed his *History* are unknown. He is said to have read it, or parts of it, at Athens, where he lived for some years before leaving as a colonist for southern Italy in 444 B.C. But he was still revising it some 15 years later, and it may be that he never put it into what he considered final form. In spite of a few minor inconsistencies, however, it seems complete.

heroic couplet: two consecutive lines of iambic pentameter verse in English whose end-words rime. (The term may come from the extensive use of this form in the "heroic" plays of the 17th and 18th centuries.) The form subdivides into the "closed couplet," whose meaning and sentence structure are complete without reference to what precedes or follows; and the "open" or "run-on couplet," which is not self-contained. *Chaucer, who learned it from the French poet Machaut, introduced it into English, and it became his favorite meter; he used both the "closed" and the "open" forms. The closed couplet achieved great popularity after its use by *Dryden and became the dominant form of English verse under the influence of *Pope. *Neo-Classical practice required not only that the two lines express a complete thought, but further that *each* line express a thought, with balance, repetition, and antithesis. The unity of rhetorical sense and meter made the form particularly apt for epigrams: "Be not the first by whom the new is tried; / Nor yet the last to lay the old aside." The poets of the *Romantic Movement and the later 19th century preferred the open couplet (*Keats, *Endymion*; *Browning, *My Last Duchess*).

Hesiod: Greek poet (probably end of 8th century B.C.). Hesiod was the son of an unsuccessful man who left his home in Asia Minor to take a farm in central Greece. When the father died, Hesiod and a younger brother, Perses, divided the farm between them; but the brothers quarreled, and Perses carried the case to the rulers, whom he bribed to decide it in his favor. Although this maneuver gained Perses the larger share of his father's property, he was an idler by nature, and his refusal to work soon reduced him to want. But Hesiod lived the hard, frugal life depicted in his poem the *Works and Days*.

The *Works and Days* is a didactic poem, and the lesson it teaches is that man must work. When the first man was created, the *Titan Prometheus stole fire from heaven and brought it to him hidden in a hollow reed. Man took the fire, although *Zeus had decreed that he should not have it; and to punish him Zeus ordered the first woman, *Pandora, to be made. He sent her to earth and with her a jar containing, as he said, her dowry; but, when she opened it, she found that Zeus had placed inside it all the evils that afflict mankind. These evils spread throughout the world, and with them came the necessity of work. Work is, therefore, the will of Zeus for man and it cannot be avoided. In fact, the need of work is greater now than in the past, for man has entered the Iron Age, the most evil period of his history, and the earth is filled with violence.

As work for most men in early Greece meant labor on the land, Hesiod first sketches the tasks that occupied an ancient peasant through the year. He does not give a complete record of the operation of a farm, and he is not interested primarily in technical details. His purpose is to inculcate diligence, and he attempts to do this by describing how an industrious man performs his work, and how his prosperity contrasts with the poverty and ultimate ruin of the idle. Hesiod had a true love of nature, and he adorns this part of the *Works and Days* with descriptions of the countryside at each season of the year. His picture of midwinter in an isolated mountain home is unforgettable.

To his account of a farmer's year Hesiod appends a brief passage on navigation for those who seek a livelihood at sea. Then he turns to the need for prudence in dealing with others and gives rules for wise conduct taken from the traditional lore of the Boeotian countryman. Finally, so that a man may know at what times the gods will bless his labor, he adds a calendar of lucky and unlucky days.

The *Works and Days* is written in the Homeric verse form, and it owes much to Homer in style and diction. But its atmosphere is altogether different. Hesiod has nothing to tell of the glorious deeds of godlike kings. His theme is the hard life of the peasants, a life made harder still by the injustice of a decadent aristocracy. For the latter Hesiod has the warning: "Make your judgments straight!" for Zeus has thrice ten thousand spirits watching the works of men, and wrongdoing will surely bring retribution from him.

As the aristocrat must be just, so the peasant must be upright in all his dealings. "Do not make base gain," the poet tells him; "base gain is as bad as ruin." Earn your living with honest work. "Work is no disgrace," and it makes for righteousness. The road to Wickedness is smooth, and she lives very near us. But between us and

Goodness the gods have placed the sweat of our brows. The path that leads to her is long and steep, and it is rough at first; but when a man has reached the height, the way is easy.

In addition to the *Works and Days*, two other poems, the *Theogony* or *Genealogy of the Gods*, and the *Shield of Heracles*, are attributed to Hesiod. The *Shield of Heracles* is an inferior production, probably an academic exercise. The *Theogony*, though of immense importance in the study of Greek religion, has less interest for the general reader than the *Works and Days*. It tells how Earth first rose out of Chaos; how the Titans, who were her breed, were overthrown by Zeus; and how each god and goddess came into being.

Little is known of Hesiod's life after his quarrel with Perses, though the legends woven around him tell how he competed in song with Homer and defeated him, and how he left his home and met a violent death abroad. His *Works and Days* was much admired by the later Greeks and the Romans, and it inspired the *Georgics*, *Vergil's poem on agriculture.

Hesse, Hermann: German novelist, critic, poet (1877–1962). The son and grandson of missionaries to India, Hesse remained a quasi-religious romantic despite self-doubts (an attempted suicide) and self-exile (to Switzerland after 1912). An early critical work (*Blick ins Chaos*—"In Sight of Chaos," 1920), envisaging half of Europe on the way to chaos, was cited by T. S. *Eliot in his notes to *The *Waste Land* and thereby assured Hesse's work the attention of the post-World War I generation. Other themes anticipated the generalizations and hopes ("artistic integrity," "relevance," "total reality") of the post-World War II generation, which feels a kinship with Hesse's attitudes: a solopsistic, involuted concern with self-identity and self-fulfillment (*Demian*, 1919), commingled with pantheistic Eastern mysticism (*Siddharta*, 1922); the credo that sincerity is the measure of artistic integrity (hence the style of a confessional); an interest in sexual ambiguity, in the depth psychology of *Jung, in the artist's banishment by a Philistine society and his split-personality—an intoxication with jazz versus love of Wagnerian music, individual consciousness versus community standards, intelligence versus intellectualism in semireligious contexts, despair versus ecstasy—dualisms which cannot be resolved through logic. Yet Hesse retains a romantic faith that reconciliation is possible in some way (the "magic theater" of fantasy? of psychoanalysis? of hashish-induced hallucination? of stoic meditation?—*Steppenwolf*, 1927; faith in a continuing pilgrimage?—*Journey to the East*, 1932). Similar dualisms receive half-aesthetic, half-religious solution in the "glass bead game," *Das Glasperlenspiel* (1943), translated title *Magister Ludi*, a sort of Utopian novel set in the future where mathematics, art, music, philosophy, etc., will be reconciled. This novel was specifically commended in the award to Hesse of the Nobel prize in 1946.

Hippolytus: the son of *Theseus, king of Athens, by the *Amazon queen Hippolyte. His beauty and innocence inflamed the passion of Phaedra, Theseus' wife, who pressed herself upon him. But he resisted her advances, and she committed suicide after accusing him to Theseus, who called on *Poseidon to punish him. The god in answer sent a sea-monster, which frightened Hippolytus' horses as he drove along the shore, and he was thrown from his chariot and dragged to death. He is the subject of tragedies by *Euripides, *Seneca, *Racine (see *Phaedra*), and *D'Annunzio.

Hobbes, Thomas: English philosopher (1588–1679). Hobbes's great work, *Leviathan, or the Matter, Form, and Power of a Commonwealth, Ecclesiastical and Civil* (1651), exerted a strong influence on political theory and psychology. He believed that the Commonwealth, which he called Leviathan, was created as the result of a "social contract." He assumed that originally men were naturally equal and lived in a state "solitary, poor, nasty, brutish, and short"—one of continuous anarchic war. For self-preservation they agreed, accordingly, to give up their "freedom" and submit to the authority of the state. The power so granted may be despotic; but, the covenant having been made, the people have no right to rebel. By this line of argument Hobbes defended absolutism in government. He was also concerned with how men acquire knowledge, and thus he became a forerunner of modern rationalism and associative psychology. He argued that man has no innate ideas, that "reasoning from authority of books . . . is not knowledge but faith." All men's knowledge he derived ultimately from sensations produced when external bodies press against organs and, by mechanical processes, bring sensation to the brain.

Hoffmann, Ernst Theodor Amadeus: German novelist and writer of tales (1776–1822). Hoffmann supported himself as a musician and lawyer and devoted his spare time to his writing. He was a striking mixture of apparently contradictory qualities—a very minor composer who was among the first to recognize and defend the greatness of Beethoven, an official in a high court of appeals who wrote volumes of meticulous legal records and volumes of fantastic tales. But his fantasy was not the superficial horrors and stage-properties of the *Gothic novel. It was a probing of the nightside of human consciousness, of the fantastic elements of ordinary reality rather than an imaginary world substituted for reality. It is for this reason that Hoffmann, who seems almost the acme of romanticism (see *classicism), was admired and imitated by men who scorned most of the romantics. Among these are *Balzac (who described him as the artist of all "that seems not to exist, and yet is alive"), *Baudelaire (who characterized one of his tales as a "catechism of advanced esthetics"), *Pushkin, and *Dostoevski.

Hoffmann's works include *The Devil's Elixirs* (*Die Elixiere des Teufels*, 1815), *Night-Pieces in Callot's Manner* (*Nachtstücke in Callots Manier*, 1817), and *Kater Murr* (1820–22). This last, to give it its full title, is *Tomcat Murr's Opinions on Life, Together with a Fragmentary Biography of Kapellmeister Johann Kreisler*, and is a remarkable performance. The musician's cat is supposed to have decided that, like his master, he will write an autobiography, and he has used the backs of his owner's scattered pages. When the manuscript went to the printer, he set up each page, front and back, in order—so that the reader has a straight life alternating with a jumbled one. Hoffmann is in earnest about his musician, who is a serious though strange creature and a mouthpiece for the author, but many passages in the tomcat's life provide a parody or ironical comment on the life of the artist. Both musician and cat are kept entirely in character.

Hoffmann also wrote a number of excellent shorter narratives. Three of these are combined to form the basis of Offenbach's opera *The Tales of Hoffmann.*

Hölderlin, (Johann Christian) Friedrich: German poet (1770–1843). Hölderlin spent most of his active life in distasteful work as a private tutor and had to give up the most congenial of his tutorial appointments because of a reciprocated passion for his employer's wife. After spending some time in Switzerland and Southern France, he returned home insane in 1802. He showed some improvement—enough to enable him to become a librarian in 1804—but in 1806 his insanity returned hopelessly and his remaining 37 years were pointless for him and the world.

Hölderlin is the most purely Hellenic of the German poets. Although he contributes an element of enthusiasm which is definitely of his own place and time, he is at his best when in contact with Greece. Thus his best prose work is *Hyperion* (*Hyperion, oder der Eremit in Griechenland*, 1797–99), a loose, philosophical novel about a young Greek involved in his country's struggle against Turkey in 1770. Other poets are likely to be imitative in classical meters, but Hölderlin is weakest in the traditional German poetic forms. His best poetry is written in the ancient meters (*To the Fates, An Die Parzen*) or in free verse on Greek themes (*Hyperion's Song of Fate, Hyperion's Schicksalslied*). Hölderlin's reputation grew slowly. He himself published only *Hyperion* and translations of two plays of *Sophocles; his friends published the rest of his work while he was insane. His lyrical pre-eminence was soon recognized in the German-speaking countries, and during the last half century he has come to be recognized as one of the world's great lyric poets.

Holy Grail (Sangreal): in medieval legend, the platter or cup used by Jesus at the Last Supper. Joseph of Arimathea took it to the Crucifixion and caught some of Christ's blood in it. During years of imprisonment, Joseph kept it and it mysteriously supplied him with food. Then he took it to Britain. Because no guardian was worthy of it, it disappeared. This tale, with its Christian mysticism, was linked to Arthurian romance, and the quest of the lost Grail was a dominating inspiration to the knights of the Round Table.

Three theories have been advanced for the origin of the story. The first, the "Christian," regards the Grail as a deliberately created symbol of the Eucharist. The second, the "ritual theory," relates the story of the recovery of the Grail (in which appear a wounded king, a waste land, and a bleeding spear) to sexual symbolism and pagan fertility cults. (Here T. S. *Eliot found much of his imagery for *The *Waste Land*.) The third theory, and the one now generally accepted, sees the seed of the Grail stories in Celtic myths of the gods Lug and Bron. That the underlying traditions were confused and confusing for the medieval narrators is apparent. In different versions the object itself may be a platter, or cup, or stone; the original guardian may be one of a number of non-Arthurian figures—Bron, or Pelles, or Amfortas, or Joseph; the hero who sees the Grail or ultimately achieves its guardianship is variously Bors, Gawain, Galahad, Perceval, all quite different in character.

The medieval Grail stories became the most widespread of the Arthurian legends, appearing in a dozen European languages. The famous versions were the French of *Chrétien de Troyes, *Perceval* or the *Conte de Graal* (c. 1180), the earliest one extant; the German of *Wolfram von Eschenbach, *Parzival* (c. 1205), the source of Wagner's opera *Parsifal*; another French version of unknown authorship, *La Queste del saint graal* (c. 1210), which was used by *Malory for *Le Morte Darthur* (c. 1470). In these versions of the story, Parsifal comes to symbolize the eternal struggle of good and evil, the purification of man and his acquisition of wisdom through suffering, the bitter psychological struggle of man for peace of mind and soul. In modern times the story is best known through Wolfram, who gave the fullest development to its symbolical aspects; through Malory; through *Tennyson, whose *Idylls of the King* is based on Malory; and through Wagner.

Homer: see *Iliad* and *Odyssey*.

Hopkins, Gerard Manley: English poet (1844–89). When Hopkins entered the Jesuit Order (1868) he burned most of his poetry. Only the small body of verse that he saved at this time, plus some poems sent later to his friend Robert Bridges, survive. None of it was published during the poet's lifetime, and his reputation developed only after the 1940's.

Hopkins was concerned with the unique, the "original, spare, strange" in persons, emotions, or nature *(Pied Beauty)*. This individualizing quality he called "inscape"; and the individual response which the "inscape" aroused in him he called "instress." His originality lies in the perception and sensuousness achieved by startling imagery, prosody, and diction: "I caught this morning morning's minion, king-/ dom of daylight's dauphin, dapple-dawn-drawn Falcon" *(The Windhover)*.

Much influenced by the metaphysical poets in analyzing his own mystic experiences, Hopkins recognized the tensions between the Jesuit and the individualist poet within himself. His best poems show an agonizing sense of frustration and suffering (*Maidens' Song* from *St. Winifred's Well*; *Sonnets: Thou Art Indeed Just, Lord*; *No Worst, Three Is None*). Although his use of *assonance and rime is reminiscent of *Swinburne and the *Pre-Raphaelites, the rhythms are new and experimental. They are based on accent only, with the foot varying from one to four syllables. Hopkins believed that this intricate pattern with alliteration and internal rime was that of common speech; he called it "sprung rhythm," the "falling paeonic rhythm, sprung and outriding." His object was, he said, to combine "markedness of rhythm—that is rhythm's self—and naturalness of expression." Elliptical syntax, word coinages, the use of an almost entirely Germanic vocabulary, terse phrasing, compound metaphors make the poetry difficult to understand, yet it gives a feeling both lyrical and dramatic, a sense of power, density, and compression. The profound self-analysis, the new feeling toward rhythm, diction, and syntax, the multiple meanings and ambiguities of reference have greatly influenced modern poets, notably *Eliot and *Auden.

Horace: Roman poet (65–8 B.C.). The life of Quintus Horatius Flaccus can be understood only in terms of the education his father gave him, an education that enabled him, in spite of his lowly birth, to develop his talents and take his place among the foremost poets of the world. Horace's father, though once a slave, would not send his son to school in the small Italian hill town of Venusia where he was born; but first at Rome and later at Athens he gave him the best intellectual training the world could provide. Horace's moral instruction his father himself undertook, shielding him from temptation during his childhood and preparing him by precept and example to make his own decisions wisely later in life. Horace never forgot the debt he owed his father; and when he had become second only to *Vergil among the poets of the Augustan Age, he looked back with love and gratitude to the humble freedman whose self-sacrifice made possible all he had achieved.

Horace was a student at Athens when the assassination of Julius *Caesar plunged the world into civil war. His sympathies lay with the Republican side; he enrolled in the Republican armies, and he endured the rout at Philippi. His life was spared by the conquerors, but his property was confiscated; and at the end of the war he returned home in poverty and disillusionment. It was at this time, when he was working as a clerk in Rome, that Horace began to write. His poetry quickly attracted the notice of Vergil, who introduced him to Maecenas, Augustus' chief minister of state. Acquaintance ripened into a friendship which grew with the years. When Maecenas became Horace's patron, the poet's future was assured; when he gave him a small estate in the Sabine Hills, there was nothing more the poet desired. He devoted the remaining years of his life to the composition of poetry; and, when he died, he was buried in Rome near the tomb of Maecenas.

Horace's chief works are the *Satires*, the *Odes*, the *Epistles*, and the *Art of Poetry*. The 18 *Satires*, published early in the poet's career, take as their theme every type of human folly, especially the insatiable desire for wealth. Written in hexameter verse skilfully suggestive of common speech, and enlivened by anecdote, dialogue, and fable, the *Satires (Sermones)* present a truly remarkable variety. Amusing sketches, like the famous journey to Brundisium, alternate with moral pieces attacking luxury and self-indulgence or calling for plain living. Types or classes of people are criticized rather than individuals; and these range from the miser who buries his head in a hole in the ground to the Stoic philosopher to whom "all the vices are equal." There is much autobiography. We see the poet as a boy on his way to school and as a young man face to face with Maecenas. We find him in the peaceful twilight of his Sabine farm listening as his neighbor Cervius tells the old wives' tale of the *Town and Country Mouse*. And we meet him one morning, as he walks on the Sacred Way, in the grip of a social climber who demands an introduction to Maecenas. This satire (I, 9) has long been a favorite, not only for the humor inherent in the situation, but also for the dramatic form in which the piece is cast and the grace and lightness of the writing. As a model for his *Satires*, Horace used the work of the old Roman poet Lucilius, although, unlike Lucilius, he wrote with sympathy and understanding for human frailty; and he avoided the personal abuse characteristic of the early poet.

Although Horace accomplished much in the field of satire, he considered the 103 *Odes* his lasting monument. In writing them he took as his models the Greek lyric poets, especially *Alcaeus and *Sappho, and he succeeded in adapting the beautiful and intricate Greek meters in which they wrote to Roman use. The *Odes* became a classic from the date of their publication, assuring Horace the place he coveted among the lyric poets of the world.

Horace had a philosophic mind, and his *Odes* contain

much comment on wise conduct. The central thought is the brevity and uncertainty of life. Death is never far away, and death ends all. The passing day alone is yours. Be wise; enjoy it. It can bring you many pleasures, but you must seize them now or they will be lost to you forever. And be content with what you have, not heaping up riches you will never use. Peace of mind cannot be bought with gems, with purple, or with gold. Setting limits to your ambition and observing moderation in all things, hold fast to the Golden Mean. In time of stress show yourself brave and resolute; yet wisely trim your sails swollen by too prosperous a gale. In his philosophy Horace is hedonistic; he teaches the wise enjoyment of the pleasures of life. But he does not look to great possessions for satisfaction, and he tempers all he says with a stern morality. Our pleasures must be harmless, and in pursuing them we must avoid excess. At times Horace is more Stoic than Epicurean.

Love songs, and songs in praise of wine and of the gods, are prominent among the *Odes*. Though the love poems show neither depth of passion nor any true affection, their polished grace places them among the most beautiful of the pieces. The favorite is probably the *Reconciliation* (III, 9), in which two faithless lovers quarrel, only to find that the quarrel itself brings back their old affection to them. But many other poems are equally good: to Chloe, who flees like a fawn before the poet, or to Pyrrha combing her golden hair for some young man soon to be shipwrecked on the sea of love.

The unreality so characteristic of the love poetry of Horace is entirely absent when he speaks of his friends. Then his feeling is deep and true, as when he mourns for Quintilius or prays that the ship carrying Vergil may come safe to Greece. His patriotic odes are also strong and good, when, as the poet of the Roman lyre, he shouts his joy at the fall of Cleopatra or calls for a restoration of the virtues that made Rome great in the days of Regulus. Horace has a keen eye for the beauty of the Italian countryside, whether in winter when Mount Soracte stands white with the deep snow or when the fierce heat of summer fails to touch the crystal fountain of Bandusia.

As a lyric poet Horace is not famed for his originality; he writes of the common thoughts and feelings of mankind. But he expresses these thoughts with such economy and beauty they seem to assume their final form in his verse. It is his talent to clothe the familiar in perfection, and for this he has been remembered through the centuries.

Horace's *Odes* were largely the work of his middle period. In his later life he returned to the hexameter to write the 22 *Epistles* or *Letters in Verse* and the *Art of Poetry (Ars poetica)*. A few of the *Epistles* are letters such as one friend might write to another, but the majority are essays in which the poet discusses life, literature, and philosophy. These latter *Epistles* differ little from the *Satires* except in their greater polish, urbanity, and mellowness of tone. The *Art of Poetry*, also written in the form of an epistle, is probably the latest of Horace's works. It is not a systematic discussion of the principles of poetic composition but a collection of random observations on poetry and the training of the poet addressed to a young friend who desired to write. The drama is given greater attention than any other form, but the qualities of good writing, whatever the type, are noted, and the beginner is advised to choose a subject within his powers, to study the best models, to seek competent criticism, and to delay publication while he revises his work with care. He must not strive for perfection, however; it cannot be attained, and small faults in a good piece will be tolerated.

The minor works of Horace are the *Epodes* or *Refrains*, a group of 17 early poems in iambic meter and varying mood, and the *Carmen Saeculare*, written to celebrate Augustus' revival of the Secular Games, in 17 B.C.

Housman, A(lfred) E(dward): English poet (1856–1936). Housman was born in Worcestershire, where the Shropshire hills are the western horizon. At St. John's College, Oxford, he gained a First in Moderations (the intermediate examination) in the classics, but failed to obtain final honors. Keenly feeling the disgrace, he withdrew into himself. For ten years he was a clerk in the British Patents Office but pursued diligently his studies and published several papers in the classical journals. Because of the excellence of his textual criticism he was appointed in 1892 to the chair of Latin at University College of London University. The rest of his life was devoted to classical scholarship (he moved to Cambridge University in 1911), with studies on Propertius and editions of *Juvenal (1905), *Lucan (1930), and Manilius (1903–30)—a negligible Latin poet whose long poem on astrology absorbed many of the best years of Housman's life. He also wrote nearly a hundred technical articles, translated odes from *Aeschylus, *Sophocles, and *Euripides, parodied the efforts of incompetent translators, and was merciless toward anything less than perfection in scholarship. Though one noted classicist of his acquaintance did not connect the poet Housman with the Latinist, Housman had achieved poetic fame early in his career. A rhymer from childhood, he had turned seriously to the writing of poetry in 1890. In 1896 he published *A Shropshire Lad* at his own expense. Critical recognition was favorable, but after two years the first edition of 500 copies was not sold out; Housman's younger brother bought the last six and realized a tidy profit on them, selling one in America for £80. In 1922 an even slenderer *Last Poems* was published. In a preface, Housman spoke his valedictory as a poet: "It is not likely that I shall ever be impelled to write much more"; and characteristically defended the printing of his book "while I am here to . . . control its spelling and punctuation." During his last years he was a famous man who made a habit of refusing the public honors which were offered him. At his death he left his brother Laurence with the responsibility for deciding which of his manuscript poems measured up to the high standards he had always set for himself, and publishing only these. Laurence published *More Poems* in 1936, and some additional ones in his *Memoir* in 1938. In 1940 *The Collected Poems* appeared.

Housman is one of the best-loved poets of the 20th century, although now, as he himself has said, his "hue is not the wear." His constancy to the themes of the brevity of life, the transience of love and beauty seemed

347

to derive from classical lyricists. But Housman denied these as conscious sources, and named *Shakespeare's songs, the Scottish Border *ballads, and *Heine as chief influences upon him. Though recalling the lyric loveliness of the first, the starkness of the second, and the deftness and insight of the third, whose *Armesünderblum'* is freely adapted in Housman's *Flower of Sinner's Rue*, Housman's manner and much of his matter were unmistakably his own. A traditional but an original poet, Housman was much imitated and parodied (the latter to his own delight). His Shropshire lads are shown ploughing, playing soccer, going to Ludlow Fair for wrestling and drinking bouts, pleading for love with timorous or false-hearted girls, or setting off to war for the Empire: "Get you the sons your fathers got/And God will save the queen."

Vivid glimpses—"the cherry hung with snow"; "the russet floors [where] by waters idle/the pine lets fall its cone"; "the smooth green miles of turf"—all show a beautiful Shropshire countryside, but the lightfoot lads and rose-lipped girls are haunted by disillusion and death. Often the melancholy deepens into pessimism, and nature becomes heartless and witless, and man's life "a long fool's errand to the grave." Sometimes the luckless lads quip wryly at the injustice; sometimes they curse "whatever brute and blackguard made the world." Age-old stoicism is expressed in Shropshire speech: " 'Tis true there's better boose than brine,/But he that drowns must drink it." Housman makes concurrent use of classical reference.

To men confronted with disaster Housman calls up Thermopylae, where, threatened with overwhelming defeat, "the Spartans on the sea-wet rock sat down and combed their hair." He shuttles easily between the colloquial and the allusive: "Malt does more than Milton can/ To justify God's ways to man."

Using the ballad stanza and even the ballad dialogue frequently, Housman is deceptively simple. Although he believed that the production of poetry is less active than passive, Housman was a conscious artist. Some of his poems were perfected years after the first drafts; of one stanza, written thirteen times, he says: "It was more than a twelvemonth before I got it right." *Assonance, alliteration, and other repetitive devices, sometimes obvious, sometimes unobtrusive, are common; accents are shifted to vary the usual monotony of the ballad stanza, resulting in a distinctive music. His diction deserves what he wrote in praise of another's poem: "It is made out of the most ordinary words, yet it is pure from the least alloy of prose." He knew the art of concealing art; he is sparse of ornamentation, believing that simile and metaphor are unessential to poetry. His output was scanty, his range limited, but within his bounds he created some of the finest lyrics in English.

Howells, William Dean: American novelist and critic (1837–1920). As editor of the *Atlantic Monthly* (1866–81), and in various critical writings, Howells exercised considerable influence over American readers. Although he overpraised such poets as Whittier, *Longfellow, and Lowell, he was a friend of the new realistic movements in literature and did a good deal to persuade his audience to read such writers as *Tolstoi, *Ibsen, and *Zola. He was himself a mildly realistic novelist, and his 40 novels and novelettes, while falling considerably below their European models, had considerable vogue in their own day. Perhaps the most interesting of them are *A Modern Instance* (1882), a study of the progress of a relationship from love through marriage to divorce; *The Rise of Silas Lapham* (1885), dealing with the attempt of a newly rich family to "crash" Boston society; and *A Hazard of New Fortunes* (1889), which treats of social problems in New York City and develops Tolstoi's idea that every man is ultimately answerable for the welfare or misery of every other.

hubris: *hybris.

Hugo, Victor: French poet, dramatist, and novelist (1802–85). The son of a Napoleonic general, Hugo gradually shifted his admiration from Bonaparte and King

Louis Philippe to democracy; for violent opposition to Napoleon III he was exiled (1851). When he finally returned to Paris in 1870, he was welcomed as a hero and prophet. In this atmosphere of adulation he spent his final years. His inordinate vanity (he thought that Paris should be renamed "Hugo" in his honor) was not entirely unjustified, for among his 50 volumes are many masterpieces.

The *Preface* to his play *Cromwell* (1827) became the manifesto of the drama of the French *Romantic Movement and established Hugo as the chief literary figure of the day. He demanded liberty in subject and versification, opposed neo-classic rules, and argued that the only essential *unity is unity of action. Defending the juxtaposition of the beautiful and ugly, he praised *Shakespeare for his combination of tragic and comic scenes. These theories Hugo put into practice in his play *Hernani* (1830). A wide variety of moods and striking scenes is developed in dialogue which mingles everyday realistic diction with elaborate figures of speech. Although *Hernani* is melodramatic and its characters unreal, the lyric outbursts are moving. Another of Hugo's plays, *The King Amuses Himself* (*Le Roi s'amuse*, 1832), is now well known because it was used as the plot of Verdi's opera *Rigoletto*.

Like the plays, Hugo's novels combine fantastic characters and sentimental exaggeration with some scenes of great emotional power. *Notre Dame de Paris* (1831) is a picturesque evocation of the swarming life of the 15th century in which Quasimodo, the hunchbacked bell-ringer, serves as a "human gargoyle." Equally sensational and melodramatic is *Les Misérables* (1862), a chaos of genres and subjects ranging from battles to the sewers of Paris. The novel is clearly a vehicle for Hugo's social ideas: men are essentially equal; the poor are crushed by the prejudices of organized society; and human misery, exemplified in the convict Jean Valjean, is its own expiation. Though the story is highly improbable and the characterization is superficial, there emerge nevertheless basic human feelings—parental love, revenge, gratitude, and compassion.

Although Hugo was widely popular as a novelist and dramatist, his lasting reputation depends on his verse. As a lyric poet he has a remarkable suppleness of rhythms and sonorities, a tremendous range of language, and striking images—characteristics of style which grew in his work until they ran to lushness. As in the novels, the romantic excesses are obvious, but Hugo's technical virtuosity and exuberance of language remained as a model and inspiration to such later French writers as *Mallarmé and *Zola, who despised his sentimental exaggeration. His collected lyrics appeared in *Songs of the Orient* (*Les Orientales*, 1829); *Autumn Leaves* (*Les Feuilles d'automne*, 1831); *Songs of Twilight* (*Chants du crépuscule*, 1835); *Inner Voices* (*Les Voix intérieures*, 1837); *Sunbeams and Shadows* (*Les Rayons et les ombres*, 1840). These volumes show increasingly Hugo's humanitarian sentimentalism and his tendency to moralize nature.

The biting satires against Napoleon III in *The Chastisements* (*Les Châtiments*, 1853) are regarded as among his greatest poems. Equally praised is his huge historical epic, *The Legend of the Ages* (*La Légende des siècles*, 1859–83). Indeed, his variety and technique were unrivaled in his time and account for his influence not only in France but on the English poets, particularly *Tennyson and *Swinburne.

humanism: an intellectual movement which characterized the *Renaissance, and the attitude of mind characteristic of this movement. Humanism represented an open break with a good many of the standard ideas of the *Middle Ages. It emphasized the dignity of man and his perfectibility. It considered this world a legitimate object of interest and love, and it tended to place reason above revelation. It stressed education (for women as well as men) and held that the goal of education is a well-balanced individual with all his capabilities fully developed. The languages, literature, and thought of ancient Greece and Rome occupied a central position in the thinking of the humanists, not because of any merely antiquarian interest or intellectual snobbery, but because the best products of these civilizations exemplified the ideals of humanism far better than did medieval literature, philosophy, or theology. They thought of *humanitas*, as used by *Cicero, to explain the goals of an intellectual and moral culture particularly befitting man. The humanists not only rediscovered classical texts and revived ancient literary types (see *pastoral), themes, and critical theories. They applied their scholarship to the establishment of accurate Biblical texts, and, especially in northern Europe, sought to reform the Church. In education they stood for physical training as well as mental, and for teaching by reason and gentleness rather than authority and brutality.

Humanism began to develop in Italy in the 14th century and spread all over Europe in the 15th and 16th. Among the most famous humanists were the Italians *Petrarch, *Boccaccio, Lorenzo Valla, Marsilio Ficino, *Pico della Mirandola, Giovanni Poggio, and Angelo Poliziano; the Germans Johann Reuchlin and Philip *Melanchthon; the Dutch *Erasmus; the French Guillaume Budé; and the English Thomas Linacre, John Colet, and Sir Thomas More (see *Utopia).

humors: see *comedy of humors.

hybris: a word borrowed from Greek, meaning "excessive pride, insolence." The Greeks accepted the maxim that "pride goeth before a fall" and considered that *hybris* demanded and would inevitably receive retribution. Thus the term is frequently encountered in discussions of Greek literature, especially tragedy. After Odysseus had killed his wife's suitors in the *Odyssey* (see *Iliad* and *Odyssey*), his old nurse was about to shout for joy; but he quickly stopped her with the warning, "It is an unholy thing to boast over slain men," for he knew the dangers of *hybris.* In *Aeschylus' *Agamemnon* (see *Oresteia*), Clytemnestra, intending to murder Agamemnon as soon as he enters his house on his return from Troy, meets his chariot and insists that he must wait for purple carpets to be spread before he dismounts, since it is unbefitting for a great conqueror like him to set his feet on the ground. This is more than an attempt to flatter him. It is a definite trap, for she knows that if he commits such an act of *hybris* he will be doomed—and that consequently her plan to murder him will succeed. Agamemnon shows that he is aware of the danger of this act of *hybris* even as he commits it.

Hypochondriac, The: see *Imaginary Invalid.*

Ibsen, Henrik: Norwegian dramatist (1828–1906). When Ibsen appeared on the literary scene, drama was almost nonexistent in Norway. In his hands a Norwegian drama developed which brought its founder international fame. He became one of Europe's most influential figures both as dramatist and as intellectual leader.

Born in Skien, a small town in southern Norway, Ibsen spent his entire youth shut off from the world. At 16 he became a pharmacist's apprentice in the tiny town of Grimstad, where he remained for six years. In his childhood and youth he displayed traits which appear in many of his chief dramatic characters. He was stubborn, self-assertive, unsociable, and rebellious, always attacking and resisting the narrow-mindedness of the times. Although Ibsen is no longer considered chiefly a social moralist as he was by his contemporaries, it was a moral and social rebellion against the stagnation of his contemporary world that first stimulated him to write. The European revolutions of 1848 strengthened and confirmed Ibsen's own efforts. A temporary interest in politics is reflected in the historical drama *Catiline* (1850), the theme of which is characteristic of many of his later works: a rebel's fight is glorified only so long as he remains true to himself and to his mission.

Catiline grew out of Ibsen's intention of studying medicine, for in preparation for admission to the university he had to study *Cicero's orations against Catiline and, like many another young student, found himself preferring the rebel to the politician. At the university he soon lost interest in medicine and attended lectures on philosophy and literature. Soon he embarked on a career in the theater. His 11 years as stage manager (Bergen, 1851–57) and theater director (Christiana—now Oslo—1857–62) provided him with a thorough knowledge of all aspects of the stage and helped him to achieve his mastery of stage technique.

Disappointed with the backwardness of his native country, whose atmosphere he felt was not conducive to free creative work, Ibsen left Norway and went to Rome in 1864. However, his first drama written in exile deeply roused all Scandinavians, for *Brand* (1866), like the succeeding drama, *Peer Gynt* (1867), was thoroughly Norwegian in character and spirit. In the figure of Brand, Ibsen created a preacher whose tragedy lies in his uncompromising devotion to an ideal that makes him blind to love and duty. Fanatically carrying out his mission as shepherd of his flock, Brand loses his family and eventually alienates his congregation. His religious fanaticism and stubbornness ensnare him and cause his downfall.

Peer Gynt, lighter and gayer in tone than *Brand*, may be considered its counterpart in character portrayal, atmosphere, and symbolism. Peer's spinelessness and weakness of character are the antithesis of Brand's determination and absolute surrender to an ideal cause. Childhood associations and the rich folklore of Scandinavia form the colorful background of *Peer Gynt*. Because of its wealth of imagery and poetry and the depth of its thought, it has become to the Scandinavians—as *Faust* has to the Germans and *Don Quixote* to the Spanish—the embodiment of their life and character, the quest for self-fulfillment and the search for a higher self.

Today Ibsen is best known for his realistic prose dramas. In order to carry conviction in his probing of social problems, he began to depict human beings, to present their inner conflicts as well as external actions, and to record their speech realistically and faithfully. Abandoning the verse form he had used in *Brand* and *Peer Gynt*, Ibsen set out to fulfill his new task with *Pillars of Society* (1877), a play which draws aside the community leaders' veil of smug hypocrisy and reveals their basic rottenness,

354

finally concluding that the real pillars of society are not self-righteous prominent men but freedom and truth. This play may be said to set the theme for much of Ibsen's later work, for again and again he returns to the idea that our society is essentially false, that it lives by a set of traditional lies and carefully hushes up everything that might reveal their falsity. It is a society which has no real principle except that appearances must be saved at any cost.

A *Doll's House (1879), in which a woman asserts her independence by finally leaving her husband, stirred up such controversy that Ibsen felt called upon to suggest an alternative ending. In *Ghosts (1881), his next drama, Ibsen presented the case of a woman who mistakenly remained with her husband—and the unfortunate consequences of her decision. This time the play caused an uproar all over Europe because of its frank treatment of venereal disease. In Norway the criticism was so severe that both liberal and conservative parties turned against Ibsen. As an answer to his critics, he wrote An *Enemy of the People (1882) in which his main attack was directed against the unthinking "compact majority."

After The *Wild Duck (1884), Ibsen returned to the theme of the individualism of women in Rosmersholm (1886) and *Hedda Gabler (1890). Both Hedda and Rebecca West are examples of women whose conflicts arise from the inconsistency of their natures with their desires.

There is hardly a play by Ibsen that does not contain some symbolic elements. The emphasis on symbolism that is evident in his early verse plays may be seen again in his later dramas—for example, the use of the wild duck, of the white horse in Rosmersholm, of the sea in The Lady from the Sea (1888). In his last plays an excessive use of symbolism and of modified autobiographical material often impedes the development of the dramatic action. In The *Master Builder (1892) and When We Dead Awaken (1899) Ibsen is apparently so much concerned with himself, his relation to his art, and his place as an artist in society that he fails to be as convincing a craftsman as he is in his social dramas.

Ibsen made his contributions to the theater by developing new techniques, while discarding old ones, and by daring to put on the stage themes and problems that had never been presented before—contributions now mostly superseded by further advances in the theater. His lasting contribution to literature, however, lies in the fact that even when he seems most concerned with the transitory complexities and pressures of "modern" life, he is dealing convincingly with eternal and universal themes—the conflict between the individual and society, between reality and illusion, between true and false idealism.

idyl(l): a descriptive *pastoral poem presenting a rural setting or incident of singing shepherds as rustic lovers in such a way as to appeal to a sophisticated, nonrural audience. The meaning of the original Greek word, "a little picture," emphasizes both the restricted scope and the pictorial quality of the type. The *Idyls* of *Theocritus established the tradition. *Vergil adopted the traditions in his *Eclogues* and *Georgics*. In recent centuries the term has been extended to include almost any work, from Izaak Walton's *The Compleat Angler* to Whittier's *Maud Muller*, which conveys an atmosphere of rural simplicity and peace. *Tennyson's use of the word for his *Idylls of the King* is not a typical one and definitely strains the meaning of the term.

Iliad and *Odyssey:* two Greek epics traditionally attributed to a poet named Homer and conjecturally dated *c.* 850 B.C. The poems are based on the legend of the Trojan War (see *Troy Tale) and are the oldest extant works of European literature.

The word *Iliad* means the *Tale of Ilios*, that is, the *Tale of Troy*. But Homer makes no attempt to tell the whole story of Troy in the poem. His theme is the *Wrath of Achilles*, a single event in the tenth year of the siege. In presenting this theme, Homer takes the details of the war and the life histories of the heroes for granted and plunges without explanation into the midst of the most critical episode of the campaign, the insult given by Agamemnon to Achilles and the quarrel which arose because of it. But this is also the most critical episode in the career of the hero Achilles. Years before, he had been offered his choice of two lives: either he could remain in Greece and live to old age without glory, or he could go to Troy, win renown on the field of battle, and die young. Achilles went to the war, and his knowledge of his approaching death makes Agamemnon's insult unendurable. When Agamemnon takes away his prize of war, the captured girl Briseis, he takes away the glory for which Achilles has sacrificed the ease and length of life he might have had. The day the quarrel arises is therefore crucial for Achilles, because it brings him the deepest humiliation of his career. And it is crucial in the story of the war because, when Achilles' anger leads him to withdraw to his hut, the Greeks lose the ablest of their champions.

When Achilles refuses to fight, the weight of the campaign falls on the other chieftains, and Homer extends his theme by describing their deeds of valor in the interval between Achilles' defection and the attempt made by Patroclus, Achilles' friend, to save the ships (Books II–XV). Nor does he hesitate to include in the account matter that properly precedes the awakening of Achilles' wrath. In Book II, when the Greek army advances against Troy, he describes the forces involved in the "Catalogue of Ships," though such a muster roll belongs to the part of the story detailiing the Greek preparations for the war. In Book III, he presents the duel between Paris and Menelaus, though this action would take place in the first year of the siege, if at all. But in a story which the audience already knew in detail, such displacement of incident from the natural time sequence would cause no embarrassment. Similarly, Homer indicates what will happen after Achilles' anger has reached its fulfillment in the death of Hector. In Book VI, when Hector says farewell to his wife Andromache, he foretells the fall of Troy and her own captivity; in Book XXII, when Hector is dying at the hands of Achilles, he relates the manner in which Achilles himself soon will meet his end. Where suspense is impossible because the audience already knows the story, there is no artistic loss in such foreshadowing.

The *Iliad*, then, is the story of the Wrath of Achilles

told against the background of the story of the siege of Troy. The two tales, advancing together, support and heighten one another; and the poem is richer in character and incident than it would be if Homer had developed his theme more narrowly. The two chief sources of interest throughout the poem are warfare and debate. The battle scenes show an astonishing knowledge of military matters on the part of the poet. The speeches, as in the assembly of warriors in Book I and the embassy to Achilles in Book IX, indicate his complete familiarity with the principles of rhetoric. And there are famous passages of other types, such as the picture of Helen among the aged men of Troy, the parting of Hector and Andromache, the making of Achilles' armor, and the ransoming of Hector's body by his father Priam.

The heroes whose words and deeds are related in the *Iliad* are ideal types whose characters were apparently established before Homer composed the poem. Achilles, the central figure, is a young man of great beauty and strength, supremely courageous and skilled in combat. As a warrior he far surpasses the other Greeks, while his mere presence, though he is unarmed, strikes terror into the Trojans. He is an excellent orator, and at the assembly he uses his skill in speech for the common good. His weakness lies in the violence of his emotions, though it should be observed that he is able to master them when the gods command him to do so. In the quarrel with Agamemnon his wrath is justified by the king's conduct. Nevertheless, when he is about to slay Agamemnon and *Athena bids him desist, he thrusts his great sword back into its sheath. But he nurses his resentment, and when Agamemnon offers him immense reparation he scornfully rejects it, though the Greeks are in extreme peril at the time. In spurning the king's attempt at reconciliation, he disregards the rights of the Greek army and destroys his position as its champion. Blinded by arrogance and the desire for vengeance, he refuses to do his duty in the crisis; instead, he sends Patroclus out clad in his armor and thus loses his friend. His grief at Patroclus' death takes him back into the battle but is so excessive that he answers Hector's dying request like a savage and abuses his corpse like a barbarian. In the end, it is true, he redeems himself, when, in obedience to *Zeus, he curbs his anger and welcomes Priam to his hut. But his self-control is strained to the breaking point. His emotions are so turbulent that he fears he may slay the old king and bring on himself the wrath of Zeus, as Agamemnon brought on himself the wrath of *Apollo. Achilles is a forerunner of the tragic heroes of Greek drama, a man preeminently noble but led by an excess of his own high nature to error and great unhappiness.

Odysseus, the hero of the *Odyssey*, is also an ideal type, though one much closer to the common man. He does not have the youth and beauty of Achilles, being now in middle age, a short, heavy man, awkward when he stands before an audience. Yet he has supreme skill in speech, and when words pour forth from his mouth like snowflakes, his listeners forget what he looks like. In conversation he is most adroit. Nothing could surpass the graciousness of his words to Nausicaa or the craft with which he deceives Polyphemus. An able, energetic man, he has courage sufficient to endure what the gods may send and wit enough to escape his manifold difficulties. Though the shrewdest of the heroes, he displays at times a lack of common prudence, as when he awaits the return of Polyphemus to his cave, or when he insults the Cyclops twice at the peril of his life after his escape. But this weakness only makes him more attractive. Odysseus does not defy the known will of the gods, as his sailors do when they slaughter the Cattle of the Sun. And he does not yield to merely sensuous temptation. Throughout his wanderings his home remains the center of his thought and affection. Though he stays eight years with Calypso, he does so unwillingly, "longing to see were it but the smoke rising from his native island." When he blesses Nausicaa, he reveals his own feeling for Penelope: "May the gods grant you all your heart's desire: a husband and a home and a mind at one with his may they give, a good gift. For there is nothing better and nobler than when man and wife are of one heart and mind in a house; a grief to their foes, and to their friends great joy, but their own hearts know it best."

Of the lesser heroes of the Homeric poems, none can

compare in interest with Hector, who is one of the noblest creations in literature. His skill in battle makes him feared by the Greeks and all but worshiped by the Trojans. His courage cannot be questioned even when he flees before Achilles. He is loyal to his people, affectionate to his family, courteous to Paris and Helen. He is beloved by the gods. But he carries a heavy burden of responsibility. He fights at home. He is on the defensive. And his mind is filled with care, as he foresees his own fate, Troy's desolation, and his family doomed to slavery or death.

The *Iliad* and the *Odyssey* are epics describing the exploits of the heroes Achilles and Odysseus. But no attempt is made in the poems to tell everything about these heroes. One specific action in their lives is taken as the theme or subject: in the *Iliad* the Wrath of Achilles and its results, in the *Odyssey* the homecoming of Odysseus after the fall of Troy. In each poem the action is serious, dignified, and of considerable magnitude. It has a definite beginning and an equally definite end; and the various events it portrays follow one another in orderly fashion, one leading naturally or inevitably to the next. A literary work composed in this way is said to have *organic unity*, that is, to be put together like a living organism, all of whose parts are necessary to it. But to say that a poem has organic unity does not mean that its structure is perfect. There are flaws in both Homeric poems, particularly in the *Iliad*.

The *Iliad* and the *Odyssey* are impersonal in tone and tell us nothing directly about the author. The only information we have concerning him is given us by writers who lived centuries after his time. They believed, almost unanimously, that both epics were the work of Homer, a poet who lived, they thought, in one of the cities of Ionia, most probably in Chios or Smyrna. They did not know when he lived. Some said as early as the 12th century B.C., others as late as the 7th. *Herodotus, the first Greek historian, places him in the 9th century, a not improbable date.

The fact that the Greeks knew almost nothing about Homer has led some modern scholars to question his existence altogether. These scholars maintain that Homer never really lived but was invented to explain the *Iliad* and the *Odyssey* after their origin had been forgotten, and that the epics are not the work of one poet, but of generations of poets, who gradually brought them into their present form by combining earlier poems, adding new material, and reworking the whole. But other scholars have not been convinced, and they have defended the traditional view. Both groups have tried to prove their position from the linguistic and literary characteristics of the epics and their references to social customs and cultural objects. But the problem, known as the "Homeric Question," has not been solved and perhaps can never be solved; the evidence is not conclusive, although it favors those who believe in the Homer of the Greeks.

The problem of the authorship of the *Iliad* and the *Odyssey* is complicated by the fact that, although we have no other literature from Greece as early as Homer, the epics clearly imply a long tradition of oral poetry. Their literary qualities admit of no other conclusion, nor does Homer's assumption that the story of the Trojan War was already known to his audience. The Greeks said that the siege of Troy took place in the 12th century B.C., a date supported by archaeology. If Homer lived in the 9th century 300 years passed between the war and the composition of the poems. During this time the history of Troy was turned into legend and expanded by the addition of myth and folklore.

As the earliest European epics, the *Iliad* and the *Odyssey* served as models for the imitative or literary epics written later, particularly the *Aeneid* of *Vergil. There are differences, however, between the two types, the most fundamental of which is that the literary epics were written to be read, while the poems of Homer were composed to be recited to an audience. They were put together, not in single words, but in word groups or phrases traditional to the oral poetry of early Greece. One interesting type of word group is made up of a noun, often a proper name, with a conventional or repeated epithet, e.g., "the loud-roaring sea," "the fleet-footed Achilles," "Agamemnon the king of men."

Though the *Iliad* and the *Odyssey* have the same general characteristics, there are a few significant differences between them. The material of the *Iliad* is warfare and debate, and the poem is highly dramatic throughout and tragic in its outcome. But the charm of the *Odyssey* arises from adventure and social life; it is less passionate than the *Iliad*, and it has a double issue, ending happily for Odysseus but tragically for the wooers. Because many of Odysseus' adventures are placed in lands unknown to the Homeric Greeks, magic becomes prominent in the story: Ino's veil supports Odysseus and the flesh of the Cattle of the Sun bellows on the spits. Since much attention is given to social life, the part played by women is far greater than in the *Iliad*. In Nausicaa Homer presents a picture of the freedom, security, and happiness of a young girl in the age of the chieftains. In Penelope he depicts not only the faithful wife, but a woman of character, intelligence, and refinement. In Arete he indicates the high respect paid to women and the large influence they wielded.

Among the literary qualities of the epics, plainness, nobility, and speed are outstanding. Homer's thoughts are simple, direct, and true to life; and he presents them in unadorned language. The result is dignified and noble. Nor is this nobility lost when the poet turns to describe some homely detail of everyday life, the taking of a bath or the preparation of a meal. Homer's swiftness has many sources; among them are the nature of the Greek hexameter in which he wrote, his refusal to be led from the point or to encumber it with unnecessary detail, and the effective alternation between passages composed with epic fullness and passages giving just enough description to assure the semblance of reality.

Homer keeps himself in the background as he tells his story. He puts as much of it as possible into the mouths of his characters; and he describes these characters, not as they appear to him, but through the effect they have on others. In the passage in which Helen appears on the walls of Troy, he depicts her beauty only as it is seen by the old Trojans whose lives have been ruined through her. When they saw her coming, they said to one another "Small blame is it that Trojans and well-greaved Achaians should for such a woman long time suffer hardships;

362

marvellously like is she to the immortal goddesses to look upon." In this passage Homer's restraint can also be seen, and the fact that he individualizes his characters in part only.

Homer does permit himself to comment on his story and his characters in the similes, which are often long and detailed. He takes his comparisons from all the experiences of life: the evening star and the snow storm; lions and eagles and flies; women wrangling in the streets and a little girl clinging to her mother's dress. The similes are never merely decorative but are used to emphasize an action the poet wishes to make unusually impressive. Sometimes two or more are presented together, as in the episode of Polyphemus where the whirling of the burning tree trank in the giant's eye is compared to the turning of an auger in a beam, and the hissing of the eyeball from the heat is likened to the sound of red-hot iron plunged into water.

The blending of divine and human action characterizes the *Iliad* and the *Odyssey* throughout. It might be thought that this feature would lessen a modern reader's interest in the poems, but it does not. Homer's gods and goddesses are thoroughly anthropomorphic. Though they have certain powers not available to human beings, in character they are much like the heroes and heroines. They never act so as to reduce the heroes to mere puppets, as Fate does in Vergil's *Aeneid.* They interfere in the action to help or hinder the heroes or to suggest what they ought to do, but they do not crush them. When Hera sends Athena to restrain Achilles in the quarrel with Agamemnon, Achilles obeys Athena of his own free will; for, as he himself says, "whosoever obeys the gods, to him they gladly hearken." The interference of the gods does not, then, destroy the interest of the story; in fact, it increases it. The human action follows no less naturally than it would otherwise do, and the divine element diversifies the tale. In the episode in which Hector is slain by Achilles, the appeal of Athena to Zeus, the weighing of the Fates by Zeus, and the deluding of Hector by Athena, are used with the greatest skill to enrich the human story.

The Homeric poems give us a picture of Greek life

that differs in important particulars from that of the later classical period. There is no single name for Greece as opposed to other lands. The Greeks are called Achaeans, Argives, and Danaans. The Hellenes are the inhabitants of a small district in Thessaly. Civilization is based on agriculture and cattle raising. Athens has no special distinction, and Sparta is comparatively insignificant. The states are ruled by kings of whom Agamemnon, the king of Mycenae, is the greatest. The kings are military commanders, judges, and priests. But they are not absolute, their power being limited by public opinion. The poems are thoroughly aristocratic, and the common people play little part in them. The chief excellences of the heroes are physical strength and courage, and their knowledge, for the most part, is of a very practical nature. But they hold wisdom and eloquence in high esteem, and they greatly reverence the bards to whom has been given "the gift of wondrous song." Outwardly their religion is not very different from what it was in later Greece, but actually it is much simpler and more naïve.

A number of ancient Greek epics dealt with the tale of Troy, and we know the titles and subjects of some of them, but only the *Iliad* and *Odyssey* have survived. To the Athenians of the 6th century B.C. these poems were already ancient classics, recited in full at a public festival every fourth year. The first real work of Latin literature was a translation of the *Odyssey*, and both epics were as well known to educated men in Augustan Rome as they had been in Periclean Athens. After the fall of Rome they dropped out of sight in western Europe, and during the *Middle Ages Homer's work was not directly known there, though his name was still revered: *Dante lists him as one of the world's supreme poets. Just as the translation of the *Odyssey* had begun Latin literature, the translation of the *Iliad* was the first real step in the revival of Greek studies during the early *Renaissance. *Boccaccio was so intent on getting a Latin version of the *Iliad* made (and improving his smattering of Greek in the process) that he actually took into his own house a pretentious, ignorant, and repulsive Greek—one Leontius Pilatus—to work on the project. Since that time six centuries ago, Homer has been an essential part of our literary tradition, and in recent times he has served as the guide and companion of men as diverse as the scholar and poet Matthew *Arnold and the adventurer Lawrence of Arabia.

Imaginary Invalid, The: a comedy by *Molière (*Le Malade imaginaire*, 1673), also known in English as *The Hypochondriac*. This is the last play Molière wrote, and the last one in which he acted. It is a stroke of irony, as paradoxical as anything Molière the playwright could have devised, that the author of a comedy about an imaginary invalid should himself have been seriously ill when he wrote it, and that as its principal actor, who so realistically dragged himself about the stage, he should die a few hours after its fourth performance, on February 17, 1673.

Molière's fight with 17th-century medicine was a long one. *The Love-Sick Doctor* (a lost farce, but one can assume something of its nature), *Love Is the Best Doctor* (*L'Amour médecin*, 1665), and *The Physician in Spite of Himself* (*Le Médecin malgré lui*, 1666) all had their barbs to throw; in fact, in *The Imaginary Invalid* one of the characters, the sensible Béralde, counsels his hypochondriac brother: "I hoped I could convince you of the error of your ways and amuse you by taking you to see one of Molière's plays on this subject." The dramatist, Béralde concludes, "has his reason for not wanting [the doctors' prescriptions] and he maintains that only vigorous and robust people are strong enough to stand them." Certainly the Molière of 1673 was a very sick man, one whom the doctors had not been able to help. But Molière's satire is not merely personal; here is for him another example of the irrationality of mankind which, gullible and discontented, will forever avoid the sensible, natural way of life.

The Imaginary Invalid is a comedy-ballet, a type favored by the pageantry-loving king. However, since Molière is, as usual, more interested in characterization than in spectacle, the ballet interludes have been made so subordinate that they are often omitted in modern performances. Molière's achievement is to derive rollicking comedy from a somber theme and to people his play with some excellent characters. There is Argan, the hypochondriac, whose chief concerns are his health and, closely related to that consuming activity, the marrying of his daughter to a physician so that he will be assured of ready and free attention. None of the other characters, including the wonderfully ridiculous, buffoonish medical suitor and the clever little maid, Toinette (who disguises herself as a doctor to make what would be to anyone but Argan incredible diagnoses), is able to dissuade the imagining but willing invalid. As the play closes he has been convinced that the only practical solution is for him to become a doctor himself. He is encouraged, for, after all, "you have but to hold forth in cap and gown, and any gibberish becomes learning, and all nonsense passes for sense." And Toinette seconds, "Just think, Monsieur, you already have the beard, and that is half the battle."

Imagists: a group of English and American poets (1909–17) who, although much influenced by the *symbolist poets (particularly Gustave Kahn, 1859–1936), desired in contrast to gain their effects by "imaging" things, by presenting the particulars exactly, making them concrete, sharply delineated, hard and clear, not blurred or diffuse. They wished also to use the exact language of common speech, to create new rhythms, to allow absolute freedom in choice of subject. Finally, they believed that "concentration is of the very essence of poetry."

These ideas they set forth in the preface to their anthology, *Some Imagist Poets* (1915). Although their imagery is more definite than that of the symbolists, the poems are frequently no more communicative, because often the image is not clearly associated with an emotion or meaning, and the concentration of the poetry is designed to suggest, not to state an idea. Indeed, Imagism has been branded "the cult of unintelligibility."

Although the Imagists soon found that their method and range of interest were too limited and gave up writing poetry that conformed strictly to their theory, they did make a significant contribution to 20th-century letters. Their passionate belief in the artistic value of modern life encouraged greater freedom in choice of subject. Their determination to use the exact, not the merely decorative, word avoided the trite expressions which so often mar symbolist poems. Their stress on newer rhythms (on composing, as *Pound said, "in the sequence of the musical phrase, not in the sequences of a metronome") exerted a liberating influence on versification while at the same time emphasizing the importance of rigorously disciplined verse. They made free verse respectable by urging that "a new cadence means a new idea." The term *imagist* had been applied to the French precursors of the movement, but the names associated with the group itself are T. E. Hulme, Richard Aldington, H[ilda] D[oolittle], John Gould Fletcher, F. S. Flint, Ezra Pound, and Amy Lowell.

impressionism: a movement in painting, music, and literature whose aim was to force the beholder, listener, or reader to participate in re-creating the experience of the artist and whose method was to suggest the "impression" or effect on the artist rather than to make precise and explicit the objective characteristics of things or events. Popularized in France in the latter half of the 19th century by the painters Cézanne, Degas, Manet, Monet, Pissarro, and Renoir, the movement took its name from Monet's painting of a sunrise, *Impression: Soleil Levant* (1874). These artists achieved their distinctive effects by their use of color and sketchy lines, in a "sort of pictorial stenography, disdainful of details which a rapid vision cannot seize."

Debussy and Ravel represent the musicians of this group. Their compositions are intended to evoke a mood rather than to present a logical structure and are marked by great delicacy and striking chromatic effects.

In literature, the term has been applied loosely to the *symbolist and *Imagist poets and to writers using the *stream-of-consciousness technique. Their method is to present through vivid peripheral details the immediate impression of experience derived from the senses without analysis or synthesis, the impression as it is seen or felt subjectively in a single fleeting moment. They do not wish to explain the essential central thought or to organize all the details explicitly into a conventional formal relationship to the central idea. By one critic or another the following have been called impressionists: *Rimbaud, *Verlaine, *Mallarmé, Valéry, *Hopkins, *Eliot, *Joyce, Virginia *Woolf.

In literary and artistic criticism, impressionism is the approach which is more interested in the critic's reaction to a work of art than in the artistic object itself. The classic statement of this point of view is the definition given by Anatole *France: "The good critic is the one who tells the adventures of his soul among masterpieces."

Indian literature: see *Jataka, *Kalidasa, *Mahabharata, *Panchatantra, *Ramayana, *Upanishads, *Vedas.

in medias res: a Latin phrase meaning literally "into the middle of things." It comes from the statement in *Horace's Ars poetica (lines 148–149) that the poet in medias res . . . auditorem rapit—"rushes his hearer into the middle of things." Thus the expression refers to a technique now conventional in epic poetry, fiction, and drama which begins a story "in the middle" and then gives the earlier action by flashbacks, as opposed to a straight, chronological narrative. For example, the Odyssey (see *Iliad and Odyssey) plunges in medias res, Odysseus being first introduced as he is about to start the final lap of his homeward voyage. Only when he recalls his experiences for Alcinous do we learn about his prior adventures with the *Cyclops, *Circe, etc. This device serves a double artistic function. It presents the story by foreshadowing and anticipation rather than surprise: the audience knows that Odysseus survived the perils of his homeward journey, and this knowledge lends both a sense of security and a special interest to learning how he managed to circumvent what often seemed insuperable difficulties. Furthermore, the narrator can secure more immediate interest by beginning well along in the story. In modern times the device has been popularized by its frequent use in films.

Industrial Revolution: term used to describe the change-over from an agricultural economy with small-scale home production and hand manufacture to an industrial economy of large-scale machine production in factories; also included in the meaning are the social and economic transformations which accompanied the new system—factories, child labor, slums, urbanization of the countryside, exploitation of natural resources. Its beginnings may be roughly placed in the last quarter of the 18th century, when the invention of the spinning jenny and the steam engine made mass production feasible and economical. Although the Industrial Revolution produced more abundant supply and wider distribution of the material goods of the world, at the same time it forced many workers into unconscionable poverty and degraded the human spirit, leaving it without pity and without hope. Pride in craftsmanship gave way to regimentation and frustration; and the uniformity required for efficiency dehumanized the worker supposed to be benefited. The insecure middle class, itself dependent on an impersonal, inhuman economic system, ignored with equal callousness the misery of the poor, the ugliness of the new cities, and the devastation of the natural environment. It was writers and artists (*Dickens, *Ruskin, *Marx, Millet, Doré, Courbet), obsessed by the misery of the workers and the ugliness of the mass products, who initiated the demand for social reform. Indeed, this humanitarianism is regarded by Sir Kenneth Clark as the significant social contribution of the 19th century.

interior monologue: see *stream-of-consciousness novel.

Ionesco, Eugène: French dramatist (1912–94). Born in Rumania, Ionesco studied in France; he became a French citizen in 1938 and in 1970 was elected to the French Academy. The presentation of *The Bald Soprano*

369

(*La Cantatrice chauve*)—a ferocious parody of contrived sentences like those one encounters in a textbook teaching a foreign language—in 1950 created a stir in the Paris theatrical world. Ionesco immediately became a controversial figure and was unanimously acknowledged as a major exponent of "the theater of the *absurd." The dialogue of *The Bald Soprano* consists in an exchange of platitudes and nonsensical statements. In the end, language breaks down completely. What is under attack beyond the inability to communicate is the emptiness of everyday life and the isolation of human beings for whom existence is nothing but a set of mechanical responses.

The Lesson (*La Leçon*, 1951) is a satire culminating in an act of brutality. *The Chairs* (*Les Chaises*, 1952), "a tragic farce" about an old couple expecting visitors who never come, explores the invasion of man's universe by objects which threaten to suffocate him and emphasizes the dehumanization of contemporary life. *Jack or the Submission* (*Jacques ou la soumission*, 1955) satirizes marriage and the domineering attitude of parents.

Ionesco's later plays became longer and more ambitious. The protagonist of *Rhinoceros* (*Le Rhinocéros*, 1960) is an individual caught up in a conformist society. A play with distinct political implications, it shows men degenerating under totalitarianism into insentient beasts. In *The Epidemics in the City* (*L'Epidemie dans la ville*, 1970), based on *Defoe's *Journal of the Plague Year*, Ionesco said he "denounces the scandal of death." Ionesco often denied being a philosopher or social reformer. But his preoccupation with the isolation, the lack of communication, and the sclerosis of modern life proves him to be a playwright dedicated to the affirmation of man's individuality in spite of the crippling atmosphere which surrounds him.

Irish Literary Revival: a movement in the late 19th and early 20th centuries, aimed at reviving the ancient folklore, legends, and traditions of Ireland, and diffusing and preserving them by means of new literary works. This movement (known also as the Irish Renaissance and the Celtic Renaissance) was the literary and cultural aspect of the same nationalistic impulse which, on its political side, demanded home rule for Ireland. In their early days, William Butler *Yeats, George Moore, and others of this group had been imitating the French decadents and *symbolists. Later they joined to channel Irish nationalism into constructive artistic achievement and to arouse a consciousness of cultural unity. Their aims were to preserve the Gaelic language, to revive Celtic myths and old folk tales, to create a legendary national character (a compound of romantic fantasy and humorous realism), to stimulate a new literature authentically Irish in spirit, to exploit the fresh, racy rhythms of native speech, and to develop a more direct and realistic verse. The group succeeded in producing some of the liveliest and most entertaining writing of the 20th century. Two major dramatists, J. M. *Synge and Sean *O'Casey, and a major poet, Yeats, were involved in the movement. Others of lesser genius were, nevertheless, writers of considerable talent: Lady Gregory (1852–1932), George W. Russell ("A. E.," 1867–1935), Lord Dunsany (1878 1957), James Stephens (1882–1950), Padraic Column (1881–1972). *Joyce, probably the most original and influential novelist of the 20th century, was influenced by the movement, though not actively a part of it.

One of the outstanding achievements of the group was the establishment of the Irish Literary Theatre (1899), and later the Abbey Theatre (1910). Some of the finest plays of the 20th century were written for and produced by the Abbey Theatre, and have exercised an important influence on British and American drama.

James, Henry: American novelist, essayist, playwright, and critic (1843–1916). Creator of the cosmopolitan novel, a fertile experimenter and theorist of fiction, Henry James emerged from the Civil War years a precocious writer and went abroad in search of his artist-peers. He is the one American novelist who devoted himself all his life exclusively to his art, lived by it, and made himself an international reputation at a time when American literature was still finding its way and was, in effect, a regional outpost of British literature. With *Melville and *Whitman, James belongs to the "flowering" of New York as distinct from the flowering of New England. He wrote for 50 years—20 novels, 112 short stories, a dozen plays, most of them unsuccessful, and several volumes of critical essays as well as travel sketches.

His fiction falls into three periods. The so-called "international" period occurred during the first half dozen years of his residence abroad and culminated in his masterpiece The *Portrait of a Lady. The second fell within the decade of the 1880's, during which he tried to emulate the naturalist school of *Zola and wrote The Bostonians, The Princess Casamassima, and The Tragic Muse. A hiatus then occurred during the first half of the nineties when he tried to become a playwright. He was a total failure. Emerging from this, he wrote a series of experimental novels dealing with English life, in which he adapted to fiction his experiences in the theater: these novels are scenic and are told through limited angles of vision or "points of view." James' experiments prepared the way for the three works commonly spoken of as representing his "major phase"—one might also call it his "modern phase." These were The *Ambassadors, The Wings of the Dove, and The Golden Bowl. They foreshadowed most of the experiments which would flow from the subjective and virtuoso school of fiction inaugurated by James *Joyce.

Large in dimension, requiring careful reading, but filled with felicities of style and invention, these novels, by exploring states of feeling and demanding of the reader "attention of perusal," foreshadow the explorations of *Proust and, in their mythic content, the myth-obsessions of Joyce. A profound believer in an "organic" novel as a work of calculated art, James infused into his fiction an important body of belief: the need for freedom, the need for observation and awareness, the need also for a morality of conduct and codes and forms of civilization, even when these must be obtained at the cost of "civilized" lies. In all his work he showed a profound belief in man's capacity to overcome the wear and tear of life and fate by understanding and facing realities. His work is that of a remarkable personality whose innovative power transcends all the demands of literary convention and the clichés of the marketplace.

James' choice of terrain was unique. No novelist up to his time had selected so much territory: his characters move between New York, London, Paris, Rome. He is an historian of manners; and in his "psychology" he is far in advance of his time. The social world he chronicled has disappeared: but the human dilemmas he treated and his symbolic and mythic imagination have reserved for him a supreme place in the history of Anglo-American fiction.

The novelist was born in New York City, in Washington Place, where New York University stands today, the second son of Mary Walsh James and of Henry James, Senior, an intellectual whose revolt against Calvinism had led him to embrace Swedenborgianism. The father was "leisured for life" by a boyhood accident in which he lost a leg and by the immigrant enterprise of the Irish-born William James, who founded the line in America after the Revolution. This gave the young Henry and his brother *William, who later became the expounder of pragmatism, a spacious and outwardly secure boyhood, with travel and schooling abroad for a five-year period during their adolescence. A shy boy, he resisted schools and tutors and went his own way as a "devourer of libraries." A young manhood at Newport, Rhode Island, where he met and was influenced by John La Farge, the painter, and formed a close friendship with another literary young man, the critic T. S. Perry, determined him in his career as a writer. His first anonymous story appeared in the *Continental Monthly* in New York, in February 1864, and his first acknowledged story in the March *Atlantic Monthly* in 1865. Between the two tales he started writing unsigned critical articles in the *North American Review*, encouraged by its editor, Charles Eliot Norton. The tales and the criticisms are precocious. By the time he had published half a dozen short stories he was hailed in 1868 as one of the most skillful writers of short fiction in the country.

The stories of this period all deal with the American scene, and nearly all foreshadow the later works: they show a careful study of James' principal models, *Balzac, Mérimée, George *Sand and George *Eliot. Of American writers, *Hawthorne provided the most important influence, but this manifested itself more clearly later. In general, however, James tended to absorb influence only in the broad sense of working methods and techniques: the texture of his fiction is woven from his own acute observation of the scene around him and his profound understanding of psychological motivations.

A strained back, suffered during the early months of the Civil War while helping put out a fire, kept him from participating in the conflict and imposed a sedentary existence for several years. In 1869–70 he made his first adult voyage to Europe, visiting Italy for the first time. While he was abroad, his cousin, Minny Temple, to whom he had formed a deep but reserved attachment, died of tuberculosis. The "passionate pilgrimage" and the shock of this loss constituted deeply felt experiences which were reflected promptly in his work. Within the next two years he had written his first important tale, *A Passionate Pilgrim*, his first novel, *Watch and Ward* (a work later disowned), and consciously set himself to writing book reviews for the *Nation* and the *Atlantic* as well as occasional art and drama criticism, seeking to support himself by free-lance writing while producing his larger fictions. A two-year residence abroad, largely in Italy, from 1872 to 1874 resulted in his first important novel, *Roderick Hudson*, and, in 1875, after another attempt to create a career for himself in America, he decided Europe would yield more material.

He went to Paris late in 1875 and there sought out the Russian novelist *Turgenev, who introduced him to *Flaubert and the group of French realists surrounding him that included Zola, *Daudet, and the young *Maupassant. The young American admired the French writers but felt them to be as provincial as the Boston Brahmins. In Turgenev alone he found that cosmopolitanism of view and sense of technique, as well as feeling for life, that had meaning for his own art. Turgenev taught James that character, not story, was important.

In 1876 the novelist settled in London. By 1879, with the publication of *Daisy Miller*, he had made an international reputation. His career thereafter was one of great and fertile productivity. Between 1880 and his death in 1916 he produced a quantity of work capable of filling more than a hundred volumes—novels, tales, travel papers, critical essays, literary portraits, book reviews, plays, drama and art criticism, autobiographies, and a series of critical prefaces that amount to a major treatise on the art of fiction. He was a voluminous letter writer, and such of his notebooks as have been preserved show his faculty for easy and voluble self-communion.

His travel books include *A Little Tour in France*, *Italian Hours*, *English Hours*, and *The American Scene*; his volumes of criticism, *French Poets and Novelists*, *Partial Portraits*, *Essays in London*, and *Notes on Novelists*. His prefaces have been collected under the title *The Art of the Novel*, and his complete plays were published in 1949. A selection from his letters appeared in 1920, and his dramatic essays have been assembled in *The Scenic Art*.

James, William: American philosopher and psychologist, founder of psychology in America and exponent of pragmatism (1842–1910). Elder brother of the novelist *Henry James, William was attracted early to problems of the will, and this led him to the study of psychological conditioning and the influence of environment and education. He was led peripherally into exploration of extrasensory perception and the spirit world. Long before modern drug addiction, James tested many drugs for what would later be called the "psychedelic" experience. A doctor of medicine, he studied abroad under Wundt, and attended Charcot's seminars in Paris shortly after *Freud had studied with the same master. At Harvard he set up the first psychological laboratory in America, and in 1889 he published his *Principles of Psychology*, long a cornerstone of psychological study. Although much of his work is out-of-date, his studies in identity and his brilliant description of *stream of consciousness still have validity today. He remains a supreme stylist among scientific writers, and his writings survive as expository literature even when their material has dated. In addition to his *Principles*, his most celebrated book is *The Varieties of Religious Experience* (1902), a work of great scholarship and wide human sympathy and precursor of modern studies of "identity crisis"; he also wrote *The Will to Believe* (1897), *Pragmatism* (1907), and *A Pluralistic Universe* (1909).

Jansenism: see *Pascal and *Racine.

Janus: a Roman divinity, the god of beginnings, whose temple was closed in time of peace and open in time of war. He was represented as having one head with two faces.

Jarry, Alfred: French dramatist and prose writer (1873–1907). In *Ubu Roi* (1896) he created a grotesque, violent puppet of a "hero," a caricature of bourgeois cruelty and greed. The same uninhibited, eccentric farce characterizes his other *Ubu* works, prose and plays, and the posthumous *Gestes et opinions du Docteur Faustroll* (1911) concerning "the science of imaginary solutions." Jarry is important because as an exponent of mannered obscurity and "absurdity" in literature he was a fruitful influence on *Apollinaire, *surrealism, and modern dramatists of the "theater of the absurd." See *Beckett, *Ionesco.

Jataka: a story, or collection of stories, about the *Buddha's earlier incarnations. The orthodox Buddhist considers these tales to be autobiographical accounts of Gautama Buddha and hence a part of the Buddhist sacred writings. One of the oldest and most important collections of folk tales extant, the *Jataka* (written in the Pāli of Buddhist scripture) comprises 547 stories. The stories are written in a common Indian form which uses prose for most of the narrative and verse for dialogue and climax; and they are usually accompanied by prose commentaries. The collection contains *fables, *fairy

376

tales, moral tales, maxims, legends. More than half the stories are not of Buddhist origin and are found in other Indian collections such as the *Panchatantra*. Many fables, like the Ass in the Lion's Skin, appear in western literature, notably in the fables attributed to *Aesop.

Jean de Meung: see *Romance of the Rose*.

Jefferson, Thomas: American statesman (1743–1826). Jefferson was a man of remarkably broad interests and abilities, and his achievements are impressive in many fields. His writings range from treatises on political theory and scientific agriculture to an Anglo-Saxon grammar. Essentially, however, his literary importance is due to a short work—the *Declaration of Independence* (1776) which he drafted for the Second Continental Congress when he was a relatively young man. (He died on the fiftieth anniversary of its signing.)

The *Declaration* is essentially Jefferson's creation, though *Franklin and Adams made some minor changes, and a few words were amended by the Congress. Long after he wrote it, Jefferson said that it did not aim at originality, though it was not copied from any previous writing but "was intended to be an expression of the American mind." *Rousseau, *Milton, and *Locke are among its begetters, but Jefferson substituted pursuit of happiness as a New World hope in place of Locke's inalienable right of property.

The *Declaration of Independence* was a justification of the American Revolution—a political, ethical, and religious argument that men have a duty to rebel when existing authority has forfeited its claim to obedience. In addition, it presented the principles on which the new state was to be founded. Basic in the argument is the philosophy of natural rights. This natural law is considered to be as old as mankind, dictated by God Himself, and superior to any other. In the state of nature men possessed equal rights to life, liberty, and the pursuit of happiness—rights which Jefferson calls inalienable. To secure these rights, governments had been instituted, but such governments "derive their just powers from the consent of the governed"; and "whenever any government becomes destructive of these ends, it is the right of the people to alter or to abolish it, and to institute new government." An impressive list of usurpations and abuses by the king is given as proof that the people of America now have this right.

The *Declaration* attains Jefferson's ideal literary qualities, euphony and strength. It has the balance and antithesis, the "sententious brevity" of 18th-century prose, combined with a dignity and stateliness befitting the occasion. This classic of democracy expresses imperishably what was at the heart of Jefferson's action and thought, his, "sworn, eternal hostility against every form of tyranny over the mind of man."

Jerome, Saint: Church Father and Bible translator (Hieronymus, *c.* A.D. 345–420). Jerome was a prolific writer who produced sermons, many Bible commentaries, lives of saints, a brief history of Christian literature, a large number of personal letters, and a great body of controversial writing in which personal abuse was an important weapon. His great work was the translation of the Bible into Latin known as the *Vulgate (c. 383–405) and still the basis of the official scripture of the Roman Catholic Church. In technical theology and Biblical exegesis his other works still have considerable authority, though they long ago ceased to influence general literature.

John of the Cross, Saint: Spanish mystical poet (San Juan de la Cruz, 1542–91). St. John was a religious reformer who preached literal adherence to the original Carmelite rule. With the aid of St. *Teresa he established a monastery of decalsced friars (1568), but his fellow Carmelites, who objected to his extreme reforms, had him imprisoned and tortured (1577–78). After nine months, he managed to escape from prison. It was during the days in prison and shortly thereafter that he wrote the 26 poems for which he is remembered today. They range all the way from descriptions of his own insufficiency and willingness "to suffer and to be despised" to fervent and intense mystic visions. The soul leaves its dark night *(The Dark Night of the Soul)* and must "empty itself of self in order to be filled with God" *(Living Flame of Love, Ascent of Mount Carmel)*. His best-known poems are paraphrases of the Songs of Solomon from the *Bible, notably the one beginning "Where hast Thou hidden Thyself, O my beloved, and abandoned me . . . ?"

Johnson, Samuel: see *Boswell.

Jones, LeRoi: American writer who adopted the name Imamu Amiri Baraka, later shortened to Amiri Baraka (1934–   ). Jones was born in Newark, New Jersey, and attended Rutgers and Howard universities. In addition to plays, he has written poetry, novels, and essays. Jones is an angry writer, his anger sparked and fueled by the plight of the American Negro in the 1960's.

His first play, *Dutchman* (1964), won the Obie Award for the Best American Play of the 1963–64 season. The setting is the subway; a white girl attempts to pick up a young black boy and stabs him when he refuses to go along with her demands. *The Toilet* and *The Slave* were presented together in 1964. The first play is concerned with homosexual love between a white boy and a black boy; in the latter a black visits his white ex-wife and her white husband and finally kills them. *The Slave* demonstrates Jones's belief in the futility of liberalism, which fails because the two races seem incapable of making true contact with one another. His novel, *The System of Dante's Hell* (1965), is based on his own youth in the slums of Newark and his experiences with the Air Force in a small Southern town. Although it is loosely patterned after *Dante's *Inferno*, what emerges is a lyrical and fragmentary picture of Jones's anger against things white.

Jones feels that it is the duty of a Negro writer to portray "the emotional history of the black man in this country: as its victim and chronicler." He is an original, talented, poetic writer, whose language and action are rough, sometimes crude, always appropriate to the characters and the situation.

jongleur: a professional wandering entertainer (minstrel) of the *Middle Ages, who usually not only sang and played instruments but did juggling and acrobatics as well. In contrast to the *troubadour, who was essentially a composer in the courtly style (although he also sang his verses), the jongleur seems rarely to have composed; chiefly he reworked songs, lyrics, ballads, stories into popular forms and disseminated these literary materials by his performances.

Jonson, Ben: English poet and dramatist (1572–1637). After receiving a sound classical education, Jonson was apprenticed to a bricklayer, so that he might learn his stepfather's trade; but he ran away to the Low Countries and fought against the Spaniards there. Later, he used to boast that he had killed an enemy in single combat between the two armies and stripped him of his arms, in the best Homeric manner. On his return he took to acting (without great success) and playwriting. In 1598 he narrowly escaped hanging for killing a fellow actor in a duel, joined the Roman Catholic Church (he left it 12 years later), and saw his first really successful play, *Every Man in His Humour*, produced (with his friend *Shakespeare as one of the cast). From this time on, his career was one of increasing eminence, in spite of occasional periods of difficulty and even imprisonment. His first success was promptly followed up with *Every Man out of His Humour* (1600). After the accession of James I in 1603, Jonson won favor, employment, and finally a pension for his skill in writing the *masque, a spectacular form of court pageantry of which James was especially fond. But the masques did not absorb his entire energy. He produced two tragedies on the classical model, *Sejanus His Fall* (1603) and *Catiline* (1611). More important, he turned from the exaggeration of his early *comedy of humors to a more mature and realistic satirical comedy in which the system of the humors was kept within reasonable bounds. In this type he produced four masterpieces: *Volpone, or The Fox* (*c.* 1606), *Epicoene, or The Silent Woman* (1609), *The Alchemist* (said by *Coleridge to have one of the three perfect plots in literature, 1610), and *Bartholomew Fair* (1614).

Jonson was always a conscious and deliberate artist, and at the outset of his real career he clearly stated his dramatic platform. The Prologue to *Every Man in His Humour* states that he refuses to court popularity by writing in ways that he cannot approve. Especially he refuses to violate the *unities by covering a span of years in a play, or to resort to cheap and sensational stage effects. He intends to be realistic, with "deeds, and language, such as men do use," and to be satirical in a comical way—to "sport with human follies, not with crimes." Such satire is to serve a useful purpose by correcting the lesser vices of society. Except that his satire later became sharper and less good-natured, his best comedies held to this program with remarkable consistency and success. The example of his realism and classical structure probably helped to temper the romanticism and diffuseness of some of his contemporaries, and his influence lived on into the comedy of the Restoration.

As a poet Jonson can be represented by his best-known work, *Drink to Me Only with Thine Eyes*, for its conciseness, brevity, ease, and formal perfection are typical of his lyrics. Even in an age when every hack playwright could turn out good lyrics, Jonson was outstanding; and his younger contemporaries, the Cavalier Poets, modeled their verses on his so openly that they gloried in the name of "the tribe of Ben."

Josephus, Flavius: Jewish historian (A.D. 37–*c.* 100). Josephus was an adherent of the Pharisees, a sect devoted to the strict observance of the Mosaic law. When the Jews revolted against the Romans, A.D. 66, Josephus was put in command of Galilee, but was unable to hold the province against the Roman general Vespasian and surrendered the next year. Immediately imprisoned by the Romans, he won their favor three years later, when his prophecy that Vespasian would become emperor was fulfilled. Josephus was present with Titus, Vespasian's son, at the siege of Jerusalem, A.D. 70, and, when the city fell, accompanied him to Rome, where he spent the rest of his life in literary work.

In addition to an autobiography or *Life*, Josephus composed a defense of Judaism called *Against Apion*, after the name of an Alexandrian anti-Semite; a history of the Jews from the Creation to the beginning of the hostilities with Rome, known as the *Antiquities*; and a *History of the Jewish War*, A.D. 66–70. The *War* is Josephus' best work both as history and as literature. In writing it he had his own experience to guide him, as well as the records of the campaign kept by Vespasian and Titus. He composed the work first in Aramaic, then translated it into Greek with the aid of secretaries.

Joyce, James: Irish novelist (1882–1941). Joyce has exerted a profound influence on modern literature, though he wrote only six books—a slim volume of verse, a play, and four books of fiction. The fiction includes a volume of short stories (*Dubliners*, 1914), a comparatively short novel (*A Portrait of the Artist as a Young Man*, 1916), and his two major experimental works, *Ulysses (1922) and *Finnegans Wake (1939).

Joyce was born in a Dublin suburb and educated in Jesuit schools. Gifted with a fine tenor voice, he was greatly interested in music for a while and might have made himself a career as a singer. His extremely weak eyesight forced him to hear the world more than to see it, and this is reflected both in Joyce's delicate ear for the nuances and cadences of language and in his predominantly auditory imagery. Early in life he turned his back on both his native city and his childhood religion, and yet wherever he went he carried with him the vision of his home and the emotions of his faith. He lived in Trieste, Zürich, Paris, teaching languages and devoting himself to writings which he had great difficulty in publishing because of their innovations, complexity, blasphemy, and use of language not then customarily seen in print. The publication (in Paris) of *Ulysses* brought Joyce to the attention of the world in spite of the book's difficulties with the British and American censorship.

Given financial aid by an Englishwoman, he was able to devote the rest of his life to his writing without having to support himself by other work.

Joyce's early fiction shows the germ of his later development. He called the short stories and sketches of *Dubliners* epiphanies, applying a religious term to the sudden insight into life granted the artist. A fragment of the first draft of *A Portrait of the Artist* (published after Joyce's death under the title of *Stephen Hero*) shows, when compared with the final version, how the novel evolved from an objective account of external experience into a subjective picture of the mind and the senses. The *Portrait* is autobiographical; through the use of the artist's sensual as well as intellectual life it attempts to show the creator as a universal figure.

The tendency toward the subjective picture of the mind and the senses is carried much further in *Ulysses*, a book which contained the first widely known use of the *stream-of-consciousness technique. Joyce did not claim that the basic idea was original; he pointed out that Edouard Dujardin had written a novel entirely in this technique 30 years earlier. In this novel also appeared, for the first time, Joyce's virtuosity in coining and compounding new words, and in setting for himself difficult technical problems (some critics have called them stunts) like the stylistic imitation of the consecutive periods of English literature in one of his chapters, or the painting of a panorama of Dublin seen through the eyes of many people in its streets at a given moment during the day.

This virtuosity had a significant influence on other writers, who learned many tricks of their craft from him. But Joyce delighted also in labyrinth-building, and in secret complexities which he leaked, however, to his acolytes. An inveterate user of myth, he created a myth about himself. It is his mythic imagination, his sense of the cycles of human life, his constant feeling for the eternal cosmic fantasies of man, that is perhaps most important in his work, especially in his word-pastiche *Finnegans Wake*, to which he devoted the last 17 years of his life. Posterity will probably attach more importance to Joyce's verbal and mythic imagination than to his labyrinth-building, however much the latter has been the delight of the annotators of our time.

In his private life Joyce seems to have been shut in; he made friends and was surrounded by a circle of admirers, but alienated them by his suspicions and his feeling that he was doomed to betrayal. His myth was that of the eternally rejected artist. Some have argued that Joyce invited "rejection" in order that he might vent his towering rage and brilliant verbal humor upon imagined enemies. Myth is woven within myth—the very title of *Ulysses* tells us this, and is blended with the myth of the Wandering Jew: so the wanderers in the modern city become the companions of Ulysses in their loneliness and despair. *Ulysses*, in spite of its protean humor, pictures urban clutter and squalor and the melancholy of men adrift and lonely among their fellows in the urban agglomeration.

As *Ulysses* was an attempt to capture a day in the life of Dublin and in the history of Ireland, *Finnegans Wake* records through the use of word-pastiche and portmanteau language the universe of word and myth that swirls around man. Its principal characters in Dublin, by the Liffey River, are asleep; and all history sweeps around them. This work cannot be read as we read ordinary books. Its music of language must be heard with the ear; it appeals to our senses and to our intellect by its word puns and verbal deformations. At first treated as a freakish and idiosyncratic work, the book has been gradually deciphered and stands as one of the fascinating experimental poems of our time in its Jungian tapping of "racial memory," its attempt to show recurrent myths and legends and use language evocatively. Many works of explication and "translation" now exist as aids to the reading of this literary "curiosity" of the 20th century.

Juan de la Cruz, San: see Saint *John of the Cross.

Jung, Carl Gustav: psychologist (1875–1961). Jung began as a disciple of *Freud, but broke with him in 1912 to found what he called "analytic psychology" in distinction to what Freud called *psychoanalysis. Jung somewhat more simplistically than Freud divided humans into extroverts and introverts. He differed with Freud's emphasis on the libido, arguing that man's immediate conflicts are more useful in understanding neuroses; in an intuitive way he argued for a relationship between the conscious and the unconscious. He also developed the hypothesis of the "collective unconscious." His emphasis on myth, his interest in cultural similarities among disparate primitive peoples, that is, his emphasis on "archetypes," have proved of great usefulness to literary theory and criticism. *Joyce in *Finnegans Wake* latched on to the Jungian idea that a "collective unconscious" exists in individuals alongside the individual consciousness.

Juno: see *Hera.

Jupiter: see *Zeus.

Juvenal: Roman satirist (c. A.D. 60–c. 140). Little is known about the life of the last Roman satirist, Decimus Junius Juvenalis. It seems probable that he was born in a village southeast of Rome, in the reign of the Emperor Nero, and it is certain he had an excellent education of the type then offered by the schools of rhetoric. But the evidence for his adult years is confusing and contradictory, though the suggestion that he turned to declamation seems plausible and finds some support in *Martial's statement that he was "eloquent." Whatever career Juvenal followed, however, he failed to achieve financial success, and his poverty filled him with frustration.

Juvenal's text, as we have it, consists of 16 satires—the last a fragment—composed in dactylic hexameters and published at irregular intervals between c. A.D. 100 and c. 128. Their purpose is to expose vice at Rome in the closing years of the first century, and the picture they present is, therefore, dark, lurid, and frequently revolting. But, although Juvenal exaggerates the evils of the society he depicts, while suppressing its redeeming features, there is truth in his description of the decay of the great noble houses, the rise of a new freedman class, the increasing admixture of Greek and Oriental elements in the population, and the contempt for morality, shown by all alike, in the pursuit of wealth.

Juvenal was well equipped as a writer of satire. He knew the city of Rome and the corruption by which it was disfigured; he was familiar with the moral teachings of the Stoics; he hated vice. He had complete mastery over the principles of rhetorical composition, vast powers of description, and an extraordinary ability to coin unforgettable phrases. Juvenal's verse is strong and good. His structure, though loose after the manner of satire, shows as clear a pattern as the type permits. His tone is merciless, but it has the support of almost all later writers in the field, who found their inspiration, not in *Horace, but in him. Juvenal's weaknesses lie in his prejudices (particularly against foreigners and women), his pessimistic conviction that Rome was incapable of reformation, and his lack of a sense of proportion, which leads him to assail foibles and affectations as savagely as crimes.

Juvenal's most famous satire is the sixth, *On Women*, but his best are probably the third, *On Life at Rome*, and the tenth, *On Prayer*. Both of these were imitated in English by Samuel Johnson, the one under the title *London*, the other under the title *The Vanity of Human Wishes*.

Kafka, Franz: German novelist (1883–1924). Kafka lived and wrote in the Prague of the Austro-Hungarian Empire. Although he was a brilliant graduate in law, he never practiced, accepting instead a minor clerical position in the department of workmen's compensation. This position gave him profound awareness of bureaucracy and red tape. His inability to assert himself in the world was marked in all his undertakings. He wrote but refused to be published, though his writings were much admired by friends to whom he read them. He could not bring himself to marry, although several times was engaged. Very early he developed tuberculosis and died leaving orders to his executor Max Brod that his manuscripts be destroyed. Brod, however, published them. None of his novels was actually completed, but even in their incomplete states *The Trial* (*Der Prozess*, 1925) and *The Castle* (*Das Schloss*, 1926) captured the imagination of a Europe caught in the 1930's in the irrationalities of dictatorship. Kafka's work deals with an incomprehensible world and authority, as when the hero finds himself inexplicably arrested. One of the earliest to have absorbed *Freud's studies in dreams, Kafka was able to translate the dream-states into his fiction—as in his celebrated short story "The Country Doctor." Unlike the *stream-of-consciousness writers, Kafka wrote of the intangible inner world of men as if it were a reality and occurring in broad daylight. One is never sure in his work whether one is inside a character's fantasies or having an actual reality described; locale and environment are left uncertain, but the writing is precise and objective. His novels document the guilt-obsessed, tripping themselves up and unaware of their identity in relation to authority. Kafka gave a vivid picture of his own inner terror in his journals and in his celebrated "letter" (*Brief an den Vater*, 1949) to his father which documents the irrationalities with which he had to cope in the parental home. His influence was pervasive, not only as a result of the unconsciously allegorical nature of his work, which adumbrated the plight of men in an irrational world of police states, but in its brilliant, precise prose, vividly captured for the English-speaking world in the translations of Edwin and Willa *Muir.

Kalevala, The: a Finnish folk epic. Though it is in many ways the most primitive of the European folk epics, *The Kalevala* ("Land of Heroes") was not put into its present form until the 19th century, when two doctors became interested in collecting the vast store of ancient songs still sung by Finnish peasants and minstrels. Zacharias Topelius began collecting this material, and although he spent the last 11 years of his life as an invalid, he managed to bring many singers to his bedside and to collect 80 fragments, which he published between 1822 and 1831. Elias Lönnrot (1802–84) continued the work of collecting, sifting, and arranging, and published his first edition (32 cantos, 12,078 lines) in 1835–36. The poem immediately attracted the attention of scholars all over Europe, and by general consent Lönnrot was the man to incorporate the new discoveries of other collectors into his own arrangement. His second edition (50 cantos, 22,795 lines), published in 1849, has remained the definitive version.

The Kalevala records the doings of five folk heroes— the minstrel, the blacksmith, the adventurer, the hunter, and the serf—all of whom are warriors in a primitive society and in a time of powerful magic. Their adventures include a number of separate stories or themes, including as a probable historical nucleus the wars between Kalevala and Pohjola (Finland and Lapland). In Finland the poem became almost a national symbol and was extensively used in the other arts, as in a number of the programmatic compositions of Sibelius. It was soon translated into the principal languages of Europe. *Longfellow's *The Song of Hiawatha* borrows its poetic form from the Finnish poem and is an attempt to *compose* (not to collect, as in the original) a *Kalevala* from the legends of the American Indians.

Kalidasa: Sanskrit dramatist and poet (4th century A.D.). Little is known of Kalidasa's life, but there is sufficient evidence to surmise that he lived at the court of Chandragupta II, a great patron of the arts. Kalidasa may not quite deserve the title of the Indian *Shakespeare, given to him by his first English translator, Sir William Jones, nor the unqualified praise bestowed upon him and his *Sakuntala* by *Goethe. Nevertheless, he is India's foremost "classical" dramatist, who wrote at least three important dramas and showed great ability as an epic and lyric poet. *Raghuvamsa*, his long poem in honor of the house of Raghu, is probably his best-known epic work. Here, as in his purely lyrical poems, Kalidasa proves himself master of the language. In his plays, too, the grace and beauty of poetic speech are most striking, especially in the descriptive and lyrical passages. These are the qualities that distinguish *Vikramorvasi*, the story of the love, separation, and final union of the king Puruavas and the nymph Urvasi; *Malavikagnimitra*, a story of court love and intrigue ending in the marriage of King Agnimitra and the princess Malavika; and *Sakuntala*, Kalidasa's best-known and most remarkable work.

Sakuntala is a seven-act drama based on the legend of the king Dushyanta, who, during a hunting party, comes to Kanwa's hermitage and falls in love with his foster daughter Sakuntala, the child of the holy Viswamitra and the nymph Menaka. After a secret and simple wedding, the king has to return to the capital and leaves his ring with Sakuntala, who is to follow him later. When Sakuntala, filled with longing for her absent husband, neglects to pay due respect to the divine sage Kasyapa—a comparatively small matter to touch off the fateful events of the following acts—he pronounces a curse to the effect that she will be forgotten by her beloved unless some token reminds him of her. When Sakuntala goes to the court, the king does not recognize her, and the ring, which might have aided her, is lost. In her plight, she is assisted by Menaka and taken to heaven, where she gives birth to a son. In the meantime a fisherman finds the ring in the stomach of a fish, and the king regains his memory and begins the search for Sakuntala. While visiting Kasyapa, Dushyanta watches a boy wrestling with a lion's cub and learns that it is his son. He is reunited with Sakuntala (in one of the most tender scenes of the play), and Kasyapa frees him of his feeling of guilt by telling him the story of the curse.

The play consists of a series of lyrical outbursts rather than of scenes marking the progression of the action. For instance, when the king searches for his wife, we are, in the main, shown various aspects of his state of inner unrest. Kalidasa's characters are not too well drawn; most of them are stylized puppets. Because the miracles of the gods determine the outcome of man's fate, there is little need to lay bare the workings of the human mind. The men are idealized; only the women seem to be somewhat closer to reality.

Sakuntala is meant for the stage, as the prologue, with its dialogue between stage manager and actress, clearly indicates. Some humor relieves the solemn and fantastic scenes, and the two constables speaking in their own peculiar language provide elements of farce. Yet the quick changes in location, the utter disregard for the element of time, the various scenes in motion—on the hunt, in the car of Indra in the air—strike anybody brought up with the traditions of Western drama as unusual.

Kawabata, Yasunari: Japanese novelist, 1968 Nobel prizewinner, author of a series of poetic novels exploring the nature of love and the alienation of the individual (1899–1972). He first attracted attention with *The Izu Dancer* (*Izu no Odoriko*, 1925). His best-known novel is *Snow Country* (*Yukiguni*, 1947), describing the passions of a country geisha and the alienated state of one of her lovers. His novel *Thousand Cranes* (*Sembazuru*, 1949) deals with the tea ceremony and the impress of the past on human lives. *The Sound of the Mountain* (*Yama no Oto*), published in 1954 and translated into English in 1970, deals with the "generation gap." *The Master of Go* (1972) records a six-month championship match of the ancient Japanese game of Go (played with pebblelike counters on a board divided into 361 squares). The defeat of the elderly, tradition-bound master by a brash young challenger marked also the more tragic difference in sensibility between the young and the old. Deeply influenced by the modern French movement and notably the *symbolists, Kawabata traveled widely and lectured in the West. During 1969 he was author-in-residence at the University of Hawaii. He committed suicide in 1972.

Keats, John: English poet (1795–1821). The son of a livery stable keeper, Keats was apprenticed to a surgeon-apothecary and studied medicine in the London hospitals. When he discovered literature, he read avidly through *Spenser's *Faerie Queen* (the influence of which is evident in most of his own poetry) and Chapman's translation of Homer. Soon after passing his medical examinations, he gave up medicine and devoted himself to poetry. He was now 21, and in the five years of life that remained to him he produced a body of work that has established him as one of the major English poets. His *Poems* (1817) attracted little attention, but *Endymion* (1818) was savagely attacked by reviewers. The attack was largely motivated by politics and was due to Keats' friendship with the violently liberal Leigh Hunt. It was also personal and in the worst possible taste; and a romantic legend grew up to the effect that Keats was killed by the derision of the reviewers. As a matter of fact, the specific charges brought against *Endymion* were largely justified: it was a lush, overexuberant, and rather formless poem. Keats can hardly have been pleased by the reviews, but they actually did not kill him. His genius matured with remarkable rapidity, and he soon rid himself of the faults of *Endymion.* During the next year (1819) nearly all his best poems were written: *La Belle Dame sans Merci,* many of the sonnets, and the great odes— *To Autumn, Ode to Psyche, Ode on Indolence, Ode to a Nightingale, Ode on a Grecian Urn, Ode on Melancholy.* These appeared in his last volume, *Lamia, Isabella, The Eve of St. Agnes and Other Poems* (1820).

After nursing a brother who died of tuberculosis, Keats contracted the disease. His condition may have been aggravated by quarrels with his guardians over his abandoning medicine; and his worry over the obstacles to his marrying Fanny Brawne, whom he passionately loved, may have made matters worse. (But Keats' mother and brother had died of tuberculosis without any such emotional crises.) A trip to the warmer climate of Italy failed to save him, and he died in Rome, where he is buried in the Protestant Cemetery. Modestly and somewhat bitterly he composed his own epitaph: "Here lies one whose name was writ in water." A more fitting tribute was paid him by *Shelley in *Adonais.*

Keats is a perfect illustration of one aspect of romanticism (see *classicism). He is probably the most sensuous poet in English, and his poetry is a riot of sounds, colors, perfumes. He even communicates sensations of touch: in *The Eve of St. Agnes* (in *Spenserian stanza), a girl undressing in a cold room after a ball "unclasps her warmed jewels one by one." But there is nothing gaudy about his richness. It is all in keeping with a subdued tone which is sometimes one of melancholy, and sometimes one of nostalgia for far-off times or enchanted worlds. Keats is not a thinker, though there is evidence that he was becoming one when he was cut off. He is a remarkably sensitive collector, organizer, and transmitter of sensations, one who tasted to the full the beauties of the world and sought to increase them, both in his poems and in his letters. The worship of beauty was both the motivation and the message of his poetry. His first ambitious work, *Endymion*, begins with the statement that "A thing of beauty is a joy for ever"; and the *Ode on a Grecian Urn* closes with the assertion that "Beauty is truth, truth beauty."

kenning: a compound metaphor, a decorative circumlocution or descriptive phrase used in place of a simple noun (from Old Norse *kenna til*, "to name after"). The kenning reflects poetic imagination (*swan-road* for "sea"); myth (*twilight-spoiler* for "dragon"); custom (*ring-giver* for "king"). Its use is one of the most interesting stylistic devices of *Beowulf* and is common to all the early Germanic literatures. By the 12th century, the kennings in Old Norse were so involved and their original meanings so remote that Snorri Sturluson, in the *Prose *Edda*, undertook to explain them for future poets.

Kierkegaard, Søren Aabye: Danish religious writer (1813–55). Kierkegaard began his career by writing various philosophical works, published under pseudonyms. These were all religious in their ultimate implications, but a more personal approach to Christianity eventually led him to attack the theologians who had made it into a philosophical system when it was essentially the personal experience of an isolated individual. An extension of this point of view led him, during the last year of his life, to an impassioned attack on *organized* religion, or "official Christianity." Among his best-known books are *Either/Or* (1843), *Fear and Trembling* (1843), *Stages on Life's Way* (1845), and *The Sickness unto Death* (1848). The papers of his final stage have been translated under the collective title of *Kierkegaard's Attack upon "Christendom."*

Kierkegaard's influence, beginning in the Scandinavian countries, has spread and grown steadily in the 150 years since his death. Not only has it affected a great many theologians and philosophers, but it has entered into a good deal of literature, being particularly important in *Ibsen, *Strindberg, and the French literature of *existentialism.

King James Version: sec *Bible.

King Lear: a tragedy by *Shakespeare (1605 or 1606). *The Tragedy of King Lear*, written at the height of Shakespeare's tragic period (1601–08), exemplifies what often happened when Shakespeare wrote a play. The materials of its plot are largely borrowed, but they are remade into a unique drama; the completed play exploits fully the capacities of its genre, often so brilliantly that no subsequent writer has gone so far; it finds its meaning by a profound exploration of the author's own time; and yet, in both plot and poetry, it develops this meaning with so much insight and comprehensiveness that it is, as Ben *Jonson said of Shakespeare generally, "not of an age but for all time."

The main plot (that of Lear) is a medieval chronicle story that was reworked by several 16th-century writers, including *Spenser and the anonymous author of a drama of 1605; the subplot (that of Gloucester) is from Sir Philip Sidney's *Arcadia* (1590). Two facts are to be noticed here. The first is that the earlier versions of these stories are relatively sketchy and afford little help in understanding Shakespeare's complex drama. The second is that the two originally independent stories of Lear and Gloucester are so thoroughly welded into one plot that we hardly feel them to have separate existences. The interrelationships of Gloucester and Lear and of their children are essential to the play, and the ironic duplication of parental experiences is a way of showing dramatically the universality of the theme. The two tragic heroes, however, do more than duplicate each other: they complement each other. Lear is a man of great force who imposes his will on the world, whereas Gloucester too much accepts the will of the world. One is violently active on wrong principles; the other's wrong principle is really passivity, a hope to get along with both sides ("I would have all well betwixt you," II, iv, 121). Between them, these principles illustrate a wide range of the human potentiality for tragic action.

A reader who wished to interpret *King Lear* entirely in terms of Shakespeare's own time would have to keep in mind the acceptance of a strong parental authority and a strong royal power, the view that bastardy implies "base" character, the privileged position of the Fool, and the conception of Nature as a universal order which has moral as well as physical manifestations. Not to understand Nature in this inclusive sense, for example, would be to miss the import of the famous storm in Act III, which would then, however striking, become merely an artificially conceived ornament instead of a dramatic representation of a distintegrating moral universe. Yet the real problem in *King Lear* is not to see it in a certain historical setting, but to understand its vision of truth which has a powerful impact long after its immediate historical setting is entirely vanished.

In a more profound way Shakespeare mirrored his age without merely relying upon its basic habits of mind. In the *Renaissance we have the transition from the medieval to the modern world, and it is precisely such a clash of ages that we see mirrored in *King Lear.* Indeed, the clash of ages is shown in terms of age: one generation is arrayed against another. But surely the play does more than present the extreme difficulties between parents and children; it is more than a "problem play." Nor can we read it simply as the unhappy story of an old man who has gone mad and in his madness turned out his best daughter and given power to evil daughters; this gives us merely a clinical record, without larger meaning. Nor do we have merely a study of filial ingratitude, for, though it certainly plays a part, the use of ingratitude as the principal dramatic force would reduce Lear from the status of morally responsible tragic hero to that of pathetic victim. Besides, ingratitude requires analysis: it may be a kind of spontaneous carelessness of obligation, or it may involve a deliberate pursuit of advantage with more or less formal rational justification. We must see what is really implied in the daughterly failure of Goneril and Regan.

In Lear the pride which so often characterizes the tragic hero and points to his "flaw" takes the form of self-will. In his self-will Lear makes several major errors: he believes that he can retain the privileges of kingship without the responsibilities; he insists that love can be measured both by words and by land; and he fails wholly to understand the language in which his daughters reply to him. The very heart of tragic error is less these specific assumptions and acts than it is their meaning: Lear has introduced into his world a spirit of calculation. In giving the country to Goneril and Regan he is not merely mistaking their quality: he is conferring worldly power upon the spirit of calculation by which he has already acted and which is their whole moral make-up. They are, then, something more than ungrateful; they represent a positive evil for the introduction of which Lear must take the responsibility. Lear's tragic flaw is their whole being. Their moral relationship to him is shown by the fact that, only a short time after he has used a mistaken calculation of love to put them in power, they use a mistaken calculation of his "need" to deprive him of the followers which are his only remaining symbol of power. When he says to them, "O, reason not the need" (II, iv, 267), he really puts a finger on the kind of rational calculation which is at the center of the Goneril-Regan world.

As parents, Gloucester and Lear are both taken in by scheming children, not as innocent victims, but because of their failure to understand available evidence. In the tremendous scope of the play, Cordelia too has the role of tragic protagonist rather than of injured bystander: like Antigone (see *Antigone*), she faces a difficult choice, with a penalty for either option. She can tell her father what he wants to hear—and violate her sense of personal honor; or she can stand on her dignity—and give the world up to her calculating sisters. She tries to compromise, answering, finally, not in the forthright measuring prose which Lear expects, but in a clipped metaphor: "I love . . . According to my bond" (I, i,

94–5). Lear's failure to understand how much this means and his acceptance of the meaningless hyperboles of Goneril and Regan show that he is suffering from a failure of imagination—the very faculty which, by affording a view of their whole lives, would produce answers to all questions about his three daughters' love. This failure of imagination recoils upon Lear when Goneril and Regan utterly fail to imagine his sense of values and on utilitarian grounds reduce him to an outcast. In all the suffering that follows—the verbal lashing from the loyal Fool, the storm, the mental anguish—Lear is really recovering his imagination; Edgar's comment upon Lear's climactic madness scene, "Reason in madness" (IV, vi, 179), emphasizes the understanding to which Lear has come and which he summarizes in images that have been used throughout the play—images of sight, smell, animals, sex, clothes, nature and justice. Most of all, he has come to value Cordelia properly, and he dies thinking that she is alive. Gloucester too dies happy, after he has learned to overcome the suicidal despair natural in a man whose habit it has been to yield too easily. What the tragedy asserts, like Greek and Elizabethan tragedy generally, is the endurance of moral values, though they may be temporarily obscured, and the ability of man to recover through suffering the moral insight which he has lost.

In the play we have a clash between an imaginative view of life (which apprehends values by their symbols) and a calculating view of life (in which value is equated with advantage). Again, there is a clash between an older order of duties and loyalties (represented by Kent, by Cordelia in her way, and eventually by Gloucester) and a newer order in which the only loyalty is to one's own prospects and profits. The double use of the word *nature* emphasizes this conflict: when Lear prays "Hear, Nature!" (I, iv) he is really addressing himself to powers of moral retribution which he considers absolute; but when Edmund proclaims, "Thou, Nature, art my goddess" (I, ii), the term means only instinct and desire. Yet Edmund, along with Goneril and Regan, is a calculator; and the insufficiency of their way of life is shown dramatically when they become ironically involved in an unplanned passion that is their only and dim approach to love and that destroys them. The death of Goneril and Regan is coldly violent, unrelieved by the illumination that comes to such tragic protagonists as Lear and Gloucester.

King Lear contains numerous wonderful scenes, notably those of Lear's disillusionment in Acts I and II, and of the storm and his madness in Acts III and IV. Some of the most powerful of all Shakespearean poetry is in these scenes. More than any other play, however, *King Lear* depends for its effects upon a particular kind of irony—namely, paradox. Gloucester is physically blinded just at the moment when he achieves spiritual insight; the central fact emerging from a wealth of imagery of sight is that it is the blind who really see. Lear strips himself, Cordelia, and Kent of possessions, and later tries to imitate Edgar's nakedness; yet it is the naked who have the warmth of love and who survive spiritually. Finally, in the Fool's raving, in Edgar's pretended madness, and in Lear's real madness there is more insight than in the most coldly sane people in the play— Edmund, Goneril, and Regan. In the former case there is "Reason in madness"; in the latter, by contrast, madness in reason. This is the final paradox that pulls all the others together. And the very prevalence of paradox makes of *King Lear* the archetypal tragedy, for in tragedy there is death, and yet victory; an "unhappy ending," and yet reassurance. For the tragic protagonist, losing a life oftenest means saving it.

Kipling, (Joseph) Rudyard: English poet and novelist, often called "poet of Empire" because he sang the glories of British rule in the world (1865–1936). He received the Nobel prize in 1907. He spent his childhood in India. After schooling in England he was a journalist in India. *Departmental Ditties* (1886) drew attention to him and his rich eastern material, and *Barrack-Room Ballads* (1892) made him famous. Many of his stories continue to be read. *Kim* (1901) and *The Jungle Book* (1894) have great vogue with children. His verse is rhetorical and declamatory and is the verse of patriotism; his prose is vigorous and vivid. He was a brilliant storyteller and his tales of India, in spite of much violence, explore profoundly human subjects. These are contained in such volumes as *Life's Handicap* (1891), *Traffics and Discoveries* (1904), *Debits and Credits* (1926). *The Light That Failed* (1891), a novel, has never been considered successful. He was at his best in the shorter medium.

Kleist, Heinrich von: German dramatist (1777–1811). Kleist came of a Prussian military family but hated the army and soon resigned his commission. He wandered to Paris and then to Switzerland, always tortured by internal conflicts and external indecision as to what he could or should make of his life. Neither his plays nor his novelettes had any real success during his own short lifetime—he never saw one of his plays performed. At the age of 34 he shot himself.

Of Kleist's eight plays, three deserve particular comment. His most widely popular one, *Katie of Heilbronn* (*Das Käthchen von Heilbronn*, 1810), is a medieval play with all the trappings of romantic medievalism, but in this loosely thrown together drama of a beautiful girl so smitten with a knight that she follows him around like a dog, Kleist has written some of his most beautiful scenes. *The Broken Jar* (*Der Zerbrochene Krug*, performed in 1808) is a comedy dealing with a lazy, slovenly local judge who has an inspector visit his court and watch the proceedings just on the day when a trivial case brings out testimony that slowly exposes the judge himself, who finally bolts from the bench. It is one of the funniest comedies in German literature and provides a fine realistic picture of village life and character. *The Prince of Homburg* (*Der Prinz von Homburg*, 1810) is generally acknowledged to be Kleist's masterpiece. This account of an officer who gained a victory by leading a magnificent charge—and thus disobeying orders—who showed abject cowardice when sentenced to death, and who recovered his manhood when made the judge of his own case, was earlier valued primarily for its upholding of rigid military discipline but is now considered remarkable for its subtle psychology and especially for the part played by the subconscious mind in the behavior of the principal character. More important than either of these special interests of the past and the present is the fact that it is a perfectly balanced and eloquently written play. In addition to his dramas, Kleist wrote several novelettes, of which *Michael Kohlhaas* (1810) is both the most ambitious and the best.

Klopstock, Friedrich Gottlieb: German epic and lyric poet (1724–1803). Klopstock's *The Messiah* (*Der Messias*, published in 20 cantos between 1748 and 1773), an epic about the life of Christ written in classical hexameters, was a famous and highly influential poem in its time, though little read today—and almost unreadable because of its length and monotony. His *Odes* (*Oden*, 1771), written in both classical and free meters, were equally influential and have endured the passage of time much better. Klopstock is usually considered the first outstanding modern German poet.

Knox, John: Scottish religious reformer (1505–72). Knox, who twice visited Geneva and established personal contact with *Calvin there, was the principal figure in the establishment of Scottish Calvinism. He preached all over Scotland against Mary, Queen of Scots (whom he called "Jezebel"), and offended Queen Elizabeth by his two *Blasts of the Trumpet Against the Monstrous Regiment of Women* (1558). He also wrote a *Historie of the Reformation of Religioun Within the Realme of Scotland* (1586). His works are models of Scots prose, and his ideas have been constantly reflected in later Scottish and Presbyterian writers.

Koran: see *Mohammed.

La Bruyère, Jean de: French social critic and satirist (1645–96). After studying law, practicing it briefly, and buying a sinecure which would support him, La Bruyère became a history tutor to one of the greatest families in France and spent the last dozen years of his life in the retinue of the Condés. Aside from the publication of his book, the only real event of his life was his reception into the Academie Française in 1693, after he had once been rejected.

In 1688 he published his only book, usually known as *Les Caractères*, or *The Characters.* The full title may be translated as *The Characters of Theophrastus, Translated from the Greek, Together with the Characters or Manners of This Age.* To a loose translation of the Greek character-sketches of *Theophrastus he had added some sketches from and observations on contemporary life. The first edition contained only about a third of the book as we know it, for as one edition followed another (nine in the eight remaining years of La Bruyère's life) he added new material of his own and relegated Theophrastus to a sort of appendix. The *Characters* contains satirical sketches of various human types (the absent-minded man, the hobbyist, the name-dropper, the aging belle, the ostentatiously busy man); general observations on types, morals, and society; and a considerable number of neat *epigrams. Though some appearance of a plan is given by a division into chapters, the work is essentially a collection of separate items (a total of 1100), most of which are less than a page long. *The Characters* is not a book to be read straight through, but is a perfect volume for dipping and skimming—an ideal book to take on a train.

In the Condé household La Bruyère was a sharp-eyed middle-class Parisian so placed that he could study the great unobtrusively but minutely. *The Characters* is the record of his observations, mercilessly but dispassionately presented. La Bruyère saw through the pretensions of the high and mighty, and in one famous paragraph he pitied the hard lot of the peasants ("beasts bound to the ground"); but he is an observer, not a reformer. His place in literature rests on his vivid colloquial style and on the precision and wit with which he captured and indicted his own times. His polish, satire, and concern with society link him with other Neo-Classical writers such as *Molière, *Addison, and *Voltaire.

La Fontaine, Jean de: French poet (1621–95) famous for his *Fables* (1668–94) Born at Château-Thierry into a wealthy, upper-class family, La Fontaine was destined for the priesthood, but his easy-going nature led him instead to Paris. Here he, *Boileau, *Racine, and *Molière became a celebrated quartet of literary friends. La Fontaine was first recognized for his *Tales* (*Contes*, 1664), sparkling narratives of light love, somewhat like *fabliaux*, distinguished by his particular gifts of speed and gracefulness.

The *Fables*, which began to appear a few years later, are compact animal *fables in the tradition of *Aesop, written with delightful humor, delicacy, and verve. It has been said that they supply different pleasures to different ages: children enjoy the vivid story; connoisseurs of literature, the consummate art with which it is told; the worldly, the subtle reflections on character and life, for each fable is in a sense a miniature human drama. The total artistic effect is one of freshness and piquancy, achieved by observation of detail, a witty merging of human and animal, remarkably precise diction which seems always to find just the right word, and an admirable versification in which cadences, meter, and rime are sensitively responsive to the mood. The latter qualities defy translation. The common-sense morality is well illustrated in the fable of the crow and the fox, who after he has attained the cheese, pronounces the moral: "Every flatterer lives at the expense of his listeners." The mastery of form, seen in the conciseness of the ingenious moralizing, in the laconic wit, in the fluent grace of the verse, has never been surpassed.

lai: see *lay.

Lamartine, Alphonse de: French poet (1790–1869). Lamartine lived a double life as a sentimental poet and a politician and statesman. His first volume, *Les Méditations poétiques* (1820), is usually considered as marking the beginning of French romantic poetry. In the year of its publication the poet also received his first diplomatic appointment. His activity both in lyric and in narrative and philosophic poetry practically stopped in 1839. His political career, which carried him to high position and important revolutionary activity, made him *persona non grata* to Napoleon III, so that from 1852 on he lived in poverty and retirement, writing prose romances, memoirs, and histories, and paying off his debts.

Lamartine's first volume contained some of his best poems: *Autumn, Evening, The Lake, Isolation.* They provoked a sensation and were an immediate popular success, for they brought intense emotion back to French poetry in verse of plaintive sweetness. Other important volumes of verse were *New Meditations (Les Nouvelles méditations*, 1823) and *Poetic and Religious Harmonies* (*Les Harmonies poétiques et religieuses*, 1830). The themes of his poetry—woman, nature, and religion—are closely interrelated by symbols of life and death, sacred and profane love, a vague pantheism and a constant idealism. The general effect is one of subjective intimacy and a reflective melancholy. The special quality of Lamartine's individuality is the combination of passion and spirituality expressed in verse of extreme suavity and limpidity.

Lamb, Charles: English essayist (1775–1834). Lamb is the unchallenged master of the English familiar essay. The success of this literary type depends on the reader's interest in the author as a person, for only such an interest can give the author's revelation of his tastes and prejudices any significance. Lamb's winning character, which made him the best beloved of the Romantics, and the heroism of his life give his essays, in which he is mirrored, a special charm, interest, and poignancy. Himself confined to an insane asylum for six weeks after a disappointment in love, he was throughout his life a willing nurse to his sister, who in one of her recurrent fits of insanity had murdered their mother. Nevertheless, Lamb faced life with resolute cheerfulness. Never affluent, he worked as a bookkeeper for the East India Company until he was retired after 33 years. Meanwhile he acquired that culture which attracted to him the principal figures of the day: *Wordsworth, *Coleridge, *Hazlitt, *De Quincey, Southey, Godwin.

Lamb had "obtruded upon the public," to use his own phrase, sundry writings to eke out his meager income, but his first popular success was a book for children, *Tales from Shakespeare* (1807), written with his sister's collaboration. His reputation as a critic was established the next year by his anthology, *Specimens of English Dramatic Poets Who Lived About the Time of Shakespeare* (1808); Lamb's appreciative comments on each excerpt were a major influence in the so-called Elizabethan Revival.

His greatness rests on the essays signed "Elia," which he contributed to the *London Magazine* (1820–25). Because his personality, his sense of form, and his interest in details transmuted any theme into a familiar essay and a work of art, all life was material for his essays. Although he often plays with "caressing littleness," what he tells us has an enduring reality: school days (*Christ's Hospital Five and Thirty Years Ago*); sprightly fantasy (*A Dissertation on Roast Pig*); nostalgic reverie (*Dream Children*); gentle irony (*Poor Relations*); his retirement (*The Superannuated Man*). The style is incisive or leisurely. Even when he affects the grand manner he does so with a gentle humor which rescues his work from sentimentality. Through the essays run warm and wide human sympathies, delicate whimsey and tenderness, and beneath the blithe surface something of the pathos which made up Lamb's life and personality. His "illumination of the lesser arts of life and the graces of character" is the quintessence of the familiar essay.

Lao Tzu: Chinese founder of Taoism (probably 3d century B.C.). Lao Tzu is credited with the authorship of the *Tao Tê Ching* (*Way of Life*) and is traditionally supposed to have been a contemporary of *Confucius. Modern scholarship, however, places him about three centuries later. His book is a short (5,000-word) description of the Way or Road of Life or Virtue. This involves a mystical and often paradoxical description of the moral universe: "Tao does not contend, yet it surely wins the victory; it does not speak, yet it surely responds." Tao is the illimitable unity which includes all things in their proper relationship, and happiness lies in and through Tao. Lao Tzu taught that the way to attain concord with this principle was by a stoical placidity in facing the temptations and hardships of the world, and an indifference to its rights and wrongs; he urged the pleasure and virtue of simple life, contemplating the harmony of nature and striving to become a part of that harmony. "Return love for hatred" was his principle for ethical, human conduct. It seems probable that a great deal of his teaching is actually intended as political advice.

La Rochefoucauld, Duke François de: French writer (1613–80). After an adventurous youth, La Rochefoucauld, who belonged to the highest French nobility, dabbled in political intrigue at court, became sentimentally attached to a succession of mistresses famous in their own right, and spent a disillusioned old age in the distinguished society of the *salons*, which he himself had helped create. His *Memoirs* (1662) records his failures in the world of action, especially his inability to destroy the power of Richelieu over the French Queen. The second book responsible for his fame is the *Maxims* (1664), a collection of over five hundred penetrating and pithy observations, cynical about man's capacities, skeptical of man's motives, remorselessly critical of his self-love: "Self-interest is the driving force of human conduct." "Love of justice is only the fear of experiencing injustice." "Virtue could not go so far if Vanity did not bear it company." "If we succeed in overcoming our passions, it is more because they are weak than because we are strong." As much as to their thought, the maxims owe their popularity to the compression and precision of their expression. These epigrams, polished and revised over the years with each succeeding edition, present the essence of sophisticated disillusionment. In exposing hidden and subconscious motivations, they anticipated the attitudes of modern psychiatry.

Lawrence, D(avid) H(erbert): English novelist (1885–1930). Lawrence's novels, written in the post-Edwardian years, helped the English world to break away from Victorian morality and taboos of class. A writer of passion, he represented a romantic strain in the novel; his works belong to the prophetic order rather than the aesthetic; his novels are formless when compared with those of certain of his fellow craftsmen, but they espouse with tenacity and temperament emotional and sexual openness, the primacy of man's primitive impulses, the benignity of the natural life. Lawrence preached the "natural man" long after *Rousseau and in a post-world-war society. There is great strength of feeling in his works, but also the lack of moderation characteristic of prophetic and didactic writers. He was the son of a coal miner. He broke the barrier of class, educated himself by scholarships and teaching. His first book, *The White Peacock* (1911), was followed by one of his most famous in 1913, *Sons and Lovers*. Here he pictured the mining village he knew intimately and those conflicts between the flesh and spirit which arise in all his work. His novel *The Rainbow* (1915) was banned for its overt sexuality, as was *Lady Chatterley's Lover* (1928), which became a *cause célèbre* in championing the use of words often spoken but seldom printed, the four-letter words *Joyce had first used. Tubercular, driven by his intensities of feeling, Lawrence traveled much in search of health and wrote continuously. Among his best-known works are *Women in Love* (1921), *Aaron's Rod* (1922), *Kangaroo* (1923). His travels in the American Southwest and in Mexico yielded *The Plumed Serpent* (1926), with its emphasis on landscape and blood rituals. He wrote an oratorical but vital study of classic American writers: they offered him a prime target for his anti-puritanism. Stronger in feeling than ideas, Lawrence shaped the feelings of an entire generation of "liberated" readers. In his assertion of primitivism, he incorporated violent and destructive elements which affected the post-Lawrentian writing. Thus his famous story of "The Woman Who Rode Away" (1928) celebrates her escape into a freedom that leads ultimately to her death at the hands of primitives in a ritual sacrifice. He remains a controversial figure.

lay (Celtic: *loid*, "song"): a medieval short story (about 1000 lines), in riming couplets of eight-syllable lines, originally intended to be chanted to the accompaniment of a harp or rote (a type of lyre). Written for the same courtly society as were the romances, the lay is a fusion of three elements: a folklore theme, a mysterious Celtic *fairy-tale atmosphere, and the ideology of the romances of *courtly or chivalric love.

Marie de France (*c.* 1165) established the name and the form in a collection of French *Lais*. Her professed sources were tales sung among the Bretons (whence the term "Breton lay"). Her lays may concern weal or woe, joy and mirth, treachery and guile, ribaldry and jest; some are of faëry, but most are about love. In the idyllic sylvan countryside, magic formulas, jealous queens, self-effacing wives, werewolves, and fairy lovers are commonplaces. Some of the lays are connected with Arthurian romance: in *Sir Launfal*, the story of a fairy mistress, Arthur and Gawain appear; *The Honeysuckle* commemorates a tryst of *Tristan and Isolt. Other themes have analogues in classical and Oriental literature. Marie's artistic achievement is noteworthy. She uses a simple unified plot, converging toward a single climactic scene.

The term "Breton lay" was used in 14th-century England for any poem set in Brittany and written in the same spirit as Marie's (*e.g.*, *Chaucer's *Franklin's Tale*). The name later came to mean any "song," and by the 19th century any short historical ballad (*e.g,* *Scott's *Lay of the Last Minstrel*).

Lear, King: see *King Lear*.

Leda: wife of Tyndareus, king of Sparta, and mother of *Castor and Pollux, Helen, and Clytemnestra. She was beloved by *Zeus, who visited her in the form of a swan.

Leopardi, Giacomo: Italian poet (1798–1837). Of noble family, Leopardi was privately educated up to a point and precociously self-educated thereafter. He injured his already frail health by excessive study. A delayed classicist in the romantic era, he wrote with restraint, clarity, and technical perfection. His central thought is profoundly pessimistic: love, knowledge, all that man seeks is essentially illusion, but he must cultivate his illusions if his life is even to seem to have meaning. Leopardi rejected alike the comforts of the ancient theologies of salvation and paradise and the promises of the new religions of science and progress. His only hope lay in love and sympathy which, though illusory and unable to improve the human lot, can make it bearable.

His important works are his poems, collectively entitled *Canti (Songs)*, and a series of prose essays, *Operette morali (Moral Essays*, 1827). The poems and the prose are similar in ideas and effect, and each illuminates the other.

Le Sage, Alain René: a versatile French writer (1668–1747). Novelist, translator, and writer of plays and comic operas, Le Sage is famous in world literature for a single work, *Gil Blas*, one of the earliest and most influential novels of manners. This novel and two plays, *Crispin* (1709) and *Turcaret* (1711), which rank with the best comedies in French literature, are the only major works among his 100 titles.

Gil Blas (1715–35) shows the influence of Le Sage's travels in Spain and his thorough familiarity with Spanish literature. Indeed, Le Sage's indebtedness to the characterization, setting, plot organization, and moral tone of the Spanish *picaresque novel was so great as to raise charges of plagiarism. Yet his treatment has a certain originality. The hero is a likable rascal, seeking his fortune in many places and attaching himself to a variety of characters from a gang of robbers to the crown prince. The plot structure is a pseudoautobiography, rambling and episodic, in a journey framework relying heavily on chance and coincidence, but rapid progression from incident to incident keeps interest at a high level. Numerous characters who wander in and out—samples of the "average sensual man"—vary only in degree and kind of ignobility, dishonesty, and moral turpitude. They tell their own histories up to the time of their meeting with Gil Blas, and the result is a conglomeration of lesser tales set into the episodic main structure. The Spanish tradition is used to satirize French people and French social conditions. Every class is realistically represented, and Le Sage's irony plays over his many illustrations of human weakness.

The influence of Le Sage is marked on the English novelists *Fielding, Smollett, and *Sterne.

Lessing, Gotthold Ephraim: German dramatist and critic (1729–81). Lessing is perhaps best known as the author of *Laocoön* (1766) and *Nathan the Wise* (1779). The first is an essay which attempts to define certain laws of aesthetic perception based on a comparative study of poetry and the visual arts. The second is a play which deals with religious tolerance and contains Lessing's religious philosophy. More generally, Lessing is considered as one of the outstanding literary critics of all time. Indeed, he has been rated as second only to *Aristotle as a critic of the drama, a judgment based on the dramatic notes and theories found mainly in the *Hamburg Dramaturgy*, which he wrote in connection with his position as critic and dramatist with the Hamburg National Theater during 1768 and 1769.

The original purpose and nature of the weekly dramatic notes which Lessing published at Hamburg was to form "a critical index of all the plays performed, and to accompany every step made by the art of either the poet or the actor." Using the *Poetics* of Aristotle as his point of departure, he amplifies, explains, and illustrates the classic theories as they are upheld or violated in selected works of the German, English, French, and Spanish dramatists of all periods, but primarily of his own. As a result of the *Dramaturgy*, the prestige of the very influential French *Neo-Classicism was pretty well demolished in Germany; and the Germans were admonished and encouraged to produce the good national drama of which Lessing felt they were capable. He must be given credit for causing a definite break with the old existing dramatic forms and giving impetus to a new drama characterized by both romanticism and reason.

In addition to his aesthetic and dramatic criticism, Lessing wrote several plays which have become classics of their kind in German dramatic literature. Of these, *Miss Sara Sampson* (1755) is historically important as the first German tragedy of middle-class life as well as the first German prose drama of any distinction. Lessing anticipates here the modern trend that considers man the proper domain of drama—man with his passions, weaknesses, and virtues, regardless of his position in life. The prose is as effective and striking an innovation as the tragic treatment of bourgeois life.

Minna von Barnhelm (1767) deals with the love of a rich girl and an impoverished Prussian officer. The play is Lessing's finest comedy and also the best German comedy of the era.

His last play, *Emilia Galotti* (1772), and the philosophical drama *Nathan the Wise* are generally agreed to be his most serious works. *Emilia Galotti*, coming 17 years after *Miss Sara Sampson*, shows a more experienced dramatist and writer of tragedy. Taking as its idea *Livy's story of Virginius' killing his daughter to protect her chastity, *Emilia Galotti* presents a classical theme in a modern setting and from a modern point of view. Emilia and her father are convincing in meeting the situation in which they are placed, and they thus support Lessing's belief that ordinary persons may well become tragic heroes and heroines. While not so obviously a middle-class tragedy as *Miss Sara Sampson*, *Emilia Galotti* strengthens Lessing's revolutionary contribution to the national dramatic literature that he felt his country could produce.

Outside Germany the most widely known of Lessing's creative works is *Nathan the Wise*, his only play in *blank verse. This five-act drama is laid in Jerusalem, with Nathan (a Jew), the Sultan (a Mohammedan), and a young Knight Templar as the three focal characters through whose conflict and consequent action Lessing expresses his plea for religious tolerance and universal love. The gist of this concept is presented through a parable which Nathan recounts when the Sultan, in a ruse to extort money from Nathan, demands that he tell him which of the three religions—Mohammedanism, Judaism, Christianity—is the true one. The wise Nathan tells the story of three rings, indistinguishable from each other, but one of them believed to have the power of bringing the grace of God and man to a wearer who believes in its virtue. It was impossible to tell which of the rings was the true one unless the conduct of its wearer showed its genuineness. In the same way, it is impossible to name the one true religion, and a man who wants to prove the truth of his religion will do best to try to prove it by his own life. All men of all religions must "Each with his might vie with the rest to bring/ Into the light the virtue of the jewel/His finger wears."

Lethe: a river of the Underworld, whose waters bring forgetfulness to all who drink them.

Lewis, Sinclair: American novelist (1885–1951). Lewis was the first American writer to be awarded a Nobel prize (1930). His reputation rests on his early novels— *Main Street* (1920), a grim satirical study of a small midwestern town; *Gopher Prairie* (1920); *Babbitt* (1922), whose hero's name added two new words, *Babbitt, Babbittry*, to the language. *Arrowsmith* (1925) concerns the medical profession; *Elmer Gantry* (1927), a midwestern religious zealot; *Dodsworth* (1929), the American business man; *It Can't Happen Here* (1935), the advent of fascism.

Lincoln, Abraham: American statesman and president (1809–65). Though Lincoln's collected writings are more extensive than those of *Shakespeare, the great majority of his production was necessarily ephemeral speeches and documents interesting only to students of political history. A few of his works, however—the *Springfield*

Address, the *Second Inaugural Address*, and especially the *Gettysburg Address*—have taken their place among the common property of mankind.

Lincoln was almost entirely self-educated, and his literary models were his early reading: Bunyan's **Pilgrim's Progress*, **Defoe's Robinson Crusoe*, **Aesop's Fables*, and, above all, the King James **Bible*. To these were added a special sort of frontier homeliness and raciness acquired around the stoves of country stores and in the rough and tumble of political campaigning.

Lincoln came early to regard his mission as the defense and extension of human freedom. After his series of debates with Douglas he commented to a friend: "I believe I have made some marks which will tell for the cause of civil liberty long after I am gone." During the war years he regarded the Civil War as a test—for all the world to see—of the possibilities of freedom's survival.

In November 1863 (the year of his *Emancipation Proclamation*), he spoke at Gettysburg National Cemetery. He was invited to speak as an afterthought, but the two-hour effort of the main orator of the occasion is forgotten, while Lincoln's few sentences are immortal. The *Gettysburg Address* answers those who say that Lincoln used no rhetorical devices. For all its difference from conventional rhetoric, it shows most skillful alliteration, **assonance, climax, balance, and antithesis. More important, of course, is the march of ideas in the simplest but best words to the solemn cadence. In this speech Lincoln's simple diction, broad humanity, and humble consciousness of his historical mission combine to produce his masterpiece.

Li Po: China's most famous lyric poet (A.D. 701–62). Like the French **Villon, Li Po was a romantic and witty vagabond, in love with wine, women, song, and good fellowship. Apparently he spent most of his life in an unsuccessful pursuit of public office; but the joys of worldly pleasures, a gentle melancholy over their transience, and a mystic sense of communion with nature form the themes of his exquisite lyrics. "By building a dam one may stop the flow of the Yellow River/But who can assuage the grief of the heart when it snows and the wind blows?" Even his death is shrouded in a legend which provides a fitting finale to a life drunk with wine and poetry. One night, it is said, while bibulously reciting verses to the moon, he attempted to grasp its reflection in the Yellow River and was drowned, and legend continues that he was then carried to the world of the immortals on the back of a dolphin.

Livy: Roman historian (59 B.C.–A.D. 17). Titus Livius was born at Padua in northern Italy, but spent much of his active life in Rome, where he was recognized as the foremost prose writer of the time. In his history Livy told the whole story of the Roman people from the foundation of the City to its culmination under *Augustus as the capital of the civilized world. He developed his theme on a grand scale in 142 books, of which 35 remain: Books I–X, the beginning to the defeat of the Samnites in 293 B.C., and XXI–XLV, the war with Hannibal and the conquest of Macedonia. Livy wrote in a rich and flowering style, embellished with the highest literary art and vivified by magnificent speeches put into the mouths of leading men. But he was interested less in preserving an exact record of the past than in providing for the moral regeneration of his own time, a fact which explains his uncritical use of earlier historians and the neglect of documentary evidence so often urged against him. Livy felt that the power and wealth of the Empire had brought a decline in civic virtue to the Roman people. He wished to revive their patriotism by composing a moving account of their rise to greatness, and to set before them living examples of the type of conduct on which a continuance of that greatness must be based. This aim Livy fulfilled. His *Ab urbe condita* or *From the City's Foundation* is a companion piece to *Vergil's *Aeneid* and a glorification of early Rome that has captured the imagination of all later generations.

Locke, John: English philosopher (1632–1704). Locke's fundamental ideas are found in two treatises, one dealing with empiricism as the basis of man's knowledge and the

412

other with political liberalism as the foundation of man's life in society.

The Essay Concerning Human Understanding (1690) examines the nature of knowledge and the basis for judging truth. At birth, said Locke, the mind is like a "white paper," a *tabula rasa* (Latin, "a scraped tablet") which through sensations acquires ideas. All knowledge, with the possible exception of logic and mathematics, is thus derived from experience. Locke's lucidity of style and avoidance of technical philosophical terminology helped to make this *Essay* the most widely read philosophical book of its generation.

Politically, Locke was a liberal who recognized that government is founded on compromise and moderation. The *Essay Concerning the True Original Extent and End of Civil Government* (his second treatise on this subject, 1690), written during the bloodless Revolution of 1688, is a milestone in the defense of representative democracy and parliamentary rule. Locke's purpose is "to make good the title [of the new king] in the consent of the people and to justify to the world the people of England, whose love of their just and natural rights . . . saved the nation." To prove his point, Locke traces man's transition from a "state of nature" to that of political society. All men, Locke holds, were by the "law of nature" born free and equal, entitled by right to life, liberty, and property, and under a moral obligation to respect these rights in others. By social contract, they delegated the function of administering this "law of nature" to the government; hence no government has "a right to obedience from a people who have not freely consented to it." Locke's stress on human liberty and on the separation of governmental powers and a system of checks and balances, his respect for man's "reason," and his lack of dogmatism *(Letters of Toleration)* greatly affected *Voltaire, *Rousseau, and *Jefferson. Not only Locke's doctrines but even his phrases are embedded in the *Declaration of Independence* and the United States *Constitution*.

London, Jack: American novelist and short-story writer (1876–1916). London is significant for his combination of primitivism (really quite idealized and false to actual nature) and socialism (a quite crude version). His wide travels as a common sailor and memories of Alaska during the Klondike gold rush (1897) supplied his narrative frames; notions emanating from *Nietzsche, *Marx, *Darwin's "survival of the fittest" (which he misunderstood), and *naturalism provided the intellectual substance. *The Son of the Wolf* (short stories, 1900), *The Call of the Wild* (1903), *White Fang* (1906) are set in the Far North. His socialistic ideas appear in *The People of the Abyss* (1903), which examines slum conditions in London, and in *The Iron Heel* (1907), which describes a fascist revolution and a Utopia. His semi-autobiographical *Martin Eden* (1909) pictured his early years of poverty, and *John Barleycorn* (1913), his "alcoholic memories." *South Sea Tales* (1911) was inspired by his voyages and a trip to Africa. His heroes—wolves, dogs, prospectors, prize fighters, sailors—all romanticized, have the same instincts. They win brutal fights, thus rise to eminence by battle, and "eventually go down under the rush of stronger enemies." Partly a reaction against the sentimentalism and "decadent squeamishness" of the Victorians, partly a development from the romanticized naturalism of Frank Norris, London's primitivism is rather a picture of man as super-brute—a powerful animal but cruel, violent, and raw; it has no relation to actual primitive societies. In *The Call of the Wild* only the Eskimo dog survives, to become a super-hound leader of a pack of wild wolves. Although London's radicalism is as näively unrealistic as his primitive superman, he was dubbed "The Prophet of the Last Frontier" and enjoyed an extraordinary vogue.

Longfellow, Henry Wadsworth: American poet and translator (1807–82). Longfellow spent most of his life as a professor of modern foreign languages (one of the first in an American university), first at Bowdoin and then at Harvard. He was extremely active as a popularizer of foreign literatures, particularly by means of his extensive translations. A huge collection of these, *Poets and Poetry of Europe*, appeared in 1845. Later, a translation of The *Divine Comedy (1867–70) gave a new impulse to the study of *Dante in America. It also inspired some sonnets which are among Longfellow's best work.

Longfellow is the most widely popular poet that America has produced, and though literary critics today place little value on The Village Blacksmith, The Wreck of the Hesperus, and The Children's Hour, these poems and others with the same simple and sentimental quality continue to be widely read and loved. In his longer narrative poems Longfellow applied some of the forms and techniques of European literature to themes from the history and legends of his own country. Thus Evangeline (1847) is inspired by the Hermann and Dorothea of *Goethe, and The Song of Hiawatha (1855) is designed to be a *Kalevala of the American Indian. The popularity of these poems was enormous: few poems have caught on like Paul Revere's Ride (1861), and The Courtship of Miles Standish (1858) sold ten thousand copies in a single day. Longfellow himself was a descendant of John Alden.

Longfellow's faults are obvious enough. He is imitative, moralizing, and inclined to sentimentality. His versification is smooth and effortless to the point of weariness, and his ideas float decoratively on the surface of things. His great virtue is his humility. His poems seldom pretend to be more than they are—sincere morality pleasantly expressed, good tales agreeably versified, and the everyday joys and sorrows of human life lovingly ornamented. Longfellow's is not the highest type of poetry, but in its own class it is unsurpassed, and has been translated into nearly every European tongue.

Longinus: the name traditionally given to the author of On the Sublime. One of the great works in the history of literary criticism, the fragmentary Greek treatise On the Sublime has been attributed for so many years to Cassius Longinus, a scholar of the 3d century A.D., that it will probably continue to be identified with his name, though it seems to have been composed, not by him, but by an unknown author who lived much earlier, probably in the 1st century A.D. Whoever the author may have been, his purpose in writing the essay was to define sublimity or *excellence of language*, to distinguish its essential elements, and to trace its sources, whether found in native ability or in training. For sublimity is impossible without grandeur of thought and intensity of feeling, both of which depend largely on innate qualities. But it also requires noble diction, skillful composition, and an appropriate use of rhetorical figures, which must be learned. Even genius, unless forewarned, is prone to fall into bombast, frigidity, or similar error, through an excessive desire for novelty, a fact which can easily be verified by examining the mistakes of the greater writers. In evaluating literature, Longinus is never deceived by what seems sublime but is not, and he exposes faults when he finds them. He is, however, enthusiastic for all that is best in literature, and he is able to impart his enthusiasm to others. Moreover he fills his work with apt illustrations, which add greatly to the pleasure to be derived from reading it. Longinus is the first pagan to quote from the Old Testament, and it is to his treatise that we owe the preservation of *Sappho's famous *Ode to Anactoria*.

Longus: author of a Greek romance (probably 3d century A.D.). Nothing is known of Longus except what can be gathered from a pastoral romance called *Daphnis and Chloe* attributed to him. This work would make it seem probable that he was a sophist or rhetorician and that in writing a novel with a bucolic setting he was attempting something new. The prologue states that a picture he had seen while hunting on Lesbos inspired the tale, but there is no way to decide whether or not Longus was a native of that island.

Daphnis and Chloe is a story of the awakening of passionate love in two foundlings who were exposed by their parents as infants and reared together in innocence by shepherds living not far from Mitylene. Unlike most of the heroes and heroines of the early romances, Daphnis and Chloe are not puppets, and the chief interest of the tale lies in the description it gives of the development of their passion. But there is also much appreciation of the sights and sounds of the country, in which they are

416

determined to live as rustics, even after their noble birth has been discovered. For the story is thoroughly pastoral in tone, though it does not dispense altogether with the adventures usual in Greek romances. War and piracy are there, as well as abduction, but they are kept subordinate, and without a change of scene, a unique feature of the composition.

Daphnis and Chloe is the best of the ancient Greek romances. Like the others, it was influenced, no doubt, by the type of theme developed in the schools of rhetoric under the Roman Empire, but its atmosphere is reminiscent of *Theocritus, and some of its characters go back apparently to New Comedy (see *Menander).

Lope de Vega: see *Vega Carpio, Lope de.

Lorca: see *García Lorca.

Lowell, Robert: American poet (1917–77). Lowell attracted wide attention with his volume of verse *Lord Weary's Castle* (1946), which won him the Pulitzer prize in 1947. A great-grandson of James Russell Lowell, and interconnected with many rooted New England families, Lowell preferred New York to Boston, and fashioned a poetry of great power and virtuosity. Perhaps his most popular work is *Life Studies* (1959), in which he helped launch, in poetry and in prose, what has come to be called the "confessional" mode in contemporary poetry—critical self-examination and reminiscence restated in visionary poetic terms. He also wrote a series of poetic plays, notably *The Old Glory* (1965). In his earlier work Lowell was staunchly Catholic but he moved from this into a modern radicalism and activism in politics. His other works include *Land of Darkness* (1944), *The Mills of the Kavanaughs* (1951), *Imitations* (1961), and *For the Union Dead* (1964).

Lucan: Roman epic poet (A.D. 39–65). Marcus Annaeus Lucanus, a public official and member of Nero's court, was forbidden to publish, possibly because of the emperor's jealousy. He joined a conspiracy and, when it was discovered, was forced to commit suicide. Lucan's only surviving work is an unfinished epic called both *Pharsalia* and *The Civil War (De bello civili)*. The latter title is preferable, since the poem deals with the whole war between Pompey and Caesar and the Battle of Pharsalia is merely the central episode. Lucan's epic was highly regarded throughout the *Middle Ages and the *Renaissance. It is the most independent of the later Roman epics, both in being less imitative of *Vergil and in rejecting the traditional supernatural "machinery" of the epic. Lucan shows considerable power as a narrative poet, though his rhetoric is often too exuberant and his descriptions too extensive for modern taste.

Lucian: Greek rhetorician and satirist (*c.* A.D. 120–*c.* 190). Lucian was born in Syria, possibly of Semitic parents. As soon as his elementary education was over, he was apprenticed to his uncle, a stonecutter, but the boy had no talent for the trade and turned to the study of rhetoric. It is not known how he supported himself, but he mastered the Greek language, learned the principles of oratory and law, and became an advocate, perhaps at Antioch. Lucian's work as counsel proved distasteful to him, however, and he set out as a public lecturer, traveling as far as Gaul. Although he gained both wealth and fame, he returned to the East in middle life and settled at Athens, where he devoted himself to literature until his appointment at an advanced age to a government post in Egypt, where presumably he died.

Lucian's chief gifts as a writer are wit and humor, and his leading passion is an intense hatred of fraud. When he examined the work of the rhetoricians, he was compelled to classify it as vanity, and, when he turned to the historians, he found them presenting the false and even the absurd as true. Nor were the philosophers better. They could not agree with one another concerning the meaning of life, and whatever school they adhered to, they failed to make their lives conform to the principles they taught. In religion also confusion reigned supreme. The state punished its citizens for committing immoral acts, yet these same acts were attributed to the gods it compelled them to worship, and in addition believers were everywhere a prey to impostors like Alexander of Abonuteichos, whose oracle duped the whole Empire. Nor were the newer faiths freer of fraud. Peregrinus gulled the Christians for profit, pretending to be one of them when he was not.

Loving the truth but finding himself surrounded by falsehood, Lucian began to attack hypocrisy wherever he found it. As a vehicle for his satire, he sometimes composed biography, as in *The Death of Peregrinus*, an interesting piece for the information it contains on ancient Christianity, and sometimes romance, as in the *True History*, a parody of the travelers' tales told by the Greek historians. This is a fantastic story, describing a voyage to the kingdom of the Moon, the Islands of the Blest, and other impossible places, and recording with an air of complete truthfulness the wonders seen and heard there. It is Lucian's most famous narrative and the ultimate inspiration of such modern works as *Gulliver's Travels* and the adventure stories of Jules Verne.

But though Lucian was skillful in narrative, he did his finest work in the satirical dialogue, a form going back to *Plato but infused with the spirit of *Aristophanes. Among the best of his pieces of this type are the *Dialogues of the Courtesans*, reminiscent of Greek New Comedy (see *Menander); the *Dialogues of the Gods*, burlesquing the absurdities and immoralities attributed to the divinities in Greek mythology; the *Sale of Creeds*, directed against the philosophers; and the *Dialogues of the Dead*. These last take as their theme the vanity of all things human. Their scene is laid in the Underworld, and their purpose is to reveal, in its unearthly gloom, all the shams and stupidities of life. Here Lucian's ridicule is no longer confined to the philosopher, the religionist, and other familiar butts. All who put their trust in the glory of this world are held up to scorn alike. Beauty, pleasure, and wealth are only for a moment; when death comes, they help us no longer, for then we are nothing except bones and skulls. In the *Dialogues of the Dead* Lucian's racy humor is at its best; his keen and delicate satire and his unsparing mockery permeate the whole. The 30 dialogues that form the series are his acknowledged masterpieces, and, although their charm has inspired many imitators, in this type of writing he is unsurpassed.

Lucretius: Roman philosophical poet (*c.* 94–*c.* 55 B.C.). Although he is one of Rome's very greatest poets, almost nothing is known of Titus Lucretius Carus. It seems probable that he belonged to the aristocracy, but this view has been challenged. It is usually thought that he lived in Rome, but a recent theory attempts to place him near Naples. His long philosophic poem *On the Nature of Things (De rerum natura)* proves his devotion to his master *Epicurus, but tells us little about himself. The condition in which the poem has reached us indicates that it was unfinished when he died. The few brief notices from antiquity concerning Lucretius are confusing and inconsistent and have given rise to endless conjecture and debate. But they enable us to fix his dates within narrow limits, and they inform us that *Cicero had something to do with editing the poem.

Lucretius' personality is as little understood as his life history. St. *Jerome (*c.* A.D. 348–420) notes in his *Chronicle* that Lucretius was driven insane by a love philter, wrote his poem in his lucid intervals, and finally committed suicide. It is generally agreed that Jerome's entry, as it stands, is jumbled, but there is no agreement as to how much of it, if any, is reliable. Scholars have advanced all sorts of theories and hypotheses, none of them capable of being clearly proved or disproved. Since *On the Nature of Things* is universally admitted to be one of the world's great poems, perhaps it is as well we are forced to focus our attention on it rather than on its author.

Luther, Martin: German religious leader (1483–1546). After a good education, Luther became a monk and a professor of biblical exegesis. A man of independent mind, he attacked the sale of indulgences by which money was being raised for the construction of St. Peter's in Rome; and in 1517 he nailed to a church door in Wittenberg 95 "theses" (propositions which he was prepared to defend against all comers) against the sale and effectiveness of indulgences. This act, intended to cause only reform, led to an open break with the Church. Luther was excommunicated, and his works were burned, in 1520; he retorted by holding his own public ceremony and burning the bull of excommunication. At the Diet of Worms (1521) he refused an opportunity to recant: "Here I stand. I cannot do otherwise. So help me God, Amen." After this he went into hiding and began work on his translation of the *Bible. In 1530 he published the Augsburg Confession, which stated his doctrines and called for the establishment of an independent church. Luther found salvation in faith alone, without the need for sacraments or intermediaries. He denied the need for celibacy of the clergy (he married a former nun in 1525) and insisted on popular education. His followers' protests against an imperial order designed to crush him gave them the name Protestants.

Luther's religious battles were largely fought with the pen. Most of his many controversial pamphlets are now of interest only to specialists, in spite of the power of their homely and racy idiom. But the translation of the Bible was a great and permanent achievement. Abandoning the Vulgate of the Church, Luther translated the New Testament from the original Greek (1522) and the Old Testament from the original Hebrew (1523–34). The influence of this work is incalculable. It went through 377 editions in Luther's own lifetime, and it remains the standard Protestant version in German, even more fundamental to the German language than the King James version is to English. It is noted for its forceful, idiomatic language, its homely sayings, and its cadenced rhythms. Three and a half centuries later *Nietzsche could still call it "the masterpiece of German prose."

Luther's musical ability and his insistence on congregational participation in the service led him to compose and adapt a large number of hymns, the most famous being *A Mighty Fortress Is Our God (Ein' feste Burg ist unser Gott)*. The *Table-Talk (Tischreden)*, containing reports by Luther's disciples of his casual conversations, is both a valuable historical source and an interesting personal document showing his irascibility, his humanity, and his absolute sincerity.

lyric: a short poem originally intended to be sung (Greek, "pertaining to the lyre"); hence any short poem whose basic qualities are those of a song. This usually implies a poem having a highly organized pattern of sound and producing the impression of an outpouring of intense personal feeling. As now used, the term does not imply that a poem has, or is necessarily suitable for, a musical setting. It is a broadly inclusive term used to designate practically any poem which is relatively short and is not a narrative.

Mabinogion, The: the title assigned to a group of 11 medieval Welsh tales in their first English translation (1838–49), made by Lady Charlotte Guest. The name comes from four of the tales, collectively called *The Four Branches of the Mabinogi*, the last word being obscure in origin, but probably referring to a tale about a hero's youth. The earliest manuscripts of these tales date from the 13th and 14th centuries, but the tales were popular much earlier. Their subject matter is a conglomeration of myths and folklore themes widespread in European fiction: allegoric representations of the annual combat of winter and summer (similar to the Pluto-*Persephone story); typical folk-tale characters like the slandered wife and the jealous stepmother; and uncanny folk heroes, like Medyr, who from Cornwall could shoot an arrow through both legs of a wren in Ireland. There are also many touches of grotesque humor and descriptions of a fairylike wonderland.

Several of the stories contain incidents and characters clearly related to Irish heroes and myths or associated with King *Arthur and his court. *Kilhwch and Olwen* is one of the earliest Arthurian romances. *Peredur* is an early version of the legend of Perceval, hero of the

*Holy Grail stories. *The Lady of the Fountain* is very much like a verse romance by *Chrétien de Troyes. *Geraint* inspired in modern times *Tennyson's *Geraint and Enid*.

Machiavelli, Niccolò: Italian statesman and dramatist (1469–1527). Machiavelli has sometimes been called the "first realist in politics." His name has also since the 16th century become a synonym for the most diabolical political cunning. Yet he was in his own day celebrated for patriotism, military skill, historical studies, and popular comedies.

Born in Florence, into a noble family of modest means, Machiavelli evidently received a good education and then went on to enjoy the frivolous life and the exciting new ideas available to a young man-about-town during the golden age of humanism under Lorenzo the Magnificent. But he was also from the first passionately concerned with his city's welfare, and the art of government was his true métier. After Savonarola had been burned, Machiavelli rose in 1498 from a minor clerk in the chancery to be Secretary to the Ten of the Republic of Florence (the committee especially entrusted with war and foreign affairs) and during the next 14 years engaged in activities of increasing responsibility. These experiences conditioned his political thinking. On varied diplomatic missions, he met princes and popes, the Emperor Maximilian, King Louis XII of France, and Cesare Borgia, who became for Machiavelli the model of effective statecraft. Although Florence was itself a republic, it was greedy for commerce; and as its representative Machiavelli was chiefly responsible for the war which resulted in Pisa's surrender to Florence. He came face to face also with the unscrupulous maneuvers of power politics by despots jockeying for control of Florence and indeed all Italy, which he recognized as the unwilling prize of the duel between two strongly national states, France and Spain. Both the commercial rivalry which kept the Italian cities from uniting politically and the papal policy unwittingly played into the hands of these foreign states.

Meanwhile the Republic of Florence itself had been

overthrown; and with the return of the Medici (1512), Machiavelli was dismissed. Desirous as he was of serving his city, he could never understand why the Medici distrusted him and did not utilize his talents; *The Prince* was an attempt to ingratiate himself with the Medici. When they in turn were expelled some 15 years later, the new Republic was similarly suspicious and refused to employ him.

In 1513 Machiavelli had been suspected of conspiracy against Florence and banished from the city for one year. Ironically, it is to this enforced leisure that we are indebted for his more important writings. The civil servant and military organizer became a man of letters almost in spite of himself. He reread the ancient historians and in true humanistic spirit illuminated their meaning and his own judgment of human affairs by the mutual reaction of one upon the other. The two political treatises which he wrote at this time reveal this new approach to the science of statecraft. The *Discourses on Livy* was planned as a comprehensive commentary on the first ten books of *Livy's History of Rome.* Actually it is an unfinished analysis of the growth of Roman republicanism. Its themes are the superiority of a democratic republic above other political forms, the ultimate reliance of even a despot upon mass consent, and finally the importance of leadership, military power, a national religion, and the will for unity and survival in explaining the rise and fall of civilizations. Like *Dante and *Petrarch, Machiavelli saw the model of Italian glory in Ancient Rome, but for him it was not imperial but republican Rome. "In every word and thought" of this book, wrote Vittorio *Alfieri, "Machiavelli breathes liberty, justice, prudence, truth, and the most lofty spirit."

*The *Prince (Il Principe,* 1513), the other political volume composed during this period and likewise a study of the mechanics of government, gives a drastically different impression from the *Discourses.* It is a plea for a strong centralized government, under the rule of a single monarch, but, in view of the *Discourses,* Machiavelli must here intend this merely as a first step toward the establishment of a sound republic. It seems likely that about this time Machiavelli also wrote *Mandragola (The*

Mandrake), a five-act play which turned out to be one of the most distinguished comedies of the Italian Renaissance. Reminiscent of classical comedy in characters, cynically licentious and crisp in dialogue, it is still popular with modern audiences.

In 1520 Machiavelli was commissioned to write a *History of Florence*; by the time it was completed five years later, his Medici patron had been elevated to the papacy as Pope Clement VII. Inspired by Livy's method, Machiavelli rejected the technique of a simple chronicle survey. Instead, he viewed his city as a living organism and attempted to analyze particularly the importance of "civil discords and internal enmities upon foreign relations." That he occasionally did violence to the facts is beyond question. But his approach represented a noteworthy contribution to the art of historiography, for it was thoroughly different from that of the medieval historians who had so often produced mere lists of events, had indiscriminately mingled fact and folklore, and had interpreted all in terms of God's purpose. Machiavelli was the author also of a historical romance, tales, essays, other plays, poetry, and letters, the latter collected and published as the *Familiar Letters*.

Machiavelli reveals many facets of the Renaissance humanist: as a government official he was primarily interested in the worldly prosperity of the Italian cities; as a Florentine gentleman and playwright he viewed life as a source of pleasure and took no interest in asceticism; as a historian he paid no attention to the teachings of the Church Fathers nor to the webs of the scholastics, but sought the solution for political problems not in moral laws but in a study of historical experience and current events.

There is no question of his devotion to his city, and, as he himself said, "his poverty was testimony of his faithfulness and goodness in such service." Of the total body of his writings it has been said that "whoever reads carefully . . . and takes the author to his heart, cannot at the end be other than a fiery enthusiast for liberty and an enlightened lover of every political virtue." If these be the true appraisals, it is the final irony that *The Prince* should seem the embodiment of wicked cynicism and that because of it Machiavelli's name should have become an adjective for wily unscrupulousness. Doubly ironic is this popular judgment, since Machiavelli thought that he could restore intellectual freedom, political independence, and integrity to Italy by summarizing his observations and describing with complete candor not the way that men ought to live but the way they do actually behave.

Macpherson, James: see *Ossianic Poems.

Madame Bovary: a novel by *Flaubert (1857). This work, probably the most famous French novel, marks a milestone in the history of this genre. Its excellences are many. The style is terse and restrained yet poetically vivid, the treatment of the country-town environment detailed and realistic, the personalities lifelike, their emotions intensely communicated despite the author's manner of disinterested objectivity. Finally, all these elements are integrated into the structure of the plot to secure a unity of tone and form seldom found in works of comparable scope.

Madame Bovary is often referred to as the first realistic novel, but Flaubert aimed at truths deeper and more complete than mere copying of the visible world. He was not concerned to copy or to instruct or condemn, but to observe and understand. Emma Bovary's life shows more singleness of motive, more plan and pattern than are usually seen in life or in the novels depicting a "slice of life." Yet she, like the other characters, grows and acts from the environment which produced her motives and plans. Emma thinks it is the social frame which constrains her and against which she rebels. Actually, she is driven by a tension between the matter of fact and the romantic—a tension which exists both in her own nature and in the structure and legends of her society. Flaubert does not ridicule her self-delusion. Objectively, he depicts her gradual downfall, her early reading in romantic novels and sentimental daydreaming, her intrigues with her lovers in her search for the soul-shattering love-experience that the novels had described, the final degradation of an affair deliberately begun in the hope of raising enough money for her creditors. Never have the disastrous results, the ironic cycle of moral and emotional deterioration, of an obsession to live in a state of sentimentalized romantic ecstasy been so pitilessly exposed.

Charles Bovary, Emma's husband, is stupid, yet he is tragic in his uncommon and sincere love for his wife. In ironic contrast is Homais, the shrewd pharmacist, who does a bit of "doctoring" on the sly while discrediting the neighborhood physicians. Although his erudition is chiefly bombast and he is in a way as self-deluding as Emma, he always manages to cover up his mistakes. It is the final irony that this petty symbol of bogus progress is awarded the Legion of Honor. He completes the gallery of portraits illustrating the dullness, vulgarity, and shallowness which Flaubert associated with the middle class.

From such commonplace, not admirable, not individually significant humanity, living literally and symbolically a provincial life, Flaubert was able to create a novel which is persistently interesting. For he saw a universal meaning in this accumulation of unimportant people. Their trivial and tawdry desires are a wry commentary on men's aspirations, and their inability to achieve even these goals is the ironic tragedy of life.

Maenads: *Bacchae.

Maeterlinck, Maurice: Belgian poet and dramatist, 1911 Nobel prizewinner (1862–1949). In his time, he was the foremost adapter to the stage of the ideas of the French *symbolists in their revolt against *naturalism. His symbolist plays include *Pélleas et Mélisande* (1892), most often seen in its operatic form with music by Debussy. *The Blue Bird* (*L'Oiseau Bleu*, 1909) is a fairy play of marked sentimentality with allegorical characters and place-names. His more conventional plays include *Monna Vanna* (1902), a tragedy reminiscent of *Corneille. His early works were gloomy and filled with brooding pessimism, and have a haunted crepuscular quality. He had an affinity with the transcendentalism of *Emerson and wrote an essay on him. His books on *The Life of the Bee* (*La Vie des Abeilles*, 1901)—"a quasi-mystical, quasi-scientific philosophical essay"—and *The*

Intelligence of Flowers (*L'Intelligence des fleurs*, 1907) had considerable vogue.

Magic Mountain, The: a novel by Thomas *Mann (*Der Zauberberg*, 1924). This long novel, considered to be one of the seminal works of our time, is on the surface the simple story of a visit paid by Hans Castorp, a German youth, to his cousin in a tuberculosis sanatorium in Switzerland. Castorp intends to remain about three weeks. He finds himself in the timeless world of the sick and the dying, who are no longer concerned with the everyday life of the outer world. They live in isolation from it and develop a different sense of values and a totally different tempo of life. The human relationships in that world have at times the rarefied quality of its rarefied mountain atmosphere. "There was no time up here to speak of, either long or short."

Castorp stays much longer than his allotted three weeks. He spends seven timeless years at Davos, observing, listening, discovering himself, discovering life, discovering above all the relationships between life and death. Mann had thought first to make the book an ironic picture of decay, showing the effect on the simple hero of "the fascination of death, the triumph of extreme disorder over a life founded upon order and consecrated to it." Amid the tensions of this novel, Castorp takes stock of the whole of life, the process of living.

The personalities Hans encounters, a Russian adventuress, a German doctor, a psychoanalyst, an Italian historian, all give him a sense of worlds beyond his own. While describing the life of the sanatorium—the medical routine, the taking of temperatures, the X-ray room—Mann at the same time is dramatizing the little events of this daily life: the vagaries of temperament among patients and physicians, the gossip, the debates on eternal questions, the heightened sexuality, the frayed nerves.

All through the book the point of view that prevails is that of Hans Castorp and his expanding consciousness. *The Magic Mountain* is a great "developmental" novel but also a classical Germanic novel of an education—an *Erziehungsroman,* or *Bildungsroman.* Some critics have seen in Hans a symbol of Man himself, as a developing and growing creature, capable of self-betterment and self-conquest, capable above all of love. It is worth noting that at the end Hans returns to "flatland" and the responsibilities of his life, but he returns a far wiser and more developed man than he could ever have become without the experience of the sanatorium. He has become mature through suffering, awareness, and confrontation of the real.

Mahabharata, The: the earlier of the two great Sanskrit epics of western India (see *Ramayana*). The "Great War of the Descendants of Bharata" is probably based on a historical fact, a struggle for the possession of the Ganges Valley about 1000 B.C. The kernel of the poem was probably in existence as early as 500 B.C. Gradually it attracted to and incorporated within itself a great variety of episodes, treatises of didactic and religious intent, and other miscellaneous materials. In its present recension in classical Sanskrit, probably achieved between A.D. 350 and 500, it consists of 100,000 couplets and is by far the longest poem that has ever existed—about eight times the combined length of the *Iliad* and *Odyssey*.

The central story concerns a war fought among cousins and rival bands of brothers for the succession to the throne. One of the brothers, Arjuna, wins the lovely Draupadi and brings her back as the wife of all five brothers. When after more than ten years of exile and war the rightful heirs gain the throne, the story ends. The finale is not that conventionally found in western poems—long life and material prosperity—but instead expiation. The victors, renouncing the world and its desires, retire to the sacred Himalayas.

The culture revealed is that of a feudal aristocracy led by contentious kings. Caste is well established and its obligations are taught. As is usual in Sanskrit poetry, the position of women is high, and the women in *The Mahabharata* are most attractive both in appearance and in character.

The main action is interspersed with moral digressions, loosely related episodes, prayers, a variety of religious, ethical, and romantic complications. There are charming narratives, full of moving tenderness and sensibility, like the tale of Savitri, whose religious learning, skill in dialectics, and devotion to her husband rescued him from death (cf. *Alcestis).

The most famous section of the poem is a long dialogue between Arjuna, the hero of the epic, and his charioteer Krishna, an avatar of Vishnu. This section of 18 chapters, often reprinted separately as the *Bhagavat Gita* ("Song of the Blessed Lord"), is the great devotional classic of Hinduism. Written possibly as early as the 2d century B.C., it represents the essence of Hinduism, much as the Sermon on the Mount presents the essence of Christianity. In this long dramatic poem there is introduced into Hindu theology for the first time the character of Krishna, "The Blessed One," who explains the single identity of all messiahs and the need for righteousness. No more climactic moment can be imagined. Arjuna's armies are drawn up on the eve of a decisive battle. Yet he hesitates, horrified before the impending slaughter of his kinsmen and the deadly sin of bloodshed. How shall he, who desires to be righteous, act? A fundamental question is posed: how can a man live without sin yet perform his manifold duties as a social being? Krishna reassures him, first explaining that no one can be killed, since the soul is immortal, and then going on to justify activism and the performance of duty if it is disinterested, without selfish desire, and does not lose sight of ultimate spiritual reality. The learned will not grieve for those who are slain or who live. So are reconciled activity and spirituality through an interpretation of man's attitude and intention. It is "open-eyed disillusionment" without the anguish of desire. This resignation, in a sense, brings peace, and Krishna's ultimate advice is: "Giving up all Dharmas [righteous and unrighteous actions], come unto Me alone for refuge. I shall free thee from all sins; grieve not." Despite some dull passages, as a philosophic poem the *Bhagavat Gita* merits comparison with *Lucretius' *On the Nature of Things*. The compatibility of the *Bhagavat Gita* with Christian philosophy has made it a favorite with Westerners, who have made more than 40 translations.

Maimonides, Moses: Spanish-born Jewish philosopher and Biblical exigete (1135–1204). Known to Jews as "the

Rambam" (acronym for *R*abbi *M*oses *B*en—"the son of"—*M*aimon), he was forced with other Jews to leave Spain in 1160; he finally settled in Cairo, becoming physician to the Sultan. His writings (largely in Arabic, but translated into Hebrew and soon thereafter into Latin) include medical treatises, *responsa* (answers to requests for interpretations of "The Law"), and the most highly esteemed commentaries on the Mishnah (1168, 1180). His *Guide for the Perplexed* (*Dux neutrorum*, 1190) is addressed to those who doubt their faith in a revealed religion. In his philosophic and interpretative works Maimonides sought to show that reason and revelation come together in the knowledge of God, that the rational method of *Aristotle (superb for corporeal earthly life) can be reconciled with the premises of the Judaic revealed religion (dealing with the incorporeal eternal). He argued that the pursuit of truth is a religious duty, that where the *Bible conflicts with reason or logic it is not to be taken literally, but only allegorically. By his subtle application of Greek and Roman medicine, mathematics, logic in interpreting the *Talmud, he has been venerated as the greatest of medieval commentators on the laws of the Old Testament. In several concepts he anticipated and influenced *Thomas Aquinas.

Mallarmé, Stéphane: French poet (1842–98). Mallarmé mastered English in order to be able to read *Poe in the original, and then spent all his active life as an English teacher, first in various provincial lycées and finally in Paris. In the 1800's he began to be known to a small circle of men of letters, and his *salon* became a gathering place for and a potent influence on the younger generation of writers. Mallarmé had begun writing as a "Parnassian" poet and a disciple of *Baudelaire, but he soon outgrew this influence and developed his own highly original manner. This style is based on the assumption that the "music" of words (*i.e.*, their sound plus vague associations) is more significant than their conventional meanings, that the hovering is preferable to the stationary, that suggestion and implication are superior to statement. Mallarmé wrote a number of brief prose articles dealing with his literary ideas, but these are almost as enigmatic—and vaguely stimulating—as many of his poems. During the latter part of his life he experimented with poems in which much of the effect was to depend on the precise use of different spacings, sizes, and fonts of type. Mallarmé became the leading figure of French *symbolism. His influence, both on French and on English and American poets, has been enormous; in fact, it is usually conceded that his influence is greater than his work. Nevertheless, he created a few masterpieces, especially the sensuous and hauntingly vague *Afternoon of a Faun* (*L'Après-midi d'un faune*, 1876), for which Debussy composed a famous orchestral *Prelude.* Other important works include *Posies* (1887), *Album de vers et de prose* (1887), and a set of short prose sketches and essays, *Divagations* (1897).

Malory, Sir Thomas: English writer (1394?–1471). Ironically the author of *Le Morte Darthur* (*The Death of Arthur*, 1469), the book which embodies the quintessence of chivalry and knightly romance, may have spent 20 years of his life in prison for unchivalric crimes. If this Thomas Malory was the author, he was of a good family, a soldier in the Hundred Years' War, knighted (before 1442), and a member of Parliament (1445). Then he entered upon a career of violence which included assaults, the plundering of an abbey, extortion, rape, poaching, and jail breaking. He was in and out of prison pretty steadily after 1451 and died in Newgate Prison.

Malory set down *Morte Darthur*, his only known writing, during his imprisonment. He must have had available English poems and long French prose versions of the Arthurian, *Tristan, and *Holy Grail stories, for these were the sources of his book. And behind them lay the whole of the Arthurian tradition as it had appeared in quasi-historical texts and in the romances of *courtly love. Malory also knew and utilized many popular folk traditions. In 1485 Caxton, the first English printer, published Malory's text, describing it in the colophon as "this noble and joyous book entitled le Morte Darthur," making a considerable number of revisions,

432

and dividing it into books and chapters without giving much thought to the thread of the narrative.

Malory's text contains eight "Tales": King Uther and the Coming of Arthur, King Arthur's War with Rome, Lancelot, Gareth, Tristram (*Tristan), Sangreal (Holy Grail), Knight of the Cart (Lancelot again), and Death of Arthur. The series starts with Arthur's birth and ends with his death and the dispersal of the Knights of the Round Table. Structurally, the book rambles, and there are long stretches in which neither Arthur nor his principal knights appear, as well as repetitious adventures with giants, sorcerers, dwarfs, and damsels in dire peril. Lacking tight structural integration, the prolix episodes are often strung together with such abrupt transitions as: "Here leaves the tale of Sir Lancelot and begins of Sir Percival of Gaul."

Yet the *Morte Darthur* is unified by its theme, the ideals of medieval chivalry: manhood (courage and chivalric adventure), courtesy (kindness and aid to ladies in distress), gentility (justice in fighting only for the right). It has been suggested that Malory was proposing that the strife-torn England of his day should return to the ideals of chivalry. Be that as it may, he certainly loved this legendary world, and he knew a good story when he found it. Also, he could build it up with complexity, depth, and reality. He pictures a whole society disintegrating as its leaders deviate from their ideals. Malory, moreover, disapproved of the adultery inherent in courtly love and felt that the courtly code was wrong when feudal service and love service came in conflict. Lancelot symbolizes this conflict, and his love for Guinevere (his second loyalty) is responsible for the fall of Arthur's court. The immorality of their conduct, its disloyalty to Arthur, and the fact that their love involves Lancelot in an unchivalrous series of murders and fights disrupts the unity of the Round Table. And Gawain becomes involved in another conflict of loyalties, as he is caught between friendship for Lancelot and devotion to the brothers whom Lancelot killed. In sharp contrast to the deeds of derring-do is the haunting elegiac tone of the latter part which, in the final book, raises the death of Arthur to true tragic proportions. Malory's vigorous language and his rhythmical prose style are especially remarkable when we consider that there were hardly any models of artistic English prose which he could have read.

Malory has special importance in the history of the Arthurian legend. He introduced the story of Gareth and Linet. He made Galahad, a knight of unblemished morality, the victor in the quest for the Grail. He gathered together and attempted to unify for the first time the Arthurian tales which had been circulating throughout the *Middle Ages. And he changed the mainspring of the action from pure adventure to emotional conflict. The book was immediately popular and Malory's version became the great wellspring of English Arthurian tradition, inspiring poets to our own day. *Tennyson's reworking of this material in the 19th century was a tremendous popular success, which, at the same time, revived interest in Malory's original "joyous and pleasant histories, noble and renowned acts of humanity, gentleness, chivalry, courtesy, friendliness, hardiness, love, cowardice, murder, hate, virtue, and sin, with many wonderful histories and adventures."

Mann, Thomas: German novelist, short-story writer, and critic (1875–1955). Mann ranks among the master novelists of the 20th century, along with such innovators and craftsmen as *Joyce and *Proust. Less a technician than his contemporaries, Mann added a new dimension to the novel by his searching inquiry into the history and civilization in which he created his fictional world. Mann's subject was Man—and it was as a philosopher in the novel that he approached his subject. In his work he studied man first within his own familiar Germanic setting. In a second stage it was Man as European, in The *Magic Mountain (Der Zauberberg), a novel that probes the mind and culture of the West. And then, with a creativity that continued into his old age, Mann sought in the Joseph series to ponder man's "origin, his essence, his goal." From the narrow national perspective Mann, over the years, moved into wider and deeper waters until he reached the all but unfathomable, the bottomless, past.

Like Proust and Joyce, Thomas Mann was preoccupied with the inner man, but not as an analyst of his stream of consciousness or as a searcher into his memories and sensations. Mann's preoccupation was rather with the mass and weight of culture and ideas, the piling up of centuries of civilization around the individual; and with a rich deliberateness and a narrative skill of unusual sensitivity and smoothness of surface, he created a body of work in which the novelist not only pictures life but adds to his picture a vein of brooding commentary. In all his writing there is, within the frame of imaginative realism, a fundamental belief in man's victory over death and timelessness, a grasp of man's mythic and symbolic imagination. Mann's work is invested with this sense of the human imagination and, as with Joyce, a feeling that man reenacts his own legends.

Like the other great novelists of the 20th century, Mann was preoccupied with Time. Indeed, *The Magic Mountain* brings into striking juxtaposition the clockless time of the sanatorium, where life is an endless succession of days, and the time-sense of the outer, goal-directed world. So, in the Joseph series, Mann pondered the "mathematical sidereal time handed down to us from ages long before" only to point out that, in the era of which he wrote, it nevertheless had an "uneven measure, despite all the objectivity of the Chaldean chronology." For the times of Joseph, as for our own, "the meaning, weight and fullness of earthly time is not everywhere one and the same."

Born in 1875, in the ancient Hanseatic town of Lübeck, Thomas Mann began his career with his long novel, *Buddenbrooks* (1901), in which the national German scene—family, home, the middle-class society—was portrayed with a narrative art that won the novelist immediate success and set him on the road that was to lead to the Nobel prize in 1929. A quarter of a century after *Buddenbrooks* came *The Magic Mountain* (1924) and then between 1933 and 1944 the four-volume *Joseph and His Brothers*. These works are the peaks in Mann's careeer. Between them and around them there are stories long and short, essays on the arts and life, and other novels of varying importance, down to the short fiction, *The Holy Sinner* (*Der Erwählte*, 1951), a masterpiece of storytelling, based on a medieval tale of a great sinner who nevertheless became Pope.

What is striking in the career of Thomas Mann is the

435

fashioning of the great European from the composed and high-serious burgher of *Buddenbrooks*. In his self-conscious examination of the artist's relation to himself and to society, Mann has a kinship with his French contemporary, André *Gide, but unlike Gide Mann has been able to step outside the charmed circle of the confessional. In his early work he reaches back to the realism of *Flaubert and *Maupassant, and in *Buddenbrooks* Mann was essentially contrasting the bleakness of 19th-century middle-class life with the soaring imagination of the artist.

In the years immediately following his first major novel, Mann wrote two novelettes which have come to be considered masterpieces of their kind: *Tonio Kröger* (1903) and *Death in Venice* (1911), a profound and humane study of man as intellect and as sensual being. He also wrote a "comedy in the form of a novel," *Royal Highness*, published in 1909, and was settling down to the story that was to become *The Magic Mountain* when the First World War interrupted his rich vein of creativity.

What followed was a period of self-probing and of analysis of the state of Western society. Mann found it difficult to write fiction in time of war. To this period belongs his book *Reflections of an Unpolitical Man*, much criticized for its conservatism and its espousal of Germanism. The writing of it seems to have acted as a kind of purgative; after it came an ever-growing awareness of the meaning of political democracy. The book can be said to mark the end of what has been called Mann's German period. What emerged thereafter was Mann the European. The novel that symbolized this emergence was *The Magic Mountain*.

The principal character of this novel, a German youth, undergoes a similar transformation, from simplicity and innocence to awareness. Deeply influencing Mann's thinking through these years had been his study of *Goethe and *Tolstoi, even as he was later to assimilate *Freud as well as certain of his English and French contemporaries. A portfolio of Biblical sketches and certain observations he found in Goethe led to his four-part retelling from the modern view—in a kind of historic past-present—of the Old Testament story of Joseph and his brothers. The parts were: *Joseph and His Brothers*

(1934), *The Young Joseph* (1935), *Joseph in Egypt* (1936), and *Joseph the Provider* (1944).

The advent of the Nazi regime led to Thomas Mann's exile from Germany. There had already been a long spiritual preparation. Mann lived in Switzerland and later in the United States, became an American citizen in 1944, and participated in the fight against fascism. After the Joseph series he wrote four short novels, *The Beloved Returns* (*Lotte in Weimar*, 1939), dealing with Goethe; *The Transposed Heads* (1940), an Indian legend; *The Holy Sinner* (1950); and *The Black Swan* (*Die Betrogene*, 1953). In 1947 appeared the last of Mann's major works, *Doctor Faustus*, a biography of an imaginary contemporary German composer, which is simultaneously a retelling of the Faust story, a return to the question of the artist and his role in the world, and a study of Germany's spiritual strength and her spiritual ruin.

After this publication Mann returned to Switzerland and from there issued his last work of fiction, the first volume of *Confessions of Felix Krull, Confidence-Man* (*Bekentnisse des Hochstaplers Felix Krull*, 1954). His selected letters were published in 1970.

Manzoni, Alessandro: Italian novelist and poet (1785–1873). Manzoni spent his early years in Paris, where he came into contact with the beginnings of French romanticism. After his return to Italy (and to Roman Catholicism) he wrote a series of fine lyrics (1812–22) under the title of *Sacred Hymns* (*Inni sacri*). These poems express the general idea that the humanitarian ideals of the French Revolution are contained in their highest and purest form in the Catholic faith. He also wrote several outstanding poems on political events, including *May 5th* (*Il cinque maggio*), on the death of Napoleon, as well as two historical plays, *Il conte di Carmagnola* (1820) and *Adelchi* (1822). These dramas are romantic in that they abandon the classical *unities of time and place. They are not very effective dramatically, but contain excellent lyrical passages.

It is remarkable that Manzoni's literary career covers only 15 of his 88 years. It really ended with the publica-

tion of his masterpiece *The Betrothed (I promessi sposi)*
in 1827. In a way, this historical novel is one of the first
results of *Scott's influence on the Continent, but both
in breadth and in depth it surpasses any of Scott's fiction.
In outline the story is obvious enough: Renzo and Lucia,
a simple pair of country lovers, are engaged at the beginning of the book and—after surmounting a terrible array
of obstacles, including a local high noble's lust for Lucia
(which leads to his forbidding the marriage and ab-
ducting her); criminal charges which force Renzo to flee;
plague, famine, and rioting in Milan; and a full-scale
war—are married at the end. So stated, it sounds like
merely another sentimental tale about the triumph of
true love, but there is far more to the novel than that.
Manzoni is a good historian with a thorough knowledge
of his period (1628–31), and passages like the long accounts of the plague hospitals in Milan are impressive
performances in their own right but gain an added interest from the involvement of his principal characters.
Nothing is oversimplified: though the story is essentially
serious and Manzoni is sympathetic with his characters,
he has a sense of humor and proportion that covers the
whole range from irony and wry wit to occasional scenes
of broad farce. He creates a fine gallery of credibly and
sharply drawn individuals. Characterization and motivation are so deftly handled that the conversion and repentance of Lucia's abductor escapes the danger of being a
melodramatic absurdity and seems both acceptable and
natural in the circumstances. All this adds up to the fact
that *The Betrothed*, though superficially a hybrid between
the typical love and adventure stories, is actually a work
of remarkable complexity and richness. Recognized as a
masterpiece from the time of its first publication (*Goethe
praised it highly), it has been a steady influence on later
historical fiction. Many Italians consider it second only to
*Dante's *Divine Comedy* in their own literature.

The version of the novel now usually read is not the
one that appeared in 1827, but a definitive revised edition
published by Manzoni in 1840. The most important change
is the conversion of the whole novel into Florentine usage,
for Manzoni had become convinced that the Tuscan dialect
of Florence should be the literary language of Italy.

Marie de France: French poetess (late 12th century). Marie lived in England most of her life and may have been the half-sister of King Henry II. She is famous for some 15 *Lais* (see *lay) written before 1189 and dealing with enchantment, chivalrous love, and folk themes. She also wrote *Ysopet*, a collection of 103 *fables.

Mark Twain: pseudonym of Samuel Langhorne Clemens, American humorist and novelist (1835–1910). Brought up in the small town of Hannibal, Missouri, on the Mississippi River, Mark Twain had less than ten years' schooling before he had to shift for himself. He was successively a printer's apprentice, a tramp printer in the East and Middle West, a steamboat pilot on the Mississippi, a half-hearted Confederate soldier (for a few weeks), and a prospector and frontier journalist in Nevada and California. All this knocking about gave him a wide knowledge of humanity. Speaking of his three years as a pilot, he later said that he recognized every well-drawn character in fiction and biography as a man "that I have known before—met him on the river." It also made him thoroughly familiar with frontier humor, especially the tall tale, and, taking the pseudonym "Mark Twain" (the riverman's cry for a sounding of two fathoms), he turned to humorous journalism. Aside from purely local fame, his first real success was the frontier tale *The Celebrated Jumping Frog of Calaveras County* (1865), published in New York. He immediately became famous, did a turn of human-interest reporting in Hawaii, and made it the basis for highly successful lectures. In 1867 he went East and published his first book, a collection of his sketches. From this time on his life was a constant round of lecturing, travel (he crossed the Atlantic 20 times and spent a total of 13 years abroad), successful books and unsuccessful business speculations, with family tragedies and increasing bitterness during his last years.

His second volume, *The Innocents Abroad* (1869), grew out of an assignment to join a tour to Southern Europe and the Near East and write back travel letters to newspapers. The formula is the application of the greenhorn humor of the frontier to both the trivialities and the glories of European civilization. At its best it is highly amusing, but much of the humor is forced, and frequently the greenhorn pose fails simply because the writer's ignorance is genuine rather than assumed. (He never quite rid himself of a rather sophomoric approach to matters about which he had no real knowledge—witness the treatment of the *Middle Ages in *The Prince and the Pauper*, 1882, and *A Connecticut Yankee in King Arthur's Court*, 1889.)

Mark Twain gradually felt his way into his real field, the scenes and life of his early years. *Roughing It* (1871) is a loosely autobiographical account of his stay in the West. In 1875 he wrote, for the *Atlantic Monthly*, a fine series of articles on ante-bellum steamboating on the Mississippi (published, with additions, as *Life on the Mississippi*, 1883). *The Adventures of Tom Sawyer* (1876) drew on his own childhood and was a new thing in boys' books, presenting real rather than model youngsters. It won an immediate and well-deserved popular success. Some years later, Mark Twain set out to write a sequel to it, but instead of a mere sequel produced his unquestioned masterpiece, *Adventures of Huckleberry Finn* (1884). The skill with which the entire story is presented through the eyes and in the idiom of an uneducated backwoods boy is only one of the secrets of the book's success. Its parody is humorous instead of merely smarty, and is richly displayed in the performances of the charlatans who call themselves the King and the Duke. Its humanitarian viewpoints are presented with simple warmth—in the person and situation of the runaway slave Jim, for example—and are thus far more effective and artistic than the shrill preaching of *The Prince and the Pauper*. The book exploits to the full the recent discovery of the literary effectiveness of local color, but without becoming merely quaint or garrulous. *Huckleberry Finn* is one of the great novels of escape: for Huck, from plaguing, genteel censors and a besotted father who terrorizes and yet fascinates him; for Jim, from physical slavery; and for the reader. It is almost incredible that Mark Twain managed to fuse so many different and contradictory elements, characters, and points of view into a simple and unified whole. Ernest

440

*Hemingway has said of it: "All modern American literature comes from one book by Mark Twain called *Huckleberry Finn*. . . . It's the best book we've had."

From the disillusionment and bitterness of Mark Twain's later years came a good deal of fragmentary work and a few good short pieces. Conspicuous among these is a short story, *The Man That Corrupted Hadleyburg*, a slashing attack on the smugness, hypocrisy, and venality of a small town. The nadir of his pessimism is marked by *What Is Man?* (published anonymously, 1906), a philosophic dialogue arguing that man is a mere automaton, mechanically determined. Although he called it his "wicked book," it did not gain the shocked attention that he feared (or courted); it is more important biographically than philosophically. *The Mysterious Stranger* (posthumous, 1916) succeeds imaginatively where *What Is Man?* fails intellectually; it has been compared, with reason, with the philosophical tales of *Voltaire.

Marlowe, Christopher: English dramatist (1564–93). Marlowe's death in a tavern brawl at the age of 29 cut short the career of the most promising Elizabethan dramatist; with 20 years more of life he might well have rivaled *Shakespeare, who, born in the same year as Marlowe, had not achieved the distinction of Marlowe when the latter was stabbed to death. But Marlowe, who in his dramas had created the most aspiring and self-assertive of personalities, suffered for two centuries the irony of oblivion. Not until the 19th century did he achieve critical esteem, and some of the major facts of his still obscure life were discovered only in the 20th century.

Comparative brevity of life and unusualness of life— in dissipation, or controversy, or violence—were shared by Marlowe with most of the "university wits," notably Greene, Peale, and Nash. Except Kyd, the wits were university trained: they all were deeply grounded in classical literature, and they had a passion to write well themselves. In fictional and nonfictional prose, narrative and lyric poetry, they did important work, but their greatest distinction lay in drama, the various forms of which they developed toward the perfection that Shakespeare achieved. And of their drama, that by Marlowe is the most intense and penetrates furthest into human emotions and experience. Technically Marlowe is known for telling a story with a mastery of dramatic form and theatrical effect, and for giving to *blank verse, which in earlier practice had been somewhat stiff and wooden, a new flexibility and sonorousness. Nor would an account of Marlowe's "mighty line" be complete without a reference to the brilliance of his imagery and his control of the secondary suggestive powers of language. Marlowe does occasionally devote his poetry to sound effects; *Tamburlaine* and *The Jew of Malta* contain a certain amount of rhetorical violence which attracts attention primarily to itself. But at its best his poetry is the agent of his insights into human passion and conflict.

Marlowe is usually praised for his grasp of the aspiring temper of the *Renaissance—its ambitiousness, restlessness, and drive. This vast striving of which humanity is capable he does capture—in Tamburlaine's pursuit of military and political power, in Faustus' quest for the ultimate power through knowledge, in the Jew of Malta's aspiration toward wealth as an ultimate end. But what Marlowe dramatizes with equal thoroughness is human limitation; his mighty aspirants find that the price of temporary success is ultimate failure, and the final dramatic note is one of nemesis. From his youth, it might be said, Marlowe distilled the energy and passion of his would-be giants; but from it, also, came a paradoxical maturity of judgment which balanced, against the wonderfully recorded human expansiveness, a sense of the bounds beyond which man cannot go. So his tragedies are more than period pieces. And having, in three plays, measured the weakness of strength, Marlowe turned ironically about and, in *Edward II*, his other major work, chose as protagonist a weakling and presented him very sympathetically. The theme of this versatile performance is friendship; that of *Dido, Queen of Carthage* (of which Nash was co-author) is love.

The plays about Tamburlaine, Faustus, and the Jew of Malta have an epiclike structure, the stage being given over almost entirely to the central character. The one-man form reflects the special talents of the actor Edward Alleyn, of the Lord Admiral's Company, with whom

Marlowe was regularly associated after leaving Cambridge in 1587. The son of a well-to-do Canterbury shoemaker, Marlowe was educated at King's School in Canterbury and at Corpus Christi College, Cambridge. All his professional career fell into the six-year period between 1587 and 1593, in which he got to know various men of letters, and in which, also, there is much mystery. There were rumors of libertinism and atheism, perhaps partly true, perhaps the result of malice or misunderstanding. Although there is marked incompatibility between any genuine atheism and the story of Faustus, a warrant was issued for Marlowe's arrest in 1593; but before action was taken, Marlowe was killed by one Ingram Frisar. It now appears that Marlowe was a government agent, and that this fact may have had some connection both with the warrant for his arrest and with his murder. An inquiry at the time reported that Marlowe and Frisar had quarreled about the tavern bill.

Dido, Queen of Carthage (published 1594) may have been either an early or a late work, it is one of the least successful of his dramas. Part I of *Tamburlaine* was written by 1587, perhaps in Cambridge; Part II in 1588. Drawing upon the "fall of princes" theme which the Renaissance carried over from the *Middle Ages, the play records the rise of a shepherd to world conquest and his eventual death. *The Tragical History of *Dr. Faustus*, probably written about 1589, was not published until 1604; the surviving texts are apparently quite corrupt. In this play the medieval story of the German scholar who sold his soul to the devil for the services of Mephistophilis is given a Renaissance interpretation.

The Jew of Malta, probably written between 1588 and 1590, survives only in an edition of 1633; the text is in very bad condition. Barabas, the title character, is in the tradition of the melodramatic Machiavellian villain who often appears in Elizabethan drama; Marlowe makes some efforts to humanize him, however, and is almost impartial in distributing evil among the other characters. There is a sharp contrast between the poetry of this play, still resonant and sweeping and often violently ranting, and the milder and less striking rhetoric of *Edward II*, written in the early 1590's and produced in 1593. Here, deserting his one-man type of play, Marlowe performs an important service in showing how historical materials may be transmuted into unified drama. *The Massacre at Paris* (probably 1593), however, is less a drama than a series of speeches.

Marlowe is also credited with writing parts of Shakespeare's *Henry VI* series. He translated *Ovid's *Elegies* and Book I of *Lucan's *Pharsalia*, and wrote the fine lyric "Come live with me and be my love" and the influential narrative love poem *Hero and Leander* (completed by Chapman and published 1598). In receiving the stimulus of classical influence, in adapting old themes to new times, and in reaching new creative heights in dramatic and nondramatic poetry, Marlowe was a representative man of letters of the Renaissance. Whatever the missing facts of his life, he was a friend of Raleigh and was referred to with affection and admiration by Nash, Chapman, Drayton, and *Jonson.

Mars: see *Ares.

Martial: Roman writer of *epigrams (*c.* A.D. 40–*c.* 104). Marcus Valerius Martialis was born in northeastern Spain. After an excellent education he came to Rome, A.D. 64, presumably to practice law, but he seems to have had little interest in pleading and he turned to the writing of epigrams. These short poems were originally memorial or dedicatory inscriptions intended to be carved on tombs or attached to votive offerings in temples. But they developed into a recognized branch of literature, and their scope was extended to include any subject capable of brief and polished expression. They had no distinctive form, however, until Martial began to construct them to culminate in a point.

The point is a comment or observation based on the subject of the epigram. It may appear as a direct statement, but commonly it involves an unexpected turn of thought, a play on words, or some rhetorical figure intended to fix attention on it. Whatever its form, however, it is almost always suspended, or kept from the reader until the last words of the poem are reached. As a literary device the point is most effective in satirical writing, and the best examples in Martial come from those of his epigrams which ridicule folly or vice. Such poems are frequent in his work and served as a model for later writers, who concentrated on this type almost to the exclusion of every other. But Martial himself composed epigrams in many different moods. His poems of mourning for children who died young are filled with sympathy and tenderness, and those addressed to his friends reveal a kind and genial spirit.

It is fortunate that Martial turned to contemporary Rome for the subject matter of his epigrams. He knew the Roman people as very few men did and he was able to write about them with realism and detachment. He reflects the life of the city in his poems as in a mirror, and the detailed information he gives forms a most valuable supplement to the general works of the Roman historians. Though some of his epigrams are obscene, and others marked by flattery of the Emperor Domitian, these faults do not touch the great majority of the pieces. And the easy flow of Martial's wit, the felicity of his language, and the variety of his themes make him on the whole one of the most entertaining of writers.

Martial's collected works include over 1500 epigrams, if his early verses are counted. These are gathered together in the *Spectacula*, or *Games*, a series of 33 poems celebrating the opening of the Colosseum, and in the *Xenia* and *Apophoreta*, or *Gifts and Favors*, a collection of 250 distichs describing various types of present.

Marx, (Heinrich) Karl: German political and economic philosopher (1818–83). Marx is one of the major influences on the sociopolitical thinking and literature of our time. Born in Germany, educated for the law, he became a professor of philosophy and then a journalist. His radical publications forced him to emigrate to Paris, to Brussels, and finally (1849) to London, where he found permanent refuge.

Marx applied to economics and history the idea (from Hegel's philosophy) that reality is a fusion of two apparently contradictory principles. He assumed that throughout history there had been two opposing classes, oppressed and oppressors. He called the oppressors of his own day capitalists or bourgeoisie ("capitalists, owners of means of social production, and employers of wage-labor"); the oppressed were the proletariat ("wage-laborers, who must sell their labor to live, not having means of production of their own"). He also analogized his doctrine of two opposing classes to biologic evolution. Ultimately, said Marx, the two classes would synthesize in a classless society. In addition to the philosophic and biologic, Marx offered a "materialist conception of history": the politics, religion, philosophy, and art of any epoch are the outcome of its methods of the production and distribution of goods.

To distinguish it from evolutionary socialism, Marx named his aggressive and international movement "communism." Unlike earlier socialists, he denied man's innate goodness. Social evolution, like all other social phenomena, he attributed only to material and economic forces, of which the most significant was class struggle. Marx held that violence is justified, that the coming of the proletariat to power should not be left to natural evolution but must be furthered by force.

His ideas were worked out in two treatises. *The Communist Manifesto* (1848), written with Friedrich Engels (1820–95), is a short, fiery essay, calling on the workers of the world to unite and revolt. Written in German as the official platform of the international Communist League, it is the simplest expression of Marx's beliefs ("the theory of the Communists may be summed up in a single sentence: abolition of private property"). *Capital* (*Das Kapital*, 3 vols, 1867, 85, 95), also written with Engels, is an excoriation of capitalism, based on a vast accumulation of data. In it he prophesied with "scientific" authority a class struggle terminating in a proletarian victory and the establishment of a collectivist society. Though often inaccurate historically and feeble stylistically, it has become a kind of bible for communists. It is ironic that Marx, who sought scientific justification for his theories, should have stimulated in his followers a pseudo-mystical veneration. Marx once revolted against the excesses of his followers by flatly stating, "I am no Marxist."

In evaluating Marx's contribution, it must be remembered that in his time working conditions were appalling.

446

His prediction, however, that the poor would get still poorer has not materialized. He did not envisage universal suffrage or the rising standard of living of the workers, nor did he fully assess the spirit of democracy. Disparaging idealism, Marx did not appreciate that the functioning of any society, even a classless one, requires ideals and moral standards. In fairness to Marx, it should be pointed out that his defenders do not think Marxism should be equated with the late Soviet government; they argue that Marx would not approve of the bureaucratic state. These defenders also argue that Marx's seeming predictions of bloody revolution were intended as warnings of what would happen if conditions for the workers did not improve peacefully.

Certain of Marx's economic and social ideas, though not entirely new, attracted considerable attention outside his immediate following. He predicted that the industrial revolution would transform the world, that there would be increasing concentration of capital and a tendency toward monopoly. He also argued that one test of the adequacy of government is what it does for the great mass of people—not for the king or aristocrats.

Marxism tended to shift moral responsibility from the individual to society. In literature, Marxist writers turned to an interest in the lower classes and to propaganda aimed to eliminate their misery and to "improve society" along Marxist lines. Marx also stimulated a school of literary criticism which interprets writers in the light of their class origins and judges them chiefly by their attitude toward the "class struggle" rather than their artistic achievement.

masque: a form of private (court) pageantry which flourished in England during the *Renaissance. The performers were members of the same circle as the audience, and masques were usually given to celebrate holidays or special occasions. The earliest surviving examples, called "disguisings" and "mummings," were written by John Lydgate about 1430. The standard masque has a prologue serving to introduce a group of actors, who enter on some sort of decorative float. They indulge in a discussion or debate which finally passes into song and dance. From about 1590 on, the literary element became important and the settings, costumes, music, and scenery lavish. The height of the form was achieved in the masques of Ben *Jonson with the costumes and settings by Inigo Jones. *Milton's *Comus* is a highly poetic example of the masque and the most valuable one from a literary point of view. After the Restoraton the form was not revived.

Master Builder, The: a play by *Ibsen (1892). In *The Master Builder* Ibsen examines the question of how far an artist may go to achieve and hold supremacy in his art. May he sacrifice love, duty, and happiness for the sake of a goal? Ibsen makes it plain that the poet or artist must face the judgment of his poetic conscience. He is working again with an old theme that has always attracted him— the pursuit of an ideal. In this drama, the architect Solness loses sight of human values in his consistent climb upward and mounts on the defeat and resignation of others—his wife, his old employer, the young draftsman in his office, and the draftsman's fiancée. Solness' consuming ambition to remain forever at the top of his profession and to shut out all others is his downfall.

The fatally tragic note of the play impresses us with one thought: destruction outweighs construction. Solness, intent on climbing higher than ever before, climbs at last into the fragile structure of his "castle in the air" of success and greatness, actually, the steeple (a symbol of the past) on his new home. Beneath him the younger generation of builders watches his ascent. None of them believes that he will reach the top, and Ragnar, the talented young draftsman long held in check by Solness and waiting for his chance to build, feels that Solness "must turn now. He can't possibly help it." But Solness does not turn; he goes too far, giddy with success and the encouragement of the young, foolish Hilda, and falls to his death.

With little difficulty, autobiographical and personal references may be detected in *The Master Builder*. Identifying the architect with the author, one sees the aging Ibsen's concern for his place as an artist, now menaced by a rising younger generation. Parts of the play are prolix and slow-moving; but it effectively develops one of Ibsen's characteristic themes—the destruction that comes from pursuing an ideal that knows no compromise.

Maupassant, Guy de: French short-story writer (1850–93). Although Maupassant became one of the masters of the short story, he did not think of a literary career until he had finished his military service and taken a position as clerk in the government. He then became a disciple of *Flaubert, who was a friend of the family and, like himself, a Norman. During the next seven years of literary apprenticeship, he mingled with Flaubert's circle of the great—*Turgenev, *Daudet, *Zola, and others—and learned much of Flaubert's technique of objectivity and precision in style.

In 1880 Maupassant's first work appeared, a volume of verse, *Des Vers*, so naturalistic in tone that the government threatened to suppress it for its "decadence" but not otherwise noteworthy. In the same year, however, Zola asked Maupassant to contribute to a collection of short stories. Maupassant's story *Butter-Ball (Boule de suif)* was a superb tale, revealing the craftsmanship which was to mark all his writing. The method, like Flaubert's, is impersonal, but the satirical portrait of human selfishness is related with ironic wit. It may be said that Maupassant began his career with a masterpiece, his artistry fully developed.

By 1886 the effects of overwork and debauchery began to reveal themselves in a general physical and mental breakdown. Paralysis was accompanied by failing reason and finally complete insanity. During his one productive decade (1880–90), however, Maupassant wrote 300 stories, six novels, and some dramatic works—enough to fill upward of 30 volumes. In the main, these stories deal sardonically with middle-class values and conventions, with the woes of the heart, with the ignoble in life, particularly the coarser aspects of sex relations. The characters, derived from Maupassant's own closely observed experience, come from all groups—the peasants and bourgeoisie of Normandy, the rising middle class in town and city, the faded nobility—and the situations in which they are placed range from the county fair to the boulevards and clubs of the city and its underworld. *A Life* (*Une Vie*, 1883), for example, is set in Normandy and shows the growing misery of a woman crushed by her husband and son, vainly hoping for a better fate with her grandson. *Good-Friend* (*Bel-Ami*, 1885) traces the success of an adventurer-scoundrel in the corrupt Parisian world of journalism and finance.

But whatever the story, it is always told with clarity and simplicity in diction, with an economy which gives only the essentials of character or situation, yet with sharp and vivid detail. It moves swiftly and logically. And like others in the naturalistic school, Maupassant never sits in judgment on his characters. His contribution to the genre of the short story was to portray the world as he, an acute observer, saw it and to give his portrayal an inevitable progression of events and a unity of effect. He also perfected the "slick" technique which can, on occasion, be used to conceal the lack of any real depth of penetration, and in this he is the founder of the modern commercial short story.

Mauriac, François: French novelist (1895–1970). He was awarded the Nobel prize in 1952 for his penetrating psychological tales, sensitive to every nuance of passion and sensuality and their conflict with religion. A fervent Catholic, Mauriac in his work reflects his religious turn of mind. By the time of the Second World War Mauriac had a solid reputation built on such works as *Le Noeud de Vipères* (*The Viper's Knot*, 1932), *Les Chemins de la Mer* (1939), *Thérèse Desqueyroux* (1927), and its sequel, *La Fin de la nuit* (1935), considered by some critics his finest work. During the Nazi occupation Mauriac worked in the French resistance as a writer, and he continued to write in the popular journals after the war, producing also some of his later fiction that included *Le Sagouin* (1950) and *Un Adolescent d'autrefois* (1969), his last work. His novels were short, tightly written, and contrived with mastery. Mauriac collected his miscellaneous writings in a series of volumes which he titled *Journal*.

They filled five volumes and covered the years 1934–53. In 1936 he wrote a life of Jesus.

Medea: a tragedy by *Euripides (431 B.C.). This tragedy—that of a passionate woman whose love turns into hatred when betrayed—is generally recognized as Euripides' masterpiece. Here the concepts of moderation and wisdom are set aside and the manifestations of passion are almost glorified.

The first reaction of an audience is one of sympathy and pity for Medea, who enters the stage as a broken woman. She has been deserted by Jason and feels desolate in a foreign city, Corinth. Plagued by feelings of jealousy and despair, she is also afraid of being humiliated by mockery. The fire of her Asiatic nature turns her once strong love for Jason into hatred and desire for revenge. After Medea has achieved the full measure of her revenge she attains a power that has an almost superhuman quality.

One of the significant conflicting forces in the play is the cultural-racial contrast between the two central characters. Medea's emotions have never been held in check by ideals of "moderation and wisdom" nor has she been spoiled by superimposed intellectual or materialistic attitudes toward life, such as Jason displays. She has obviously been used to giving her emotions free rein, both in the positive sense (in the vigor and absoluteness of her love for Jason, a love for which she gave up everything she possessed) and in the negative sense (for she does not hesitate to shed blood to get what her passion demands). Jason, on the other hand, is a cold and calculating character. Worldly ambition has made him forget his early love for Medea, and he now abandons her for his own selfish goals. He neither loves nor hates her now but feels only a cold indifference, unmoved by the passion and despair of this woman whom he had loved as long as he found it convenient.

In the course of the play revenge becomes the dominant theme, replacing the note of despair which prevailed in the beginning. It drowns out all other human emotions. Medea's desire for vengeance makes her violent and murderous, intent on destroying everything dear and meaningful to Jason. At the beginning of the play Jason had no claim to sympathy either from the audience or from the other characters. He is openly condemned by Medea, by the chorus of Corinthian women friendly toward Medea, by both servants (the nurse and the male attendant of the children); he is not even defended by Creon. However, Medea's increasing brutality arouses some compassion for her real victim, Jason. Horror at Medea's deeds—her planned murder of Jason's second wife and of her own children—supplants the audience's feeling of pity for her plight.

The climax of the tragedy is reached when Jason discovers that his children have been slaughtered. The victory of this passionate woman crushes Jason and strews his feeble curses to the wind. Denying him even his last pitiful wish, to touch his dead children once more, Medea further triumphs over her victim by prophesying his death and leaving him to live—and suffer.

medieval romance: a type of fictitious and frequently supernatural adventure story written in the vernacular, which was at its prime in western Europe from the 12th to the 15th century. The earlier romances are all in verse; those in prose are late. Based on the conventions of feudal chivalry, the romances relate the activities of famous kings and knights who go on quests or engage in combat to please a lady, who is often in distress and sometimes the object of their *courtly love. The most important pseudohistorical material in the romances came from three sources: the *Matter of Greece and Rome*, which retold classical legends about Troy (as *Chaucer does in *Troilus and Criseyde*), Thebes, Aeneas, and Alexander; the *Matter of France*, which dealt in *chansons de geste* and later romances with Charlemagne and his peers; the *Matter of Britain*, which related legends of King *Arthur and the Knights of the Round Table. A fourth group of romances described the adventures of such English heroes as King Horn, Bevis of Hampton, Havelock the Dane, and Guy of Warwick. A fifth group, largely derived from Oriental tales, included *Amis and Amiloun* and *Floris and Blanchfleur*.

When a number of tales deal with the adventures of a single hero (*e.g.*, *Arthur, Lancelot, Gawain, *Tristan) or with a single quest (*e.g.*, the *Holy Grail), the group of related romances is called a "cycle." The Arthurian poems elaborated in French prose in the 13th century are known as the "Vulgate Cycle" or "Vulgate Romances." French was the language of the early romances; and it is likely that French poets were the first to join courtly love with pseudohistorical narrative marvels, folklore, mythological themes, Celtic and classical tales, and occasionally (as in *Tristan*) even the *fabliaux.

The romance suggests comparison with the *epic, since both deal with idealized heroes engaged in battles. In the romance, however, the motivations for fighting are comparatively trivial; the stories have less unity of action and are looser in structure (*Sir *Gawain and the Green Night* is a notable exception). Romances also tend to be deficient in psychological insight (although some attempted to develop character and motivation by such devices as soliloquies), and the heroes are barely differentiated. Yet the form remained enormously popular for centuries. The most important of the later romances is *Le Morte Darthur,* *Malory's prose summary of the *Matter of Britain*.

During the *Renaissance the humanists scorned the romances because of their exaggeration, repetitious formlessness, false values, and often immorality; and the general condemnation of the decadent romances inspired *Cervantes' satire in *Don Quixote*. Few new romances were written after the *Middle Ages, but the old ones were read for many years, and the best of them still hold their audience. After all, they were concocted from the standard and perennial ingredients of popular literature—adventure and love.

meistersingers ("master singers"): German writers of the 14th to 16th centuries, of whom Hans Sachs (1494–1576), the cobbler of Nuremberg, is the most celebrated. Their poetry grew from *Volkslieder* ("folk songs"),

Sprachdichtung ("gnomic poetry"), and the lyric poetry of their predecessor *minnesingers. By the 15th century the term *meistersingers* was applied to organized social groups of professional poets (by vocation craftsmen, weavers, smithies, etc.). They aspired, by the regulations of their "guild," to be distinguished from wandering, footloose minstrels and, by their elaborate rules for poetic composition, to write in conformity to the spirit (often also satiric and sardonic) and tonal and strophic patterns of their earlier compatriots (*e.g.*, Walther von der Vogelweide). Wagner's opera *Die Meistersinger von Nürnberg* (1868) both depicts the elaborate rules of the group and satirizes the critics.

Melville, Herman: American writer of fiction (1819–91). "Call me Ishmael," the first words of Melville's masterpiece, might well be applied to him, for he was a wanderer, physically and spiritually, throughout his life. He rebelled against many of the social and literary standards of his day and in turn was rejected. His major novel, *Moby-Dick, was reprinted only once in the 40 years between its publication and Melville's death. After producing first-rate tales and the novel called "our sole American epic," Melville wrote no fiction for over 30 years toward the close of his life. *Moby-Dick* has been more intensively studied than any other American novel, but Melville's contemporary critics paid little attention to it. His death attracted scant notice in the *New York Times*; the editorial writer had even forgotten his Christian name.

Nothing in Melville's early life pointed toward a literary vocation: When his father failed in business and died, the family moved to Albany, where Herman spent his later childhood in genteel poverty, working at various odd jobs. At the age of 20 he signed on a merchant ship and made a voyage to England. On his return, he again tried odd jobs, until in 1841 he signed as foremast hand on a whaler. The next few years saw him as a deserter, guest of a cannibal tribe in the Marquesas, whaler again, mutineer, prisoner, farmer, harpooner, probably beachcomber, and sailor in the U. S. Navy. In October 1844, he returned to Boston, collected his pay and discharge, and symbolically threw his white jacket into the river.

Practically all Melville's writing is based on the experiences of these few crowded years. *Typee* (1846) is a fictionalized version of his experiences in the Marquesas. *Omoo* (1847) is a still freer account of his life among the Tahitians. *Mardi* (1849), an out-and-out Polynesian romance, is a long, uncontrolled romantic allegory, incoherent and murky, but containing some mature political comment. *Redburn* (1849), a potboiler—he described it as "beggarly"—is based on his first voyage to England. *White-Jacket* (1850) mingles his experiences in the Navy and sharp protests against its brutality with increasing allegorical implications. Melville now moved to Massachusetts, where he became a friend of *Hawthorne and began work on "a strange sort of book" which was published in London as *The Whale* and in New York as *Moby-Dick; or, The Whale* (1851). *Pierre* (1852) was a sort of psychological romance. *Israel Potter* (1855), a serialized historical novel, was a mere piece of hack work; but *Piazza Tales* (1857) contained some of his finest short fiction in *Benito Cereno*, *Bartleby*, and *The Encantadas*. The last novelette published during Melville's lifetime, *The Confidence Man* (1857), is strongly satirical and misanthropic. Some years of gloomy drifting followed before his first volume of verse, *Battle Pieces and Aspects of the War,* appeared in 1866. In the same year he received a long-sought government appointment and began 19 years' service as a customs official in New York. The philosophical poem *Clarel* (1876) was a fruit of the relative leisure of this position. Some modest legacies enabled Melville to resign in 1885 and from the "unfinished work at his desk" to complete two more books of poems, *John Marr and Other Sailors* (1888) and *Timoleon* (1891). At his death he left the unpublished manuscript of a short novel, *Billy Budd*, which was finally published in 1924 and which formed the basis for Benjamin Britten's opera *Billy Budd* (1951).

The first serious biography of Melville was published on the centenary of his birth, and since that time his fame has risen in a manner that can only be described as a literary boom. In 1910 a standard British reference work which devoted 40 lines to Hawthorne concluded its 8 lines on Melville with the statement, "He was a very unequal writer, but occasionally showed considerable power and originality." Recent American critics have considered him one of the major figures of world literature. The final estimate will doubtless come to rest between these extremes.

Menaechmi: a comedy adapted (*c.* 200 B.C.) by the Roman playwright *Plautus from an unknown Greek original of the type composed by *Menander. The title of the play is the Latin plural of the proper name Menaechmus, given successively to the twins about whom the action revolves.

The situation is as follows. A merchant, living at Syracuse in Sicily, had two sons, Sosicles and Menaechmus, who were identical twins. While they were still small boys, he took Menaechmus to Tarentum in southern Italy, where he was kidnapped and brought across the Adriatic Sea to Epidamnus on the Illyrian coast. Here Menaechmus grew up in the home of his kidnapper, who adopted him and made him his heir, so that in time he became wealthy. Meanwhile the father died, and the grandfather, who took charge of the family, renamed Sosicles Menaechmus to honor the boy who was lost. He is the Menaechmus II of the play. When he came of age, he set out to search for his brother and, after wandering six years, he and his slave Messenio arrive in Epidamnus and walk along the street where Menaechmus lives with his wife, a typical comic shrew, whose violent temper is aggravated by the wiles of her husband's mistress, Erotium ("Little Love"), who occupies the house next door. From the moment Erotium's cook Cylindrus ("Rolling Pin") mistakes Sosicles for Menaechmus, confusion reigns supreme, and while Sosicles enjoys the best of everything, Menaechmus is locked out by both his wife and his mistress, certified insane by a quack physician, and rescued only by the timely arrival of Messenio, who brings about the recognition with which the play ends.

Though simple farce, the *Menaechmi* is probably the

favorite Roman comedy with modern readers. The plot is unusually well constructed. The prologue gives the information necessary to follow the action. The entrances make it completely clear which twin is on the stage in any scene. The weak point in the action—Sosicles' failure to realize that his search is ended—is masked first by the suspicion with which he views everyone in Epidamnus and later by the anger that overcomes him when he is accosted by strangers he considers villains. The two lives Menaechmus is leading are brought together skillfully when the parasite Peniculus ("Crumbbrush") betrays Menaechmus to his wife in revenge for an outrage Sosicles does him. The characters are competently drawn, especially the ridiculous physician and the faithful slave Messenio, though the twins themselves are kept comparatively colorless, lest distinctive traits of temperament lead prematurely to their recognition as different people. The pace of the *Menaechmi* is rapid, the dialogue witty, the songs spirited and very amusing. In fact the only adverse criticism which can be made of the piece is the undue length of the recognition scene.

Plautus' *Menaechmi* has been much imitated by later writers in the various languages of Europe. In English it inspired *Shakespeare's *Comedy of Errors*, which in turn formed the basis for George Abbott's production *The Boys from Syracuse*.

Menander: Greek writer of comedies (342–291 B.C.). The comic poet Menander was born at Athens in 342 B.C., four years before the conquest of Greece by Philip II, king of Macedon. He grew up during the reign of Philip's son, Alexander the Great, and spent his adult life under the rule of the generals who gained control of the Macedonian empire when Alexander died in 323 B.C. Menander was the greatest of the writers of Greek New Comedy, and his reputation in antiquity was immense. But one of his comedies, the *Dyskolos*, has survived complete, found as recently as 1955 in a papyrus of the late third century B.C., the only complete Greek dramatic text to survive in a manuscript of the Hellenistic period. Also extant are more than half of the *Epitrepontes*, or

Arbitration, and considerable fragments of a few other plays, as well as many short passages and individual lines.

New Comedy as written by Menander and other playwrights presents material selected from private life in carefully constructed plots, which are often explained to the audience in formal prologues after the manner of *Euripides. It uses fictitious characters intended to depict classes of people rather than particular persons. Though given individualizing traits, especially by Menander, who is famous for his character drawing, they generally represent such common types as the harsh father, the wayward son, the indulgent uncle, the miser, the soldier, the cook, the slave dealer, and the slave dealer's victims, the *hetairai* or dancing girls, who acted as the mistresses of the well-to-do. These *hetairai* were frequently women of good birth forced into servitude by war or the mass transfers of population characteristic of Macedonian rule; or they were women abandoned by their parents in infancy and reared by slave dealers for a profit. They are often presented sympathetically by the dramatists, and when cast as heroines are rescued from their environment before any real harm has come to them. The chorus in New Comedy usually consists of a band of revelers whose performances are reduced to mere interludes so little connected with the action they are not even included in the manuscript.

The language of New Comedy is clear and simple, yet highly artistic; the meters are fewer and less complex than those of *Aristophanes. Political comment and satire directed against persons in high position are avoided, and the gross indecency of Old Comedy is modified or omitted altogether. There is much moralizing: St. Paul's admonition to the Corinthians that "evil communications corrupt good manners" is taken from Menander. To help the audience recognize the various types of persons presented in a play, conventional masks and costumes were used and standardized names were often given the characters. In *The Arbitration*, Habrotonon ("Pretty Thing") is a *hetaira*, Pamphila ("Altogether Lovable") a young matron, and Pamphila's father, Smicrines ("Small"), an old man too close with his money. Because it was impossible to show interior scenes in the

Greek theater, the action took place in the street in front of the houses of the principal characters.

The favorite theme with the writers of New Comedy is romantic love, the plot turning about the attempts of the lovers to solve the difficulties that are destroying their happiness. Usually they are seeking a way to marry in the face of almost hopeless odds, but in *The Arbitration* they have been married happily for a short time when the play begins. Their joy vanishes, however, when the young husband Charisius learns that, while he was away, his wife Pamphila gave birth to a baby, which she exposed in order to conceal the fact that she had been raped at a night festival some months before her wedding. Though she did not recognize her attacker in the darkness, she was able to seize his ring; and this she put with the infant when she exposed him. The baby was found by a goatherd named Davus, who gave him to Syriscus, a charcoal-burner. But when Syriscus demanded the ring in the hope that someday it might establish the baby's identity, Davus refused to give it to him. While the two argue, Smicrines comes along the road, and they ask him to arbitrate the dispute. He decides, as is right, in favor of Syriscus.

In the meantime, Charisius, who is fond of his wife and unwilling to publish her shame, takes refuge in his sorrow with a *hetaira* named Habrotonon. But Smicrines discovers what he is doing—without, of course, knowing the cause—and he urges Pamphila to consent to a divorce. She clings stubbornly to her husband, however; and the entanglement in all their lives is brought to a conclusion only when it is discovered, by tracing the ring to Charisius, that it was he himself who had attacked Pamphila without knowing who she was—or realizing clearly in his intoxication what he had done. With Charisius' repentance, the restoration of affection within the family, and the return of the baby, the play appropriately ends.

Because the writers of New Comedy worked and reworked the same material, there is much repetition of incident and character in their plays. And though variety is provided in minor details, the endless succession of irascible fathers, rebellious sons, seduced maidens, and infants exposed with their birth tokens, wearies the reader, as do those knavish slaves who first abet their young masters' misdeeds, and then extricate them from all difficulty by sheer cleverness. Incredible coincidences and gross improbabilities also mar even the better plots. But the plays of New Comedy were written in great numbers—Menander alone is credited with more than a hundred—and when any type of literature is mass-produced from what amounts to a formula, a certain monotony results, and the writers, conscious of their hackneyed themes, begin to use fantastic episodes in an effort to outdo their rivals in ingenuity.

When the word "comedy" is used to describe the work of Menander, Diphilus, Philemon, or any other of the writers of New Comedy, it does not carry the same meaning as when it is applied to the dramas of Aristophanes. The purpose of New Comedy was different. It sought "to hold a mirror up to nature," that is, to depict human beings as they are, and to entertain while so doing. It deals with the gay and the amusing; but though its tone is light and it insists on a happy ending, it has a place for the pathetic and the sorrowful also. In fact, it is not so close to Old Comedy as to the tragedy of Euripides, from which its form, its diction, its interest in romantic love, some of its favorite motifs, its moralizing tone, and much of its general atmosphere are largely derived.

New Comedy exercised an immense influence on later literature. Transferred first to the Roman stage (see *Plautus and *Terence) and passing from the Romans to the peoples of Europe, it is the prototype of the modern *comedy of manners perfected by *Molière.

Mercury: see *Hermes.

metaphysical poetry: a type of poetry written especially by John *Donne and his followers in the 17th century and revived in England and America in the 20th. Its most conspicuous characteristics are a deliberate combination of different types of emotions, the use of elaborate and far from obvious comparison ("conceits"), and harshness of versification. The mixture of emotions and attitudes is precisely what the romantic poet usually seeks to avoid: he permits no jesting in a serious poem, no carnality in a spiritual song, no financial concerns in a love poem. The metaphysical poet accepts the fact that "pure" feelings do not actually exist and hence are artificial—that a man may be genuinely and deeply in love and at the same time may objectively analyze his feelings and be aware of (and amused by) the antics of lovers, including himself. The figures of speech are intellectually conceived rather than merely ornamental. The romantic love poet compares himself and his lady to turtledoves, to flowers, to anything ornamental, without too much concern for the strict accuracy of his comparison. (Ornithologists tell us that turtledoves are not especially loving or faithful.) But the metaphysical poet tells us that he and his lady are like a geometrical compass: they are two things joined by a bond that makes them one; they are often separated, one traveling while the other remains stationary; but the stationary one inclines toward the traveler and is the center of his motions (Donne, *A Valediction, Forbidding Mourning*). The prosaic, unpromising-looking comparison throws a good deal more light on the actual relationships of the lovers than would a pair of cooing doves. Another example, short enough to be directly quoted, shows the same features. Donne, attacking all ideas of "platonic" or unconsummated love, compresses a great deal into a witty metaphor: "Who ever loves, if he do not propose/The right true end of love, he's one that goes/To sea for nothing but to make him sick."

The habitual harsh versification of the metaphysical poet is partly a result of putting the idea above the sound, and partly a deliberate device reflecting the combination of incongruities and the shifts of viewpoint found in the poetry. It is also in keeping with the colloquial style used by the metaphysicals.

Donne's immediate followers were the religious poets George Herbert, Richard Crashaw, and Henry Vaughan, but the metaphysical style also appears in Cavalier poets like Richard Lovelace and satirists like John Cleveland, as well as in Abraham Cowley, who does not fit into any neat category. In recent times the manner of the metaphysical poets has been effectively revived in England and America, especially by T. S. *Eliot and his disciples. In fact, a good deal of recent poetry may be described as a fusion of the metaphysicals of the 17th century with the French *symbolists of the late 19th.

Mickiewicz, Adam Bernard: Polish poet and dramatist (1798–1855). At the age of 26, Mickiewicz was banished from Poland because of political activities. He spent the rest of his life in Russia, Italy, Switzerland, and France, where he wrote, taught, and always plotted for Polish independence. He died in Turkey, where he was organizing Polish forces.

Mickiewicz is the leader of Polish romanticism (see *classicism) and Poland's greatest poet. Although he wrote a number of loosely organized romantic plays, his reputation rests largely on his poetry, which ranges from sonnets, lyrics, and patriotic songs to full-scale epics, or, as they are sometimes called, novels in verse. One of these, *Konrad Wallenrod* (1828), is a romantic treatment of a patriotic theme and deals with a long-sought and ultimately successful revenge on the enemies of Poland. Another epic, *Pan Tadeusz* (1832–34), is an idyllic picture of the life of the Polish aristocracy in the time of the poet's youth. It is generally considered his masterpiece.

Middle Ages: a period of European history extending from the end of *classical antiquity (about A.D. 500) to the *Renaissance, or approximately to 1450. This period of nearly 1000 years is far from static and includes widely divergent types and levels of civilization at different places and times. In general, however, it can be said to fall into two almost equal halves, with the transition about the year 1000.

The first half of the Middle Ages is frequently and unfortunately called "the Dark Ages." This period covers the collapse of the international trade and government of the Roman Empire, the overrunning of Europe by a group of barbarian tribes (most of them Germanic), the Christianization of these tribes, the development of local government and local economic self-sufficiency, and the beginnings of a new form of large-scale organization in the feudal system. Though this system, which was both political and economic, could be perverted into a form of exploitation, it was essentially a bargain by which, in precarious times, the weak worked for the strong so that it would be to the interest of the strong to protect them.

During the second half of the Middle Ages the institutions of the modern world begin to take shape. The re-establishment of large-scale transportation and communication makes possible the rise of great cities and the production of goods for exchange rather than merely for local consumption; and these developments in turn lead to the rise of a prosperous, independent middle class of merchants and artisans. Feudalism thus becomes more important as an organization of political power than as a system of land tenure, and the king becomes more a ruler and less a great landowner than before. Gradually, the modern idea of the nation is formed, and a struggle ensues in which the Church, the one great power of the early Middle Ages, loses most of its temporal authority to the secular rulers.

During the first half of the Middle Ages relatively little literature was produced. For a time the classical heritage was strong enough to inspire Latin works of learning like those of the philosopher *Boethius or the encyclopedist Isidore of Seville, but this tradition gradually faded. The vernacular modern languages had not yet achieved a literary existence. The two great forces of change were the continued migrations of the Germanic tribes and the incursions of Islam. The various tribes of Germanic stock had long been on the move— in fact, they had been the principal external reason for the collapse of the Roman Empire—and the fact that Lombardy, France, England, and Russia are named for tribes of these invaders is sufficient evidence of their extensive activity. Shortly after the death of *Mohammed in A.D. 632, his followers set out on a career of conquest which took them, in a single century, as far as the Loire valley in France. Charlemagne's grandfather turned them back near Tours in 732, but they were not finally expelled from Spain (where they overthrew a Gothic kingdom) until 1492. Thus in both northern and southern Europe the Dark Ages were a time of troubles.

The history of England during this time may be cited as a typical case of the sort of troubles usually encountered. The Roman legions which had kept order there for some 350 years were withdrawn in A.D. 410. Within a generation the Germanic tribes from the Continent were beginning to take over the country, driving out the Celtic inhabitants and wrecking the last vestiges of Christianity and Roman civilization. By A.D. 600 they controlled all England and were themselves beginning to be Christianized. The learning and institutions of the Church advanced so rapidly that during the late 7th and 8th centuries England was the acknowledged intellectual leader of Europe, and her monasteries produced a series of distinguished scholars. Then another wave of Germanic pagans struck. At first the Vikings came merely to burn and plunder, but later they stayed to conquer and settle. King Alfred tells us that when he came to the throne in A.D. 871 there were very few priests in England who could read a simple letter in Latin (the language of the Church and its Bible)—and this in a country which, before the Vikings came, had supplied scholars and educators to the rest of Europe.

During all this period, the one force working for learning, communication between peoples, large-scale order, and the traditions of civilization was the Church. The Holy Roman Empire, established with Charlemagne as its "emperor" in the year 800, was—as the old quip says—neither holy nor Roman nor an empire; but it was an attempt to give the medieval world, under the leadership of the Church, the order, peace, and civilization which the Roman Empire at its best had given to the ancient world. Like any other institution, the Church had its faults, but for centuries it was the only really civilizing force at work. If its zeal occasionally led it to destroy pagan works which we should like to have, it is also true that it preserved most of those that we do possess. Practically the entire body of Old English literature was committed to writing by monks, and the same holds for most literature of the Dark Ages.

This literature falls into two classifications. There is an unbroken tradition in Latin, and many purely secular works (see, for example, *beast epic) were written in this language throughout the Middle Ages. Some types new to European literature, like the stanzaic hymn, were developed in medieval Latin before they were transferred to the vernacular tongues. Alongside this writing in Latin there was a literature in the modern languages which were now in the process of formation. At first this folk literature was entirely oral and hence does not now survive, but soon some of it began to be recorded (often with both artistic and theological revision) by the monks. The earliest of the modern vernacular literatures which we possess is that of Old English (Anglo-Saxon), dating from about the year 700. The latest in western Europe is Italian, dating from the 13th century. Thus it will be seen that some languages have no literature during the Dark Ages. In most of the others, the literature of this period is little more than a groping toward a real literature which was to come later. English is the outstanding exception: Old English literature was well developed in epic (see *Beowulf*), lyric, and general narrative poetry, as well as in a deliberately artistic prose used in chronicles and sermons.

During the second half of the medieval period the great national literatures begin to emerge. The French *Song of Roland* probably dates from the very beginning of this epoch, about the year 1000. The first literature to reach its full stature, however, was the Provençal poetry of southern France during the 11th and 12th centuries (see *troubadour). The poets writing in Provençal achieved a high standard, especially in the lyrical poetry of *courtly love, but the brutal Albigensian Crusade (a piece of feudal conquest carried out under cover of extirpating a heresy) wrecked their literature and civilization in the years following 1309. But through its influence on the *trouvères* of northern France, the poets of the Sicilian School, the "sweet new style" of *Dante and his group, and the *minnesingers of Germany, medieval Provençal poetry was the beginning of all modern poetry. Alongside this elegant court poetry, the folk song continued on its way and presumably flourished, though it was only occasionally that some literate person took the trouble to record it for posterity.

As lyric poetry developed in Provence, narrative poetry of a new style spread from northern France. The *Song of Roland* was only the first (or at least the earliest that has survived) of a long series of *chansons de geste* concerning first the exploits of Charlemagne and his peers,

465

and later those of various other heroes. These led in their turn to the *medieval romance, which was characteristically a tale of love, adventure, chivalry, and often enchantment. It has been observed that the romance stems from an age of chivalry as the epic does from a heroic age. A medieval French poet comments that there are three subjects of romance: the matter of France (Charlemagne and his peers, and the other heroes of the *chansons de geste*), the matter of Britain (*Arthur and his Round Table, with other loosely attached stories like that of *Tristan and Isolt), and the matter of "Rome the Great" (all *classical antiquity, from historical figures like Alexander the Great to the *Troy Tale). The romances spread over all Europe and included some fine works like the Middle-English *Sir *Gawain and the Green Knight*. They also exerted a considerable influence on the great epic writers in Austria about 1200—the anonymous author of the *Nibelungenlied*, *Wolfram von Eschenbach, Gottfried von Strassburg, and Hartmann von Aue. Ultimately the romances degenerated into the turgid, tedious, exaggerated prose fictions satirized in *Don Quixote*.

The medieval mind was essentially allegorical, seeing the visible and material world as a reflection of an invisible moral or spiritual order. This characteristic led to the development of a number of types of allegorical literature. The *dream-allegory is the most elaborate of these purely symbolic forms, but types such as the *bestiary and lapidary, in which the alleged facts of zoology and the properties of precious stones were given allegorical interpretations, belong to the same class. Another widespread type, the debate, represented a contention between two contrasting or opposing forces—body and soul, flower and leaf, knight and priest, etc. We can readily see its allegorical nature in the Middle English *Owl and Nightingale*, where the two birds berate each other and praise themselves but essentially are used to represent two different points of view: the owl is a utilitarian who boasts that he catches rats; but the nightingale is an aesthete who cheers men by his song. *Allegory could be used not only to make the abstract presentable, but to make the indiscreet safe, and thus we get the veiled political satire of the beast epic.

It is an interesting fact that until about 1300 medieval

literature is largely anonymous and that its tone and themes are international—or, since nations in the modern sense of the word are just coming into existence, perhaps we should say interlingual. The anonymity may arise in part from the dearth of records, but not entirely. It reflects a point of view which paid scant attention to worldly achievements or individual ambitions. We no more know who designed the Gothic cathedrals than we know who produced the statues and glass that ornament them or who wrote most of the metrical romances. The common tone and subjects of much medieval literature reflect the single Church and the basic unity of Christendom, which, in spite of endless bickering, made a joint enterprise like the Crusades possible. The common tongue of Latin (still spoken fluently by scholars) spread learned materials from one end of Europe to the other and doubtless spread a good deal of lighter material by word of mouth. At any rate, the same themes were treated in much the same way in many literatures. The originally Celtic tale of *Tristan and Isolt was popularized in French, and medieval versions of it appeared in Icelandic and Czech and in most of the languages lying between these limits.

After about 1300 we not only know the names of more individual authors, but—far more important—authors come to be much more individual. *The *Divine Comedy* of *Dante (finished about 1321) deals with standard ethical, moral, and theological ideas in a not unusual type of framework, but it bears the stamp of an individual mind in a way that the *chansons de geste* and the romances and *fabliaux* do not. The irrepressible *Chaucer breaks through even the conventionality of his early dream-allegories, but he is much more distinctly himself in *Troilus and Criseyde* and The *Canterbury Tales*. This individual note is one of the principal ingredients in the new humanism of *Boccaccio and *Petrarch, and this fact, together with their enthusiasm for the revival of classical studies (especially Greek), has often led to their being considered as the first men of the Renaissance. Actually, they are transitional figures whom it is not inconsistent to consider as belonging both to the waning Middle Ages and to the dawning Italian Renaissance. (This fact points up the time lag in intellectual movements, for

Chaucer, who outlived them both by a quarter of a century, is definitely a man of the Middle Ages and cannot be considered as belonging to the Renaissance.)

During the last few centuries of the medieval period the growth of the cities and the rise of the middle class proceeded rapidly and left their mark on literature. Much of it was still written—as it would be for centuries to come—for the patronage of kings, nobles, and the princes of the Church, but the tone and content of such types as the fabliau and the beast epic imply a middle-class audience. So does the whole of the medieval drama. Not only were the great cycles of *mystery plays sponsored and performed by the trade guilds, but such other dramatic types as the *miracle plays and the *morality plays are clearly written for a middle-class town audience. This audience did not necessarily know how to read, but the complexities of international trade and credit were producing a highly literate group of merchants and master artisans. These began to provide a middle-class group of *readers*, for increasing literacy meant that literature was more likely to be read silently to oneself instead of being recited or read aloud to a group. With the rise of a literate middle class, the stage was set for the art of printing and the beginning of the Renaissance.

Miles gloriosus (Latin: "braggart soldier"): a play by *Plautus in which one of the chief characters is a boastful soldier. The term connotes a cowardly, vainglorious braggart, usually parasitical and likely to be easily victimized by practical jokers. The character type had appeared even earlier in Greek comedy and was later imitated in Continental and English drama, notably in *Shakespeare's Falstaff (*Henry IV*, Parts 1 and 2).

Miller, Arthur. American dramatist (1915–   ). Like the hero of his play *A Memory of Two Mondays* (1955), Arthur Miller had to earn the money for his studies in a warehouse for automobile spare parts. After leaving the university he worked for the Federal Theatre Project and for the radio in New York. His first play performed on Broadway, *The Man Who Had All the Luck* (1944),

468

was a failure; but three years later the New York theater critics declared *All My Sons* the best play of the season. Miller's most important work, *Death of a Salesman* (1949), for which he received the Pulitzer Prize and the New York Drama Critics' Circle Award, unmasked with anti-illusionistic techniques everyday reality as a deceptive surface appearance of lies and false values and pushed to a deeper dimension of reality. It formed a modern tragedy out of the stuff of an average life. In 1955 he repeated this experiment with *A View from the Bridge*, but less convincingly, although—or because—he evidently strove to link up with Greek tragedy.

His drama *The Crucible* (1953), while dealing with the witch trials at Salem, Massachusetts, in 1698, reveals his concern with problems of individual conscience and guilt by association—social and political problems of his own time. His presumably autobiographical play, *After the Fall* (1964), examines a man's right to hope in a world where incredible horror and violence repeatedly present themselves. A domestic drama, *The Price* (1968), uncovers, layer by layer, the story of two generations of loveless family life as two sons reflect upon their concern for their dead father, yet realize that they needed to live lives of their own. Thematically Miller's plays attest a pronounced sympathy for the hapless victims of society; technically they show the influence of *Ibsen's realism.

Milton, John: English poet and controversial writer 1608–74). Milton was a man of remarkably strong and consistent character, though if we try to put him into any conventional classification he seems to be a mass of contradictions. He was both a *Renaissance humanist and a Puritan. He was a retiring poet who devoted 20 years of his life to public service in a period of turmoil. He was a devout Christian who, during his later years, participated in no formal religious observances, either public or private. In epic poetry he wrote in the grand style, and in political controversy he was a master of scurrilous personal abuse. He loved study and quiet but condemned the "fugitive and cloistered virtue" which evades the battles of life; and he himself was a tireless and fearless fighter for anything he thought right, and for nothing else, no matter how expedient it might be.

Milton was educated at St. Paul's School and Christ's College, Cambridge, where he remained for seven years (1625–32) and began his career as a poet. From his Cambridge days date his first known original poem (*On the Death of a Fair Infant Dying of a Cough*, occasioned by the death of his sister's baby), and such well-known works as the hymn *On the Morning of Christ's Nativity*, and the poems *At a Solemn Music* and *On Shakespeare*. At the university he was known to his fellow students as "the lady of Christ's." There has been some debate as to whether this nickname implied admiration or derision—possibly it reflected a mixture of these attitudes.

After leaving Cambridge, Milton spent six years in self-directed study at his father's country place at Horton, where he read widely, studied languages, continued to write, and in general prepared himself for the career in poetry which had already become his goal. At Horton he wrote some of his best lyrics. *L'Allegro* and *Il Penseroso* (possibly written during his last years at Cambridge) are two companion pieces, describing in detail the day and night of two types, the cheerful man and the reflective man, and thus presenting what are really two sides of the author's own personality. *Lycidas*, probably the finest example of the *pastoral *elegy in English, is a lament for a Cambridge fellow student who had drowned. Edward King, the ostensible subject, seems to have been no more than an acquaintance of Milton, but in the poem he became a symbol of all lost hopes; and the fact that he wrote poetry and was studying for the ministry enabled Milton to include fine passages on the triviality of much contemporary verse and the general corruption of the clergy. To the Horton period also belong Milton's two *masques, *Arcades* (1633) and *Comus* (performed 1634, published 1637), the latter furnished with music by the eminent composer Henry Lawes. The works of this period are perfect illustrations of the "simple, sensuous and passionate" language which he demanded for the best poetry.

In 1638 Milton left England for the period of Continental travel that was part of the education of an English gentleman. After some time in France and Italy (where

470

he met *Galileo), he cut short his tour because of the culminating troubles between the Puritans and the Royalists in his own country. It was in 1639 that he returned, settled in London, tutored his two nephews (teaching he found to be a burdensome occupation), and began to give serious thought to the writing of a great poem. Since his student days he had had this ambition, and during his travel on the Continent he had reached the conclusion "that by labor and intense study (which I take to be my portion in this life), joined with the strong propensity of nature, I might perhaps leave something so written to aftertimes, as they should not willingly let it die." But this project had to wait nearly two decades, for Milton was drawn into the religious and political controversies connected with the English Civil War. For the next 20 years, first as a private citizen and later as Secretary in Foreign Tongues to the Council of State (a position somewhat like that of Secretary of State) under Cromwell's Commonwealth, he wrote controversial prose in English and, for the purposes of international diplomacy, in Latin. In 1641 he began to attack the hierarchical organization of the Church of England, and in 1643–44 he wrote several tracts demanding more latitude in the matter of divorce. (These last were doubtless conditioned by the fact that after a month of marriage his first wife went home to her father, where she stayed for two years. She returned to Milton in 1645, and later bore him three daughters. His other two marriages were happier.) In 1644 he published two important pamphlets, a *Tractate on Education* and *Areopagitica,* an impassioned plea for a limited freedom of the press. The full title is *Areopagitica: A Speech of Mr. John Milton for the Liberty of Unlicensed Printing to the Parliament of England.* Milton opposed the system by which a work had to be licensed *before* it could be published and could thus be kept from ever appearing; but he did hold that the author, although having the right to decide what he would publish, was liable after the event. Famous is its plea: "Give me liberty to know, to utter, and to argue freely according to conscience, above all other liberties." During this period of prose controversy Milton's only poetic activity was the writing of a few fine sonnets, mainly on political and religious subjects—an innovation which broke the tradition that a sonnet must be a love poem. However, he did collect his earlier verse in a volume entitled *Poems* (1645).

In the meantime, the breach between the Puritans and the Royalists had widened into open war. The struggle was partly religious and partly political, for, in general, the Puritans opposed the established Church of England, and supported the rights of a democratic Parliament against the claims of an autocratic king. After seven years of fighting, the Puritans decisively got the upper hand, tried King Charles I, and beheaded him (1649). Milton took it upon himself to justify this act to a Europe which had been accustomed to accepting the idea of the divine right of kings. In *The Tenure of Kings and Magistrates* (1649), he argued that all public officials are directly responsible to their own people, who have the right and duty of passing judgment on their acts. This work led to Milton's appointment as Secretary. It was followed by a *Defence of the English People (Pro populo anglicano defensio)* in 1650, and a *Second Defence* (also in Latin) in 1654. But these treatises were only the high points in the onerous job of Secretary in Foreign Tongues which Milton held from 1649 until the Restoration of the Monarchy in 1660. His eyesight had been impaired as early as 1644, and in 1652 it entirely failed him, so that he was totally blind during the greater part of his term in public office, and during the later years when all his major poetical works were composed.

He had finally decided on the subject for his great poem. Rejecting the earlier idea of a national epic based on King *Arthur, he decided to write a universal epic based on Adam and centering on the fall of man. He began work on it in 1658, and after the Restoration relieved him of all public duties (and sent him into hiding for a brief period) in 1660, he was able to devote all his time to it. *Paradise Lost* was finished in 1664, and published in 1667. (The publisher paid Milton £20, in four installments, for an edition of 4,500 copies.) This poem raised Milton from the position of a good poet to an eminence which was great in his own time and has constantly increased, so that now, when the average English-speaking person thinks of poetry in the grand style, *Paradise Lost* is almost invariably his standard of excellence. But the poem, though offering a promise of redemption, actually closed with the expulsion of man from the Garden of Eden. A Quaker friend who read the manuscript handed it back to Milton with the remark, "Thou hast said much of Paradise lost, but what hast thou to say of Paradise found?" Milton's reply was *Paradise Regained* (1671). In many ways this poem represents a decline from the level of *Paradise Lost*, especially in the character of Satan, who fades from a magnificent rebel in the first poem to an ineffectual shyster in the second. But the majesty of language, the wealth and splendor of detail, and the impact of the deepest convictions of a powerful mind are still there; and Milton's decline still leaves him on a level to which few poets have attained. Furthermore, another masterpiece, the classical tragedy *Samson Agonistes* ("Samson Combatant"), was published in the same volume. Though there is no direct evidence as to when this play was written, it seems reasonable to assume that it was after the Restoration, for Samson is a perfect counterpart of Milton during his last years. He, supposed to be a deliverer of his people, is now blind, helpless, enslaved by his triumphant enemies. The play tells how Samson, even in these circumstances, arranged to destroy both himself and the Philistines—and any student of Milton's life and character feels that Milton would have grasped any opportunity to pull the props out from under the dissolute and frivolous court of Charles II and would have been happy, if necessary, to destroy himself in the process. However we may speculate about the autobiographical element in *Samson Agonistes*, the play remains one of the most eloquent and solidly constructed works of English poetry and unquestionably the finest English tragedy written on the Greek model.

Perhaps the key to Milton's greatness lies in an unusual combination of splendid and magnificent language with absolute sobriety and integrity of character. All too frequently the poet who has a great command of all the resources of language becomes (as one British statesman said of another) "inebriated by the exuberance of his own verbosity" to such an extent that he uses language for its own sake to say nothing in particular, or is at least tempted to exaggerate, to inflate, to write bombastically.

Milton had the linguistic power, but his major subjects were matters of the highest importance, on a universal scale: only Miltonic rhetoric could be worthy of a character like Satan, as he is drawn in *Paradise Lost.* Furthermore, Milton was always in earnest about his subjects, which were not themes chosen merely to provide poetic opportunities, but matters on which he held fundamental convictions. Thus there was little temptation to exaggerate, for to exaggerate is necessarily to falsify.

In much the same way, his impressiveness as a character may be said to come from the harmony of the apparent contradictions in his make-up. He was a Puritan in a sense, but he felt a real humility before the wonder of God's creation instead of despising this world as a thing of naught. He was a humanist who loved music and the great classical poets, who affirmed the glory of the world and the holiness of sex, who defended human dignity and freedom and free will in both church and state. From the study of the classics he accepted the ideals of intellectual freedom and the models of poetic style. From the Hebrew prophets he acquired a moral passion, and from his Protestantism a sense of the immediacy of God. His humanism fused these elements and gave practical and poetic direction to his genius. As he himself said, he was inspired "to imbreed and cherish in a great people the seeds of virtue and public civility, and to allay the perturbations of the mind, and set the affections in right tune; to celebrate in glorious and lofty hymns the throne and equipage of God's almightiness."

Minerva: see *Athena.

minnesingers (German: "singers of love"): medieval German lyric poets who, like the *troubadours, were members of the knightly chivalric class. Composing under similar feudal conditions, they too adored their ladies in *courtly-love fashion; but they frequently added a spiritual and mystical note. Although the name *minnesinger* implies that the subject of the verses was exclusively love, they actually wrote on all the themes (lament, crusade, nature, dawn, politics) and in all the styles made popular by the troubadours, who were their artistic inspiration. The most famous of the minnesingers was Walther von der Vogelweide (1170?–1230), whose poetry is distinguished not only for its euphony but for its sincerity, social idealism, and love of nature. The "leader of a choir of nightingales," as his contemporary Gottfried von Strassburg called him, Walther was the greatest lyric poet in German before *Goethe.

miracle play: see *mystery play.

Misanthrope, The: a comedy by *Molière (1666). Most of Molière's plays illustrate the folly of those who deviate too freely from the norm of conduct that society has established; in *The Misanthrope,* Molière demonstrates that even a seeming virtue practiced immoderately gives rise to absurdities. Alceste, the leading character (a role acted by Molière himself), is a misanthrope, hating mankind for the deceit and affectation which he sees universally practiced and condoned. He believes in complete honesty—naked truth—in social relationships, and he attempts to apply this principle in his encounters with an amateur poet, with some fashionable courtiers, and with the young coquette of whom he is enamored. The results are disastrous—and amusing.

Molière's artistry is to be seen in the complexity of the characterization of Alceste. We can sympathize with a good deal of his point of view: empty compliments and the hypocrisy of much of social amenity can be distasteful. And there are aspects of his character which attract us just as they attract the loyal, sane Philinte and the intelligent Eliante. Yet Alceste is a comic figure: Philinte's speeches assert it and Alceste's own actions bear out the contention. Alceste is foolish in his zeal; for example, not to secure counsel in a lawsuit is to confuse idealism with folly. Moreover, a great part of his attitude is prompted by selfishness and a lack of understanding of human nature. His infatuation with Célimène and his hopeful suggestion that such a social butterfly renounce the world with him are patent absurdities.

The play is simple, the plot negligible, and yet *The Mis-*

anthrope is a masterpiece. Molière's insight into character is the important thing, and this ability to see the individual against the frame of human nature and society is the source of his comedy. Although *The Misanthrope* is a humorous play with abounding wit, it also illustrates the narrow division between great comedy and tragedy. "In this world we need a more pliable virtue. By being too wise we may be quite at fault. Common sense avoids all extremes and bids us be soberly wise. This unbending stiffness of the virtues of ancient times clashes too much with the ordinary customs of our own. . . ." This advice of Philinte to his friend is very similar to warnings made by another great exponent of the golden mean, *Sophocles, who in *Antigone* speaks of "minds too stiff" which "most often stumble" and of "the trees that bend before the storm" and "save their last twigs." Excess and refusal to compromise lead to disaster, and whether the disaster is comic or tragic will depend on the circumstances—and the poet.

Miser, The: a comedy by *Molière (*L'Avare*, 1668). This typical comedy of Molière illustrates his comic genius as well as his weaknesses. With the casualness common to so many of his contemporaries, he dipped liberally into other authors for his material and much of *The Miser* derives from *Plautus' *Aulularia*. But like another famous "plagiarist," *Shakespeare, what Molière borrowed he made his own. With its social satire of a rising, money-conscious middle class and the excessive control of 17th-century parents over their children, with its complicated plot and its improbable ending in an all's-well-that-ends-well turn of events, with its humorous revelation of miserliness through numerous details as well as through broad characterization, with its sympathetic attitude toward youth and young love—*The Miser* becomes, in its totality, uniquely Molière's, regardless of his sources.

Harpagon, the miser, wishes to marry his daughter Elise to a rich, middle-aged man, although she has already made her choice of Valère, who is secretly introduced into the household as a servant. Not only does Harpagon interfere in his daughter's romance, but he is willing to disown his son, Cléante, because of a young woman in whom they are both interested and who actually does love the son. Torn between love for money and love for the attractive but dowerless Mariane, Harpagon succumbs to the stronger passion when his precious money box is stolen. To gain its return he reluctantly gives the two young couples permission to wed, Mariane and Valère having been revealed to be the long-lost children of Anselme, the man to whom Harpagon would have married his daughter.

If the ending is weakly contrived, the body of the play is filled with laughter. Molière wished above all to amuse and entertain, and his dialogue and stage action accomplish this end. The sickly, repulsive Harpagon preening himself before the flattery of an adventuress (one can imagine Molière, ill himself, with a persistent cough, playing the role very realistically), Harpagon almost unconsciously snuffing out the second candle when two are lighted, Harpagon fumbling in his pocket to produce not the expected tip but a handkerchief—these are the little details which, with the extensive comedy of the banquet plans (Harpagon would woo his lady but not expensively!) and the loan that he is unsuspectingly negotiating with his son through a broker, make the play still alive and lively after the passage of some three centuries.

Mishima, Yukio: Japanese novelist, born into a Samurai family, imbued with the codes of control over physical and mental capacities (1925–70). He disciplined himself in his craft and produced a series of vivid novels that included the tetralogy *The Sea of Fertility* (posthumous), *The Temple of the Golden Pavilion* (1959), *Forbidden Colors* (1968), *Thirst for Love* (1969), and other works. A nationalist opposed to modern trends in Japanese life, he committed ritual suicide on November 25, 1970, after failing to rally the Japanese military to his conservative ideas.

Moby-Dick; or, The Whale: a novel by *Melville (1851). Early in the composition of *Moby-Dick* Melville wrote to a friend that it was hard to get poetry out of blubber.

For nearly ten years thoughts of his whaling experiences had been simmering; these he fortified with wide reading in the literature of whaling. He originally planned a romance of whaling adventure, but in progress the work, influenced by Elizabethan dramatists (especially *Shakespeare) and by *Hawthorne, grew into a parable of the author's new philosophical convictions in heightened style. A vast amount of other reading underlay the writing: the influence of the *Bible, *Milton, *Goethe, *Byron, *Carlyle, and *Emerson is evident.

Moby-Dick may be read on several levels. It is a thrilling adventure story, "the world's greatest sea novel," compounded of search, pursuit, conflict, and catastrophe. It is the plot of unceasing search for revenge, the "Americanized Gothic" of mystery and terror, crowded with omens and forebodings from the cracked Elijah's warnings to the prophecies of Fedallah, which are reminiscent of the witches' croakings in *Macbeth*. Clear throughout is a mastery of suspense and horror, of both subtle and broad humor, of exciting narrative in vigorous prose. Readers for the story's sake are dismayed by the numerous chapters on whales and whaling, but this lore serves as the ballast of verisimilitude to uninitiated readers. When the book was published, the catastrophe was met with skepticism; coincidentally, less than a month later a whale actually did ram and sink a ship. The chapters on whaling not only prepare the reader for the unfamiliar events, skillfully retard the swift action, and present an authentic, full way of life; they also serve for leisurely exploration of ideas in the manner of the familiar *essay.

The more important levels, of course, are those of characterization and meaning. A veritable gallery of unique portraits emerges. In spite of their few, brief appearances, Peter Coffin, Captains Bildad and Peleg, and the officers of passing vessels are vividly delineated. Melville most convincingly individualizes Starbuck, Stubb, and Flask. Starbuck's wary courage and "right mindedness" are fully developed to make him a foil to Ahab. The three harpooners are also individualized: the lithe American Indian, Tashtego; the unbroken African, Daggoo, physically admirable and truculent, so unlike the minstrel-show Negroes in the literature of Melville's day;

and Queequeg, the Polynesian heathen who "must help these Christians," whose characterization is a masterpiece of understanding and revelation. The characterizations of the semi-autobiographical Ishmael and of Ahab are the most important, and they are inextricably tied up with the book's meaning.

Ishmael's name, of course, connotes the wanderer and outcast. He shares the malaise and restlessness of the romantic hero, but he rises above them. He is no mere escapist or misanthrope. Himself inclined to melancholy, he recognizes that Ahab's concentration on woe is madness. Midway of the book, Ishmael, the participant and narrator, merges with the omniscient author. At first caught by the fever of the oath on the quarter-deck to hunt Moby-Dick to the kill, he alone has the intelligence and will to recognize and oppose the madness of it. Starting out somewhat as a philosophical anarchist, repudiating society and those in power, he grows in real democracy, in deep respect for and insight into the secrets of human life. Regarding both believer and infidel with equal eye, he is no agnostic about the dignity of man and the imperative need of fellowship. And he alone of the *Pequod* is saved.

The biblical Ahab worshiped false gods: he was slain in battle and the dogs licked up his blood. Melville's Ahab has numerous counterparts in literature: Prometheus, *Milton's Satan, *Doctor Faustus, and *King Lear, but is nevertheless one of literature's great originals. On his long-prepared-for entrance, "reality outran apprehension." Branded like Milton's Satan, sturdy, erect on his bone leg, but "with a crucifixion in his face," Ahab has all the "overbearing dignity of some mighty woe." His actions are of one piece, for he is driven by a force stronger than himself, though of his own creation. Right after Moby-Dick had sheared off his leg on a previous voyage, his "torn body and gashed soul bled into one another," and the final monomania seized him. With feline cunning he did his best to conceal the madness, but from the frenzied oath on the quarter-deck the steps to destruction are sure: a man never known to kneel swears he would strike the sun if it insulted him; he throws overboard his pipe (symbol of serenity); smashes the quadrant (symbol of scientific aid); defies the lightning, breathing the kindred fire of his spirit back at it; and, tempering a forged harpoon in the blood of his pagan harpooners, baptizes it in the name not of the Father, but of the devil. Isolation, pride, obsession with revenge, reliance on the unaided self, and blasphemy make up his tragic flaw. But as his old friend Peleg said: "Ahab has his humanities." His scenes with the cabin boy Pip recall Shakespeare's moving scenes of Lear and the Fool. But the "humanities" get short shrift: Captain Boomer, who lost an arm to Moby-Dick, wants no more of the monster, but such common sense shocks Ahab as poltroonery.

In a letter to Mrs. Hawthorne, Melville said that only Hawthorne's insight had revealed to him "the part-and-parcel allegoricalness of the whole." Later commentators have not agreed on any correct and final interpretation of a single allegory, but all point out Melville's obvious penchant for symbolism. He has a habit of underscoring the spiritual meaning of physical details: "some certain significance," he says, "lurks in all things." The monkey-rope tying Ishmael to Queequeg becomes the bond of brotherhood; "loose and fast fish" produce thoughts of privilege, of Russian serfdom and American slavery. The nine "gams" (conversations) with other ships are generally symbolic: the misnamed *Delight* has just suffered humiliating defeat from Moby-Dick, and the *Rachel*, like her Biblical namesake, seeks her lost children.

Various scholars have interpreted the white whale as representing various forces and evils—sometimes throwing more light on themselves than on the book. Safer ground than such subjective criticism of an inexhaustibly suggestive but highly elusive novel lies in Melville's own explication. To Ahab, the whale is "the monomaniac incarnation of all those malicious agencies which some deep men feel eating in them," is "all evil, visibly personified" against which he piled "all the rage and hate felt by his whole race from Adam down." But to Ishmael, Ahab is insane. Less bluntly and plainly, Ishmael states what the whale means to him: he is appalled chiefly by the hideous whiteness, which suggests the demonism in the world, the co-ordinate visible love and invisible terror, the charnel house giving the lie to the allurements of deified Nature. Starbuck, at sea to hunt whales, not his commander's vengeance, considers the whale a dumb beast, smiting from blindest instinct. Other seamen believe in the malice behind the tremendous strength, but assume no self-appointed mission to destroy it. In the last chase Starbuck calls to Ahab that it is not too late, that Moby-Dick seeks him not: "It is thou that madly seekest him." But bound by more than oaths on the quarter-deck, Ahab is forever Ahab, the Fates' lieutenant, acting under orders.

Crucial to Melville's study of evil are the words from Father Mapple's sermon early in the book: "If we obey God, we must disobey ourselves; and it is in this disobeying ourselves, wherein the hardness of obeying God consists." Ishmael sees the madness and foresees the disaster of self-willed Ahab, who smuggled his own destruction aboard with him. So Melville's intelligence, his imagination and emotion, however, seem to echo Stubb's pride in the way Ahab, having been dealt certain cards, plays out the hand without complaint. To Hawthorne, Melville wrote that the book's secret motto was the baptism of the harpoon *in nomine diaboli*. His fondness for his unreconciled, insuperable *Titan hero, whose defiance and tragedy he vicariously shared, probably explains why he wrote to Hawthorne: "I have written a wicked book, and feel spotless as a lamb."

Mohammed (or Muhammad): religious leader and author of the *Koran* (A.D. 570–632). The religion frequently called Mohammedanism by outsiders is properly known as Islam ("submission" to the will of God). Its followers, Moslems (more properly Muslims, "those who have submitted"), today number one sixth of the world's population. Mohammed was a caravan driver who at 40 received his first revelation: "Thou art Allah's messenger, and I am Gabriel." As other visions followed and Mohammed began to preach and convert, he aroused the enmity of Mecca, the city where he was born and lived. He fled in A.D. 622 to Medina. This flight, known as the *Hegira*, marks the beginning of the Mohammedan calendar (just as the year of the birth of Jesus begins the Christian calendar). But eventually Mecca and the Bedouin tribes vowed loyalty to him, and Mohammed became not only a preacher but the ruler of a state. Within a generation after his death the revelations which he had made to his followers from time to time, and which they had memorized, were collected; it is these which make up the *Koran*, the sacred text of the religion.

The *Koran* ("reading") is composed in Arabic of 114 chapters, *Surahs*, of cadenced prose and rime. Their arrangement, presumably Mohammed's own, depends on length, with the longest first, or, according to another theory, moves from "inmost things to outward things." The subject matter is a combination of traditional history, promises to the faithful, and admonitions moral, religious, and political. The core material is indebted to the Old Testament and the traditions of the Hebrew Talmud, with some use of Christian and Zoroastrian legends.

The *Surahs* include commands to proselytize, to be ethical and honest, to give alms. Although polytheism and idolatry were current among his people, Mohammed preached monotheism: "there is no God but Allah and Mohammed is his prophet." Recognizing 28 earlier prophets, including Abraham, Alexander the Great, and Jesus, Mohammed asserted that he, Mohammed, was the greatest and last of them. He also believed in angels and in an intermediate group between man and angels, the jinn, some good, some wicked. The most powerful of the wicked jinn is *Shaiton* (Satan). Mohammed prophesied a final Day of Judgment when the faithful, equal before Allah, would enter upon a bodily resurrection and an eternal life of bliss with the ever-virgin "damsels with large dark eyes" in a garden Paradise. The evil would be tortured by "burning wind and scalding water" in a fiery Hell.

Mohammed's concept of his religion as both a spiritual and a political organization gave social solidarity to the tribes of Arabia, who until his time had been utterly disorganized. The new religion led them to a breath-taking political and cultural expansion in which the diverse peoples who embraced Islam produced one of the world's great civilizations.

Molière: Stage name of Jean Baptiste Poquelin, French writer of comedy (1622–73). Like *Shakespeare,

Molière was an outstanding figure in a great age of drama. What the Elizabethan period was to English dramatic history, the *Neo-Classical 17th century was to the French. This age of *Corneille, Molière, and *Racine—like that of *Marlowe, *Jonson, Shakespeare, and Webster—was a pioneer period for the theater. The medieval amateur guilds and their religious productions had given way in the second part of the 16th century to professional touring companies which, in the 17th century, settled in Paris under the patronage of the crown. Cardinal Richelieu's interest in drama and his influence on Louis XIII in support of these troupes, together with the later favor of Louis XIV and Cardinal Mazarin, greatly encouraged the development of an art which was in disrepute with the clergy in general and with society.

Theatrical conditions were still primitive. When Molière came on the stage in 1643, there were only a few permanent buildings for the performance of plays, and these were often rather crude affairs, frequently converted indoor tennis courts. The typical playhouse was long and narrow, with galleries lining three sides, the stage on the fourth and an open pit in the center where the lower classes could stand. Later in the century the audience of court gallants was to invade the stage itself, sitting along its edges and often disrupting the course of the play. Lighting was poor and scenic effects were meager. But a greater problem in the development of the theater was the ambiguous position of the actor. Favored by royal approval and often very popular with the general public, the man of the theater still followed a profession which was condemned by the clergy and not officially sanctioned by society. An actor was not respectable; he was automatically excommunicated and was denied the rites of Christian burial unless he renounced his career.

In these circumstances, it is quite remarkable that Jean Baptiste Poquelin chose to become Molière: there was everything against such a move, nothing in favor of it. The son of a prosperous upholsterer, the future Molière was given an unusually fine education at the Jesuit college of Clermont and everything pointed to his following in his father's steps as *tapissier ordinaire du roi,* a member of the king's household for some three months of the year. But in 1643 he turned his back on this promising career and became one of the founders of a company of actors calling themselves the *Illustre Théâtre*. Whether Molière was influenced by the personable actress Madeline Béjart, one of the company and a close associate all his life, or whether he had contracted a passion for the stage from the productions he had seen in his native Paris is conjectural; the fact remains that he was off on the course he was to pursue throughout his lifetime.

The Illustrious Theater venture was not successful, and after several failures and subsequent brushes with creditors, the company took to the provinces, where it became one more in the growing number of traveling troupes. There, "in the field," for 12 years Molière served his apprenticeship as actor, manager, and playwright. When he returned to Paris in 1658, he had a great deal of experience behind him and at least two plays to his credit: *The Blunderer* (*L'Etourdi,* 1655) and *The Love Tiff* (*Dépit amoureux,* 1656). These two comedies and his first Parisian offering, *The Love-Sick Doctor* (a piece which has not survived), are typical of the prevailing farces, plays patterned on Italian comedy, with stock characters, prankish intrigue, and buffoonery. Molière was to refine this slap-dash type into a thoughtful comedy unrivaled until George Bernard *Shaw.

His next play, *The High-Brow Ladies* (*Les Précieuses Ridicules,* 1659), already shows development; here is a brilliant satire on the affectations of a blue-stocking cult then in fashion. The modern *comedy of manners was born, and Paris began to take note of its new author. The king himself approved, and Molière enjoyed his favor almost continuously from that point on. Although Louis' support was a bulwark for the playwright against the forces which were to oppose him from time to time, this patronage also meant that much of Molière's time and energy were to be dissipated in arranging various spectacles and ballets for his royal master.

Molière seems to have had a serious ambition to become a great tragedian, but his *Dom Garcie de Navarre* was a miserable failure the following year, 1660, and he finally settled down to developing his genuine talent, comedy writing. The next few years saw many successful pieces:

The School for Husbands (*L'Ecole des maris,* 1661), with its suggestion that women should be trusted and given more freedom; *The Bores* (*Les Fâcheux,* 1661), a satirical aggregation of all sorts of annoying courtiers; *The School for Wives* (*L'Ecole des femmes,* 1662), a companion to *The School for Husbands* and a commentary on the control of guardians over their wards. In the meantime, just before his last play, Molière had married Armande Béjart, Madeline's younger sister. Much younger than her husband and reportedly coquettish, Armande was not a very suitable wife, and their married life may well have given Molière a wry perspective for his domestic farces.

In 1664 appeared that important satire on religious hypocrisy, **Tartuffe,* so violently attacked by religious groups as a burlesque on piety that even the tacit support of the king was not sufficient to quell the opposition. Molière had to rewrite the play two times, and it was not until five years later that he finally succeeded in getting it publicly performed in Paris. His next satire, *Don Juan,* first performed in 1665, was also denounced as sanctioning libertinism, though actually it is a damning portrait of the unscrupulous courtier type found in Louis' own court.

Undaunted by all this criticism, Molière continued writing, and much of his best work still lay ahead. In 1666 he presented *The *Misanthrope,* his masterpiece of "thoughtful" comedy. A play of very little action, it is a brilliant exposition of Molière's rational philosophy of life, where moderation and good sense are the keynotes and any deviation is fair game for comedy. In close succession followed *The Physician in Spite of Himself* (*Le Médecin malgré lui,* 1666), a rollicking farce with barbs for the medical profession; two years later *The *Miser* (*L'Avare),* one of his best-known works, a social comedy on miserliness and parental authority; *The Would-Be Gentleman* (*Le Bourgeois gentilhomme,* 1670), a comedy-ballet on the social aspirations of the rising middle class; and *The Learned Women* (*Les Femmes savantes,* 1672), another devastating attack on ostentatiously learned females.

Meanwhile, Molière's health, which had always been poor, became worse. Throughout his career he had leveled his biting wit against a profession too unskilled or incompetent to help him. In 1673 he hurled his last defiance at doctors with *The *Imaginary Invalid* (*Le Malade imaginaire*). Not only did he write this paradoxically merry play in ill health, but, dying, he played its title role himself, ironically portraying a perfectly healthy hypochondriac. A few hours after the fourth performance, on February 17, 1673, he died. It is further irony that France's great—if not greatest—playwright was to be denied Christian burial because of his art. Since priests would not attend the author of *Tartuffe* and allow him the privilege of renouncing his profession, it was only at the intercession of his widow and friends that the king prevailed upon the archbishop to permit a quiet ceremony.

There are some striking similarities between Molière and Shakespeare: both were actors as well as authors, both were successful businessmen in their literary enterprises, and both were from good middle-class stock. But these are only biographical parallels. If Molière and Shakespeare have any significant similarity it must be in their attitudes toward life, people, and the theater—their insight into character, their humanity and their art—and in these fields the contrast between them is greater than the resemblance.

Although Molière's genius is more restricted than Shakespeare's, his achievement in his domain of thoughtful comedy has been supreme. The difference in structure between the comedies of the two men is significant. Shakespeare bases a comedy on a plot which will give an opportunity for various amusing scenes and situations; but Molière bases a comedy on a single comic or incongruous idea. We can say that Molière's comedies are about hypocrisy, avarice, or other such qualities, but the only way to tell what a Shakespearian comedy is about is to give a résumé of the plot.

As a practical, secular man who believed in the right of the individual to develop his nature under the guidance of reason, Molière was not a zealous reformer but a laughing, urbane commentator. Humane but not sentimental, he selected the absurdities of mankind as his target with comedy as his weapon, for, as he himself stated in his introduction to *Tartuffe*, "people do not mind being wicked; but they object to being made ridiculous . . ." Molière's interest, therefore, is in character, and he depicts persons who are at the same time 17th-century individuals and universal figures. And if in his interest he considers his plot secondary, often contriving an abrupt, artificial ending, it is not because he did not know better (there was his classical training at the College de Clermont, his acquaintance with the contemporary Italian drama performed in France, and his own experience in the theater), but because he considered plot merely the framework for all the Tartuffes, Harpagons, Alcestes, Dorines, Toinettes—one could continue the listing indefinitely—who are the real source of his comedy.

Montaigne, Michel Eyquem de: French essayist (1533–92). Montaigne was born at his family's ancestral castle in southwestern France. As soon as he was able to babble a few syllables, he was placed under the tutelage of a German preceptor who knew no French and who was required to use Latin exclusively when instructing his infant pupil. "As for the rest of the household," says Montaigne, "it was an inviolable rule that neither my mother, nor my valet, nor the maid used in my presence anything but those Latin words which each had learned, to be able to converse with me. . . . I was more than ten years old, and yet I knew no more French than Arabic. . . ." This insistence on the learning of a classical tongue shows how rapidly the *Renaissance, which was little more than a quarter of a century old in France, was progressing. It is not surprising that Montaigne became one of the chief exponents of the New Learning, not only in his own country but in the whole of Europe.

After studying law, he held important assignments in the Parliament of Bordeaux. He married in 1565 and had six daughters, five of whom died young. At the age of 37, he retired to his château of Montaigne in order to begin writing his *Essays*, the first two books of which were published in Bordeaux in 1580. Montaigne then undertook a voyage by slow stages to Rome, making stops at Paris and Venice en route. While in Rome, he learned that he had been elected mayor of Bordeaux. He was re-elected in 1583; two years later he retired once more to his château to continue the writing of his *Essays*. Locked up in his tower-library, which he called "the seat of his domination," he read, dreamed, and wrote. During his last years he prepared a third edition of the *Essays*, which appeared posthumously in 1595.

The continual modifications which Montaigne made as he reworked his *Essays* would seem to indicate that he had no set plan when he began to write. In the late 16th century, scholars delighted in applying quotations from classical authors to themselves and their own times and thus developing short moral dissertations or lessons. In the same way, Montaigne jotted down the reflections which his reading inspired; gradually he developed the idea of portraying himself: "Everyone recognizes me in my book," he wrote, "and everyone recognizes my book in me." By this method he hoped to come to know himself, to "assay" or test his character in the many circumstances of life. This he announces in all sincerity at the beginning: "Reader, this is a book of good faith. My intention is that everyone see me in my book just as I am, without any sham or artifice."

What, one may ask, is the value of these personal observations? Montaigne himself answers the question: in any single man one recognizes all humanity, for each individual bears all the characteristics of the species. Montaigne's *Essays*, although essentially personal, have the universality of all great literature. Montaigne did not plan, like *Rousseau, to give his readers some conceited "confessions" in which his intolerable ego displays and imposes itself; Montaigne speaks of himself only insofar as this self-revelation can be controlled by his sound common sense and by his own experience, supplemented by the recorded experiences of others. "What a brilliant idea to give us a portrait of himself," says *Voltaire, "for in portraying himself he has portrayed human nature."

Montaigne observes that he is, at one and the same time, timid and brave, an egotistic father and a devoted friend; in brief, he is torn asunder with contradictions, and this, he believes, is the fundamental trait of humanity. These contradictions at first amuse him; as he proceeds in his thinking and writing, he founds on them his philosophy of life, which is basically skeptical.

Montaigne's skepticism is the result of his observation that man is essentially changeable, an "undulating and diverse" being, incapable of attaining truth. Neither science, nor reason, nor philosophy can guide him. Man is the obedient servant of customs, prejudices, self-interest, and fanaticism; he is the victim of circumstances and of the impressions which these circumstances make upon him. This prosecution of man is found throughout the *Essays* and is their central theme; its vehemence attains the virulence of a strong and continuous indictment in the famous *Apology of Raymond Sebonde* (Book II, Essay XII).

Yet Montaigne is neither an iconoclast out to shatter the idols of humanity nor a satirist ridiculing human stupidity and gullibility. He is rather a very intelligent and conservative thinker who, when everyone else is shouting "I know!" and cursing or killing his neighbor for disagreeing with him, murmurs softly to himself, "*Que sais-je?*"—What do I know? All extreme and dogmatic opinions offend him. Most so-called obvious truths are, in his opinion, mere guesses. Above all, we should reserve judgment, and we should be especially suspicious of the slogans of our own time. "Since a wise man may be wrong, or a hundred men, or several nations, and since even human nature (as we think) goes wrong for several centuries on this matter or on that, how can we be certain that it occasionally stops going wrong, and that in this century it is not mistaken?"

Montaigne is essentially an epicurean; he sides with nature and is opposed to all forms of discipline. Along with his own "*Qu sais-je?*" he could very well have adopted *Rabelais' motto: "*Fay ce que voudras*"—Do as you please. In the last chapters of his *Essays* he makes his thought unequivocal on this score: "The wisest attitude to take toward nature is to abandon oneself to it purely and simply. What a soft and wholesome headrest ignorance and intellectual indifference make for the well-made head! Merely allow nature to take its course; she understands our concerns much better than we." Thus Montaigne tries to make us consider nature as the hidden source of every type of moderation and peace.

Because of his easy-going morality, Montaigne was hardly acceptable to *Pascal and all the preachers who, realizing that man is feeble and sinful, attempt to correct and discipline him. On the other hand, the freethinkers in the 17th–18th centuries, Bayle, *Voltaire, the Encyclopedists (see *Diderot), and the rationalists in the 19th century looked upon him as their master. It may seem inconsistent for these authors to admire Montaigne and still believe in progress and devote all their energies to it. Yet their conduct and pronouncements are quite logical; they prized Montaigne primarily as the ironical and implacable enemy of cocksureness. It was he who said: "The bane of man is the illusion that he has the certainty of his knowledge." By thus undermining dogmatism Montaigne paved the way for modern thought.

Montaigne's entire pedagogical system was far in advance of its time and pointed the way to educators of a later day. The ultimate aim of education in the true sense, according to Montaigne, should be to enable us to understand men and things as they are and to live a more harmonious life. And this objective cannot be attained without a certain perspective of values, without a certain mental equilibrium. Rabelais, Montaigne's predecessor in the French Renaissance, stressed the importance of the accumulation of learning, and wished to see in his pupil "a deep well of knowledge"; Montaigne stresses rather the paramount importance of acquiring judgment, as against merely memorizing facts. If possible, one should choose a teacher who is both wise and learned, but if a choice must be made, one should "choose a teacher who has a well-made head rather than a well-filled head. . . . This great world is the large mirror in which we must look at ourselves in order to know ourselves as we are; in a word, I wish it to be the textbook of my pupil." The lessons taken from life itself and from nature are more valuable than all the books in the world.

Montaigne's theories on education stress the importance of character training as well as intellectual achievement, though his moral code is, of course, somewhat different from ours. This is quite logical if we remember that *Seneca and *Plutarch are the two authors from whom Montaigne drew most of his own philosophy of life. Seneca treats ethical and moral questions in an easy-going manner and is seldom doctrinal; his moderate stoicism makes virtue human and attractive. Plutarch in his *Parallel Lives sum-

490

marizes all antiquity and reduces history to moral teaching. The commonsense philosophy and ethics of Seneca and Plutarch find a ready recipient in Montaigne: "Virtue is not, as Scholastic philosophy asserts, planted at the summit of a steep, rugged and inaccessible mountain; those who have attained it assert, on the contrary, that it is to be found in a beautiful, fertile, blooming plain from which it can contemplate all things below; if once you know where virtue abides, you may reach it easily by following shady, green, flowery roads which are smooth and have an easy slope, just as does the vault of heaven." The fundamental trait of Montaigne's character is a congenital dislike of straining. He would have been the last man to "take up arms against a sea of troubles." Study is to be a valuable diversion, not a burdensome task. Knowledge, however useful and important, should not disturb one's physical or mental equilibrium.

Montaigne's *Essays* reflect the character of their author. They consist of whimsical excursions of a mind that is as unrestrained as it is engaging and that represents the apparent inconsistency of an unerring judgment following the dictates of an uncontrolled imagination. He drifts from one topic to another, is led into digressions, sometimes writes about something else instead of what the title announces. Some of the titles are fantastic—*On Fleas*, for example, and *On the Habit of Wearing Clothes*—and there is no attempt to arrange the 94 essays in any logical order. Montaigne is an author to be browsed in, not read consecutively. In his casual disorder, however, he comes sooner or later to almost every topic of human interest. He deals with leisure, friendship, cannibals, women, solitude, prayer, books, sleep, and his opinions on these matters always enlighten us both about the author and mankind—and about ourselves. Montaigne was the first to write this type of personal essay, and his followers— *Lamb, *Bacon, *Addison, *Emerson, *Thoreau—are all heavily in his debt.

Emerson in his *Representative Men* summed up the appeal of Montaigne. "There have been men with deeper insight; but, one would say, never a man with such abundance of thoughts: he is never dull, never insincere, and has the genius to make the reader care for all that he cares for."

Montesquieu: Charles de Secondat, baron de la Brède et de Montesquieu, French satirist and political philosopher (1689–1755). After becoming a lawyer (in the tradition of his family) and rising to be president of the parliament of Bordeaux, Montesquieu abandoned the practice of law for more literary and philosophical activities.

In 1721 he published his *Persian Letters (Lettres persanes)* anonymously. They had an immediate and resounding success in all Europe because, precisely at this time, a philosophical movement, headed by *Voltaire and the other Encyclopedists (see *Diderot), was getting under way, its chief aim being the reform, or, more exactly, the overthrow, of the Old Regime, of which absolute monarchy was the odious symbol.

In his *Persian Letters* Montesquieu gives us a biting satire on European, especially French, customs. The correspondence of several Persians living in Paris, Venice, and Ispahan allows the author to contrast the manners and institutions of the West with those of Persia, to the obvious detriment of the former. A somewhat voluptuous seraglio intrigue serves the dual purpose of giving the book some semblance of unity and keeping the morbid curiosity of the reader on the alert. Against this Oriental background, Montesquieu unfurls a glowing picture of all the real or imagined shortcomings of European society in matters of religion, philosophy, government, commerce, finance, agriculture, political economy, marriage. No phase of human activity escapes his sarcasm.

In order to become better acquainted with men and nations, and the institutions under which they live, Montesquieu decided to travel. He spent the years from 1728 to 1731 visiting all the important cities in Europe, conferring with outstanding personalities, and, above all, gathering documents and making direct observations which were to serve as a basis for his more mature works. He went to England in the company of Lord Chesterfield and remained in that country for almost two years. In London he studied at close range the functioning of a constitution which combined monarchial and democratic features and which was, in his estimation, the ideal form of government. Upon returning to France, he lived the life of a scholar in his Château de la Brède, reading, reflecting, and putting his notes and impressions in order.

In 1734 Montesquieu published *Les Considérations sur les causes de la grandeur et de la décadence des Romains*, the results of a profound and personal study of the decadence rather than the greatness of Rome. He attributes the downfall of Rome to political rather than moral causes. In this work he also tested his particular historical method and political theories on one great and admirable race before applying them to humanity as a whole in his most important book, *The Spirit of the Laws* (*L'Esprit des lois*, 1748).

The 18th century has often been called the Age of Reason and the Age of Enlightenment. The names of Voltaire, Helvétius, d'Holbach, *Rousseau are associated with the *Encyclopédie* and with a reform movement characterized by its boldness, impetuosity, and excesses. Montesquieu's name and work are representative of a philosophical movement more discreet in its methods and more modest in its results; it was less boisterous, but not less efficient. *The Persian Letters* had marked the beginning of this campaign; *The Spirit of the Laws* was its culminating point.

Montesquieu's manner of approaching his subject is in itself a proof of his genius. The law is not considered, as heretofore, the result of the arbitrary will of one man or of a nation. "Laws," he says, "in their broader sense, are the necessary relations which derive from the nature of things, and in this sense, all beings have their laws. . . ." Yet Montesquieu does not allow himself to be distracted by this rather metaphysical general statement. Instead of looking for these *necessary relations* in the realm of ideas, he finds them in the positive study of facts. He does not look upon man as an abstract being; but rather as an actual flesh-and-blood individual who has both influenced history and been influenced by it. He examines the laws which govern men in their relation with government, customs, climate, religion, and commerce, not only in France, but in all countries and in all

493

ages. After a thorough analysis of the various types of governments, he concludes that in any country the laws must conform to the temperament and historical background of the people whom they are intended to govern.

The spirit of moderation and tolerance which characterized Montesquieu's theories on government and religion was not appreciated in a century when the iconoclasts of the *Encyclopédie* were at work. Yet Voltaire himself, a decided enemy of Montesquieu, was forced to speak favorably of this book, and in all parts of Europe it was well received. Its influence was great, but not immediate. Most of the world's constitutional governments today are indebted to it.

morality play: a type of medieval drama in which the characters are personified abstractions: Everyman, Good Deeds, Faith, Mercy, Anger, etc. The morality play is a fusion of two streams—medieval allegory, as in the *Romance of the Rose*, and the religious drama of the *mystery plays. It developed in the last quarter of the 14th century and spread over all western Europe, being especially cultivated in England and France. The two main themes of the religious moralities are the struggle between good and evil powers for man's soul, and the journey or pilgrimage of life, with its choice of eternal destinations. Vices, devils, etc., gave a considerable opportunity for low comedy, and the farcical element was especially developed in France. Though the morality was essentially religious, it was also used to inculcate ethical or educational ideals and to provide thinly disguised political commentary or satire. After about 1550 the morality play practically disappeared, though vestiges of it found their way into the regular theater as in the Good and Evil Angels and the parade of the Seven Deadly Sins in *Marlowe's *Doctor Faustus*. The outstanding English morality play is *Everyman* (c. 1500).

Mörike, Eduard: German poet (1804–74). A rather idle and weak-willed man as well as a hypochondriac, Mörike entered the ministry but eventually gave it up and lived on a small pension, supplemented by teaching German literature in a girls' school. His works include narrative poetry with a rich vein of country humor (*Idylle vom Bodensee,* 1846); an unfinished two-volume novel about the development of a painter (*Maler Nolton,* 1832), typically romantic in its formlessness and preoccupation with the artist, but in some ways looking toward realism; and a prose masterpiece in the sketch *Mozart on the Way to Prague* (*Mozart auf der Reise nach Prag,* 1855). He is chiefly remembered as a lyric poet, however, for his *Poems* (*Gedichte,* 1838). He manages to express or imply profound feeling with the most direct and simple language, much in the manner of the folk song. His reputation grew slowly; in fact, he was to some extent discovered and popularized by composers, in the settings of his poems by such men as Schumann, Franz Schubert, Brahms, and especially Hugo Wolf. Today he is accepted as one of the greatest of the German lyric poets.

Morris, William: English poet (1834–96). Morris was the author of *Defence of Guenevere and Other Poems* (1858), *Earthly Paradise* (1868–70); a translator (Icelandic sagas, medieval romances); a novelist of socialist propaganda (*News from Nowhere,* 1891); a *Pre-Raphaelite, printer (Kelmscott Press), painter, decorator (his designs for textiles, furniture, and homes revolutionized English taste and domestic architecture), and liberal social theorist (organizer of the Socialist League, 1884).

Moschus: Greek *pastoral poet (*fl. c.* 150 B.C.). Moschus was long believed to be the author of the beautiful *Lament for Bion,* a poem now considered the composition of an unknown writer, who made his home in southern Italy, perhaps during the early part of the 1st century B.C. (See *Bion.)

Muir, Edwin: Scottish poet, critic, novelist, translator (1887–1959). Although his name is not widely known, Muir is an important poet and translator (with his wife, Willa) of *Kafka's *The Trial* and *The Castle.* His own poetry (collected 1921–58) is of remarkable beauty and clarity, and of them T. S. *Eliot said Muir found almost "unconsciously the right, the inevitable way of saying what he had to say." He wrote three novels, a series of critical essays, an autobiography (*The Story and the Fable*, 1940, 1954), and was director of the British Institute at Rome in 1949 and professor of history at Harvard 1955–56.

Mulciber: see *Hephaestus.

Murasaki, Lady Shikibu: see *The Tale of *Genji.

Muses: nine beautiful daughters of *Zeus, who inspire literature, science, and the arts. Each had her particular field of activity: Calliope, epic poetry; Clio, history; Erato, love poetry; Euterpe, lyric poetry in general; Melpomene, tragedy; Polyhymnia, sacred poetry; Terpsichore, choral song and dance; Thalia, comedy and idyllic poetry; Urania, astronomy.

Musset, Alfred de: French lyric poet and dramatist (1810–57). The most passionate French lyric poet in an age of passionate lyric poets, Musset is celebrated for his poignant portrayal of the ecstasies and despairs of love. He entered Parisian literary circles as a gay, sparkling prodigy and became the spoiled darling of the older Romantics. An adolescent genius, he published before he was 20 a volume of brilliant poems, *Tales of Spain and Italy* (*Contes d' Espagne et d'Italie*, 1829), full of Byronic passion, daring, and ironic wit. He proceeded to write excellent comedies and a long narrative poem, *Rolla* (1835), the "last night of a rake"—another Byronic effusion, whose cynical gloom is set against exotic backgrounds.

The most decisive experience of his life was a tempestuous love affair with the authoress known as George *Sand, whom he met when he was 23. Their relationship crystallized his genius; but her infidelities, and their violent quarrels, reconciliations, and final parting destroyed his gaiety forever. She came through the experience unscathed. The best-known records of his love and grief are the prose autobiography, *Confession of a Child of the Age* (1836), *Souvenir* (1841), and the four poems of the *Nights* (*Nuits*, 1835, 1837). The *Nights*, in May, December, August, October, are poems developed in dialogues with the poet's Muse, who urges him to forget his sorrow. But Musset is inconsolable; the bruised heart must continue to love and suffer forever. Frank in their confession of the experience and in exaltation of the poet's own personality, his poems are intense expressions of his love, vehement even in memory. When he failed to make romantic love a continuing experience in life, he immortalized his ardor and misery in a few great poems written with "swooning beauty." Musset believed that feeling is more important than form. Hence he did not seek finish and polish in versification and diction. The poems are carried by the white heat of their emotion.

Musset's position in the French theater is perhaps even more secure than his reputation as a poet. Between 1833 and 1845 he wrote a series of tragedies and comedies, all marked by elegance of sentiment and language and combining serious implications with lightness of touch. Several of these used proverbs as their titles: *One Mustn't Jest with Love* (*On ne badine pas avec l'amour*, 1834) and *Don't Swear to Anything* (*Il ne faut jurer de rien*, 1836). His plays of this sort are frequently referred to as his *Proverbs*.

He spent his last ten years seeking forgetfulness in debauchery. *Sainte-Beuve summarized his life: "What a light! What an eclipse!"

mystery play: a name given to any of the Biblical plays performed (usually in groups or cycles) during the late *Middle Ages and early *Renaissance. The name is ultimately derived from Latin *ministerium* ("service, occupation"), not from *mysterium* ("mystery"). It probably refers to the performance by occupational guilds, and it has no connection with the "mysteries" of revelation. These plays developed from a great expansion and elaboration of the *trope, which moved outdoors and lost its ecclesiastical sponsorship. Each guild performed one play, often choosing one that was appropriate to its profession, or for which it would have the necessary properties or equipment (*e.g.,* the water-carriers would perform Noah's Flood). The plays were performed on "pageants" (stages built on large wagons) before reviewing stands, so that the spectator could take up his position at one place and all the plays of the cycle would come to him in order. The four great surviving cycles of English mystery plays, the Cornish, Chester, York, and Towneley (or Wakefield) Cycles, date from the 14th and 15th centuries and total some 150 plays.

A distinction is frequently made, as in French, between mystery plays, which are based on the Bible, and miracle plays, which are based on saints' lives, apocryphal miracles of the Virgin, etc.; but the distinction is not consistent and the two terms are sometimes used interchangeably.

myth: a traditional tale common to the members of a tribe, race, or nation, usually involving the supernatural and serving to explain some natural phenomenon. The story of *Persephone is a clear example: it was common to the peoples of *classical antiquity, and its account of how Persephone (daughter of *Demeter, goddess of grain) was carried off to the Underworld by *Hades but was allowed to return and visit her mother for half of each year, supplied an explanation of the alternation of the seasons. The explanatory purpose of many myths is now obscure, for a myth often continues to live as a tale in its own right after its explanation has been supplanted.

It must be emphasized that a myth is not a specific literary work, but a floating tale. Myths are often given literary treatment (as in *Aeschylus' *Prometheus Bound* and *Oresteia*), but the myth is the raw material for these plays, not the plays themselves.

The myths of a people, taken all together, form a mythology. (This term is also used to designate the study of myths.) A mythology is usually taken for granted as part of the common background of writer and reader, and most Occidental writers assume that their audience will understand allusions to classical and Scandinavian mythology. The European or American who begins to read Sanskrit or Arabic literature soon finds himself handicapped by his ignorance of the myths which the writers assume that he knows. All peoples everywhere have always had their mythologies to explain such things as the origin of the world and of man and woman, the rising and setting of the sun, birth, death, and the alternation of the seasons. One almost universal mythical figure is the culture-hero, the man who, soon after the beginning of things, first invented or discovered or stole (like Prometheus) such necessities as fire and the art of weaving and gave these blessings to his people.

Nabokov, Vladimir: Russian-American novelist (1900–77). He is best known for his popular novel *Lolita* (1958) and has written fiction both in Russian and in brilliant English, which he learned during his polyglot childhood in Russia and later cultivated as a student at Cambridge, England. His first novel written in English was *The Real Life of Sebastian Knight* (1941), and it was followed by a series of works that included *Bend Sinister* (1947) and an autobiography, *Speak, Memory*. He translated and edited *Pushkin and wrote on entomology—of which he was an ardent amateur. His late novel *Ada* (1969) displays his multilingual verbal improvisations, some of which match in their humor, wit, and sexuality the verbal compounds of *Joyce.

naturalism: a literary method and school of the later 19th century, stemming in literary history from *Balzac and developed by the Goncourt brothers and *Zola, who formulated its principles and objectives. Thomas *Hardy and George Moore were additional influences upon American naturalism—Stephen *Crane, Theodore *Dreiser, Jack *London, Frank Norris. Its purpose was to dispel superstition and idealization. The method was to apply to literary subjects scientific objectivity: to observe closely, to put no limitation on choice of subject, and to be more widely inclusive of details than were the realists (see *realism). It wished to "tell everything," to show the environment exactly as it is by the technique of a "brutal photography," to present "a slice of life," to "experiment" with the characters as if in a laboratory and trace their development as it is dictated by heredity and environment; for the basic assumption of these novelists with respect to any one individual character is a pessimistic determinism in which free will becomes almost nonexistent, human responsibility altogether denied, with "conditions, not men, at fault," the individual but "a pawn on the chessboard" of nature, subject to the indifferent laws of a fatalistic, mechanistic universe. Such a theory, by denying human choice or dignity, makes tragedy in the classical sense impossible (see *Aristotle). The naturalists stressed the materialism of men's motives, the coarser, ignominious aspects of their characters, where Fate leads them to evil and cruel ends (so a Jack London prospector, discovering a rich vein of gold, can with easy conscience bury alive a rival prospector who comes along quite by accident). Many used the novel as a study in social problems, combining their naïvely romantic idealism about a future perfect socialistic society with "objectivity" toward their own society—a "naturalistic" view which was bitter and satirical (cf. Henry *Adams, *Democracy*, 1881). As happens with many other writers, the naturalists are often at their best when they are least "clinical," "objective," "naturalistic"; when moved by intense personal involvement—grief, fury, bewilderment—they transmute their emotions into a literature of passion.

nectar: see *ambrosia.

Nemesis: a Greek divinity, daughter of Night. Although she punished crimes and rewarded virtue, she was generally thought of primarily in her punitive function. She is the avenger of the gods and is particularly concerned with the punishment of impiety and *hybris*.

Neo-Classicism: a period of European literature primarily during the 17th and 18th centuries, though its chronological limits vary from country to country. It is characterized by a conscious effort to attain the restraint, polish, and objectivity of *classicism.

It often happens that a human institution is gradually arrived at by experimenting within the framework of an earlier tradition, that it proves remarkably effective for a time, that because of its effectiveness it becomes enshrined in custom and law, and that this fact preserves it as a burdensome legacy long after it has lost all real vitality or effectiveness, until eventually a successful revolution against it ushers in a new period of experiment. This is exactly what happened with Neo-Classicism in European literature.

During the latter years of the *Renaissance a decline in individualism and a tendency toward conformity began to appear. The remarks that critics had been making as observations about literary practice came increasingly to be considered and stated as rules for the writing of literature. In the drama, for example, the three *unities were first stated as rules by Italian critics late in the Renaissance, and throughout most of the Neo-Classical period writers occasionally complained of these restrictions but generally followed them.

The desire to regulate and to accept regulation is perhaps most clearly seen in the extremely personal matter of language. The Renaissance was a period of linguistic freedom, of wide experimentation with what were essentially rather new vernacular tongues. Gradually, however, the concept of language as etiquette, with a series of do's and don't's, took shape—and with it came academies, often with governmental sanction, to police the language. The first of these, the *Academia della Crusca,* was founded in Florence in 1552 for the purpose of sifting impurities out of the language. Many similar ones followed in France, Spain, Portugal, and Germany, largely during the 17th century. The most important and influential of these has been the French Academy, which was recognized by the king in 1635. Its function was "to give our language certainty by rules and to make it pure, eloquent, and capable of dealing with the arts and sciences." These purposes were to be achieved by compiling a dictionary, a grammar, a treatise on poetics, and a rhetoric. The dictionary first appeared in 1694 and the grammar in 1932; but the Academy has not got around to the poetics and the rhetoric yet. In England an academy was often proposed (especially by *Swift in 1712) but was never quite formed.

The creation of academies was, however, only a symptom of the general desire to have fixed standards and to be able to conform to them with the certainty of being right. Basically, it was our modern yearning to unload our personal problems on "experts" and let them tell us what to do. This was the essential point of view of the Neo-Classical Age, with the modification that the place of the expert was frequently taken by "reason" or "common sense," whereas now it is "science." For this reason a part of the Neo-Classical period in the 18th century is frequently known as the Age of Reason, or, even less modestly, the Age of Enlightenment. These characteristics were reinforced by Newtonian physics and mathematics, which revealed that the whole universe was rational, systematic, and consistent, operating by its "laws" with mathematical precision. As Alexander *Pope's witty epigram put it: "God said let Newton be, and all was light."

The central nation in the Neo-Classical movement was France, and French literature dominated Europe during this period. We may say, if a date must be chosen, that the period begins in 1635, the year of the royal sponsorship of the Academy, and of the first significant play by *Corneille, a tragedy on Medea. In the next year his play *The Cid* stirred a storm of debate and criticism that showed how far the idea of literary "correctness"—as opposed to mere effectiveness—had already established itself. Though Corneille won a great popular success and though the attacks on him were in part dictated by Cardinal Richelieu's jealousy, Corneille's subsequent plays did not take the liberties that had marked *The Cid*.

But the paradox of Neo-Classicism (as it always seems to Romantics) lies in the fact that these stricter plays that followed—*Horace, Cinna, Polyeucte*—are fine tragedies and are Corneille's masterpieces. At its best, Neo-Classicism gains in polish, speed, and concentration at least as much as it loses in caprice and scope by its voluntary confinement. *The Cid* actually introduced one of the most glorious periods of modern literature, the Age of Louis XIV. This monarch's amazingly long reign (1643–1715) produced the writings of such men as *Racine, *Molière, *La Fontaine, *Pascal, *Boileau, and *La Rochefoucauld, to name only some of the greatest.

The spirit of this literature is, in general, that of classicism, but it is by no means a slavish imitation of the ancients. For example, the chorus was one of the most conspicuous features of an ancient tragedy, but the typical Neo-Classical tragedy has no chorus. It is a new literary type inspired by an older one, but not directly imitated from it.

The two dominant aims of the Age of Louis XIV were to produce the illusion of reality and to follow the dictates of decorum. Frequently they came to the same thing, as in the tendency to characterize types more than individuals and to avoid eccentricities. Since the literary rules of French Neo-Classicism were neatly codified in *The Poetic Art (L'Art poétique)* of Boileau in 1674, this poem will serve to illustrate some of the typical attitudes of the age. For example, Boileau tells the dramatist what a young man is like and warns him not to characterize one differently. He demands the strict observance of the *unities because without it there can be no illusion of reality: in Spain, it is true, a character can be a child in the first act of a play and a graybeard in the last, but a French audience cannot be taken in by such a crude improbability. But this insistence on the unities is not merely the acceptance of a dogma. It follows because "reason leads us to accept these rules." Above all, everything is to be elegant and decorous—at least, on the surface. "The most indecent love will not offend if it is chastely expressed." Here we have art clearly reflecting society, for the Neo-Classical period was a licentious but socially correct age.

Most of the 18th century in French literature was marked by a stubborn clinging to a Neo-Classical tradition which had ceased to be really productive. Tragedies continued to be made by substituting in the established formula, but they had no power. Even as mercurial a spirit as *Voltaire, when writing in this form, is correct, polished, and almost dull. In the theater the only really new development is the middle-class tragedy, or sometimes merely problem-play—the result of an increasing democratic revolt against the assumption that only kings and mythological characters could be tragic heroes. Outside the theater, the 18th century saw the rise of a school of social criticism and political theory which finally built up to the explosion of the French Revolution at the end of the century. It is a striking paradox that this radical thought was often combined with extreme artistic conservatism. Voltaire furnishes an outstanding example. While demanding that the miraculous claims of religion be judged by everyday reason, and while constantly fighting for equal justice and defending the victims of the inequities of the old order, in his plays and poems he himself still stubbornly clung to the old order. The outstanding exception to this paradox was *Rousseau, the Frenchman of the 18th century who was equally radical in politics, in literature, and in human sensibility in general, but his history belongs with the beginnings of the *Romantic Movement.

Neo-Classicism came late to England, with the return of the courtiers who had spent the period of the Commonwealth in France. When the monarchy was restored with the recall of Charles II in 1660, a new era dawned in English letters. (It is true that *Milton, a man of the Renaissance, wrote his greatest works after this, but he was a holdover from an earlier age.) The change was immediately evident in the theater, for plays had been forbidden during 18 years of Puritan domination. Hence there was no tradition left to be overcome, and Neo-Classical drama arrived almost overnight. Since the English sense of decorum was at this point of history (and only at this point) weaker than the French, Restoration comedy is far more licentious than that of Molière. It is also more obviously brilliant, and more superficial. Restoration tragedy, though it produced some good plays, is feeble indeed in comparison with its French models. What tragic genius there was went into the "heroic play," a type of dramatized epic which was spectacularly produced and highly successful in its own time. John *Dryden, who was equally effective in tragedy, the heroic play, criticism, and satire, dominated the English literature of the Restoration.

Satire proved to be the most distinctive literary undertaking of 18th-century England, satire in prose and verse ranging from the tolerant amusement at human foibles shown by *Addison, through the venomous personal attacks of *Pope, to *Swift's blasting of the "little odious vermin" which constitute the human race. And this satire was always skillful, always neat, whether in polished *heroic couplets or in lucid, straightforward prose. In fact, it is the writer's complete control of both his medium and himself which not only enables him to damn an enemy without raising his voice, but which gives a good deal of its effectiveness to all Neo-Classical literature. The essential characteristics continued throughout' most of the 18th century, and the only entirely new development was the rise of the *novel.

During the last half of the 18th century, England as well as France was tending toward the *Romantic Movement. Thomas *Gray, whose *Elegy Wrote in a Country Church-Yard* is probably the most "classical" poem in English, began to write poems inspired by ancient Celtic and Scandinavian legends. In 1765 Bishop Percy published a number of old ballads which he had collected, and James Macpherson (see *Ossianic Poems) had already begun to forge ancient bardic songs. Sentiment and sensibility began to come into their own again, and the voice of untutored genius electrified the country in the songs of *Burns. All this, however, is properly not a part of Neo-Classicism, but of the first stirrings against it, which the French literary historians have named Pre-Romanticism.

French and English literature have been considered individually because the great achievements of Neo-Classicism are theirs. Most of the other European nations were blinded by the glory of Louis XIV's court at Versailles and imitated its literature, just as most of the rulers of the German principalities imitated his formal gardens and elaborate entertainments. Although Spain and Italy produced some distinguished work, it was essentially a reflection of that of France.

The modern German literature of importance outside its own country really begins with the revolt against French Neo-Classicism. This was primarily the work of two men, *Lessing and *Herder. Beginning about the middle of the 18th century, Lessing introduced the new middle-class tragedy to Germany, attacked the imitative poets and the borrowed French type of drama, and held up *Shakespeare as a better model. Herder, in a number of works (largely fragmentary), and even more by his personal influence, set the vogue of folk literature and primitive myth—of the elemental and powerful generally as opposed to the refined and polished. These two men created the intellectual and literary climate in which the early works of *Goethe and *Schiller appeared, and the *Sturm und Drang movement of which they were a part made the 1770's in Germany one of the crucial points of the Romantic Movement. Even though philosophers earnestly hoped to tidy up society by the use of reason, the violent reaction against the Neo-Classical closed universe and its "sweet smile of reason" also is to be seen in art, for example, in Goya's (1744–1828) etching "The dream of reason produces monsters" (*El sueño de la razon produce monstruos*).

Neo-Platonism: a philosophical school giving a mystical development to the teachings of *Plato. The founder of the school was Plotinus, a Greek-speaking Egyptian who began teaching in Rome about A.D. 244. His pupil Porphyry edited his works in six books of nine chapters each, which are consequently known as *Enneads*. Porphyry also wrote a life of Plotinus, who, he tells us, was such a spiritual man that "he seemed ashamed to be in a body." Plotinus' philosophy discounts the physical and material world by arranging the phenomena of existence in an ascending order: matter, soul, reason, God. God is pure existence, having neither form nor matter. Plotinus had considerable influence on Christianity, both through Saint *Augustine and *Boethius and through medieval philosophers. He was also an important element in the literary Platonism of the *Renaissance.

Neo-Platonism later degenerated. It is easy to pass from spiritual conceptions to an array of spirits, and this is precisely what happened. During the early *Middle Ages elaborate hierarchies of angels and demons were developed from the ideas of these philosophers (plus Oriental influences), together with appropriate spells, rituals, etc. A good deal of both learned and popular demonology eventually comes from this source.

506

Neptune: see *Poseidon.

New Comedy: see *Menander.

Nibelungenlied: a Middle High German narrative poem (*c.* 1200), one of the most popular and celebrated monuments of German literature. The unknown author (from the region now called Austria) drew his materials from the mythology of prehistoric Scandinavia and the semi-historical legends of the tribal migrations of the Germanic peoples, centering around the defeat of the Burgundians by the Huns in A.D. 437. These are the same materials which inspired the Icelandic *Volsung Saga* and parts of the *Poetic *Edda.* In the *Nibelungenlied* the setting and motivation are made contemporary with the author, so that a story originally dealing with Germanic paganism is presented as taking place in a Christian and feudal culture. The poem (which is almost the same length as The *Aeneid*) is divided into 39 chapters, or "Adventures." It is written in four-line stanzas riming aabb, with a clearly marked pause in the middle of each line, and the last half-line of the stanza longer than the others. The style is direct, without rhetorical imagery, but the poet complies with the epic tradition by giving the beginning of his story through the technique of the flashback and by adumbrating the outcome by means of anticipations and warnings.

The poem falls into two distinct parts. The first half deals with the mythical Nibelungen, the nurture of Siegfried (Icelandic Sigurd), his winning the Nibelung hoard, his relation to Brunhild, his marriage to Kriemhild (Icelandic Gudrun), and his murder by her brother's retainer. The second half is concerned with the revenge which Kriemhild takes on her family and her husband's murderers at the court of Etzel (Attila the Hun).

Although the characters are presented as 12th-century knights, their actions are essentially those of a much earlier story. Revenge for a slight or a murder is a solemn obligation. Loyalty is personal rather than political, and it would be unworthy for a retainer to question the justice of his master's or mistress's cause. Although a good deal of the supernatural remains from the early story, all the motivation of the action is eminently human and understandable. There is no attempt at psychological subtlety or analysis: the characters are boldly drawn, larger-than-life figures strongly moved by the fundamental passions of love, hate, loyalty, pride, and greed.

One remarkable feature of the poem is the complete reversal of sympathy between the two halves. At the end of the first part, Kriemhild is a grievously wronged woman whose husband has been treacherously murdered and whose heritage has been insolently snatched from her so that she can be kept too helpless to plot any revenge. Both the poet and the reader are then pleased when Attila sends an emissary to woo her and when her marriage to him at last puts her in a position to avenge her wrongs. But she pursues her revenge so ruthlessly and her victims make such a magnificent fight against odds which they know to be insuperable that the villains of the first part become the heroes of the second. In a final crescendo of horror, all the characters of the first part are wiped out in what has been called the "most awful bloodbath of all epic poetry." Then, when Kriemhild has her captured brother killed, and with her own hands and her murdered husband's long-guarded sword beheads her husband's bound and helpless murderer—and when one of Etzel's retainers, as an act of simple justice, cuts down the screaming Kriemhild—the reader suddenly realizes that his own wishes have been carried out. In the course of the poem, he has sympathized with each side, and wished for the destruction of the other, and in the last few stanzas he joins the Huns in a sort of respectful grief for all the slain.

Nicomachean Ethics: a treatise written by *Aristotle and named after his son Nicomachus, who may have edited it for publication (4th century B.C.). The *Nicomachean Ethics* is an inquiry into the nature of the Good, which Aristotle defines as the ultimate end or purpose of all action and which he identifies with happiness, though not with happiness as it is commonly conceived to be. For he believes that the Good is to be found not in externals like wealth and honor, as people imagine, nor yet in pleasure, but in that activity which is most becoming to man as a rational being. This, he concludes, is contemplation or philosophy, and therefore he considers the contemplative life of intellectual virtue the best and happiest for man, as it is the most appropriate to him. In the nature of things, however, few men can lead this type of life, and Aristotle therefore adds that, although it is first, the practical life of moral virtue is second; and he devotes a large part of his discourse to its examination. In doing so, he discovers that moral virtue is a disposition of the will, developed by practice, to choose the mean between extremes of conduct, as for example, to choose courage, the mean between cowardice and recklessness, rather than either of these extremes, both of which are vices. The mean is, of course, not arithmetical, but normally lies closer to one extreme than to the other, as courage lies closer to recklessness than to cowardice. But the beginner will find it most easily in any case if he aims at the extreme farthest from his own predisposition. And with practice anyone will be able to find and follow it effortlessly or almost so, such is the force of habit and training in us.

The Doctrine of the Mean is central in Aristotle's ethical thinking, and under it he examines the great moral virtues—courage, justice, temperance, gentleness, liberality, and the others. The point of view it represents is not, of course, original with him, being found in the traditional Greek concept of *nothing too much*. Nor does he look upon it as a solution to all the problems of life. There are actions to which it obviously does not apply. And yet, for the most part, there is a right way to perform a given action, and the wrong ways are wrong because they fall short of the right way or go beyond it. Moreover, the right way is always the most efficient way, as the most efficient way to meet danger is by courageous action, for it cannot be overcome best by recklessness, and still less by cowardice.

Nietzsche, Friedrich Wilhelm: German philosopher and poet (1844–1900). When Nietzsche was only five, his father died, and the boy was brought up by his pious female relatives—a fact which has been associated with his later attacks on both women and religion. He was a brilliant and model youngster, and, although he had leanings toward both music and theology, he finally specialized in classical philology at the Universities of Bonn and Leipzig. His achievements were such that he became Professor of Greek at Basle in 1869—a remarkable distinction for such a young man at one of the most conservative universities. Ten years later he resigned his post because of poor health and for the next ten years led a solitary life in southern Germany, Switzerland, and Italy. Then, in January 1889, he suffered a complete mental collapse from which he never recovered, although his body lived on for 11 years more.

Soon after achieving his professorship, he had published a brilliant little book, *The Birth of Tragedy from the Spirit of Music* (*Die Geburt der Tragödie aus dem Geiste der Musik,* 1872), not an antiquarian study of the mechanical details, but an intuitive philosophical investigation into the spiritual background of Greek tragedy. This was followed by *Untimely Opinions* (*Unzeitgemässe Betrachtungen,* 1873–76), which dealt scathingly with the smug conceit of the new Bismarckian state. Among the important books of the rest of his career are *Thus Spake Zarathustra* (*Also sprach Zarathustra,* published 1883–92), a rhapsodical series of sermons of an imaginary prophet, written in a poetic prose modeled on that of the *Bible; Beyond Good and Evil* (*Jenseits von Gut und Böse,* 1886); *The Genealogy of Morals* (*Zur Genealogie der Moral,* 1887); *The Will to Power* (*Der Wille zur Macht,* which was left incomplete at the time of his collapse); and a posthumously published autobiography, *Ecce Homo* (1908). He also wrote a small body of distinguished poetry.

Nietzsche is an extremely complicated figure. He sharply attacked all the cherished ideas and ideals of his age—Christianity, conventional morality, sympathy for the weak and helpless, rationalism—and yet he warned a friend that it was neither necessary nor desirable for his readers to agree with him; the best attitude for the reader was a mixture of curiosity and ironic resistance! There are points on which his doctrine is essentially fascistic, and Hitler's minions were ready enough to claim him as their prophet and inspirer—but to see the perversion of truth in this claim we have only to remember that Nietzsche was strongly opposed to nationalism, standing armies, the German Empire, racism (especially anti-Semitism), and power politics. The interpretation of Nietzsche is made more difficult by the fact that he often deliberately overstated his case in order to make some impression on those who were already strongly committed to the other side. His ideas are expressed with remarkable verve and caustic wit; they are always exciting and sometimes dangerous. His exaggerations and extremes are probably the result of his own background and temperament, as well as his own particular moment of history. Society had become smugly ossified and narcissistic, and, like *Ibsen, Nietzsche was determined to show it how hollow many of its idols were.

Nine Worthies: a group of illustrious men widely praised in medieval times. The list included three Gentiles (Hector, Alexander the Great, and Julius Caesar), three Hebrews (Joshua, David, and Judas Maccabeus), and three Christians (King Arthur, Charlemagne, Godfrey of Bouillon).

Nobel prizewinners in literature:

1901 **Sully Prudhomme.** *French poet.*

1902 **Theodor Mommsen.** *German historian.*

1903 **Björnstjerne Björnson.** *Norwegian novelist, poet, and dramatist.*

1904 **Frédéric Mistral.** *Provençal poet and philologist.* **José Echegaray y Eizagaitre.** *Spanish dramatist.*

1905 **Henryk Sienkiewicz.** *Polish novelist.*

1906 **Giosuè *Carducci.** *Italian poet.*

1907 **Rudyard *Kipling.** *English poet and novelist.*

1908 **Rudolf Eucken.** *German philosopher.*

1909 **Selma Lagerlöf.** *Swedish novelist.*

1910 **Paul von Heyse.** *German poet, novelist and dramatist.*

1911 Maurice *Maeterlinck. *Belgian dramatist.*

1912 Gerhart *Hauptmann. *German dramatist and novelist.*

1913 Rabindranath Tagore. *East Indian poet.*

1914 No award.

1915 Romain *Rolland. *French novelist.*

1916 Verner von Heidenstam. *Swedish poet.*

1917 Karl Gjellerup. *Danish novelist and poet.*
Henrik Pontoppidan. *Danish novelist.*

1918 No award.

1919 Carl Spitteler. *Swiss poet and novelist.*

1920 Knut Hamsun. *Norwegian novelist.*

1921 Anatole *France. *French novelist.*

1922 Jacinto Benavente y Martinez. *Spanish dramatist.*

1923 William Butler *Yeats. *Irish poet.*

1924 Wladyslaw Stanislaw Reymont. *Polish novelist.*

1925 George Bernard *Shaw. *Irish dramatist.*

1926 Grazia Deledda. *Italian novelist.*

1927 Henri Louis *Bergson. *French philosopher.*

1928 Sigrid Undset. *Norwegian novelist.*

1929 Thomas *Mann. *German novelist.*

1930 Sinclair *Lewis. *American novelist.*

1931 Erik Axel Karlfeldt. *Swedish poet. Posthumous award. Karlfeldt had refused the award ten years before on the grounds that he was not read outside of Sweden.*

1932 John *Galsworthy. *English novelist and dramatist.*

1933 Ivan Alexeyevich Bunin. *Russian novelist and poet.*

1934 Luigi *Pirandello. *Italian novelist and dramatist.*

1935 No award.

1936 **Eugene *O'Neill.** *American dramatist.*

1937 **Roger Martin du Gard.** *French novelist.*

1938 **Pearl S. Buck.** *American novelist.*

1939 **Frans Eemil Sillanpaa.** *Finnish novelist.*

1940
1943 } **No awards.**

1944 **Johannes V. Jensen.** *Danish novelist and poet.*

1945 **Gabriela Mistral (Lucila Godoy y Aleayaga).** *Chilean poet.*

1946 **Hermann *Hesse.** *Swiss novelist and poet.*

1947 **André *Gide.** *French novelist, essayist, philosopher, and poet.*

1948 **T. S. *Eliot.** *English poet and critic.*

1949 **William *Faulkner.** *American novelist.*

1950 **Bertrand *Russell.** *English philosopher and mathematician.*

1951 **Pär F. Lagerkvist.** *Swedish novelist, poet and essayist.*

1952 **François *Mauriac.** *French novelist, journalist, and poet.*

1953 **Sir Winston Churchill.** *English historian and statesman.*

1954 **Ernest *Hemingway.** *American novelist.*

1955 **Halldór Kiljan Laxness.** *Icelandic novelist.*

1956 **Juan Ramón Jiménez.** *Spanish poet.*

1957 **Albert *Camus.** *French novelist and dramatist.*

1958 **Boris L. *Pasternak.** *Russian poet and novelist (declined the award).*

1959 **Salvatore Quasimodo.** *Italian poet and critic.*

1960 **Saint-John Perse (Alexis Léger).** *French poet.*

1961 **Ivo Andric.** *Yugoslavian novelist.*

1962   **John Steinbeck.** *American novelist.*

1963   **Giorgos Seferiades.** *Greek poet (see George *Seferis).*

1964   **Jean-Paul *Sartre.** *French philosopher, novelist and dramatist (declined the award).*

1965   **Mikhai1 Sholokhov.** *Russian novelist.*

1966   **S. Y. *Agnon.** *Israeli novelist.*
      Nelly Sachs. *German poet.*

1967   **Miguel Angel Asturias.** *Guatemalan poet.*

1968   **Yasunari *Kawabata.** *Japanese novelist.*

1969   **Samuel *Beckett.** *Irish dramatist and novelist.*

1970   **Aleksander *Solzhenitsyn.** *Russian novelist.*

1971   **Pablo Neruda (Ricardo Eliezer Neftalí Reyes y Basoalto).** *Chilean poet.*

1972   **Heinrich Böll.** *German novelist.*

1973   **Patrick White.** *Australian novelist.*

1974   **Eyvind Johnson.** *Swedish novelist.*
      Harry Martinson. *Swedish novelist, essayist, poet, and short-story writer.*

1975   **Eugenio Montale.** *Italian poet and essayist.*

1976   **Saul Bellow.** *American novelist.*

1977   **Vicente Aleixandre.** *Spanish poet.*

1978   **Isaac Bashevis Singer.** *Jewish-American novelist.*

1979   **Odysseus Elytis (Odysseus Alepoudhelis).** *Greek poet.*

1980   **Czeslaw Milosz.** *Polish poet, essayist, novelist, and translator.*

1981   **Elias Canetti.** *Bulgarian novelist, dramatist, and essayist.*

1982   **Gabriel García Márquez.** *Colombian novelist and shorty-story write.*

1983   **Sir William Golding.** *British novelist.*

1984 **Jaroslav Seifert.** *Czech poet.*

1985 **Claude Simon.** *French novelist.*

1986 **Wole Soyinka.** *Nigerian novelist, dramatist, poet, and lecturer.*

1987 **Joseph Brodsky.** *American poet.*

1988 **Naguib Mahfouz.** *Egyptian short-story writer, novelist, and dramatist.*

1989 **Camilo José Cela.** *Spanish novelist and poet.*

1990 **Octavio Paz.** *Mexican poet and essayist.*

1991 **Nadine Gordimer.** *South African novelist and short-story writer.*

1992 **Derek Walcott.** *West Indian poet and dramatist.*

1993 **Toni Morrison.** *American novelist.*

1994 **Kenzaburo Oe.** *Japanese novelist and essayist.*

1995 **Seamus Heaney.** *Irish poet.*

1996 **Wislawa Szymborska.** *Polish poet.*

1997 **Dario Fo.** *Italian dramatist and actor.*

1998 **Jose Saramago.** *Portuguese novelist.*

1999 **Günter Grass.** *German novelist, poet, dramatist, essayist, and short-story writer.*

2000 **Gao Xingjian.** *Chinese novelist and dramatist.*

novel: a prose narrative on a large scale. Like the *short story, the novel defies accurate definition both because of the essential but unfixable element of length and because it includes so many different types and possibilities. In fact, even the insistence on prose is arbitrary: not only is *Chaucer's *Troilus and Criseyde* (*c.* 1385) essentially a novel in verse, but a number of works describing themselves as "novels in verse" have been published within the past century.

This problem of definition makes it extremely difficult to give any real history of the novel because we cannot

515

be sure just what works are a part of its history. Extended narratives in prose have been known almost since the dawn of literature. The ancient Egyptians had them, though the surviving works would indicate that they did not go much beyond the scope of the *novelette. We are on surer ground with the *Satyricon* of *Petronius (*c.* A.D. 50) and *The Golden Ass* of *Apuleius (*c.* A.D. 150), as well as the whole school of Greek romances of about the 3d century A.D. (see *Longus). These romances are sometimes discounted on the ground that they are merely strung-together series of episodes, for the general theme is that of the course of true love upset by pirates, shipwreck, kidnapings, etc. But if we exclude them for this reason we shall have to exclude also the novels of *Cooper, a great many current "Westerns," and many other works which, whatever else we may think of them, are unquestionably novels.

The basic nature of the impulse to write novels is attested by the fact that the first full-fledged novel, by modern standards, was written outside the Western world and was unknown to it until comparatively recently. Lady Murasaki's *Tale of *Genji* (*c.* 1000) is not approached in its type until Madame de Lafayette's *La Princesse de Clèves* (1678), which is also a novel of sentiment. When Lady Murasaki was writing, Europe was just beginning to exploit the narrative in verse, in the *chansons de geste* and the later *medieval romance. Prose narrative returned with the Italian collections of tales, of which *Boccaccio's *Decameron* (1348–53) is the most famous example. The word *novel* is derived from the Italian name for such a tale, *novella* (plural, *novelle*). Most other European languages derive their word for "novel" (French and German *roman*, for example) from the name of the medieval *romance*; and thus the names of the form recall its two principal forerunners.

A basic division of novels into love stories, adventure stories, and fantastic stories has been suggested. This classification seems particularly valid because these types seldom combine. The woman—if any—in an adventure story is a stereotyped and colorless figure, and the first great novel of adventure, *Defoe's *Robinson Crusoe* (1719), has no "female interest" whatsoever. Similarly, whatever adventure there may be in a love story is not there for its own sake, but usually merely to help characterize the hero. (W. H. Hudson's *Green Mansions* is probably the most successful effort to combine the love and adventure interests.) The fantastic story stands apart from both love and adventure in that it is deliberately unreal if not impossible and uses a fantastic plot and setting as a vehicle for ideas. *Gargantua and Pantagruel*, *Don Quixote*, *Gulliver's Travels*, and *Candide* fall into this category.

One indispensable condition for the flourishing of the novel is the existence of a large public able to read with some fluency. This condition began to be met during the *Renaissance, when printing brought mass production to books, with a consequent lowering of price and a more uniform product. For the first time, it became both possible and desirable for everyone to learn to read. During the 17th century, the novel began to establish itself as a standard literary type, and by the early 18th century it was well on its way to its present triumph as the dominant literary form.

Though the basic separation into fantasy, love, and adventure holds up reasonably well, the variety of the modern novel is astonishing We speak of epistolary, *picaresque, *Gothic, and *Utopian novels—of Western, detective, and science-fiction novels—of psychological, *stream-of-consciousness, and even psychoanalytical novels—of religious, sociological, and "escape" novels—of romantic, sentimental, realistic, naturalistic, and surrealistic novels, and also of semi-autobiographical novels (Maugham's *Of Human Bondage*) or of *romans à clef. It is this variety which makes real definition impossible. We are tempted to say that a novel must describe a course of events, but a minor French novelist boasted that he had written the perfect naturalistic novel—in which nothing whatsoever happened (Henry Céard, *Une belle journée*, 1881). We may say that it must have characters, but a stream-of-consciousness novel may easily have only one real character. The one requirement of which we can be certain is imagination, which is clearly required in the composition of even the most documentary or reportorial novel. We can therefore agree on the vague definition that a novel is a book-length piece of imaginative fiction.

The novel is unquestionably the dominant literary form

at present, both in quantity and in quality. In quantity its only rival is the magazine short story. Millions of people who would not think of reading any other form of literature regularly read a considerable quantity of novels and short stories. This demand results in a tremendous amount of commercial writing of no literary interest whatsoever. But qualitatively, too, the novel is in the lead. When one thinks of present-day writers who are likely to be future "classics," it is almost invariably men like *Mann and *Faulkner—novelists—who come to mind. If the late-19th and 20th centuries had to have a special designation, they might well be called the age of the novel.

In the decade of the 1950's, French writers of "the new novel" (*le nouveau roman*), e.g., Natalie Saurraute (1900–99), Alain Robbe-Grillet (1922–   ), Michel Butor (1926–   ), seeking to intensify our awareness of "reality," argued that we now know so much about the complexity of human personality that earlier novelists, though great in their own day (e.g., *Balzac), created characters who today appear too simplified and too artificial. The "new novel" deals with inner, compulsive, detailed reactions which cross the consciousness very rapidly, almost imperceptive reactions concealed by gestures and language, a "sub-conversation" operating on a deeper psychic level than the stream-of-consciousness and interior monologue. The author's use of fragmentary details to convey this deep psychic activity often makes it difficult for the reader to determine exactly what is happening in the novel and to whom.

novelette: a form of fiction intermediate between the *short story and the *novel. (The cumbersome term "long short story" is sometimes used as a synonym.) No exact limits can be set as to length, but the novelette differs from the short story in that it is not only longer but is more elaborate and has greater scope. It is not only shorter and less elaborate than the novel but is designed to be read at a single sitting and to produce a single, concentrated effect. Practically speaking, the novelette can be defined as a piece of prose fiction between 50 and 150 ordinary pages long.

The novelette has been more popular and effective on the Continent than in the English-speaking countries. Germany especially has cultivated the form in a long line of distinguished writers from *Goethe to Thomas Mann and Ernst Wiechert. The relative neglect of the novelette in England and America is partly due to the economics of publishing: it is too long for inclusion in the average periodical and too short to justify (in the average reader's mind) the cost of a hard-cover book. The trend toward publication of paper-backed originals may change this situation. In spite of publishing difficulties, the novelette has been cultivated to some extent in English. Outstanding examples are Henry *James' *The Turn of the Screw* (1898) and Ernest *Hemingway's *The Old Man and the Sea* (1952).

oblique rime: see *assonance.

O'Casey, Sean: Irish playwright (1880–1964). O'Casey spent his early life as a pick-and-shovel laborer in Dublin—humiliated, poverty-stricken, and bitter. He took from the Dublin slums the setting for three realistic plays produced at the Abbey Theatre, *The Shadow of the Gunman* (1923), *Juno and the Paycock* (1924), *The Plough and the Stars* (1926). His later dramas, which employ *symbolism, fantasy, and *expressionism, have not won the critical acclaim accorded to his early realistic work. *The Silver Tassie* (1928) was rejected by the Abbey Theatre. But *Within the Gates* (1933) had a successful New York run in 1934, and *Red Roses for Me* (1942) in 1955. The satiric wit and ironic comedy with which he often parallels and points up his tragic plot leave little distinction between comedy and tragedy. The recurrent tragic theme is a double conflict—within the individual, who wishes to preserve his personality and integrity, and between him and the group in which he must seek his salvation. O'Casey began a series of brilliant prose autobiographical works with *I Knock at the*

Door (1939). Other volumes in the series are *Pictures in the Hallway* (1942), *Drums under the Window* (1945), *Inishfallen Fare Thee Well* (1949), *Rose and Crown* (1952), *Sunset and Evening Star* (1954). Pungent in humor, resolute in spirit, overflowing in compassion, moving in a gorgeous dance of words, he has described himself as "a Shelleyan Communist and a Dickensian one and a Byronic one and a Miltonian one and a Whitmanian one and one like all those who thought big and beautifully and who cared for others, as I am a Marxian one, too."

ode (Greek: "song"): an extended lyrical poem dealing in a dignified tone with a serious theme. In ancient Greece the odes of *Pindar and of Greek drama were sung by a chorus who danced at the same time. The metrical and stanzaic forms are extremely complicated, following a pattern and rhythms which could also be paralleled in the dance. The basic pattern was threefold—a strophe, antistrophe, and epode: the strophe (one series of dance steps) and antistrophe (the steps of the strophe reversed) had the same metrical structure; the epode (during which the dancers stood still) was a closing section and had a different scheme. This pattern could then be repeated as often as the poet wished. In English the term is used flexibly to include close imitations of the Pindaric pattern (*Gray, *The Bard*) and poems which have lines and stanzas of varying lengths or one stanzaic form (Collins, *Ode to Liberty*; *Coleridge, *Ode to France*; *Wordsworth, *Ode on Intimations of Immortality*; *Shelley, *Ode to the West Wind*; *Keats, *Ode to a Nightingale*).

Odyssey: see *Iliad* and *Odyssey*.

Oedipus the King and **Oedipus at Colonus:** two tragedies by *Sophocles (430 B.C. and 406 B.C., respectively). The fatefully tragic story of King Oedipus is one of the great legends that Western culture has inherited from ancient Greece. Not only has it penetrated into the legend and literature of all ages, but it has left its mark on the psychoanalytic theories of *Freud. The term "Oedipus Complex" (meaning an unnatural love for one's mother)

520

has become as widespread and common to modern man as the ancient legend must have been to the old Greeks.

Sophocles was not the only Greek poet to create a tragedy from the Oedipus story; both *Aeschylus and *Euripides treated this material in dramatic form. It is, however, Sophocles' version that we know today.

Oedipus the King is often claimed as the greatest of all Greek tragedies, for its action rises in one great crescendo, making it a drama of extreme tension. As in *Antigone*, Sophocles allowed one single person—King Oedipus—to rule the action, thereby unfolding the whole measure of a tragic fate to his audience. The profoundly human value of this tragedy lies in the fact that Sophocles does not, like his predecessor Aeschylus, treat the crucial events of the story (King Oedipus' murder of his father and his marriage with his mother) but rather deals with the even more terrible aftermath: the gradual disclosure of dreadful deeds performed in ignorance. Sophocles shows a true sense of the dramatic when he presents Oedipus in the act of learning about his guilty deeds rather than in the act of committing them, for the tragedy lies in the hero's knowledge of his guilt rather than in the guilt itself. Thus he catches man in a situation capable of revealing the essence of his being, the duality of his nature wherein his strength and his weakness war with each other. There is an element of the sublime in Oedipus as he first suspects and then realizes what the outcome of his investigation will be, and yet insists in pushing on to the full truth and the full proof.

To Sophocles, man has become an emancipated individual with a free will who cannot excuse his deeds by blaming Fate, the gods, or oracles. Reason is thus man's highest possession and greatest power. Yet in *Oedipus the King* Sophocles shows how man's strength may become his weakness. The more assiduously everyone, including Oedipus, tried to prevent the fulfillment of the terrible oracle—that Oedipus was destined to kill his father and marry his mother—the sooner its fulfillment was brought about. Every step of investigation draws the net tighter until man is finally caught in it, helpless within the clutches of fate and his own incorrigible deeds. This drama is essentially a symbolic portrayal of the thorny path a human being must tread until he gains insight into the nature of his own being and his place on earth.

When Oedipus realizes his own helplessness and incapacity against the oracle of the gods and the visionary power of the priest, he deprives himself of his eyesight, an act which has a deep symbolic undertone. For having once believed his own insight superior to the revelations of the blind priest, Oedipus finally has "nothing beautiful left to see in this world" and thus desperately deprives himself of his own power of vision.

Oedipus the King ends with Oedipus' acts of contrition, his self-inflicted blindness and eventual banishment from his country. The ancient spectator might have felt that the time had now come for the gods to decide whether to redeem him or to condemn him. Sophocles in *Oedipus at Colonus*, like *Goethe in Part II of *Faust*, completed his story after an interval of many years. Both poets were near the end of their lives (Sophocles was approaching his 90th year) when they brought to a conclusion the dramatic struggle of their heroes.

The play of *Oedipus at Colonus* is a beautiful lyrical postlude to both the poet's and the hero's stormy life. As the desolate and blind Oedipus rests from his wanderings in the grove of the *Eumenides, tidings of a new oracle arrive: he will be sought after "to bring salvation to the Theban race" and his person, both in life and in death, will be of sacred importance. Oedipus, however, refuses aid to both factions (represented by Creon and Polynices); he wanders to Athens to end his life in the place predicted for his death. Thunder and lightning, signs predicted by an earlier oracle and understood by him alone, bring about a miraculous transformation in Oedipus: proud and erect, the once blind and humiliated sinner guides the others, who are stupefied, to the place appointed for his grave. There he dies, in mysterious splendor.

Old Testament: see *Bible.

Omar Khayyam: Persian poet (died *c.* 1123). Omar, famous in his own day as mathematician (he wrote one of the best medieval treatises on algebra) and Astronomer Royal, is memorable to Westerners for his avocation, as the author of some 280 *Rubáiyát* ("Quatrains").

The brief verses vary in theme from skepticism about the orthodox conceptions of the afterlife to mystical yearnings addressed to the Deity; from sophisticated satires on the unreasonableness of human reason to passionate lyrics on the joys and sorrows of love and wine and on the wisdom of grasping pleasure while we can. This epicurean delight in the sensuous joys of the world is intertwined with a prevailing sense of melancholy. For the apparently beautiful world is ruled by an imponderable fate ("The Moving Finger Writes; and having writ, / Moves on"). Much of the poem's appeal comes from this paradoxical nature of the theme—the passion for physical beauty and its irresponsible pleasures contrasted with the uneasy knowledge that it must be relinquished; the weariness of spirit that comes from the recognition that both beauty and passion are transient: "Never bloomed so red / The rose as where some buried Caesar bled."

For Western readers, Omar's poem was reborn in the brilliant and deservedly celebrated translation by Edward Fitzgerald (1809–83), published anonymously in 1859. He had previously rendered into English the plays of *Aeschylus, *Sophocles, and *Calderón, but it was his translation from the Persian which made him famous. Fitzgerald's version is a free rendering in the original form (quatrains riming aaxa) of the *Rubáiyát*, an attempt to capture their spirit by "transmutation." In more than one sense, however, it is an original creation. The exotic imagery is moulded into quotable phrases by Fitzgerald's haunting cadences, and the skeptical, epicurean qualities of the original are. emphasized by his selectivity. Furthermore, he arranges the originally independent quatrains as stanzas of a coherent larger poem. His call for "A Jug of Wine, a Loaf of Bread—and Thou" became a literary mood. It was one answer to the questionings and melancholy of the late 19th century. In our own age, which shares with Omar and Fitzgerald intellectual skepticism, a sense of fleeting values, and a longing to solve the unconquered mystery of life and death, the poem voices common yearnings and disillusionments.

O'Neill, Eugene (Gladstone): American playwright (1888–1953). Eugene, the son of the actor James O'Neill, spent his early life as a seaman, a gold prospector, a sewing-machine repair man and at other odd jobs in various corners of the world. For a while he tried his hand at reporting, and from time to time he worked as a stage hand and acted small parts with his father's company. In 1916, after a year at Princeton and a course in Professor Baker's workshop at Harvard, he helped to organize the Provincetown Players, who were (first in Provincetown, later in New York) to perform most of his short plays. In 1920 his first long play, *Beyond the Horizon*, was produced and won the Pulitzer Prize. Since then he has written such plays as *Anna Christie* (1920), *All God's Chillun Got Wings* (1924), *The Iceman Cometh* (1939), *Long Day's Journey Into Night* (produced 1955), and *More Stately Mansions* (American premiere 1967). In 1936 he received the Nobel Prize for Literature. This award was the official recognition of the American dramatist by the outside world; O'Neill was honored because (to quote from the official statement) "he has been successful in interpreting universal human experiences in terms of the drama."

O'Neill made various contributions to the American theater. He brought into it a strength and a vitality lacking in earlier American drama. He used native material, and yet he was able to give his plays a universal appeal which has made him a lively force in the theater of South America, Europe, and Asia. Although not responsible for great innovations, he did attempt to make new and interesting use of established devices and techniques. Thus he employs masks in *The Great God Brown* (1925) and *Lazarus Laughed* (1927), systematically uses the aside (in order to reveal the unspoken thoughts in people) in *Strange Interlude* (1928), has the double appearance of the same character in *Days Without End* (1934) and builds a whole play, *The Emperor Jones* (1920), around the soliloquy.

In addition, O'Neill shows a great deal of versatility. He is the author of one-act plays as well as of some of the longest plays in the history of the American drama. He has written stark tragedies (*Desire Under the Elms*, 1924), satires (*Marco Millions*, 1928), light farce-comedies (*Ah, Wilderness!*, 1933), expressionistic as well as realistic plays. Frequently, as in *The Hairy Ape* (1922), he has mixed realism and symbolism. He has even succeeded in writing a trilogy, *Mourning Becomes Electra* (1931), in which he attempts "a modern psychological approximation of Greek sense of fate, which an intelligent audience of today, possessed by no belief in gods or moral retribution, could accept and be moved by." This work is a modern adaptation of the *Oresteia of *Aeschylus, with the American Civil War replacing the Trojan War as background for the action. For his advances in technique, his insight into the soul of modern man, and his versatility and originality of expression, O'Neill may be considered one of the foremost playwrights of the 20th century.

On the Nature of Things: a didactic poem in six books written by the Roman poet *Lucretius (*De Rerum natura,* c. 94–c. 55 B.C.) to expound the philosophy of *Epicurus and free men's minds from religious fears. The philosophy of Epicurus is based on the single principle of the infallibility of the senses. Whatever the senses tell us is true, and we must accept it. Where they give us no information, we may adopt any view consistent with what they do tell us. But our senses tell us of nothing except matter and motion. We therefore accept matter as the one reality; and, so that matter may have room in which to move, we accept empty space, which we conceive as infinite in extent.

The senses do not inform us of the nature of matter, but it is not inconsistent with what they do tell us to suppose that matter is composed of atoms. We are free therefore to adopt this explanation; and we conceive of atoms as small, indivisible, eternal particles of solid matter. They differ in size, shape, and weight; they are infinite in number; and out of them the universe and all that it contains are built.

If then the universe is composed of atoms, we as part of the universe are composed of atoms also. Therefore, like the world and everything else in it, we are mortal. For all things can be divided into the atoms of which they are composed, and things which can be divided cannot endure forever. When we die our bodies cease to exist, because they disintegrate into the atoms of which they are made. But the atoms themselves do not perish; being solid and indivisible and therefore eternal, they merely become separated and may be brought together again to form new bodies. Our souls, like our bodies, are made of atoms. Therefore they too must be mortal, though the atoms of which they are composed survive to be used again to make other souls.

As our souls do not survive death, we reject the idea of a future life. And in doing so we gain much, for we free our minds of those fears of punishment in another world implanted in us by religion: we now know that such punishments are altogether impossible for us. Nor does death bring us any loss. It removes the possibility of enjoying the good things of life, but this is not a real loss because after death we can neither desire nor miss these things. Death therefore is nothing to us. While we live, it does not exist for us. When it exists for us, we cease to exist. In the very nature of things, it and we cannot exist together.

Fear of the gods is as empty as our former fear of death and the torment of *Hades. It is true that the gods exist. They live in the interspaces between the worlds, where their bodies, constantly renewed by the atom streams, never suffer dissolution. But they have no interest in us. We cannot win their favor by piety or rouse their indignation by neglect or crime. Knowing no trouble themselves and causing none to others, they live in perfect peace, lost in the contemplation of their own happiness.

The phenomena of the sky—sun and moon, storm cloud and lightning—have nothing to do with the gods, but are a part of nature and proceed in accordance with natural law, though without design. Nor when we say this are we substituting for the tyranny of the gods the even greater tyranny of scientific determinism. We feel free, and our senses never deceive us: therefore, we are free. Moreover, we can conceive how, in a world of atoms and empty space, this can be so. We assume that in the atoms themselves there is a tendency to swerve which makes their precise movements unpredictable. This element gives us free will, explains chance in inorganic matter, and accounts for the origin of things. For it tells us how the atoms, carried by their weight through empty space, were able to meet and by meeting to form the universe.

Having asserted our freedom from determinism and gods alike, we are now ready to establish our way of life. Our feelings always inform us that pleasure is good and pain is evil. We will therefore direct our lives so as to gain the maximum amount of pleasure possible to us.

But in seeking pleasure we will not act so as to involve ourselves in pain either now or later. We will avoid all overindulgence. We will never glut our stomachs with a superfluity of rich fare from which we will suffer afterward. We will eat just enough plain food to satisfy our hunger and keep our bodies healthy. In all else concerning the body we will proceed in the same way, for absence of pain is more important in the state of well-being we seek than active pleasure is.

Painlessness of body alone is not sufficient, however. We also desire tranquillity of mind and soul. We will therefore shun those situations in life most likely to disturb us. We will take no part in the public conduct of affairs, and we will not marry. We will, however, cultivate the friendship of like-minded persons; friendship adds greatly to the pleasure of life without binding us too closely, as love does. And we will devote ourselves to the study of nature, not in the spirit of science, but to free our minds from religious fears. For by learning "what can come to pass and what can not," we attain *ataraxia*, the tranquillity of soul or absence of mental pain we value most in life.

Such is the philosophy of Epicurus. It is easy to point out its flaws. It makes no attempt to prove its fundamental concept, the infallibility of sense perception. But all philosophic systems must begin with certain assumptions which are by definition unprovable. A more serious charge is that it does not come to grips with real pain—with the problem of evil in general. But in it Lucretius found deliverance from the religious fears that preyed upon him, and he was filled with a desire to convince others of its truth.

Lucretius begins his poem with an invocation to *Venus as the creative force in nature and the mother of Aeneas and therefore of Rome. (Mythology may be used as poetic embellishment provided there is no belief in it.) Next he urges his reader to study Epicurean philosophy, presents Epicurus as the deliverer of a world overwhelmed by religious fear, and denies that his master's teaching is unholy. Religion, not Epicureanism, leads men to sin. The chosen leader of the Greeks, persuaded by a priest, stained the altar of a goddess with his own daughter's blood: "such are the crimes to which religion leads" (I, 102). After this introduction, Lucretius proceeds to develop his philosophy along the lines already indicated. Books I and II establish his fundamental position. Book III explains the atomic structure of the human soul and its relationship to the mind and body. Book IV is devoted to an exposition of Epicurean psychology as expressed in the theories concerning sensation and thought. Book V describes the history of the world and of the human race, and Book VI, after a consideration of such natural phenomena as lightning, earthquakes, and epidemics, concludes the poem with an account (based on *Thucydides) of the plague at Athens during the Peloponnesian War.

The difficulties involved in writing *On the Nature of Things* were enormous, but the poet was well equipped to deal with them. He was passionately devoted to Epicurean doctrine and driven by a consuming desire to teach it. He was able to develop his arguments logically step by step and to express his thoughts precisely. He was familiar with the literature of Greece and the writings of his own countrymen. He had large poetic gifts, and, seeing the beauty in the common things of life, he used that beauty to adorn his scientific theories with a wealth of illustration. And while he himself speaks of his poetry as mere honey to sweeten bitter medicine, *On the Nature of Things* is the one great literary achievement of the Epicurean sect and the supreme didactic poem of *classical antiquity.

Oresteia: a trilogy by *Aeschylus (458 B.C.). The regular entry in the dramatic festivals of Athens consisted of a trilogy, or group of three tragedies on a single large theme, followed by a *satyr-play. The *Oresteia*, which won a first prize for its festival, is the only complete trilogy to survive to modern times. It consists of the plays *Agamemnon*, *Choephoroe (The Libation-Bearers)*, and *Eumenides*.

In the *Oresteia*, as in his earlier *Seven Against Thebes* (467 B.C.), Aeschylus makes skillful dramatic use of the theme of a family curse. The curse on the house of Atreus functions both as a unifying core (notice the use of net and web images) for the three plays and also as a focus for the playwright's views on the problem of evil. Although the first play opens with the close of the Trojan War and the return to Greece of Agamemnon, the great king and military leader, the Greek audience was well aware of the background of the legend. Atreus, the father of Agamemnon and Menelaus, had quarreled with his brother Thyestes, who in revenge killed his brother's children and served them to the unsuspecting father at a great banquet. The blood feud then lay dormant over a number of years, during which time Menelaus' wife, Helen, was taken to Troy. Her abduction was the major cause of the outbreak of the Trojan War (see *Troy Tale). In the absence of Agamemnon, who had been made leader of the Greek warriors, Clytemnestra, his queen and Helen's sister, took as her lover Aegisthus, the son of Thyestes. She rationalized her action by citing Agamemnon's sacrifice of their daughter Iphigenia to gain fair winds for the becalmed Greek fleet and his later infidelity to her at Troy. The curse on the house of Atreus is a significant force throughout the trilogy; however, there is one other important consideration that makes Agamemnon as well as the other Greeks liable to retribution, independently of this curse. Again and again Aeschylus raises the moral question of the justification of a war which he looks upon as a destructive evil—a war that cost innumerable Greek lives on the plains of Troy.

The trilogy opens with the return of the conquering hero-king, who is met by a resolute and crafty Clytemnestra. She murders both him and Cassandra, whom he has brought back from Troy as his slave. The second tragedy, *The Choephoroe*, concerns the revenge of Agamemnon's son Orestes for his father's death. Encouraged by his sister Electra, he kills Aegisthus as well as his mother, Clytemnestra. The third play traces the wanderings of Orestes as he is pursued by the Furies in vengeance for the matricide. The long account of murder is finally balanced when Orestes is tried at the newly established court of justice in Athens, the Areopagus. *Athena, casting the deciding vote, frees him of his guilt and terminates the curse. The Furies are propitiated by being made the protectors of the new city and are thereafter known to the Athenians by the placating name the *Eumenides, the Well-Intentioned. It is in this third play that Athena and *Apollo emerge as representatives of *Zeus. Zeus, at the beginning of the trilogy a god of strict, retributive justice, has been replaced in that function by the Furies. The concept of Zeus as combining justice (moral retribution) and compassion is given con-crete evidence through the figures of Athena and Apollo and expressed in the closing lines of the *Eumenides*: "The Law that is Fate and the Father, the All-Comprehending, / Are here met together as one."

Thus the *Oresteia* is more than a series of revenge tragedies motivated by relentless fate—a force which the chorus in the *Eumenides* thus acknowledges: "woe springs from wrong, the plant is like the seed." Aeschylus' concept of fate does not merely refer to what is inevitably to be but also indicates a moral force that springs from human nature itself. Clytemnestra's individual responsibility is strictly in accord with what Aeschylus means by fate. Aegisthus' illicit love affair; his complicity in the murder of Agamemnon, and Orestes' matricide, all part of the machinations of divine fate, are never completely removed from the whole question of individual guilt. The complex workings of fate in his plays together with the philosophy that "man by suffering shall learn"—this source of wisdom being a divine gift—are striking features of Aeschylus' art.

Orpheus: the greatest singer and musician of Greek mythology. He made a journey to the Underworld to rescue his wife Eurydice but failed through disobedience to *Hades.

Osborne, John: English dramatist (1930–94). After leaving school at sixteen, Osborne first tried his hand at journalism but soon turned to acting, a profession that he pursued for ten years during which time he was also writing. In 1956 he suddenly became famous when *Look Back in Anger* was produced. This play made Osborne head of the angry-young-man movement and a one-man insurrection against the Establishment.

In *Look Back in Anger* and in his other plays Osborne rebels against society in all its forms. In *The Entertainer* (1957) he satirizes the political situation and shows the family outside society. *Luther* (1961) is Osborne's inter-pretation of Martin Luther's struggle with his sense of guilt and his search for a personal relationship with God. In his *Plays for England* (1962), which includes *The Blood of the Bambergs* and *Under Plain Cover*, he is angry at the affectations and excesses of royalty and the haughty attitude with which the bourgeoisie views the lower classes. *Inadmissible Evidence* (1964) denounces the older generation for its failure to find solutions to its problems.

Interested in historical themes, he wrote about the Austro-Hungarian Empire during the years before the First World War in *A Patriot for Me* (1965) and about the 1842 trial of George Jacob Holyoake, the last person tried for blasphemy in England, in *A Subject of Scandal and Concern* (1960), another indirect attack on the Establishment.

Osborne's characters and dialogue possess tremendous vitality. This vigor, along with his themes—rebellion against parents and wives, refusals to conform to a sick society, protests against historical incidents which could possibly recur—established Osborne as one of the leading English playwrights of the 1950's and early 1960's.

Ossianic Poems: a series of works published by James Macpherson (1736–96), purporting to be translations from the legendary 3d-century Gaelic bard Ossian (or Oisin). Macpherson's *Fragments of Ancient Poetry, Collected in the Highlands of Scotland, and Translated from the Guelic or Erse Language* (1760) aroused so much interest that money was collected to finance the author on further trips to collect similar material. The results were *Fingal, an Ancient Epic Poem, in Six Books* (1762), and *Temora, an Epic Poem in Eight Books* (1763). These were followed by a collected edition of *The Works of Ossian* (1765). All these poems were presented in a poetic prose which expressed lofty sentiments, a romantic love of the wilder aspects of nature, and a pervasive melancholy. They immediately became the center of a controversy, with some critics hailing them as an invaluable literary discovery and others (e.g., Samuel Johnson) denouncing them as a pure fake. The truth probably lies somewhere between these two extremes, but nearer to the latter. Macpherson apparently did collect some fragments of early Gaelic poetry and legends, but they seem to have served largely as suggestions for the tone and themes of what was essentially his own work. The Ossianic Poems did not have any great importance in English literature, though they did help to stimulate some of the romantic trends of which they were themselves a product. On the Continent, however, their impact was much greater. They were soon translated into the principal languages and were highly esteemed by Napoleon. *Goethe admired them tremendously (in his youth), and his *Werther* owes a great debt to them. In both France and Germany they were frequently cited and left their mark on the whole of the *Romantic Movement.

ottava rima: a stanza of eight lines riming abababcc. In English the lines are 10-syllabled (iambic pentameter); in Italian 11-syllabled. *Boccaccio (in *Il Filostrato*) is credited with the invention of this stanza, which became a favorite with Italian *Renaissance poets, including *Ariosto. Ottava rima was introduced into English by Sir Thomas Wyatt (1503–42). *Byron's *Don Juan* is a brilliant example of the form.

Ovid: Roman poet (43 B.C.–A.D. 17 or 18). Publius Ovidius Naso belonged to a wealthy equestrian family residing at Sulmo, some 90 miles east of Rome. His parents wished him to enter the service of the state and sent him to Rome for the rhetorical education then given young men of the upper classes, but, after holding a few minor offices, Ovid abandoned all thought of a political career to become a poet. His brilliant wit and social charm made him a prominent figure in fashionable circles until A.D. 8, when his life was suddenly shattered by an edict from the Emperor Augustus ordering him to leave Italy and take up residence at Tomis, a Roman outpost on the Black Sea. The reason for this action is not completely understood. Ovid refers to it as "a poem and an error." But while the poem is undoubtedly the *Ars Amatoria (Art of Love)*, a textbook in seduction which angered Augustus, the error has thus far defied analysis, though it seems reasonably sure Ovid found out something personally affecting the Emperor, which he ought to have reported and did not, and that when this fact became known, he was banished. As long as Augustus lived, Ovid apparently felt pardon was not impossible, but, when Tiberius succeeded to the throne, he gave up hope and after almost 10 years in the wilderness, died an exile.

Ovid won his reputation as a poet with the *Amores*

(Loves), a series of brief erotic sketches professedly based on his own experiences; the *Heroides (Heroines)*, a set of imaginary letters in verse from such famous ladies as Penelope, Medea, and Dido to their absent loved ones; and the *Art of Love*, a book which provides the reader many fascinating glimpses of Roman life in its lighter moments, at the theater, the races, and the games. The *Art* is filled with wit and humor and was extremely popular in antiquity. Though immoral and antagonistic to Augustus' program of social reform, it is probably not particularly corrupting. These works and others of less importance made Ovid the greatest of contemporary poets before he turned to narrative verse in the *Fasti,* an unfinished calendar of Roman festivals, and the *Metamorphoses,* a vast collection of *myths and legends unified by the fact that each story involves some supernatural transformation, as when Daphne is changed into a laurel, or Ceyx and Alcyone into sea birds. The *Metamorphoses* was almost complete when Ovid was banished from Rome. His later poems, the *Tristia (Sorrows)*, the *Epistulae ex Ponto (Letters from the Black Sea)*, and others, are interesting chiefly for the biographical detail they contain. The best known among them is *Tristia I, 3*, describing the poet's last night in Rome.

Ovid composed the *Metamorphoses* in hexameter verses, but he used *elegiac couplets for his other works. His meter is smooth and easy, and his language, though artificial, is brilliant. His narrative is clear, rapid, and very highly adorned, for Ovid was a writer of great ability and excellent training in both rhetoric and literature. He was not a man of deep feelings, and he could not compose long narratives; epic was therefore beyond his powers. But he excelled in telling short stories, which he set down with enough realism to hold the attention of the reader without disturbing his emotions. In all he wrote, Ovid sought only to amuse or entertain, but though he was not a serious author like *Vergil, he was popular all through the *Middle Ages and extremely influential on the poets and painters of the *Renaissance. Indeed, even today, when his minor works are probably not so well known as formerly, the *Metamorphoses* is still universally recognized as one of the truly great books in the history of Western literature.

Paine, Thomas: English political writer and radical pamphleteer (1737–1809). Though not an original thinker, Paine gave inflammatory publicity to the libertarian ideals of the 18th-century thinkers. He held official positions and worked for the American Colonies during the Revolution but later fell out of favor in this country. He was banished from England as a traitor because of his aid to the Colonies. He participated in the French Revolution and once again gained and lost favor, being imprisoned during the Reign of Terror. He died in poverty in the United States, where he was refused burial in consecrated ground because of his religious rationalism. His principal works are *Common Sense* (1776), *The American Crisis* (1776–83), *The Rights of Man* (1791–92), and *The Age of Reason* (1794–95).

Palatine Anthology: see *Greek Anthology.*

Pallas: a title of *Athena, often used as a name for her.

Pan: a Greek god of shepherds and herdsmen, part man, part goat in appearance, identified by the Romans with Faunus.

Panchatantra (Sanskrit: "Five Headings"): a collection of *fables in Sanskrit (*c.* A.D. 300–500). There is no way of dating the collection beyond the fact that it was translated into Pehlevi (a literary language of Persia) by order of a king who died in A.D. 579. The individual fables had doubtless been current for centuries before the collection assumed its present form; and though this collection is Hindu, the tales seem to belong to the Buddhistic tradition of the *Jatakas.

The work is enclosed in a *frame-tale about a king who despaired of educating his three stupid and idle sons, until he finally found a Brahmin who taught them wisdom through the fables of the *Panchatantra.* A portion circulated as the *Fables of Bidpai*, by legend an Indian scholar who told the fables to reform a king.

From the Persian version the tales were translated into Syriac and Arabic, and the Arabs apparently brought them into Spain. They also entered Europe by way of Constantinople, so that the medieval *beast epic—and consequently most modern fables—derives ultimately from the Indian tradition. (Whether *Aesop is indebted to the Indian tradition is a matter of debate.) Indian fables (though not this particular collection) had also spread to China by the 7th century.

The tales themselves are compressed, dramatic, and humorous. The animals have all the characteristics of men—even studying the *Vedas and indulging in religious disputes. Their conduct and experiences are used to point morals, both private and political.

Pandora: in Greek mythology, the first woman, created by *Hephaestus to punish man for accepting fire, which had been stolen from heaven and given to him contrary to the will of *Zeus. When Pandora came from heaven, she brought with her a casket containing the afflictions that beset humanity, though she did not know its contents, Zeus having told her merely that it contained her marriage portion. He did warn her, however, not to open it; but she did so, and the evils in the box spread across the earth. The name *Pandora* means *all gifts*, and she is probably in origin a goddess of the earth, which is the giver of all. See *Hesiod.

Paradise Lost: a poem by *Milton (1667), usually accepted as the greatest epic of modern times. In the first edition the poem did not have the "argument" (summary of the action) and was divided into 10 books. The publisher added the argument (presumably written by Milton) to the copies remaining in his stock in 1668. In the second edition (1674) the poem was divided into 12 books.

The scope of the theme is the universe itself—the dealings of God with the human race. The poem tells "Of man's first disobedience and the fruit / Of that forbidden tree whose mortal taste / Brought death into the world, and all our woe, / With loss of Eden." Such a subject—the meaning of evil in a universe created by a benevolent God—is significant not only to English-speaking peoples and to Western culture, but to the whole of humankind. The drama was not finished in Eden, is not yet finished. The world may well be lost again unless the poet can "assert Eternal Providence, / And justify the ways of God to Man."

The story adopts the simple narrative in Genesis, the tempting of Eve and Adam and their expulsion from Eden; to this account it adds other Biblical allusions to Satan as an adversary of God. But the story is fleshed out to encompass the whole range of man's experiences—history, theology and mythology, passion and discipline, love and hate, pride and humility. Plunging *in medias res*, the opening describes the activities of Satan and his cohorts, former angels who have fallen with him into the flaming lake of Hell after their rebellion against God: "Him the Almighty Power / Hurled headlong flaming from the ethereal sky." Unable to defeat God in battle, Satan determines to war against God indirectly: "All is not lost; the unconquerable will, / And study of revenge, immortal hate, / And courage never to submit or yield." The first division of the poem (the first four books) ends with Satan's passage from Hell past Sin and Death, and his arrival on earth. The next four books are a flashback of preceding events, the revolt of the angels and the creation of earth and man. In the final four books Satan enters the newly created Garden of Eden and persuades Eve, and, through her, Adam, to taste the fruit of the forbidden Tree of Knowledge. For his sin Satan is reduced to the mean estate of the serpent and the couple are expelled from the Garden: "They, hand in hand, with wandering steps and slow, / Through Eden took their solitary way." They have been comforted, however, by the prophecy that a Saviour, God's own Son, will redeem mankind. Salvation can come by atonement.

Milton did not arrive at this theme without much thought. A list of nearly a hundred subjects (in Milton's own handwriting) shows how carefully he explored the possibilities, seeking always one which would have "universality." He wavered between a Biblical theme and legendary national history, such as had inspired Homer and *Vergil. Finally rejecting Arthurian legend, he chose instead an event which was of the highest importance in Biblical history and a subject of theological controversy in Milton's own day—the meaning of the Fall of man from his original state of holiness.

In the Fall, Milton saw the issues of knowledge, freedom, and free will, the very problems which concerned him all his life. He regarded man's impulse for knowledge and for freedom as admirable. But he felt that since all created things have freedom of will, they must accept moral responsibility for their acts. Adam and Eve, when they sought to escape divinely imposed limitations on humanity, were not moved to defiance of divine restrictions by love of knowledge. Rather it was the sin of *hybris—"pride," which impelled them; in this sense Adam and Eve are guilty of a moral lapse, the same flaw that led in Greek tragedies to the downfall of the protagonist. But Adam (Man) is also a tragic hero whose human frailty can be remedied by repentence and faith. The titanic figure of Satan, like all evil guile under disguise, seems at first a magnificent and innocent victim. His libertarian sentiments are seductive when he cries, "Better to reign in Hell than serve in Heaven." He appears superior to time and place in his conclusion that "The mind is its own place, and in itself / Can make a Heaven of Hell, a Hell of Heaven." Gradually the extent of his egotism and debasement is revealed, until his villainy is apparent long before he becomes a hissing serpent.

Whether or not one accepts Milton's interpretation of Biblical myth and Christian doctrine, one can appreciate the gifts he brought to the story: psychological understanding of the impulse to freedom and its rejection when it becomes license; breadth of imaginative vision as the story moves from Hell to Chaos, from Pandemonium to the Garden of Eden, from Heaven to Earth; and a perception of the interrelations between knowledge and morality. Certainly the universal theme he chose was worthy of a great poem.

Since Milton desired to rival Homer and Vergil, many

details of his poem are modeled on their epic formulas—the invocation, the roll call of leaders, elaborate similes, the device of beginning in the middle of the action and using flashbacks to present the antecedent action. Even the structure of Milton's sentences sometimes strains the English idiom to follow Latin syntax. Yet his genius succeeds in creating an effect that seems not awkward but dignified and serious. And its distance from ordinary idiomatic speech makes it suitable for its timeless theme. Even more important, Milton fully grasped the major lesson of classical art, the need for a central, predominating, unified theme into which every detail of image and story can be integrated. Magnificent as are separate sections of *Paradise Lost*, such as the account of the rebel angels in the first two books, or the later descriptions of the Garden of Eden, or the prayers and hymns of Adam and Eve, they are always held strictly subordinate to the main theme.

In addition to the Greek and Latin epics and the Bible, Milton drew on the Greek tragedians, on the Apocrypha (see *Bible), on rabbinical traditions, the Church Fathers, the Italian and French *Renaissance poets, the English dramatists, and *Spenser. These assembled treasures of learning, the wealth of allusions, the charm of reminiscence in the analogies and similes give an added complexity and concentration of meaning. Yet the inclusive richness is kept under control, just as Milton sees the luxuriance of the Garden of Eden rich but disciplined and man's own opulent emotions moderated by reason. In sum, Milton achieved a poetry that was, in his own phrase, "simple, sensuous, and passionate." The *blank verse with its shifting cadences is expertly manipulated to give the movement of the ideas and to achieve the greatest musical values. From Vergil, Milton caught the effectiveness of running the thought and structure of the phrase past the end of the line (enjambement), and thus combining lines to form "verse paragraphs." The control and discipline of the verse paragraph paradoxically permit greater freedom in the line, producing an effective combination of flexibility and restraint which secured the union of sustained thought and varied rhythm. Milton's blindness may have contributed to this

538

technique by forcing him to compose and revise mentally and therefore to retain long sections of the poem in his memory.

This variety in unity runs through every aspect of the poem and deepens its meaning. Unity is achieved between the Renaissance and Reformation aspects of Milton's own learning, between the classical and romantic aspects of his art, between much that can be traced to conventional literary sources and more that grew from the climate of ideas and passions in Milton's own day and culture. It is at once the story of the loss of mankind's spiritual innocence and the parallel story of the loss of the Commonwealth Utopia. England and the world were not a land of saints able to deepen their spiritual understanding or control their passions by reasoned discipline, just as Adam was not a saint able to hold on to Paradise. The poem thus becomes a parable of Milton's day and of ours, the inner, but also the outer, history of mankind. Yet as Milton surveyed this world with his range of knowledge and experience ("Greatly in peace of thought"), he saw that "suffering for Truth's sake / Is Fortitude to highest victory," that the world will yet be "Founded in righteousness and peace and love, / To bring forth fruits Joy, and eternal Bliss."

Parallel Lives: a series of biographies of famous Greeks and Romans, written by +Plutarch in Greek, apparently during the first two decades of the 2d century A.D. The *Parallel Lives* is so named because the biographies were published in pairs, each consisting of the life of a Greek, the life of a Roman who is in some way a parallel to him, and a brief comparison of the two. For example, Themistocles, the Athenian general who saved Greece from the Persians, is matched with Camillus, the Roman dictator who saved Italy from the Gauls. Lycurgus, who established the Spartan constitution, is bracketed with Numa, who, the Romans said, first organized their religious usages. Pericles is presented with Fabius, Alcibiades with Coriolanus, *Demosthenes with *Cicero, Alexander the Great with Julius *Caesar. The series is confined to soldiers and statesmen, because Plutarch wished to demonstrate that the exploits of the Greeks in war and politics were equal to those of the Romans in these fields, a fact which had been all but forgotten. For the great age of Greece had long since passed and with it her men of action, whereas the achievements of Rome were recent and very spectacular, including even the subjugation of Greece itself. Patriotism, then, influenced Plutarch in composing the *Parallel Lives*. But he did not flatter his fellow countrymen in it, nor did he disparage their conquerors, for he knew that the Roman Empire was necessary to preserve law and order in the world.

Not all the biographies Plutarch wrote are extant, but 23 pairs have survived, a few without comparisons, and four single lives, making a total of 50 pieces. Together they form a work of vast learning, the product of years of study, yet suffused throughout with sympathy and understanding, and marked by an unfailing love of the task. Plutarch derived much enjoyment from their composition, as people usually enjoy doing the things that they do best. Though not a great stylist, he had the narrative skill and the insight into character necessary for this type of writing, and he was endowed besides with a strong sense of the dramatic and that love of a good story which is perhaps his most notable characteristic. Plutarch fills his *Lives* with anecdotes, though it is only proper to observe that he tells them for the light they throw on the men he is depicting. His biographies are studies in ethics rather than studies in history, being intended primarily, not to narrate events, but to portray character, a purpose well served by the recording of minor incidents. Plutarch therefore emphasized material of this nature, while he passed quickly over occurrences of greater historical importance that did not further his objective, particularly if they had been adequately presented already. He intended his biographies to supplement the work of the historians, not to rival or replace it. The use of the *Lives* today as a source for ancient history is, therefore, an accidental result of the loss of other authors, though much valuable historical information can be extracted from them. Some caution is necessary, however, for if Plutarch consulted the best authorities on important points, he often went to secondary sources for detail. But it is frequently possible to separate the reliable from the unreliable material in his writing. In general, the lives of Romans are more dependent on oral tradition than the lives of Greeks, and of course the biographies of the earliest figures of both peoples are tissues of myth and folklore.

*Shakespeare based his *Coriolanus*, *Julius Cuesar*, and *Antony and Cleopatra* on Sir Thomas North's *Plutarch* (1579), the most famous of the translations of the *Lives* into English.

para-rime: see *assonance.

Pascal, Blaise: French mathematician and religious philosopher (1623–62). Pascal's name is inseparably associated with Jansenism, a religious movement which inspired much of the literature of his time and attracted many of the most prominent families of the kingdom. During the 17th century there were few important writers or distinguished people at court or in society who were not at some time or other involved, directly or indirectly, with Jansenism.

The first half of this century in France was characterized by a number of movements—all of which tended to discipline human activity in literature, society, philosophy, and religion. The French Academy, Préciosité, Descartes, Jansenism belong to this period and give to the entire century its particular idealistic and formal character.

Jansenism was essentially a reform movement within the official state religion, the Catholic Church. It derived its name from a Dutch bishop by the name of Jansen, who in 1640 published in Latin a book entitled *Augustinus*. Jansen's book purported to be a restatement of the doctrine of Saint *Augustine on divine grace and free will. Man does not merit God's grace by his works, it was asserted; but divine grace which makes salvation possible is a free gift of God. The obvious inference is that man is predestined to be saved or to be damned. Jansen evidently found it difficult to reconcile this doctrine with the orthodox teaching that man is free to choose between right and wrong, thus making salvation a matter of his own choice. There was no doubt in Jansen's mind, however, that man is free to live a life in close conformity with God's precepts; indeed, a Christian's assurance of being predestined to be saved was in proportion to the austerity of his life.

At the time when Jansen's theories on grace were being discussed in religious and social circles in Paris, Mother Angélique Arnauld, the superior of a convent at Port-Royal, some 15 miles southwest of Paris, was attempting to introduce reforms in her religious community. During the four centuries since its founding, the convent had become somewhat worldly and lax in its observation of monastic obligations. Mother Angélique invited Saint-Cyran, a priest converted to the Jansenist doctrines, to come to Port-Royal as father confessor of the nuns. Before long the entire convent was won over to the new beliefs, and men and women from the social and intellectual world of Paris were drawn to Port-Royal to live a more austerely Christian life. The men lived in separate houses and were called *Messieurs* or *Solitaires*; among these were the famous Arnaulds, Nicole, Hamon, and Pascal. They devoted much of their time to meditation and prayer; some of them were scholars and wrote valuable books on logic, Latin, Greek, and French; these texts were considered standard works at the time and were used at the University of Paris. The *Solitaires* opened a school for destitute boys at Port-Royal; *Racine, the future great dramatist, was one of their pupils.

It was not long before the Jansenist doctrines were challenged by the Jesuits, who, through their influence at Court, caused them to be condemned by the Sorbonne and later by Rome. Port-Royal later enjoyed some years of intermittent, relative peace with the short-lived tide of favor at the Louvre or in Rome, but in 1704 the monastery was destroyed by order of Louis XIV.

Pascal was without doubt the most brilliant of the Jansenists. He attained a reputation as a great mathematician and physicist and became one of the outstanding writers of his age. His first conversion to Jansenism occurred in 1646, but his faith was more theoretical than practical for some years; from 1652 to 1654 he even led a rather worldly life in high Parisian society, where he was honored as a great scientist, and he associated with the most noted freethinkers of the day.

After this fling at frivolous social life, Pascal was definitely converted to Jansenism and retired to Port-Royal. Two years later, in 1656, his brother Jansenists called upon him to defend the cause of Port-Royal against the persistent attacks of the Jesuits. He complied by writing his famous *Lettres provinciales*, a series of letters addressed to a Provincial, or Superior of the Jesuit Order, containing an ironical, indignant, and at times comical attack on the presumed easygoing and accommodating procedure of Jesuit confessors in matters of casuistry— that is, in the application of ethical or theological precepts in determining the degree of guilt in questions of conduct. In spite of the general interest of minute discussions on severe or lax morality, the *Provinciales* would now belong to the great mass of dead polemical literature were it not for Pascal's great qualities as a writer. *Voltaire observes that "all types of eloquence are contained in these letters."

After he began his association with Port-Royal, Pascal jotted down reflections which were ultimately to serve as the material for an apology for the Christian religion. In 1670, eight years after his death, his Jansenist friends and relatives decided to publish these fragments under the title *Thoughts of Monsieur Pascal on Religion and Several Other Subjects Which Were Found Among His Papers After His Death.* Pascal's editors deemed it prudent, in the interest of religious peace, to attenuate the extremely Jansenistic tone of many of the fragments. It was not until 1844 that a completely reliable edition of the *Pensées (Thoughts)*, based on the original manuscript, was published. All subsequent editions have been based on this standard text.

Students of Pascal's *Pensées* have ingeniously rearranged his 924 single reflections according to a plan which Pascal himself no doubt would have approved. In his *Pensées* Pascal really writes an apology for the Christian religion directed primarily to the freethinkers and rationalists of the age who, like *Montaigne in the preceding century, mocked those who smugly believed that they were in possession of the truth. Pascal meets these rationalizing skeptics on their own ground, bases his argumentation on scientific and philosophic premises, and seeks to prove that man, left to his own reasoning powers, is weak, that the various philosophic systems are of little help, and, finally, that only the dogma of Redemption gives meaning to the high aspirations of man, who can do little for himself because of the consequences of original sin.

More important than the economy of Pascal's *Pensées* are the questions he raises and his persuasive style. He brought before the reading public philosophical and theological problems of deep concern to everyone. Here as well as in his *Lettres* Pascal displays the power of a polemic genius and a vehement orator. His lively imagination colors his style with figures of speech that in many instances make him comparable to some of the greatest lyric poets. It might be added that his physical and moral sufferings have left their imprint on his spontaneous and sincere expressions of anguish and hope. Thinking of time and space, he frankly admits: "The eternal silence of these infinite spaces terrifies me."

Two of Pascal's concepts deserve special mention. The first is his distinction between "*l'esprit de géométrie*," or the deductive argumentation of the scholar and scientist who bases his conclusions exclusively on reasoning, and the "*esprit de finesse*," which is the instinctive or intuitive perception of the most cogent proofs. Pascal's keen intelligence made him realize that there are more things in Heaven and Earth than are dreamed of in a proposition of Euclid and that the emotions very often have a logic of their own which reason itself cannot fathom.

Second, and closely akin to this reliance on intuition when reason does not avail, is Pascal's notorious "*règle du pari*," or "law of the wager." Though the existence of God cannot be proved by pure reason, argues Pascal, the mere instinct of security and self-preservation would prompt us to wager that God does in fact exist; in which case, we are likely to conduct our lives accordingly; then, he continues, even though God does not exist, we have everything to gain, nothing to lose. On the other hand, if we wager that there is no Supreme Being, our lives lack the most cogent motive for right living; then, if there is a God, in the end we lose all.

Pascal applied these principles to his own living and thinking. No author was ever more honest with himself and with others. His style is the most spontaneous of his age and is the result of deep meditation, rigid logic, and keen psychological insight.

Pasternak, Boris Leonidovich: Russian poet and novelist (1890–1960). A lyric poet of sharp vision, philosophic reflectiveness, and intense passion, Pasternak published six volumes of distinguished verse between 1914 and 1932. These included two epic poems extolling freedom and the revolutionary movement, but pressures demanding ideological conformity silenced his poetic publication. Instead he translated *Shakespeare, *Shelley, Goethe, and in the forties commenced a novel, *Doctor Zhivago* (1946–53?)—banned in the Soviet Union, but published in Milan in 1957. Awarded the Nobel prize in 1958, he declined it under pressure from the authorities. His other prose includes *I Remember—Sketch for an Autobiography. Doctor Zhivago* is conceived in epic proportions. Set against a background of Russian history of the 20th century and the vastness of the land itself, the novel's philosophic concerns are with life, mature love, and the cruelty of revolution, which surrounds life with death. Although it does not attack Soviet standards, the novel places its emphasis on other values—individual integrity, compassion, and spiritual understanding. This sensitivity and mystic feeling dominate the poems appended to the novel.

pastoral: a literary work which, under the guise of a rustic author using shepherds as characters and an idyllic rural life as setting, actually presents a clever, sophisticated point of view. The convention is artificial, for the values of the society pictured are not rustic, nor are dress and speech those of actual shepherds. The pastoral was cultivated in classical times by such writers as *Theocritus and *Vergil and was revived in the *Renaissance by the Italian Sannazzaro (*L'Arcadia*, 1501), the Frenchman Marot (1496–1544), and the Englishman *Spenser (*The Shepheardes Calendar*, 1579). The typical classical pastoral poem was the *eclogue. Since *pastoral* refers to content and not form, in modern times it is often combined with another term, as in *pastoral romance* (Montemayor, *Diana enamorada*, 1552; Sidney, *Arcadia*, 1590); *pastoral play* (Guarini, *Il Pastor fido*, 1590; Fletcher, *The Faithful Shepherdess*, 1608; *Shakespeare, *As You Like It*); *pastoral elegy* (*Milton, *Lycidas*; *Shelley, *Adonais*). The term is also used loosely to refer to rural scope and setting in general; thus, Robert *Frost has been called a pastoral poet.

Pearl Poet: see *Gawain and the Green Knight, Sir.*

Pegasus: a winged horse ridden by the Greek hero Bellerophon. Because his hoofprint produced the inspiring Hippocrene Fountain, in modern times he has been considered to be sacred to the *Muses and has become a symbol of the art of poetry.

Père Goriot, Le: see *Father Goriot.*

Persephone: the daughter of Demeter and the wife of *Hades, king of the Underworld, called Proserpina by the Romans.

Perseus: one of the greatest of Greek heroes, the son of *Zeus and Danaë, and the slayer of the Gorgon Medusa.

Petrarch, Francesco: Italian poet and scholar (Italian: Petrarca; 1304–74). Petrarch was born in Arezzo, where his family had moved after being expelled from Florence by the same enemies and the same decree that exiled their friend *Dante. Soon after Petrarch's birth, the family settled in Avignon, where the self-exiled Papal Court was established. Petrarch's career was largely determined by this cosmopolitan city, and, although it is inaccurate to call any one place his permanent residence, he kept returning to Avignon's suburbs all his life. After studying law at Montpellier and Bologna, he abandoned it for literature. In order to be eligible for appointment to religious benefices, he took minor clerical orders, but to secure the comforts of life he relied primarily on his genius for friendship and his reputation as a writer. And justifiably so. He became the idol of aristocratic society, who felt honored by his presence. Kings, princes, and popes vied for the distinction of having him in their retinue or in their dominions. They placed at his disposal their homes and every luxury they could offer. And when Petrarch became restless, as he often did, these patrons provided the means for his numerous comings and goings. These trips—to Gascony, Paris, the Netherlands, the Rhineland, Bohemia, northern Italy, Rome—broadened his horizons.

But it was Rome, with its ancient monuments and sacred relics, that really stirred him. His first visit (1337) made him realize how much he loved Italy. He had never lived in Florence and felt none of the local attachment which was the core of Dante's patriotism. As an outsider from Avignon, Petrarch could love Italy as a whole, and particularly Rome, symbol of Italy's traditional glories. When he received two invitations on the same day—one from Paris, one from Rome—to accept the poet's crown of laurel, he of course chose Rome, home of *Cicero and *Vergil, eloquent monument of the ancient empire and center of Christianity. A revived Rome, unifying Italy, from which would radiate a new Golden Age—that was Petrarch's dream. But neither the Emperor at Prague nor the Pope at Avignon shared his enthusiasms. The rebel tribune Cola di Rienzo, whom Petrarch vigorously supported during his brief period of political activity, failed to remain in power.

Petrarch's first literary fame was won by his Italian verses, most of them inspired by his passion for Laura. But about Laura we cannot be sure. Was she the wife of Hugues de Sade? Was she the sole object of his "keen but constant and pure attachment"? Was there in fact a lady Laura at all—or is she an abstraction for the laurel crown which Petrarch so avidly sought? Was Petrarch merely following a *troubadour tradition solidified by Dante's idealization of Beatrice? According to his own account, he had seen her for the first time in his early twenties, in church, on Good Friday, 1327; she was destined to die on the very same day 21 years later, in the plague of 1348. When he first knew her, she was already married. (We do know that she was not the mother of Petrarch's two illegitimate children.) In any event, Petrarch says that his first sight of Laura made him a poet. And his primary poetic theme is hopeless love, a spiritualized passion for the unattainable.

Through most of his life, Petrarch kept writing and rearranging the verses for Laura in Life and Laura in Death, a total of 366 poems. They are in varied forms. The *sonnets, which form the majority, have been described as the most polished verses in western European literature. There can be no doubt that their form is perfect, but their lasting appeal comes from the combination of form and content. Petrarch is permanently in the center of the stage, exploring indefatigably all the delicate phenomena of his emotions. His sentiments come from the discord between the senses and the soul, the flesh and the spirit, the sensuality of his love and a mystic acceptance of its spirituality. His inner struggle between the sensuous and the ascetic is reflected in subtleties and antitheses of expression. He does not fight or rebel against the conflict but records it with tender melancholy in plaintive tones, clear, sweet, with the elegance of technical perfection. The musical qualities are developed with the greatest sensitivity. No wonder the poems swept Europe and immortalized their author. Their mood, imagery, and rime scheme (see sonnet) dominated literary circles for centuries, and the names of Petrarch and Laura became symbols of passionate love constrained by spirituality. The sonnets are the only works of Petrarch which are still widely read outside Italy.

Linguistically, his Italian provided supple and varied music; and since the *Renaissance he has been called "the father of the Italian language," a title which he shares with two other Florentines, Dante and *Boccaccio. Yet he always referred to these poems as his juvenile

548

trifles and was convinced that literature worthy of the name must be written in Latin. Expecting to be judged by students of classical Latin literature, he believed his own Latin works to be his best claim to fame. He was wrong in more ways than one. *Africa*, an epic poem in Latin hexameters, modeled on *The *Aeneid* and relating the triumph of Scipio over Carthage, was never completed and never publicly circulated. He must have realized that he had no real talent for this sort of sustained heroic verse. His Latin prose did, however, enjoy for a time a wide audience: The *Lives of Illustrious Men* (*De viris illustribus*, 1338) is a collection of 24 biographies of illustrious Romans whose combined lives make up a history of Rome. The *Secretum* (*c.* 1342) is a series of imaginary dialogues with St. *Augustine, in which Petrarch explained the most intimate conflicts of his life. His letters (over 600 are extant) were circulated by his correspondents and were adjudged in his age superior in style to Cicero's. Knowing that they would be widely read, Petrarch made them substantial essays, carefully polished their literary form—and kept copies.

But it was not so much Petrarch's own writings in Latin as his influence upon the revival of the classics that is important. When he was crowned poet laureate in Rome in April 1341, the laurel wreath (sacred to *Apollo, the god of poetry) honored Petrarch the poet, but even more Petrarch the humanist and classical scholar, recognizing him as the most vital force in the re-education of Europe. Throughout his life, he urged the study of Greek and Latin literature as a form of intercourse with great men which would open up a new life. He looked to *classical antiquity for an expansion of the spirit. He searched out old manuscripts, preserved, copied, and annotated them, collected ancient coins, rediscovered some letters and speeches of Cicero, and made Cicero one of the formative influences on humanism. He persuaded Boccaccio to study Greek and to write in Latin, and himself translated Boccaccio's last tale of *The *Decameron* into Latin, thus putting the story of Griselda into international circulation. Petrarch assembled an extensive library of such rare and wonderful items that even in his own day its value was recognized, and Venice granted him a home on condition that he should leave this library to the city.

Petrarch's own spirit was divided between Christianity and classical antiquity, but there were already plenty of Christians, and his intense devotion to classical studies was something new which he communicated to the rest of Europe. Therefore his importance in the history of ideas lies in the fact that he inaugurated the Revival of Learning and was himself the first example of the *humanism of the Renaissance. In literature, however, his works of classical inspiration have now only a historical interest, whereas his sonnets—the elegant trifles of his early years—not only served as the starting point for modern lyric poetry, but are still widely read and very much alive. •

Petronius: Roman satirist (died A.D. 66). The Roman satirist Gaius Petronius Arbiter ("Arbiter of Elegance") was famous among his contemporaries, not as a literary figure, but as an intimate friend of the Emperor Nero, whose favor he secured through his discrimination in the art of pleasure-seeking. Though potentially a man of vigor and capacity, Petronius realized that serious effort was futile during Nero's reign, and he spent his time at court as a kind of Master of the Revels, until he incurred the Emperor's suspicion and was forced to commit suicide. *Tacitus has a description of Petronius in his *Annals*, and Sienkiewicz an idealized study in his novel *Quo Vadis?*

Petronius' chief literary work is the *Satyricon*, a *picaresque novel dealing with the seamier side of Roman life and surviving only in fragments. It is written in the *Menippean* form (that is, in a medley of prose and verse) and consists of a series of loosely connected episodes recording the adventures of three young scamps named Encolpius, Ascyltus, and Giton as they wander through southern Italy. It describes their carousals and love affairs, their quarrels with outraged citizens, and their difficulties with the authorities as they try to live by their wits. And it introduces a large number of picturesque

550

minor characters such as those who appear at the Banquet of Trimalchio.

The description of this dinner party is the longest and best-known episode in the *Satyricon*. The host, Trimalchio, is an egotistical and vulgar man, who was once a slave but is now enormously rich and who aspires, therefore, to be considered a person of culture and refinement. But he can think only in terms of wealth, and his efforts to ape the aristocracy turn his banquet into a long parade of ostentation. Course follows course in fantastic array; hands are washed, not in water, but in wine; a silver dish, dropped accidentally to the floor, is swept out with the rest of the garbage. Trimalchio loves to display his learning, and, as the meal proceeds, he explains how Agamemnon eloped with Helen and how Hannibal took part in the siege of Troy. The crossroads Latin spoken by his guests marks them as men and women of his same general type. It was no doubt amusing to a courtier like Petronius to satirize such upstarts as Trimalchio, but perhaps beneath the surface there is a current of ridicule directed against the whole age, which was excessively interested in the accumulation of material possessions.

Phaedo: the dialogue of *Plato that concludes the story of the trial and death of *Socrates began in the *Apology* and the *Crito* (4th century B.C.). The dialogue is presented, not as it takes place, but as it is reported by Phaedo, a disciple who was with Socrates in the prison on the last day of his life and who, at the request of Echecrates, describes what was said and done there. The account begins with the arrival of the disciples very early in the morning and continues until the afternoon, when Socrates drinks the poison while "the sun is still upon the hills." If read simply as a story, Phaedo's description exerts an emotional appeal hardly equaled in the whole range of Greek literature. But it is important as philosophy also: its discussion of the immortality of the soul involves a presentation of the Theory of Ideas, which is the central doctrine in Platonic metaphysics.

It is impossible to determine the historicity of the various elements in the *Phaedo*, for although it seems unlikely that anyone would challenge the essential truth of its narrative parts, some scholars consider its philosophical sections characteristic of Plato rather than of Socrates. The discussion attempts to show that a belief in immortality is rational. The first argument, which presents the soul as passing through a succession of many lives, is based on two considerations: (1) existence takes the form of an endless alternation of opposites, and therefore life must spring from death as death from life; and (2) knowledge is really reminiscence, the soul being stimulated by the imperfect objects of sense perception to recall the perfect Ideas with which it was associated before its imprisonment in the body. The second argument finds support in the observation that death results from the division of the composite and does not, therefore, affect the soul, which is simple and uncompounded, like the Ideas. The third shows that the soul partakes of the Idea *life* and therefore cannot admit its opposite, the Idea *death*, nor yet perish when assailed by it. And therefore "when death attacks, the mortal portion of a man may be supposed to die, but the immortal goes out of the way of death and is preserved." Other considerations are advanced, objections answered, and a description given of rewards and punishments after death. Socrates confesses that he is not certain that everything he has told his friends is literally true, but he is confident that something of the sort must occur.

At the close of the discussion Socrates bathes and, after saying farewell to his wife and children, sits down to await the attendant with the poison. When it is given him and he drinks it, one of the disciples utters a loud cry, but Socrates rebukes him, saying it was to prevent this sort of thing that he had sent the women away. He walks about a little until his legs become heavy and then lies down. In a few minutes the poison reaches his heart and he dies—"a man," as Phaedo describes him, "whom I may truly call the best of those of his time, the most righteous, and the most wise."

Phaedra: a tragedy by *Racine (1677). Racine excelled in the creation of tragic roles for women, and Phaedra is one of his masterpieces. Caught in the web of her emotions, entangled in a ruinous infatuation, Phaedra is a great characterization created out of the powerful themes of passion and sin. Although the play is considered by many to be Racine's best, it is the work which marks his withdrawal from the "worldly" stage. Here was a heroine, damned by a fatal love and a consciousness of her sins, suitable to pave his return to the Jansenist (see Racine and *Pascal) fold, and here was a production whose history was such as to warrant the retreat. Racine's enemies had commissioned a rival play on the same subject, and when in 1677 the two dramas were presented almost simultaneously, they bought up blocks of seats for both plays and then went to the other one, leaving Racine's theater discouragingly empty.

Like most 17th-century tragedies, *Phaedra* is based on classical sources: *Euripides' *Hippolytus* and, to a lesser degree, a play of *Seneca. But as Racine's title suggests, he shifted the emphasis from the youth Hippolytus to the woman Phaedra, for to Racine women demonstrate best the weakness of human nature when confronted with powerful, fatal emotions. So Phaedra—somewhat akin to her Euripidean counterpart, who was helpless in the hands of *Venus—is driven to her ruin all aware of her sins but powerless to overcome them. She is not a despicable character: she has tried to curb her illicit love for her stepson, and it is only when she believes her adventuring husband to be dead that she reveals her feelings to Hippolytus. There are, however, weaknesses in Phaedra's character, which her passion intensifies: she can be swayed by her maid to act against her reason; and, when her husband returns unexpectedly and is made suspicious of his son, she fails to save Hippolytus because she learns of his love for another. In her jealousy (like *Shakespeare's Othello), she kills what she loves most.

The Greeks believed that such flaws of character necessarily brought destruction; the Jansenists held that any virtues without "saving grace" were inconsequential. Racine was indoctrinated in both traditions: "In no other of my plays have I given virtue so exalted a place as in this. The slightest evil is severely punished. The very thought of crime is made as horrible as the crime itself. The weaknesses of love are treated as veritable shortcomings. The passions are exhibited only with the purpose of showing the disorder into which they lead us; vice is painted in such colors as to make us recognize and hate its deformity" (from his preface to *Phaedra*). But even the reader who is not at all interested in the philosophic concepts behind the play finds *Phaedra* a fascinating and beautifully executed study of a woman consumed by an unusual passion which she can neither approve nor control.

philippic: in modern usage, any speech of bitter accusation, denunciation, and invective. The term originated as the name of any of a group of speeches in which *Demosthenes, the self-styled watchdog of the state, berated Philip of Macedon, in whose conquest of Athens (338 B.C.) he correctly foresaw the end of the independence of the Greek city-states.

Phoebus: see *Apollo.

picaresque novel: the life story of a good-natured rogue (Spanish: *picaro*), a clever and amusing adventurer of low social class who makes his way by tricks and roguery rather than by honorable industry. When he does work, he begins with petty, menial tasks (often as household servant, valet). His immoral rascality manages somehow (even when he takes up with thieves) to fall a hairbreadth short of actual criminality—or so at least he himself maintains.

The story is usually told by the *picaro* in the first person, as autobiography. Episodic in nature, the loose plot consists of a series of thrilling incidents only slightly connected and strung together without organic relationship. Usually it is a novel of the road, and the hero wanders from place to place as well as from job to job, rushing headlong from one impossible situation to another. (Even *Tom Jones, for example, who is not a real *picaro*, spends roughly one-third of his time at home, one-third on the road, and the rest in London.) When the story ends with the rogue's seeming reform and his marriage (to a rich widow or an heiress), the change is purely external, no real development in his character having taken place, except that he has learned to conform outwardly to the ways of society.

The adventures and wanderings in different social settings permit the *picaro* to meet, at moments not governed or inhibited by social etiquette, people of all social classes—bankers, politicians, society folk, the clergy, doctors, lawyers, actors. He is thus provided with the opportunity of satirizing the corruption and hypocrisy, folly, injustice, and brutality, of a whole society and epoch. The picaresque novel is in consequence a study of manners, both morally provocative and entertaining.

The earliest example of the type is the Spanish *Lazarillo de Tormes* (c. 1554), which became one of the most popular books of the century (and gave the type its name). It was imitated by Thomas Nash in *The Unfortunate Traveller; or the Life of Jack Wilton* (1594), the first English picaresque novel. The French *Gil Blas* (1715), by *Le Sage, is the most famous and most influential of such works. And *Defoe increased the stature of the form by *Moll Flanders* (1722), the history of a female rogue. The novels of *Fielding, Smollett, and *Voltaire contain many picaresque elements, as does *Mark Twain's *Adventures of Huckleberry Finn*. A major picaresque novel was cut short by Thomas *Mann's death in 1955, after he had completed only the first volume of his *Confessions of Felix Krull, Confidence Man (Bekentnisse des Hochstaplers Felix Krull)*.

Perhaps first inspired in reaction against the decaying conventions of an idealistically conceived knight, the picaresque novel is "anti-pastoral, anti-chivalric, anti-aristocratic"; it is important because it first gave a realistic picture of a whole age. Moreover, it popularized a literary type in which people of low and humble origin were treated honestly and, even when wicked, sympathetically. The broad social canvas, the vivid descriptions of trades and professions, the mingling of all social classes, the ironic survey of morals and manners—all these materials were later drawn into the nonpicaresque novel, to the immeasurable enrichment of its scope and effectiveness.

Pico della Mirandola, Count Giovanni: Italian humanist and member of the Platonic Academy of Florence (1463–94). Pico's special contribution to world literature is his Latin *Oration on the Dignity of Man* (*Oratio de hominis dignitate*, 1486), one of the earliest and most eloquent statements of that faith in the equality of men and in their infinite capacity for perfectibility through reason which was characteristic of *humanism. The son of a petty prince, Pico became one of the most learned and original thinkers of his day. To his solid study of the medieval interpretations of *Plato and *Aristotle, he added a knowledge of the Arabic commentators on Aristotle. And he was one of the earliest modern Christian scholars to study Hebrew and the cabala. (His Hebrew work was, in fact, one of the first books to be printed in Hebrew characters.)

Inspired by one of his feudal titles, Count Concordia, he was fascinated by the thought of being "the great reconciler" and felt not only that Plato could be reconciled with Aristotle and both of these philosophers with Christianity, but that there was a basic harmony of all religions and all philosophies. He hoped to be the one to make the synthesis. His early death, however, cut short his *Symphonia Platonis et Aristotelis.* During his lifetime, two of his published works were condemned as heretical. He was, nevertheless, one of the most important influences on the enlightened religious attitudes of the English humanists, notably on John Colet and Sir Thomas More (see *Utopia*).

The *Oration on the Dignity of Man* proclaims man a free and self-reliant spirit. Man was made at the close of the creation so that seeing it whole he could "ponder the rationality of so great a work" and learn to understand the laws, the beauty, and the vastness of the universe. To man alone was given the power of choice and the capacity to reason intelligently. "To you alone, man, was given a growth and a development depending on your own free will. You bear in you the germs of universal life." The all-embracing aspirations of the *Renaissance find their expression in Pico: "Not content with the mediocre, we shall pant after the highest."

Piers Plowman (The Vision of William Concerning Piers the Plowman): a dream-vision *allegory in unrhymed alliterative verse (1370?–1387?) by William Langland (?). Despite lack of orderly development from episode to episode, the poem achieves intellectual and artistic force, and some 60 extant manuscripts (falling into three versions in terms of length, content, and dating) attest its early popularity. Within a dream-frame, the dreamer-narrator, called "Will," sets out on a journey toward salvation, a pilgrimage in quest of Truth (the true meaning of the Christian life) to discover how a man may save his soul. There are momentary awakenings, dreams-within-dreams, allegorical debates, sermons, "complaints," exhortations (e.g., by Conscience and Theology), visions (e.g., of a rat parliament—"who will bell the cat?"; of the *Seven Deadly Sins—Glutton in the tavern is one of the high marks of the poem). At the beginning the dreamer learns from Lady Holy Church that a worthy Christian must practice charity, love, and especially truth. The next dreams are satirical visions of "middle-earth," the world as it is, monstrously abused by Church and State, corrupted by individual pride and greed, enervated by spiritual sloth. Society, working and wandering, is castigated by being shown in its typical activities: "a fair field full of folk," barons and burgesses, friars and clergy, pilgrims and palmers, tailors and tinkers, king, knights, commons. The characters have tag-names (like Robert the Robber) or are allegorical personifications, e.g., Clergy, Concupiscencia-Carnis, Conscience, Meekness, Patience, Peace, Reason, Repentance, Scripture, Study, Wit, Wrong.

When Piers the Plowman appears, he offers to help the pilgrims find their way if they will wait until he plows his half-acre. More than just an honest laborer, devout and hardworking, he comes to represent the disciple Peter (the rock of the Church), the Church, and ultimately Christ himself—*Petrus id est Christus*. And it is Piers whom Conscience seeks at the end. Humble and pious, Piers and Will hope that the discovery of Dowel (Do well), Dobet (Do better), and Dobest (Do best) will reform society. (Allegorically their search represents the cumulative process of spiritual growth.) Dowel is honesty and labor; Dobet is humbleness and charity (understanding the life of Christ); Dobest is above both and bears the Bishop's cross (understanding the Church). Not Thought, not Wisdom, not Study can point to where Dowel, Dobet, Dobest dwell among the people, or the friars, or the clergy. Sloth and Knavery, deceitful confessors, Hunger, and Death are so powerful that Piers succumbs. In another version the search for Dowel resumes, and Piers is apparently still alive; Will's dreams become more intellectual, and the definitions shift: Dowel, the active life, becomes a life of humble, patient poverty. The search for Dobet includes Ymaginatif's discourse on false wealth and learning. The narrator, learning more about Faith, Hope and Charity, love, contrition, confession, experiences a mystic apocalyptic vision of the Passion, the Harrowing of Hell, and the Church Militant (Dobest). Seizing his pilgrim's staff, Conscience prepares to seek Piers that together they may destroy Pride and the friars, flatterers who benumb Contrition. The cry of Conscience beseeching God's help ends the poem by awakening the dreamer into a world still unredeemed. Conscience must continue the quest, apparently never-ending, for justice and love among men redeemed by God's grace.

Pilgrim's Progress, [The] (1678; second part, 1684): a prose dream-vision *allegory by John Bunyan (1628–88). *Pilgrim's Progress* is a journey toward salvation (see *The *Canterbury Tales*, *The *Divine Comedy*, *Piers Plowman*). By trade a tinker (that also of his father), Bunyan became by "a miracle of precious grace" a self-styled "mechanik" lay preacher (working man turned preacher) and an author. His inner religious struggles he described in an autobiography, *Grace Abounding to the Chief of Sinners, or the brief Relation of the exceeding Mercy of*

God in Christ to his poor servant John Bunyan (1666).
Here he confesses a youthful propensity to cursing,
swearing, lying, and dancing; then, after tormenting
doubts, he was persuaded, by "a miracle of precious
grace," that he had been specially chosen to spread the
word of God. Since he was not ordained and his beliefs
did not conform to those of the Established Church of
England, with the return of the Stuart monarchy he was
refused a license to preach. But preach he would, and
he was promptly arrested in 1660. During the next dozen
years, although legally a prisoner, he was paroled intermittently to attend church meetings, to travel, to write
(some 60 separate works, all religious instruction, of
which three are narrative fictional allegories). In 1672 he
was formally pardoned. Under the terms of the government's *Declaration of Religious Indulgence*, he was licensed to preach to those "who are of the persuasion
commonly called Congregational." The *Declaration* was
withdrawn in 1675, and Bunyan was again clapped into
jail, this time for about six weeks, during which period
Pilgrim's Progress is believed to have been written. The
book was Bunyan's fictional dramatization of spiritual
experiences already recorded in *Grace Abounding* and,
like it, intended as a vehicle of spiritual instruction.

The full title is *The Pilgrim's Progress from This
World to That which is to come: delivered under the Si-
militude of a Dream Wherein is Discovered, The manner
of his setting out, His Dangerous Journey, and safe Arrival at the Desired Country.* One of the masterpieces of
"prison literature" (see *Boethius, *Socrates), the *Progress* became Everyman's purposeful journey through life
seeking peace of mind and eternal life (the Second Part,
a story of the pilgrimage of Christiana and their children,
under the guidance of Greatheart and Mercy, to join
Christian, is vivid and humorous, but lacks the suspense
of the First Part). The work opens with the narrator's
dreams of the central character, Christian, asking "What
shall I do to be saved?" Bearing a pack (his burden of
original sin), Christian rejects his own City of Destruction, his family and society, and walks his earthly "journey
through the Wilderness of the World" on a pilgrimage to
God's Promised Land. Although "all is of Grace, not of

Works" and all men predestined either for salvation or damnation, Christian's journey is beset by temptations, dangers, difficulties: "A Christian man is never long at ease./ When one fright's gone, another doth him seize." Accompanied at times by Evangelist, Faithful, or Hopeful, Christian is mired in the Slough of Despond, learns not to trust Mr. Worldly Wiseman of Carnal City, is nearly crushed to death by the fiend Apollyon (spiritual doubt), finds himself in a dungeon of Giant Despair of Doubting Castle, visits the town of Vanity and its Fair (the "pride and show of the acquisitive life"; see *Thackeray), where the chief commodity is "the ware of Rome," is tried and convicted (the judge is named Hategood, the jury foreman, Blind-Man), escapes the jail, sees the gaping mouth of Hell, and finally, after a near-drowning in the dark river, is welcomed to the Celestial City.

Spiritual instruction and allegorical characters notwithstanding, the homely imagery and descriptions are full of humor and of pervasive social satire. The different skills of the narrator reinforce one another. The illusion of a literal journey is sustained by the realistic obstacles of a country road, ditches, stiles, dark forests; and the traveler meets real people (with allegorical names) who go directly to the point in plain everyday colloquial speech, Obstinate, Pliable, Talkative from Prating Row, and Ignorance from the country of Conceit, Flatter, and Mr. By-ends argue and walk away, as any villagers might when Christian's catechism and evangelical fervor gets too hot for them. So pungent is the talk that the language and imagery have become part of our vocabulary, so realistic are these allegorical portraits that attempts have been made to identify the originals. The great crowds and bustle of Vanity Fair have been identified with the great Stourbridge Fair, held annually at Cambridge. The book was an immediate popular success, a classic of the English Puritan tradition. Second and third editions (with expansions) appeared within a year, and altogether 12 editions were published in the decade before Bunyan's death (the book made a fortune for the printer). Subsequently translated into a hundred foreign tongues, the book's appeal has penetrated different cultures and races and non-Christian religions.

Pindar: Greek lyric poet (518–438 B.C.). Pindar was a professional poet and spent his life in composition, but of all his works, except for fragments, only the *Epinicia* (or *Victory Odes*) are extant. There are 44 of these odes, the majority less than 100 lines in length, written for athletes who had won prizes in the great national games and intended to be sung by a chorus, usually during the celebration that followed the victor's return to his home. For a crown gained at Olympia or in some other contest by a man's strength and skill shed glory, the Greeks believed, on his whole city and demanded public recognition of his accomplishment.

Though Pindar celebrates athletic victories in his poems, he seldom describes the contests in which the prizes were won. After giving the essential facts concerning the victor, he takes some legend connected with him or his city and develops it as the main theme of his ode. For example, in the *First Olympian*, written to extol Hiero, tyrant (ruler) of Syracuse and winner of a horse race at Olympia, Pindar devotes his attention largely to the story of the hero Pelops, who gave his name to the Peloponnesus, the southern part of Greece, from which came the colonists who founded Syracuse. Pelops was a friend of the sea-god *Poseidon, with whose winged horses he gained his bride in the first great race at Olympia. His grave overlooks the field, and his spirit inspires the games in which Hiero won and will win again if the gods are with him. Thus, by means of mythology, Pindar links the glory of the past to the glory of the present, while at the same time he creates an appropriate atmosphere for the moral and religious instruction he weaves into his verses. For in all his writings Pindar shows his devotion to the gods, and particularly to *Apollo, with whose priests he enjoyed the closest friendship.

Although an aristocrat writing largely for aristocratic patrons, Pindar maintained his position as the greatest of lyric poets through all the political changes that swept over the Greek and Roman worlds. The elevation of his thought, the brilliance of his language, the beauty and insight of his ethical maxims combined, the ancients thought, with the torrent of his eloquence to leave him without a rival. And yet, of the major classical writers, Pindar is probably the least read today. His verse is too difficult for our taste and his themes too remote from our experience. But the Pindaric ode has been imitated in English, with varying success, by *Dryden, *Gray, and other poets.

Pinter, Harold: English dramatist (1930–   ). Pinter was born in Hackney, East London. After training for the stage at the Royal Academy of Dramatic Arts and the Center School of Speech and Drama, he acted and held a variety of small jobs. He also did work in films, radio, and television before turning to playwriting in 1957 with *The Room*.

An underlying theme of violence and suspense pervades Pinter's plays. Oftentimes the characters are not aware of what it is that they fear; they only know that it is something from outside their small realm. In *The Dumb Waiter* (1957) it is the unseen person who sends messages on the dumbwaiter; in *The Birthday Party* (1957) and *A Slight Ache* (1958) there is again an unseen threat to the safety of the room. In general, Pinter's women are either possessive mother figures or prostitutes or both, and so they are almost impossible to possess. His men often are ignorant of what they want from the girl and sometimes give her up after fighting for possession of her. In *The Homecoming* (1965) the bridegroom takes his wife to England, then returns to America, leaving her to be a whore for his father and brothers. In *The Basement* (1967) the last lines of the play are identical to the opening lines, but the roles of the two men are completely reversed. Throughout his plays Pinter remains an outside observer, recording the illogical, often one-sided conversations of his characters and the mysterious, menacing situations which confront them and often overtake them. This existential quality shows the influence of Samuel *Beckett's *Waiting for Godot*.

Pirandello, Luigi: Italian novelist and dramatist (1867–1936). Pirandello was born in Sicily, the son of a well-to-do mine owner. He attended the University of Rome and Bonn University, from which he received his doctorate in philology in 1891. Back in Rome, he married a Sicilian girl chosen for him by his father (she was to become mentally ill several years after their marriage), taught for a while at a girls' college, and started writing novels and short stories, some of which he dramatized later.

Pirandello must be acknowledged as an original playwright. He rejected the theories of *naturalism, which claimed that art should be an imitation of life. To his anti-realistic dramas, he gave the name *Naked Masks* (*Maschere Nude*). The first of Pirandello's plays to attract wide recognition was *It Is So!—If You Think So* (*Così é se vi pare*, 1917), which deals with the problem of the relativity of truth. Among the numerous plays which followed, the best are *Six Characters in Search of an Author* (*Sei Personaggi in cerca d'autore*, 1921) and *Henry IV* (*Enrico IV*, 1922). In the former work the rehearsal of a play is interrupted by six characters who insist upon acting out their own drama. In the course of this "play within a play," Pirandello explores one of his favorite themes: the contrast between life, which is movement and chaos, and art, which is form and order. Concerned on the surface with the interplay between madness and sanity, *Henry IV* treats the conflict between reality and appearance, self-recognition and self-deception. For Pirandello, illusion is a necessary means of survival.

Although Pirandello's is a theater of ideas, it is not abstract or allegorical, and his characters never become mouthpieces for their creator. Possessing genuine dramatic intensity, they probe into their psyches not for the sake of psychological analysis, but as a means of getting at the root of the sufferings inherent in the human condition. Pirandello has expressed his ideas on artistic creation, the function of dramatic characters, and the conflict between life and art in his preface to *Six Characters in Search of an Author*.

Plato: Greek philosopher (*c.* 428–347 B.C.). Like many other young Athenians of the upper classes, Plato attached himself to *Socrates early in life, and his writings show the extraordinary influence their association

563

had upon him. When Socrates was executed in 399 B.C., Plato, now almost 30 years old, left Athens to live at Megara, though it is not known whether he also undertook the journey to Egypt and Cyrene attributed to him by tradition. He did visit Italy, however, where he was much influenced by the Pythagoreans, and Sicily, where he formed a lasting friendship with Dion, a member of the court of Dionysius I, then tyrant (ruler) of Syracuse. Plato returned to Athens about 386 B.C. and established a school called the *Academy*, in which he taught until his death, interrupting his work only twice, on both occasions to visit Syracuse at the invitation of Dionysius II, who succeeded his father in 367 B.C. But, although Plato had reason to hope that with Dion's help he would be able to guide the young tyrant in reforming the government of the city, he met with no success. This was the philosopher's only attempt to influence practical politics; he did not enter public life at Athens, being repelled both by the excesses of the later democracy, which culminated in the trial and death of Socrates, and by the cruelties of the Thirty, as the oligarchical government which ruled the city for a time after the Peloponnesian War was called. But the Academy flourished, continuing as a center of learning until A.D. 529, when the Emperor Justinian closed the schools of philosophy; and at least in its early years it was much concerned with political science.

From time to time during his long career Plato published the dialogues on which his fame as the greatest of ancient philosophers is now established. These are writings of a popular type treating particular points in ethics, metaphysics, or epistemology which he wished to elucidate. They do not set forth his philosophy systematically, nor are they free of inconsistencies. There are 42 dialogues in the collection, including seven considered spurious and at least four others suspected in antiquity. Probably 25 to 28 are genuine. They fall into three groups, the earliest consisting of short pieces such as the *Euthyphro* and the *Crito, which describe Socrates overthrowing the contentions of his opponents rather than advancing views of his own. These dialogues are noted for their dramatic setting and vivid style as well as for their great biographical interest, for

Socrates seems to act and speak in them much as in real life, though doubtless he is somewhat idealized. The second group, written in Plato's middle period, contains such famous works as the *Phaedo*, the *Symposium*, and the *Republic* and presents Socrates attempting to establish positive doctrines, sometimes with the aid of myths. Changes in literary technique also appear; the dialogue is narrated rather than reported directly, and the scene is at times thrown back into Plato's childhood. There is much debate as to whether the views Socrates expresses in these dialogues belong historically to him or to Plato, but the question is so complex that it is impossible to do more than note it here. Finally, there is a third group of late compositions such as the *Timaeus* and the *Laws*, in which Socrates is less prominent than before, or entirely absent.

The central point in Platonic philosophy, as it is found in the dialogues, is the Theory of Ideas, according to which each thing we perceive in this world is an imperfect imitation of a perfect original called the *Idea* or Form. Not that an Idea exists corresponding to each individual object of sense, but that an Idea exists corresponding to each class of such objects that is distinguished by a common name. There is, for example, the Idea *man*, and every man *partakes of* or *participates in* that Idea, though each fails, of course, to reflect it completely, because each is imperfect and changing and therefore essentially unreal. For the sole realities in the world are the Ideas, *which are not ideas such as pass through the minds of men* but entities existing forever in a region outside time and space, changeless themselves, and unaffected by changes in material objects.

But, in the nature of things, there can be no true knowledge of that which is subject to change, and therefore the Ideas, which alone of all things are changeless, are the only real objects of knowledge in the universe. Concerning all other things we have only opinion, which is changeable, fallible, and irrational, whereas knowledge is enduring, infallible, and rational. For the Ideas are incorporeal and therefore invisible, and a knowledge of them can be attained only by the reason unaffected by sensation and proceeding by dialectic, though Plato states that things of sense may remind us of the Ideas which they imitate. They can do this because the soul, before entering the body, has encountered the Ideas in another world. The soul has forgotten much that it learned about them then, but it has not forgotten all; and, if it struggles to remember, it will find that the Imitations, faint and distorted though they are, serve, like bad portraits, to suggest to it the realities that it once knew. This is Plato's doctrine that *learning is recollection*. It is called *anamnesis*; and it involves belief in the immortality of the soul, which passes from life through death to life again according to the theory of *transmigration* or *metempsychosis*.

Proof that knowledge is recollection and that the soul has met the Ideas before its imprisonment in the body is found in such phenomena as our instantaneous recognition of mathematical truths. The Ideas are not confined to natural kinds like men and horses, dogs and cats and mice, and all the manifold species of animals and plants. They extend to anything that is thinkable, to mathematical figures like circles, triangles, and squares, and to moral concepts like courage, justice, temperance, and goodness. There is such a thing as a perfect circle, and we know what it is, though we have never seen it. And there is such a thing as absolute goodness, even if it is not to be found on earth. It is the Idea of the Good, the supreme Idea in the hierarchy of the Ideas, and the true lover of wisdom will spend his life in contemplating it.

By virtue of this magnificent theory, Plato became the first of the great idealistic philosophers of Europe, and as such his influence on subsequent thought has been immense. This is no doubt his true glory. But it should be noted that, from a literary point of view, he also stands high among the foremost writers of the world, his style, which lies on the borderland between prose and poetry, being almost infinite in its variety, as he moves from passages marked by conversational ease and grace to bursts of soaring eloquence, or from flashes of wit and humor to the noblest pathos in pagan literature. The *Republic* is the greatest of Plato's works, though the story of the trial and death of Socrates, told in the *Apology*, *Crito*, and *Phaedo*, surpasses it in emotional appeal, and the

Symposium is the literary masterpiece among the dialogues.

Plautus, Titus Maccius: Roman writer of comedies (*c.* 254–184 B.C.). Plautus was born in northern Italy but in his youth went to Rome, where he was connected in some way with the performance of plays—a fact borne out by the mastery of practical stagecraft exhibited in his comedies. Plautus seems to have saved a considerable sum of money, which he risked in trade and lost, so that he was forced by poverty to turn to manual labor in a flour mill. During this period of hardship he began to compose his dramas, translating and adapting them from *Menander and the other writers of Greek New Comedy. But we do not know how many plays he wrote, and we can date only a few of the 20 that have survived.

Roman plays were given regularly at the great public festivals throughout the year and sometimes on other occasions. They were presented by troupes of actors, whose managers purchased the scripts and arranged with the magistrates in charge of the festivals for their production. In Plautus' day the performances were staged on a long, temporary, wooden platform equipped with an altar and a background which, in comedy, usually represented two houses with a passageway between them. No seats were provided the spectators at first, but in 194 B.C. chairs were placed for the senators in the orchestra, the semicircular space immediately in front of the stage. (The Romans cut the round dancing-place of the Greeks in half.) About 50 years later wooden benches began to be built for the audience as a whole, and more adequate staging was introduced. But it was not until 55 B.C. that Pompey constructed Rome's first permanent stone theater.

On the Roman stage, as in ancient Greece, an actor played more than one part. Four or five actors were therefore sufficient to present any of Plautus' comedies. They seem not to have used masks, although the point is disputed; but they wore traditional costumes that indicated at a glance the stock characters they represented. The action of the play took place in the street in front of the houses of the leading characters, a convention that explains the awkward entrances and exits sometimes found in Roman comedy. By another convention, the stage door on the spectators' right led to the forum in the center of the city, that on their left to the country or abroad.

In adapting Greek comedies to the Roman stage, the dramatists normally abolished the chorus, and to compensate for the loss of its music, they presented much of the action of the play itself in song. This technique became increasingly popular. In the later dramas of Plautus, who perfected it, lyrical passages, composed in a variety of meters and sung to the music of the flute, make up about a third of the comedy, while additional scenes were written in recitative verse and chanted against a soft musical background.

By omitting the chorus the Roman dramatists were able to present a continuous, or almost continuous, performance; and the emphasis on the lyrical element gave their plays a new form closely resembling that of modern musical comedy. But despite these changes, Greek drama, as adapted at Rome, maintained its foreign atmosphere. The scene was laid in a Greek city, usually Athens; the characters kept their Greek names; and the traditional costumes the actors wore were cut in the Greek style. It was necessary for the Romans to present New Comedy in this way. No author could possibly identify the reckless young men who play the major roles in Menander and Philemon with the disciplined youth of Rome or attempt to portray their wild and licentious conduct as characteristic of life in the early Republic. Drama so constructed would have been false to the point of absurdity and so offensive to Roman morals that the censors would have suppressed it before it reached the stage. For Plautus' Rome was in no sense the rich and dissolute city of the later Republic. It retained much of the stern morality that marked its infancy, it was impoverished by the Punic Wars, and it was subject to sumptuary laws that limited clothing to homespun and food to the simplest fare.

But, although the Romans would not tolerate New Comedy in Roman dress, they accepted it in its original setting. The parasite displayed his wit, the slave abetted his young master's misdeeds, and the other stock characters played their parts without offense at Rome, provided it was clear that they were Greeks. There was one exception: a dramatist could not depict a Greek *hetaira* sympathetically when Plautus wrote, though he could do so later, in the time of *Terence. Marriage was on a high plane at Rome, the wife was the husband's equal, and a prostitute who possessed redeeming virtues would have shocked the audience.

As social usage at Rome affected Greek New Comedy, so did the need for simplification. Some details in the original dramas would have been incomprehensible to a Roman and consequently had to be altered by the substitution of more familiar material. If a scene portraying a process of Greek law was beyond the grasp of the spectators but required by the action, Plautus rewrote it in Roman terms, even though by so doing he put the Roman legal system and Roman magistrates where they did not belong. Nor did the incongruity involved in this procedure seem to trouble him. In fact, he often added Roman details to the plays merely for the sake of their humor. It is quite possible that the spectators enjoyed the confusion. Local references inserted in a script by a modern actor seldom fail to please an unsophisticated audience.

And the Romans who stood before Plautus' stage were still largely untutored, their grasp of drama was superficial and their taste unformed. They had no long cultural tradition behind them and were little inclined to criticize an amusing piece for artistic flaws. In playing to them Plautus was free to shape his material as he wished, always provided he made it entertaining.

Plautus' comedies are amazingly uneven in both structure and characterization, but we have no way of knowing whether he was sometimes hasty and careless in his own work, or whether he merely reproduced the faults of the Greek plays which he adapted. At any rate, some of his plays have a masterly construction and some are slipshod. Some of his characters are fine portraits: the deceived wife in *Amphitryon*, the miser in *Aulularia (Pot of Gold)*, the boaster in *Miles gloriosus (The Braggart

Soldier), and even some of his minor characters. But in some plays—the *Asinaria (Comedy of Asses)* is an example—the figures are mere caricatures.

Though Plautus took his plots and characters from Greece, his style is all his own. He composed his plays in colloquial Latin, an idiom he used with unsurpassed skill. His language is spontaneous, rapid, and brilliant with wit and humor. He is a master of every conceivable type of joke and word play. He loves alliteration, *assonance, and comic redundancy, and he uses them with full effect. He cites long comic lists and coins new comic words in great numbers. He addresses and abuses the audience directly. He descends to the coarsest of banter at times, and he depicts some atrocious scenes, though he does make the worst vices repulsive. He is a hearty, boisterous, exuberant poet, and though a lesser artist than *Aristophanes, he reminds one of him.

The most influential of Plautus' plays are the *Menaechmi* (on which *Shakespeare based *The Comedy of Errors*); the *Pot of Gold* (which inspired *Molière's *The Miser*); the *Braggart Soldier*, whose hero, the swaggering poltroon Pyrgopolynices, seems to enjoy perennial appeal; and the *Amphitryon*, a travesty on the Greek myth describing how *Zeus seduced Alcmene, Amphitryon's wife, by assuming the form of her husband. This last comedy has been much imitated in modern times; Molière's *Amphitryon* is based on it, but the contemporary *Amphitryon 38* by Jean *Giraudoux has little in common with the Latin version. *Captivi (The Prisoners)* is an especially noble play. Plautus himself tells us that "dramatists find few comedies like this one which make good men better," and the German critic *Lessing called it the finest comedy ever staged. Its structure is excellent, its characters well drawn, and its theme, the devotion of a slave to his master, is unusual in New Comedy. But *The Prisoners* is a very quiet play. It has "no low intrigue, no illicit love-affair, no scheming courtesan, no braggart warrior," or desperate young man. It therefore gains in decency and freshness but loses in gaiety and speed.

Plautus was the most popular of the Roman comic dramatists during his lifetime, and his plays were often staged under the late Republic. He was much read in the period of the Empire, especially during the 2d century A.D., when the educated classes had a lively interest in the earlier Roman writers. Plautus passed out of fashion in the *Middle Ages but returned to favor at the *Renaissance; and he has remained a storehouse of amusing situations and comic characters to the present day.

Pléiade: the name given to a group of 16th-century French writers who joined under the leadership of *Ronsard to create a new French poetry as great as that of *classical antiquity by applying to French the lessons learned from the classics. The name (taken from a constellation of seven stars called the Pleiades) was originally applied in the 3d century B.C. to a group of seven Alexandrian poets (including *Theocritus). Ronsard was probably thinking of this group when he referred to his own literary intimates as the Pléiade.

The literary manifesto of this "school" was Du Bellay's *Defense and Illustration of the French Language* (1549), the "illustration" of the title meaning both explanation (elucidation) of the powers of the language and an indication of the means of making it "illustrious," of ennobling it. The essay, analogous in spirit and ideas to *Dante's defense of Italian in *De vulgari eloquentia (The Illustrious Vernacular)*, stressed the high function of the poet and patriotically defended the inherent beauty and "nobility" of the French language, as potentially equal to the classic tongues. Du Bellay proposed a conscious creation of diction and style by coining words and imitating Greek and Latin, and he suggested specific reforms for the enrichment of vocabulary and rhythms. Superiority could be achieved by "devouring, digesting, and converting into blood and nourishment" the themes, myths, diction, and stylistic devices of classical literature. The great current of medieval French literature in the vernacular was to be abandoned.

Although the Pléiade started as an original and energetic movement to infuse new spirit into French poetry, the suggestions of its members were gradually interpreted more and more rigidly by conservative Neo-Classicists, grammarians, and others devoted to standardization of form. The ideas of the Pléiade are also expressed in Ronsard's critical writings, especially the preface to his *Odes* (1550) and the *Summary of French Poetic Art* (*Abregé de l'art poétique françois*, 1565). Ronsard's last roster of the group lists himself, Du' Bellay, de Baïf, Jodelle, Pontus de Tyard, Bełleau, and Dorat. The Pléiade had an important and constructive influence on English Elizabethan poets, notably *Spenser.

Pliny the Elder: Roman encyclopedist (*c.* A.D. 23–79). Gaius Plinius Secundus was born in northern Italy but educated at Rome, where he became the friend and confidential adviser of the Emperor Vespasian and his son Titus, who succeeded him. Pliny spent his life in the service of the Roman government, first as a soldier in Germany, and later as an administrator in Gaul, Africa, and Spain. In A.D. 79 he was in command of a Roman fleet stationed not far from Naples when Mt. Vesuvius erupted on August 24. Pliny desired to view the phenomenon close at hand and at the same time to bring assistance to those civilians who were in immediate danger. He therefore set sail with part of the fleet and disembarked near the mountain, where he was suffocated the following morning by the poison gas thrown off in the eruption. Pliny's death is described in a famous letter written by his nephew and adopted son, *Pliny the Younger, to the historian *Tacitus.

Despite Pliny's official duties he became the most learned Roman of his age. He had a passion for collecting information, he considered time not spent on study as wasted, and he worked all day and most of the night reading, excerpting what he read, and dictating. He seems to have required very little sleep, and during his waking hours he followed a routine in which not a moment was lost, his secretary accompanying him at all times and reading to him even while he ate. Pliny composed works on grammar, rhetoric, biography, history, and military tactics, but only his great compendium of ancient science, the *Naturalis Historia (Natural History)*, is extant.

The *Natural History* is prefaced by a dedication to Titus, followed by a table of contents and a list of authorities, which together make up Book I. Books II–VI discuss astronomy, meteorology, and geography; Book VII, anthropology and human physiology; Books VIII–XXXII, zoology, botany, pharmacology, and medicine; Books XXXIII–XXXVII, mineralogy and the use of minerals in the fine arts. The preface states that the work contains 20,000 facts collected from 2,000 volumes, and the indexes give the names of 473 authorities. But it would seem probable that Pliny based each section on a comparatively few of these and that he used the others chiefly for illustration. He himself speaks of 100 authors as his principal sources.

The *Natural History* is a digest and, like any other book of the type, its value depends on the reliability of its sources and the discrimination shown in using them. Only a few of Pliny's authorities are extant, but it is clear that they varied greatly in trustworthiness and, as a compiler, he himself had two chief faults, credulity and hastiness. His reading was so extensive that he had little time for reflection, and his preoccupation with marvels led him to include the false with the true in his volume and to elevate the curious to a level with the significant. Nevertheless, Pliny's love of the curious has preserved much valuable detail that would otherwise have been lost, and at least some of his statements, once condemned as absurd, have been confirmed by investigation. His *Natural History* marks the highest point reached in scientific writing by the Romans, it was extremely influential throughout the *Middle Ages, and its importance in the history of science seems likely to increase. Pliny was not a trained observer, but he did have a sincere desire for knowledge. He was a Stoic, but he was not tightly bound by his philosophy. He was conscientious in assembling his facts; and, while he made errors at times, particularly in translating from Greek into Latin, he was generally accurate.

Every section of the *Natural History* contains much of permanent interest, but the books on zoology are especially entertaining, and those describing the fine arts are important for information not preserved elsewhere concerning painting and sculpture in antiquity.

Pliny the Younger: Roman orator and statesman (A.D. 61 or 62–c. 113). Gaius Plinius Caecilius Secundus was born in northern Italy but educated at Rome, where he enjoyed unusual success as a pleader and held various magistracies under the emperors Domitian, Nerva, and Trajan. Pliny had great administrative ability and wide experience in business, and in A.D. 111, when it became necessary to reorganize the finances of Bithynia, he was chosen for the task and made governor of the province. His official correspondence with Trajan is extant and gives an excellent picture of his administration. There is no record of his return to Italy, and it is thought that he died at his post, probably before A.D. 114.

Pliny lost his father in childhood and was adopted by his maternal uncle, *Pliny the Elder, who taught him to love literature and to study it with diligence, so that he became one of the most learned men of the age. His ambition was to follow in the footsteps of *Cicero, whom he admired more than any other writer, and to attain fame, as his model had, first in oratory and then in other branches of composition. With this in mind, Pliny revised his orations with elaborate care before he published them. But, except for the *Panegyric on Trajan*, which is little read, they have perished, and Pliny's reputation depends almost entirely on the ten books of his collected letters.

The letters in Books I–IX are addressed to relatives and friends. They were written as models of literary style and intended for publication; for this reason they are somewhat lacking in spontaneity and vividness, though very entertaining. Each is a little essay on a single theme, a trial perhaps, or a debate in the senate, an illness, a death, or a murder, a conversation, a ghost story, a description of a country home, a gift, or any subject likely to interest the reading public. These letters paint a pleasant picture of life under the Empire; they throw a strong light on Pliny's character, which was amiable, though vain; and they introduce us to many prominent

574

individuals, including *Tacitus, *Suetonius, and *Martial. The best are probably the two describing the eruption of Mt. Vesuvius, in which Pliny the Elder lost his life; but all are good, and those to Calpurnia, Pliny's wife, are charming.

The letters in Book X are addressed to Trajan and are often accompanied by the Emperor's replies. Almost all were written during Pliny's governorship. They are historical documents of great value, and two of them concerning Christianity in Bithynia are famous, but as a group they are probably less interesting than the private letters.

Plotinus: see *Neo-Platonism.

Plutarch: Greek biographer and essayist (*c.* A.D. 45–*c.* 125). Plutarch was born at Chaeronea, a country town in Boeotia, not long before the middle of the 1st century A.D. He was educated at Athens—for his parents were wealthy—and he supplemented his formal studies by extensive reading and travel in Greece, Italy, and Egypt. He lived for a time at Rome, partly to conduct a diplomatic mission with which he had been entrusted, partly to deliver a series of lectures that won him many friends among those interested in philosophy. But though he might have remained permanently in the city and may have been tempted to do so for the sake of its libraries if for nothing else, pride in his country eventually drew him back to Chaeronea. Here he became a local magistrate, a priest of the god *Apollo, a teacher instructing his friends and their children, and a writer from whose works the modern world has drawn more of its concept of antiquity than from any other single source.

Plutarch's works, as we now have them, are gathered together in two great collections, the *Parallel Lives*, on which his reputation chiefly rests, and the *Moral Essays (Moralia)*, a group of some 80 treatises on a wide variety of subjects, cast in the form of addresses, dialogues, and letters. About half the *Essays* discuss philosophy, particularly ethics, largely from the Platonic point of view, while the rest are on such subjects as history and litera-

575

ture, religion, education, and antiquities. The essays were intended to be popular and, though neither original nor profound, are most entertaining, being relieved everywhere by illustrations and anecdotes. They are also most valuable for the information they have preserved and for the light they throw on the *Parallel Lives*, to which they form a kind of companion piece. For just as the lives were intended to show what the Greeks had done in the world of action, so the essays were designed to set forth their accomplishments in the world of thought. Almost all make good reading, but among the best are *On Bringing Up a Boy*, *On the Student at Lectures*, *On Fawner and Friend*, *On Talkativeness*, *On Superstition*, *On the Control of Anger*, *On Instances of Delay in Divine Punishment*, *On the Cessation of the Oracles*, and *On the Genius of Socrates*.

Pluto: see *Hades.

Poe, Edgar Allan: American short-story writer, poet, and critic (1809–49). Edgar Poe was born in Boston of actor parents, but his father deserted the family and his mother died in Richmond, Virginia, when the boy was only two. John Allan, a Richmond merchant, took the child into his home and christened him Edgar Allan Poe, though he did not legally adopt him. Allan's childless wife was extremely fond of Poe, and he was given good schooling in Richmond and in England. He attended the University of Virginia for less than a year, making a good record scholastically; but because of his drinking and gambling Allan refused to pay his debts and put him to work. In 1827 Poe ran away to Boston, where he published *Tamerlane and Other Poems*, "by a Bostonian." He served for two years in the U. S. Army before Allan (whose wife was now dead) got him an appointment to West Point—where he soon provoked his own dismissal. Allan's anger at this, and his second marriage, produced a final break, and Poe was now on his own.

He had published other slim volumes of verse in 1829 and *Poems* (second edition) in 1831, but his first literary success was a prizewinning story, *MS. Found in a Bottle*, which gained him useful literary friends and secured him an *entrée* to the *Southern Literary Messenger.* Within a year he was its editor. In 1836 he married his 14-year-old cousin and forsook the *Messenger* for New York. For the last dozen years of his life he eked out a meager living in Philadelphia and New York as journalist, editor, and general hack writer, his work ranging from excellent to wretched, from bold originality to shameless plagiarism. His creative writing ran concurrently with his journalism, occasionally overlapping with it. Except for *The Narrative of Arthur Gordon Pym*, all his fiction was of a length and type designed for magazine publication. Many of his stories were collected in *Tales of the Grotesque and Arabesque* (2 vols., 1840), and he scored great popular successes with a short story (*The Gold Bug*, 1843) and a poem (*The Raven*, 1845). Two important collections, *Tales* and *The Raven and Other Poems*, appeared in 1845. His wife died in 1847 after a lingering illness endured in conditions of dire poverty. In the two years remaining to him, Poe had three love affairs. He was preparing for a second marriage when, in circumstances never explained, he stopped in Baltimore and was found in a stupor in a polling booth. He died without fully regaining consciousness.

In an evil hour Poe had named the Rev. Mr. Rufus W. Griswold his literary executor. Two days after Poe's death this man published an article about Poe compounded of half-truths and whole lies; he later enlarged this into a malicious *Memoir* in which he even went so far as to publish letters from Poe—containing damaging sentences forged by Griswold. Literary friends, including *Longfellow (whom Poe had publicly and consistently abused), came to his defense, but Griswold had confused the record so effectively that nearly a century elapsed before a reasonably accurate biography and a just estimate of Poe's character could emerge. Both his detractors and his defenders produced a legendary figure, and the bravado and falsity of many of Poe's own autobiographical statements did not help to set the record straight.

As a poet, Poe left a small body of distinguished and influential work. Most of it is essentially romantic, though there are examples of compression and symbolic meaning, as in *To Helen*. Most of his better poems, however—*The Raven*, *Annabel Lee*, *Lenore*, *Ulalume*—are examples of virtuosity in the manipulation of sound. Poe's poetry was of narrow range, but of consummate artistry within that range. He revised tirelessly—there are 16 versions of *The Raven*. A student of prosodic devices, he sought to attain a more felicitous verbal music by use of repetition in the forms of alliteration, *assonance, echoes, repetends, refrains, and onomatopoeia. Sound was more important than meaning to him and was used to reinforce his characteristic effects of melancholy, mystery, terror, and horror. Not a poet of great thought or broad humanity, he is at his best a magical conjurer of mood and the creator of an original music.

Among Poe's most striking tales are those of horror, based on the *Gothic novel, but far more concentrated and direct in their effect. He used the conventional properties—old castles, lavishly bizarre chambers, charnel houses, and clanking irons—but he expanded the possibilities of the type, demonstrating that terror was "not of Germany, but of the soul." *The Pit and the Pendulum* reproduces the anguish of a victim of the Inquisition subjected to the *expectation* of fiendish tortures. *The Assignation*, somewhat conventionally Gothic in setting and plot, has one of the very few love stories in which Poe deals with normal passion between the sexes. In *Berenice*, *Morella*, and *Ligeia* he has heroines of otherworldly beauty and rare erudition, all doomed to an early death. His heroes are aristocratic, wealthy, learned, isolated, mysteriously branded, and neurasthenic to the verge of insanity. The supernatural abounds, but instead of mere conventional ghosts there are disembodied spirits seeking reincarnation, revenants from premature burials, or Death himself, as in *The Masque of the Red Death*. *The Fall of the House of Usher* is perhaps Poe's masterpiece in this field.

In his prose-poems—*Silence*, *Shadow*, and *Eleanora*, for example—Poe used pronounced prose rhythms, tone color, and a considerable amount of symbolism. But some of his tales stand in direct contrast to the ornateness and occasional theatricality of the stories mentioned so far. *The Cask of Amontillado*, *The Tell-Tale Heart*, and *The Black Cat* are all spare and vigorous tales of murder revealing a deep insight into the nature of abnormality. The horror comes from the workings of the criminal mind, impelled to evil by a perverse, irrational force which Poe called an elementary impulse in man. The influence of tales of this sort, which are definitely not out of this world, has been greater than that of such fantasies as *Ligeia*, which Poe considered his best. The "tales of ratiocination," in which he displayed his analytic and constructive skill, have also had a wide influence. These include *The Gold Bug* (one of the first and best tales of finding treasure through a cryptogram) and three tales illustrating the acumen of the French amateur detective Monsieur Dupin: *The Murders in the Rue Morgue*, *The Mystery of Marie Roget*, and *The Purloined Letter*. The long line of successful practitioners of the detective story owes much to Poe's pioneering. He is still superior to most of them in that he is concerned not only with discovering the perpetrator of the crime, but also with the analytic steps by which the discovery is reached. Poe also wrote two other types of tales. His attempts at humor and whimsey are at best feeble, but he was more successful in such literary hoaxes as *The Unparalleled Adventure of One Hans Pfaall* and *The Facts in the Case of Mr. Valdemar*. Here his scientific curiosity and skill in achieving verisimilitude helped to establish the beginnings of science fiction.

Poe's *burlesque, *How to Write a Blackwood's Article*, travesties so clearly the recondite, pedantic extravagance of the contemporary horror story that a question naturally arises as to how seriously he took his own fiction. He often stated quite frankly his canny awareness of the market value of sensationalism. Yet many find the compulsion for Poe's tales in his unconscious, and certain psychoanalytical critics have read into his fiction meanings far beyond Poe's wildest dreaming. It remains an open question whether the stories are uncontrollable fantasies or the skillful contrivances of an artist who, as Poe insisted, always knew what he was doing, but there is no gainsaying the technical skill or the depth of insight into abnormality in Poe's best tales.

His literary criticism is of larger bulk than his poetry and fiction. Much of it is ephemeral book reviewing, often marred by favoritism and prejudice but frequently giving remarkably just estimates of new authors. His general ideas are, however, more important. His attack on "the heresy of the didactic"—the prevalent stress on moralizing in literature—was a distinct and much-needed service. His general critical theory is largely influenced by *Coleridge—and slanted to exalt the sort of writing that Poe himself did. Poetry is "the rhythmical creation of beauty," and truth (by which he meant moralizing, factual science, logic—"the satisfaction of the intellect") is only incidental in poetry. A long poem is a contradiction in terms, since unity of impression is essential to the concept of poetry and can be secured only in a work read at a single sitting. The best known of his general critical statements are *The Poetic Principle* and *The Philosophy of Composition*, in which he pretends to tell how *The Raven* was written. It is really less an actual account of the writing of a poem than a defense of his type of poetry. He used the same arguments of unity and intensity to exalt the short story above the novel. In his review of *Hawthorne's *Twice-Told Tales* Poe stated the basic requirement of the modern short story: "In the whole composition there should be no word written of which the tendency, direct or indirect, is not to the one pre-established design."

Poe is one of the most seminal influences in modern literature. His aesthetic theory and conscious craftsmanship influenced the devotees of art for art's sake, especially in France after *Baudelaire's translation in 1852. Poe's dislike of didacticism, his stress upon suggestive indefiniteness, his verbal music, and his confusion of sensory impressions appealed to *Verlaine, *Mallarmé, and the *symbolists in general. *Dostoevski was also impressed by Poe's "fantastic realism" and published translations of *The Black Cat* and *The Tell-Tale Heart* in his periodical. Poe's influence upon his own country followed his discovery by Europeans. His science-fiction tales, influencing H. G. *Wells and Jules Verne, and his detective stories, influencing A. Conan Doyle, have begotten two most popular, though subordinate, types of modern fiction. In the narrow sense, his disciples in the tale of terror would be little-known figures like Fitz-James O'Brien and H. P. Lovecraft, but in the broader sense his concern with abnormal states of mind and the subconscious self anticipates an important contemporary trend. Of international repute and influence today, he was a critic more feared than followed in his time. *Emerson dismissed him as "the jingle man," and Lowell—with some justice—considered "three fifths [of him] genius and two fifths sheer fudge." It is one of the ironies of Poe's story that the only man of letters to attend the dedication of his monument in Baltimore in 1877 was Walt *Whitman, whose theory and practice of literature were in such marked contrast to his.

Poetic Edda: see *Edda.

Poetics: a treatise on literary principles by *Aristotle (4th century B.C.). Like Aristotle's other surviving works, the Poetics is not in a form designed for publication but is probably a set of lecture notes. Nevertheless, it has been used as a kind of handbook for writers and critics from ancient times to the present. It has undergone changes of emphasis and differences of interpretation as each age demanded. Although Aristotle set down a theory of poetry based on a literature already "classical," modern writers, not obeying all his precepts, still regard the Poetics as a statement of certain basic principles which have meaning and application today.

The Poetics begins with a discussion of poetry in general, continues with a broad consideration of its various modes, and concludes with a more detailed account of *epic and *tragedy. Aristotle's basic premise is that "imitation" is the common principle of all arts and that the differences which distinguish artistic imitation—the medium, the objects, and the manner—produce the various art types: epic and dithyrambic poetry, tragedy and *comedy, flute- and lyre-playing, dancing, etc. As the title indicates, Aristotle's chief interest is in poetry and its forms—dramatic narrative, pure narrative (including lyric poetry), and pure drama. He discusses at length the techniques of language and poetic diction for all forms. He finds that some of the devices of poetry can be neither taught nor learned. One of these is a command of metaphor. "This alone cannot be imparted by another; it is the mark of genius, for to make good metaphors implies an eye for resemblances." Of the specific forms which poetry takes, epic and tragedy are those most closely analyzed.

Aristotle's theories of tragedy have decisively influenced the drama of the Western world, for almost all tragic dramatists have written with an eye on the ancient Greek's theories. This is not to say that all subsequent tragic drama conforms to Aristotle's rules. The strict adherence of the French Neo-Classical school to the *unities sometimes resulted in a rigidity which Aristotle could hardly have intended. Other tragic drama, notably that of *Shakespeare, may obey the spirit but not the letter of the Aristotelian concept of tragedy. Modern tragedy, while deviating considerably from the classic canon, still acknowledges the truth or universality of Aristotle's fundamental concepts, especially the recognition of the basic elements in human nature that go into the making of tragedy. Maxwell Anderson and Arthur *Miller are two contemporary tragic dramatists who acknowledge this debt to Aristotle. The worth and greatness of Aristotle's *Poetics* lie not in establishing rules for tragic drama, but in setting forth certain universal principles of tragedy which define its spirit rather than its techniques.

Aristotle begins his account of tragedy by pointing out that differences in aim give rise to tragedy and comedy; comedy aims at representing men as worse, tragedy as better, than in actual life. His definition of tragedy thus follows: "Tragedy is an imitation of an action that is serious, complete, and of a certain magnitude; in a language embellished with each kind of artistic ornament . . .; in the form of action, not of narrative; with incidents arousing pity and fear, wherewith to accomplish its catharsis of emotions." In order to fulfill these requirements, tragedy must have six parts: plot, character, diction, thought, spectacle, and melody. Of these the most important is the plot, or action—the structure of the incidents. It is the soul of a tragedy; without action there cannot be a tragedy, though there may be one without character. Any dramatic action must be of sufficient length to admit a change from bad fortune to good (comedy) or good fortune to bad (tragedy) and must be so constituted that all parts combine to make an organic and unified whole. Distinguishing between simple and complex plots, Aristotle states that the greater and nobler tragedy results from the poet's skillful manipulation of the complex action. Complex action achieves its greatest impact through "surprises" or, better, as Lane Cooper translated it, through "astounding revelations." These depend primarily upon two devices. "Reversal" of the situation is a change by which the action veers round to a direction opposite to its original course; this change must stay within the limits of probability or necessity, and it produces an effect of dramatic irony. "Recognition" is a change from ignorance to knowledge, producing love or hate in the characters destined for the good or bad fortune.

The personages in a tragedy must be morally good, of fitting character, true to life, and consistent in their actions. The change of fortune for the tragic hero must be from good to bad and come as a result of a flaw in character or an error in judgment. The poet, choosing suitable characters and placing them in a carefully constructed plot, should aim at the imitation of actions which will excite pity and fear, the distinctive effects of tragic imitation. The downfall of a noble, highly renowned, prosperous, and morally good person will arouse pity (for his misfortune) and fear (for the misfortune of a man like ourselves) and thus effect a catharsis (or purgation) of those emotions.

Aristotle's remarks on the epic further define the nature of tragedy. The two forms differ in their length: epic action has no limits, while that of tragedy "endeavors to confine itself to a single revolution of the sun" (unity of time). Though both forms imitate the highest type of action and character, it is felt that tragedy is superior to the epic in that it can use all the resources of the epic

583

plus some which are peculiarly its own, and it achieves its proper effect with greater economy and unity.

Politics: A treatise by *Aristotle (4th century B.C.). The *Politics* discusses government from the point of view of the city-state, which, Aristotle explains, developed from a union of villages, as the village developed from a union of families. It is the best type of political organization for man, the end or consummation of community living, and if the family and the village are natural, it is natural also, and man is a political animal. The purpose of the state is to provide its citizens the means for living the good life, and it alone is able to do this, for the good life cannot be lived in isolation. Moreover, as this purpose is moral rather than material, government should rest in the hands of the good. When we examine states, we find three types of government that we may regard as *true* (monarchy, aristocracy, and constitutional government or *politeia*) and three that are perversions (tyranny, oligarchy, and democracy). Ideally, the best of these six types is a monarchy in which absolute power is exercised by one person for the good of all, but this is unattainable, and in actual practice a constitutional government is the most effective, since it is the most stable. It is to be noted also that, of the perversions, tyranny is the worst and democracy the best, though neither looks to the common good of the whole citizen body (a mark of any true government), tyranny considering the welfare of the tyrant only and democracy the welfare of the poor.

In reading the *Politics* it is necessary to remember that Aristotle is dealing throughout with the Greek city-state, a small community, numbering typically a few thousand people, and that all Greek city-states, whether democracies, oligarchies, or tyrannies, were slave-owning societies, a fact which alters their political nature considerably. It is also necessary to remember that when Aristotle uses words, he uses them with the meaning they had then, which is not necessarily the meaning they have now. Aristocracy to him meant the rule of the best, not the rule of the high-born, and democracy the rule of the poor, not the rule of all the citizens.

Pollux: see *Castor and Pollux.

Polo, Marco: Italian traveler (1254?-1324?). Marco Polo was a Venetian merchant whose account of his trip to the Far East is the most famous of travel books. Marco, his father, and his uncle set out in 1271 on a trading expedition to Cathay (China). Warmly received by the Tartar emperor Kublai Khan, they remained attached to his court for 17 years, finally returning home in 1295. Soon thereafter, during a war against Genoa, Marco was captured (1298). By a lucky coincidence, in prison he met a professional author, Rustician of Pisa, to whom he dictated the account of his travels. Although Marco has been proved amazingly accurate, to his contemporaries the splendors he described seemed the wildest exaggeration. Marco's book, the first significant addition to Western knowledge of Asia during the *Middle Ages, was the first record of a medieval traveler to China, Mongolia, Burma, and Sumatra, and an invaluable reservoir of history, geography, and folk customs. It is, moreover, often brilliant in its observations and storytelling. A copy of the travels owned by Columbus, and marked with his notes, shows it as a continuing stimulus to Western imagination.

Polybius: Greek historian (*c.* 201–*c.* 120 B.C.). Polybius served the Achaean League in Greece, was a hostage in Rome, was present at the siege of Carthage (147 B.C.), and helped to reorganize the administration of the Achaean cities after the Roman conquest. His *History* set out to trace the rise of Rome to a dominant position in the Mediterranean world by the conquest of Carthage, Macedonia, and Greece. The work is in 40 books, of which only the first five survive entirely, though there are fragments of most of the others.

Polybius was admirably fitted for his task. He was a soldier and statesman with a firm grasp of earlier history.

He had traveled widely and had a personal knowledge of many of the battlefields and men he discussed. He had a deep respect for the truth and a desire to understand the causes of the events he reported. Though he admired Rome, he did not distort history in Rome's favor. The one serious criticism that has been made of his book is his inferior style of writing, which has made him more a source book than a literary figure in his own right.

Polydeuces: see *Castor and Pollux.

Pope, Alexander: English poet (1688–1744). Pope was the greatest English poet between *Dryden and the Romantics, and his poetry is the epitome of the *Neo-Classicism of 18th-century England. Didactic, satiric, witty, technically superb, his verse approaches his own goal—"True wit is nature to advantage dressed,/ What oft was thought, but ne'er so well expressed."

The elusive elements which produce genius can never be anticipated. Pope was crippled, he was only 4'6" tall, and his Roman Catholicism barred him from the universities. This combination so soured his disposition that he earned the epithet the "wicked wasp of Twickenham" (his home); yet he acquired a knowledge of classical and English poetry, and before he was 25, he was himself acknowledged England's greatest living poet. Indeed, his proposal to translate the *Iliad* was a national event, the subscriptions netting Pope a fortune of £5,000. When he finished this task in 1720, he undertook an equally successful translation of the *Odyssey* (1726) and followed this by bringing out an edition of *Shakespeare. Greatly enriched by these ventures, he returned to his own original poetry. He was now a famous figure, and the leading men of the time—*Swift, Gay, Bolingbroke—were proud to be numbered among his friends.

His poetry concerns itself with what is "correct," whether in literature or social conduct. In this broad sense, the didactic and the satiric merge. In his *Essay on Criticism* (1711), in *heroic couplets, he formulated an aesthetics of poetry for his age as *Horace had for Augustan Rome and *Boileau for Neo-Classical France. "Learn for ancient rules a just esteem/ To copy nature is to copy them."

His real greatness lay in his satiric verse, sharpened to the stiletto's point. England had already produced a master satirist in Dryden. Pope recognized his genius and proposed to surpass it. *The Rape of the Lock* (1712, 1714) started off as a clever trifle which Pope broadened into a charming piece of mock-heroic persiflage on the foibles of fashionable society. *The Dunciad* (an "Epic of Dunces" as the *Iliad* is an "Epic of Ilium"; 1728–43) is likewise a mock-epic, but it is a personal satire on all sorts of "dunces," a dunce being any person with whom Pope had quarreled. By the irony of fate, many of them are remembered only because Pope made them the victims of his venomous invective. The best sections of *The Dunciad* are, nevertheless, those which rise above personalities to ridicule pretentiousness and pedantry.

Pope's *Essay on Man* (1733–34) abandoned satire for pseudophilosophy. A summary of 18th-century generalizations about a rational universe, optimism, and deism, it proclaims that "whatever is, is right" and "the proper study of mankind is man." Yet the poem lives not for its thought, which is neither profound nor systematic, but for its expert workmanship and wit. (A complete rejection of the ideas which formed the substance of Pope's poem is to be found in *Voltaire's *Candide.*) The *Moral Essays* (1731–35) and *Imitations of Horace* (1733–38) are again generalizations on social conduct.

Sharpening his wit on the whetstone of the heroic couplet, Pope has given the English language more familiar quotations than any other poet except Shakespeare. He remains unsurpassed for coining just the right phrase to distill a doctrine into an *epigram. With all the lucidity, mental agility, and cleverness of the best prose, Pope's poetry has the added values of compression, glitter, and musical effect which only a master craftsman in verse can produce.

Portrait of a Lady, The: a novel by Henry *James. Published in serial form in 1880, *The Portrait of a Lady* appeared as a book in the following year and established James' reputation as one of the great novelists of his time. In this work the novelist assimilated the lessons of two of his masters: *Turgenev and George *Eliot. From Turgenev, James had absorbed the idea of allowing the character to determine and shape the story. From George Eliot he had gained a sense of tight and logical structure, of the organically constructed novel.

Isabel Archer shapes and determines the story of this novel. She is the "lady" and it is her portrait that James paints. The plot itself is not complicated. James conceived the book as the story of an American girl of high spirit and intelligence who, given free choice to live her life as she will, makes a fundamental error and must in the end pay the price for it. The error is not entirely hers. She is the victim of certain clever but wicked persons. But her inner resources and moral fiber are such that she plucks a victory out of seeming defeat. She is able to go on to a difficult life at the end because she understands her actions and is ready to take responsibility for them.

Without propounding the question of the freedom of the will, without discussing determinism, James adheres to the simple facts of his story and leaves the reflection upon its moral values to the reader. Isabel Archer is endowed with a fortune in England by a beneficent and curious relative, who wants to see what she will do with it. Of three suitors, she chooses the worst, a deeply corrupt figure, who covers his corruption with a façade of European civilization.

The novel derives its rich texture from the portrait of Isabel's mind and the manner in which she matures despite her tragic error. What James is saying in this book, and he repeated it with greater subtlety in his last works, is that, given the hard knocks of life, the civilized being can come to terms with it only through mental fortitude—and through understanding. To understand is to feel, and to know, and to be able to face one's problems. The inner life of Isabel is unfolded for us with great analytical and psychological power, and it is through her lucid mind that James finally knits all the elements of her drama.

In this novel, as in most of his other works, James endows his American girl with a quality of innocence that rises above the civilized complexities of the Europeans and establishes the essential distinction of the American woman as he was to portray her in his successive works.

Poseidon: the Greek god of the sea, identified by the Romans with Neptune.

Pound, Ezra L.: American poet (1885–1972). Whatever the judgment of posterity on Pound as a poet, he will always be regarded as having been at the very center of the "modern movement" of 20th-century literature. He came out of the Northwest, was educated at the University of Pennsylvania, and in 1907 went abroad as a crusader on behalf of poetry. He promptly found himself involved with the leading moderns. He aided young poets and, in a deep concern with craft, formed friendships with the older ones, including *Yeats. In his position as foreign editor of *Poetry, A Magazine of Verse*, he became a friend of the early Robert *Frost and helped T. S. *Eliot, whose major poem *The *Waste Land* he revised for publication. He helped *Joyce by his practical sense of publishing, and was also of assistance to Wyndham Lewis. A founder of the *Imagists, he wrote a poem of modern disquietude in *Hugh Selwyn Mauberley* (1920), an earlier volume, *Homage to Sextus Propertius* (1917), having attracted the attention of the poetic world. For years he worked on a series of Cantos; they are recondite and colloquial, contain many styles and languages, and seem to be a kind of shoring up—a passage through a poet's mind—of segments of life and culture of the modern world, East and West, and of intellectual history. His literary essays are rhetorical; his letters published in 1950 are bellicose and lively. Possessing an erratic, venturesome mind, he seems to have found himself always in relation to the sponsorship of talent and to the pursuit of a high ideal of craft. He broadcast on behalf of the Italian fascists during the war and was ruled mentally unfit to stand trial on the charges

589

of giving aid and comfort to the enemy. From 1946 to 1958 he was confined to St. Elizabeth's Hospital in Washington. When he was released he returned to Italy, where he had lived for many years. His poems are of a high competence; but they betray his erratic intellect and at the same time display his keen poetic ear.

Pre-Raphaelite Brotherhood: a group of 19th-century English writers and painters, of whom Dante Gabriel *Rossetti was the most influential. Others in the group were William Rossetti and the painters Holman Hunt, Edward Millais, and Burne-Jones; and later Christina Rossetti, *Swinburne, and William *Morris.

The movement began in 1848 as an organization of painters who called themselves Pre-Raphaelites and had an exhibition of their pictures. They insisted that a painter should paint whatever he sees, regardless of the formal rules of painting. Nature was to be portrayed just as it was experienced, without being altered because of the traditional methods of previous painters. The group were *Pre-Raphaelite* not because their style derived from earlier Italian painting but because they insisted on freedom from the rules and requirements laid down by Raphael for painting ideal figures. In their efforts at fidelity to nature and experience, they achieved sharply realized details; but their conception of nature and experience was exceedingly limited. They took not the least account of the ugliness or the vitality of contemporary England and its problems, turning instead to a heroic and decorative world of the *Middle Ages, and to a poetry which by *symbolism, imagery, and music created a pictorial impression or a vague mood from which all ideas sometimes disappeared. For the sensual elements ("fleshly mysticism") of such poems as Rossetti's *The Blessed Damozel* they were condemned as the "fleshly school."

The Pre-Raphaelites rendered a distinct service to art by insisting that it is *not* the business of the artist to instruct or to solve social problems. But their complete withdrawal from contemporary life into mere sensuous and decorative beauty left their experiences and their poetry thin and bodiless. Their aesthetic goals influenced the *symbolist poets.

Prévost, Antoine-François: French novelist (1697–1763). The Abbé Prévost is the author of the first modern "novel of passion," *Manon Lescaut* (*L'Histoire du chevalier Des Grieux et de Manon Lescaut*, 1731). During a stormy youth he ran away from his Benedictine abbey, saw service in the army, and visited England. There he discovered his talent as a novelist and translator. Impressed by Richardson's novels, he made excellent translations of them into French and thereby started the vogue of sentimental novels which reached a climax in *Rousseau's *La Nouvelle Héloïse*. He also wrote a number of minor novels which were very popular, tragic stories developed in the autobiographical method, featuring wild plots and exotic backgrounds.

The celebrated *Manon Lescaut*, which forms a part of an eight-novel series, *Memoirs and Adventures of a Gentleman of Quality Who Has Withdrawn from the World* (1726–32), is remarkable for a combination of qualities. Noteworthy is its simple structure; it is short and concise, without extraneous episodes. The unified action, moreover, grows inevitably from the chief characters, who are real and appealing. Des Grieux, the hero, may be weak and Manon perfidious, but they are so very young (17), and their passion is so overpowering that Prévost succeeds in making them thoroughly sympathetic characters. A pervasive tone of pathos and fatality adds a unifying element and increases the meaning of each scene, carrying it forward with the suspense of impending tragedy. The novel gains depth by ironic similarities and contrasts, by the ambivalent forces which pull the characters together and then cause their separations, particularly in the relations of the ever-faithful Des Grieux and the pleasure-loving Manon.

A certain tension is secured by a contrast between the subject of the novel and its tone. The subject is a violent and devastating passion, but the narrator is represented as an old man reporting the fatal love affair of a practical stranger, as the stranger had told it to him after it was all over, long ago. Thus there is no incongruity in handling the violent passion with painstaking and deliberate restraint. This restraint contributes to the moral purpose announced in the preface, for the novel is allegedly not a glorification of passion, but a warning example.

Manon Lescaut has been used as the basis of well-known operas by Massenet and Puccini.

Pride and Prejudice: a novel by Jane *Austen (1813). Though a contemporary of the major Romantics, Jane Austen is a child of the 18th century, particularly in its Neo-Classical aspects; she is a witty and ironic observer of human inconsistency and ludicrousness rather than a painstaking recorder of consuming passions. As a writer of *comedy of manners, she is concerned with a world in which the problems are of good form rather than of subsistence, of the ill-bred rather than the undernourished, of manors rather than slums, of matrimony rather than careers, of gracious gregariousness rather than aggressive worldliness—in short, of bread-and-butter letters rather than bread and butter. To say as much is to risk suggesting that Jane Austen's world is basically a rather trivial and frothy one. But no discerning reader of hers could hold such an opinion, for she is a serious writer of comedy. In her world the relative unimportance of economic, professional, and political problems permits a concentrating of attention upon personal relations and the quality of living which they make possible. The issue is the uniting of moral and social graces, the reconciliation of form and spontaneity.

To present this world, she uses a kind of farce of character familiar in comic drama and 18th-century fiction—that is, caricature, though less for the sheer fun of the grotesque than for satire. We see this in the stupidity and servility of Collins, the snobbery of Lady Catherine de Bourgh, and the pedantry of Mary Bennet, and to a lesser extent in the malicious Miss Bingley, the silly youngest Bennet girls, and the literal-minded Mrs. Bennet. Jane Austen also draws upon popular literary conventions in writing an occasional melodramatic episode: when she wants to demonstrate active badness in a character, she nearly always falls back upon seduction. Yet if Wickham is in this respect cut rather mechanically and not very plausibly from an old pattern, the author achieves variety by endowing him with a somewhat engaging effrontery, and rare meaningfulness by making Lydia an insensitively pleased little adventuress rather than the usual dismal victim.

At its best, comedy of manners is concerned not merely with good manners but with manners in an older sense—conduct exhibiting character. The central comedy of *Pride and Prejudice* is rooted in maturely conceived character—that is, character observed with a sense of human realities and a sense of values that extends the significance of the imagined individuals beyond their immediate sphere in the book and thus beyond the book itself. Bingley is more than a pleasant suitor for a nice girl; his amiability is there, indeed, but qualified by a negativeness and suggestibility that differentiate him from the mere type of the sought-after eligible youth. As a sardonic observer of human follies, Mr. Bennet is a considerable departure from a mere father of a heroine; but Austen goes still further and joins his shrewd perceptiveness to a fundamental inertia that makes his life a symbolic comment on intelligence without will or drive (just as his wife is all will or drive without intelligence). In Jane Bennet we see initially only the sweet and good heroine. Yet her sweetness is saved from insipidity by the fact that she has convictions and always tries to act by them; and her goodness is saved from implausible idealization by the fact that she is entirely passive and has an inadequate view of the motives of other people. All these characters Jane Austen thus sees in perspective; what is much more remarkable, however, is that she sees Darcy and Elizabeth equally in perspective. With an allegorical title, she is clearly in danger of creating a pair of simple opposites, one to be detested, the other admired. It is perhaps less of a feat to identify in Darcy the core of individual character that is overlaid with class superciliousness than to take in Elizabeth a person of her own sex and age and background, endow her with independence and sharpness of mind, and then portray fully her liability to prejudgment, wrongheadedness, and self-satisfaction in the midst of error. The final mark of imaginative insight and wisdom in an author is his remaining coolly distant from his leading character, especially when that character is very much like himself.

The comic incongruities of these characters, and of the situation created by the characters, are given a multiple development which could have become quite chaotic had not Elizabeth and Darcy been given a thoroughly dominant position. In fact, the creation of unity from diversity takes place in three different ways. Looking at the story technically, we see that virtually all of it is told from the point of view of Elizabeth: we are interested primarily in her own affair, and our awareness of other affairs is really a sharing of her awareness of them. We are not carried from one situation or set of characters to another; rather we see them as they impinge upon Elizabeth—the marriage of Miss Lucas, the distress of Jane, the elopement of Lydia, the eccentricities of her parents, the activities of the Gardiners. The focus of attention upon her is aided by the attitudes of the more serious characters—Charlotte Lucas' desire for her esteem, Jane's reliance upon her, Mr. Bennet's respect and confidingness, the Gardiners' attentiveness. Secondly, the dominant position of Elizabeth and Darcy is secured by a quite subtle device of characterization: they are the only characters who have a complete self-awareness which permits them to assess themselves and act accordingly. Though all characters have their imperfections, only Darcy and Elizabeth have a "comic flaw" (to adapt the term "tragic flaw" used of the tragic hero) which they come to understand and to try to make amends for. In thus arriving at self-knowledge (an experience also comparable to that of the tragic hero), they are morally active in a way that not only differentiates them from all the others but makes them preeminent. Third, the diverse parts of the story are held together by means of the theme, which is a little less simple than it may look at first glance. We can hardly say that Elizabeth conquers prejudice, and Darcy pride; it is more accurate to say that both of them conquer prejudice, and that pride in the best sense is vindicated. In the latter part of Chapter 16, Wickham, who, though unscrupulous, is not stupid, speaks a key line on Darcy's pride: "It has connected him nearer with virtue than any other feeling." In fact, the book may best be read as a brilliant study of pride in all of its manifestations, a demonstration that what Elizabeth had taken to be one thing—social snobbery—is really many things. Only Miss Bingley and Lady Catherine justify Elizabeth's narrow definition. In Miss Darcy, what had seemed pride is really shyness. In Darcy himself, pride is essentially self-respect and a sense of responsibility—a virtue shared by Elizabeth and Jane, and, in the background, by the Gardiners. Then we should observe how skillfully the other characters are brought into the picture. Some of them suffer from a perverted pride—Mary in her conceited bookishness, the Lucases in the perpetual bowing and scraping which they take to be courtliness, and most of all Collins in his gross servility. The others suffer from an absence of pride—Charlotte Lucas in her acceptance of Collins, Mrs. Bennet and her youngest daughters in their lack of dignity, and even Mr. Bennet in his general irresponsibility.

This pride is not the tragic *hybris* which devours the individual and threatens the whole world; rather it is a social grace or a social failing, to be seen in perspective and admired with moderation or deflated with ridicule. Whether admiring or deflating, Jane Austen is uniformly detached, witty, and good-humored; maintenance of tone is a final way of unifying her materials. Even when she is hitting off lack of moderation by an appropriate caricature, or with epigrammatic phrase and wry irony identifying folly in her own creatures or envy and malice in the world at large, she is closer to placidity than disillusionment. For the disturbances she sees are in the foreground; in the background there still lies an unshaken moral universe. To this stable order of things comedy does not refer, but because of it comedy can exist—to point out the whole range of human frailties and yet not despair.

Prince, The: a treatise on politics by *Machiavelli (*Il Principe*, written 1513, published 1532). In our own times *The Prince* has been condemned as the guidebook of dictators and with equal extravagance praised as the first realistic primer of government based on the observation of men's actual motivations, passions, and conduct. But blamed or praised, the volume has been universally recognized as "one of the half dozen books that have done most to shape western thought."

Written while Machiavelli was in temporary exile from Florence, it was put together in a spirit of opportunism to win a friend among the Medici, for Lorenzo de' Medici (not Lorenzo the Magnificent, but a minor member of the family, the Duke of Urbino) was governor of Florence. The attempt failed. Lorenzo, to whom it was addressed, paid it not one whit of attention; the fiery exhortation of the final chapter had not the least effect on him—if he ever read it. But the volume did circulate and gain for its author a sort of underground fame during his lifetime, though it was not published until five years after his death.

The Prince is a short treatise, an informal, loosely organized essay on the science of statecraft, divided into 26 brief chapters (the first chapter, for example, has but one paragraph, the second three, and the longest not more than 19). Machiavelli's broad purpose was to analyze a technical idea, a theory of the state. Since, however, he saw Italy being despoiled by invaders, he actually presented a theory of how to create and maintain a unified national state. He thus became concerned with the machinery of monarchic government rather than with its fundamental nature. The dominating tone of the treatise is one of personal exhortation; its dominating spirit is enthusiasm for the freedom and unity of Italy; its doctrinaire morality is the immoral thought that the state is undeterred by morality and is free to do anything necessary to strengthen itself.

Machiavelli was convinced that a strong government for Italy could be achieved only through a ruthless leader (his candidate was Lorenzo, the "boss" of Florence), that all men desire power and a clever man can obtain it. The first half of the essay, therefore, deals with the various types of governments by princes, hereditary and acquired, how governments are gained and defended and why they are lost, with numerous specific illustrations garnered from history and Machiavelli's own experiences. There is never the slightest allusion to the divine right of princes to rule. These chapters assemble a number of shrewd maxims and methods by which a ruler may eliminate rivals (there is no need to use force if fraud will do it), avoid revolution (a national religion is a stabilizing force and should be exploited), overcome foreign invaders (the essential activity for a prince is to maintain and augment his state). Two chapters (9 and 20) exhort the prince to win the esteem of the populace, for the best fortress of a prince is the love of his people; three (10, 12, 14) teach the nature of military defenses, with a pointed observation of the superiority of native militia over mercenaries.

Superficially the middle section (15 to 23) follows the conventional medieval patterns of "advice to rulers" on domestic and foreign policy, with such familiar catch-titles as the need for liberality, whether it is better to be loved or feared, how to select ministers and avoid flatterers. Deeply indebted as Machiavelli was to a great body of predecessors in this genre of "mirror-of-princes" literature, he abandoned their traditional views in his attitude toward morality. It is his striking subordination of moral principles to the necessities of political existence which has made his little book notorious. Previous writers had demanded that the good ruler be a good man. Machiavelli found that the precepts of morality played little part in the practical politics of Italian cities, and he defines a good ruler as one who is good for the people. To be sure, self-discipline and conventional virtues are important—but only in so far as they will contribute to the well-being of the people. In seeking justice and welfare for them, the intelligent ruler must keep his goal always in mind and must possess the force of character to utilize whatever means are necessary to achieve it, not allowing ethical considerations to swerve or hinder him: "a good prince is moral rather to benefit his people than to obey the laws of God." He can be immoral for the same object. In other words, pragmatic success in securing goals, not moral law, is the only test of whether the means are proper. The ultimate good of his people may require, says Machiavelli, that a prince lie, cheat, and murder.

Machiavellli was convinced that in thus subordinating ethical principles he was merely recognizing the world as it is and men as they are. He saw society ruled not by superhuman or mystical forces but by the passions and interests of men. For Machiavelli, to govern is to understand how to regulate these passions and interests for the ruler's aim. Machiavelli finds most men simple-minded, greedy, and wicked. To be spectacular and attractive to such people, the prince should *appear* to be religious, compassionate, and just: "It is not necessary for a prince really to have virtues, but it is very necessary to seem to have them." Among so many who are not good, however, the prince must learn to be not good, and will actually have to be knavish and cruel. Machiavelli never gives approval to the self-centered tyrant; he always condemns the bad ruler. Thus his only ethical problem is whether a ruler whose purposes are good may engage in acts usually regarded as immoral. His answer is an unequivocal *yes*. "The prince should not depart from what is morally right if he can observe it, but should know how to adopt what is bad when he is obliged to." The prince cannot act as if the world were a paradise of virtuous men. If all men were good, the prince could be faithful, for it is an honor to keep one's sworn word; but, because most men are wicked, the prince must learn to break faith for the good of the state. "The princes who have done great things are the ones who have taken little account of their promises and who have known how to addle the brains of men with craft." (Machiavelli's unmasking of the mechanism by which a despot operates is indeed so complete that *Spinoza concluded that the book, though dedicated to a tyrant, was ironically intended for the people, to inspire them to hate the prince and seek republicanism.)

The concluding sections are a disquisition of the power of Fortune in human affairs and an appeal for a strong new ruler. Although the book is permeated with the concept that Fortune's power cannot be denied, Machiavelli argues that "Fortune governs but half our lives," and if a man keeps to his inner spirit and yet adapts himself to circumstances, Fortune may favor him at any moment. The final chapter glows with a spirit of nationalism and a patriotic prophecy from *Petrarch—"In Italian hearts the ancient valor is not yet dead."

Wherein lies the inherent greatness of this volume, setting aside its phenomenal influence and its vigorous life as a symbol? In many ways it anticipated and heralded new ideas. The *Middle Ages had rested content with the conviction that life in this world was an unimportant shadow of the other world. Like many a modernist, Machiavelli is concerned only with life on earth. His analytical spirit and his courage in setting forth his conclusions were revolutionary in political writing. In subordinating moral principles and humanistic idealism, he moved toward political realism and the kind of secular truth which he had observed. He made a fundamental contribution by bringing political theory into touch with the practical by examining closely things as they are and drawing deductions. "Florence and Siena, France and Germany, were the countries he looked at, not Utopia or Atlantis or the City of God."

He furthermore perceived, if only dimly, the beginnings of the modern Western nation-state system (as opposed to innumerable petty dukedoms) and recognized realistically the need for concentration of power in a central authority in order to achieve this unity. He then went on to explain without euphemisms or embarrassment the methods (often callous and cruel) by which such unity could be achieved. It is unfortunate for the world but a credit to Machiavelli's perception that the techniques of power which he evaluated are the very ones which have been used effectively to carve out political communities. The greatness of the book rests in part on this unabashed and startling exposé of hardheaded, ruthless power-politics, and even more on the spectacular illustrations, the clarity of presentation, and the polemical intensity. Others may have thought all this; Machiavelli said it clearly, vigorously, passionately.

By the heyday of the Elizabethan drama, Machiavelli had become a name for grotesque wickedness and hypocrisy, even murder, extortion, and torture, as we see in *Marlowe's *Jew of Malta*; and *Shakespeare and Ben *Jonson were similarly fascinated by this symbol of unconscionable corruption. It is therefore surprising to realize that Elizabethan England had scarcely read Machiavelli (*The Prince* was not translated until 1640) and that the Elizabethan ideas about him came chiefly from a French version distorting and attacking him. But the symbol remained, and *Machiavellian* continues to be a term of opprobrium to describe unscrupulous and diabolical intrigue.

Procrustes: "the stretcher," a fabled robber of Ancient Greece who stretched or shortened his guests to fit his guest bed; hence *Procrustean*—producing, by ruthless violence, conformity to an arbitrary standard.

Prometheus Bound: a tragedy by *Aeschylus, of uncertain date. As Greek drama was religious in origin, the dramatic contests themselves being part of a religious festival, it is not surprising to find that the plays are concerned with fundamental theological problems: the relationship of gods to men, the conflicting role of free will and fate, the presence of evil in a divinely controlled universe. Such matters particularly interested Aeschylus and are at the heart of his *Prometheus Bound*. This play, the first and only extant part of a trilogy, deals with the punishment of the *Titan Prometheus ("Forethought"), who stole fire from the gods in order to preserve mankind. The Prometheus portrayed here is the savior of man and a rebel against an oppressive god. As the forger of his chains says to him, "A god yourself, you did not dread God's anger, but gave to mortals honor not their due, and therefore you must guard this joyless rock. . . . *Zeus has no mind to pity. He is harsh, like upstarts always."

From the opening scene, in which Prometheus is chained for eternity by Power, Force, and *Hephaestus, to the conclusion, in which he stands defiant though helpless before the thunder of Zeus, he is firm in his disobedience, comforted by the foreknowledge that Zeus will eventually change.

Contrasted to the strong character, Prometheus, are his visitors, Oceanus, Io, and *Hermes—whose comings and goings provide some motion, though in this play, the binding of the hero greatly restricts action. Oceanus, a somewhat comic figure and a fellow Titan sympathetic to Prometheus, advises a conciliatory course toward Zeus. Io is another victim of the god, an innocent maiden who is persecuted by the jealous goddess *Hera and whose descendant, *Heracles, is destined to release Prometheus. Hermes is the "lackey" of Zeus, who tries first to persuade and then to threaten Prometheus into divulging the secret of who will oppose Zeus.

Though the play rises to a climactic close with the storm which Prometheus' obstinacy has provoked, *Prometheus Bound* was meant to be more than a drama of rebellion. Aeschylus' overall plan has been lost, but one can surmise that the first play was to present a world in which evil exists, for Prometheus says of Zeus, "You are but young in tyranny, and think to inhabit a citadel unassaulted of grief." From elements in *Prometheus Bound* and the nature of the *Oresteia*, one may gather that the Prometheus trilogy probably developed the concept of a Zeus whose character combined wisdom with authority maintained by force, and who evolved from the tyrant of the first play into a benevolent deity, the enlightened ruler of the world. (For another dramatic incident of the Prometheus legend, see *Shelley.)

Prose Edda: see *Edda.

Proserpina: see *Persephone.

Proteus: the shepherd of *Poseidon's herd of seals. He could change his shape at will and also prophesy the future—a perception he would disclose reluctantly only when he could no longer shift his shape because held tightly by a powerful and persistent questioner. As an imaginative symbol, Proteus reveals that truth can be discovered "behind the countless shifting disguises of mutability."

Proust, Marcel: French novelist (1871–1922). Proust became a legend in French literary circles long before his death. A social lion turned recluse, a delicate, frail individual who suffered from crippling asthma, he gradually withdrew from the drawing rooms of the Third Republic to spend long periods in bed during which he wrote his remarkable work. He was allergic to noise, to light, to dust: his room was soundproofed and overheated; he remained in semi-darkness; and here he wrote the long novel whose creation alone seemed to keep him alive. In the end Proust seemed to exist as an isolated vessel of feeling, an apparatus for his bold literary experiment, that of putting on record what has come to be regarded as one of the most truthful artistic searches ever undertaken by an individual into his sensory and imaginative experience.

À la Recherche du temps perdu can be literally translated as "The Quest for Lost Time." In the Scott-Moncrieff translation it is called *Remembrance of Things Past.* In its original French it appeared in 16 volumes between 1913 and 1927, the last, five years after Proust's death. Proust sought, as the title suggests, to write the past—time lost and seemingly irrecoverable—into the permanence of art. Like James *Joyce and T. S. *Eliot (and Henry *James and his "sense of the past"), Proust is preoccupied with time. Indeed, Time is an ever-present fact as the memory of the narrator shuttles back and forth without regard to chronology or the mechanical time of a clock. Indebted to *Bergson, who developed the distinctions between mechanical and psychological time, Proust dredged up from his personal past the heritage of his own experiences. This process of rendering actual again what seemed lost is exemplified in the celebrated passage in the first volume about the cup of tea and bit of cake. The taste of the cake Proust has dipped into the tea gives him a feeling of intense joy. He asks himself why taste should thus make him so happy and evoke so complex a series of emotions. Step by step he is led to the revelation that the sensory experience is a "trigger" which awakens what he calls "involuntary memory"— and by the time he had finished his long novel he had reawakened his personal past, and refashioned into art the social and artistic world of his youth, revealing the ways in which one's inner world can color total experience. Proust created a highly original and moral work that gives us a brilliant picture of a decadent society. Through the multiple channels of memory, the life of the small town, the hypochondriacal aunt, the boy's attachment to his mother, the story of Swann's marriage, his life in Paris take their place in flowing narrative. We see people in their youth and then catch them grown old—past and present juxtaposed to make us aware of the passage of time. Proust, by exhibiting them, shows us that the values of this high society are a fraud, and as he strips the mask of glitter from it he makes us aware of certain great themes—love, art, man's way of seeing and feeling life, homosexuality, the rituals of aristocracy, architecture; indeed all civilization passes in review.

Proust was born in Paris, the son of a doctor. His father was professor of public health in the Faculty of Medicine at the University of Paris. His mother was a member of a cultivated and well-to-do Jewish family. From the age of nine Proust began to manifest those allergies which finally immured him in his womb of cork, from which he issued at night when the city's noises were subdued and the cold moonlight and glitter of the stars replaced the brightness of the sun. Illness made of Proust a spoilt child. His parents indulged his whims. He had a lazy, pleasant youth, casual studies, long summers in the country, and, in those years when his health still permitted, he became the dandy of certain Paris salons. He was the Third Republic's precocious child and he evolved into an aesthete, eccentric, curious, cultivating and cultivated by a fashionable literary set. In one salon he met Anatole *France, who wrote the preface to Proust's first book, *Les Plaisirs et les Jours* (1896), a precious piece of writing. Later France remembered Proust as "a charming and witty fellow with a keen sense of observation."

At about the time of the publication of this volume, Proust was already writing a long novel, the existence of which was not discovered until more than 25 years after his death. A large work, written in the traditional manner, it contained much of the material later converted into the subjective pages of *À la Recherche du temps perdu*. Discovered among Proust's papers, it was published in France in 1952 under the title of *Jean Santeuil*. It reveals that the young and seemingly frivolous Proust possessed a mastery of the art of fiction. He could have produced, had he wished, novels of the conventional type that would have been, as a result of his acuteness of observation, highly successful. But as he developed his characteristic form and his search for the inner workings of the mind, he discarded this early work and undertook the difficult task that preoccupied him to the end. *Jean Santeuil* is an autobiographical novel, although Proust gives it a careful setting to make it seem a work of fiction. But it is the record of external events. He discarded it in its entirety; happily he did not destroy it. Its resurrection showed the single-mindedness with which Proust converted what he had already written from an objective into a subjective novel, an autobiography of the mind.

Proust always denied that his long novel was autobiographical; although much of the material in it stems from his own experiences it has been imaginatively reworked. "I have invented everything to suit the requirements of my presentation," Proust asserted in the last part of the book, describing how he borrowed from life the smile of one person and the eyebrow of another in order to create, in the end, fictitious personages.

Between the writing of his early discarded novel and the rewriting of it, during a visit to Venice, Proust discovered the work of John *Ruskin. He translated Ruskin's *Bible of Amiens* and *Sesame and Lilies* and was profoundly influenced by him and by the reading of certain English novelists, among them George *Eliot. The death of his parents and the return of his illness brought about his gradual withdrawal, and during the early years of the 20th century a great part of his long novel was written. The first, and perhaps most celebrated portion, *Swann's Way* (*Du côté de chez Swann*, 1913), was privately printed after several publishers had rejected it. He had planned the novel as a three-volume work, but it continued to grow. *Within a Budding Grove* (*A l'ombre des jeunes filles en fleurs*, 1918) won the Goncourt prize, bringing celebrity to the recluse, and *The Guermantes Way* (*Le côté de Guermantes*, 1920–21) found an interested public awaiting it. Proust died in 1922 and the last portions of his work appeared in 1927. Difficult in style, with sentences long and elaborated, with long qualifying phrases and rich metaphor, the work nevertheless found a brilliant translator in Charles K. Scott-Moncrieff, who turned into English all but the last part, which was translated by Stephen Hudson. The novel's influence in the English-speaking world has been very great, among the earliest writers to be inspired by it being Virginia *Woolf.

Like Joyce, Proust discovered that when it was necessary to catch the play of mind and the flow of thought, the use of metaphor, symbol, image—the language of poetry—was essential. Thus in trying to re-create the atmosphere of the mind both Proust and Joyce found themselves in the camp of the *symbolists.

psychoanalysis: a system of psychology developed by Sigmund *Freud for treatment of mental and nervous disorders. This was characterized by his seeking a view of all aspects of mental life, conscious and unconscious, but placing special emphasis on the exploration of the "unconscious." Freud began by using hynotism, but he found this insufficient and developed thereafter the use of "free association" in an attempt to arrive at the symbolic and mythic statements contained in the dream histories and psychical life of his patients. His quest for the "train of thought" contributed to the creation of *stream-of-consciousness fiction. Freud's theoretical and clinical uses of his psychoanalytical techniques were subsequently elaborated by *Jung, who explored the mythical side and originated the hypothesis of the "collective unconscious." In America Harry Stack Sullivan, building on the work of William *James and others, developed theories of interpersonal relations in psychoanalysis, while Karen Horney emphasized the social and environmental world of the patient. Earlier, Alfred Adler, branching off from Freud, focused on ego-association and power. These and other figures were concerned with the clinical side; but certain of the psychoanalytical ideas, as they relate to symbolic representation and the prevalence of myth in man's imaginative history, have been used in the study of man's creative imagination. In literary criticism Lionel Trilling has been the expositor of Freud; Northrop Frye has used Jung in developing his "anatomy" of criticism, while Leon Edel has used psychoanalytical concepts in his biographical writings and in his studies of the psychological novel.

Pushkin, Alexander: Russian poet and dramatist (1799–1837). Pushkin was the first of the major Russian writers to become widely known outside his own country. At home, his work is regarded as the quintessence of the national genius, and the Russians love him with special affection, much as the Scots esteem *Burns. Of an old aristocratic family, Pushkin wrote his first prose, a historical novel, about his maternal great-grandfather (a Negro), who had been an Abyssinian general. Then, he began a short-lived career of dissipation and poetry. In Byronic fashion Pushkin's lyrics lauded freedom and defied oppressors. His reputation as a liberal caused his demotion in the Foreign Office, then his transfer (really a form of banishment) to the remote south (1820–24), and finally his dismissal from the service. Three long exotic narrative poems, *The Caucasian Prisoner*, *The Gypsies*, *The Brother Robbers*, set in Crimea and the Caucasus (to which Pushkin had been "exiled") confirmed his reputation as the "*Byron of Russia" and made him a literary lion. His marriage to a dazzling and flirtatious beauty (by his own count, Woman No. 113 in his life) did not make either of them settle down. Six years later, at the age of 38, he was killed in a duel brought on by his wife's infidelities.

During his years in south Russia, Pushkin had begun a long romantic-satiric novel in verse, *Eugen Onegin* (1833), modeled on Byron's *Beppo* and *Don Juan.* For this poem, Pushkin invented a 14-line stanza which admirably sustains the tone and narrative. *Eugen Onegin* has been called the first Russian novel because of its firm grasp of character and its realistic presentation of scene, both on the great estates and in St. Petersburg. Another work, *Boris Godunov* (1825), a historical tragedy in *blank verse, based on the life of a 16th-century czar, was patterned after the chronicle plays of "our father *Shakespeare," as Pushkin called him. Pushkin's other writings include lyrics on a wide variety of subjects, paraphrases of the *Song of Songs* and the **Koran*, and adaptations of native folk tales. His lyrics and narratives attracted composers of the first rank: Glinka based an opera on *Ruslan and Ludmila* (1820); Tschaikovsky used *Eugen Onegin* and the *Queen of Spades* (*Pique-Dame*, a short story from the collection *Tales of Belkin*, 1830); Moussorgsky, *Boris Godunov*; Rimski Korsakov, *Le Coq d'Or* (*The Golden Cockerel*).

Pushkin's greatness lies essentially in his lyric gifts, for, as Tschaikovsky said, Pushkin's lyrics "sang themselves." His precise, energetic, lyrical language expresses the poetic impact of commonplace things and suggests their deeper symbolic meaning. His intrinsic qualities and his seminal influence make him one of the most significant of Russian writers.

Quintilian: Roman rhetorician and critic (*c.* A.D. 35–*c.* 95). Marcus Fabius Quintilianus, the most famous of Roman schoolteachers, was born in northern Spain but educated at Rome, where he was the first rhetorician to establish a public school and to receive a salary from the state. In his later years he composed a treatise, the *Institutio oratoria (Training of the Orator)*, in which he describes the education necessary for success in public speaking. Though the work is noted for common sense and enriched by the experience gained in a lifetime of teaching, much of it is necessarily technical, and its permanent value lies in individual passages. Among these the remarks on elementary education in Book I and the comparative survey of Greek and Roman literature in Book X are probably the best known today. In reading the latter passage, however, one must remember that Quintilian is judging the writers he discusses solely for their value to an orator.

Rabelais, François: French writer (*c.* 1495–1553). Although the author of **Gargantua and Pantagruel* became a celebrity and a friend of some of the great men of his time, few of the facts of his life are established beyond dispute. His biography is pieced together like a patchwork quilt from scattered records supplemented by inferences drawn from his own writing. He was born in the Loire valley, the son of a country lawyer. In early youth he entered a Franciscan monastery as a novice, and in due course he was ordained a priest. Always a diligent student, he devoted himself to scholastic philosophy and to the Greek studies which were just beginning to be revived in France. These activities led to constant friction between Rabelais and the head of his monastery, who had little use for erudition in general, and still less for humanistic studies. Finally, Rabelais secured papal permission to transfer (in 1524) to the more liberal and scholarly Benedictines, who encouraged Greek studies. But even this arrangement was not satisfactory, and it would seem (for we have little information about the next six years) that he traveled and studied, much as his hero Pantagruel did (Book II).

In September 1530, he entered the University of Montpellier; and by November 1 he had become a bachelor of arts. Apparently in the years for which we have no biographical records he had acquired, along with his theology, a familiarity with Paris and its student types and a knowledge of medieval philosophy, of jurisprudence, and especially of medicine. Early in 1531 he lectured publicly on the ancient Greek physicians Galen and Hippocrates. He had found his calling and was to be known thereafter as a doctor of medicine. He never left the Church, but was granted permission to practice medicine while wearing his priestly garb, provided only that he did not engage in surgery. The next year, 1532, he moved to Lyons, was appointed physician at the city hospital, and lectured on anatomy. At the same time he began a career as editor, reviser, and translator of medical treatises, including those of Hippocrates and Galen, and the *Medical Letters* of the Italian Manardi. Lyons was at this time the publishing and intellectual center of

France, the meeting place of the patrons of the new learning. In this cultivated society Rabelais was sought after and at home, and the humanists whom he met in these days became friends powerful in Church and state, who may more than once have saved him from the stake. And at Lyons he wrote the first works which were to make him immortal. He was now nearly 40.

In November 1532, he published *Pantagruel* (which was promptly censored by the theological faculty of the University of Paris). Two years later a quarrel between his father and a neighbor over fishing rights provided the main episode (The Pichrocholine War) for *Gargantua*, which is now printed as the first part. Out of simple everyday life Rabelais thus shaped a "perfect picture of rural manners" and one of the world's masterpieces of rollicking satire. The year 1532 also saw his publication of a facetious almanac, *Prognostication Pantagrueline*, the first of a long series which survive only in fragments. Like *Pantagruel*, this was published under an anagrammatic pseudonym, "Alcofribas." The condemnation of *Pantagruel* as sacrilegious and obscene may in part explain why in 1534 Rabelais abandoned his post in the Lyons hospital—and apparently his monastic garb—without permission, to go as personal physician with Jean du Bellay (later a cardinal) to Rome, where he received absolution for this act of "apostasy." This friendship was to be of the greatest importance to Rabelais, who under the protection of one or another of the du Bellay brothers subsequently made four visits to Italy and met the learned and important at the French and papal courts. In 1536, through the successful efforts of his friends, Rabelais was granted papal authorization to doff his Benedictine habit for that of a secular priest, and du Bellay appointed him a canon. Rabelais continued to practice medicine, however, taking the degree in 1537 at the University of Montpellier. He became increasingly famous for his dissection of cadavers, for lecturing directly from the Greek text (humanist that he was), and for his cures. Tales of his medical marvels spread; he was hailed as "the glory of the healing art."

During the next decade, papal, French, and imperial relations were strained. In the cross fire of fears, accusations, and heresies Rabelais "ducked" (as he said) and made no effort to bring his work before the public until 1546, when, having obtained a royal "privilege," he published Book III of *Gargantua and Pantagruel*. Although the volume was dedicated to the king's sister, Queen Marguerite of Navarre, like its predecessors it was condemned by the theological faculty of the University of Paris. Again Rabelais took no chances; he left France and went to Metz until the commotion blew over. In 1552 he resigned his curacies, probably in order to publish Book IV, which appeared during the same year, with less risk. He must have died shortly thereafter, probably in Paris, as tradition says, though the date and place of his death, like those of his birth, are debated. His great work was concluded by the publication of Book V in 1564. The authorship of this last book is questionable, but the present consensus is that it is essentially the work of Rabelais, though doubtless edited and expanded from his notes by another hand.

As physician, scholar, educator, and humanist, Rabelais is now of only historical interest, but he remains as one of the world's foremost humorists and satirists. Though his name is usually associated with a frank and exuberant treatment of the facts of human physiology and reproduction—as when we speak of a Rabelaisian story—it might more significantly be associated with his two fundamental propositions: "All men desire to know" and "Laughter is a proper function of man."

Racine, Jean: French writer of tragedy (1639–99). The 17th century saw great changes take place in France. The exuberant, individualistic period of the *Renaissance gave way to the more disciplined era of absolute monarchy, when classical regulation was the spirit of the day (see *classicism). From a feudal land torn by civil war and religious strife, France became a great unified nation, the glittering and urbane cultural center of Europe. The growth of Louis XIV's sophisticated court was paralleled by a similar development in literature; and just as *Molière evolved a mature, intellectual comedy from the rude popular farce, so did Jean Racine refine tragic drama.

Earlier in the century, *Corneille, France's first important tragedian, had prepared the way by instituting his great dramas of psychological crisis. His heroic characters, caught in an energetic struggle between will and emotion, were strong, rational figures, counterparts of the Frenchmen of the age of Louis XIII. But in another generation, this "Roman" type no longer reflected the contemporary aristocrat, nor did Corneille's plays suit the taste of a more cultivated audience. "Sensible" drama was required: tragedy to express the emotional rather than the rational attitudes of a day greatly concerned with love and passion, tragedy to be written in lines that were polished rather than majestic—in short, an elegant, ordered theater was necessary for the ladies and gentlemen of Versailles and the Parisian *salons*. To fulfill these requirements and yet save tragedy from degenerating into a completely artificial form, a playwright of genius and sensibility was needed; this was Racine.

Two dominant influences in Racine's life combined to produce his great tragedy of passion, with its helpless victims and its inevitably fatal consequences: his Jansenist education and, derived from that, his thorough and sympathetic knowledge of Greek drama. The Protestant Reformation had roused Catholics to the need of a countermovement, so that the 17th century saw the rise of many organizations, secular as well as clerical, to strengthen faith and combat the increase of freethinking. Among these groups were the Jansenists (see *Pascal), who believed in a predestination theory of salvation.

Port-Royal, near Paris, was the center of Jansenism, and the "gentlemen of Port-Royal" developed an excellent educational system, based on a firm foundation in Greek language and literature, and indoctrinated many distinguished pupils—among them Jean Racine. It was natural that Racine was sent to Port-Royal, since he came from a family of deep Jansenist conviction, with strong personal ties to Port-Royal itself. Orphaned at an early age, Racine had been raised by devout grandparents and had been enrolled at the College de Beauvais, a school with Jansenist affiliations, until 1655, when he entered Port-Royal. This was just a year before the school was officially closed for a time, but as Racine had family connections there, he was able to remain and receive an unusual amount of attention and affection. Though he left Port-Royal in 1658, those three years left their mark: that paradoxical combination of austere religiosity and Hellenism in which he had been saturated was to be a lasting influence.

On first consideration, however, the subsequent years seem a complete contradiction of this training. After leaving the sheltered Jansenist community, Racine launched into an existence that was to become more and more worldly. First he lived in Paris, attending the Collége d'Harcourt while staying with his uncle, a substantial man of affairs who introduced him into society; then he spent a year in Southern France, preparing for a church preferment and taking note of the beautiful women of Provence. The good inhabitants of Port-Royal began to worry about their protégé—and not without reason, for when his pursuit of a benefice proved unsuccessful, Racine returned to Paris in 1663 and entered a career which in the 17th century was highly questionable—the theater. Consorting with actresses, mingling with worldly, artistic friends, Racine led a life that brought upon him the censure of his pious aunt and her Jansenist associates. And Racine in anger retaliated with two open letters in savage indictment of his former teachers and counselors.

But though Racine's activities during the period from 1658 to 1677 were undoubtedly a reaction against his earlier experiences, they were not—however much he might consciously rebel—a negation of them, for the very plays with which he was achieving popular fame were a product of his youthful indoctrination. If his years "in the world" gave him the knowledge of feminine psychology which his plays demonstrate, his years at Port-Royal conditioned this insight. Racine is a great—if not the greatest—creator of female roles in the theater, for women, as the weaker sex, supplied the best illustrations of the natural weakness, irrationality, and cruelty of the human race. It was from a severe, fatalistic religion that Racine derived his tragedy of passion.

The Jansenists provided not only the fiber of Racine's drama but, indirectly, its matter, form, and style. In the Greek literature in which they had grounded him, Racine found his great models. The French 17th century is known as a Neo-Classical period; in Racine the classical influence bore perhaps its happiest fruit. The regulation of the three *unities, which Corneille had found so shackling and at which he had youthfully rebelled, was thoroughly appropriate for Racine's drama, which turned on psychological crisis and required concentration. The subject matter of Greek and Roman tragedy was often adaptable to his purpose and had the important advantage of being sufficiently distant for poetic perspective. And the simplicity and order of Racine's style can be traced to the classic masters, too. This is not to suggest that Racine is merely an imitator; as writers of genius have always done, he absorbed all influences and evolved a drama that is his own—a drama that is specifically of his century in its aristocratic men and women and courtly lines and yet is universal in its concept of the emotional aspect of man's nature.

Although Racine had achieved some youthful success with occasional verse (an ode honoring Louis XIV's marriage and a poem commemorating the king's recovery from illness), he had early become interested in the stage. In 1660, two years after leaving Port-Royal, he had written two plays, neither of them extant. Then in 1664, he finished *The Thebaïde* and had it played by Molière's company. Largely indebted to Corneillian drama, it is not a very significant work, nor is his second tragedy, *Alexander the Great*, except that it marks the end of his association with Molière. Though Racine made lasting friendships with *La Fontaine, the famous fabulist, and *Boileau, the critic and poet, he suffered throughout his career from the hostilities which his hotheadedness and pride were quick to incur. He alienated the generous Molière by arranging for the Hôtel de Bourgogne, a rival troupe with a better reputation for tragedy, to produce *Alexander* at the same time as Molière; and with the same play he antagonized Corneille by his anger over the old master's failure to be very enthusiastic about the drama.

Racine was still nothing more than a promising young artist when 1667 brought *Andromache* to the boards. An amazingly mature piece, it is one of his best dramas, typical of his later work in its powerful exposition of love and hate. The play heralded Racine's genius and was followed in the next ten years by other great classics of the French theater: *The Litigants* (*Les Plaideurs*), his sole comedy, a clever adaptation of *Aristophanes' Wasps*; *Britannicus*, a tragedy of ambition and intrigue in Nero's court; *Bérénice*, his triumph over Corneille, whose current play on the same subject was far less favorably received; *Bajazet*, a contemporary drama of the popular Turkish scene; *Mithridates*, another success in the Corneillian manner; *Iphigénie*, a play on the same subject as *Euripides' Iphigenia at Aulis*; and then, in 1677, *Phaedra*.

Usually considered Racine's best work, *Phaedra* was the last of his secular plays. That a popular playwright should retire from the stage at the height of his achievement is not surprising in the light of *Phaedra*'s stage history and Racine's temperament. For his enemies— many of them Corneille's offended supporters—had commissioned a rival play and supported its production at the same time that they emptied Racine's theater by buying up blocks of seats. A humiliated Racine, also involved in financial problems and an unhappy love affair, was ready to return to the Jansenist fold. *Phaedra* itself made a good gesture of reconciliation, for here was a play based on moral considerations very much in the Jansenist spirit. The tragedy of Phaedra demonstrated that sin must be expiated and that virtue without "saving grace" was futile. Port-Royal welcomed back its prodigal and he sedately married a pious and well-dowered lady, who had never read a single one of his wicked plays.

As if to confirm his actions, Racine that same year accepted with Boileau the post of historiographer to the king. To all intents and purposes his dramatic career was at an end. However, Madame de Maintenon, Louis' devout mistress, later prevailed upon him to write two Biblical plays for production at St. Cyr, a school for young ladies which she had founded. These religious plays, *Esther* and *Athalie*, are very different in theme and treatment—being more philosophical and religious than psychological—from his great dramas of passion and hate, but they have merits of their own, including Racine's characteristically fine verse. Mme. de Sévigné—that famous 17th-century commentator—was moved to declare: "Racine loves God now the way he used to love his mistresses."

So it was as a religious, respectable gentleman, father of a large family, that Racine passed the rest of his life. Unfortunately, his friendship with the king, which *Esther* and *Athalie* had helped strengthen, was marred in his last days by disagreement over political statements that he had made. But though he was currently out of favor at court, Racine was a respected man when he died in 1699. The Jansenist influence, which had played so important a role throughout his lifetime, endured to the very end; Racine was buried at Port-Royal, where he had requested that he be laid at the feet of his favorite teacher.

Ramayana, The: an epic of India ("The Lay of Rama"), begun about 500 B.C. and probably completed in its present forms (there are three different versions) about A.D. 200. It was probably the work of many authors, although it is traditionally ascribed to the poet Valmiki (4th century B.C.), and it is quite possible that the core of the poem is his work. As the poem now stands, it contains about 24,000 couplets, divided into seven books.

The heart of the work is the two-part story contained in Books II–VI. In the first part, Prince Rama wins Sita for his wife and is named heir-apparent to the throne. But another of the king's wives, who wants her own son (Rama's half-brother) to rule, plots against him and has him banished. The king dies; Bharata, the half-brother, refuses the throne, finds Rama in the forest in which he and Sita had lived during the banishment, and offers him the throne; but because of a vow he has taken, Rama refuses the throne and sends Bharata back to rule. This part of the epic is purely human and natural in both its motivation and its events.

The second part is of an entirely different sort, for its story is full of supernatural marvels and its characters include demons and talking animals and birds—the god and the commander-in-chief of the monkeys play a prominent role. Sita is abducted by the demon-king Ravana, and carried off to Lanka (Ceylon). After many marvelous adventures Rama, aided by the monkey-nation, kills Ravana and wins Sita back. Sita clears herself of all suspicion of infidelity, and Rama returns with her to share the throne with his half-brother and bring his subjects peace and prosperity. (In one version the earth goddess then disappears with Sita.)

To this story have been added an introduction and a conclusion (Books I and VII) designed to attach it to the worship of Vishnu. Book I explains that Rama is a reincarnation of Vishnu, born at the request of the other gods for the specific purpose of destroying Ravana. Book VII returns to the gods, who come to Rama and reveal to him that he is an incarnation of Vishnu. This religious framework has given *The Ramayana* the status of a sacred text, constantly recited throughout India and familiar to millions of Hindus who take Rama and Sita as their models and strive to follow them in love, friendship, heroism, truth, and justice.

realism: an artistic creed which holds that the purpose of art is to depict life with complete and objective honesty—to show things "as they really are." To this end, it values concrete, verifiable details more than sweeping generalizations, and impersonal photographic accuracy more than the artist's individual "interpretation" of experience. As a recognizable literary creed, realism began in the 18th century with the novels of *Defoe and *Fielding, but its triumph as a literary school came in the 19th and early 20th centuries, under the double influence of the growth of science and philosophical rationalism and of a revolt against the emotional and stylistic excesses of the *Romantic Movement. Because the realist sought to avoid idealism and romantic prettifying of his subjects, he often seemed to stress either the commonplace and trivial or the sordid and brutal aspects of life.

Fiction and painting were the artistic activities in which realism found its greatest scope and most systematic exploitation. The great realistic novelists include *Balzac, *Flaubert, George *Eliot, *James, *Tolstoi, *Dostoevski, *Mark Twain, and *Verga. The extreme form of realism is often called *naturalism.

Remus: see *Romulus and Remus.

Renaissance: a period of European history largely in the 15th, 16th, and early 17th centuries, though its limits are indefinite and vary from country to country. Its beginnings in Italy are often pushed back to approximately 1350, with the poetry and the classical studies of *Petrarch and *Boccaccio, though as a general European movement the Renaissance does not begin until about a century later.

Two events make it convenient to consider the true beginning of the "rebirth" (for that is the meaning of *Renaissance*) as coming about 1450. After the fall of Rome, the eastern part of the Roman Empire, with Constantinople as its capital, had remained intact for nearly a thousand years and had preserved the learning and works of ancient Greece, which had been lost in western Europe (see *classical antiquity). But on the morning of May 29, 1453, the Turks breached the walls and Constantinople fell. The result was a diffusion of fugitive scholars, bringing valuable manuscripts with them; and the most obvious haven was Italy. (There is a striking resemblance between this wave of refugees and the influx of scholars, writers, composers, and artists who fled the police-states of Europe in the mid-20th century and sought sanctuary in the United States.) A revival of humanistic and classical studies had already begun in Italy, and the fugitives stimulated and assisted it. Thus, although some Latin writers like *Vergil and *Ovid had never fallen into neglect, Latin writers like *Catullus and *Lucretius were rediscovered, as was almost all Greek literature as we know it today. It used to be the fashion to explain the whole of the Renaissance as the impact of the resurrected writings of antiquity. This is an obvious exaggeration, for it not only ignores other important influences, but it ignores the fact that the Greek classics could not have been revived at all unless something of their spirit had already been in the air. Nevertheless, the revival of learning was an important part of the Renaissance and helped to determine the forms in which the new spirit manifested itself. For example, in most countries except England the loose dramatic structure of the *Middle Ages was abandoned for the tighter structure of classical drama.

The second event which marks the dawn of the Renaissance is the European invention of printing from movable type. Printing from blocks (as in the woodcut) was nothing new; and books had been printed from type for centuries in Chinese, Korean, and Japanese, but the technique had not been passed on to Europe. Then, in or near Mainz, within a few years of 1450, someone made the great discovery that cutting a separate type for each letter made it possible to set the type in any desired arrangement and run off rapidly as many identical copies as were needed. In other words, the hand-crafted manuscript was replaced by the mass-produced book, and the result was, of course, a more uniform and a cheaper product. The effects were revolutionary. General popular education became both possible and desirable, and a really large reading public appeared. Thus literature began to have a commercial aspect, and to be not only democratic, but often vulgar. The chapbooks and broadsides of Elizabethan England were addressed to the people who read "comic" books today. There was, however, a great diffusion of the art and knowledge which up to this time had been the property of a fortunate few. The printing press was also one of the chief instruments of social and religious change, for the pamphlet made it possible for a reformer or agitator to broadcast his views over a large area and to do it with far greater personal safety than if he had to spread his ideas by public speeches or sermons. Without the printing press, the Reformation would probably have come to little more than various similar movements before the invention of printing (see *Wyclif).

The Renaissance, then, was a general new spirit, stimulated by the revival of learning and diffused by the art of printing. The chief ingredients of the new spirit were individualism and worldliness, and these characteristics manifested themselves in many forms. We may note, to begin with, that it was doubtless these same ingredients in classical Greek literature which attracted the men of the Renaissance. The ancient Greek was a worldly man in that his whole life and hope were centered on this present world rather than some future one; and in this he was the direct opposite of the medieval man who was constantly told, and who at least felt that he ought to believe, that this life is merely a short but annoying placement test to determine his eternal status. The ancient Greek, as revealed in literature, was also a strong individualist, for the voice of this literature was, of course, that of democratic and individualistic Athens rather than the regimented ant hill of Sparta.

One of the principal forms which the individualism of the Renaissance took was the rejection of authority—the determination to make one's own decisions, right or wrong. Thus the central position of the Reformation was that a man could deal directly with his God without going through the channels of the Church, and that he should have the *Bible in his own tongue, to read and interpret for himself, instead of merely accepting official dogma without going to its source. In much the same way, *Aristotle, whose word (in Latin translation) had been law in the Middle Ages, came to be considered as a wise, but necessarily fallible, philosopher. The beginnings of modern science can be found in this same rejection of authority, for it automatically involves a new look at the evidence. So we find *Rabelais editing the ancient medical authorities, but, not content to take their word on faith, studying anatomy by making his own dissections.

Another important facet of individualism was the insistence on the well-rounded man. If a man is only a unit in a social mass, there is a strong obligation to be as much like the other units as possible. But if a man is an individual, an end in himself, then there is a value in his differences, in his uniqueness. Furthermore, he should be complete, with all his potentialities developed,

619

instead of being a mere specialist who must be completed by other specialists. The accomplished courtier of the Renaissance is supposed to be able to fence, to ride, to read Latin and Greek, to organize the siege of a city, or to write a graceful sonnet to a lady. And in actual fact we find figures like Leonardo da Vinci, painter, sculptor, engineer, and inventor; like Sir Walter Raleigh, explorer, freebooter, courtier, poet, and historian; like Thomas Campion, physician, poet, and composer.

Worldliness is connected with all-round development in that it takes the form of a hunger for all the experiences that this world has to offer. The man who is merely an athlete misses all the intellectual and aesthetic pleasures of life, and the mere intellectual or aesthete never knows the pleasure of skillful and strenuous physical effort. The ascetic never knows the joys of the flesh, and the sensualist never knows the exultation of the spirit. All the arts of the Renaissance flower into a richness of color, of emotion, of response to the beauty and excitements of the physical world.

About 1195 Pope Innocent III had written a famous book *On Contempt for the World (De contemptu mundi)*; but in 1580 *Montaigne, writing *On the Education of Children*, says that "this great world" ought to be "the book my young gentleman should study with the most attention." The attitude has been completely reversed.

Since the Renaissance and the Reformation were two different aspects of the same intellectual ferment, the two movements are more or less complementary. In Italy, where the Renaissance was at its strongest, the Reformation was hardly felt. In Germany, where all energy went into the Reformation (either for or against it), there is really no Renaissance. In France and England both movements were felt, but neither in its full concentration.

Because of the time lag in the spread of the new literature from its center in Italy, it is more useful to consider the literature of the Renaissance by types than to arrange it chronologically. One of the most typical activities of the Renaissance is the writing of *pastoral poetry based on classical models. The vogue was so great that in *Don Quixote* playing at being a shepherd is clearly the next best thing to playing at being a knight-errant.

Furthermore, the Renaissance created a new combination, the pastoral play, heralded by Poliziano's *Orfeo* (c. 1482) and reaching its full development in *Tasso's *Aminta* (1581) and Guarini's *The Faithful Shepherd* (*Il pastor fido*, 1590). It also developed, as a parallel form, the sentimental pastoral romance—Montemayor's *La Diana* (1559), Sir Philip Sidney's *Arcadia* (1590), and Honoré d'Urfé's *L'Astrée* (1607). The influence of these types is seen in the pastoral scenes in many Elizabethan tragi-comedies, and in such comedies as *As You Like It*.

Another typical product of the period was the Renaissance epic, which was essentially a fusion of the heroic classical epic with the color, pageantry, love interest, and marvelous episodes of the *medieval romance. The number of such epics is astonishing—Lope de *Vega Carpio wrote some half a dozen—but most of them are now known only to specialists. The principal ones still widely read are the *Orlando furioso* of *Ariosto, the *Jerusalem Delivered* of Tasso, *The Lusiads* of *Camoëns, and *The *Faerie Queene* of *Spenser, all written during the 16th century.

Being a personal expression, lyric poetry always flourishes in an individualistic age, and the Renaissance was no exception. The lyrics of this period were particularly fortunate in combining the tumultuous joy of life of their own period with the perfection of form and workmanship of the admired Latin and Greek models. This combination is plainly visible in the poems of the French members of the *Pléiade, and their critical writings show that it was a deliberate achievement rather than a mere historical accident. The greatest model of the Renaissance lyric, however, was the Petrarchan *sonnet. This poetic form spread all over Europe (the first English examples were published in 1557 but were written about a quarter of a century earlier), and the content and spirit were adopted along with the form. So was the custom of writing sonnets in an organized series, and the sonnet sequence became a fashionable poetic type.

The revival of interest in Latin drama and the discovery of Greek tragedy were bound to react on the loosely organized drama which had evolved independently during the Middle Ages, but the degree of the influence varied with the strength of the Renaissance. In the Romance countries the drama soon went over to an essentially classical form and spirit. The first tragedy in French, for example, was the "classical" *Cléopâtre captive*, written by Etienne Jodelle and performed before the king and his court in 1552. The progress of the classical type of play was probably facilitated by the fact that Renaissance schoolmasters took to writing tragedies in Latin on the classical model for performance by their pupils, some of which became celebrated and widely known. (Montaigne tells us that at school he "played the chief parts in the Latin tragedies of Buchanan, Guerente, and Muret.") In England, where the native dramatic tradition was stronger, the classical influence was weaker. Some scholars like Ben *Jonson prided themselves on adhering to the *unities and some of the other conventions, but in general the classical tradition contributed little beyond a certain tightening of form and some useful devices borrowed from the plays of *Seneca. Much the same thing happened in Spain, where the great drama of the Golden Age continues an indigenous tradition only slightly touched by the plays of classical antiquity. The classical drama was hard to assimilate, and the great plays of the Renaissance are those of the relatively independent English and Spanish theaters. Only later, in the period of *Neo-Classicism, did Europe master the classical form sufficiently to use it for new triumphs.

Though it was primarily an age of poetry, the Renaissance produced distinguished works in prose as well. Aside from the prose of information and controversy (one writer remarked that the "dissension in divinity" was "fierce beyond God's forbid"), it produced distinguished translations of most of the great Latin and Greek writers and something of a new type in the essays of Montaigne and *Bacon. The greatest achievement of prose, however, lay in the development of the fantastic fiction—an utterly unrealistic tale containing a good deal of food for serious thought. Three outstanding examples are More's *Utopia, *Rabelais' *Gargantua and Pantagruel, and *Cervantes' *Don Quixote.

One of the strangest phenomena of the later Renaissance was the development in several countries of highly artificial styles of writing which for a time became fads. The Gongorism of Spain, the Marinism of Italy, and the *euphemism of England were such styles (named for writers or works responsible for their popularity), and the slightly later *préciosité* of France had a good deal in common with them. The vogue of these styles, which were necessarily imitative for most writers who used them, is an evidence that in the late 16th and early 17th centuries the individualism of the Renaissance is beginning to give way to that spirit of conformity to preestablished rules and standards which is the most conspicuous feature of *Neo-Classicism.

Renan, Ernest: French scholar and philosopher (1823–92). Eminent savant of ancient cultures, historian of Judaism and of Christianity, philologist of the Semitic languages, student of Celtic literature, literary critic, master skeptic, Renan was one of the influential men of his age. Although he was educated for the priesthood, he turned from orthodox religion to a faith in science and in social regeneration under the guidance of the intellectually elite (*The Future of Science*—*L'Avenir de la science*—1848, published 1890). For him the unpardonable sin was dogmatism, since he believed that neither religious, nor historical, nor scientific knowledge is wholly accurate.

His historical studies of the Old and New Testaments, which attempted to explain their origins by their geographic, racial, social, and political environment, popularized the use of scientific and historical methods in the study of the *Bible (*History of the Origins of Christianity*—*Histoire des origines du Christianisme*—8 vols., 1863–83). The first volume in this series of histories, *The Life of Jesus* (*Vie de Jésus*, 1863), created a sensation. Rationalistic in its point of view, it was nevertheless written in a charming style and with a sincerity, sympathy, and poignancy that marked it as a work of genius.

But Renan is noteworthy not as a literary man but as a profound influence on literary men (particularly Anatole *France); he influenced modern views of religious history and presented studies of comparative religious origins in an original and captivating style, sentimental yet ironic and skeptical.

Republic, The: a dialogue by *Plato (4th century B.C.). In this, the greatest of the dialogues of Plato, *Socrates, while seeking an answer to the question *What is justice?*, describes an ideal or perfect society, the republic after which the book is named. The scene of the dialogue is laid at the Piraeus, the port of Athens, about five miles from the city, and the chief speaker is Socrates, who repeats the conversation for an unnamed group the day after it occurs. Those taking part besides himself, he says, were his friend Cephalus, now far advanced in years, Cephalus' son Polemarchus, Plato's brothers Glaucon and Adeimantus, and a sophist called Thrasymachus.

The conversation begins with a discussion of old age, but this is soon abandoned in favor of an attempt to define justice, a virtue Cephalus unhesitatingly equates with speaking the truth and paying your debts. But though his concept is based on the honesty of his own life, when examined by Socrates it is found wanting, as is that of Polemarchus, who draws on traditional ethics to explain that justice consists in doing good to your friends and evil to your enemies. Nor is Thrasymachus' cynical opinion that justice is the interest of the stronger found acceptable, however correctly it may describe the actual practice of governments, after which it is patterned. Not that Socrates persuades Thrasymachus he is wrong. To him, injustice is preferable to justice, and the unjust man happier than the just, provided of course that he is successful in his injustice. Thrasymachus is an extremist, violent in his opinions and abusive in his speech, and Socrates is content merely to silence him. But when Glaucon and Adeimantus point out that, though men praise justice, they do so largely for the rewards it brings, and add that they would like to hear it defended for its own sake, Socrates accepts the challenge. Beginning in Book II and continuing through Book VII, he creates an ideal republic—a procedure which, he believes, will be of no small advantage in searching into the meaning of justice. For as an inscription can be deciphered with greater ease when written in large characters, so the nature and value of justice will appear more clearly if presented on a grand scale in a state than if confined to the actions of an individual.

In constructing his ideal republic, Socrates begins with a Greek city-state, a community of no great size surrounded by others both Hellenic and barbarian. His purpose is not to concoct some imaginary culture in the clouds but to indicate how Athens, for example, might most easily be brought to perfection and so become the embodiment of the justice he and his friends are attempting to define. He begins with the principle of the division of labor, which seems to be a part of the order established by nature for humanity, at least when based on innate aptitudes. In it he finds not only an explanation of the origin and growth of states but an approach to an understanding of justice, which appears in a community *when each man does the work for which he is suited best.* Socrates therefore applies this principle to his commonwealth, dividing its citizens into three classes, the philosophers who rule the state, the warriors who defend it, and the producers (farmers, artisans, and tradesmen) who satisfy its economic needs. These groups correspond, he finds, to the reason, the will, and the appetites in man, who must be ruled by reason, if he is to attain that justice of the soul which results in each of his faculties' performing its appointed task.

When Socrates describes the classes in his ideal state, he says little about the producers, for he intends no radical change in their way of life; but he focuses attention on the warriors and the philosophers, whom he called *guardians*, explaining the abolition of private property and the community of wives and children to which they will be subjected. He also sets forth a vast educational system designed primarily to equip the philosophers to rule the state, though the warriors and perhaps even the general population share its benefits to a lesser degree. At the elementary level it consists of music in the Greek sense and gymnastic, though the music is purged of the myths and fables of the poets, and the gymnastic is directed toward the welfare of the soul as well as of the body. At an advanced level it includes arithmetic, geometry, astronomy, harmonics, and dialectic, that is, the study of the Ideas; and those who succeed in mastering it will be prepared to govern with justice, for they, and they alone of all mankind, will understand the nature of the Good. But until they take office, states will never rest from the evils brought upon them by the separation of political power and philosophy. The only solution for their difficulties is to make it possible for philosophers to become kings or kings philosophers.

The education of the rulers is completed in Book VII, and with it the ideal state of *aristocracy* is fully established. Socrates therefore turns in Book VIII to study those cities which have deviated from the ideal, considering, in the order of their degeneracy, (1) *timocracy*, or the state devoted to honor, (2) *oligarchy*, or the state devoted to wealth, (3) *democracy*, or the state in which each man does as he pleases, and (4) *tyranny*, or the slave-state in which the tyrant rules alone. Then, by contrasting tyranny, which is the triumph of injustice, with the ideal republic, in which justice reigns supreme, and the tyrant, who is the completely unjust man, with the philosopher-king, who is altogether just, Socrates is able to defend justice when stripped of its rewards, as Glaucon and Adeimantus asked him to do. For he can now show that to say that injustice is preferable to justice is to say that disease is preferable to health and misery to happiness. For injustice is that internal discord which is the sickness of the soul, as disease is the sickness of the body, and the tyrant, who suffers from it more than any other man, is the most wretched of the human race. In Book IX the study of the tyrant is complete, justice is equated with health and happiness in state or individual, and the purpose for which the *Republic* was written is fulfilled. Book X follows as a kind of appendix containing a further attack on poetry and a vision of the hereafter which presents the doctrine of reincarnation and describes the rewards and punishments of the soul after death.

The *Republic* is Plato's masterpiece and one of the greatest books in literature, but it was not composed in a vacuum, and if it is to be understood, its historical background must be kept in mind and modern political and sociological thinking not allowed to distort its meaning. Plato was a Greek, writing about the Greek city-state. When he speaks of timocracy and oligarchy, he has in mind the better and the worse aspects of Spartan civilization. When he satirizes democracy, he means democracy as practiced at Athens after Athens had been ruined in the Peloponnesian War. (Indeed, this great conflict is ever before Plato's eyes, and *Thucydides' History is therefore an excellent commentary on his work.) The reader must also remember that Plato's object in writing the Republic was to frame an ideal toward which mankind might struggle, not to prepare a constitution for submission to a legislative assembly. Some of his statements are not to be taken literally, and some of his proposals are not completely thought through. The community of wives and children, for example, was reluctantly given up as impossible in his later writing.

Among the famous passages in the Republic are the picture of the naturally good old man in Book I, the analysis of the four cardinal virtues of wisdom, courage, temperance, and justice in Book IV, the simile of the divided line used to explain the theory of the Ideas in Book VI, the allegory of the cave at the beginning of Book VII, the sketches of corrupt men and states that occupy Book VIII, and the vision of the soul's destiny revealed to Er, the son of Armenius, with which Book X closes.

Return of the Native, The: a novel by *Hardy (1878). In The Return of the Native Hardy shows the conflicts and realignments produced by adding a new and different element to a statically balanced combination. The novel devotes its first chapter to an account of the timeless and unchanging wasteland of Egdon Heath—an environment so impressive and influential that the heath has often been called one of the principal characters of the story. On this heath live a number of superstitious and ignorant rustics who are hardly presented as individual characters, for they are almost as primitive and eternal as the heath itself. Against this ancient natural and human background Hardy presents a group of what might be called modern individuals. Diggory Venn and Thomasin Yeobright are essentially of the heath in their patient endurance and ultimate survival. In contrast with these, other characters are already trapped when the story opens. Eustacia Vye—"the raw material of a divinity"—can find no scope for her beauty and passion and wildness of spirit on the heath, and her affair with the unstable, pleasure-loving Wildeve (also at odds with his surroundings) is only a temporary indulgence and a dream of escape.

Into this situation comes the "native," Clym Yeobright, who has forsaken a business as a jeweler in Paris to return to his native heath. From this point on, irony is piled on irony. Wildeve's reason and better nature urge him to a marriage with Thomasin, but this marriage is only a hollow form, for he cannot free himself from his infatuation for Eustacia. Eustacia pursues and marries Clym, partly for the novelty of the thing and partly on a calculated assumption that she can maneuver him into returning to Paris, and can thus make her own escape from the heath.

As in Hardy's other novels, chance—or "hap," as he sometimes calls it—plays a decisive role at several points, notably in Wildeve's sudden wealth which tempts Eustacia away from Clym, and in Clym's failure to wake up when his mother knocks at his door for a reconciliation. But this chance is not merely random events; it is more of a malicious power which arranges the details of things that were already logically fated to happen. Eustacia and Wildeve can neither escape from the heath nor adapt themselves to it, and their death is the inevitable resolution of their problem. Clym, somewhat arbitrarily saved from death, carries on his original idea of a return to his own place and people, but he can do this only after the dislocation of local life caused by his return has been healed. The marriage of Diggory and Thomasin was not part of the original plan of the story but was finally included more or less as a concession to readers who demanded a happy ending. But it is reasonable and appropriate that, after the inexorable tragedy has been played out, these two—the most patient, most simple, most heathlike of the principal characters—should survive and flourish, as do the heath and its minor inhabitants, to represent the triumph of the timeless, unreasoning, indomitable spirit of life.

Rilke, Rainer Maria: German poet (1875–1926). Rilke spent most of his life as a rather unattached wanderer and observer, with residence and extensive travel in Russia, Paris, and Italy as well as Germany. His early lyrics are in the general tradition of *Heine and the German folk song but already show some tendencies toward the highly personal style which he later developed. He published various poems and tales from 1896 on, but his first work of major importance was *Stories of God* (*Geschichte vom Lieben Gott*, 1900), a work which overlapped the composition of the religious poems of the *Book of Hours* (*Stundenbuch*, 1905). His poetic masterpieces followed: *New Poems* (*Neue Gedichte*, 2 vols., 1907–08), *Requiem* (1909), and *Die Sonette un Orpheus* and *Duineser Elegien* (*The Sonnets to Orpheus* and *Duino Elegies*, both 1923). Other prose works include a book on the French sculptor *Auguste Rodin* (1903); *The Tale of the Love and Death of Cornet Christopher Rilke* (*Die Weise von Liebe und Tod des Cornets Christoph Rilke*, 1906), an impressionistic account of a military ancestor; and his prose masterpiece, *Notebook of Malte Laurids Brigge* (*Aufzeichnungen des Malte Laurids Brigge*, 1910), a study of a character's development seen entirely from the inside. Various other works, including letters, have been published since Rilke's death.

Rilke's personal style and syntax somehow managed to avoid the danger of becoming merely mannnerism. His use of nouns as verbs and verbs as nouns, of everyday words in highly lyrical contexts, of abstractions in concrete senses, etc., provides a special atmosphere that seems to suit his probings of existence. One critic has spoken of his habit of contrasting "the agitation of the *I* with the peacefulness of things." Yet this is a partial view, for his insight makes things come alive. The taste of an apple becomes, not an everyday affair, but a carefully studied, accurately described experience with philosophical implications. Few poets have shown so deep or intuitive an understanding of children and animals. Rilke can be summed up as a man for whom nothing was obscured by daily habit. Everything was freshly seen and fully savored as an experience valuable in its own right. He is one of the few poets of obvious first rank in the 20th century.

Rimbaud, Jean Arthur: French poet (1854–91). Rimbaud, important as a forerunner of the *symbolists and *surrealism, abandoned literature before he was 20. A perverse and rebellious genius, he ran away from home at the age of 15 and entered on a life of dissolute wandering. After a brief relationship with *Verlaine he forsook writing, supported himself precariously by various activities in Germany, the East Indies, and Egypt, until he finally settled in Abyssinia, where he traded in coffee and slaves, with gun-running as a sideline. The only work which Rimbaud himself published was *A Season in Hell* (*Une Saison en enfer*, 1873), a psychological autobiography. *The Illuminations* (*Les Illuminations*, written *c.* 1871, published 1886) consists of both verse and prose-poems. His best-known poem is *The Drunken Boat (Bateau ivre)*.

Rimbaud's contribution was to make the role of poetry one of mystic release and revelation and to devise a technique which gave the immediacy of direct sensation to the morbid dream, hallucination, or vision, by the juxtaposition of symbols and images. He deliberately cultivated his world of unreality. "I accustomed myself to simple hallucination" before going on to double and triple hallucination. His whole life was a flight from the everyday and the "real"—his early vagabondage, his brief period of literary activity, and his final years, during which "the adventurer in the real replaced the adventurer in the ideal." His extreme sensibility to the "deep and eternal wound" inflicted by life is condensed into sharply drawn images grouped about central metaphors. His elliptical compressions and complex rhythms, his use of words for their tone color, his distortions of common meaning and syntax, his use of free verse are characteristic techniques deliberately employed to produce the overtones of the vague, mysterious, intuitively sensed complexities of the life of the mind.

rime royal: a seven-line stanza, usually of iambic pentameters, riming ababbcc. It was used by *Chaucer in *Troilus and Criseyde* and has been a common English stanza since that time. The name was conferred because of its use by King James I of Scotland in his poem *The Kingis Quair* (1423).

Rolland, Romain: French novelist (1866–1944), Rolland is best known for his serial-novel *Jean Christophe* (1903–12), a ten-volume novel dealing with the life and work of a musical genius of German birth who, however, lives in France. Rolland thus tried to suggest that on the ground of art a meeting was possible between these two divided nations. Rolland began by studying history, but he won a fellowship to Rome in archaeology and here was exposed to classical art and had as friends German votaries of Beethoven and *Goethe, *Nietzsche and Wagner. Influenced by *Tolstoi, Rolland returned to France and wrote essays on music and plays; he found his first success with a life of Beethoven, and later would write equally successful works on Michelangelo and Tolstoi. The writing of *Jean Christophe* won him an international audience and he received the Nobel prize in 1916. A confirmed pacifist, he remained in Switzerland during the First World War. In later years he was interested in Oriental religion and in communism. He also wrote a seven-volume serial-novel, *L'Ame enchantée*, between 1922 and 1933. His work is romantic; he belongs not so much to literature (for he was neither a stylist nor an innovator) but to the humanistic movement of which Tolstoi was the founder. While less involved with religion, Rolland felt deeply that the intellectuals of this world must commit themselves to antiwar activity and remain "above the battle."

roman à clef: "novel with a key," in which actual historical persons are depicted, disguised (and often satirized) under fictional names. For example, in *Point Counter Point* (1928) by Aldous Huxley (1874–1963), Philip Quarles is Huxley himself and Mark Rampion is based on D. H. *Lawrence. In *The Moon and Sixpence* (1919) by Somerset Maugham (1874–1965), Charles Strickland is based on the French painter Gauguin; the same author's *Cakes and Ale* (1930) details gossipy tidbits from the life of Thomas *Hardy. *The Mandarins* (1954) by Simone de Beauvoir (1908–86) concerns, among others, *Sartre, *Camus, Algren, Koestler.

Romance of the Rose: French allegorical and satirical poem (*Le Roman de la rose, c.* 1235; 1280). This narrative was the most widely read poem of its period and one of the most influential. It has been said that to understand the *Middle Ages it is necessary to read three books: *Dante's *Divine Comedy*, *Chaucer's *Canterbury Tales*, and the *Romance of the Rose*. Written in the verse form of French romances, eight-syllable rimed couplets, the *Romance* is the work of two authors. Guillaume de Lorris (*c.* 1235) wrote about 4,000 lines, leaving the project incomplete but probably very close to its intended conclusion. Some fifty years later Jean de Meung added more than 18,000 lines. Both versatile; the two poets were in every other respect virtually antithetical. The poem in many ways constitutes two separate works—the first part a well-constructed allegorical description of a courtly lover's difficult and prolonged pursuit of his lady, personified as the Rose; the second, a prolix satire on *courtly love and the society which cultivated such unreasonable and unnatural conventions. As a result of this combination of points of view, "This, the Romance of the Rose, / Does the whole art of love enclose."

The entire poem is a *dream-allegory, with considerable sexual symbolism, of the discovery and winning of the Rose, symbol both of love and of the lady herself. The other characters are mainly moral and emotional abstractions like Fear, Shame, Chastity, and Pity. The dreamer-lover enters an idyllic garden from which are excluded Hypocrisy, Avarice, Envy, and similar evils. He accepts an invitation to join in a dance with Courtesy, Cupid and Beauty, Candor and Youth, Mirth and Delight. Later, he sees in a fountain the reflection of a fascinating Rose. His heart is pierced by Cupid, who instructs him in the blessings of love; and Fair Welcome invites him to approach the Rose. When, through the intercession of Venus, he has kissed the Rose, Evil Tongue, Shame, and Jealousy prevent him from further approaching her. Then the dramatic struggle begins. Reason has tried in vain to divert him from the folly of love. Fair Welcome is confined to a tower by Jealousy. At this crucial point Guillaume died and his part of the poem ends. He had captured the vividness of the dream experience, created lively personifications, described his scenes with clarity and color, and worked them all into a rapid and well-constructed plot.

Jean de Meung at this point takes up the narrative. After thousands of lines of digressions, the tower is successfully assaulted by Cupid and his allies, Fair Welcome is freed, and the Lover is allowed to pluck the Rose. Jean de Meung abandoned Guillaume's tone and attitude for a realistic view of middle-class people, thus sacrificing poetic unity to social analysis. The main thread is so frequently forgotten that the poem has been described as "a work of chaos and Babylonian confusion."

The popularity of this poem and its unique quality lie in the originality of the combination of romantic fervor, descriptive charm, and constructive skill of the first part with the philosophic skepticism, vast knowledge, and ironic wit of the second—in the very contrast of the two parts in theme and style.

Individual elements of the poem—the dream, spring, romantic love, the spiritual conflict represented as a physical battle, the allegory of vices and virtues, the symbol of the rose—were not new. But the combination was. For the first time a dream was used to present a large-scale allegorical analysis of the mind and feelings of a lover and his relations to his beloved; and so successful was the result that *The Romance of the Rose* was both the inspiration and the model of the many dream-allegories that followed during the next three centuries.

Jean de Meung's encyclopedic treatment of every possible topic of manners and belief included knowledge of the physical world, geography, and astronomy. There are disquisitions on Friendship and Fortune, Predestination and Free Will (much in the manner of *Boethius' Lady Philosophy), on the superiority of Reason to Love and of the virtues of the Golden Age to the present vices of the human race. Most bold are the speeches of Venus, Nature, and her envoy Genius, which give a daring apology for sensuality: Nature, for example, laboring at her forge against death, asserts the superiority of science over superstition and bemoans the degeneration of man, the only one of her creatures who defies Nature's law of procreation and instead praises chastity and celibacy. The political and social scene are also cynically surveyed by Nature and Reason in trenchant tirades. There are brilliant characterizations of a jealous husband and an Old Woman whose "advice" is a scathing exposure of woman's presumed beauty and virtues. These passages, moreover, are decorated with epigrams and maxims so quotable that many have become proverbial.

The juxtaposed points of view are another element of appeal. One long speech of Genius, for example, is a striking combination of sensuality and mysticism. The poet envelops love in symbolism and allegory, thus satisfying the medieval imagination while masking the medieval defiance of the Christian ideal of chastity. Courtly love contrasts with sensual cynicism, a whole-hearted emotional idealism with a hard-headed realism.

The poem achieved immediate and continued popularity, as hundreds of manuscripts attest. It was the inspiration for innumerable French poets, was soon translated into Flemish, Italian, and English (by Chaucer), and influenced distinguished authors of the 14th century, including *Boccaccio, Chaucer, and the unknown author of *Sir *Gawain and the Green Knight*. It provided a limitless storehouse for later literary adapters and stirred up all manner of controversy in the 15th century. In the 16th century, its language was modernized by Clement Marot, who also provided a moral commentary for an exquisitely printed edition; and it was highly praised by the poets of the *Pléiade. This excitement alone is proof of its vitality.

romanticism: see *classicism; see *Romantic Movement.

Romantic Movement: the name given to the triumph of romanticism (see *classicism) in European and American literature during the first half of the 19th century. The Romantic Movement is the result of a deliberate revolt against the now impotent tradition of *Neo-Classicism. Furthermore, this revolt is carried on, in its early stages at least, as a definite campaign against the individual elements of the Neo-Classical tradition. Instead of portraying great or typical characters, writers would seek out lowly and eccentric ones. Instead of using an established type of lofty poetic diction, they would cultivate the everyday speech of actual people. Instead of confining themselves to a few established verse forms like the English *heroic couplet and the French *Alexandrine, they would experiment with every conceivable type of meter and stanza. Instead of trying to be objective, they would revel in their own unique personalities. Although they could not quite reject *classical antiquity, they would draw more of their inspiration from folk literature and the *Middle Ages. And they would overthrow the ideals of both conformity and decorum by openly—and rather enthusiastically—dealing with taboo themes like incest.

The beginnings of the Romantic Movement lie in various manifestations of Pre-Romanticism during the latter part of the period of *Neo-Classicism. The origins of the new literature can be traced in an interesting series of interrelationships involving France, Germany, and England; and it is not hard to grasp the general lines of the development. In 1750 *Rousseau had won a prize with an essay contending that unspoiled nature is good and that what passes for progress is actually corruption. This was the beginning of a literary career which never stopped meeting every cherished dogma of Neo-Classicism with a flat contradiction. The second paragraph of his last and most influential book, the *Confessions* (published 1781–88), contains a statement which might well serve as the battle cry of the entire Romantic Movement:

"I am not made like anyone I have seen; I dare believe that I am not made like anyone in existence. If I am not better, at least I am different." By the time these words were published, Rousseau's name was a household word in western Europe and his earlier works had already combined with the intellectual currents which had helped to produce them, to make a broadening stream of revolt. Folk literature was being collected in England and praised in Germany. In the early plays of *Goethe and *Schiller, the German theater was not only rejecting the Neo-Classical form for the Elizabethan (as *Lessing had urged) but was glorifying the typical romantic hero, the rebel. Goethe's *Werther* was giving an immense vogue to a type of self-pitying romantic sensibility. Other adherents of the *Sturm und Drang*, like Bürger, were writing new ballads, using the ancient ones as models. This movement in Germany in the 1770's did not lead directly to the Romantic Movement, although it is really a part of it. Goethe moved into a classical period, and Schiller's plays, while retaining many romantic features, became less revolutionary and more formal. The German trends, however, reacted on England and France. Romantic elements had been increasing in English literature for nearly half a century before the publication of *Wordsworth and *Coleridge's *Lyrical Ballads*, and especially the second edition with Wordsworth's *Preface* (1800), marked what may be called the official beginning of the Romantic Movement in England. By this time Coleridge had spent some time in Germany, and Wordsworth had been in France on the eve of the Revolution. In the later work of the English romantics we find German literature and philosophy of the *Sturm und Drang* and of the early 19th century as a large and overt influence on such writers as Coleridge, *Scott, *De Quincey, and *Carlyle. So prevalent was this German influence that it permeated even the works of writers who had no direct contact with it.

About the turn of the century, the Romantic Movement proper began in Germany with a large group of gifted writers. Although it had high achievements in almost all departments of literature, its greatest distinction lay in lyric poetry (Goethe, *Eichendorff, *Heine) and

636

in fantastic fiction. This latter type owed something to the vogue of the *Gothic novel but went considerably deeper both in its fantasy and in its humor. In this vein the writings of Jean Paul Richter and E.T.A. *Hoffmann had an international vogue and influence. During this period Germany also continued the work begun by *Herder in the collection of folk songs and began to collect folk tales and to lay the foundations for the study of *folklore as a form of literature.

As might be expected, the country which had produced Neo-Classicism had the greatest difficulty in throwing it off. Though Rousseau had in a way touched off the Romantic Movement, France was late in joining it. This delay may be partly due to the amount of energy that went into the political romanticism of the Revolution. However this may be, the fact remains that the beginnings lie in two books of Mme. de Staël, both written after the triumph of English romanticism. *On Literature* (*De la littérature*, 1800) sees a literature as the product of a society and hence strikes a heavy blow at the idea of unchanging rules and eternal principles. *On Germany* (*De l'Allemagne*, 1810) reveals the world of recent (romantic) German literature to France for the first time. In fact, one chapter, "On Classic and Romantic Poetry," is the first use of the words *classic* and *romantic* to designate two fundamentally different types of literature. These two books were "un-French" in their desire for change and their praise of a foreign—an enemy—culture: Mme. de Staël was banished from Paris for the first one and from France for the second. Nevertheless, the ideas in them made gradual progress, and the romantic triumph in France is dated from 1820 in poetry, with *Lamartine's *Les méditations poétiques*, and from 1830 on the stage, with Victor *Hugo's *Hernani*. Even this late, the stronghold of Neo-Classicism, the theater, did not fall without a struggle; and the "Battle of *Hernani*," with its public commotion and disorderly conduct in the theater, is an amusing chapter of French literary history.

At the height of the Romantic Movement the literary commerce among the nations of northern Europe was lively. Some aspects of this mutual influence have already been mentioned. Others include the tremendous vogue of *Byron on the Continent, where his influence extended as far as Russia (see *Pushkin), and the rapid spread and wide popularity of the historical novel after Scott practically invented it. One of the striking facts of the Romantic Movement is that the example of *Shakespeare dominated and revivified the theater in France and Germany, but that England (because it had already produced Shakespeare and the other dramatists of the Renaissance?) produced no theatrical works of any importance, though there were some distinguished poetic plays (by Byron and *Shelley, for example) intended primarily to be read rather than acted.

The Romantic Movement is at its greatest in lyric poetry, for romanticism is basically an emphasis on individuality, and the lyric is the ultimate in direct personal expression. Lyric poetry had not flourished under Neo-Classicism because of the strong tendency toward the submergence of the individual, but now it burst into a chorus probably never equaled in the world before. Many of the romantic poets are familiar names even to people who have never read them, as Wordsworth, Coleridge, Byron, Shelley, *Keats, and *Poe are to all English-speaking people. In the same way Goethe, Heine, Hugo, *Musset, Pushkin, *Mickiewicz, *Leopardi are invariably known in their own countries, and often beyond. In a similar vein, the familiar essay, especially in England, dealt with the author's own quirks and foibles and set out to give information about the writer's reaction to a subject rather than to the subject objectively considered. Charles *Lamb was the greatest master of this form, though *Hazlitt and De Quincey were also eminent.

The Romantic Movement centered in France, Germany, and England, but it spread to all of Europe and to the Western Hemisphere as well. Thus we find distinct Romantic Movements in countries like Italy, Poland, and Russia, though they are not always so intense or so clearly marked as the romanticism of the leading nations. The most interesting aspect of the diffusion of this literary school is its spread across the Atlantic. American literature had begun, of course, as a transplanted English literature in North America and a transplanted Spanish and Portuguese literature in Central and South America. After beginning an independent existence, the new literatures were for some time merely imitative. It takes a specialist or a chauvinist to develop much enthusiasm about Colonial American writing, though Latin America, with a much earlier start, did somewhat better. With the Romantic Movement, for the first time, the Americas, especially the United States, began to produce literature which, while fitting into the European spirit of the times, had enough power and originality to command attention and respect outside their own boundaries. Except for extraneous reasons (such as Benjamin *Franklin's personal popularity in France), the first American writers to make a European impression were the generation of *Cooper, Irving, *Hawthorne, Poe, *Longfellow, and *Emerson—the American Romantics.

International though it was, the Romantic Movement ends or fades out at various times and in different ways. In France it gave way before the middle of the century to *realism and then *naturalism in fiction and to Parnassianism and then *symbolism in poetry. In Germany it gradually gave way to realism in fiction and to the problem play in the theater, although in poetry it lasted, with some modifications, into the 20th century. In English literature it is customary to make a distinction between the Romantic Movement and the Victorian period, with the year 1832 as the dividing line, but the distinction is not very significant. Although the Victorian writers added some new elements such as humanitarian social ideals and a strait-laced sense of decorum, they are essentially a continuation of the earlier movement until about the end of the 19th century. American romanticism held sway until the time of the Civil War. Sometimes literary historians terminate it with the first edition of *Whitman's *Leaves of Grass* in 1855; sometimes they allow it to continue until the triumph of the local-color writers about 1870. Here again the shift is far from definite, for, in spite of a certain amount of realistic description, a man like Bret Harte is as complete a romantic as can be found. The essential shift in fiction comes with Stephen *Crane in the 1890's and with *Dreiser early in the 20th century. In spite of the more or less isolated figure of Whitman, American poetry was primarily romantic until the advent of the *Imagists about 1913 marked the rise of "modern" poetry.

From these various terminations of the Romantic Movement it is evident that no similarly international trend has followed it, though we can see a tendency for it to give way to some type of realism. It may be that we are still too close to distinguish the main current from the eddies and backwaters—or it may be that the general turbulence is such that there is no main current. However this may be, since the end of the Romantic Movement, the literary history of the Western World is a welter of transient and often conflicting trends and theories—of realism, naturalism, symbolism, imagism (see *Imagists), regionalism, *expressionism, *impressionism, *surrealism, *existentialism—and journalism. The "cult of nature," a worship of nature as almost a divinity, even in its oldest, harshest aspects of lightning, mountains, torrential streams, was to become one of the hallmarks of the Romantic Movement and to affect art, *e.g.*, Constable, Turner, *Ruskin, as well as literature.

Romeo and Juliet: a tragedy by *Shakespeare, probably his first (*c.* 1596). The play's subject matter, young love, and its setting, an Italian city-state, suggest romantic comedy rather than tragedy. However, Shakespeare turned the merely melodramatic plot which he inherited into an inevitably tragic action by maintaining complete sympathy for his hero and heroine, emphasizing the framing action of the family feud, and building up a foreboding atmosphere.

The foreboding atmosphere is not merely a matter of statements such as the Prologue's "star-cross'd lovers" and "their death mark'd love" or Romeo's misgivings of "Some consequence yet hanging in the stars" (I.iv.107) and Juliet's "ill-divining soul" (III.v.54); it permeates the language of the whole play, for the Capulet-Montague feud forces the reversal of certain key terms in the normal equations assumed by the lovers and the Elizabethan audience alike. Normally, day, light, order, good, life, and love would be equated, and they would be opposed, term for term, to night, dark, chaos, evil, death, and hate; but the family feud forces Romeo and Juliet to equate their love with night and ultimately with death, although they attempt, in the extensive lyrical passages for which the play is noted, to substitute the light of their love for the light of day (*e.g.*, Romeo's "Juliet is the sun . . ." and Juliet's "come Romeo; come, thou day in night . . ."). The public feud flares most hotly by day, whereas at night it is suspended in favor of the private, or rather necessarily secret, love action. Both the love and the hate are associated not only with light but with its destructive forms—fire, lightning, and the explosion of gunpowder—all of them appropriate to the violence, suddenness, and destructiveness of the action, which concludes with the restoration of order in Verona at the cost of the lives of the principal characters.

Besides, the pervasive conflict of love and hate, the play works with conflicts between various pairs of five different attitudes toward love and marriage. The parental attitude, which subordinates love to social convention, is most clearly exemplified in the Capulets. The bawdy jests of Mercutio, the Nurse, and the servants exemplify the earthy reduction of love to physical appetite. Friar Laurence represents the attitude of the church, although it must be pointed out that his speeches are not to be taken out of context and used to reduce the play to a simple moral allegory. Finally, there are the immature, romantic attitude of Romeo and Juliet themselves and their later mature, realistic attitude; both attitudes spiritualize their love as something holy (note the imagery of the famous kiss-sonnet when the lovers first speak to one another). The major stages in the growth of the lovers from adolescence to the maturity that makes them tragic rather than merely pathetic figures are marked by the passionate, oxymoronic outbursts from each when the family feud impinges on their love (I.i.183–189, spoken by Romeo while he is still in love with Rosaline, who is of the Capulet faction; and III.ii.73–82, spoken by Juliet upon learning that Romeo has killed Tybalt) and by the heroic resolution each acquires after their separation by Romeo's banishment. Their final resolutions, to be united in death, make even their suicides sympathetic.

The artificial contrivances of the plotting, especially in the last acts of the play, should be seen—as they would have been seen by Shakespeare's audiences, especially in the speed and intensity of performance—as ever greater ironies resulting from the love-hate situation rather than as technical ineptness on the part of the author or mere melodrama to be condemned for its lack of "truth to life." Like Shakespeare's other tragedies, perhaps like tragedy generally, *Romeo and Juliet* is not "true to life" as audiences expect or wish life to be; instead it is true to a vision of life as audiences fear it may indeed be.

Romulus and Remus: twin brothers, the sons of *Mars and Rhea Silvia, a Vestal Virgin; the mythical founders of Rome.

rondeau: a medieval French verse form, revived in the 19th and 20th centuries, primarily for light verse. The history of the rondeau is an almost exact parallel to that of the *ballade. Originally it was intended to be sung, and the musical form paralleled that of the verse. (The *rondo*, as a musical form, is the ultimate development in instrumental music.) There are a number of special forms of the rondeau, varying from eight to 14 lines, but the principle is the same in all: only two rimes are used, and the beginning of the poem must be repeated in the middle and at the end. The amount to be repeated varies from two or three lines to the first half line in one popular form (McCrae, *In Flanders' Fields*); sometimes, as in one example by *Villon, it may be only a single word. The triolet is a special eight-line form which repeats the first line in the middle and the first two at the end. In the best rondeaux, the grammar or meaning of the repeated section is usually shifted with each recurrence. The terms *rondel* and *roundel* have both been used as synonyms for *rondeau*.

Ronsard, Pierre de: French poet (1525–85). Ronsard was the preeminent poet of 16th-century France, celebrated for his odes, his love sonnets, and his leadership of the literary group known as the *Pléiade. Ironically, Ronsard turned to literature only because illness at the age of 16 left him too deaf to continue at the royal court the diplomatic career for which his birth, good looks, and personality had destined him. He plunged into the study of classical literature. A group of friends joined him in efforts to make a synthesis between classic models and French poetry, and du Bellay issued a statement of their aims, *Defense and Illustration of the French Language* (1549). In the following year appeared Ronsard's *Odes*. This collection of 94 odes was modeled in the main on *Pindar and *Horace. With their picturesque imagery, classical metaphors and allusions, metrical innovations, and rich rime, they exemplified the principles of du Bellay's essay and demonstrated that French was a vehicle capable of elevated lyric poetry. If the *Odes* lacked the complexity and real enthusiasm of their classical prototypes, they injected a new quality into French poetry by their elaborate and meticulous form. Then followed Ronsard's *Amours* (*Loves*, 1552), a collection of 181 sonnets, imitative of *Petrarch, yet occasionally revealing true passion. His *Hymns* (1555) were mythological and philosophical poems in praise of his patrons. These and other poems of this decade (1550–60) were modeled on Pindar, *Theocritus, Horace, *Vergil, and Petrarch, in part no doubt because Ronsard, with his *carpe diem attitude, shared their love of freedom and their joy in the sensuous and beautiful in life.

Ronsard enjoyed a meteoric rise to popularity. He boasted that he rivaled Pindar and surpassed Horace, and his contemporaries confirmed his self-evaluation. The years between 1560 and 1574, when he was official court poet to two successive French kings, mark the height of his fame. He wrote elegies and an unsuccessful epic, as well as ironic advice on the government of France. Ronsard was already a model for English writers and was to be increasingly imitated by them as well as by his own countrymen. His spirit and style lived on into the 17th century in Herrick's lyrics.

In his later years, when he had retired from public life, he turned from the themes of sensual love and youthful ardor to a more contemplative and elegiac view of life and of nature as a symbol of universal change. The note of melancholy became stronger, and to this period belong his memorable *Sonnets for Helen*, of which the most famous begins "When you grow old, at evening, in the candle-light." The English poets Landor and *Yeats have imitated Ronsard's use of this theme.

Ronsard survives as the greatest poet of the Pléiade. His poetic genius was equal to their theorizing, and he was able to introduce many new words and stylistic devices into a body of poetry which is effective rather than merely experimental. The subtleties of his versification inspired his fellow poets, and his consciousness of a classical tradition enabled him to write with a precision that made the serious lyric a French art form. His own lyric qualities were not equaled until the French romantic poets of the 19th century.

Rossetti, Dante Gabriel: English poet and painter (1828–82). Rossetti was one of the founders of the *Pre-Raphaelite Brotherhood and was well educated both in literary studies and in painting. As a painter he tended toward the illustration of literary subjects, and as a poet toward sensuous, and especially visual, description. His best sonnets and ballads, however, achieve a strong dramatic impact. His most successful poems are *The Blessed Damozel* (1847), the ballads *Sister Helen* (1870) and *The King's Tragedy* (1881), and the sonnet sequence *The House of Life* (1881). His translations from *Villon and from early Italian poets (*Dante and His Circle*, 1861) helped to enlarge the literary horizons of Victorian England.

Rousseau, Jean-Jacques: French writer (1712–78). Rousseau was one of those rare individuals who, by some strange alchemy, become the voice of mankind at a crucial moment in history. He told once, in a letter written to a friend, how he quite suddenly had the extraordinary inspiration that served to guide him to his triumphs in literature and philosophy. He had set out to visit his friend *Diderot, who had been jailed at Vincennes for one of his writings. Rousseau bought an issue of the *Mercure de France* and read it as he walked along the highway. He came upon an announcement that the Dijon Academy would bestow a prize for the best essay on whether manners had been improved and purified by the arts and sciences in France.

This subject sounds simple enough, but it seems to have aroused in Rousseau's mind a train of thought that was crucial. Manners, the role of man, the relation between environment and man's problems, all these thoughts for the first time in his vagabond life seemed to add up to a total, a sum, and that sum was to be reflected in all his future writings. He had not been a writer, but now he became one and carried off the Academy prize. The emotion and the inspiration had indeed been extraordinary. As he described it in his letter: "All at once I felt myself dazzled by a thousand sparkling lights; crowds of vivid ideas thronged into my head with a force and confusion that threw me into unspeakable agitation; I felt my head whirling in a giddiness like that of intoxication."

He said that he sat down under a tree to collect himself, so great had been the force of the emotion and the surge of ideas about the human state. When calm returned he discovered the front of his waistcoat was wet with tears he couldn't remember having shed. "Ah, if I could ever have written the quarter of what I saw and felt under that tree, with what clearness should I have brought out all the contradictions of our social system. . . ."

He was to write down much of what stemmed from these extraordinary moments of vision. Indeed, he was to write words that moved worlds. Many of the basic ideas in modern democracy stem from the rhetoric he first set down, and it was he who generated the *Romantic Movement in literature, which is still a great living force in the writing of our time. Neither a philosopher nor a literary man in the strict sense of the word, author of ideas often confused and ambiguous, he nevertheless was able to express certain inner feelings about man and society which corresponded to the feelings of his fellow men in the 18th century. In him they found dramatic utterance, and in his works they discovered the meaning of their hidden longings and their striving for betterment.

The man who had this singular experience and whose accomplishment was so remarkable was a vagabond, a strolling musician, one who often broke moral codes and led a life that hardly commends itself as that of an inspired thinker. Yet he cut his way through to certain homely truths that we today take for granted. In his time, however, they were revolutionary. He was the son of a Swiss watchmaker and was born in Geneva in 1712. Of French descent, he had a difficult childhood, but we know of it only from what he wrote in his *Confessions (Les Confessions)*. Some biographers feel that these contain an enlargement of the truth. But in the absence of documents no other version of Rousseau's early days exists. His candor, however, and the incidents he relates (whatever embellishment there may have been) do give us a picture of an unstable boyhood which foreshadowed the unstable life he was to lead. At times what he tells of himself is not flattering. When Jean-Jacques was ten he was placed under the teaching of a clergyman and then apprenticed to an engraver, from whom he ran away. He went to a little Catholic town nearby and there met Mme. de Warens, herself a recent convert to Catholicism, a woman of wealth and intellectual pretensions. She shipped the youth off to Turin to be converted, but he, in due course, abandoned the religious circles to become a lackey and then a tramp, wandering in and out of Switzerland and France and residing for a time in Paris. In the intervals between these wanderings he returned to Mme. de Warens and seems to have been her ward, her lover, and for a while the manager of her estates. It was she who made of him a student of music.

In 1741 he settled in Paris, where he remained, with interruptions, for the next 15 years, composing and teaching music, figuring in the salon of Mme. d'Épinay, and acquiring the friendship of Diderot. While thus moving in high circles he conceived an attachment for an ignorant scullery maid in the hotel where he stayed, Thérèse le Vasseur. According to his memoirs, she bore him five children. All were consigned to a foundling home.

The future author of a major treatise on education never had the problem of the education of his own children.

Rousseau had his great vision on the road to Vincennes in 1749, and the following year he submitted his discourse on the sciences and arts and their relation to manners to the Dijon Academy. He won the prize and became famous. Fame did not render this vagabond happy, nor did it bring him peace. Although he could have had excellent employment, he chose to continue his desultory life and supported himself by copying music. He presented an opera at the French court in 1752, and it was well received. He could have had a royal pension, but never went to court, and by this act spurned it. Instead he returned to Geneva in 1754 and re-embraced Calvinism. In 1755 he published his second discourse, *On the Origin of Inequality (Discours sur l'origine et les fondements de l'inégalité parmi les hommes)*, and although it did not win a prize, it proved to be extremely popular.

For several years Rousseau lived with Thérèse le Vasseur in the Hermitage, a cottage provided by his patroness, Mme. d'Épinay, and it was here that he wrote most of *The New Eloise (Julie, ou la nouvelle Héloïse)*. In 1757, after a series of bitter quarrels, he broke with Diderot and his patroness and retired to a cottage near the forest of Montmorency. Here he achieved his greatest work. He completed *Eloise* (published in 1761), and wrote **Emile (Emile ou de l'éducation)* and *The Social Contract (Le Contrat social)*, both of which appeared in 1762. These two last works were condemned in Paris, and Rousseau accepted the generous offer of asylum in England made to him by the philosopher David Hume. In 1766 he arrived in London. There he met **Boswell and was lionized by British society. Once again a royal pension seemed likely, and once again Rousseau's conduct cut short the opportunity. Suffering from feelings of persecution, he broke with Hume and, returning to the Continent, made new friends, only to break with them. In England he had written the greater part of his *Confessions*. In 1770 he was back in Paris copying music for a living. A new patron installed him in a house at

Ermenonville, where he lived, his mind unsettled, until his death in 1778. The ideas he had launched continued to gain force and became the core of Jacobin thinking during the French Revolution.

In essence Rousseau argued that the "natural man" is happy and good and that society, which abuses the benefits of civilization, tends to deprave him. He preached the recognition of man's true nature. These ideas represented Rousseau's revolt against the indifference to human misery shown by the feudal aristocrats of his age and his hatred of his dependency upon them for patronage. His expression of them led to the enunciation, in bold rhetoric, of a theory of the rights of all men. "No citizen should be rich enough to buy another, and none so poor that he is obliged to sell himself" was one of the declarations of the *Social Contract*. Its opening sentence is: "Man is born free; and everywhere he is in chains." And while great thinkers could pick flaws and illogicalities in Rousseau's theorizing, they could not stop the force of his rhetoric, for he spoke the language of the heart. "In *Voltaire," said *Goethe, "we see the end of a world; in Rousseau the beginning of a new one."

Rousseau's "infinite introspections amid the solitudes of the heart" of which Lytton Strachey speaks were new to the 18th century, and although the Encyclopedists and Voltaire, who placed reason above the heart, disagreed with Rousseau, the multitude of his readers did not. They responded to his glorification of "sensibility," "feeling," "passion." It may be said that he inspired a new cult: "I feel, therefore I am." (cf. Descartes, "I think, therefore I am.") Today *The New Eloise* seems like a tedious and long-winded novel to some of its readers: but women two hundred years ago rushed to buy it and with palpitation read the love story in it. In the *Confessions* Rousseau accomplished what other men had feared to do: he talked of his intimate self, of the inner workings of his spirit. Unashamedly he spoke of matters—such as his sexual experiences—which men hitherto had preferred to bury in silence and forgetfulness. Uneducated in any formal sense, he nevertheless wrote a great book on education. Long before our psychologically aware era, he was a shrewd psychologist. A man of paradox, a bundle of contradictions, he nevertheless enunciated a bundle of truths.

His eloquence and his insistence upon the thoughtful man and the man of natural feelings, and upon the importance of the individual influenced the literature of Germany, France, and England. His writings not only helped to touch off the French Revolution but led, says Morley, to "that glow of enthusiastic feeling in France" which brought French aid to the American Revolution. Rousseau was a man who had a sense of his own unusual mind in the society of his time. That is why he wrote some of the most persuasive books ever set down in the Western world.

Ruskin, John: English art critic and social critic (1819–1900). Ruskin's life and work were colored by a thorough knowledge of the King James Bible and a need to be sheltered from the rough and tumble of ordinary life—both due to his mother. He began his literary career with excellent textbooks on drawing and perspective and went on to criticism of art in *Modern Painters* (1846–60). This work, which defended modernism in art, and especially the work of Turner, began to appear anonymously but was completed under Ruskin's name. It is now appreciated that his unique genius lay in his understanding and defense of a new art, with its emphasis upon light instead of forms, on color instead of picturesque people. Turner heralds Monet and *Impressionism. In the past Ruskin's most important work had been considered his sharp criticism of Victorian society, which he regarded as immoral in its acquisitiveness, materialism, and exploitation. Much of this work was in the form of lectures, collected and published after delivery. Among the works of social criticism are *Unto This Last* (1860–62), *The Crown of Wild Olive* (1866), *Sesame and Lilies* (1871), *Munera Pulveris* (1872), and *Fors Clavigera* (1871–84). Ruskin represented the extreme form of the point of view that art is essentially and inevitably moral, that art is conditioned by the morality of its producers, that a bad man cannot write a good book. This idea is applied to architecture in *The Seven Lamps of Architecture* (1849) and *The Stones of Venice* (1851–53) and to literature in various works. Ruskin also left an unfinished autobiography, *Praeterita* (1885–89). His views on the arts were widely influential, especially as a counterpoise to the opposite and equally extreme views of the cult of "art for art's sake." A great many of his proposed social reforms have been widely adopted and are now taken as matters of course.

Sa'di (also Sadi, Saadi): Persian poet and mystic (1194–1282 or 1292). Of the many works of Sa'di, the best known are a profound moralizing poem, the *Bustan* ("Fruit Garden," 1257) and a miscellany in rhymed prose, the *Gulistan* ("Rose Garden," 1258). One of the wittiest passages in this latter work tells how, on a visit to the Holy Land, he was captured by the Crusaders and held until ransomed. The *Gulistan* contains many aphorisms covering every aspect of public and private life. These epigrams have become popular proverbs in their own land. Sa'di's works have been frequently quoted and paraphrased in the West, notably by *Goethe and *Emerson.

saga: any medieval Icelandic prose narrative. The word means, literally, "a saying" and thus records the fact that many of the sagas were handed down by oral tradition for some time before they were written down, generally in the 12th and 13th centuries. Sagas deal with European Scandinavian kings; with the earlier histories of Icelandic individuals, families, and districts; with notables contemporary with the authors. Many of the sagas of these types are sober and accurate history, and others, like *The Saga of Grettir the Strong (Grettis Saga)*, consist of history ornamented with folklore. There are also two types of nonhistorical sagas: those dealing with a legendary past, such as the *Volsung Saga*; and those which are merely translations of foreign romances.

The best sagas are remarkable literary works. They are written in a bald, simple, factual prose, and the author does not intrude with explanations or interpretations. He tells simply what any eyewitness would have seen and heard, putting it down in simple sentences in the order in which it occurred. Yet this matter-of-fact telling of a tale is highly artistic and succeeds in producing a suspense and emotional impact often lacking in works which seem to try for them much harder. (Some of Ernest *Hemingway's short stories seem to be not-too-successful attempts to imitate the sagas.)

Most of the sagas are available in good translations. One of the best and most widely read, in addition to those already mentioned, is *The Story of Burnt Njal (Njáls Saga)*.

In recent times the term *saga* has sometimes been applied to any fictional history involving several generations of a family. Sometimes it is the title of a series of novels, as in John *Galsworthy's *The Forsyte Saga* (1906–21).

Sainte-Beuve, Charles Augustin: French critic and writer (1804–69). The great French literary critic Sainte-Beuve was successively the spokesman for the *Romantic Movement, the initiator of a biographical-psychological school of criticism that studied a work of literature through the personality and individuality of the author, and the popularizer of a "social" criticism that (like *naturalism in the novel) emphasized the family, social, and historical background in which an author wrote, as well as his literary and philosophic environment. Sainte-Beuve was studying medicine when a former teacher, now a newspaper editor, invited him to contribute some literary articles (1824). When these pieces on the romantic tendencies of the 16th century were printed as *Historical Sketch of French Poetry in the Sixteenth Century (Tableau de la poésie française au 16ème siècle*, 1827), they established Sainte-Beuve as the leading expositor of Romanticism. During the following years he was the sympathetic critic of the Romantics, introducing, formulating, and legitimating their theories while trying to moderate their excesses. He wrote brilliant analyses of *Chateaubriand, *Musset, *Hugo, *Vigny. In addition to his critical books and articles, he wrote a somewhat autobiographical novel and collections of verse. His best-known poetry is *The Book of Love* (*Le Livre d'amour*, 1843), a recounting with painful frankness of his early love affair with Victor Hugo's wife. His novel, *Volupté* (1834), strikes a reader today as surprisingly modern.

His critical articles to the number of a thousand fill 48 volumes. The most famous are the weekly articles *Causeries du Lundi* ("Monday Chats," 1851–62) and *Nouveaux Lundis* ("New Mondays," 1863–70), the *Literary Portraits* (*Portraits littéraires*, 1862–64), and *Contemporary Portraits* (*Portraits contemporains*, 1869–71). The basic standards he employed in his mature criticism were taste, truth to life, and artistic unity. His ideas were developed in a style of great charm, with urbanity and ironic humor; and his studies were enriched by his diversified use of religion, science, politics, and history to deepen critical analysis. The best known of his critical essays is *What Is a Classic?* (*Qu'est-ce qu'un classique?*, 1850).

Sand, George: pseudonym of Amandine Aurore Dupin, French novelist (1804–76). After a marriage of convenience by which she had two children, George Sand left her husband and embarked on a variegated career. Amid a series of notorious love affairs (with Alfred de *Musset and Frédéric Chopin, among others), she continued to pour forth novels as if, she herself said, "from a faucet." Their themes are passion, free love, and the "misunderstood woman" (1832–40); social and humanitarian ideas (1840–48); nature and bucolic scenes (1849–70). The social novels, although superficial and slowed up by too much declamation on their theses, have importance because of the problems that they introduced. The pastoral novels, written after Sand had returned to her native province, are the century's best French stories of country life because of their sense of reality, their love of nature, and their sympathetic understanding of simple people. Among her more interesting works are *Lélia* (1833), *Consuelo* (1842–43), *La Mare au diable* (1846), and *Elle et lui* (her version of her affair with Musset, 1859).

Sangreal: see *Holy Grail.

Sapphic (also Sapphic stanza): a four-line stanza named from its use by the Greek poetess *Sappho. Each of the first three lines consists of two trochees, a dactyl, and two more trochees; the last line is shorter and is made up of a dactyl and a trochee. The most successful English use of this stanza is in the *Sapphics* of *Swinburne, a stanza of which will illustrate the form:

> By the gray sea-side, unassuaged, unheard of,
> Unbeloved, unseen in the ebb of twilight,
> Ghosts of outcast women return lamenting,
>   Purged not in Lethe.

Sappho: Greek lyric poetess (born *c.* 615 B.C.). On her native island, Lesbos, Sappho gathered around her a group of girls interested in poetry and organized perhaps as a cult in honor of *Aphrodite. With these girls she seems to have spent much of her life; certainly she felt a deep affection for them and composed many of her poems in their honor. Sappho was married and had a daughter Cleis, whose name survives in a famous fragment. Besides these few facts, little of any importance is known of her life, for, though tradition wove many tales about her, they are altogether improbable. In particular, the story of her love for a young man named Phaon and her leap from a cliff into the sea when he rejected her is fiction.

Sappho's poems are *monodies*, that is, songs for a single voice; their favorite theme is love and their occasion typically some event important to the writer, as, for example, the marriage of one of the girls in her group. Sappho's poems carry the personal lyric to the highest point it attained in ancient Greece and perhaps in all Western literature. They are unique, not only for the intensity of the emotion they express and the truth with which they express it, but for their simple, though tempestuous, language, their absolutely perfect form, their exquisite melody, and the profound feeling for the beauty of the world which they reveal.

These qualities can be clearly seen even in the meager fragments of Sappho's work now extant, and they justify the praise lavished on her by all antiquity. But they depend on combinations of sense and sound hard to transfer to another language and on intricate metrical forms utterly foreign to English. Occasionally, it is true, something of the original effect can be captured, as in *Rossetti's translation of the lines on a young bride who is "Like the sweet apple which reddens upon the topmost bough, / A-top on the topmost twig,—which the pluckers forgot somehow,— / Forgot it not, nay, but got it not, for none could get it till now." But these successes are brief fragments. The two longer poems extant have proved the despair of every translator who has attempted them: the *Ode to Anactoria*, in which Sappho is overcome by emotion as she gazes at a young bride who sits laughing next to her bridegroom, and the *Ode to Aphrodite*, beginning "Throned in splendor, immortal Aphrodite, / Wile-weaving child of Zeus, I supplicate you, / Break not my heart with suffering and sorrow. . . ."

Sartre, Jean-Paul: French philosopher, novelist, and dramatist (1905–80). Sartre was born in Paris, studied at the École Normale Supérieure from 1924 to 1929, and taught philosophy at Le Havre in 1931. In 1932, he studied in Berlin. Returning to France, Sartre taught for a few more years in French lycées; following the end of the Second World War he devoted himself exclusively to writing.

As a philosopher, Sartre is indebted to Husserl and Heidegger. However, his own version of *existentialism constitutes an original philosophical system. It rests on the premise that "God is dead"; therefore atheism is a necessary basis for ethics. In Sartre's view, man's destiny is not predetermined, and there is no universal moral law; thus, as a moral agent, man is free; indeed he is condemned to freedom, so that his commitment remains his own choice and responsibility. He cannot, however, exist as an individual without recognizing the role played by others in his own evaluation of himself.

Sartre has applied his philosophical tenets to the place of the writer in modern society. His conclusion is that artistic creation must be a moral activity and that literature, if it is to exist at all, has to be committed.

Sartre's early psychological essays, *Outline of a Theory of the Emotions* (*Esquisse d'une théorie des émotions*, 1939) and *The Psychology of Imagination* (*L'Imaginaire: psychologie phénoménologique de l'imagination*, 1940) remained relatively unnoticed; but his first novel, *Nausea* (*La Nausée*, 1938), and his collection of short stories, *Intimacy* (*Le Mur*, 1938), brought him immediate recognition. Both works dramatize the existentialist notions of alienation and commitment, and of redemption through art.

In his major philosophical work, *Being and Nothingness* (*L'Etre et la néant*, 1943), Sartre explores the condition of man with regard to himself, the exterior world, and other individuals. He popularized these preoccupations in his essay *Existentialism* (*L'Existentialisme est un humanisme*, 1946) and illustrated them in his trilogy of novels, *The Roads to Freedom* (*Les Chemins de la liberté*, 1945-1949).

Sartre's central notion of the committed writer is made clear in his plays, which deal with moral issues without being *pièces à thèse*. In *The Flies* (*Les Mouches*, 1943), the young killer's freedom is pitted against the powerless Jupiter. *No Exit* (*Huis Clos*, 1947) presents hell as the inescapable but necessary judgment of others. Sartre wrote numerous critical essays, including two full-length studies on *Baudelaire (1947) and Jean Genêt (1952). A biography of his early years, *The Words (Les Mots)*, appeared in 1964. He was awarded the Nobel prize in 1964, but declined it.

satire: a term applied to any form of literature whose manner is a blend of criticism, wit, and ironic humor and whose immediate aim is the ridicule or rebuke of someone or something. The target may be anything from a philosophical system (*Voltaire's *Candide*) or a social evil like hypocrisy (*Molière's *Tartuffe*) to an individual person (*Dryden's *Mac Flecknoe*). It is often maintained that the ultimate purpose of satire is to reform society by exposing its vices. If that be true, in the long run a satire can be a literary success only by being a sociological failure. If *Tartuffe* had put an end to religious hypocrisy, it would now be a "dated" piece; but it is still effective and interesting because religious hypocrites still flourish.

Satire can take almost any literary form and use various approaches and techniques. Often there are specific references to topical and political subjects, concrete descriptions, realistic pictures of the seamy side of a society or a personality—sometimes scurrility or obscenity. Nevertheless, a sharp line can be drawn between invective or mere insult and satire. If *Pope had written, "No matter how hard you try, you can't write anything intelligent," he would have been merely insulting. But when he writes, "You beat your pate and fancy wit will come: / Knock as you please, there's nobody at home," he is being satirical. The difference lies in the wit of the presentation, which is an essential quality of satire. This is not a literary convention, but a psychological truth. We may defy or curse things that we fear, but we do not laugh at them. To laugh at something is a sign of the laugher's feeling of superiority. Hence the satirist makes his attack without doing his victim the honor of taking him seriously. A very fat, very drunk man might inspire disgust or revulsion or moral indignation, but when Dryden describes the "Og" of *Absalom and Achitophel* as "rolling home" from the tavern, "Round as a globe, and liquored every chink," Dryden makes himself superior to Og: we laugh *with* Dryden *at* Og. Satire is not necessarily "funny." It may be bitter, as in *Swift's *A Modest Proposal*, in which the exploitation of Ireland and the resultant poverty of the peasants, who cannot feed their children, are attacked under cover of a proposal that Irish children should be bred for the English market, to be butchered and eaten—thus providing income for their parents and saving the children from lives of misery. Even here, however, the principle is the same: it is a grim jest, but the fact that Swift can jest gives him a certain superiority.

Satire appears in every period of literature—among the Greeks in *Aristophanes, among the Romans in *Martial, *Petronius, and the greatest of them, *Horace and *Juvenal. The concentrated satirical lyric, with frequent epigrammatic lines, is said to be the only form of poetry invented by the Romans. In the *Middle Ages the *beast epic, *fabliau, and certain forms of *allegory (e.g., *Romance of the Rose) were popular types used to convey satire. The *picaresque novel, *Erasmus' Praise of Folly, the novels of *Rabelais and *Cervantes are striking examples of *Renaissance satire. The *Neo-Classicism of the 17th and 18th centuries marks a high-water mark of modern satire composed according to the Roman manner; such are the verse satires of Dryden, *Boileau (Les Satires, 1666), and Pope (Rape of the Lock, Dunciad). Satire appears also in the writings of Steele and *Addison, Swift, *Fielding, Voltaire. In the 19th century the most famous satirists were *Byron in England, *Mark Twain in America, and Anatole *France in France. Among the outstanding satirists writing in English during the 20th century were Sinclair *Lewis, James Thurber, E. B. White, and C. S. Lewis.

satyr-play: a form of grotesque Greek play dealing with an absurd part of a myth or treating a serious part in a burlesque fashion. The name comes from the fact that the chorus were dressed as satyrs, the part-man, part-beast followers of *Dionysus. The satyr-play was largely buffoonery, frequently reinforced by obscenity. In Periclean Athens the regular entry in the dramatic competitions consisted of three tragedies and a satyr-play. The only one of these plays which survives entire is the Cyclops of *Euripides.

Schiller (Johann Christian) Friedrich: German dramatist (1759–1805). Schiller was the first German dramatist to gain a hearing abroad—over 200 translations of his individual dramas were published in English between 1792 and 1900. In 19th-century Germany he was not only the representative of high drama but also the most popular poet of the middle class; he has remained to this day the favorite poet of the German schools. He owes this popularity to three qualities: the fervent idealism of his thought, the sonorous pathos of his style, and the prevalence of the theme of freedom in all his works.

Schiller was a superior craftsman, schooled in the Mannheim and Weimar theaters. Inspired primarily by the conflict and tension which existed within his own high-strung character, he created in each of his nine dramas a masterwork. He composed his first drama, *The Robbers* (*Die Räuber*, 1781), while he was an unwilling student in the military academy of the Duke of Württemberg. After its great success, the duke forbade him to continue writing, but Schiller made a sensational escape across the frontier—an action considered high treason. The robbers are a band of young noblemen and students who withdraw to the Bohemian Forests to strive for the betterment of society. Their leader, the warm-hearted Karl Moor, has been supplanted at home by his brother Franz, an envious, spiteful, and destructive person. Karl, too much of an idealist, uses criminal means to attain good ends; he robs the rich in order to give to the poor. This drama, unrestrained in language and form, was the climax of the turbulent *Sturm und Drang* movement of the young generation of German authors. But *Love and Intrigue* (*Kabale und Liebe*, 1784), Schiller's only middle-class tragedy, still championed "Storm and Stress" ideas. The dramatic tension is created by the steadily growing social conflict between the aristocracy and the rising bourgeoisie of the time.

The central period of Schiller's life is flanked by the two dramas *Don Carlos* (1787) and *Wallenstein* (1800). Schiller becomes the herald of a new kind of human being—an individual who attains perfection by the pursuit of moral duty. In each drama it is not the hero, but a contrasting character (Marquis Posa, Max Piccolomini), who becomes the representative of this concept. Schiller arrived at these ideas by a laborious self-discipline, first through the study and writing of history (*History of the Revolution of the Netherlands*, 1787; *History of the Thirty Years War*, 1791; professorship of history at the University of Jena, 1789–99), then through the study of the works of Kant. It was this study that made

Schiller the dramatic spokesman of the philosophy called "German idealism." He came to believe that art or aesthetic beauty is the mediator between the sensual and the spiritual. Through aesthetics, man can learn to discipline his natural inclination and thus develop his instinct for that which is right and good until it becomes inherent in him, *i.e.*, until *duty* becomes a *habit*. The drama—because of its possibilities of combining poetry with didacticism—seemed to Schiller the most suitable manifestation of art to convey his ideas to the public. Thus, the process of winning spiritual freedom from the bonds nature inflicts upon man becomes the underlying idea in Schiller's classical dramas. But before embodying it in his later dramas he formulated it in several essays, of which the *Letters on Aesthetic Education* (1795) and *On Naïve and Sentimental Poetry* (1796) are most famous.

Although his whole life was a struggle against poverty and the last five years were embittered by his battle with tuberculosis (he died at 45), the last ten were enriched by his friendship with *Goethe, in rivalry with whom he wrote poetry, especially ballads; it was Goethe who made him move to Weimar. In the last dramas, the influence of Goethe the realist is noticeable only insofar as they strive for a synthesis between the realistic and the idealistic, the antique and the modern, the rational and the romantic, and for a harmony between content and form. It is this synthesis or harmony which has been called "classical." His last dramas, indeed all after *Don Carlos*, are in blank verse; only in the early days did Schiller use prose.

In *Mary Stuart* (1801), Mary of Scotland as a tragic heroine achieves true greatness by overcoming in her mind the injustice she suffers from Elizabeth of England. Willingly she goes to her death on the scaffold, convinced that God has given her this chance to atone for her past sin, the murder of her husband. Thus, Mary has freed herself of her nature and has gained complete spiritual freedom.

In the "romantic tragedy," *The Maid of Orleans* (*Die Jungfrau von Orleans*, 1802), Joan of Arc cannot reach a higher level of understanding until she first experiences all that which she must overcome. She must renounce all claims to human happiness. Her strong will—symboli-

659

cally represented by the breaking of the chains that imprison her in the enemy's fortress—helps her transcend her physical nature. Having thus attained the highest degree of spiritual and moral freedom, Joan is able to save her people from the tyranny of the invader. Her death on the battlefield is the triumph of moral will, the victory of the spirit over the senses. It was Schiller who rehabilitated Joan of Arc, who had been portrayed as a witch by *Shakespeare *(Henry VI)* and ridiculed by *Voltaire *(La Pucelle)* as the French national saint.

It was Schiller also who gave the Swiss their national festival play, *William Tell* (1805), a drama dealing with their struggle to gain—or rather to preserve—their liberty, the hero representing the united spirit of a freedom-loving nation. This drama, together with *Don Carlos*, was the political legacy of Schiller to the liberal and democratic movements of the 19th century.

What has kept Schiller alive on the German stage (in the 1900's he ranked first, before Shakespeare and *Hauptmann; in the 1920's second, between Shakespeare and Goethe) is less the rigorous idealism of his thought than the eminently stage-worthy and colorful action of all his plays. Although *Kleist had a more powerful dramatic gift, *Grillparzer a subtler psychology, *Hebbel a more profound philosophy, and Hauptmann a greater fecundity in the creation of characters, Schiller surpassed them all in that his work shows a synthesis of all these qualities. What has kept him alive in world literature, however, is his rare combination of critic and creator. He was a conscious poet capable of giving articulate accounts of his tendencies in profound treatises; he was a thinker able to translate his theories fully into living works of art. And, whereas the 19th century had no doubt that his lasting contribution lay in his dramas and poems, the critics of the 20th asked whether he has not an equally lasting monument in his essays or in his *Correspondence* with Goethe.

Schopenhauer, Arthur: German philosopher (1788–1860). Schopenhauer spent a good deal of his childhood in France and England. After some ventures in business and a period of tutoring, he spent almost the last 30 years of his life in more or less solitary seclusion at Frankfurt. The basic work of his philosophy, *The World as Will and Idea (Die Welt als Wille und Vorstellung)*, appeared in 1819 but attracted no attention. Much the same thing happened with *Will in Nature* (*Uber den Willen in der Natur*, 1836) and *The Two Basic Problems of Ethics* (*Die beiden Grundprobleme der Ethik*, 1841). By 1851, however, the pessimism which Schopenhauer had been expressing for more than 30 years was the prevailing mood, and his final book, a collection of essays entitled *Parerga und Paralipomena*, at last secured serious attention and even a measure of popularity for his views.

Schopenhauer considered that the visible and phenomenal world is not reality but only idea *(Vorstellung)* and that the ultimate reality, both in the universe and in man, is the will. But the will is put into action only by a deficiency or a feeling of some lack—in other words, by a form of suffering. Struggle involves suffering, but the absence of any struggle involves tedium, which is also a form of suffering. The only alternative to suffering is the abandonment of the "will to live," or nonexistence.

Schopenhauer's pessimism did not remain a merely academic theory, primarily because he was a master of effective and impassioned prose, so that he communicated not merely a philosophy, but a personal reaction to the miseries of existence. For this reason he is as much a literary figure as a philosopher. The important place which his philosophy assigned to the arts was another feature of especial interest to 19th-century Germany. Since the 1850's he has been a pervasive literary influence, especially on such men as Wagner, *Nietzsche, *Mann, and *Gide.

Scott, Sir Walter: English novelist, poet, and antiquarian (1771–1832). Scott was educated for the law and practiced for some time, while collecting popular ballads as a private interest. His activities gradually shifted to literature and he became famous for his adventure stories in verse. Later he went over to the novel (writing anonymously at first, so as not to get by on his reputation as a poet). In recognition of his literary work he was made a baronet in 1819. In 1826 a publishing firm in which Scott was a partner failed. Though he could have gone bankrupt, paid his creditors a few pence on the pound, and recouped his own fortunes with his next books, he chose to assume the full indebtedness and wrote feverishly for the rest of his life to pay it off.

Scott's literary importance is impressive in three different fields—the study of ballads, the poem of action, and the historical novel. His *Minstrelsy of the Scottish Border* (3 vols., 1802–03) is not a mere hobbyist's collection but a work of pioneer scholarship. With its historical researches into the events which gave rise to the ballads, its publication of variant versions and study of their significance, and its careful comparative and historical method generally, it laid the foundations of the serious study of folk poetry.

Scott's interest in both Scottish antiquities and the ballads which recorded them led him to try his own hand at narrative poems of adventure and action with historical settings. His three outstanding successes in this type—which he practically created—were *The Lay of the Last Minstrel* (1805), *Marmion* (1808), and *The Lady of the Lake* (1810). These and other similar poems made Scott a great reputation as one of the leading poets of his time. He abandoned this type of writing, however, because, as he said, *Byron had begun to do the same sort of thing much better. Probably also he was beginning to tire of the limitations of the adventure tale in verse.

Waverley, a novel which Scott had begun some years before, was completed and anonymously published in 1814. Scott's anonymity was maintained until the failure in 1826, the subsequent novels appearing as "by the author of Waverley," and hence Scott's novels are often collectively called "the *Waverley* novels." Some of the more widely read ones are *Old Mortality* (1816), *Rob Roy* (1817), *The Heart of Midlothian* (1818), *Ivanhoe* (1819—one of three novels published during that year, all dictated while Scott was too ill to sit up and write), and *Kenilworth* (1821). During Scott's last years there was some decline in the quality of his work under the pressure of his prodigious activity, but he accomplished enough literary work for several lifetimes, in addition to capably holding various official positions. He published biographies, editions of *Swift and *Dryden, tales, lyric poetry, and various antiquarian and historical studies. In fact, while the authorship of the *Waverley* novels was still a secret, Scott was sometimes suspected, but it was always argued that he was doing so much other work that he could not possibly have time to be secretly writing novels.

In the *Waverley* series, Scott practically invented the historical novel. It promptly spread all over Europe and has remained one of the most popular literary types right up to the present. Furthermore, it has remained essentially as Scott created it, with its historical minor characters and fictitious principal ones, its historical color in speech and costume, its crowds and sweep and pageantry, its emphasis on suspense and action rather than subtlety or analysis. Both at its best and at its worst, Hollywood owes a great debt to Scott.

So does world literature. Scott removed the ballad from the province of sentimental nostalgia and unrealistic idealization of the folk element and placed it in a context of historical and literary knowledge. He created a type of verse narrative which, taken up by Byron, spread as far afield as Russia and *Pushkin. And, finally, he invented, in the historical novel, one of the principal types of fiction, both "literary" and popular, of the past 125 years.

Scylla: see *Charybdis.

Seferis, George: Greek poet and 1963 Nobel prizewinner (1900–71), a diplomat whose real name is Georgios Seferiadis. He studied law and early became involved in diplomacy. He was Greek ambassador to London 1957–62. His earliest poems in 1931 won him wide fame, and he has been translated into many languages. He has also translated T. S. *Eliot into Greek. He brought to Greek verse great complexity but a directness of statement in the modern idiom, a profound feeling for his country's past, and a melancholy which at the same time is highly humane and sensual. His *Poems*, translated by Rex Warner, appeared in 1960.

Seneca, Lucius Annaeus: Roman dramatist and essayist (*c.* 4 B.C.–A.D. 65). The Stoic philosopher Seneca was born at Cordoba in southern Spain but was educated at Rome, where for a time, during Nero's reign, he was the virtual ruler of the Empire. As a writer he is now remembered chiefly for his philosophical essays, among which the *Epistulae morales (Moral Letters)* is probably the most interesting. But he also composed tragedies on the familiar themes of Greek mythology, which, though little read today, were much admired at the time of the *Renaissance and exercised considerable influence on European drama. His plays are marked by a certain cultivation of horror for its own sake and the habitual use of condensed, pithy, usually moralizing sayings *(sententiae)*. Seneca left behind a slight work, sometimes studied as an example of Roman satire, lampooning the deification of Claudius, and implying by its title *Apocolocyntosis* that the dead emperor had been turned, not into a god, but into a pumpkin. Seneca was charged with treason and forced to commit suicide, A.D. 65. His death is described in the *Annals* of the Roman historian *Tacitus.

seven arts, the: the core of the medieval university curriculum, consisting of the *trivium* (threefold way) and the *quadrivium* (fourfold way). The *trivium*—grammar (of Latin), rhetoric (including public speaking), logic— occupied the four-year course of study for the A.B. degree. The *quadrivium*—arithmetic, music, geometry, and astronomy—supplied the subjects of the three-year course leading to the M.A. The threefold way to eloquence and the fourfold way to knowledge together made up the seven liberal arts.

seven deadly sins: pride, envy (which includes malice in general), wrath, lust (or lechery), gluttony, avarice (or covetousness), and sloth. Pride, the sin of Satan, was the worst. These sins are deadly because they entail spiritual death unless they are atoned for by repentance. They appear as allegorical figures in innumerable theological, literary, and artistic works of the *Middle Ages, and they determine not only the themes but the sevenfold structure of many works or parts of works (*Dante, *The *Divine Comedy*; Gower, *Confessio Amantis*).

seven virtues: the four cardinal (or temporal) virtues of the Greeks—justice, temperance, fortitude (courage), and prudence (wisdom)—plus the three Christian (or theological) virtues—faith, hope, love (charity). The four temporal virtues are analyzed in Book IV of *Plato's **Republic.* On one level of meaning, *Dante's *Purgatory* (in his *Divine Comedy) is organized around the seven virtues.

seven wonders of the ancient world: the Pyramids of Egypt, the Hanging Gardens of Babylon, the statue of *Zeus by Phidias at Olympia, the Temple of *Artemis (Diana) at Ephesus, the Tomb (mausoleum) of Mausolus at Halicarnassus, the Colossus (statue of *Apollo) at Rhodes, the Pharos (lighthouse) at Alexandria.

Shakespeare, William: English dramatist and poet (1564–1616). Although there are gaps in the biography of Shakespeare—as in the lives of most Elizabethan dramatists—the principal facts about him are clearly established by unimpeachable contemporary testimony and documents. He was baptized in the parish church of Stratford-on-Avon on April 26, 1564. As his father was a prominent citizen of the town, it is usually assumed that he attended the excellent local grammar school. We next hear of him in 1582, when a special action made it possible for him to marry Ann Hathaway (eight years older than he) without delay. The reason is clear enough: five months later their daughter Susanna was born. The twins Hamnet and Judith followed after two years.

We do not know just when Shakespeare went to London, nor in what capacity he was first connected with the theater, although there are unverified and unconvincing legends on both points. Three professional theaters were operating in London, but we know very little of either their business or their offerings until about 1592, which is the year of the first public mention of Shakespeare. At this time he had won enough success as a playwright to provoke a malicious comment from another dramatist, Robert Greene. After this there are many records of his activities as dramatist, actor, and businessman. In addition to turning out a steady stream of plays, he won himself a reputation as a narrative poet with *Venus and Adonis* (1593), a work which was popular enough to go through nine reprintings within a few years. Another narrative poem, *The Rape of Lucrece*, appeared a year later. After a few other minor poems, Shakespeare's standing as a lyric poet was established in 1609 by the publication of 154 *Sonnets*, probably written, for the most part, between 1593 and 1598.

In 1594 Shakespeare was one of the organizers of the Lord Chamberlain's Company, a theatrical firm in which he played the triple role of actor, shareholder, and playwright. In 1599 this company built its own theater, The Globe; and when James I came to the throne in 1603 it came directly under royal patronage and consequently changed its name to The King's Company (informally called The King's Men). Various records show that Shakespeare prospered. In 1596 he obtained an official coat-of-arms in his father's name, a grant which allowed him the use of the arms and the title of "Gentleman." In 1597 he bought New Place, one of the finest houses in Stratford; this was the first of a number of purchases of houses and land both in Stratford and in London. Early in 1598, when there was some shortage of food, a survey of stocks showed that Shakespeare had large holdings of grain and malt in Stratford. Later in the same year Francis Meres published a book entitled *Palladis Tamia* in which he singled Shakespeare out for particular praise as one of the best English writers, and in the course of his commendation he named a dozen of Shakespeare's plays. Other records tell of his receiving legacies from fellow actors and Stratford friends, of his appearing as a witness in lawsuits, of his acting in specific plays, etc. Sometime before the end of his life, probably about 1612, he retired to Stratford. On the 25th of March, 1616, he executed a long and detailed will leaving most of his property to his daughter Susanna, and less than a month later, on April 23, he died.

These facts have been given in some detail—though by no means all of them were mentioned—because many people have the idea that we "know nothing about Shakespeare." The simple fact is that actors and playwrights had a position rather low in the social scale, and their doings were not the matters of public interest that they have since become. Actually, we know a good deal more about Shakespeare than we do about most of his contemporaries in his profession. The numerous attempts to prove that someone else really wrote Shakespeare's plays trade on this relative ignorance and are usually traceable to one of two prejudices. The first is a confusion of genius with learning—the idea being that a great writer must be a great scholar, a university man, etc. This notion is stimulated by the fact that it now requires learning to interpret some references and allusions which were very unlearned when they were first made. There is no learning in Shakespeare's plays which could not have been readily acquired in Stratford grammar school and in a quarter of a century of busy life and work in Renaissance London. The second prejudice is less creditable and seems to be merely a sort of social snobbery which insists on trying to assign the plays to *Lord* Bacon or the *Earl* of Oxford or some other titled dignitary. Actually, Shakespeare's authorship of his plays is so well attested that the people who attempt to deprive him of it are forced to assume that, for some fantastic reason, the whole thing was an elaborate hoax in which Shakespeare collaborated. They use fanatically misplaced ingenuity in an attempt to discredit simple and clearly established facts.

Shakespeare's plays fall into three distinct types—comedies, tragedies, and histories (or chronicle-history plays). The first two require no explanation here beyond the statement that comic scenes may appear in tragedy and vice versa; but the histories are a special Elizabethan type. The prosperity and rising greatness of England, accentuated by the defeat of the Spanish Armada in 1588, led to a popular interest in English history, and the history plays were large-scale dramatizations and glorifications of the events falling roughly between 1200 and 1550. Many of Shakespeare's tragedies—*Julius Caesar*, for example—are based on history, but his "histories" in the special sense can be readily identified by the fact that their titles are all the names of English kings—*Richard III*, *Henry V*, etc. (Note that *King Lear*, whose hero is a *legendary* king of Britain, is a tragedy, not a history.)

The chronology of Shakespeare's plays presents considerable difficulty, largely because plays were usually not published until some time after they were introduced on the stage. Single plays published during the author's lifetime appeared as quartos, and the first collected edition was the *First Folio*, seven years after his death (1623). (*Quarto* and *folio* are terms of the book trade designating the size of the page.) The gap between production and publication might be as much as 30 years, or as little as two or three. (Part I of *Henry VI* was first performed in 1592 and first published in 1623.) The evidence used in dating the plays includes records of performance, references in the plays themselves to contemporary events, references to the plays in other writings (the dozen titles listed by Meres, for example), and general considerations of style and versification. Using all these criteria, scholars have constructed a good general chronology of the plays.

Shakespeare began with histories and light comedies in the early 1590's, though some plays may go back to the end of the 1580's. To this first period belong *Henry VI* (in three parts), *Richard III*, *Love's Labor's Lost*, *The Comedy of Errors*, and *The Taming of the Shrew*. To the middle 90's belong *Romeo and Juliet*, *A Midsummer Night's Dream*, *Richard II*, and *The Merchant of Venice*. The last few years of the century saw the production of *Henry IV* (in two parts), *As You Like It*, *Julius Caesar*, and *Henry V*. During the first five or six years of the 17th century Shakespeare wrote *Hamlet*, *Twelfth Night*, and *Othello*, and between about 1606 and 1609 added *King Lear*, *Macbeth*, *Antony and Cleopatra*, and *Coriolanus*. There seems to have been a lull in his activity before the production of his last group of plays, dating from about 1611: *Cymbeline*, *The Winter's Tale*,

The *Tempest, and *Henry VIII*. This list includes only the better known of the 35 plays (not counting parts separately) that are attributed to Shakespeare.

We can see a definite development in the course of Shakespeare's career. The early plays have an exuberance of word-play and rhyme not surprising in a young genius learning how to manipulate the tools of his craft. Then his comedy becomes more thoughtful, and his tragedy more the working of human forces and less dependent on an arbitrary fate. In the later tragedies, especially *King Lear*, he achieves a concentration of language and a compression of meaning that sometimes lead to obscurity; and he finally emerges in a serene, philosophical view best exemplified in *The Tempest*.

The circumstances in which Shakespeare wrote his plays are reflected in various aspects of the works themselves. As an actor he had a practical knowledge of stagecraft which meant that he would make his plays good theater as well as good drama. His own standards were high enough to protect him from mere commercialism, but as a stockholder he naturally wanted plays that would appeal to the general public—he could not afford the snobbery which sometimes assumes that a popular success must be an artistic failure. Because he wrote for his own company, his roles are sometimes conditioned by the strong and weak points of the actors who would be called on to play them.

Above all, his plays were written for the Elizabethan theater, which was very different from the modern one. First of all, it was a small building—the interior of *The Fortune* (built in 1600) was only 55 feet square. This gave an intimacy to the performance which is unattainable now except in arena stagings, and it made asides and soliloquies seem natural. The commercial theaters were open to the sky and the plays were presented by daylight, so that lighting effects were impossible. Costumes were often lavish, but scenery was practically nonexistent. As a result, lighting and scenery were often written into the speeches, in references to the sun, moon, and darkness, to forests, castles, and streams. The main stage projected out into the theater and could not be concealed by a curtain; therefore a scene had to begin with entrances and close with exits, and if bodies were left lying about—as frequently happened—someone had to be instructed to carry them off. This main stage served for open country, city streets and squares, and large rooms, but two other playing areas were also used. At the back of the main stage was a small space which could be closed with curtains. This inner stage was used for small rooms, shops opening on a street, a hovel on the heath (in *King Lear*), the tomb of the Capulets (in *Romeo and Juliet*), and other similar localities. Above it was the upper stage, which served for windows above the street, or a hilltop overlooking the battlefield (in *Julius Caesar*), for Juliet's balcony. Any information about the locale of a scene which the audience needed was worked into the dialogue. The absence of scenery and the use of several playing areas meant that the action was unbroken, and this gave a better illusion of reality and a greater sense of speed and concentration than can be achieved in a production which must be constantly held up while elaborate "realistic" scenery is installed or removed. In recent years there has been an increasing tendency to stage Shakespearean plays more or less as was originally intended. Not the least of the advantages of this practice is that the elimination of scene-shifting increases the time available for acting, and there is consequently no need for drastic cutting of the text.

Shakespeare was recognized in his own time as an eminent writer, and though his plays were often modified and "improved" to suit contemporary taste during the Restoration and the 18th century, his fame has increased fairly steadily. During the period of *Neo-Classicism, he was often regarded as something of an inspired barbarian because he did not follow the conventions of classical drama. With the reaction of the *Romantic Movement, the worship of Shakespeare may be said to have begun, with *Coleridge as the chief prophet of the cult. Shakespeare had already become an international figure under whose banner *Lessing, *Herder, *Goethe and *Schiller in Germany and, much later, *Hugo in France revolted against Neo-Classicism. There is no question that the deification of Shakespeare during the 19th century went too far, and many people even today prefer an attitude of ignorant worship to an informed appreciation of his greatness; but it is both more profitable and more respectful to read, understand, and perform his works than to speak of him in hushed tones.

Shaw, George Bernard: English dramatist and critic (1856–1950). Although born in Dublin of a middle-class, Protestant family, Shaw took no part in the *Irish Literary Revival but went to London and is consequently identified with British social and literary movements. His activities as a London newspaper critic of music and drama produced his best-known nondramatic works, The *Quintessence of Ibsenism* (1891) and *The Perfect Wagnerite* (1898). His interest in Henry George, Karl *Marx, and other social theorists led to his affiliation with the Fabian Socialists, for whom he wrote numerous tracts. He was also much influenced by Samuel Butler and *Ibsen.

Ingenious and witty, Shaw's comedies present a fearless intellectual criticism of his age, sugar-coated by a pretended lightness of tone. Aware of the discrepancy between the accepted conventions of life and what really lies underneath, Shaw rebelled against muddled thinking and smug prudishness. He hoped to puncture men's hollow pretentions and restore their intellectual courage. The objects of his satire included conventionalized religion and philosophy (*Androcles and the Lion*, 1912; *Back to Methuselah*, 1921); social attitudes toward sex relations (*Mrs. Warren's Profession*, 1894; *Candida*, 1895; *Man and Superman*, 1903); military heroism (*Arms and the Man*, 1894; *The Devil's Disciple*, 1897); high society and the Cinderella theme (*Pygmalion*, 1912); professional charity (*Major Barbara*, 1905). In all these plays, although characters are mere mouthpieces for ideas, and situations are highly artificial, Shaw's sense of the theatrical and his witty paradoxes achieve his ends. His dialogue is as brilliant as *Congreve's or *Wilde's. It is a combination of the dramatic, the comic, and the social corrective that gives Shaw's comedies their special flavor. The plays, it must be admitted, often suffer from too much talk. Their arguments spilled over into extended prefaces to the published versions, and these critical analyses of a wide range of social and literary subjects are famous in their own right. He was awarded the Nobel prize in 1926.

Shelley, Percy Bysshe: English poet (1792–1822). Shelley is the visionary idealist of English Romanticism and its most ecstatic lyric singer. An aristocrat by birth (his son succeeded to the title of baronet), Shelley nevertheless had radical ideas, especially a complete faith in the perfectibility of mankind and an anarchistic love of freedom. These ideas (largely derived from William Godwin) were connected with the study of Greek poetry and Platonic philosophy. While at Oxford he wrote a pamphlet, *The Necessity of Atheism* (1811), which caused him to be expelled. He soon made a rash marriage to Harriet Westbrook (1811) but within a few years deserted her and ran off to the Continent with Mary Godwin (1814). They were married after his first wife's suicide. Indignant over the refusal of the courts to give him the custody of his two children and worried about his health, he left England permanently. Not long thereafter, he was drowned while out sailing. When his body was washed ashore, his pockets held two volumes, *Sophocles and *Keats. In his brief 30 years Shelley had moved näively through a series of unconventional acts that caused much suffering. Yet he had desired to reform the world, and all who knew him agreed that he was "the least selfish man," motivated always by the highest integrity.

Shelley remained constant to his faith in the progress and perfectibility of man (*Hymn to Intellectual Beauty*, 1816; *Ode to the West Wind*, 1819). Once tyranny and cruelty had been removed and man's reason and love substituted, then the Soul of the Universe, the Spirit of Love, would be revealed. This is the theme that runs through all his work. *Prometheus Unbound* (1818–19), a lyrical drama, modifies the legend of Prometheus as told by *Aeschylus to show what man (Prometheus) can be when he refuses to tolerate tyranny (*Zeus) and is made free by nature and love (Asia). An idealized social philosophy also runs through *Queen Mab* (1813), *The Revolt of Islam* (1818), and *Hellas* (1821). In *The Cenci* (1819), another verse-drama, the tragedy is the defeat of love by incest and revenge.

In his shorter poems, Shelley achieves a rare combination of prophetic message, precision of imagery, and captivating melody (*Ode to the West Wind*, 1819, in **terza limar; To Night*, 1821). Something of the same tone infuses *Adonais* (1821), a pastoral *elegy in *Spenserian stanzas, lamenting the death of Keats. The fate of genius is to be misunderstood, and Shelley was quite aware of adding pathos by making much of what he writes about Keats applicable to himself also. It was the critics, said Shelley, who, hating instead of loving, had killed Keats; the irony of their criticism lay in the greatness of Keats, which Shelley was able to recognize.

*Arnold's picture of Shelley as the "beautiful and ineffectual angel beating in the void his luminous wings in vain" is a narrow judgment even on his poetry. And his prose is clear, vigorous, and brilliant, certainly never ineffectual or in vain, or in a void. Yet we can see Arnold's point: Shelley moved in a world of abstract ideas, without reference to practical considerations or the everyday world, and he was utterly without a sense of proportion or (what is really the same thing) a sense of humor. His *Defence of Poetry* (1821), although incomplete, is a stirring manifesto of the poet's function: "poetry is the record of the best and happiest moments of the happiest and best minds. . . . Poets are the unacknowledged legislators of the world." Another aspect of Shelley's versatility should be noted: he was an excellent linguist, whose translations from Greek, Italian, Spanish, and German transmuted the spirit of one literature into the language of another.

Shelley's command of the sound effects of his verse is nothing short of marvelous. To this melody he brought other qualities of greatness—a sense of form, intensity, and sensuousness. His images give concrete pictures though they deal with insubstantial things like winds, dead leaves, or "an enchanted Boat, / Which like a sleeping swan doth float / Upon the silver waves of thy sweet singing." Together with these gifts his idealism gave his verse a rhapsodic quality. "The desire of the moth for the star, / Of the night for the morrow, / The devotion to something afar / From the sphere of our sorrow."

short story: a prose narrative of limited length. In one sense the short story is as old as any literary form and must have existed for thousands of years before the art of writing was known. Stories of gods and demons, accounts of the day's hunting, even the more elaborate bits of local gossip are restricted prose narratives. Possibly the oldest recorded example is the Egyptian tale of *The Two Brothers*, dating from about 3200 B.C., and from that time to this the flow of short narratives has been unbroken. The birth-tales of the *Jataka*, the fables of the *Panchatantra* and of *Aesop, the stories of Daniel, Jonah, and Ruth in the Old Testament and the Parables of the New, *Apuleius' story of *Cupid and Psyche*, the bawdy tales of the *Gesta Romanorum* and the saints' lives of the *Golden Legend*, the *Arabian Nights* and The *Decameron*—the list of tales is inexhaustible. And, in one sense, all these tales are short stories. In another sense the term is considerably less inclusive. Frequently a distinction is made between the folk tale, fable, parable, anecdote, etc., and the carefully contrived literary form known as the short story. According to this view, the short story is a form dating from the 19th century and closely related to the rise of general periodicals. It requires more than the mere reporting of a series of events, for it must have characterization, unity, cumulative interest, climax, resolution. The difficulty here is twofold. In the first place, no definition can be made that will include the stories of *Maupassant and O. Henry and exclude *Chaucer's tales of the miller and the reeve, unless Chaucer is ruthlessly ruled out for being in verse. In the second place, during the past fifty years the consciously literary short story has developed in so many directions that it defies definition, for no definition will fit all the possibilities without being so broad as to include almost everything ever written.

674

A further attempt is sometimes made to draw a distinction between the commercial and the artistic short story. The distinction certainly exists, but the difference is more a matter of quality than of kind. A man like William Saroyan produced quantities of commercial short stories and a few artistic ones in much the same way that a poet like *Wordsworth wrote quantities of poor poems and a few excellent ones. The difference that makes the commercial short story appear as a separate type is simply the fact that there is a huge market for mediocre fiction and none for mediocre poetry.

sirens: creatures of Greek mythology (half women, half birds) who lure sailors to shipwreck with their enchanting song.

Sisyphus: one of the great sinners of Greek mythology, condemned to spend eternity trying to roll a stone up a hill. Whenever he came near the top, the stone got away from him and he had to start over. Hence, a labor of Sisyphus is any unending task.

Socrates: Greek philosopher (469–399 B.C.). Socrates was born at Athens 10 years after the battle of Plataea brought the Persian Wars on the mainland of Greece to an end. He grew up during the Periclean Age, apparently in a prosperous family, with sufficient leisure, while still a young man, to master the philosophy of the time. This philosophy consisted largely of various attempts to provide a scientific explanation of the origin and structure of the universe, in contrast to the mythological accounts commonly accepted by the people. Scholars do not agree how long Socrates maintained an interest in physical philosophy or what distinction he achieved in its pursuit. But before the Peloponnesian War began in 431 B.C., he had abandoned its study to devote the rest of his life to an examination of conduct.

This change in the direction of Socrates' thought would seem to reflect increasing dissatisfaction on his part with the results of scientific speculation, but it was precipitated by the oracle of *Apollo at Delphi. When an Athenian named Chaerephon inquired at the shrine, he was informed that "no man is wiser than Socrates." Now Socrates knew that Apollo could not lie, but he also knew that he himself possessed no wisdom. He therefore considered the god's words a kind of riddle and set out to seek a man wiser than himself, intending, as soon as he found one, to ask Apollo what he meant. But though he examined many persons in all classes of society, questioning them about justice and courage and temperance and those other qualities on which right conduct depends, he was able to discover nothing more in what they told him than a mass of confused and contradictory opinions, derived from examples, maintained by tradition, and modified at will to suit changing times and circumstances. Such opinions were not knowledge and did not entitle their possessors to a reputation for wisdom. And yet, by virtue of them, many believed themselves wise and often seemed so to others.

When Socrates observed these facts, he no longer regarded himself as investigating the oracle, the truth of which was becoming apparent. Instead, he began to entertain the belief that he had been chosen by Apollo to destroy the false conceit of knowledge blinding the Athenians to their real ignorance. In this new service to the god, he continued conversing with all who would listen. Day after day he would ask the same question, *What is justice?*—or piety or friendship, as the case might be. And as often as a definition was given, he would proceed to demonstrate, by a series of adroitly put questions, how utterly worthless it was. Not that he had something more adequate to suggest. He was, he confessed, completely ignorant in these matters. But he admitted his ignorance, and because he did so, Apollo had judged him the wisest of the Athenians. The god had used his name, however, merely as an example, and his fellow citizens could win the same commendation on the same terms. For the true meaning of the oracle was clearly that *he is the wisest of men who knows, as Socrates knows, that his wisdom is nothing.*

When a man realizes his ignorance, he sets out on the search for truth, as Socrates had done, and as he wished the other Athenians to do also. To help them, he had exposed the folly of their traditional ideas of virtue and urged them to examine their moral concepts until they could define them in terms admitting no exceptions, for only definitions which possessed universal validity could provide a sure foundation for a science of human conduct. Once that science was established, it would lead invariably to right conduct. Socrates was convinced that to know the good is to do the good; that *knowledge is virtue*, just as its opposite, ignorance, is vice; and that if a man does wrong, he does wrong because his knowledge is faulty and never for any other cause. For to do wrong is to oppose one's own welfare, as to do right is to promote it; and all men seek, by their very nature, that which benefits themselves.

Thus what began as an investigation of the oracle became a search for universal truth, conducted by a method of question and answer known as *dialectic*, the only way, in Socrates' view, by which men would ever find knowledge. For the action of mind on mind was required to reveal the nature of moral concepts and in the end to make clear the fact that *all the virtues are one*. Socrates realized that the method was unpopular. People resented being questioned in public by a man who said he knew nothing, when the result invariably seemed to prove their ignorance and his wisdom. They were bitter, too, at his influence on the young men of the city, who watched their elders cross-examined, learned the technique of dialectic, and turned it against the code of ethics in which they were reared. As a result Socrates was regarded as a corrupter of the youth, who, like some of the sophists, taught successful argument without regard for truth or justice. He seemed to *make the worse appear the better reason and to teach others to do the same.*

Moreover, Socrates and those who kept company with him were commonly considered antidemocratic. His disciples came for the most part from wealthy families with oligarchical sympathies. Alcibiades turned traitor to Athens during the Peloponnesian War, and Critias was one of the Thirty Tyrants set over the city by the victorious Spartans. Socrates himself fought with conspicuous bravery at Potidaea, Delium, and Amphipolis, but he did not go into exile with the democratic leaders after Athens' defeat, and all through his career his political views were in complete disagreement with those of his fellow citizens. He believed that in government, as in medicine, expert opinion alone is of value and that only those trained to do so should rule. He disapproved of the democratic concept of popular election to public office, particularly election by lot. And he never advised the assembly, although his silence could be interpreted as hostility to it.

Socrates was also suspected of impiety. His interest in physical science had not been forgotten. Many people thought he was still *searching into things in the heavens and beneath the earth*, as they had seen his caricature do in *Aristophanes' comedy The *Clouds a quarter of a century before. And the physical philosophers were considered atheists by the general population. But even if Socrates could show his long dissociation from this group, he was subject to attack on other grounds, for he claimed to be guided by a *daimonion*, that is, a divine sign or warning, which came to him in the form of a voice and forbade him to undertake this or that action, sometimes although it was of the simplest sort.

In 399 B.C., when he was more than 70 years of age, Socrates was accused of corrupting the youth and believing not in the gods of the city but in gods of his own. (An amnesty law passed by the restored democracy prevented his political views from being called in question.) He was tried by one of those immense juries characteristic of Athenian legal procedure, found guilty by a vote of 281 to 220, and condemned to die by drinking poison hemlock. The story of his trial, imprisonment, and execution is told by his disciple *Plato in three short dialogues (*Apology, *Crito, and *Phaedo); there is an excellent portrait of him in the *Symposium; and he is the chief speaker in most of Plato's other works. Some information is also preserved about him in *Xenophon's *Memorabilia* and elsewhere, but the world will always think of Socrates in terms of Plato's description, for Socrates himself wrote nothing.

Late in life Socrates married a woman named Xanthippe, who is famous for her evil temper, a phenomenon traceable perhaps, at least in part, to the poverty in which her husband's activities forced her to live. Socrates did not charge his young friends for what they learned from him, nor did he often accept their presents. He had three sons, but none of them attained distinction. Socrates was odd in appearance, short and thickset, but possessed of great strength and courage. He was utterly indifferent to the cold, going dressed in a ragged cloak winter as well as summer, and marching on at least one occasion barefoot through the snow. Socrates was kind and genial in disposition, and he had a keen sense of humor. But he baited those he cross-examined with his famous *irony*, a sly pretense of ignorance which delighted the company as much as it enraged the victim who took it at face value and was trapped. And he was subject to strange fits of brooding, when he would remain silent for long periods of time. Socrates never left Athens except on military service, and in his later years he was still unfamiliar with common sights near the city. He was not interested in worldly possessions, and he could not manage even the little property he owned. His concern was for the perfection of the soul, and this he sought with diligence, firm in the belief that to a good man no harm can come either in life or in death.

Many of the schools of Greek philosophy, including the Stoics and the Epicureans as well as the followers of Plato and *Aristotle, traced their origin to Socrates.

Solzhenitsyn, Aleksander I.: Russian novelist and playwright (1918–   ). He achieved fame in the Soviet Union for his anti-Stalinist novel *One Day in the Life of Ivan Denisovich* (1962). His other writings, *The First Circle*, *The Cancer Ward*, and *August 1914*, published in the U.S. after 1966, have never been published in Russia, but have the status of bestsellers in many countries. *August 1914* (American translation 1972); a "polemical" novel about Russian participation in World War I, has inspired comparison to *Shakespeare and *Tolstoi for its sweep, power, and compassion. Imprisoned after war service for an alleged slur on Stalin, the novelist has focused on the Soviet prison system and written of it not only from firsthand experience but in a profound and humane way, and in a style that has caused many to regard him as the one "classic" Russian novelist of this time. Solzhenitsyn was expelled from the Soviet Writers Union in 1969 for publishing his works abroad and for the "radical" views they express, which he defined in his undelivered acceptance speech for the Nobel prize (1970): the indivisibility of truth and the "perception of world literature as the one great heart which beats for the concerns and misfortunes of our world."

Song of Roland: the earliest extant poem of substantial length in Old French and the best-known *chanson de geste* (c. 1100). The French regard it as the characteristic expression of their early spirit. The oldest complete version (the 12th-century Oxford MS. in Anglo-Norman) was probably derived from a poem now lost written in the preceding century; the "warlike example" of chivalrous Roland was said to have been sung by the Normans at the Battle of Hastings (1066).

As in many another medieval poem, the core of history is slight, but there is some confirmation in chronicle records. Charlemagne (742–814) had led a few minor campaigns against the Spanish heathen. Then, according to the narrative of Eginhard, Charlemagne's friend and biographer, Charlemagne went to Spain in 778 to guarantee his frontiers by alliance. The main body of his army withdrew after a relatively peaceful expedition. As the rear guard was passing through the narrow passes of the Pyrenees at Roncesvalles, it was ambushed and destroyed by Christians, Gascon (Basque) mountaineers. Among the dead was one Roland, prefect of Brittany. So much for history. But this obscure skirmish was to prove rich material for the storyteller.

By steps which cannot be traced, the legend evolved until in the *Song of Roland* the original Gascons were transformed into Saracens and the insignificant rearguard action into a major catastrophe set in the atmosphere of a crusade. A noble friendship binds two of Charlemagne's vassals, Oliver and Roland, the latter identified as the king's nephew, his "right arm" and renowned retainer. Roland, moreover, possesses a horn whose distinctive blast can be recognized 30 leagues away. Charlemagne, who is regarded with religious as well as feudal devotion, is a hoary longbeard nearly 200 years old (he was actually only in his thirties at the time of the expedition). In close attendance upon him is the Angel Gabriel, who appears at critical moments to warn and advise. And the cause of the destruction of the flower of the army is the treachery of Roland's stepfather Ganelon, who is sent as a negotiator, but who instead conspires with the heathen to destroy the rear guard led by Roland.

In what circumstances this transformation occurred is still matter of scholarly debate. Was this anonymous poem a piece of ecclesiastical proselytizing? Was it an exhortation to a crusade? Or a poetic lure contrived in some monastery that boasted relics of Roland and Charlemagne and that hoped by the poem to "interest, attract, retain, educate, and amuse" pilgrims? Or is the poem merely secular and military, glorifying feudal values and infused with the wonder and praise of "la douce France"? Whatever the answer to these questions, the work survives not because of its local color, historical details, patriotic spirit, crusading propaganda, or religious tone, interesting as all these are. It holds us because of its literary merits, its synthesis of poetry, mood, and heroic characters.

The verse, intended to be sung or chanted, consists of 4,001 10-syllabled lines bound together by *assonance and arranged in stanzaic paragraphs of from 5 to 35 lines. This form produces a series of dramatic vignettes—tableaux such as the scene of Ganelon defying Roland, of Charlemagne receiving in the garden, of Roland attempting to shatter his sword. There are lyric passages of strong feeling, such as Archbishop Turpin's dying benediction, Roland's farewell to Oliver, the dying Roland's feudal proffer of his glove to his Lord God.

Terse and laconic, the style achieves dramatic effect by suggestion more than by direct statement. Similarly the characters show emotion by speech and action, not by reflective self-analysis. The physical descriptions are stark. Only one formal simile occurs: "Even as a stag before the hound goes flying" (lines 1874–5; contrast this with some 180 similes in the *Iliad*).

The blending of piety with feudal loyalty produces a unity of theme, a steady faith in the values of the social order. The knights accept without question and seek with valorous persistence the ideals of their society. They know that they are fighting for God, king, and country—and these three are one, the glory of Christian France. Charlemagne is the symbol of this triple loyalty, religious, feudal, and national. The inner rumblings of discontent with royal authority, faintly implied, never erupt. If Ganelon's treachery represents the ambivalence of the feudal knights toward the growing power of the king, the ranks of feudalism are still consolidated to fight outsiders, especially pagans. Even Ganelon plots in the belief that he can confine his treachery to Roland without endangering king, country, or religion.

This political naïveté is paralleled by what may seem like emotional simplicity when viewed in the light of modern attitudes toward love. Charlemagne announces bluntly to Alde that her betrothed, Roland, has been killed, and in the same breath offers her his own son instead. The role of women is so unimportant that Alde is dead within 10 lines of her first appearance.

Interest is maintained by conflicts on several levels: between Christian truth and heathen error; between Ganelon and Roland as individuals, as symbols of treachery and loyalty, and as symbols of private revenge and the public good which that treachery endangers. The contrast in character between two heroes—"Roland is brave and Oliver is wise"—creates the dramatic climax of the poem, when Oliver urges him and Roland twice refuses to sound his horn for help. When he finally blows, the call brings back Charlemagne and the army, but too late to save the rear guard.

Like a doomed Greek hero, Roland in his proud pursuit of glory was at first blind to the tragic results of his recklessness: his desire for future military fame induced him to disregard the immediate crisis. Thus he suffered no inner conflict when making his choice to risk destruction rather than the possibility of being called a coward.

That is his code. Only when he sees the calamitous outcome does he feel sorrow. At the opening of the poem, he is proud, insensitive, and headstrong; at the end, he recognizes that his behavior was not heroic, but vain. And although he never deplores his pride in that bravery which is the mark of his class, he develops a new humility in his compassion and his sense of responsibility for the dead. With the *warrior* virtue of valor and the *feudal* virtue of loyalty, he has now achieved the *Christian* virtue of humility. The Angel Gabriel finds him worthy of heaven.

Although the glamorous Roland is the only character who shows development, it is Charlemagne who elicits our compassion. Like Hrothgar (see *Beowulf*), he is venerable and sage, subject to prophetic dreams that indicate his wisdom and piety. Like Aeneas (see *Aeneid*), he has acted with a selfless integrity, serving only the common good, willing to sacrifice himself for his land and his religion. Yet even when his dearest men have been slain and their slayers punished, there is no rest. The divine messenger sends him on a new mission against the heathen. "God!" said the king: "my life is hard indeed!" Tears filled his eyes. But we know that he will go on, for he is the symbol, the embodied ideal and destiny of his people.

sonnet (Italian, "a little song"): a lyric poem of 14 lines. In English sonnets these lines are always iambic pentameters. Although poets have exercised great freedom within the form, most sonnets fall into one of two basic patterns—the Italian (Petrarchan), riming abba abba cde cde (the pattern of the last six lines may vary); and the English (Shakespearian), riming abab cdcd efef gg. The development of the theme in the Italian sonnet is indicated by the changes in the rime scheme: the first eight lines (octave) present the theme, raise the issue, doubt, or query; the last six (sestet) answer the query, resolve the problem, drive home the point by an abstract comment. Frequently the octave is subdivided into two quatrains and the sestet into two tercets. In the English form, the closing couplet is an epigrammatic comment or summary. The balanced structure, unifying rime scheme, and parallelism between form and content have made the sonnet one of the most popular and exacting of poetic forms. In most countries and periods, the Italian form has been predominant, as it is today. Of Italian origin, the stanza was developed to its highest point in Italian poetry by *Petrarch, whose themes and manner were widely imitated. It captivated the *Renaissance after its introduction in the 16th century into England (by Wyatt and Surrey) and France (by Marot and by *Ronsard and the other poets of the *Pléiade). The form has attracted the greatest poets—*Spenser (abab bcbc cdcd ee), *Shakespeare, *Milton, *Keats, *Wordsworth. Many have followed Petrarch's example of linking sonnets in a series (called a "sonnet sequence") around a single theme—Sidney, *Astrophel and Stella*, Spenser, *Amoretti*, Elizabeth Barrett Browning (see Robert *Browning) *Sonnets from the Portuguese.* Throughout the Renaissance the sonnet was essentially a love poem. But Milton enlarged its function to political and moral criticism, and his lead has been followed by later poets. Today the sonnet is used for any subject for which a short concentrated lyric would be appropriate.

Sophocles: Greek dramatist (*c.* 496–406 B.C.). Sophocles was to the Greeks a kind of "tragic Homer," hailed as the favorite of the gods and honored by the state with sacrifices long after his death. His tragedies are representative of an era of democracy and the emancipated individual. His heroes are not mere victims but develop during the course of the drama into proud bearers of their tragic fate because they learn to accept it with courage and strength. They are indeed symbols of tragic, human fate: a guiltless guilt, an ancient curse that it is not within man's power to escape. The ancient traditions of myth and ancestry, which make man the innocent victim, seem superficial compared to Sophocles' conception. Now the weaknesses lie mostly within man himself, and the gods are simply the helpers of the righteous and the cursers of those who overstep their human limitations. Yet Sophocles is deeply aware of the disproportion between the dignity of his human creations and the destructiveness of the forces which produce tragedy.

Oedipus, as treated by Sophocles in *Oedipus the King*, is not chiefly the cursed victim of an old prophecy but an example, a symbol of human weakness in general, who atones for his tragic, guiltless guilt—having unknowingly killed his father and married his mother—by the responsibility with which he accepts this guilt and by a voluntary, courageous, though desperate, deed: he blinds himself. In *Antigone* the heroine is even more an individual. A daughter of Oedipus, and thus connected with his misfortune, she frees herself from all conventional bonds by following her determination to bury her dead brother, even though the burial violates the highest law of the state. Her instinct for eternal human right and dignity is paramount and leads her to greatness as an individual, for it makes duty more important than life, love, or death.

In his oldest extant tragedy, *Ajax* (c. 445–440 B.C.), Sophocles presents a religious message in the fate of a hero who spites the gods and thinks himself their equal because of his enormous strength. But because he possesses only physical strength and lacks the balancing spiritual insight, he oversteps the proper boundaries of mankind; he lets his boldness get the better of him and incurs the wrath of the goddess *Athena. In the prologue Athena pronounces his punishment and the moral of the tragedy. Ajax is punished with madness, for it is man's duty to respect the omnipotence of the gods and to realize his own limitations. All earthly things are fleeting, and, although great strength may be man's possession one day, the next his glory may turn into humiliation.

Of Sophocles' 123 plays only 7 are extant. Besides those already mentioned, there are *Trachiniae* (c. 413 B.C.), *Electra* (c. 410 B.C.), *Philoctetes* (409 B.C.), *Oedipus at Colonus* (401 B.C.), and the *satyr-play, *Ichneutae*.

Sophocles easily made his way to the top as a public administrator and as a poet. He received first prize several times in the annual dramatic festivals, and once won the victory over the old master *Aeschylus, the younger poet's language being more restrained and at the same time more powerful and more suggestive.

In many ways Sophocles improved the dramatic technique of ancient Greece. He enlarged the importance of a third major actor, whom Aeschylus had allowed to appear only in a single scene. He individualized his heroes and made them more human. He was so daring as to portray a suicide on the stage in order to give the hero (in this case, Ajax) a chance to speak his innermost thoughts to the audience. He substituted three separate play-units for the usual three parts of the trilogy, a device which loosened their former, often forced, connection. He enlarged the chorus from 12 to 15 members.

But in spite of these improvements (which were deviations from older traditions), Sophocles followed in the footsteps of his master, Aeschylus. He regarded himself not only as a poet but also as an educator of the people. With harmony and balance he united political, religious, and personal elements into moving, tragic drama.

Spenser, Edmund: English poet (1552?–99). The author of *The *Faerie Queene* is the least read of major English poets, even by specialists in English literature. His own generation, however, revered his skill in forging a new alloy from the classics, *Chaucer, and the French and Italian *Renaissance poets. By Spenser's time, Chaucer's verse had become archaic; Spenser was by general consent Chaucer's successor. In one sense Elizabethan judgment has been confirmed. Spenser has been a continuing influence on craftsmen in verse; the vividness of his scenes, the richness of his imagery, and the variety of his sound effects taught—to name only a few—*Milton, *Pope, *Burns, *Keats, and *Tennyson. But his chief poem hardly satisfies the modern taste for narrative movement and realism of character as do Chaucer and *Shakespeare. Thus the praise so often accorded Spenser in *Lamb's epithet that he is "the poet's poet"—reveals both Spenser's subtlety of appeal and his limited audience.

Born in London of middle-class parents, Spenser was well educated in the conventional humanistic discipline of classical studies and in such then unconventional subjects as English composition and dramatic art. For the "sage and serious" Spenser (in Milton's phrase), this mixed curriculum was a rich infusion. Seven years at Cambridge University, from which Spenser received two degrees, confirmed his enthusiasm for poetry and won him a group of friends, intellectually stimulating and politically useful. He came to know the Earl of Leicester, Sir Philip Sidney, and even Queen Elizabeth.

A career seemed to be opening, if not at court at least under the patronage of one of the humanistic wealthy aristocrats. Because it was regarded as not quite the thing to make money by poetry, Spenser published *The Shepheardes Calendar* (1579) anonymously and dedicated it to that gentleman of learning and chivalry, Sir Philip Sidney. With some originality, Spenser made this series of 12 *eclogues correspond to the calendar, one for each month of the year. The poems are peopled by shepherds who represent Spenser and his friends. Spenser appears as Colin Clout, whose love affair and rejection by Rosalinde (a lady who has not yet been identified) centralize the poem artistically. In their ideas about love, poetry, and religious feeling these pastorals draw unabashedly on classical eclogues and the long succession of Renaissance *pastoral allegories. The work was, however, deliberately designed to continue an English poetic tradition whose master Spenser correctly recognized to be Chaucer. But the true Chaucerian quality Spenser did not understand, and it is copied only in externals, in occasional rhythms and the "old rustic language." Chaucer's diction (the "well of English undefyled") charmed Spenser and inspired his use of archaic words and obsolete spellings intended to restore "to their rightful heritage good and natural English words." In form, *The Shepheardes Calendar* is meticulously symmetrical, even in minute details. Spenser's impulse to experiment is revealed in the variety of verse types, all used with conscious virtuosity. The result, quaint and occasionally charming, heralded the appearance of a new poet. It was an artistic and even something of a financial triumph.

But Spenser still lacked a steady income, what his friend Harvey called "ordinary wages." Then a job materialized, not in England but in Ireland. Spenser went there in 1580 as private secretary to the new Governor, Lord Grey of Wilton. Ireland was to be Spenser's home for the rest of his life, and although he achieved the position of Sheriff of Cork, he never ceased to regard himself as an exile. Despite his sensitivity as an artist (he noted that the Irish bards had "sweet wit and good invention"), he was curiously insensitive to the plight and problems of the Irish and was uncompromising with their customs and manners. Indeed, Spenser endorsed Grey's cruel policy of military plunder, portrayed the harsh governor as Artegall, *i.e.*, Justice, in *The Faerie Queene*, praised him in a report on the *View of the Present State of Ireland* (not published till 1633).

Spenser had been working for some time on "hymns" to love and beauty, on *Mother Hubberd's Tale*, and on *The Faerie Queene*. Although the poems were not immediately published, their circulation in manuscript (along with others now lost) enlarged Spenser's reputation. In the fall of 1589, he returned to London with Sir Walter Raleigh, who had read in Ireland the first three books of *The Faerie Queene* and saw in them for Spenser (and perhaps for himself) a way to patronage and position. When these first books of *The Faerie Queene* were published in 1590, they were dedicated to the "most mighty and magnificent" Empress Elizabeth, "the greatest Gloriana," heroine of the poem. The poem made Spenser immediately famous and won him the tangible reward of a pension of £50 a year. But it failed to secure for him either a government post in England or a rich patron who would keep him there. He returned to Ireland disillusioned. His bitterness he voiced in the lament of *The Tears of the Muses* and the satire of *Mother Hubberd's Tale*, both published in *Complaints* (1591), and in *Colin Clout's Come Home Again* (1595).

Meanwhile he had married Elizabeth Boyle (1594) and presented her with an unusual wedding gift, the *Epithalamion*. This poem, a song of their marriage, described the whole of the wedding day from the dawn which lights the day to the night which leaves the bride and groom together. As the poem and the day progress, the meaning of their love is deepened, spiritualized, and extended by allusive references. Conveying a sense of intense joy, a richness of tone, a deeply felt theme, and an intricate pattern of echoes from mythology and the *Bible, it is Spenser's finest poem.

Other works soon went to press: The *Amoretti* (1595), a sequence of "Spenserian" sonnets (the rime scheme is abab bcbc cdcd ee), written in large part for his wife; *The Four Hymns*, two in praise of earthly, two in praise of heavenly, love and beauty; and the *Prothalamion* (1596), a marriage poem for the double wedding of the daughters of the Earl of Worcester. Less intense in feeling than its predecessor, the *Prothalamion* is nevertheless memorable for its musical quality, particularly in the refrain, "Sweet Thames, run softly till I end my song." In 1596, when the next three books of *The Faerie Queene* were published, they were likewise received with critical acclaim and favorably compared with the most famous epics of ancient and modern times.

But this fame in no way improved Spenser's material fortune. He remained stationed in Ireland. Not long thereafter, in the summer of 1598, the Irish rebelled. Spenser's home, Kilcolman Castle, was burned and pillaged. He fled with his wife and four children to Cork, then to England. Exhausted emotionally and physically, he died suddenly, not long after his arrival in London. Even in death his fame and ironic ill-fortune went together. Poets accompanied the body to a grave near Chaucer's in Westminster Abbey and covered it with elegies, but a monument ordered by Queen Elizabeth was never erected.

Spenserian stanza: a stanza composed of nine lines, the first eight iambic pentameters, the ninth an iambic hexameter (an *Alexandrine). The rime scheme is ababbcbcc. The name is derived from *Spenser, who created this pattern for his *Faerie Queene*. Other notable poets have used the form: *Burns, *Cotter's Saturday Night;* *Shelley, *Adonais;* *Keats, *Eve of St. Agnes;* *Byron, *Childe Harold*.

Sphinx: a winged monster having the body of a lion and the head of a woman. In Greek mythology she perched on a rock outside Thebes asking each passer-by her famous riddle, "What creature alone changes the number of its legs, going in the morning on four, at noon on two, and in the evening on three?" When Oedipus answered, "Man," the Sphinx in exasperation slew herself.

Statius, Publius Papinius: Roman epic poet (*c.* A.D. 45–*c.* 96). Statius was born at Naples but spent much of his active life in Rome, where his literary talent made him for years a favorite of the people and the emperor Domitian. Statius' most important work is the *Thebaid*, an epic in 12 books describing the strife between the two sons of Oedipus, Eteocles and Polyneices, for the overlordship of Thebes. His lesser works are an unfinished epic, the *Achilleid (Story of Achilles)*, and the *Silvae*, a collection of 32 occasional poems including the famous invocation *To Sleep* (V. 4). Though little read today, Statius was the most eminent poet of his time and was popular throughout the *Middle Ages. *Dante places him in the Purgatory of *The *Divine Comedy*, and *Chaucer not only imitates his *Thebaid* in *Troilus and Criseyde*, but places him with *Vergil, *Ovid, Homer, and *Lucan as one of the world's great poets.

Spinoza, Baruch de: Dutch-Jewish philosopher (1632–77), "the noblest and most lovable of the great philosophers. . . . Ethically he is supreme" (Bertrand Russell). Learned in the Hebraic Scriptures and the *Talmud, Spinoza nevertheless denied free will and a personal God—views which prompted his expulsion from the Jewish community of Amsterdam. He accepted the deterministic physics of Descartes but rejected Descartes' concept of duality of spirit and matter. Instead, Spinoza argued, both were attributes of a One-ness, God, immanent in nature, of which finite objects are interconnected "modes," limitations, aspects of the Divine Being. "We are part of universal nature, and we follow her order"—a pantheistic doctrine. The *Ethics* (written 1665; published posthumously 1677) is Platonic in considering that morality is man's perfecting his knowledge and love of God, and that such knowledge will produce love of one's fellow men and perfect happiness. Like *Socrates and *Plato, Spinoza believed that all wrong action is the result of intellectual error: "He who clearly and distinctly understands himself and his emotion loves God." Spinoza, who did not minimize the difficulty of acquiring this habit of thinking, ends his treatise—"all excellent things are as difficult as they are rare." It is certainly not easy to endure the evil and cruelty of the world with patience, but Spinoza's reflections may help us to avoid what Russell has described as "the paralysis of utter despair."

Stein, Gertrude: American experimental writer (1874–1946), one of the few so-called primitivists (see *naturalism) who had a scientific-realistic interest in what later came to be called "the unconscious." While a student of William *James at Radcliffe College, she experimented with automatic writing, a type of experiment which later would become very common among the *surrealists. She attempted to capture the half-formed thoughts, word pictures, and repetitions as these came into consciousness, seeking to render quiescent in the process the rational and logical mind which imposes order on the irrationalities and symbolic forms of the unconscious. Her first and most important book was *Three Lives* (1909), a trio of tales. One of these, "Melanctha" has been called the first genuinely primitivistic study in American literature. In combining the theories of modern psychology and of the *symbolists, Miss Stein recognized that emotional associations, shifting syntactic patterns, and rhythmic repetitions load words with special sensual significances far beyond the denotative dictionary meaning, as in *Tender Buttons* (1914) and *Four Saints in Three Acts*, an "opera libretto" (1934) with music by Virgil Thompson. The effect of these theories on modern writers can be seen in Sherwood Anderson, Dos Passos, *Hemingway, and Ezra *Pound. In addition to her influence on "the lost generation," Miss Stein was a patron and discriminating critic of modern artists: Braque, Cezanne, Juan Gris, Matisse, Picasso. She also published, as presumably written by her lifelong companion, a witty tongue-in-cheek autobiography, *The Autobiography of Alice B. Toklas* (1933).

Steinbeck, John: American novelist (1902–68). The judges who awarded Steinbeck the Nobel prize (1962) called attention to "his sympathetic humor and sociological perception." Acerbic critics have condemned his sentimentalism and thin philosophizing. Both comments can be justified. Born in California of middle-class parents, Steinbeck used his native state as background, and the laborers working its lands as the subject, for much of his best fiction: *Tortilla Flat* (1935), *Of Mice and Men* (1937), and *The Grapes of Wrath* (1939). The latter novel, which awakened America to the plight of its poverty-stricken dispossessed, is the "anchor" of Steinbeck's fame. It is a compassionate, realistic narrative of the Joad family, impoverished victims of the "Dustbowl" drought in Oklahoma. They seek in California their "promised land" but find instead exploitative migrant labor camps, which compound the misery of their poverty and dislocation. Not by heroic individualism but by cooperation and adaptation are they able to survive. The book was awarded the Pulitzer Prize in 1940. The novels which followed did not achieve the imaginative power or forcefulness of Steinbeck's early work. *The Winter of Our Discontent* (1961), a sermon more than a novel, about America's declining moral standards was, however, also cited by the Nobel prize judges because of its "instinct for what is genuinely American, be it good or bad."

Stendhal: pen-name of Henri Beyle, French novelist (1783–1842). Beyle was one of the first of the great psychological novelists and in the first great tide of the modern European novel—that is, he was a contemporary of *Scott, *Balzac, and *Goethe. In two significant novels Beyle dissected with considerable finesse the psychology of love. These two realistic novels are *The Red and the Black* (*Le Rouge et le noir*, 1830), which deals with the restoration period, and *The Charterhouse of Parma* (*La*

Chartreuse de Parme, 1839). These works, like the great novels of Balzac, depict a society in which power and rapacity dominate. Stendhal also kept a journal and wrote many fugitive pieces and critical essays. His work *De l'Amour (On Love)* appeared in 1822; he did a study of *Racine and *Shakespeare (1823–25); his other novels are *L'Abbesse de Castro* (1839) and the unfinished *Lucien Leuwen*, published posthumously. There are also two autobiographical fragments, *La vie de Henri Brulard* (1835–36) and *Souvenirs d'Egotisme*. His "complete works" occupy 18 volumes.

Le Rouge et le noir created a certain kind of European hero in Julien Sorel, a worker's son who has great sensitivity but also great ambition. This drive to power in one lowly born finds its outlet in the church, which alone offered to the bright young men of the lower classes opportunity for advancement. Critics believe that the "red" in the title symbolizes the republicanism of the French Revolution, and the "black," reactionary clericalism. Julien advances by tutoring in noble houses and by seduction of noblewomen; the drama becomes then a drama of passion used for power, involving an act of violence by Julien which brings him to the scaffold. *La Chartreuse de Parme* deals with intrigues in a small Italian court in the period of Napoleon's final exile. Fabrice del Dongo, the hero, participates in the Battle of Waterloo—scenes brilliantly depicted and said to have influenced *Tolstoi in his writing of *War and Peace*. Fabrice embraces a clerical career and again passion complements and interferes with his drive to power; he is imprisoned, pardoned, achieves high ecclesiastical position, carries on a love affair, but in the end, after a series of personal disasters, retires into a monastery. Balzac hailed this novel as a masterpiece.

Stendhal was born into a provincial (Grenoble) professional family, but he sought to escape the bourgeois environment. Joining Napoleon's army in 1799 he went to Milan and was captivated by Italian life. He spent some years in Paris but returned to the army (in services of supplies) as a means of earning sufficient money for his needs. Later he lived in Italy very much the life of one of his heroes—a life in which passion dominated.

After Napoleon's death, he was mostly in Paris, and his novels belong to this period. Still later he was appointed French consul at Trieste, but then was shifted to a little port near Rome from which he absented himself frequently through boredom. He believed that man's actions spring from a quest for gratification of his deepest desires. He was also among the earliest of the "observers," an acute student of human motive and character. The word *Beylisme*, which he himself coined, is used to suggest Stendhal's strong belief in the life-energy man uses to pursue his ends—love and power.

Sterne, Laurence: English novelist (1713–68). After his education at Cambridge, Sterne spent the rest of his life as a clergyman, an occupation in which he seems to have had no particular interest. Late in his life he began his literary career, publishing the first two volumes of *The Life and Opinions of Tristram Shandy, Gent.*, in 1760. They immediately made him famous, and he practically absconded from his parish, although he continued nominally to serve it. He kept on adding to his novel, the final part of which appeared in 1767. The next year—the year of his death—he published *A Sentimental Journey Through France and Italy*, a fictionalized account of a tour which he took after becoming a celebrity. (It is from this book, not, as most people think, from the *Bible, that the saying, "God tempers the wind to the shorn lamb," is taken.) He also published some sermons.

Sterne is noted for a highly personal brand of whimsicality and indirection, with deliberate incoherences and digressions. He reaches the third volume of *Tristram Shandy* before he gets around to having his hero born. He has practically no plot but develops a gallery of delightfully eccentric characters. His sentiment—often deliberately exaggerated—is one of the early symptoms of a revolt against the intellectualism of the 18th century. Sterne owes a good deal to *Rabelais (though Sterne's indecency is snickering rather than exuberant) and has himself been constantly imitated from his own time to the present.

stichomythia: a device in Greek drama by which two characters in a lively or heated scene exchange speeches consisting of only one line each (Greek, "line-speech"). It usually involves a sort of contention or verbal sparring, and sometimes the speeches are reduced to only half a line each. Typical stylistic devices in stichomythic dialogue are antithesis and parallelism, picking up the words of one's opponent, and phrasing the argument into philosophical maxims. Later drama has frequently used this device, usually in direct imitation of the Greeks.

Stoicism: a philosophy founded in Athens *c.* 315 B.C. by *Zeno and later expounded, with some modifications, by *Seneca, *Epictetus, and Marcus *Aurelius. Stoicism held that the universe was an organized whole consisting of intelligence (God) and matter and that events went in a long cycle which, when finished, started over and repeated itself exactly. It taught the universal brotherhood of man (including barbarians and slaves). The end of man is a life of virtue, since virtue is obedience to the law of the universe; and happiness comes from virtue. This being true, it is a mistake to make one's happiness depend on fortune or external accidents, and the true Stoic is moved neither by good nor by bad fortune.

Storm and Stress: see *Sturm und Drang.*

stream-of-consciousness novel: a novel in which the story is presented through a discontinuous succession of images and ideas, connected by association rather than logical sequential thought. The metaphor was used originally by William *James in his *Principles of Psychology* to define the flow of continuity of perceptual experience and describe the ways in which man's consciousness is in a constant state of flux. The attempt to "narrate" "thought" and give an illusion of inner flux involved novelists in large changes of the temporal and spatial form of fiction. Because the reader is confined to a given consciousness, the "point of view" methods of Henry

*James must come into play; time is always the present, since the author tries to put the reader into the actual moment of thought or of perceptual experience. Discontinuity occurs because inner attention jumps from one thought to another; and finally the novelists realized that they had to render simultaneities of experience, the orchestra of the senses. The first to employ the technique systematically, but awkwardly, was Edouard Dujardin in *Les Lauriers sont coupés* (*We'll to the Woods No More*, 1887). Dorothy M. Richardson (1873–1957) in her 12-part novel *Pilgrimage* focused on camera "point of view" and discontinuity early in the century, while *Proust was exploring memory and association. James *Joyce with his verbal virtuosity first showed how swiftly the reader might be carried from inner to outer reality and developed complex modes of subjectivity in *Ulysses*, using many mimetic and parody devices, with close attention to sensory material. The second wave of writers in the movement, Virginia *Woolf and *Faulkner, brought modifications to the Joycean techniques. Conrad Aiken's novels, especially *Blue Voyage*, adapted the methods of Joyce and Woolf. Faulkner in a highly original way attempted to render sensory and "triggered" experience in his picture of an idiot, following in this the method of the opening section of Joyce's *Portrait of the Artist as a Young Man.* Certain forms of stream of consciousness have been called "interior monologue," a designation first used by Russian critics to describe *Tolstoi's early attempts to capture moments of consciousness in their flowing state (as in *Anna Karenina*, when Anna's troubled thoughts at the end of the book are rendered discontinuous by the smell of fresh paint, or in certain hypnagogic passages in *War and Peace*). The *surrealists and before them Gertrude *Stein experimented with automatic writing in an attempt to capture moments out of the "unconscious." Stream-of-consciousness fiction presupposes the use of thoughts and sensations brought into consciousness. While there have been two or three treatises on the techniques and history of this movement, the work which defines it in the sense of both thought and sensory perception is Leon Edel's *The Modern Psychological Novel* (1955).

Strindberg, August: Swedish dramatist (1849–1912). Strindberg is Sweden's foremost writer and one of the representative men of his age. The scope of his work includes almost every aspect of human thought and existence. Although best known for his dramatic works, Strindberg wrote as many as eight autobiographies. His prose writings, extending into the fields of religion, history, science, sociology, and politics, include one of the finest histories of the Swedish people and some of the most violent criticism of the decadence of his time—a decadence of which he himself was a victim. In his dramatic works Strindberg was equally comprehensive. Here he displayed himself as a naturalistic psychologist, as a folklorist, as a religious expressionist, and as a historian. His dramas range from one-act plays to long dramatic cycles, almost Wagnerian in scope.

Strindberg's most characteristic feature was dissent. He was an unfortunate child of nature, always regarding himself as the tragic victim of fate, environment, and heredity. His attitude toward the world and his fellow human beings was hateful and vindictive. A great split divided his personality so that his whole life consisted of oscillation between extremes. One day he could be a humble and devout Christian; the next he would think himself God's equal and try to upset the social order by making gold and to overthrow the divine order by making a Homunculus.

With a naturalist's eyes, Strindberg saw the "spectacle of life . . . so brutal, so cynical, so heartless," as he writes in his revolutionary preface to *Miss Julie* (1888), a play which made Strindberg the forerunner of a new kind of drama. The helplessness of human beings in their chains of social, physical, and psychological predetermination inspired him to write this play, the story of a girl of noble birth who succumbs to her physical desire. She is unable to resist the butler, Jean, and kills herself with his razor out of shame and humiliation. The characters of this play are victims of their time, like their creator; "I have made my figures vacillating, out of joint, torn between the old and the new . . . and the type indicates degeneration."

One of the gravest results of Strindberg's conflicting

nature was his hatred of women—a feeling which probably had its origin in his attitude toward his mother. He was always most conscious of the fact that his father had married below his rank. Never could he forget that he was "the Son of a Servant" (the title of one of his autobiographical works, 1886).

Strindberg married often and unhappily. Woman was a necessary evil to him: he hated her and was at the same time bound to her. This terrible conflict reaches a typical Strindbergian overintensification in the well-known play *The Father* (1887). Here the two sexes are at war. Woman is portrayed as exploiting everything she possesses—her frailty, her children, her womanhood—to enslave her natural superior, her husband. Love is the trap in which a man is caught and ruined. The man is portrayed as aspiring and kind, the woman soulless and cunning, a real she-devil. The husband, forever struggling to escape his wife's snare, is finally caught and carried away in a straitjacket both figuratively and literally.

Another drama which deals with the battle of the sexes is the "masterpiece of horror," *Dance of Death* (1901). This time Strindberg does not take sides; in fact, the husband is portrayed as more destructive than his wife. The misery and horror of this play stem from Strindberg's own experience; in his own words: "Life was so alien, so contrary, so cruel, right from my childhood, and people were so cruel that I became so too."

There were periods when this oversensitive poet's strained and persecuted mind almost reached a breaking point. In Paris during the years 1894–96 Strindberg underwent a severe mental crisis, which is recorded in his autobiography *Inferno* (1897). Haunted by evil spirits, Strindberg became an occultist and Swedenborgian. His strange scientific experiments also date back to this time.

As this crisis passed, Strindberg found new light and thus began his greatest productive period. Understanding and repentance came to him and in this frame of mind he wrote the Parisian tragicomedy *There Are Crimes and Crimes* (1899), published, together with his mystery play *Advent* (1898), under the common title, *In a Higher Court*. A play inspired by his past experiences of the power of evil, *There Are Crimes and Crimes* shows that guilt cannot be eradicated by the fact that a man is cleared in court, for there is a higher judgment, man's conscience.

With greater understanding of himself and with repentance for his past egotistical life, Strindberg now set out to write one of his most important works, the trilogy *To Damascus* (1898–1904), a kind of purgatory drama. He himself appears as the Stranger, symbolically reliving his past life and thereby ridding himself of its horror, a process which reminds one of *psychoanalysis. Strindberg often speaks with the voice of many characters; he is both protagonist and spectator. Simultaneously he appears as the Stranger, the Writer, the Beggar, and the Madman who are his doubles. Through the techniques employed in this trilogy, Strindberg has become known as the father of the expressionistic drama.

Strindberg continued this form in *A Dream Play* (1902), perhaps his greatest play. With its dreamlike atmosphere and surrealistic sequence of events, it transcends the realm of reality entirely. As he pointed out in the preface, this play is a kind of continuation of *To Damascus*. It revolves around the secret of a locked door. The young officer, who is the leading character, forever waits and forever wonders—he waits for his imaginary girl and wonders about the inside of the eternally locked door. The result is disillusionment: the girl is not his and there is nothing behind the door. Strindberg is saying that if one violently forces open the door to life, as the officer is trying to do with the help of a locksmith, then he will be disappointed and disillusioned. One might even become a Nihilist as a result. His answer is to let life go past like the colorful pageant of a dream, to look at it, but not to judge it. Every bad dream will bring a fresh awakening with it, a new reconciliation with life, just as all sorrow and despair, no matter how bad, will be relieved by a ray of light.

Strindberg's works—like those produced by the *existentialism of our own time—are outcries in the agony of existence. They are expressions of a man's long and terrible struggle for self-realization in a chaotic world.

Sturm und Drang: German literary movement of the 1770's. *Lessing's appreciative articles on *Shakespeare helped to inspire the movement and its leaders, *Herder, *Goethe, and *Schiller. The name (not applied to the period until much later) comes from *Wirrwar, oder Sturm und Drang (Confusion, or Storm and Stress)*, by Friedrich Klinger (1752–1831). Produced in 1776, this play was a literary declaration of independence intended to liberate German drama from French Neo-Classical rules. Enthusiasm for Shakespeare broadened into a passion for the *Ossianic Poems, *Rousseau, *Diderot, folk *ballads, "natural impulses," and freedom from any rules or conventions. This German version of romantic impetuosity and emotional fervor was the artistic environment during the youth of the greatest German dramatists. Essentially, it was a movement of youthful revolt. In its strictest sense the period of *Sturm und Drang* extends from Goethe's *Gotz von Berlichingen* in 1773 to Schiller's *The Robbers* in 1781.

Styx: the chief river of the Underworld. Oaths sworn by it were inviolable.

surrealism: "super-realism," an artistic and literary movement in France between the two World Wars. During the First World War dadaism had arisen as a protest, by means of infantile language, against all established logic, institutions, and values. André Breton (1896–1966), a medical student, broke away from dadaism and launched the new school with his first surrealist manifesto in 1924: "pure psychic automatism . . . free from the exercise of reason and exempt from any aesthetic or moral purpose," an aesthetic mysticism seeking total liberation of the unconscious, in the magic of art to "create an evocation freed from time and space and movement." The basic idea, derived from a combination of dadaism with *Freud, is that the automatic, illogical, uncontrolled fantasies and associations of the mind represent a higher reality than the realistic, deliberately manipulated world of practical life and ordinary literature. Essentially, the surrealist strives to present a dream-world, leaving the interpretation of the dream to

700

his audience. He cultivates free association and automatic writing, decries any concept of art or talent (since these terms imply a deliberate control on the part of the artist), and delights in the illogical and inexplicable. The tendencies and humor can be briefly illustrated by the *Surrealistic Proverbs* of Paul Eluard and Benjamin Péret: "Elephants are contagious," and "Stupid like sausages whose sauerkraut has already been eaten away"; or in André Breton's idea of love: "Your flesh sprinkled by the flight of a thousand birds of paradise/Is a high flame lying in the snow." As a concerted movement, surrealism broke up at the beginning of the Second World War, largely as a result of political dissension among its adherents. Although the aspiration of transposing a dream directly and "by-passing the conscious awareness of the artist" did not work in practice, the movement exerted considerable influence on a good deal of modern and contemporary thought, literature, and painting (as on Giorgio di Chirico, Max Ernst, Joan Miró). Probably the most widely known manifestations of surrealism are the limp watches and clocks of the painter Dali. (See Balakian: *The Literary Origins of Surrealism*.)

Swedenborg, Emanuel: Swedish mystic (1688–1772). Swedenborg was an official at the Swedish department of mines for 31 years and during this time published a large body of scientific, mathematical, and philosophical work. As early as 1743 ideas of spiritualism had appeared in some of his scientific works. Ten years later he passed through a religious crisis. In 1747 he resigned his position and spent his remaining 25 years writing and publishing his mystical works. He was on terms of familiarity with angels and had direct orders from Christ to explain the true significance of the *Bible. His mystical works, like the earlier scientific ones, are written in Latin. They include *The Heavenly Arcana* (*Arcana coelestia*, 1749–56), *The Doctrine of Life for the New Jerusalem* (*Doctrina vitae pro Novo Hierosolyma*, 1763), and *The True Christian Religion* (*Vera christiana religio*, 1771). After his death his followers organized a Swedenborgian Church, and his ideas influenced writers as different as *Goethe and *Balzac.

Swift, Jonathan: English satirist (1667–1745). Born in Ireland of English parents, Swift lived a life that might almost be described as a continual flight from Ireland and a constant return to it, as if the fugitive were impelled by an unalterable destiny. His greatest disappointment was his failure to become a bishop in England and his being given, instead, the deanship of St. Patrick's Cathedral in Dublin (1713). In 1714, then, he returned to Ireland as if to exile; but in the remaining 30 years of his life he became thoroughly identified with Irish life, and, through such brilliant pamphlets as the *Drapier Letters* and *A Modest Proposal*, became virtually a "national hero." And there he wrote his greatest work, *Gulliver's Travels.*

After attending Kilkenny Grammar School and Trinity College, Dublin (where, refusing to study logic, he received a degree only by "special grace"), Swift first left Ireland in 1688. He spent a considerable part of the 1690's as secretary to Sir William Temple at Moor Park, Surrey, where he had time to read and to try his hand at writing. His first efforts were in the Pindaric *ode, a complicated form which he executed heavily, with results quite unlike the banter, lively humor, irony, satire, and even pungent realism variously achieved later in such works as *Description of a City Shower* (1709), *Description of the Morning* (1709), *Verses on His Own Death* (1731), *The Lady's Dressing Room* (1732), and *On Poetry, a Rhapsody* (1733). Resenting his dependent status and distressed at his lack of advancement, Swift in 1694 made his first flight back to Ireland and by being ordained in the Anglican church laid the foundation for his final return to Dublin as Dean Swift 20 years later.

After an unsuccessful effort to marry an heiress with whom he had fallen in love, Swift left Ireland again in 1696 for a second venture with Temple at Moor Park. Aside from editing Temple's correspondence, he now began to find himself as a writer of satirical prose, creating his first two works of permanent interest—*The Battle of the Books*, a digressive mock-epic version of the "Quarrel of the Ancients and Moderns," a dispute over the relative merits of ancient and modern literature in which Temple had been engaged, and *A Tale of a Tub* (both published 1704), a mixture of satirical essays and a narrative which burlesques the historical development of the Christian sects. Here he exhibits the keen insight and develops the unusual objectivity that characterize so much of his work. In these years, also, he tutored Esther Johnson, perhaps Temple's illegitimate daughter; thought by some to have become Swift's wife, she was at least a lifelong friend; and for her he wrote from London the *Journal to Stella* (1710–13), which not only gossips entertainingly about the literary and political great of London but reveals the capacity for affectionate devotion in a man often and inaccurately labeled a "misanthrope."

Temple's death in 1699 drove Swift back to Ireland and minor church appointments. But he made various visits to London, and eventually an ecclesiastical mission grew into an almost continuous stay from 1708 to 1714. Here he wrote with sharp irony on church questions (*Letter Concerning the Sacramental Test*, 1709; and *The Abolishing of Christianity*, 1711), playfully ridiculed the astrologer John Partridge with a series of pamphlets by "Isaac Bickerstaff," and, after initial collaboration with the Whigs, became in 1710 a powerful Tory publicist (editing the *Examiner* for a time in 1710 and writing such pamphlets as *The Conduct of the Allies*, 1711, *Some Remarks on the Barrier Treaty*, 1712, and *The Public Spirit of the Whigs*, 1714). In this most brilliant period of his life Swift was the associate of the ministers Oxford and Bolingbroke and, in the Scriblerus Club, of such literary figures as *Pope, *Congreve, Gay, Parnell, and Arbuthnot. Yet the excitement and promise of the period ended in anticlimax and disappointment: the Tories went into a decline, and in 1714 Swift, with only the deanship of St. Patrick's as reward, retired again to Dublin—with but a few visits to England to break his long final Irish sojourn.

But he reconciled himself to his destiny, won the love of the Irish, and did some of his most distinguished writing. *A Modest Proposal* (1720), urging the Irish to solve their problems by raising children for the English food market, is one of the finest pieces of irony in English. *Gulliver's Travels* (1726) makes highly original use of fantasy to comment both on contemporary society and on the foibles and failures of humanity generally. He wrote other pamphlets on Irish affairs. A related side of him appears in the instructive but by no means solemn *A Letter to a Young Clergyman* (1721), *A Letter of Advice to a Young Poet* (1721), and *A Letter to a Very Young Lady on Her Marriage* (1729). And he is primarily the humorist in *Directions to Servants* (1731) and *A Complete Collection of Genteel and Ingenious Conversation* (1738). *Cadenus and Vanessa* (1726) is a verse account of and commentary on his relations with Esther Vanhomrigh, who had fallen in love with him many years before.

Swift underwent a mental decline before his death in 1745. Mourned then as a vehement and slashing defender of the underprivileged Irish, he has constantly grown in stature as one of the most uncompromising but not cynical observers of "the animal called man," as a master of irony that could be playful or fierce but was always straightfaced to the end of whatever daring literary or rhetorical game he chose to play. If it is true, as has been suggested, that an artist's greatness is allied to his not "belonging" wholly to some social group and to his being essentially an observant outsider, it may be that in Swift's movements back and forth across the Irish channel and in the temporariness of his allegiances and identifications we can see a partial explanation of his detached and piercing insight, of his ability to carry to an ultimate, beyond any limitation that might be imposed by the commitments of a person completely in harmony with some local or social order, his vision, gracefully aloof or deeply passionate, of human capability and failure.

Swinburne, Algernon Charles: English poet (1837–1909). Educated at Eton and Oxford, Swinburne was a brilliant, erratic, and undisciplined student. His *Atalanta in Calydon* (1865), a tragedy on the classical model, showed an amazing lyrical gift, especially in the choruses. The first series of *Poems and Ballads*, published the next year, confirmed the impressions of the poet's skill and manifested two tendencies for which the Victorians could never forgive him: he openly despised Christianity, and he was fascinated by sex, especially in its violent and perverted forms. But even in poems like *Laus Veneris* and *Anactoria* and *Dolores*, deliberately written to shock his audience, there was fine poetry. Some of the poems have never been surpassed in their type: *A Leave-Taking* and *The Triumph of Time*, both growing out of an unrequited love; *The Garden of Proserpine*, a dreamy picture of "the sleep eternal / In an eternal night," which follows death and is better than any resurrection; the *Hymn to Proserpine*, in which a Roman of the old school laments the fine ancient gods who have been displaced by the "gray" world of Christianity. Later, Swinburne wrote political poetry (especially on the theme of Italian independence), historical plays, and a considerable body of distinguished criticism, but essentially he continued to repeat his earlier poems.

All his verse is written with amazing technical skill and a great richness of sound, with complex rhythms, intricate patterns of alliteration and *assonance, and rich riming. Sometimes the sound is so enthralling that it becomes cloying or hypnotic, and the reader suddenly realizes that he is reading along happily without the least notion of what is being said. He may even go back and find that nothing is being said. At his best, though, Swinburne has a good deal to say and says it with remarkable effectiveness. In fact, some of the condemnation heaped upon him was directly due to the fact that he was effective in saying some things that needed to be said.

symbolism: a conscious and deliberate technique of the use of symbols, brought to the status of a literary school (which became international in scope) in the late 19th century by a group of French poets, including *Mallarmé, *Verlaine, and *Rimbaud.

The underlying philosophy of the symbolists was a conviction that the transient objective world is not true reality, but a reflection of the invisible Absolute. Moreover, correspondences exist between impulses derived through different senses (*Baudelaire's *Correspondances*).

The symbolists therefore rebelled against the techniques of *realism, and *naturalism, which were designed to capture the transient. They believed that the inner eternal reality could only be suggested: "to name is to destroy, to suggest is to create" (Mallarmé). Intensity and complexity were to be achieved by condensed syntax and minor images clustered around one main metaphor, until one sense impression was translated into another and both became symbols of the original impression. Their symbolism was occasionally trite and more often deliberately vague or esoteric. However, they were satisfied that their poems should be "an enigma for the vulgar, chamber-music for the initiated." Critics have in consequence charged them with substituting the "rimed rebus for poetry." Accepting *Poe's definition of a poem—"the rhythmic creation of beauty"—the symbolists emphasized the primary importance of the sound of the verse and the need for fastidious craftsmanship in creating the effects of music through words.

The symbolists rejected sociological and ethical themes, insisting that art pursues the "sensations of beauty" apart from moral or social responsibility. For them any theme, any individual perception, was right so long as it captured the poet's subtle intuitions and contributed to a total design; in short, they subscribed to the doctrine of "art for art's sake."

Contemptuous of their environment and of middle-class morality, some of them flaunted their perversions and despair, a "new shudder" (the phrase was first applied to Baudelaire) deliberately induced through drugs, alcohol, and sadism. Verlaine and Rimbaud welcomed as an accolade the name *Decadent*, the term by which *Gautier had characterized their idol Baudelaire, whose *Flowers of Evil* (*Les Fleurs du Mal*, 1857), combining depravity, mysticism, and Christian love, had given a major impetus to the movement. In addition to freeing writers from conventional subject matter, the major contribution of the symbolist movement was its emphasis on a technique—the allusive symbol and the music. The line of primary influence runs from Poe to Baudelaire to Mallarmé. From France the movement spread to influence such writers as the Englishman *Yeats, the German

*Rilke, and the Russian Andrey Bely. (See Balakian: *The Symbolist Movement*.)

Symposium, The: a dialogue of *Plato describing a banquet held at the home of the tragic poet Agathon and reporting the speeches in praise of love that were made there by *Socrates and others (4th century B.C.). The narrative is put into the mouth of Apollodorus, who heard it from Aristodemus, a disciple of Socrates who accompanied him to the banquet, for Apollodorus himself was a child at the time. Aristodemus said that, when the dinner was over, Eryximachus, the physician, had suggested that the professional entertainer provided by Agathon be dismissed and that the guests speak in praise of love instead. And he added that, although he did not remember all the addresses that were made, he could repeat some, at least in part. Phaedrus, he knew, spoke first and extolled love as the most helpful of the gods toward the attainment of virtue; but Pausanias was more cautious, distinguishing between the higher love of the soul and the lower love of the body and thus making love not one but two. Eryximachus, who accepted this distinction, then identified the two forms of love with health and sickness, not only in men, but in animals and plants and all things, after which *Aristophanes devised a grotesque fable presenting love as a quest conducted by every person for his other self. Finally Agathon eulogized love again in exquisite phrases adorned with antithesis and rhythm and all the flowers of rhetoric, and after he had finished, it was Socrates' turn to speak.

Socrates began by pointing out that love is always manifested as a desire for some good which the lover does not possess, or which, if he does possess, he fears that he may lose; for his wish is to have it forever. Moreover the object of his desire is always beauty in some form; and beauty is eternal; therefore love is really the aspiration for immortality through possession of, or union with, the beautiful. On the bodily level it is fulfilled by the begetting of children; on the higher level of mind and soul by the fame that comes from great achievements; but its truest manifestation is found in mystic union with the Idea of Beauty itself.

These facts, Socrates says, he learned from a prophetess Diotima of Mantinea.

Socrates pauses and Aristophanes is about to reply, when Alcibiades bursts in half-drunk and is invited to join the others in praising love; but he sees Socrates and declares that he will praise him instead, as he proceeds to do in one of the best-known passages in Plato. After he has finished, a band of revelers enters and throws everything into confusion. Some of the guests go home and others fall asleep, among them Aristodemus, who awakens just before dawn to find Socrates discussing the nature of the drama with Aristophanes and Agathon.

Synge, John Millington: Irish dramatist (1871–1909). A new Irish theater was probably the most important outgrowth of the *Irish Literary Revival, and Synge was the chief dramatist of this theater. He, more than any other member of the group, was able to blend Celtic romanticism with modern realism, and his best plays— *Riders to the Sea, The Playboy of the Western World,* and *Deirdre of the Sorrows*—have become classics of the modern stage.

It was *Yeats who discovered Synge in Paris (where he had gone after graduating from Trinity College, Dublin) and persuaded him to return to his homeland and absorb the native tradition. Synge's subsequent period in the Aran Islands, in the isolated, westernmost part of Ireland, gave him his knowledge of the Irish peasantry and their speech, two important elements in his drama. As he explains in his preface to *The Playboy*, "in countries where the imagination of the people, and the language they use, is rich and living, it is possible for a writer to be rich and copious in his words, and at the same time to give the reality, which is the root of all poetry, in a comprehensive and natural form."

This combination of the poetic and realistic is excellently demonstrated by *Riders to the Sea* (1904), a very simple but powerful one-act play about a mother who loses her sixth son to the sea. The characters are peasants of the type Synge lived with in the Aran Islands, a rude people, and yet the tragedy of their struggle against

708

a relentless nature is beautifully told in poetic prose based on their common speech: "They're all gone now, and there isn't anything more the sea can do to me."

In comedy also Synge found richness in a peasant setting. *The Playboy of the Western World* (1907) is the ironical story of Christy, a young weakling who flees to an isolated public house after a family quarrel and is accepted as a dashing figure by all the country folk, on the basis of his boast that he has just killed his father. He becomes the local hero, center of female admiration, especially pursued by a widow and finally engaged to the pub owner's daughter Pegeen, when his domineering father, bandaged but alive, appears. Christy fells him again only to learn that the mob is fickle and that "there's a great gap between a gallous story and a dirty deed." But this is a comedy, and old Mahon has a stout skull; he rises for a second time and is proud to be led off by the son who has become a man. Although contemporary patriots read into the play a satire on Ireland, it is rather an exuberant folk tale in which the humorous is curiously blended with the poetic.

Synge's third significant play, *Deirdre of the Sorrows*, has been acclaimed the masterpiece of Irish romanticism. Based on an old legend popular with Irish writers (see *Deirdre), it is an outstanding version of this famous story of love and passion, although Synge's early death from Hodgkin's disease in 1909 prevented a final revision of the play.

Tacitus, Gaius (or Publius) Cornelius: Roman historian (*c.* A.D. 55–*c.* 117). Little is known about Tacitus, except what can be gleaned from his own writings and those of his friend *Pliny the Younger. These sources indicate that he belonged to the upper classes, that he was given the rhetorical type of education popular in the early Empire, and that he achieved unusual success as a lawyer and government official. Tacitus was a brilliant orator who pleaded in many famous cases and, after

709

holding the consulship and various other offices, was entrusted with the highest administrative post open to a senator, the proconsulate of Asia. He married the daughter of Agricola, governor of Britain under the Emperor Domitian, and his life with her was happy. But beyond these few facts, almost everything concerning him is obscure.

Tacitus' major works are the *Histories* and the *Annals*, the *Histories* tracing events in the Roman Empire from A.D. 69 to A.D. 96, the *Annals* treating the earlier period from A.D. 14 to A.D. 68. Both books were written when Tacitus' powers were at their height, and, though much has been lost from them, what remains provides by far the best source we have for Roman history during the first century of our era. Tacitus' minor works, composed earlier in his life, are the *Dialogue on Orators*, a discussion of the decline in eloquence that followed the establishment of the Principate of Augustus, the *Life of Agricola*, a laudatory biography containing much interesting material about ancient Britain, and an ethnographical treatise usually referred to as the *Germania*, describing the tribes who lived across the Rhine and the Danube beyond the frontiers of Rome. Of these brief works, the *Germania* is the best known, as all serious study of Central Europe must begin with it; but the *Agricola* is also widely read, being regarded by common consent as the finest Roman biography extant.

Although Tacitus is undoubtedly a great historian, there are certain flaws in his work. He presents his material at times as if he were concerned chiefly with its didactic value, a tendency particularly apparent in the *Germania.* He centers attention on the corruption of the court and the city, often to the neglect of the provinces, which were on the whole ably governed. And he supports the Roman nobility in their opposition to the Caesars, as can be observed, for example, in his account of Tiberius' reign in the *Annals.* For Tacitus' experience with the tyranny of Domitian had embittered him against the whole imperial system, and he was ready at all times to attack it, although he did not willfully falsify the facts in order to do so, and the essential truth of his history is incontestable.

But Tacitus is more than a great historian. He is a supreme literary artist. His style is marked by dignity and elevation and is unique in Latin literature for its bold condensation and brilliant use of epigram and innuendo. His ability to analyze human emotion is remarkable, his dramatic skill in the portrayal of character astonishing. His vast descriptive powers, which seem peculiarly adapted to the depiction of disaster and crime, have fixed the dark period following the death of Augustus forever in the memory of mankind.

Talmud (= teaching): an interpretive commentary on the Old Testament, and particularly of the Pentateuch, which was, according to Jewish tradition, given to Moses verbatim (see *Bible). There are two versions of the Talmud—the shorter compiled in Jerusalem and the other, compiled in Babylon (150 B.C.–A.D. 250; additions 250–600 A.D.), considered more authoritative The Talmud states the binding laws (*Halakhah* = manner of life) and their interpretation (*Haggadah* = telling), the latter an extensive collection of ethical maxims, scientific observations, folk tales, semi-historical narratives, and comic anecdotes. Originally oral, these commentaries by the third-century A.D. were reduced to a writing called the *Mishnah* (= repetition), which itself stimulated further commentaries, called the *Gemarrah* (= completion). Since the 7th century the text of the Talmud has been stable, but it continued to inspire the reflections and commentaries of distinguished medieval Hebraists and philosophers, notably *Maimonides and *Aquinas.

Tantalus: one of the great sinners of Greek mythology, condemned to stand forever in a pool of water that recedes when he stoops to drink, while trees hang above his head laden with fruit that withdraws when he reaches for it. His name gives us the verb *tantalize*.

Taoism: like *Confucianism, at the core of Chinese thought and life for more than 2000 years and pervasive in Chinese culture. It has been described as the twin of

711

Confucianism, that is, as the mystical side in opposition to the practical side. As a philosophy it stands for spiritual freedom, naturalism, simplicity. First mentioned during the first century B.C., it seems to have been germinating long before. The founder of Taoism was Lao-tzu; and central to Taoism, as developed by him and subsequent thinkers, is a profound idea of *laissez-faire*: things must be allowed to follow their natural course. In some of its tenets it bears a resemblance to Western anarchistic philosophy; but in its Eastern concept the word *anarchism* would not apply because the Taoists focus on high ethical feeling and an idea of goodness and virtue: thus a strange mixture of active feeling and passive conduct, while at the same time the very tenets of the belief require active rather than passive attention. And within its doctrines of quietude and unworldliness it offers a practical way of life. Taoism influenced the development of *Zen. In spirit it seeks natural harmony and peace, and while in subsequent centuries there were elaborations and a Neo-Taoist school, the fundamentals have never lost their deep roots in Chinese culture.

Tartuffe: a comedy by *Molière (1669). Molière's great satire on religious hypocrisy is interesting in itself, for its history, and for the insight of 17th-century France which that history provides. The play which we know today, and which was produced in 1669, is a third version, the first two having been suppressed by religious groups. For five years before the final five-act version was released, *Tartuffe* was the subject of a bitter controversy. In an age which took its religion seriously and which had seen the establishment of religious associations dedicated to preserving the faith against any free-thinking, Molière's comedy was attacked as a satire on the pietism then in vogue and on religion itself. Although the king, the all-powerful Louis XIV, sympathized with Molière and had seen the original play without questioning it, the pressure from religious factions headed by the Archbishop of Paris himself was strong enough to bar *Tartuffe* from public showing for five years and to force Molière to rewrite much of it.

The 1669 version of the play is the only one extant, but from all the evidence, it may be assumed that the 1664 comedy focused on the credulity of Orgon rather than on the hypocrisy of Tartuffe, without any final defeat of the hypocrite. Orgon, enthralled by Tartuffe and his pretended devoutness, brings him into his home, where Tartuffe gains control, tries to seduce his host's wife, and—except for the intervention of the king—would expel the family when his villainy is disclosed. It is not difficult to ascribe the long didactic passages in the later play to Molière's determination that there be no confusion in the satire. The distinction between genuine religious feeling and hypocrisy is made specifically and repeatedly, apparently to the satisfaction of the religious critics if not to the pleasure of a modern audience. The fifth-act intervention of the king, in the manner of the classic *deus ex machina*, is also another outgrowth of the struggle. One might question the consistency of Orgon's characterization and the propriety of including in the play a glorification of Louis' omniscience, but no one could complain that evil had been allowed to triumph or that Molière did not venerate his king and appreciate his support.

Molière's primary interest was in character rather than moralizing, and these changes undoubtedly made *Tartuffe* a different play from what he had intended. Though the revisions probably weakened the play, *Tartuffe* is still an excellent comedy, one of Molière's best. The satire is seriously conceived, yet even the passages in which Tartuffe appears most despicable are relieved and given comic character by the sprightly maid, Dorine. And if Orgon seems incredibly gullible, he has his humorous counterpart in his mother, the very credible and imperious Madame Pernelle. So it is that Molière derives amusing but thoughtful satire from what has on occasion been matter for a Restoration drama of seduction or an Elizabethan melodrama of villainy.

Tasso, Torquato: Italian poet (1544–95). Tasso's *Jerusalem Delivered* (*Gerusalemme liberata*, 1575, published 1581) is the best-known romantic epic of the *Renaissance. It was first published without Tasso's permission, and his later revisions (1593), undertaken between attacks of lunacy, spoiled it. The general story concerns Godfrey of Bouillon and the first crusade. The substance of the poem deals with the unsuccessful efforts of the devil, assisted by a beautiful sorceress, Armida, to prevent the crusaders from capturing Jerusalem. Though the poem is modeled on *Vergil, it is entirely distinct in its tone and interest. It presents a series of love affairs between beautiful pagan heroines and Christian knights, interwoven with scenes of battles and religious allegories. The nature scenes and the passions and plaints of the tenderhearted mistresses are full of charm. The imagery and tone greatly influenced *Spenser and *Milton.

Tasso's other works include an early epic, *Rinaldo* (1562); a charming pastoral play in blank verse, *Aminta* (1573, published 1580); and an unsuccessful sequel to his great epic, *Gerusalemme conquistata* (1593). Tasso himself became the hero of *Goethe's poetic drama *Torquato Tasso* (1790) and *Byron's dramatic soliloquy *The Lament of Tasso* (1817).

Tempest, The: a comedy by *Shakespeare (c. 1611). *The Tempest* was acted at court in 1611 and 1613, and various evidence indicates that it was probably written not long before the first of these performances. The unusual spectacular elements of the play—storms, a mythological masque, a magic banquet, the use of a pack of dogs to pursue Caliban and his associates, and, above all, the lavish use of both vocal and instrumental music—made the play particularly suitable for court presentation.

This comedy has two other particular distinctions. It is the only play by Shakespeare for which there is no known source, and it seems likely that the plot may be his own invention. If so, this fact may reinforce the speculation about the second distinction. *The Tempest* may well be the last play that Shakespeare wrote, and it has been suggested that it was designed as a deliberate farewell to the theater—that Shakespeare is Prospero, the magician, commenting on the basic identity of illusions,

714

plays, and life itself: "We are such stuff / As dreams are made on, and our little life / Is rounded with a sleep" (IV, i). If this is the dramatist's farewell, the appropriateness of Prospero's act of freeing his spirits and renouncing his magic at the end of the play is obvious.

Interesting as such biographical speculation may be, however, it is entirely independent of the value of the play as a work of art. Here too, this play is unique among Shakespeare's productions, for it presents a systematic view of all the range of life that bears any relationship to humanity. Shakespeare here uses the old idea that life is arranged in a "chain of being," each link of which shares something of the nature of the links on either side of it. Caliban is a subhuman creature, something halfway between brute and man. Stephano and Trinculo are man at his lowest, and it is significant that Caliban greatly admires them: they are the next stage above him, and hence superior, but not beyond his comprehension, whereas Prospero is quite out of the range of Caliban's understanding. Next in the scale we have a wide variety of ordinary people of varying degrees of effectiveness and imperfection. Sebastian and Antonio are vicious, but dangerous to any merely mortal power. Gonzalo is honest and faithful, but old and powerless, and a bit ridiculous. The officers and crew of the ship are mere technicians, useful as sailors, but of no interest as human beings. Ferdinand and Miranda are perfect in their way, but young, impulsive, and too innocent to be very effective. Prospero is slightly past the edge of perfect humanity. He has full experience, knowledge, and wisdom, together with tolerance and detachment; and although he cannot himself go beyond the limits of humanity, he commands spirits who can. Ariel at the upper end of the scale balances Caliban at the lower: he is not really human but has some characteristics in common with humanity. Just as Caliban is too brutal to be touched by human sorrows, Ariel is too spiritual.

The play abounds with balances and parallels. Caliban's contempt for apes "with foreheads villainous low" is like the contempt of Trinculo and Stephano for Caliban. The stupidly ineffective plot of these three against Prospero's life is almost a burlesque of the dangerous plot of Sebastian and Antonio against Alonzo's life. Just as Caliban mistakes drunkards for gods, Miranda at first takes Ferdinand for a spirit, and he takes her for the goddess of the island. And if we laugh at Caliban's imbecility when he admires buffoons, we smile at Miranda's inexperience when for the first time she sees a miscellaneous group of people—including two who have just plotted and attempted two murders—and exclaims, "How many goodly creatures are there here! How beauteous mankind is!" Yet it is part of the wisdom of the play that we really accept her inexperienced view as truer than our own jaded one. Finally, we note that Prospero, who had let a kingdom be taken from him while he studied the magic arts, renounces these arts and goes back to rule his kingdom—thus accepting his own humanity and obligations even while he regards all human life as a grave but transitory comedy.

Tennyson, Alfred, Lord: English poet (1809–92). Poet Laureate for over 40 years, Tennyson is representative of the Victorian age. His skilled craftsmanship and noble ideals retained a large audience for poetry in an age when the novel was engrossing more and more readers. Tennyson's early works (*Poems, Chiefly Lyrical*, 1831; 1832) were markedly influenced by *Keats, *Byron, and *Scott. Exquisitely melodious, they nevertheless reveal the defects of much of Tennyson's poetry, superficial thinking and excessive artificiality of style. They provoked the criticism that the words were too good for the meaning.

But the next volume, *Poems* (1842), assured Tennyson's popularity and reputation. It contained rewritings of the earlier *The Lady of Shalott* and *The Lotus Eaters*, immeasurably improved in pictorial and symbolic qualities and in their caressing music. Two new poems, *Morte D'Arthur* (later to be revised as *The Passing of Arthur*) and *Locksley Hall*, expressed the sentimental optimism of the era. Another poem, *Ulysses*, symbolized the Victorian conception of the ideal heroic spirit. This distinguished volume was just what the age desired. Here was a moral poet-teacher, no disconcerting rebel, who was also a meticulous artist.

Meanwhile Tennyson had suffered a severe emotional shock in the death (1833) of his dearest friend, Arthur Hallam. To his memory Tennyson wrote 181 poems during the course of the next 17 years. They were published as *In Memoriam* (1850). These lyrics (in the stanza form abba) deal with doubts and suffering (" 'Tis better to have loved and lost / Than never to have loved at all"), problems of death, the evidence of science, and a hard-won faith in a God of Love and a life eternal ("believing where we cannot prove"). With an odd humility, Tennyson said, "*I* is not always the author speaking of himself, but the voice of the human race speaking through him." It is certainly the voice of Victorian England.

The *Idylls of the King* (1859–85) is a series of 12 narratives in *blank verse. Based on *Malory's *Morte Darthur*, they attempt to give the illusion of a distant and picturesque era, but they remain Victorian, didactic, allegorical. It is perhaps no exaggeration to say that King Arthur's knights are modeled on Prince Albert. The moral lessons are sentimental and not very penetrating. This poem and *Locksley Hall* have lessened his reputation among the modern critics who despise a moral message and demand a social one; Tennyson seems often to have closed his eyes to the ugliness of the Victorian period or to have been deluded by the mirage of material prosperity. Yet sometimes, as in parts of *Maud* (1855), he is scathingly aware of the evils and false values of Victorian society.

Tennyson's real contribution lies in his shorter poems (*The Lady of Shalott*, *Oenone*, the songs from *The Princess, Ulysses, A Dream of Fair Women, The Palace of Art*), where the sensuous image is molded with fastidious restraint and intensified by complexity and irony. Romantic passion is refined, perhaps overrefined, but its distinctive melodies are disciplined with impeccable taste. Tennyson's fame rests on his perfect control of sound, the synthesis of sound and meaning, the union of the pictorial and the musical.

Terence: Roman comic poet (*c.* 195–159 B.C.). Publius Terentius Afer was born at Carthage, but while still a child he was brought to Rome as the slave of a senator named Terentius Lucanus, who educated him and later set him free. This act of generosity enabled Terence to develop his talent as a dramatist and gave him entrance into the Scipionic Circle, an aristocratic coterie interested in furthering the spread of Greek culture at Rome. Under their patronage, Terence adapted four plays from *Menander, the chief of the writers of Greek New Comedy, and two others from Apollodorus of Carystus. These comedies have all been preserved. After producing the last of his plays, *Adelphoe* (*The Brothers*, 160 B.C.), Terence set sail for Greece, where he died, under unknown circumstances, the following year.

In adapting Greek New Comedy to Roman use, Terence discarded the expository prologue used traditionally to reveal the outcome of the action and divulge the hidden identities of the characters involved in it. By this change he introduced new elements of suspense and surprise into his dramas and gave them a more modern tone than the comedies of Menander or *Plautus, in which the audience was told the secret of the plot from the beginning. At the same time, however, the omission of the prologue weakened the part played by dramatic irony in Terence's compositions; for this depended on the spectator's knowing in advance who the characters really were and how their difficulties would be solved. Although Terence used foreshadowing within the body of the play itself to keep as much irony as possible, the loss is noticeable, especially in a comedy of discovery like the *Hecyra (Mother-in-Law)*.

Terence made a practice of combining characters and scenes from different dramas to form a single comedy. He based his earliest play, *Andria* (*The Woman of Andros*, 166 B.C.), on the *Andria* of Menander, but he added certain elements from Menander's *Perinthia* to it; and he constructed *Eunuchus* (*The Eunuch*, 161 B.C.) and *The Brothers* in a similar way. Terence used this method of composition (known as *contamination*) to give his plays increased complexity of plot and added variety of characters. For Greek New Comedy was often thin and trite. But the practice offended those who insisted on a faithful adaptation of the Greek, and the attacks they made

718

on him forced Terence to answer their charges in literary prologues.

Terence's literary prologues bear no resemblance to the expository prologues he had previously discarded. They neither outline the action, nor comment on the characters. Instead, they carry a direct appeal from the poet to the audience on some point connected with the composition of his plays. For besides the accusations brought against him on grounds of *contamination*, Terence was charged with pilfering characters and scenes from earlier translators and with depending on his friends more than on himself in composing his comedies. Because of the nature of Terence's prologues, they can be omitted without affecting the plays to which they are prefixed; and this is done in some modern translations. Historically, however, they are of great value for the information they contain on the poet's sources and methods of work.

Terence's material is that of his Greek originals, but the workmanship is his own, and it is excellent. His language is pure and highly polished, his dialogue easy yet pointed, his whole style perfectly adjusted to the type of comedy he wrote. His plays are humane, refined, and filled with proverbial wisdom. The ideal they present is that of moderation. The Greek atmosphere is kept by avoiding Roman allusions, and the elaborate Roman lyrics characteristic of Plautus are reduced in scope. There are touches of realism, too, not found in the older poet. Sometimes Terence begins a scene in the middle of a line, and except at the end of *The Woman of Andros*, he does not break the dramatic illusion by direct address to the audience.

But Terence is lacking in comic power, and his plays seem tame beside those of Plautus. They are not without humor; but the humor is delicate and subtle and requires study for its appreciation. Terence wrote for the educated classes, and his comedy did not command much popular support. But he was read through the Roman period and the *Middle Ages, and he has been influential since the *Renaissance, especially in France.

The favorite plays of Terence today are *The Woman of Andros* and *The Brothers*, both adapted from Menander. *The Woman of Andros* describes the intrigue by which Pamphilus won Glycerium as his bride, although at first his case seemed hopeless. She was supposedly an orphan of foreign birth, and her reputation was doubtful; for she lived with a *hetaira* named Chrysis, who was believed to be her sister. He was engaged by his father to marry an Athenian girl of good social standing and unquestioned virtue, Philumena, the daughter of Chremes, an old family friend. The action of *The Woman of Andros* is therefore typical of New Comedy. But Terence enriched it by adding the story of the true love of Charinus for Philumena, an episode in which he approaches the modern theme of honorable courtship in a way all but unique in ancient literature.

The Brothers is the most intellectual of Terence's comedies and probably also the best. It describes how a countryman named Demea gives his elder son Aeschinus to his citified brother Micio to rear, but keeps his younger boy Ctesipho at home on the farm. Demea is a stern man by nature, and he rears Ctesipho under the strictest supervision; but Micio, who is very lax, gives Aeschinus the fullest liberty. Each brother is convinced that he is right, and that in the end his boy will turn out the better man. But when the test comes, it reveals that both alike have failed to develop good character in their charges. The point of the play thus becomes clear. In the rearing of children, neither discipline alone nor indulgence alone is desirable. Liberty and control are both equally necessary; but they must be used with moderation.

In addition to *The Woman of Andros* and *The Brothers*, Terence borrowed two other comedies from Menander: *The Eunuch*, his greatest stage success, though now condemned on moral grounds; and the *Heauton Timorumenos* (*Self Tormentor*, 163 B.C.). *The Self Tormentor*, named after a father who imposes penance on himself when his harshness drives his son from home, is a well-constructed play filled with dramatic irony. Its opening scene is famous. From Apollodorus, Terence adapted *Phormio* (161 B.C.), a lively play of love intrigue, and *The Mother-in-Law*, a sentimental drama with a plot similar to that of Menander's *Arbitration*.

Teresa of Jesus, Saint: Spanish mystic (1515–82). Saint Teresa has given the world one of its most remarkable spiritual autobiographies. *Life, Interior Castle, Way of Perfection* record her trances and visions, fear of Hell, and spiritual marriage with the Lord, and because she was acutely self-analytical, she explained her inner experiences with clarity and vividness. A mystic in religion, she was a forceful administrator in the world of practical affairs. In spite of violent opposition (her *Conception of the Love of God* was banned by the Inquisition), she founded the first convent of discalced Carmelite nuns (1562), then organized numerous other such convents, and enlisted the aid of St. *John of the Cross to establish similar groups for friars. In a modern play, *Four Saints in Three Acts*, Gertrude *Stein has tried to capture Saint Teresa's paradoxical combination of practicality and mysticism.

terza rima: a rime scheme in which three-line groups, usually of iambic pentameter lines, are held by interlocking rhymes each of which (after the first) occurs three times: aba bcb cdc, etc. This would form an endless sequence if it were not normally concluded by the use of a four-line group, the last line of which rhymes with the second: dede. This is the poetic form of *Dante's *Divine Comedy*. In English it has been used in such poems as *Shelley's *Ode to the West Wind* and William *Morris's *The Defence of Guenevere*.

Thackeray, William Makepeace: English novelist and essayist (1811–63). Thackeray was a voluminous writer and one of the masters of English *realism. He began with essays and sketches and all his life wrote primarily for periodicals, but the beginning of the serial publication of novels enabled him to move into large-scale fiction without changing his writing habits or having to seek new markets. Though some of his smaller works are excellent, especially some of the humorous sketches and satirical light verse, he is remembered primarily for a few novels: *Vanity Fair, A Novel Without a Hero* (1847–48), *The History of Pendennis* (1848–50), *The His-

tory of Henry Esmond (1852). His later novels, while excellent in some ways, fall slightly below the level of these three. The fact that Thackeray has been accused of both sentimentality and cynicism is a tribute to the balance that he keeps between the subjective and the objective, between feeling and thought. He was essentially a blend of humorist and satirist, a man who watched the world with sympathy tempered by ironic amusement.

Theocritus: Greek pastoral poet (*c.* 310–*c.* 250 B.C.). Almost nothing is known about the life of Theocritus except that he was born in Syracuse and that he made his home for a time at Alexandria and on the Aegean island of Cos. Twenty-four *epigrams and 30 short poems called *Idyls (Sketches)* are attributed to him, although a few of them are certainly by other hands. The *Idyls* are of various types, some developing epic or lyric themes, some panegyric, but the most interesting are the *mimes*, which present dramatic pictures of town and country life in monologue or dialogue form. Of the urban mimes the best is the *Women at the Adonis Festival*, describing a visit made by two Syracusan ladies to the palace of Ptolemy, which had been thrown open to the public for the rites of the dying god. But the *Spell*, in which a girl named Simaetha resorts to magic to win back her lover, is almost as great. Despite the fame of these pieces, however, Theocritus' most influential work consists of the rural mimes, known traditionally as *pastorals* or *bucolics*, and based on the rustic lays of Sicilian shepherds and herdsmen. These poems were the first of their type ever written, and in composing them Theocritus both invented pastoral poetry and perfected it. None of his imitators, not even *Vergil, was as able as he was to retain the freshness and vigor of rural song in the finished form demanded by literature. And none remained as true as he did in his descriptive passages to the realities of country life. Theocritus also introduced almost all the motives that became traditional in this type of poetry. He developed the refrain and the inserted song, and he used the lament, the serenade, the contest for a prize, and the coarse but friendly banter of rustics. Among his good rural pieces are the *Thyrsis*, mourning the death of Daphnis, the traditional shepherds' hero, and the *Harvest Home*, presenting himself and his friends as countrymen.

Theophrastus: Greek writer and philosopher (*c.* 372–*c.* 287 B.C.). Theophrastus studied under *Aristotle and was his successor as president of the Lyceum. His wide interests are reflected in his list of publications on many subjects, particularly botany, which he established as a science.

To the student of literature, Theophrastus is above all else the author of the *Characters*. This work consists of a dedicatory letter followed by 30 brief sketches on such common human failings as tactlessness, officiousness, distrustfulness, and greed. Each of its sections consists of the definition of a single fault illustrated by concrete example of the behavior in which it results. The surly man curses the stone he stumbles over. The stupid cannot find what he has put away himself. The children of the loquacious man say to him at bedtime, "Talk to us, father, we want to go to sleep."

The plan of the *Characters* is simple and the style unpretentious, but the matter is very interesting. The examples, which make up the bulk of the work, are shrewdly selected, true to life, and often most amusing. They show how permanent the little weaknesses of human nature are and at the same time provide a glimpse into the social life of the Athenian people, with their different social conventions. In Theophrastus, only the boor answers the door himself.

The *Characters* deals with types rather than individuals and represents the first systematic attempt at personality description in Greek literature. It was probably suggested by Aristotle's studies of the ruling traits in human nature, but because it is essentially humorous, it resembles the work of the writers of New Comedy (see *Menander) more closely. It is not known for what purpose the *Characters* was composed, but possibly it was intended for reading at dinner parties. It inspired the *Caractères* of the 17th-century French author *La Bruyère.

Theseus: a great Greek hero, the son of Aegeus, king of Athens, husband of Phaedra, the father of *Hippolytus by the Amazon queen Hippolyta.

Thomas à Kempis: German mystic and ascetic (1380–1471). Born of peasant stock, Thomas à Kempis entered an Augustinian monastery in Holland, seemingly little different from thousands of other pious men who devote their lives to God. He too produced pedestrian tracts on monastic life and copied manuscripts in an exquisite hand. It had been said of him that he was "no theologian and no humanist, no philosopher and no poet, and hardly even a true mystic." Yet he is believed to be the author of the Latin *Imitation of Christ (Imitatio Christi)*, which became the most influential work of its kind, translated into every major language of the world. It is a book of confessions and mystic exaltations, prayers to God, and personal exhortations to the reader. Its unique quality comes in part from the simple directness and clarity of style; but more important is its paradoxical combination of otherworldliness and common sense. Thomas joins a mystic vision of the good life, which needs no material pleasures, with a realistic understanding of the external distractions which keep men from the "upward way" to the "land of everlasting clearness." Those who go often on pilgrimages, says Thomas, rarely become saints. He knows that pride and ambition mask themselves by seeming to be other motives, that it is not the "deep words" of self-righteousness that make a man holy and upright but the good life: "Even if you should see your neighbor sin openly or grievously, do not reckon yourself better than he, for you do not know how long you will keep your integrity." Only in self-effacing meekness and obedience to God's will, in continence and poverty so complete that it frees the spirit, can man enjoy the undistracted contemplation of the Deity. To Thomas—and this is his message—this way of life was

Christ's way: those who would be true Christians must imitate Christ.

Thomas Aquinas, Saint: theologian (1225–74). Thomas Aquinas, surnamed the Angelic Doctor or the Angel of the School, was born near Aquino in the province of Naples. His family was one of the most influential in southern Italy; his brothers held high ranks in the imperial army, and most of his sisters had contracted illustrious alliances. All his family objected when, after receiving a good education, he became a Dominican monk in 1243.

A few years later Thomas Aquinas was in the schools of Paris and Cologne, studying under Albert the Great. Because of his huge physical stature and his silent, meditative disposition his comrades referred to him as "the great, dumb ox of Sicily." In a public debate his argumentation was so logical and persuasive that Albert the Great commented that "the roaring of this ox would echo in the entire universe." In 1248 he started to teach as a lecturer under the guidance of his master. During this period he composed his first works, *On the Principles of Nature* and *On Being and Essence.* In 1252 he received his degree of Bachelor of Arts at the University of Paris and was given a chair of theology. At this time he delivered numerous sermons in various churches of the French capital; little is known of the quality of his preaching except that it cultivated the subtleties which characterized the period.

Aquinas' great distinction as a scholar outweighed certain differences of opinion between him and the authorities of the University; in 1257 he received his Doctorate in Theology. His fame had, by this time, extended over all Europe; disciples from all parts of the civilized world flocked to his lectures on philosophy and theology. He wrote his *Summa contra gentiles* to help convert the Moors in Spain. King Louis IX invited him to take part in the private deliberations of his Council. In 1261 Pope Urban IV called Aquinas to Rome, where he strove to effect a reconciliation between the Greek church and the Church of Rome: his treatise *Against the Errors of the Greeks* was written for this purpose. Meanwhile, he taught theology in Rome and accompanied Urban IV and his successor Clement IV on their missions.

In 1265 Aquinas refused the archbishopric of Naples and began to compose the work which he had been planning for many years, the *Summa theologica*. Disgusted, as he himself avers, with the exuberance, obscurity, and lack of economy in the scholastic theologies written up to that time, he conceived the plan of a substantial summary, which would be clear and methodical and would include all that is important in Christianity, beginning with the existence of God and at the same time not neglecting the most humble precept of Gospel teaching. The composition of this monumental work occupied much of Aquinas' time during the last nine years of his life. Nevertheless, he continued to teach theology intermittently in Paris, Bologna, Rome, and Naples. He died in the winter of 1274 at the age of 49, while on the way to a church council at Lyons. He was canonized in 1323 and declared a Doctor of the Church in 1567.

Aquinas was endowed with a complex genius. His writings are marked by a powerful dialectic and animated by the ardor of mysticism and theological poetry. The breadth of his intelligence and the solidity of his reasoning were aided by an unusual mental acuity. He is said to have dictated at one time to four secretaries on entirely different subjects. Yet his style is not entirely devoid of some of the defects which characterize most of the writing of his century. The Latin in which he composed his works contains obscure passages which have occasionally misled scholars to conflicting interpretations.

These are relatively negligible shortcomings when we consider that Aquinas' philosophical system is one of the most important products of the *Middle Ages, both because of its intrinsic value and because of its almost unrivaled influence on philosophy and theology, which then formed an inseparable whole. The *Summa theologica* is the culmination of scholastic philosophy and its formulation into a cohesive system of thought. For centuries the *Summa* was in the hands of all theologians and philosophers; the Fathers of the Council of Trent placed it on the desks of their secretaries beside the

Scriptures, since it contained, in their estimation, the solution to all the problems under discussion.

The *Summa* is divided into three parts which have been briefly summarized as dealing successively with God, man, and God in the form of man (Christ). Part I treats of the existence, nature, and attributes of God and His angels, together with God's creation and government of the world. Part II first deals with general morality and the nature of man (this section is based on *Aristotle's *Nicomachaean Ethics*), and then goes on to special moral problems, particularly those of a theological or Christian nature. In this part Aquinas devotes considerable space to a discussion of the help by which God directs man to his immortal destiny. (Aquinas' theories on divine grace resemble closely those of *Augustine in that God's nature and not man's will is the source of good. This theory was the cause of extended disputes between Thomists and Scotists.) The third part of the *Summa* deals with Christ and the plan of Redemption and develops a theory of the sacraments. Aquinas had conducted his study as far as the fourth sacrament, penance, when death ended his career in 1274. Disciples of Thomas Aquinas have attempted to complete the *Summa* with the aid of materials taken from his other works; but it is obvious that the master's touch is absent from this posthumous part.

Aquinas applies the same method of argumentation in each of the more than 3000 articles which the *Summa* comprises. First he proposes the problem which he is about to solve or the theorem which he plans to develop; then follows an enumeration of the difficulties that have been brought against the teachings of the Church or against the articles of faith that concern this problem. A succinct proposition offers a solution of these difficulties; then come the proofs taken from the Scriptures, from tradition, and from theological reasoning. Aquinas adheres invariably to this technique in his attempt to answer more than 10,000 objections to points of Christian dogma. One recognizes in this procedure the direct influence of Aristotle, for in unfolding the vast panorama of religion, Aquinas follows the peripatetic method, as Augustine, nine centuries earlier, adapted the philosophy of *Plato to the same purpose.

Thomism, in a broad sense, is the name given to the theological and philosophical doctrines taught by Aquinas and embodied in his works. In a more restricted sense the name is applied only to certain theories proper to the Angelic Doctor and to the school of which he is the standard-bearer. The renewal of interest in the philosophy and theology of Aquinas, which was prompted in more recent times by the encyclical of Pope Leo XIII, *Aeterni Patris* (1879), bears the name of Neo-Thomism.

Thomas, Dylan: English poet (1914–53). Thomas was a writer of vigorous musical and incantatory poems, which he made famous by chanting and declaiming in reading tours, notably in America. His poems contain vigorous if complex imagery. He lived briefly, without care for his person, and had a large following and influence on younger poets. His collected poems were published in 1952. A prose work, *Portrait of the Artist as a Young Dog*, appeared in 1940; a second prose work came out posthumously in 1955, *Adventures in the Skin Trade*. A play for voices, *Under Milk Wood*, was first performed publicly in 1953, when he read it in an unfinished version. He completed it before his death that year.

Thoreau, Henry David: American philosophical essayist and nature writer (1817–62). Even in a group of nonconformists such as *Emerson, *Hawthorne, and Bronson Alcott, Thoreau stands out as the extreme individualist. After an impecunious youth and an education at Harvard (which "taught all the branches and none of the roots"), Thoreau supported himself by making pencils, working as a hired man, writing, tutoring, lecturing, surveying—anything that would make a simple living for him without dominating his life. His best-known period is the 26 months (1845–47) when he lived at Walden Pond in a hut he had built there (with a borrowed ax), growing vegetables to feed himself, observing the wild life about him, thinking out his own ideas, and laying the foundations for his best book. His purpose in this experiment is so simple and obvious that many people have found it impossible to accept and have attributed all sorts of ulterior motives to him, but there seems to be no reason for doubting his own statement: "I went to the woods because I wished to live deliberately, to front only the essential facts of life, and see if I could not learn what it had to teach, and not, when I came to die, discover that I had not lived." As he puts it in another place, "a man is rich in proportion to the number of things which he can afford to let alone," and among these things, for Thoreau, were voting and politics, regular employment, and churches and preaching. On his deathbed, asked if he had made his peace with God, he replied that he was not aware that he and God had ever quarreled, and to another's speculation about the other world he answered, "One world at a time." He was jailed for refusing to pay a poll tax to a proslavery government, and his first major essay, *Resistance to Civil Government* (1849; later called *Civil Disobedience*) developed the idea of passive resistance. This essay later influenced *Tolstoi and Gandhi.

His first volume, *A Week on the Concord and Merrimac Rivers* (1849), is the story of a trip taken with his brother, but the thread of the narrative is at times almost lost in a mass of original and quoted poetry, antiquarian anecdotes, literary criticism, and transcendental speculation. *Walden* (1854) was the only other book published during his lifetime. It is better constructed and more mature, the fruit of seven years of his best thinking and writing. It describes his life and thought at Walden Pond and develops most of his essential ideas. A number of travel books and books of essays were published posthumously: *Excursions*, *The Maine Woods*, *Cape Cod*, *A Yankee in Canada*.

Essentially, Thoreau is valuable for a completely fresh approach to the world. Even when his ideas were not really new (and what idea ever is?) they were not secondhand; he had arrived at them independently, and he expressed them in a vigorous and pithy style which, in spite of a fundamental earnestness and occasional moral indignation, never really lost its bearings or its sense of humor.

Thousand and One Nights: see *Arabian Nights.*

Thucydides: Greek historian (471?–400? B.C.). When the naval forces commanded by Thucydides were defeated at the Battle of Amphipolis (424 B.C.), the Athenians banished Thucydides. He devoted the 20 years of his exile to studying the Peloponnesian War as it happened and to writing his only work, *History of the Peloponnesian War.* "I lived through the whole of the war," he says, "being of an age to comprehend events and giving my attention to them in order to know the exact truth about them" (V, 26). About 404 B.C. he returned to Athens, and there, according to tradition, he was assassinated.

Thucydides was well equipped "to know the exact truth" about the war. He had naturally an objective and judicious mind; as a banished Athenian he was partial neither to his own countrymen nor their enemies; he had a firsthand knowledge of both sides; and he lived with the events as they unfolded. To these accidental advantages he added painstaking research by traveling about Greece, examining documents, questioning eyewitnesses, and admitting no facts to his *History* until they had been carefully checked. He was thus the first historian who set out to be meticulously accurate in his facts and objective in his point of view.

Thucydides leads up to his real subject by briefly filling in the background of Greek history, and then goes on to study both the superficial and the underlying causes of the war. Next he analyzes the campaigns chronologically by summers and winters. He planned to cover the whole 27 years of the war but did not live to complete the task; the *History* breaks off three quarters of the way through, while describing the events of 411 B.C.

Thucydides was not content merely to establish the facts. He sought to understand them. Thus he studies character and is as much concerned with the motives of statesmen and generals as with their acts. And his approach is purely rationalistic: human events are not to be explained by invoking chance, fate, or divine will; they spring from human causes. In seeking to define these causes, Thucydides becomes the first historian critically to appraise and analyze psychological, economic, and social forces.

All these qualities explain Thucydides' eminence as a historian, but they cannot account for his literary reputation. This derives from the skill and power with which he presents his facts and analyses. He has a strong dramatic sense. Thus, at climactic points, he reports important speeches—speeches which he had to compose himself, always, as he tells us, sticking to the general sense of what was actually said, and considering what was demanded of the speaker by the situation. One of these speeches, that delivered by Pericles at the end of the first year of the war (II, 34–46), in honor of the Athenian dead, is a memorable defense of the Athenian way of life, with its democratic institutions, its spirit of free inquiry, and its artistic interests. With his usual sense of dramatic contrast, Thucydides follows this magnificent tribute with a vivid account of a plague that devastated Athens. He is a master of rhetoric and can gain his effects by restraint as well as by eloquence. His account of the ill-fated Sicilian expedition (Books VI and VII), describing how the young Athenians set sail as gaily as if they were going on a picnic, how they suffered incredible hardships and finally died like flies as prisoners in the quarries near Syracuse, was considered by John Stuart Mill to be "the most powerful and affecting piece of narrative perhaps in all literature." By his literary skill Thucydides breathes life and significance into the dry bones of his careful facts.

This significance is, as he points out, "a possession forever." "It will be enough for me if my work is useful to those who want a clear understanding of the things which happened in the past and which (human nature being what it is) will sooner or later and in much the same way be repeated in the future." Certainly the central events of his history have been repeated often, for his work is essentially a study of the degeneration of a great people. Evil passions—especially greed—beget war, and war brutalizes those who practice it, until, win or lose, they destroy the values of their own civilization.

Titans: in Greek mythology, the six sons and six daughters of Uranus (Heaven) and Ge (Earth). In a long and intricate series of events, they overthrew their father and set Cronus on his throne. Later *Zeus, son of Cronus, overthrew *his* father and the Titans who supported him. Ancient writers sometimes confuse this war between Zeus and the Titans with the war between the gods and the giants. The name *Titan* is also given to some of their descendants, such as Prometheus.

Tolstoi, Count Leo (Lev Nikolaevich): Russian novelist (1828–1910). Tolstoi grew up on his family manor in the heart of European Russia and, after desultory university attendance, returned home, hoping to better the lot of the peasants. But they only became suspicious of his good intentions. In 1851 he joined the army. From his experiences in the Crimean War came *Sketches of Sevastopol*, which, with an earlier volume, *Childhood* (1852), earned Tolstoi a reputation. He, however, had little liking for the writers he met in Russian literary circles. A trip to western Europe confirmed his distrust of Western materialism; the reform of Russia by imitation of the West was not for him.

Again (1860) Tolstoi took up residence at his country home, working with the country people and teaching them. The primer, graded reader, and arithmetic which he wrote had an enormous circulation. During the next 20 years he also composed two great works, the historical novel *War and Peace* (*Voyna i mir*, 1862–69) and a novel of contemporary manners, *Anna Karenina* (1875–77). Signs of the later "converted" Tolstoi are apparent in both these works. He showed the decadence and ineffectuality of the nobility and intellectuals, their mad pursuit of diversion, their inability to cope with practical problems, and their tendency to brutalize the peasants.

By 1879, Tolstoi's so-called "conversion" was complete. He was no longer interested in producing literature, but in conveying a message. He spoke out on religion, social problems, and art. In *A Confession* (1879), he described his "transformation," a kind of mystic fervor combined with a glorifying of work. He now preached a primitive Christianity purged of ritual, church organization, and priesthood. The important thing was that men should love one another. In *What Is to Be Done?* (1884), he attacked the evils of money as such and demanded that the leisured and professional classes "get off the necks of the people." In *What Is Art?* (1897) he denounced art for art's sake, excoriated many of the world's greatest writers, and insisted on religion and social purpose as the test of all art. He even condemned his own greatest works. But he continued to write fiction, notably *The Kreutzer Sonata* (1889) and *Resurrection* (1900).

Tolstoi's emphasis on spiritual reawakening and his obvious sincerity won him numerous followers. Although Russian Czarist censorship barred many of his essays, he was not molested, for he had an international reputation. Later, the Russian Bolsheviks tolerated his work even though he had rejected the economic interpretation of history and scorned violence or revolution as a method of social reform. Not only is Tolstoi usually considered as Russia's greatest novelist, but he is one of the very few writers who have been widely read and acclaimed both in the Orient and in the Occident.

Tom Jones: a novel by *Fielding (1749). *Tom Jones* is one of four great works (*Swift's *Gulliver's Travels*, Richardson's *Clarissa*, and *Sterne's *Tristram Shandy*) which dominate English fiction of the 18th century and make, in their vastly different ways, great contributions to the form of the novel, which was then in its infancy. Starting virtually from scratch, with no examples of the novel as we know it, Fielding created in *Tom Jones* one of the great fictional comedies of Western literature. Not that he was entirely without literary examples: he was well read in comic drama, *picaresque fiction, and classical *epic, and from all of them he did some borrowing. *Tom Jones* is really a further development of the "comic prose epic" which Fielding felt that he was writing in *Joseph Andrews* (1742). Yet the 17 informal, and usually playful, critical chapters which he distributes throughout the novel show that he had a wide knowledge of world literature and drew on all literary types for his materials.

But the sign of his genius is the air of originality that pervades even recognizable plot mechanism. Fielding asserts, half-seriously, that he is founding "a new province of writing" and claims the right "to make what laws I please therein." Yet his originality appears rather in the variety and sharpness of his imaginative grasp than in the prescribing of new "laws" for literary practice. Indeed, in the matters of form which are suggested by the word "laws," Fielding really picked up older concepts and naturalized them in prose fiction and did this in a way so accessible to many subsequent novelists that to the experienced reader he seems technically quite orthodox. Despite his digressions and despite a large and complicated cast of characters, Fielding achieves unity of action: in a story twice the length of the usual 20th-century novel, he has successfully subordinated a mass of complex activities to the central business of reestablishing Tom in the good graces of Squire Allworthy and Sophia. In fact, this denouement is inseparable from the resolution of the situations of all the other characters. The various interrelated actions are managed so skillfully that suspense and a sense of movement are always present; at the same time all the major developments of the plot are so well prepared for in advance that, despite Fielding's addiction to coincidence, we have always a sense of a logical unfolding of what the author often calls a "history." For such reasons Fielding's plotting has been admired by critics from *Coleridge to the present.

But the plot is more than a skillful manipulation of conventional narrative counters; rather it is a placing in dramatic tension of extraordinarily individualized and realized characters. Perhaps we can best grasp Fielding's achievement in character by noting how well he has distinguished apparently similar individuals. There are two country squires, Allworthy and Western, each presented largely as a devoted guardian, each with a single sister, each liable to deception by selfish schemers; yet Western's tempestuousness, inconsistency, and addiction to hunting (which provides metaphors for every phase of his existence) wholly set him apart from the more disciplined, moderate, and mature Allworthy. Allworthy's sister, though important to the plot, appears mostly in rather colorless household schemings, but Miss Western, besides being as tempestuous as her brother, is a "bluestocking," proud of her knowledge of the world, especially in its political aspect. Similar pairings appear in Lady Bellaston and Mrs. Waters, in Mr. Fitzpatrick and Lord Fellamar. Several young ladies in love are differently drawn—Nancy Miller, the sweet but rather conventional victim of seduction; Mrs. Fitzpatrick, who after an unhappy runaway marriage is well on the way to a managing worldliness; and Sophia, whose problem is to be true to her love and dutiful as a daughter. When we consider the authenticity of these portraits as well as those of the tutors Thwackum and Square, with their antagonistic humanism and Anglicanism, held with equal inflexibility, and of numerous doctors, lawyers, servants, soldiers, and riffraff, we can conclude that Fielding the practitioner achieved the "nature" upon which Fielding the theorist laid primary emphasis.

Characters have meaning as well as life, however, and in setting forth his main theme Fielding depends primarily upon three sharply differentiated young men—Nightingale, a very ordinary fellow whom convention may impel at different times to less admirable or more admirable conduct; Blifil, almost entirely a calculator who can feign the appearance of good while actually engaged in malicious plotting; and Tom Jones, a contrastingly spontaneous and spirited youth whose impulsiveness leads mostly to kindness and generosity but can also lead into serious predicaments and morally questionable situations. In part, Fielding is counterbalancing the morality of the "prescribed act" with that of the "good heart," that of the thing done with that of the attiude maintained. Fielding's sympathy is all with the "good heart," though he is detached enough from his hero to understand that the reliance upon impulse may lead, not only to something qualitatively better than the prescribed act, but also, on the other hand, to the proscribed act. The evidence of Tom's growth is that he comes to recognize the need for a kind of conscious discipline to complement the valid promptings of the heart: this crowns the recognition theme which provides the central structure of the book. At the simplest, Jones must escape his anonymity: he comes to be recognized as Allworthy's nephew. At a more meaningful level, he must be morally recognized by Allworthy, who, misled both by appearance and by the machinations of Blifil, has thought him a villain. (Allworthy's change of attitude is parodied by that of Western, for whom Tom becomes admirable merely by being discovered to be Allworthy's nephew.) Finally, he must recognize himself: his eventual self-understanding is marked by his acceptance of the analysis which Fielding significantly puts into the mouth of Sophia, who, though she admires his "great goodness of heart," declares that "an entire profligacy of manners will corrupt the best heart in the world" and produce only "a good-natured libertine."

All the recognitions, including Tom's renunciation of good-natured libertinism, are accomplished rather neatly and with a great surge of amiability among the characters; even Blifil (whose rationally executed malice puts him in a direct line of descent from *Shakespeare's Goneril, Regan, and Iago), though banished from the family circle, is not driven to despair but carries on with an apparently successful worldliness. This way of doing things is of the nature of comedy, which is concerned, in the broadest sense, with the social life rather than the spiritual life. Though it may introduce ethical problems, as Fielding does, it aspires rather to comfortable adjustment than to that confrontation of irreconcilables (the driving passion and the persistent moral awareness) which defines the orbit of tragedy. Fielding's concern with good and evil is focused not in the ultimate terms of the spirit, with its indelible marks and its awareness of nemesis, but in terms of society, where things are manageable and accommodations may be reached.

Within the comic mode Fielding achieves the greatest possible variety. He has a sharp power of satirical observation—of London life, for instance: of urban self-satisfaction, of the morality of high life, of the insolence of servants. There is comedy of character—such as that which springs from the smugness of Miss Western. There is the comedy of intrigue—servants such as Honour scheming in terms of the profit motive. There are numerous farcical scenes—especially those in bedrooms of inns. Mock epic appears in the churchyard battle. And over everything hangs the flexible, jocular style of the author, who can shift at will from humorous periphrasis to clipped anticlimax, from casual essay to sharp quip, from a characteristic hyperbole to occasional understatement, from a jocose circumlocution—his favorite manner—to sharper irony and paradox. He has a fine ear for a dozen kinds of speech, most notably for the truculent and exacerbated vulgarities of Western. All the chattiness and the zestful enjoyment of chattiness, all the joking and expounding, are the style of one who neither knew nor aspired to the streamlined form of the modern novel: Fielding is ever present, an indulgent and genial impresario, crossing and recrossing the stage, sometimes pushing his story ahead briskly, sometimes, as witty observer or flamboyant showman, mock-earnestly discussing its points or twitting its participants. As a master of the practical joke, the satirical thrust, or amused raillery, he had that ease which was possible in an age when the certainties still outnumbered the uncertainties.

tragedy: a type of drama in which the chief character undergoes a morally significant struggle which ends disastrously. Probably tragedy originated in Greek religious rituals to celebrate *Dionysus, in whose honor the chorus, dressed as goats (the animal sacred to the god), or satyrs (his mythical half-goat, half-human companions), danced and chanted verses. (The word *tragedy* means "goat song.") To these choral beginnings speakers and plots were added as *Aristotle explains in the *Poetics*, until Greek tragedy became the highly developed poetic form we know in *Aeschylus, *Sophocles, and *Euripides (see also *classical antiquity). In Greek tragedy (and in most great tragedies written since) the hero is essentially a superior person and is treated sympathetically; his destiny or choice is to go down fighting rather than submit, and thus to pluck a moral victory from a physical defeat. The hero's recognition of his role and his acceptance of his destiny constitute the climax of the tragic structure. His "tragic flaw," as Aristotle calls it, is some defect which helps to involve him in ruin, for the spectacle of entirely undeserved suffering would be merely depressing. Consequently, the hero must have ordinary human failings or limitations, and must fall short of ultimate perfection. Ironically, the noblest efforts of the hero involve him in guilt and lead to his misery. The struggle may be between one character and conflicting forces which he can in no way control. In the greatest tragedies, however, there is also conflict within the character himself, although it may be symbolized in external form. Tragedy thus assumes that humanity has a sense of its own dignity and free will and of a moral law and forces which are outside of and bigger than any individual. In defining tragedy, Aristotle described its moral and psychological effect on the spectator—a catharsis (purgative) of "pity and fear"; he who hears the tale will "thrill with horror and melt with pity."

In a nontheatrical sense, tragedy during the *Middle Ages meant any narrative in which a person of high rank (either through ill fortune or his own error) fell from high estate to low (*Chaucer's *Monk's Tale*, Lydgate's *Fall of Princes*). *Renaissance tragedy was influenced by classical theory, the example of *Seneca, and medieval definition. In the 16th century, however, English tragedy did not keep its types and forms separate but regularly mixed tragedy and comedy, verse and prose. *Shakespeare's *King Lear* and *Hamlet* are nevertheless tragedies never surpassed in poetic and dramatic power. French Renaissance tragedy (*Corneille, *Racine), on the other hand, observed the classical "rules" of the *unities strictly.

In modern times, the writers of tragedy have exercised the greatest freedom with respect to characters, diction, and the meaning of the tragic theme. More and more tragedies have dealt with ordinary people faced with dilemmas of ordinary situations—a development which began in the 18th century. The tragedy lies in the hero's courage or sense of the futility of courage in a world in which he believes nature operates blindly and observes no moral rules; or in his feeling of the unfairness of his struggle when he is pitted against social conventions and forces which, by their very mass, will destroy not merely his life but his individuality. Great modern writers of tragedy are *Hauptmann, *Ibsen, *Chekhov, *Synge, *O'Casey, and *O'Neill.

Tristan and Isolt: the hero and heroine of one of the world's greatest love stories. (Variant forms include Tristram, Iseult, Isolde, Isoud, Yseult, etc.) The story of Tristan and Isolt "is of a love which passed all other love, of love from whence came wondrous sorrow, and whereof they died together in the self-same day." Originally the record of a 9th-century dragon-killing hero of the Picts, the story developed to tell how the youthful Tristan killed but was himself wounded by the Irish knight Morholt; how Tristan's wound refused to heal; how he was set adrift, landed in Ireland, and, without being recognized, was cured by Isolt, the niece of his victim; how he returned home to his uncle King Mark, then made a second voyage to Ireland to win Isolt as a bride for his uncle; and how on the return voyage they unwittingly drank the love philter intended for Mark and his bride. Thus were they condemned to a life of surreptitious meetings, discovery, separation, exile. The drink plunged them into a passion which conscience and circumstances forbade their indulging and yet which they could not resist. Cries Isolt's maid-companion: " 'You have drunk not love alone, but love and death together . . .' [but] the lovers held each other . . . and Tristan said, 'Well, then, come Death.' "

If we judge by similar episodes in old Irish legends (see *Deirdre), the core theme was a Celtic tale of the elopement of the wife and nephew of a king, their wandering in the wilderness, pursuit by the king, and death at his hands. French courtly poets added the atmosphere of chivalry, attached it vaguely to King *Arthur by naming Tristan one of the Knights of the Round Table. In the process of accretion Tristan becomes the most versatile hero of legendary history. He is not only death to dragons, but a first-rate harpist and singer, an expert linguist, a cunning huntsman, an imitator of bird songs, an excellent seaman, the supreme lover, and, it must be admitted, an accomplished liar. As the legend swelled in retellings, it added to the folklore themes of the Voyage of Healing, the Princess of the Swallow's Hair, the Separating Sword, the Ambiguous Oath, the Hero's Leap, various other episodes which were circulating in Greek legends, Oriental tales, *fabliaux—with the theatrical trappings of secret messages, fake bird calls, disguised lepers, spying courtiers, last-minute escapes. Yet in every retelling the lovers continue fresh and eager, moved by an exaltation both extraordinarily passionate and sorrowful. The tragic element was no doubt emphasized by the French meaning of the word *triste* ("sad"). The frenzied, uncontrollable passion and the ingenious deceptions which facilitate the lovers' meetings are far from the usual episodes of dignified *courtly love or heroic narratives. Yet the human appeal of the story was immediate and widespread, and it continues to be so, although no complete version by a major poet survives.

The oldest extant texts, in Anglo-Norman of the late 12th century (by Béroul and Thomas), are, though incomplete, full of the suspense and feeling which remain the hallmark of the legend. The tale was retold in verse and prose in various languages throughout the *Middle Ages, but no single medieval version combines all the episodes, not even *Malory's *Morte Darthur*. The account of the lovers' death also varies—sometimes Tristan dies when he is told that the vessel bringing Isolt to cure him of a second wound has black sails in token that she is not on it; in fact she is coming, and the sails are white. In other versions he is killed by King Mark.

A French narrative, perhaps the lost one of *Chrétien de Troyes, was the source of Gottfried von Strassburg's unfinished medieval German poem (*c.* 1210). This mature, urbane version stresses the psychological conflict between all-consuming love and honor—the feudal and familial loyalty due to a devoted and upright husband and uncle-king. Gottfried penetrates not only into the tragedy of the lovers but also into that of the deceived and humiliated husband. Deeply moving in its sympa-

740

thies, unified and lyrical, this masterpiece has been termed "a high song of love."

Modern audiences too have found distinguished interpreters—in the passionate music drama of Wagner (first performed in 1865), and in the poems of *Tennyson, *Arnold, *Swinburne, *Hardy, Masefield, and E. A. Robinson. A 20th-century French reconstruction by the great medieval scholar Joseph Bédier (translated into English by Hilaire Belloc) conjured into life the major details with such grave and charming felicity that it has itself become a minor modern classic, retaining for all "who are cast down in heart and troubled or filled with desire" the delicate nuances of beauty and fatality.

Tristram Shandy: a novel by *Sterne.

Troilus and Criseyde: a narrative poem by *Chaucer (c. 1385). Chaucer's second masterpiece (see *Canterbury Tales*) is the earliest psychological love story of English fiction. It is an 8,000-line poem about a purported incident of the Trojan War—the love and betrayal of Troilus, son of King Priam of Troy, by Criseyde, widowed daughter of the seer Calchas. Troilus' first meetings with Criseyde are arranged through the efforts of his friend Pandarus (whence the meaning of the modern word *pander*). The lovers swear eternal fidelity. When Criseyde is suddenly ordered to the Greek camp in exchange for Trojan prisoners, she vows to return. Instead, she becomes the mistress of the Greek Diomede. Troilus, in desparing and deliberately rash bravery, soon meets in battle the death he so ardently seeks.

There is no trace of such an incident in Homer (see *Iliad*), who barely mentions Troilus and Pandarus. In spurious Latin histories by Dares Phrygius and Dictys Cretensis, Troilus underwent a heroic expansion and became second only to Hector. A 12th-century French poet, Benoît de Sainte-Maure *(Roman de Troie)*, created a love story between Troilus and Criseyde (he spelled it Briseida), but Benoît started in the middle of the romance when the lovers were about to separate. In the

13th century Benoît's version was translated into Latin by Guido delle Colonne *(Historia Trojana)*. When *Boccaccio used this material in a long narrative poem, *Il Filostrato* (designed primarily to express his passion for his own mistress), he added an account of the wooing and winning of Criseyde. Chaucer derived his narrative from this Italian poem of Boccaccio.

In Chaucer's hands the tale underwent an artistic metamorphosis. Borrowing and translating less than half (some 2,700 lines) of Boccaccio's poem, Chaucer expanded the text to create an entirely different kind of story. His interest was not in voluptuous passion, as was Boccaccio's, but in character and in the ironic and philosophic implications of the fate of these lovers. To the practical question of the modern reader as to why Criseyde did not marry Troilus, the answer is in large part that the story is in the literary convention of *courtly love, in which marriage, children, and a family are incompatible with real love.

The typical Chaucerian skills in narrative, metrics, and characterization produced an entirely novel effect. Chaucer improved and expanded details of the plot and its lyric features, shifted interest from Troilus to Criseyde, and made the setting at once more courtly and more vivid. Troilus' conduct and the coloration of his speeches conform to the conventions of courtly love: he swears loyalty, secrecy, complete and humble obedience to Criseyde's every wish. Even his timidity about declaring his feelings is a standard symptom of the courtly lover. But within this conventional frame Troilus' overwhelming passion and the scenes of the meetings and parting are realistic. In another characteristic change, Chaucer enriched the intellectual meaning of the poem—and retarded its passionate action—by introducing reflections on free will, predestination, foreknowledge, and fate, problems which had been raised centuries before by *Boethius and were still subjects of discussion among Chaucer's contemporaries.

Sure in technique and verse, the dialogue is subtle, natural, and humorous, capturing the tone and idiom of colloquial speech, of witty repartee. It is well to remember also that the long monologue dilating on one's miseries

742

and raptures was a popular literary device. Chaucer's greatness lies in part in the skill with which he uses this literary convention of the "complaint" at dramatic moments. With an easy naturalness whose deceptive smoothness may blind us to the difficulties overcome, Chaucer harnesses into the structure of *rime royal a variety of sources—including prayers from *Dante, philosophy from Boethius, a sonnet from *Petrarch, all molded into passionate avowals by Troilus, introspective self-questionings by Criseyde, homely proverbial wisdom and witty commentary by Pandarus.

But more significant than these qualities, noteworthy as they are, is Chaucer's treatment of the characters. Boccaccio's rather simple and sensual protagonists—the young man about town, his shallow mistress, her dissolute young cousin who is the confidant of the lover—are subtly transformed into a complex trio. Troilus remains, on the whole, the languishing lover, yet he becomes more profound and more deeply serious than a mere voluptuary. Criseyde and Pandarus are fundamentally changed. Criseyde is in love, but skeptical and dignified, aware of her high place in society, and yet tremulously fearful of love, of entanglements, and of her equivocal position in Troy, which her father has deserted because he foresees its doom. And Pandarus becomes the fulcrum of the poem, an older man and Criseyde's uncle, a change which at once complicates his role and his character. He is no mere go-between but a philosophic adviser gushing proverbs wise and humorous and an ironic observer. His sophistication and urbanity have not destroyed his delight in the youthful love affair which he is promoting; but his worldliness and riper experience have also confirmed his ironic pessimism about the tragic difference between illusion and reality. In the scene on the walls of Troy, as he and Troilus futilely await Criseyde's return, the young man continues to hope, but the ironic intelligence of Pandarus, sympathetic but long since disillusioned, realizes the truth. Chaucer pities Troilus' tragic disillusionment and recognizes the human need for faithfulness in this changeable world; yet Chaucer is never bitter with Criseyde. Her weakness and infidelity he treats with a tender understanding of human

743

frailty. Whatever component of irony exists in his compassion for Criseyde, he feared and would not have favored the subsequent deterioration of her reputation. By the time of Chaucer's follower Henryson (*The Testament of Cresseid*, 1493), she had sadly fallen; and in *Shakespeare's *Troilus and Cressida* (*c*. 1602) she became a byword for infidelity: "As false as Cressid."

To Chaucer it is not ultimately Criseyde's unfaithfulness which is responsible for Troilus' misery, but his own false standards of felicity. Throughout the poem Chaucer has accepted the conventions of courtly love and has viewed the human passion of his lovers with a kindly, though detached, sympathy. In an amazing passage just at the end, however, he twice rejects the point of view of the whole poem. When Troilus is killed, his soul ascends to the heavens, and as he looks down on "this litel spot of erthe" from the viewpoint of infinite time and space, he laughs at the sorrow of his friends who are mourning his death—whose minds are entirely taken up with trivial and transitory things. And then Chaucer, in his own person, addresses the reader from a specifically Christian point of view: "O yonge fresshe folkes, he or she / In which that love up groweth with your age, / Repeyreth hoom from worldly vanitee . . ."— set your hearts, not on a lover or a mistress, but on Christ, whose love never betrays. And so, with a prayer translated from *Dante, the poem closes.

trope: a group of spoken lines interpolated into the sung portions of the Easter Mass of the Roman Catholic Church. A trope is like a minute drama, a bit of dialogue. The most famous as well as the earliest of tropes (9th century) is four lines dramatically spoken by the Angels and the three Marys. The first line is *Quem quaeritis in sepulchro, o christicolae?* ("Whom seek ye in the sepulchre, O Christian women?"). When additional speakers and lines were added, the interpolated play of the Easter story became an important part of the service. Soon other scenes were acted out on other holy days, until much of Biblical story was so dramatized during the regular service. The trope, a tiny play, was the seed

744

of medieval drama, which thereafter moved out of the Church and developed into miracle (Biblical story), *mystery (saints' lives), and *morality plays (allegorical characters representing vices and virtues).

In rhetoric, *trope* is also a technical term used to designate a figurative expression or figure of speech.

troubadour: an aristocratic lyric poet of the feudal society of southern France (Provence), in the 12th and 13th centuries. The word is adapted from a Provençal word meaning "finder, inventor." The troubadours were aristocratic composer-poets, as distinguished from the *jongleurs*, the paid wandering minstrels. Nearly 2,500 of the troubadours' poems have survived, many of them with their music. The sources of this poetry were primitive native verse flourishing among the peasants since pre-Roman times and Latin and Spanish-Arabic lyrics. From these, the troubadours created highly artistic forms of intricate versification, "finding" and exploiting every lyric possibility of accent and rime. This technical dexterity is one of the outstanding qualities of troubadour verse. Certain of the lyric forms were widely imitated: the *chanson* (dance-song), *alba* or *aubade* (dawn song), pastoral wooing song, lament, dialogue, political satire. But among the troubadours it became an unwritten law that the poet would not repeat a stanzaic form which had been used before. Hence the variety of verse schemes is almost incredible, but the form deteriorated when intricacy of pattern became an end in itself. The subjects were at first limited to three—war, love, honor. Of these love became the most popular theme; and it was *courtly love which was described, the love for a married lady *(dame)*, whose patronage the poet sought. Troubadour poetry thus figures importantly in the development and dissemination of courtly love not only in France and England but in Germany (see *minnesingers). The earliest troubadour is Duke William IX of Aquitaine (1071–1127), grandfather of Eleanor of Aquitaine (who became Queen of England as wife of Henry II), herself famous in literature for encouraging courtly love. The celebrated troubadour Bernart de Ventadorn followed Eleanor to

England. Eleanor's daughter Marie de Champagne cultivated courtly-love literature at her court with *Chrétien de Troyes and Andreas Capellanus. Eleanor's granddaughter Blanche of Castile received such fervent lyric homage from the leading troubadour of her day, Count Theobald of Champagne, that it caused a state scandal. Another famous troubadour, Arnaut Daniel, whose poetry was much admired by the Italian lyricists, was immortalized by *Dante in *The *Divine Comedy.*

The poetry of the troubadours achieved such standing that many Spanish and Italian poets chose to write in Provençal rather than in their own tongues. It was the starting point of modern literary lyric poetry, and its influence was essential in the work of the *trouvères* of northern France, the German minnesingers, and especially the poets of Sicily and Italy.

Troy Tale: the legend of the siege and destruction of Troy, on which the two great Greek epics, the *Iliad* and the *Odyssey* of Homer, are based.

The Troy Tale begins with a sea-goddess Thetis whom *Zeus loved and would have married, had he not known she was destined to bear a son who would be greater than his father. For this reason Zeus decided that Thetis should marry a mortal; and he chose Peleus, king of Phthia, to be her husband. All the gods and goddesses were invited to the wedding except Eris, the goddess of Strife. She was enraged at the slight and, coming unexpectedly into the banqueting hall, threw among the guests a golden apple inscribed "For the Fairest." At once a debate arose: *Hera, the wife of Zeus, and two of his daughters, *Athena and *Aphrodite, claimed the Apple of Discord. They appealed to Zeus for a decision, and he sent them to Paris, the son of King Priam of Troy. But not one of the goddesses was willing to rest her case on her beauty. Each offered the judge a bribe. Hera promised him royal power, Athena military successes, and Aphrodite the most beautiful woman in the world to be his wife. Tempted by Aphrodite's bribe, Paris awarded the apple to her.

The most beautiful woman in the world was Helen,

the wife of Menelaus, king of Sparta. With Aphrodite's help, therefore, Paris sailed across the Aegean Sea and came to the Spartan court, where he wooed Helen and finally induced her to return with him to Troy. But years before, when the kings of Greece were paying court to Helen, they had sworn that, if anyone should injure her or, because of her, the husband she should choose, they would avenge the injury. When Menelaus, therefore, found that his wife was gone, he could call on all the rulers of Greece to prepare ships and men for war with Troy.

Menelaus' brother Agamemnon, king of Mycenae, was chosen to lead the expedition, and he made elaborate preparations for it. Many years were spent assembling an army, but at last 1,000 ships gathered at Aulis to carry 100,000 warriors across the sea. When all was ready, suddenly the wind changed and the fleet was stormbound. Calchas, the priest of the army, consulted the omens and revealed that Agamemnon, who had been hunting to pass the time of waiting, had killed a deer sacred to the goddess Artemis and that only by sacrificing his daughter Iphigenia could he win the goddess' favor and continue the campaign. Agamemnon, therefore, was forced to choose between his army and his daughter's life. After a difficult struggle he consented to the sacrifice and sent Odysseus, king of Ithaca, to Mycenae to bring Iphigenia to the camp. Odysseus informed Clytemnestra, Agamemnon's wife, that her daughter was to become the bride of Achilles, the son of Peleus and Thetis and leader of the Myrmidons; and so he enticed her away. But when she reached Aulis she was sacrificed.

A fair wind carried the Greeks to Troy. They drew up their ships on the beach and constructed a camp. At one end they put Achilles and at the other end Aias (Ajax), for these two were the greatest warriors. Agamemnon had his quarters in the center. Between the camp and Troy there was an open plain on which the Greeks and Trojans fought, one army trying to capture the city and the other to burn the fleet. And so nine years passed by and Troy remained unconquered, though the Greeks took many smaller cities and gained much plunder, which they divided among the warriors. After one such raid, in the tenth year of the war, Achilles received as his prize a young woman named Briseis, and Agamemnon another named Chryseis, the daughter of Chryses, a priest of *Apollo. It is at this point that the *Iliad begins.

The *Iliad begins with a plague in the Greek camp. For when Chryses came to ransom Chryseis, Agamemnon sent him roughly away. And the old man was afraid and went and prayed to Apollo to take vengeance on the Greeks. And Apollo heard him, and for nine days the plague continued; but on the tenth day Achilles called an assembly, at which Calchas declared that the insolence of Agamemnon to Chryses was the cause of the pestilence. And Agamemnon was forced to restore Chryseis, but he took Briseis from Achilles in her place. And Achilles withdrew from the war in anger and prayed to his mother Thetis to intercede with Zeus to bring destruction on the Greeks until they admitted his worth.

The plague abated, and the Greek army advanced against Troy. But as they were about to engage the Trojans in battle, Paris challenged Menelaus to single combat to decide the quarrel. A truce was made and the champions came forward to fight. But when Menelaus had disabled Paris and was about to give him the death wound, Aphrodite caught him away to the safety of his home. The truce was broken and the war continued. The Greeks, inspired by the valor of the hero Diomedes, pressed the Trojans so hard that Hector returned to the city to bid the Trojan women supplicate Athena, Troy's most implacable enemy. As he reached the Scaean Gates, his wife Andromache came running to meet him with their little son Astyanax. Andromache begged Hector not to leave the safety of the city; but though Hector could not do as she asked him, he felt great pity for her, for he was filled with a presentiment of Troy's ultimate destruction, his own death, and her captivity.

In answer to Thetis' entreaty, Zeus now began to give victory to the Trojans. Under Hector's leadership they drove the Greeks before them and encamped on the plain near the ships. At an assembly Agamemnon admitted his wrongdoing in taking Briseis from Achilles and offered to return her at once with enormous gifts. An embassy was sent to Achilles, but the hero contemptuously rejected their proposal. That night Odysseus and Diomedes succeeded in slaying Rhesus, the Thracian leader, who had just arrived to strengthen the Trojan side. The next day Agamemnon, Odysseus, and Diomedes were disabled and retired from the field, and Hector opened the way for his troops into the Greek camp. Though delayed by *Poseidon and Hera, with the help of Zeus the Trojans reached the Greek fleet and began to set fire to the ships. In the crisis Patroclus, Achilles' retainer and closest friend, begged permission to take the Myrmidons and enter the battle. Achilles agreed; but he ordered Patroclus to return as soon as he had driven the enemy away from the ships. Patroclus now went forth, clad in Achilles' armor and leading his troops. The Trojans, thinking he was Achilles, fled before him in panic, and he pursued them to the city gates, where Hector turned and slew him and took Achilles' armor from him and put it on. But the Greeks succeeded in recovering the body.

When the news was brought to Achilles, he was overcome with grief. New armor was made for him by *Hephaestus, the smith god. At an assembly he renounced his anger, and Agamemnon apologized publicly for his conduct. Achilles now re-entered the battle and in his fury slew the Trojans or drove them back into the city. Only Hector dared to remain outside, and even he felt his courage leave him when he saw Achilles approaching; and he fled three times around the walls of Troy. Then, doomed by fate and grossly deceived by Athena, he stood and fought; and Achilles thrust him through the neck with his spear and stripped the armor from him and dragged him in the dust to the Greek camp. On the next day the funeral of Patroclus was held; but Achilles continued to mistreat the body of Hector until Zeus commanded him to permit its ransom. At the same time Zeus sent a message to Priam to go to the Greek camp and bring back the body of his son. Guided through the night by *Hermes, the messenger god, the old man was received with kindness by Achilles, who gave him the body and granted a truce for the funeral. Hermes then conducted Priam back to Troy; and the *Iliad* ends with the mourning of the Trojans for Hector and a brief account of his burial.

But after the death of Hector the myth goes on to tell how other warriors came to the defense of Troy, the Amazons under their queen Penthesilea and the Ethiopians commanded by Memnon. These too Achilles conquered. But at last the day came on which the hero was fated to die. He was invulnerable except in the heel; to this place Apollo guided an arrow shot by Paris, and he perished of the wound. Other heroes also were dying. Paris, like Achilles, lost his life by an arrow wound; and Aias committed suicide because Achilles' armor was awarded, not to him, but to Odysseus. All seemed lost to the Greeks when, with the help of Athena, they devised a plan that enabled them to capture the city. They abandoned their camp and set sail, pretending they were returning to Greece, although they went only to the island of Tenedos, a few miles distant. On the beach they left behind a huge wooden horse, the work of Epeius, within which their bravest warriors lay concealed. The Trojans were deceived into thinking the horse a magic talisman which would keep their city from destruction; and they drew it into Troy amid wild rejoicings. But that night the Greeks inside the horse made their way into the streets, killed the Trojans guarding the gates, and admitted their comrades who had sailed back to Troy in the darkness. In the sack of the city that followed, Priam and Astyanax lost their lives and Andromache was taken into slavery. The Trojans who escaped gathered under Aeneas and set sail the next spring for Italy, there to establish the Roman people, a greater Troy beyond the seas. Their adventures form the theme of *Vergil's *Aeneid*. As for the Greeks, Helen and Menelaus were reunited and returned together to Sparta. Agamemnon arrived safely in Mycenae, only to be murdered by Clytemnestra in revenge for the sacrifice of Iphigenia. Odysseus wandered ten years before he came to Ithaca, his island kingdom. His adventures at sea and on his homecoming are told in the second great Homeric poem, the *Odyssey*.

The *Odyssey* begins in the tenth year after Troy was taken by the Greeks, All the heroes except Odysseus were now at home. He was kept a prisoner by the nymph Calypso, though he longed to return to his wife Penelope and his son Telemachus. In Ithaca meanwhile the noblest princes of the kingdom had gathered in the palace to woo Penelope. Insisting that Odysseus was dead and urging her to remarry so that the island might have a king, they vexed her and Telemachus and wasted Odysseus' wealth in revelry.

Meanwhile on Mt. Olympus, the home of the gods, Athena begged Zeus to permit Odysseus to return. He received her petition with favor; and she descended to Ithaca where, disguised as a friend of Odysseus, she urged Telemachus to expel the wooers and go in search of his father. Telemachus was afraid to take action against the wooers; but he did set out secretly from Ithaca, going first to Pylos, the home of Nestor, the oldest of the kings who fought at Troy, and later to Sparta where Helen and Menelaus informed him his father was a prisoner on Calypso's isle. When the wooers discovered Telemachus' absence, they plotted to kill him as he returned.

In answer to Athena's entreaty, Zeus now sent Hermes to Calypso commanding her to release Odysseus; and the nymph helped him build a raft on which he set sail from her island. But just as he came within sight of Scheria, the land of the Phaeacians, the god Poseidon destroyed his raft and cast him in the sea. But the goddess Ino gave him her veil, which buoyed him up until he landed on the shore at the mouth of a river near an olive grove, in which he slept. That night Athena sent a dream to Nausicaa, the daughter of Alcinous, king of the Phaeacians, as a result of which she went the next day with her attendants to wash her clothes in the river. The shouting of the girls awakened Odysseus, and he begged Nausicaa for food and clothing. She provided for his needs and directed him to the palace of her father and her mother Arete. He asked them for a ship to take him home, and they granted it without inquiring who he was. The next day the Phaeacians held athletic games at which Odysseus distinguished himself. During the feast that followed, the blind bard Demodocus sang of the fall of Troy, and Odysseus turned his head aside and wept. Alcinous now asked him who he was; and when Odysseus told him, the Phaeacians begged for the story of his wanderings.

Books IX–XII of the *Odyssey*, in which Odysseus tells his tale to Alcinous, contain some of the best stories in literature. How Odysseus came to the land of the one-eyed giants, the Cyclopes, and entered the cave of Polyphemus; and how he blinded the giant and escaped, though he won the hatred of Poseidon by doing so. How the god Aeolus showed him much kindness, binding in a leather bag all the winds except the one that would blow him home; and how the sailors while he slept undid the bag, thinking that it contained treasure. How Circe, the daughter of the Sun, turned his men into swine, and how with the aid of Hermes he overcame her. How he descended into the Underworld and talked to Agamemnon and Achilles, and what they told him. How he alone of all men heard the Sirens' song and lived. Of the Cicones, the Lotus-eaters, and the Laestrygonians; the monster Scylla and the whirlpool *Charybdis; and the Cattle of the Sun whose slaughter led to the loss of his ship and all his men.

The Phaeacians loaded Odysseus with presents and sent him home on a magic ship. The hero was asleep when the ship reached Ithaca, and the sailors carried him ashore and left him. When Odysseus awoke he did not recognize his native island. But Athena came to him and told him of the wooers and disguised him as an old man and sent him to Eumaeus, his faithful swineherd. Here he remained until Telemachus returned from Sparta. For Athena warned Telemachus in a dream to come home, instructing him to avoid the wooers' ambush and to go, not to the palace, but to the swineherd's hut. Father and son were reunited here and together they plotted to kill the wooers, As part of the plan Telemachus went openly to the palace, while Odysseus came there later disguised as a beggar.

Meanwhile Penelope, at her wits' end as to what to do, announced that she would marry the man who could string the bow of Odysseus and shoot an arrow through the openings in a line of 12 ax-heads. She talked to Odysseus in his beggar's disguise, but did not recognize him. He did not make himself known to her, but he approved of the contest, seeing in it a means of killing the wooers. To facilitate their slaughter Telemachus removed the weapons that hung on the palace walls; and when the contest began, Eumaeus and another faithful herdsman, Philoetius, closed the doors and stood on guard. One after another the wooers attempted in vain to string the bow. When all had failed, Odysseus asked permission to try. After some opposition the bow was handed to him. Without rising from where he sat, he strung it and shot an arrow through the axes. Telemachus belted on his sword and grasped his spear. Odysseus announced who he was and began to shoot down the wooers. In the struggle that followed, with the aid of Athena, he and his friends were able to kill them all. Then the hall was cleansed and the unfaithful servants punished; Odysseus made himself known to Penelope and his old father Laertes; Hermes conducted the souls of the dead to the Underworld. The *Odyssey* ends with Odysseus' preparations to defend himself against the kinsmen of the wooers, their attack on the palace, and the intervention of Athena, who brings peace to the island.

Turgenev, Ivan Sergeyevich: Russian novelist (1818–83). Turgenev's role was a double one. He was the literary voice of the "Westernizers" in Russia and at the same time he made Europe aware of the Russian genius.

Son of a wealthy landowning family, he attended the universities of Moscow and St. Petersburg, and then, as was fashionable, went on to Berlin. He also spent fruitful years in Paris, where he met and learned from *Flaubert and other leading writers. This cosmopolitanism gave him the detachment necessary to see Russian life in relation to Western progress.

A Sportsman's Sketches (1852) made him famous. It showed his skill in catching revealing detail and in characterization. Moreover, it was a pioneer work, giving an unsentimental presentation of the serfs, who nevertheless contrasted favorably with their owners. The book aroused the critical attention of government officials, and an obituary of *Gogol added to their suspicion. Turgenev was in consequence banished to his country estate for 18 months. Upon his return to St. Petersburg he found himself a literary lion and the dictator of Russian letters.

The novels of the next decade—*Rudin* (1855), *A Nest of Gentlefolk* (1858), *On the Eve* (1861), and *Fathers and Sons* (1861)—show the high quality of Turgenev the artist. *Fathers and Sons*, however, aroused the intelligentsia and radicals, who did not like the hero, Bazarov. Turgenev was so sensitive to the criticism of this group, of which he felt himself a part, that he entered upon a self-imposed exile which lasted for nearly 20 years, until his death.

During this long stay in western Europe, broken only by brief visits to his native land, he drew materials for his writing from his recollections of his youthful experiences in Russia, notably in *Smoke* (1867) and *Virgin Soil* (1876). His awareness of social problems makes his novels a kind of chronicle of the middle decades of 19th-century Russia, a period when Russian economy was moving from serfdom to free labor.

Of himself he said, "I am, above all, a realist, and chiefly interested in the living truth of the human race. . . . I don't believe in absolutes and systems; I love freedom better than anything. . . . Everything human is dear to me." This living truth, in terms of individual lives, Turgenev described with a scrupulous sense of form and meticulous attention to detail.

Twain, Mark: see *Mark Twain.

Ulysses: a novel by James *Joyce (1922). *Ulysses* is the story of a day in Dublin, from early in the morning of June 16, 1904, until about 2:30 the following morning. Originally planned as a short story for inclusion in *Dubliners*, it grew in Joyce's hands to become a 767-page modern "epic." The actual events of the story are simple enough: Stephen Dedalus (the artist of *A Portrait*

754

of the Artist as a Young Man) has returned to Dublin from his studies in Paris, to be at the deathbed of his mother. He is haunted by a sense of guilt; his revolt against Catholicism has been so strong that he refused to kneel down and grant his mother's dying wish that he pray for her.

The first three episodes show Stephen having breakfast in the Martello tower where he lives, giving a history lesson at Mr. Deasy's school, and walking along the beach at Sandymount. The next 12 episodes relate the day of Leopold Bloom, the "Ulysses" of the book, his breakfast in his Eccles Street home, the funeral at Glasnevin Cemetery, the newspaper office, Davy Byrnes' pub, the library, the streets of the city and the viceregal cavalcade, the music at Ormond Hotel, the clash with the citizen at Barney Kiernan's, the flirtation with Gerty MacDowell on the beach, the maternity hospital where Bloom finally meets Dedalus (who is the "Telemachus" of the book), and finally their adventures at Bella Cohen's brothel. The third section has three parts to balance the first three—Bloom and Dedalus at the cabman's shelter, the return to Eccles Street, and finally the bedroom and Molly Bloom's erotic reveries.

In the first section we are largely in the mind of Stephen. In the middle section we move in and out of the *stream of consciousness of Leopold Bloom, who is preoccupied with his wife's infidelities, and in the very last chapter we are wholly in the mind of Mrs. Bloom.

The chapters parallel the *Odyssey* (see *Troy Tale). Thus Bloom, who is an advertising solicitor, visiting the newspaper, is acting out a parallel to the Aeolus episode, that of the Palace of the Winds. Past and present thus merge. Stephen, as Telemachus, searches for his wandering father. His meeting with Bloom symbolizes the reunion of father and son. Mrs. Bloom is an unfaithful Penelope. Stuart Gilbert, in his *James Joyce's 'Ulysses'* (1930), outlined in detail the manner in which the novelist placed his modern epic on the frame of the ancient work.

The difficulties of *Ulysses* reside not so much in the book's structure as in its style. To create his Homeric picture of Dublin Joyce indulged in constant and sometimes seemingly arbitrary displays of technique, and once these are grasped much of the book's narrative becomes clear. Some of the virtuoso displays are designed the better to render the minds of the characters. Others are simply the exercises of the greatest literary craftsman of our time. In the hospital scene, Joyce parodies the great writers in English literature. He uses a cinematic technique to give the reader a panoramic sense of Dublin, writing a series of short scenes as if his pen were a roving camera in the Irish capital. He writes an entire chapter as if it were a catechism, parodies sentimental novels in the Gerty MacDowell episode, and uses both dramatic and cinematic effects to render the drunken night-town scene at Bella Cohen's.

In the entire book Joyce seems to be saying that life and time are continuous and the heroic wanderings of Ulysses in Homeric times are re-enacted in the unheroic wanderings of men upon the face of the earth in our times, that life is made up of recurring cycles, that birth, life and death are surrounded by legends that grow out of the life-and-death process, past and present as well as future, and that these cycles occur in the vastness of eternity.

Underworld: see *Hades.

unities: three specific conventions of Neo-Classical drama. Unity of *time* demands that the time of the play's action should not extend beyond 24 hours. Unity of *place* requires, in the strictest sense, that only one setting be used, or sometimes, more liberally, that the action remain within a single general vicinity. Unity of *action* excludes irrelevant episodes or important subplots. *Aristotle, in his *Poetics*, had demanded unity of action and had remarked that the action of a tragedy was usually confined to a single day. Italian critics of the *Renaissance kept the unity of action, made the unity of time a fixed rule, and from it deduced the unity of place. The "three unities" were first formally stated as rules of drama by Castelvetro in 1570.

The rule of the unities applies only to drama on the

classical model (see *classicism). English drama of the Elizabethan and Jacobean periods (until the Puritans closed the theaters in 1642) is largely independent of it. *Shakespeare and *Marlowe, for example, pay little heed to these "rules," although Ben *Jonson (with his classical leanings) strictly observed them in *The Alchemist* (1610). After the newly formed French Academy attacked *Corneille's *Le Cid* (1636) for not perfectly following the "rule" of the unities, they became firmly established in French drama and remained for nearly two centuries, until they were finally overthrown by Victor *Hugo's *Hernani* (1830), which replaced classical theories with romantic ones. Since then dramatists have not considered themselves under any obligation to observe the unities, although they have been actually observed in some very effective plays (several of *Ibsen's, for example) and films *(High Noon)*.

In general, the unities reduce the scope of a play and make it extremely difficult to present any convincing development in a character. On the other hand, they lend concentration and a sense of speed and inevitability to a tragic action.

Upanishads: a series of mystical and philosophic prose works constituting the chief theological documents of ancient Hinduism. The title means "a sitting down [at the feet of a master]," hence "secret or esoteric doctrine." They cannot be exactly dated, but probably the earliest do not antedate 600 B.C. These 108 discourses are designed to guide the hermit on the path to union with Brahma. They give an explication of Hindu belief in the form of prayers, observations, dialogues, and narratives. The contribution of the *Upanishads* to Hindu philosophy is the new emphasis on Brahma as the supreme creating God, a conception that approaches monotheism. Other gods, as described in the *Rig *Veda*, are here reduced to the status of names of the various powers of Brahma, an indescribable being or spirit which created and rules the universe, "makes all, knows all, the self-caused, eternal, immeasurable, indestructible, breath by name when breathing, speech by name when speaking, eye by name when seeing, mind by name when thinking." With Brahma is equated the concept of *Atman*, the Universal Soul or Universal Self, which existed before all else and is the source of all life. By devotion to the Self (or Spirit, or Absolute, or God within us) which is our real being, by meditation, by renunciation of all worldly desire, one may ultimately achieve union and identification with Brahma. Thus partaking of the eternal and infinite, one may avoid the misery of repeated rebirths. For evil-doers and the righteous there emerges in the *Upanishads* (as also in the **Mahabharata*) a clear statement of a hell and a heaven, inhabited by the soul during the intervals between rebirths. This conception of Brahma was denied by Buddha.

The *Upanishads* came to be known in Europe during the 18th century. Since that time they have exerted considerable influence on the thought of such men as *Schopenhauer, *Carlyle, *Emerson, and *Yeats.

Utopia: a work by Sir Thomas More describing an imaginary ideal commonwealth (1516; 1551). More coined the name from Greek elements meaning "no place," in recognition of the fact that no ideal society actually exists; and the point of the book lies in the ironic contrast between Utopia and More's own society and civilization. Written originally in Latin (1516) for scholars, *Utopia* was translated into English in 1551. It is presented as the report of a traveler, Raphael Hythloday ("Nonsense-Talker"), who has been to an ideal state where all must work and each (except the slaves) may take the goods of society according to his needs. Because of this work, the adjective *utopian* has come to be applied to any idealistic, but visionary or impractical, idea or scheme.

"Utopia" has also come to designate any literary presentation of an ideal commonwealth. Some of the principal utopias were written by *Plato (*The *Republic*, to which all the others are indebted), *Rabelais, Campanella (*The City of the Sun*, 1623), *Bacon, *Voltaire, Samuel Butler (*Erewhon*—a reversal of "Nowhere"—1872), and H. G. Wells (*A Modern Utopia*, 1905).

Vedas: the earliest scriptures of Hinduism (*veda* means "knowledge"). The dates assigned to them are conjectural and vary by as much as 2,500 years. The period between 1300 and 1000 B.C. seems probable. The *Rig Veda* is the earliest and the most important of the four, and the others are in part derived from it. They are the *Yajur Veda* (prayer-formulae and litanies), the *Sama Veda* (a hymnbook), and the *Atharva Veda* (730 spells of blessings and curses which are more a part of popular practices and folklore than of religion).

The *Rig Veda*, hymns of "praise" resembling the Psalms, contains 1,028 poems of some 10,000 stanzas, making it longer than the *Iliad* and *Odyssey* together. It glorifies 33 gods, who, it declares, had not existed from the beginning of time but were created along with the sky, earth, and the creatures of the earth. Like the gods of the Greeks, these gods often personify the powers of nature—sun, moon, dawn, stars, forest. Many come from the culture of the Indo-European invaders of India: the sky-god Dyaush bears a functional and linguistic relationship to *Zeus. There is in the *Rig Veda* only the briefest mention of *caste*, the system later to become so important a part of Hindu religious beliefs. This early poetry, which is often questioning, allegorical, and metaphysical, is also often joyful, vigorous, and pictorial, describing nature vividly. Developed before the Hindu religious spirit had been molded by authoritarianism, the poetry has a tone of deep humility combined with a sense of wonder and awe. The celebrated pantheistic Creation Hymn is typical. It asks: "Who verily knows and who can here declare it, whence was it born, and whence came this creation?"

Vega Carpio, Lope Félix de: Spanish dramatist (1562–1635). Lope de Vega (as he is usually called) was indeed the "prodigy of nature" that *Cervantes labeled him. How better could one characterize the man whose plays numbered over 2,000 (about 500 have survived) and whose loves were almost as numerous—the adventurer who went off on the Spanish Armada and who brought back, if not victory, at least the larger part of an *epic—this literary giant whose worldly escapades were effected with as much exuberance as the scourgings which he gave himself in penitence? Lope the writer, Lope the soldier, Lope the priest, Lope the lover—he filled all roles with a vigor and flamboyancy that have made him one of the most colorful personalities in literature.

The career which was to establish him as a master of the Spanish world of letters began precociously early. It is reported that at the age of five he could read Latin and perform other prodigious feats. By 14 he was at the Jesuit Collegio Imperial in Madrid, completing his education (after an interlude of fighting against the Portuguese) at the University of Alcala de Henares, where the Bishop of Avila sponsored him. Afterward, his life included a turbulent succession of military expeditions to the Azores and on the Armada, romantic adventures, and both clerical and secular careers. In and out of scrapes, at one time a fugitive eloping in the face of imprisonment, and at another a priest of the Inquisition, he lived 73 full years, and only the loss of a favorite son and daughter toward the end of his life was able to dampen his ebullient spirit.

Lope invaded the literary world with characteristic energy and versatility: epics, *pastorals, *odes and *sonnets flowed from his ready pen, but it was in drama that his genius found itself. He must be considered the founder of the Spanish theater; not only did he contribute to it a huge bulk of plays, but he took its poorly organized drama and gave it form and scope. Establishing the three-act comedy and practically inventing the "cloak and sword" romance of intrigue and manners, he also wrote significant sacred plays (autos), melodramas, histories, and plays with peasant characters that might be considered forerunners of proletarian drama. As his talents spread widely, it is not surprising that they do not penetrate deeply; and writing as rapidly as he did, he naturally produced very unequal and generally unpolished work. But he had a genius for plot construction, and with this inventiveness and a good dramatic instinct, he established the types that his successors perfected.

Lope is better known for a large number of successful

productions than for any masterpieces. *The Madrid Steel* (*El acero de Madrid*, the source of *Molière's *Physician in Spite of Himself*), *The Languishing Lady* (*La dama boba*), *The Gardener's Dog* (*El perro del hortelano*), *Punishment Without Revenge* (*El castigo sin venganza*), *The Sheep-Well* (*Fuente-Ovejuna*, a play about the peasantry)—these are only a few titles from his extensive repertory. *The Star of Seville* (*La estrella de Sevilla*), a well-known work long attributed to him, is now considered of doubtful authorship, but it might well be his, since it has features typical of his plays: a skillfully contrived plot turning on situation and developing unexpectedly; aristocratic characters embroiled in issues of love, honor, and loyalty; and a spirited blend of tragic and comic elements.

Verga, Giovanni: Italian writer of fiction (1840–1922). Verga began his career as a highly successful writer of commercial romances, but the reading of a ship's log, with its unadorned truth, led him to abandon the artificially prettified love story. Henceforth he wrote about the peasants and fishermen of his native Sicily, and in so doing he became the leader of the school of writing which, coming late to Italy, combined *realism and *naturalism under the name of *verismo*. His later work, then, presents a completely unadorned, non-"literary" account of the lives of a poor, simple, hot-blooded people, in a style often as powerful and brutal as the characters it describes. The first works after Verga's shift to *verismo* were two collections of short stories and sketches, *Life of the Fields* (*Vita dei campi*, 1880) and *Country Tales* (*Novelle rusticane*, 1883). He then set out to write a series of novels to be entitled *I Vinti (The Conquered)* and to deal with those who have been crushed in the modern stampede toward material progress. Only two works of the series were written, both of them named for the characters in them: *I Malavoglia* (1881), Verga's masterpiece, deals with a family of fishermen; and *Mastro Don Gesualdo* (1889) treats the social ascent from the peasantry to the petty aristocracy. Verga also wrote plays.

One of his short stories, *Cavalleria rusticana*, was rewritten in the form of a play and then served as the basis for Mascagni's opera of the same title.

Vergil: Latin poet (70–19 B.C.). Publius Vergilius Maro, the greatest of the Roman poets, was born near Mantua in northern Italy and educated in the schools of Cremona, Milan, and Rome. His ill health and sensitive, retiring disposition, together with a certain rustic awkwardness that clung to him through life, unfitted him for the public career for which his education had formally prepared him; and when his schooling was over he returned to his father's farm to devote himself to the writing of poetry. The confiscations that followed the Civil War brought this period of Vergil's life to an end. After the battle of Philippi in 42 B.C., large tracts of land in the north were seized for the veterans, and Vergil's property was included. The details are obscure, though attempts have been made to reconstruct them from the *Eclogues (Bucolics)*, a group of 10 pastoral poems composed by Vergil between 42 and 37 B.C.

Vergil wrote the *Eclogues* in imitation of the *Idyls*, or *Sketches*, of the Sicilian Greek poet *Theocritus. In them idealized shepherds sing their songs against a dreamlike background of mountain, grove, and stream. There is great beauty in the *Eclogues*, but it is beauty separated from reality: no shepherd ever sang as Vergil's do; no countryside can be found like his. Nevertheless, these poems show a true love of nature and a deep sympathy for humanity. Some of them are single songs by individual shepherds; some are in dialogue, the result of a chance meeting; others are singing matches in friendly rivalry or competition for a prize. The traditional themes Vergil used are the love song, the lamentation or dirge, and the friendly banter of rustics; but to these he added others taken from contemporary events and his own personal experience. Thus the *First* and *Ninth Eclogues* refer to the confiscations near Mantua, and the rustics Tityrus and Menalcas who appear in them are traditionally believed to represent Vergil himself. But the attempt to reconstruct actual events in Vergil's life from these poems is of uncertain value.

The *Fourth Eclogue*, addressed to Vergil's earliest protector, Pollio, is one of the most famous poems in the world. In it the poet celebrates the birth of a child during whose lifetime the Golden Age of peace and innocence will come again, while all the world rejoices. No one knows what child Vergil meant; but for centuries it was believed he spoke of the child Jesus—an interpretation of the poem that made him a pagan prophet of the birth of Christ.

Because of certain statements in the *Eclogues*, it is believed by some scholars that Vergil's farm was restored to him through a personal appeal to Augustus. Whether or not this is true, it is certain that before the *Eclogues* were published he was fully established in the literary circle of the Emperor's chief minister, Maecenas. He was given an estate in southern Italy; his financial needs were met; and, equally important for one so lacking in self-confidence, he was urged to write. At the time, Augustus was attempting to revive Italian agriculture, long ruined by civil war; and Maecenas encouraged Vergil to compose a poem in support of the Emperor's agrarian policy. The result was the *Georgics (Poem on Agriculture)*.

Vergil did not write the *Georgics* as a practical guide to farming. Though modeled professedly on the *Works and Days* of *Hesiod, the poem is more national and philosophical than didactic. Its purpose is to blend Vergil's ideal of human life as part of universal nature with his concept of the beauty of Italy and the greatness of Rome. Not that the advice Vergil gives the farmer is impractical; it is incidental. The profit that comes from reading the poem lies not so much in technical details concerning field crops, orchards and vineyards, flocks and herds, and bees—the stated topics of the four books—as in Vergil's exalted patriotism, his love of nature, his sympathy for all living things, and his preoccupation with the mystery of life. In all these things the *Georgics* goes far beyond the *Works and Days*; but Vergil insists, as Hesiod insisted before him, on the necessity of work if man is to be the victor in the struggle with nature.

Vergil took seven years to write the *Georgics*, and the poem is polished with lavish care. The "Praises of Italy" (III, 136–176) is perhaps the most famous single passage.

While Vergil was working on the *Georgics*, if not from a still earlier date, he had planned to write a national epic to glorify Rome and Augustus. On this poem, the *Aeneid (Story of Aeneas)*, he spent the remaining years of his life. By 19 B.C. the epic was complete, although still lacking final revision, a task which the poet thought would require about three years. At this time Vergil also desired to visit Greece and Asia Minor, where some of the scenes of the *Aeneid* are laid. At Athens he met Augustus and agreed to accompany the Emperor to Rome. But he took ill at Megara and grew worse as the journey proceeded. He died shortly after the ship reached Italy and was buried near Naples, where his tomb, the exact location of which is now unknown, quickly became an object of both reverence and superstition. At the time of his death Vergil was much troubled by the imperfections in the *Aeneid* and desired to burn the poem; but Augustus refused permission, and two years after the poet died it was published with minor revisions.

From the time he published the *Eclogues*, Vergil's fame was assured. He was esteemed by the Emperor, the court, and the literary men of his generation. He was held in great reverence by the people. Through the generosity of his patrons he amassed a fortune. He wielded immense influence on later Roman writers in prose as well as poetry. He was read all through the *Middle Ages. He brought the Latin hexameter, in which he wrote his works, to its highest possible development. In the *Eclogues* he gave *pastoral poetry its permanent direction. In the *Georgics* he created a type of poem completely new. In the *Aeneid* he not only expressed the hopes and aspirations of a whole nation; he went beyond this to reveal the mystery of the sadness that lies at the heart of life. (In addition to the *Eclogues, Georgics*, and *Aeneid*, a number of minor poems are traditionally attributed to Vergil.)

Verlaine, Paul: French poet (1844–96). Paul Verlaine's musical sensitivity and delicate suggestion of mood made him one of the best of the *symbolists. It is ironic that poetry so delicate in charm should have been written by one whose life was in so many ways violent and crude. The son of an army engineer, Verlaine was educated and worked in Paris (as an insurance clerk) until his association with some of the leading writers of the day (*Flaubert, *Gautier) turned him to poetry as a vocation. He also became friendly with the wild boy-poet *Rimbaud, and thereafter his life was an uneasy vagabondage in Belgium and France, and a vacillation between the cafés, the gutter, and charity hospitals. He took drugs to induce sensation, was proud to be called "decadent," and spent a term in prison for attempting to murder Rimbaud, with whom his relationship had become notorious. After his release he tried to earn a living in England by teaching French, but his irregular habits made steady work of any sort impossible. As the symbolist creed began to attract more poets in the 1890's, Verlaine became something of a celebrity, but even this fame did not save him from an obscure and squalid death.

A paradoxical unevenness is reflected in his poems, in the perverse disillusionment of *Saturnine Poems (Poèmes saturniens*, 1866); the exquisite elegance of *Fêtes galantes* (1869), like a Watteau 18th-century painting; the joyous lyric sweetness of *The Good Song* (*La Bonne Chanson*, 1870), which Verlaine wrote for his bride; and the religious mysticism, dreamy suggestions, and poignancy of *Wisdom* (*Sagesse*, 1881). His symbolist manner reached its fullest flowering in *Romances Without Words* (*Romances sans paroles*, 1874; published 1887), whose title indicates the emphasis on music, rather than clear-cut ideas. Elusive, vague sensations, subconscious ideas, a mystical and cynical temper are conveyed by the musical flow of the lines and the juxtaposed symbols. Verlaine is not so powerful as *Baudelaire nor so intense as Rimbaud, but better than any other symbolist, he expresses a mood of gentle, vague melancholy, of "tears that have no reason."

Vigny, Count Alfred de: French poet, novelist, dramatist (1797–1863). Vigny was the most philosophical and stoical of the French romantic poets. Born into the aristocracy, he found the nobles, the army (in which he served for 13 years), and a fickle mistress a series of cumulative disappointments. Disillusioned thereafter by the *Romantic Movement, he withdrew from society to his writing, to an inner life, an "ivory tower"—the now-famous cliché first applied to his emotional retreat by *Sainte-Beuve. Vigny translated *Shakespeare's *Othello* and *The Merchant of Venice* into French verse and wrote the first French historical novel, *Cinq-Mars* (1826), as well as short stories and a play.

His lasting fame, however, rests on his verse: *Poems* (1822); *Eloa* (1824); *Poems Ancient and Modern* (1826); *The Fates* (*Les Destinées*, published posthumously 1864). His chief literary sources, the *Bible, Homer, *Byron, he regarded through the prism of his own disillusionment and pessimism. He perceived that evil often triumphs, that the laws of nature are impersonal, that the poet is by his ideals and character isolated and a martyr. In short narrative poems he concretizes these philosophic ideas through symbols which give them universality. So, for example, Samson, in *The Anger of Samson*, symbolizes the betrayal of man's strength; the prophet in *Moses* typifies the loneliness of genius; the message cast overboard in a shipwreck *(The Bottle in the Sea)* represents an indestructible force, science. Although he shared with his French and English romantic contemporaries melancholy, individualism, and a sense of unappreciated genius, he does not sink to the depths of despair or self-pity we see, for example, in *Musset. A famous poem, after praising a wolf that fought to the last and died in silence, draws the conclusion that "groans, tears, prayers are equally cowardly," that "silence alone is great; all else is weak" *(La Mort du loup)*. His verse, constantly reflecting his stoicism and restraint, gives a sense of classical polish and perfection.

Villon, François: French poet (1431–after 1462). "The sorriest figure on the rolls of fame," François Villon led so disreputable a life and was so excellent a lyric poet that he has become a legend. Born into a poor and un-lettered family, Villon took his surname from a relative, a kindly priest who proved a patient and devoted patron to his brilliant, reckless young protégé. By the time he was 21, Villon had both Bachelor's and Master's degrees from the University of Paris, but apparently he led a vagabond life with ruffians and sharpers in the taverns of the Latin Quarter. The details of his life, meager as they are, are chiefly details of his scrapes and crimes. He was arrested several times for complicity in murders and robberies, was banished and forced to flee Paris. Pardoned by a general amnesty (1461), he returned to Paris, but in 1462 he was again imprisoned and sentenced to be hanged. The punishment was later commuted to ten years' banishment. Villon was then only about 30 years old. Thereafter he disappeared completely from view. By 1489 his works had appeared in print.

The most vivid account of Villon's life is to be found in his poetry, which records his poverty, loves, and satisfaction in his adventurous life. Jollity and wit mingle with an ironic recognition that much of this gay confidence is only bravado. There is regret for wasted youth and anguished hopes for ultimate salvation. His career stimulated *Hugo and Robert Louis Stevenson to write romanticized stories about him, and he has been the hero of plays and films. But his real importance lies in his verse, which has inspired distinguished English poets—*Rossetti, *Swinburne, and Henley—to serve as his translators.

The *Little Testament* (*Petit testament*, 1456) and the *Great Testament* (*Grand testament*, 1462) show both the traditional and the original aspects of his genius. He rejected allegory, asceticism, and narrow moralizing, but he accepted the conventional eight-syllable verse and followed the popular medieval device of the literary last will and testament, with its imaginary legacies to friends and foes. His originality, realism, and technical skill infuse this frame with life. *Ballades and *rondeaux are dexterously introduced as part of the well-organized central plan. The complex form of these poems contrasts

767

with their direct language. The simple adjectives which describe the famous ladies and the allusive refrain—"But where are the snows of yesteryear?"—give a tender irony to the *Ballade of Dead Ladies*. Nor can one forget "the exquisite ache of its music."

Villon's originality is to be seen also in a new note of personal feeling, in his self-analysis and deep pathos. The sharp, realistic picture of bodies on the gallows scorched by the sun and torn by birds of carrion produces the unforgettable horror of the *Ballade of the Hanged*. The poignancy of these lines is increased by realization that Villon wrote them in grim expectation of this same imminent fate.

Through the imaginary bequest, Villon was also able, "laughing through tears," to give a detailed view of the charm and variety of Paris—its teeming vitality, its great churches, and its great ladies, and also its chimney sweeps, petty thieves, and whores. Gay or mocking, solemn or penitent, his poems are remarkable for the life which is crammed into them, for their lyric quality, their biting realism, their sense of personal sincerity. "Trouble has ground my wits," he said, "and taught me more than any thing in Aristotle."

Volsung Saga: a 13th-century Icelandic prose narrative. This saga has historic importance as the earliest complete and unified tale of the Volsungs and Nibelungs, heroes of the myths and historic legends dating back to the Teutonic migrations (Atli is Attila the Hun, d. 453). The story of Sigurd the Volsung was in the *Middle Ages the best-loved legend among the Scandinavian peoples. The saga supplements the incomplete narratives of the *Eddas*, skillfully ironing out their inconsistencies and making an essentially human story out of a mixture of legendary history, folklore, and mythology. Having described the founding of the family, it presents a unified narrative of the birth of Sigurd (German Siegfried), his slaying of the dragon Fafnir, his winning of the Nibelung gold, his rescue of Brynhild from her circle of fire, his marriage to Gudrun (Kriemhild), his death at the hands of his kinsman, and then the final catastrophic destruc-

768

tion of the dynasty at the court of Atli (Etzel). In this dramatic culmination of greed and deception, the proud heroes foresee their unhappy destiny but nevertheless will not succumb passively to it. With philosophic pessimism and heroic grandeur they refuse to be intimidated by their fate and go unflinchingly to their doom.

The greatness of the tale lies in its exalted emotions, its lyric and dramatic intensity, the psychological complexities of the characters. They fully realize their tragic dilemmas: Brynhild demanding the death of Sigurd, the only man she can love; Gunnar torn between his love for Brynhild and his oath to Sigurd.

The legend forms the subject of one of the greatest of the Middle High German epics, *The *Nibelungenlied*. A number of modern works of genuine artistic value are also indebted to this saga: William *Morris's *The Story of Sigurd the Volsung*, *Ibsen's *The Vikings at Relgeland*, *Hebbel's dramatic trilogy *The Nibelungs*, and Wagner's cycle of four operas, *The Ring of the Nibelungs*, particularly *The Valkyrie*.

Voltaire: pseudonym of François-Marie Arouet, French satirist (1694–1778). The name Voltaire awakens the image of a sharp-featured, ugly old man, weak in health but hardened enough to live through most of a century. Active in mind to the end of his 83 years, he hobbled around with his cane during a rather large portion of that long lifetime. Blended with the physical image there is one of a keen, inquisitive intellect, an ironical skepticism, an ambition that tolerated no rivals for public favor or consideration. Almost any general statement about Voltaire's views must be accompanied with many a reservation. He is equally complicated, even bewildering, whether one considers his ideas or his personality, his philosophy or his behavior—or misbehavior. It has been said of him that he darted about Europe like a nervous fish in a tank. Let us follow him as we may, remembering always that his name is a symbol of revolt against intolerance and superstition and that during most of his life he was a refugee from his own country.

At 20 Voltaire was already well known, and from that

age until his death he was the brilliant popularizer of the most advanced philosophy in a century of revolt against every restraint. It was a time of remarkable progress in science. Voltaire was no inventor of new ideas, but a facile assimilator of new thought, a charming elucidator, a leader, and a reformer. He was, at the same time, an interpreter of his age and, finally, a revered patriarch to whom every prince paid homage.

Voltaire is remarkable for his style. No man ever wrote more lucid French. He is said to have remarked that "one word in the wrong place can completely ruin an idea." The witty turn of his genius gave every page of his prose interest, and whatever other criticisms may be leveled against him, he is never dull. But he was not satisfied with writing brilliant prose; he was a graceful and successful poet as well. He left no form of literature untried and, in his day, received the commendation of the best critics. While still a young man, Voltaire was considered the greatest writer of tragedy then living. He even wrote an epic poem which was so well received that its sale formed the beginning of his large fortune.

It was only natural that Voltaire, the satirical analyst, should have often found himself at odds with *Rousseau, the sensitive emotionalist. When the latter sent Voltaire a copy of his *Discourse on the Origins of Inequality*, Voltaire's acknowledgment was typical: "I have received, sir, your new book against the human race, and thank you for it. . . . No one has ever used so much intelligence to make us out stupid animals. The examples set by us have made savages almost as vicious as we are."

Voltaire was schooled by clever freethinkers and patronized by powerful nobles. He became so arrogant that he was whipped by the Duke of Rohan's lackeys and imprisoned. Voltaire's letter of protest to the government at Rohan's attack was in his best manner: "I affirm humbly that I have been murderously attacked by the brave Chevalier de Rohan, supported by six thugs, behind whom he boldly took his stand. I have constantly sought since then to repair, not my honor but his. The task has been too difficult." The upshot of this episode was that Voltaire was exiled to England for three years. Here he learned English and made the acquaintance of the philosophers *Locke and Hume. His quick intelligence recognized the superiority of English government and society over the tyranny, snobbery, bigotry, and intolerance of his own country under Louis XV. His literary appreciation revealed to him the worth of English literature, and the achievements of English science aroused his admiration. After those three years in England he became the interpreter of English culture to his countrymen, beginning the influence which brought back to France a new vigor of inspiration. Voltaire published the results of his observations in his famous *Philosophic Letters on the English* (*Lettres philosophiques* or *Lettres anglaises*, English version, 1733; French edition, 1734). These letters wittily present a point of view that is especially fresh today, in view of world conditions. They give a notion of English literature, science and society, religion and government. The authorities quickly sensed the implied attack on French institutions. The book was burned, and its author again barely escaped imprisonment.

Thereafter, Voltaire sought comfortable, luxurious freedom, first at the court of Frederic the Great of Prussia. But he gained little experience and knowledge there. He enjoyed a huge fortune won by clever speculation. Finally he established himself at Ferney, just inside the French border from Switzerland, where, if necessary, he would be able to slip out of the country. From this safe retreat he rained a never-ceasing torrent of pamphlets on Paris. He used a great variety of pen names, always denying his authorship. But no one was deceived: his wit and style betrayed him. Nevertheless, his anonymity made it possible for the indulgent and amused authorities not to prosecute him. Among these works in pamphlet form was the *Philosophical Dictionary* (*Dictionnaire philosophique*, 1764), published first in a pocket edition but gradually enlarged to six volumes. Here were collected in alphabetical order very short articles on every possible subject.

Voltaire radically altered the writing of history by introducing a new concept: history is not merely the story of a king's life and deeds or a general's battles; it treats the spirit of the age, every human interest, insisting especially on the artistic and literary, but, at the same time, presenting the economic. History thus becomes, to Voltaire, a gradually unveiled picture of humanity, from its first gropings to the spiritual and material fruits of what we are pleased to call modern civilization. In his *Essay on Manners* (*Essai sur les mœurs et l'esprit des nations*, 1756) Voltaire was the first to present such a vista of the succession of ages and nations.

Voltaire's brilliant intellect, his ability to work hard and long, and the unusual length of his life resulted in his production of some 70 volumes of literature. In all this mass of material, the best and most enduring works are the philosophical tales, especially *Zadig* (1748) and *Candide* (1759). This type of writing, as Voltaire developed it, skillfully performed two difficult tasks at once— it enabled an author to say dangerous things safely, and it tricked light-minded readers into thinking. These goals were achieved by telling an entertaining and often absurd story in a flippant way, but at the same time making it serve as a vehicle for serious moral or philosophical ideas.

Voltaire was, essentially, a champion of progress and liberty. Above all, he believed in freedom of speech and free discussion. He is often quoted as having said: "I may not agree with a word you say, but I shall defend to the death your right to say it." Actually he never really said exactly this, but one of his biographers cited it as a speech which would have summed up his attitude and conduct in matters of controversy.

Many have been repelled by his cynicism. To them the mocking smile on his ugly, impish face has been an unendurable leer. His insolent and loud skepticism has been to many an unpardonable exaggeration. Yet the world has excused it. Dominating a hundred years, he typifies the 18th century and all it did for the liberation and enlightenment of the human intelligence.

Eleven years after his death the French Revolution broke out. It was in part the result of his campaign against the Old Regime. His remains had been resting very inappropriately in a convent. They were transported with great pomp to Paris and placed in the Panthéon beside those of his arch-enemy, Rousseau. On the hearse one read this inscription: "Poet, philosopher, historian, he gave wings to the human intelligence; he prepared us for freedom."

Vulcan: see *Hephaestus.

Vulgate: the Latin version of the Bible translated from the Greek by St. *Jerome in the 4th century. The name, a past participle of *vulgare* ("to make general or common, to spread abroad") refers to the fact that it made the Scriptures available to the Romans in their own language. This, the version read throughout the *Middle Ages, exercised an incalculable influence on life and literature. It was the first book printed by movable type. It has remained with few modifications the standard version of the Roman Catholic Church. (See also *Bible.)

Walther von der Vogelweide: see *minnesingers.

War and Peace: a novel by *Tolstoi (*Voyna i mir*, 1862–69). This picture of Russian life, set against a background of Napoleon's invasion, is one of the great novels of world literature. In scope, organization, and variety of character studies, *War and Peace* defies limitation to any particular category of fiction. To classify the book as a historical, sociological, psychological, political, epic, or panoramic novel, or as an *exemplum* for a philosophy of history arbitrarily limits a breadth of treatment which combines all these elements. Yet the work has angered many. Historians quarrel with the appraisal of Napoleon and with Tolstoi's theories of history; military strategists find fault with the accounts of battles; non-Russian readers are confused by the many classes and groups; and literary critics have decried the loose episodic structure. The answer to all these critics is that the sweep of the novel and the force and interest of its characters are enough to carry the reader through the difficulties and win the respect of the critics in spite of the flaws.

The problem for the reader is orienting himself. At first he is lost amidst faces and names. Some figures make a vivid impression at once; others hover nebulously in a marginal area of recognition. The reader must pick up threads of continuity in the lives of the characters and fit together pieces of the jig-saw picture. Gradually each locale takes definite form; personalities seem richer with each contact until the reader is at home in each group. With the ease of familiarity he is able to move about in the social circles of Moscow and Petersburg, to make quick visits to estates in the provinces, and to live with the armies at the front.

The people in *War and Peace* are worth knowing. Napoleon is met face to face only a few times, but his personality permeates the story and he is seldom out of the thinking of the chief characters. But he is not the hero. Indeed, there is no one hero but a half dozen, each making a bid for the chief interest. There are Dolokhof, a man of personal fearlessness and cold cynicism, and Anatol Kuragin, the son of Prince Vasili and one of the most convincing debauchés in literature. In contrast to the unprincipled Prince Vasili is old Prince Bolkonsky, rigid in his routine and principles. About his son Andrei hovers an aura of impending doom even in his most triumphant moments, and his potentialities are wiped out by a horrible death from a wound received in heroic but fruitless effort at the indecisive battle of Borodino. Then there are Nikolai Rostof and Pierre Bezukhoi, unlike in almost every respect. Nikolai, a dashing extrovert, reveled in the life of a soldier. When he marries the wealthy Princess Mariya, sister of the ill-fated Andrei, Nikolai finally finds contentment in family life and an outlet for his energy in the management of the estate. Pierre, introvert, ungainly, fumbling for the right values, is the illegitimate son of Prince Bezukhoi but is made legal heir to the Prince's title and fabulous wealth. Accepted as a well-intentioned fool, he mixes with all the Russian groups from the highest aristocrats to the bedraggled mob rescued from the French. But finally he too finds self-respect and contentment in a love-marriage and family life with Natasha Rostof. The story ends in peace, with a visit of Pierre's family to Nikolai and Mariya at their provincial estate and Tolstoi makes it plain that though Napoleons, empires, movements, and ideas may come and go, human love, trust, and everyday domestic life are the abiding values.

Considerable parts of the book (including all the final chapters) are devoted to Tolstoi's theory of history. This theory is essentially fatalistic. Free will is an illusion, and hence it is an illusion to attribute the events of history to the efforts of great men. This idea is worked out in the contrast between the two historical figures in *War and Peace*, Napoleon and the Russian commander-in-chief Kutuzof. Napoleon won the battles but lost his army in Russia. Kutuzof spent a large part of his time reading novels, lost the battles, lost Moscow, but saved Russia. Napoleon was a blunderer who does not deserve the credit for his successes; hence he was not a great man. Kutuzof was great, not because of personal ability, but because he happened to be the embodiment of the forces of *necessity* and was wise enough not to try to shape the course of history. (The obvious inconsistency here is apparently inspired by patriotism, though Tolstoi does develop the idea that the difference in greatness between the two men lies more in what they were—in their own characters—than in what they did.) In general, Tolstoi opposed the idea of the great man or leader. Since the will is not free, events shape the man: he is governed by the manifold natural and supernatural forces which combine to produce *necessity*. And man's tragedies and disasters are the result of his inability to read the signs of this necessity.

The greatness of *War and Peace* does not lie in its philosophy or in any contribution to the facts or theory of history. It depends on the budding of a vast panorama of a whole society out of innumerable minute realistic details. These details of events, settings, and characters make every part of the story vivid and interesting, but without artistic organization they would merely overwhelm the reader. *War and Peace* does have plan. Unlike many long 19th-century novels, the sprawling story has structure. Individual episodes and groups of characters are not merely episodes; they turn out to be blocks functioning as parts of a larger structure. In the finished work the design of related movements, events, and personalities becomes apparent. The total picture is an unforgettable vision, distinguished by its depth and scope.

Warren, Robert Penn: novelist and poet (1905–89). Best known for his novel of American politics *All the King's Men* (1946), Warren is also a gifted poet, author of such works as *Brother to Dragons* (1953) and other volumes of verse including *Audubon* (1969). Professor of English at Yale, he won the Pulitzer Prize for his writings and received the National Medal for Literature in 1970.

Waste Land, The: a poem by T. S. *Eliot (1922). *The Waste Land* is not a long poem, running to only 403 lines (plus several pages of notes). But its imaginative power, its borrowings from myth and legend, its assimilation of a long poetic tradition, and its elaborate annotation—as if it were an ancient manuscript requiring explanation to the modern reader—give it a very special place in the poetic history of our time. With the world now being rendered waste literally, by pollution and ecological disturbance, the poem may indeed acquire a meaning far beyond that which the poet intended.

The poem is divided into five parts. In "The Burial of the Dead" Eliot describes the stirring of life in the land with the coming of spring, when fertility prevails over the sterility of winter. "The Game of Chess" begins with the splendors of Cleopatra and contrasts them with contemporary uneasiness and despair. "The Fire Sermon" conjures up a picture of the ugliness of cities and the mechanization of modern life and emotion. "Death by Water," a brief lyric threaded into the poem, suggests the irony that water can bring death not only through drowning but through its absence, which causes drought, and the final passage, "What the Thunder Said," is a picture of drought—the decay and emptiness of modern life—"voices singing out of empty cisterns and exhausted wells."

This picture of desiccation and gloom reflects the

mood that followed the First World War but contains also the record of the poet's personal melancholy. The poem's striking characteristics are varied rhythms and meters, borrowings from many writers, use of material from the legends of the *Holy Grail and Frazer's monumental anthropological work *The Golden Bough.* Eliot introduces into the poem the blind seer Tiresias of Greek tragedy, whose function is to act as a central consciousness who "*sees,* in fact, the substance of the poem" as Strether sees his situation in Henry *James' *The *Ambassadors.* Eliot calls him in his notes "the most important personage in the poem, uniting all the rest."

The key image of *The Waste Land* is that of sterility; throughout the work there are symbols of drought, disintegration, dryness, decay—dusty trees, muddy streets, desert rocks, dry bones, empty cisterns, exhausted wells. Water relieves drought but can also be destructive. Fire is a destroyer. It is also a purifier. Eliot thus is using the universal symbols—air, earth, fire, water—to evoke the "waste" of a world. And with this, Eliot seeks to evoke the dreariness of modern cities in which people work and make love in a kind of mechanical sleep-walking routine. The poet constantly alternates his setting between time present and time past.

In spite of its obscurities, the poem creates a brooding atmosphere and marked tension; even if we ignore Eliot's scholarly notes, with their ironic pedantry, and do not grasp the full meaning of the poem, we catch a profound emotion in its overtones. The manuscript, long thought lost, is in the Berg Collection of the New York Public Library, with its original notes and the emendations scribbled on it by Ezra *Pound, to whom *The Waste Land* is dedicated.

Wells, H(erbert) G(eorge): English novelist and social critic, creator of "space fiction" (1866–1946). Wells was born into the English servant-class, but rose by his ability to learn post-Darwinian science under Huxley and to write a fascinating series of science fiction novels, which went far beyond Jules Verne in predicting "the shape of things to come," as Wells put it. He made his reputation with *The Time Machine* (1895) and in fast succession produced *The Invisible Man* (1897), *The War of the Worlds* (1898), and *The First Men on the Moon* (1901). His fanciful forecasts of the future led to his assuming the role of prophet and in this he was highly successful, making himself a social commentator and analyst of current affairs in the press and on the lecture platform for almost half a century. After the turn of the century he wrote a series of social novels, which were widely read and reflected his idiosyncratic flirtation with socialism. His science fiction was eventually utopian; but his early poverty gave his novels a Dickensian flavor. He had an alert and witty mind, and he easily dominated the world of ideas and the journalistic-literary scene beyond the Edwardian period and through the two world wars. His other works include among the social novels *Love and Mr. Lewisham* (1900), *Kipps* (1905), *Tono-Bungay* (1909), *Ann Veronica* (1909), *The History of Mr. Polly* (1910). His nonfiction includes one of the great bestsellers of modern times, his *Outline of History* (1920), and such utopian books as *Anticipations* (1902), *The New Machiavelli* (1911), and *The Shape of Things to Come* (1933).

Wesley, John: English religious leader (1703–91). Wesley was a man of great learning who devoted his long life to the cause of Methodism. His brother Charles had founded the Methodist Society, and John became its leader in 1729. He never considered himself a man of letters, and his extensive literary activity was merely one aspect of his religious leadership. From our present vantage point we can see that Methodism was in one sense the religious aspect of Romanticism (see *Romantic Movement), particularly in its emphasis on emotion and intuition as opposed to ritual and analysis. It also advocated a specific humanitarian, moral, and social code. Wesley's literary productions include a number of concise works written for the use of his followers, most of whom came from the poorer and uneducated classes. These include grammars of the classical tongues and of English; handbooks on logic, medicine, physics; works on ancient, English, and church history; Bible commentaries; 50 theological works, and editions of earlier religious classics like the writings of Bunyan. Wesley's place in literature depends on the collections of hymns (both original and translated) that he published in collaboration with his brother Charles (author of *Jesus, Lover of My Soul*) and on his *Diary*. The hymns had a strong influence on the subsequent history of English religious poetry, replacing the involved metaphysical images of the 17th century with the simple statements of the chorales of *Luther—and of the modern hymn. The *Diary* presents Wesley's experiences with a combination of unswerving faith in his mission, an ironic sense of humor, and personal humility.

Whitman, Walt(er): American poet (1819–92). Praising Whitman's *Leaves of Grass* on its appearance in 1855, *Emerson surmised "a long foreground somewhere, for such a start"; but the foreground does little to explain the start. Whitman was brought up on Long Island, where he had five years of schooling and a great deal of loafing, rambling, and reading. Then he worked as an office boy, printer's apprentice, schoolmaster, printer, editor, journalist. During this period he produced some lurid tales, a tear-jerking temperance novel, and some conventionally metrical rimed verse which is merely sentimental doggerel. His humanitarian and nationalistic editorials for the Brooklyn *Eagle* and his book reviewing give more of an indication of his future course. In 1848 Whitman made a trip down the Ohio and Mississippi to New Orleans, returning by Chicago, the Great Lakes, and the Hudson. This experience opened his eyes to the country and its people. A few more years of drifting and odd jobs followed before the appearance of *Leaves of Grass*, a book of 12 poems, partly set up in type by the poet himself.

Basically new in thought and style, *Leaves of Grass* was savagely attacked. Whitman later said, "I expected hell, and I got it." Reviewers said that he was a criminal monster, "as unacquainted with art as a hog is with mathematics," and demanded that he be publicly flogged. A kinder and more perceptive review called the book "a mixture of Yankee transcendentalism and New York rowdyism." Emerson, however, wrote a letter of generous praise—which Whitman promptly used for advertising purposes without Emerson's permission. In spite of all the commotion, the book did not sell, and Whitman went on with his journalism. While visiting a brother who had been wounded in Virginia in 1861, Whitman realized the desperate need for male nurses in the Civil War hospitals, and for the rest of the war he served in this capacity in Washington, seeing the full horror of war, but also seeing in the common soldiers "the plentifully-supplied, last needed proof of democracy." *Drum-Taps* (1865) is the outgrowth of this experience; after the assassination of *Lincoln he added to this collection the unrepresentative *O Captain, My Captain* and the magnificent *elegy *When Lilacs Last in the Dooryard Bloom'd.*

From this point on his biography is largely that of *Leaves of Grass*, which he continued to revise and enlarge through nine editions. An appointment in the Indian Bureau was terminated when the Secretary of the Interior read a few lines of Whitman's poetry. William D. O'Connor came to Whitman's defense in a rhapsodic pamphlet entitled *The Good Gray Poet*; the sobriquet stuck, and Whitman was appointed to a sinecure in the Attorney-General's office. He had been in poor health since he had contracted malaria during his hospital work. In 1873 he suffered a paralytic stroke, but in spite of fluctuating and never really good health, he continued to work at his writing until his death 19 years later. In 1881 *Leaves of Grass* was for the first time brought out by a reputable publisher and ironically was banned; but to top the irony the banning increased the sales, and Whitman began to realize money from his poetry. Moreover, William Rossetti, *Tennyson, and *Swinburne had spoken in his praise in England, and in America a Whitman cult had grown up. *November Boughs* (1888) contained an interesting autobiographical essay, *A Backward Glance O'er Travel'd Roads*. In his last months he prepared the "Deathbed Edition" of *Leaves of Grass*, "for future printing, if there should be any."

Whitman's thought contains elements drawn from many

sources, Emerson being the most important. "I was simmering," he said; "Emerson brought me to a boil." Perhaps the two strongest single currents in his work are nationalism and democracy. He insisted on rejecting a great deal of European tradition and culture, urging the *Muses to migrate from Greece, to "cross out those immensely overpaid accounts," to "placard 'Removed' and 'To Let' on Parnassus" *(Song of the Exposition)*. The more extreme statements of his nationalism and his faith in the common man give point to Sidney Lanier's jibe: "As nearly as I can make it out, Whitman's argument seems to be that . . . because the Mississippi is long, therefore every American is God." Whitman's identification of himself with the common man frequently led to an appearance of conceit—"I celebrate myself and sing myself"—but "I" here is everyone, "for every atom belonging to me as good belongs to you." He has a remarkable power of empathy by which he *becomes* whatever he looks upon: "I was the man, I suffered, I was there." He was not deluded into unrealistic idealization of the people, but he put his final trust in them because he saw that they had not only the "cruel, beastly, hoggish qualities," but also the admirable and spiritual. As he told Horace Traubel, the disciple of his latter years, "Everything comes out of the dirt—everything comes out of the people . . . not university people, not F.F.V. people: people, people, just people."

The range of Whitman's subjects is remarkable and intentional, for he set out to include and celebrate everything. He finds nothing too ignoble for his senses to discover. He excludes nothing from his boundless sympathy, including the felon, the slave, the prostitute, the diseased, as well as the healthy and beautiful. He boasts of being the poet of the body as well as of the soul. Against the Victorian reticence concerning sex, he blurts out physiological catalogues. Against romantic love-poets "forever occupied in dyspeptic amours with dyspeptic women," he urged honest recognition of sex, without shame. (It was this attitude which caused many of his contemporaries to condemn him.) Essentially, he accepts everything. Grief-stricken with the nation at the murder of Lincoln, Whitman still sings a chant of fullest welcome to death, "Dark mother always gliding near with soft feet." The praise due to the fathomless universe is not only for life, joy, and love, "for objects and knowledge curious," but also for "the sure-enwinding arms of cool-enfolding death." This acceptance is, however, an attitude toward life rather than a reasoned philosophical system. For such systems, and for consistency as an end in itself, Whitman had little sympathy. "Do I contradict myself? / Very well, then, I contradict myself: / (I am large, I contain multitudes.)"

Whitman's description of his poetry as a "barbaric yawp" is simply bravado. He evolved his own type of free verse for his own type of expression, but he was neither careless of technique nor indifferent to it. *The Prayer of Columbus*, for instance, was rewritten 20 times. Although he rebelled against regular meters, other standard poetic devices of sound—alliterations, *assonance, balance and repetition (initial, within the line, and terminal)—give abundant evidence of his conscious artistry. In fact, he was strongly influenced by music, especially by Italian opera, on which he based some of his poetic devices. He was not uniformly excellent, of course, and he was not a good critic of his own productions, which contain stretches of flat prose and inflated rhetoric, along with occasional sudden lapses. *Come Up from the Fields, Father*, an otherwise simple and moving poem, contains the appalling line: "See, dearest mother, the letter says Pete will soon be better."

Two of Whitman's characteristic poetic techniques deserve special mention. One is his habit of using vignettes—snapshots, as some critics have called them—brief pictures, often complete in a single line. These are often combined in long series, the "catalogues" for which his poetry is also noted. Often these give a cumulative effect, a general picture arrived at without having to abandon realistic detail, but sometimes they run away with him and produce merely an effect of uncontrolled prolixity. It was the occasional abuse of this cataloguing technique which led Emerson to deplore his making not the songs of the nation but its inventories.

Whitman's best work has become part of the common property of Occidental civilization. Not only do almost all modern American poets owe something to him, but poets in England, France, Italy, and Latin America are in his debt. His influence is general and pervasive, for he had no direct followers and founded no school. His real service, through his honest inclusiveness in portraying himself and America, was to enlarge the province of literature.

Whitman's prose fills a large volume. Often sprawling, a kind of improvisation with the dash serving for almost all punctuation, it is still rewarding in a study of the man and the poet. The most important prose works are *Specimen Days* (1882), a kind of notebook kept over many years, the major part dealing with his hospital experience, wartime Washington, and Lincoln; and *Democratic Vistas* (1871), a sober casting up of accounts in which Whitman, without uncontrolled optimism or unrestrained enthusiasm, takes his stand firmly with democracy.

Wild Duck, The: a play by *Ibsen (1884). In many ways *The Wild Duck* seems to be Ibsen's own answer to *An *Enemy of the People.* There he had portrayed a character, not especially sensitive or great, who was able to risk security, happiness, and even his life for the sake of the truth. In *The Wild Duck* he found it necessary to examine the question of whether it is possible for human beings to bear up under the disillusionment and bitterness that truth often brings. Is not man so weak and so lazy that he prefers to seek shelter in the easy, comfortable life of illusion? Ibsen shows us a man who makes such a choice, Hjalmar Ekdal. Smug and well-fed, he pursues—often boastfully—his dreams of greatness. Hjalmar thinks of himself as a great inventor, but his dreams are vague and unsubstantial. Just as his profession of photography is *re*productive rather than *pro*ductive, his whole life lacks creative originality; it is based upon pretense.

Gregers Werle, Hjalmar's old school friend, at times seems to be a caricature, the tragic figure of a potential artist without real artistic and creative qualities. Highstrung and neurotic, he gives the impression of having been crippled by life. The hatred for his father seems to have crept into his soul. To atone for his father's sense of guilt toward the Ekdals, he throws himself wholeheartedly into his so-called "mission"; to pursue the "claim of the ideal." As noble as this quest for truth may sound, it becomes an escape, a substitute for something life cannot give him. In his anxiousness to fulfill his "mission" Gregers achieves nothing but tragedy. Lacking the creative power of an artist, the strength to follow his "ideal" to full realization, Gregers must fail in his mission. As he also lacks the instinct for the right psychological moment, his revelations to Hjalmar about the latter's family strike too hard and fail to effect the desired change.

Ibsen's doctor-psychologist, Relling, is a complete opposite to Gregers Werle. He regards the possession of an Ideal (or the quest for Truth) as a luxury which only certain people can afford and for which the poor have neither time nor means. The average man does not care to be "pestered with the claim of the ideal," to be constantly handed its "confounded duns" by a man like Gregers Werle. Relling's answer to Gregers' "mission" amounts to this: people need their life of illusion and pretense to brighten their dull everyday routine, and for people like the Ekdal family truth will prove disastrous.

A large part of *The Wild Duck* consists in the portrayal of life isolated from the world of reality, self-sufficient in its pretense. To broaden and deepen the meaning of the play, Ibsen used the symbol of the wild duck. According to an old legend, a wild duck, when wounded, does not return to its flock but dives to the bottom of the sea and fastens itself to the seaweed. In a symbolical sense, Gregers Werle and all the Ekdals except Gina are wounded. The wild duck which the Ekdals keep in their garret creates the atmosphere of the play; it becomes a kind of pervasive symbol which ties all the characters together.

The Wild Duck abounds in subtle and skillful methods of character portrayal and plot movement. For instance, the climax of the play—the crucial awakening of Hjalmar Ekdal—comes *between* Acts III and IV rather than in the play itself. Ibsen combines tragic and comic elements and fuses reality with symbolism in order to bring into clear focus the great conflict between truth and illusion.

Wilde, Oscar (Fingal O'Flahertie Wills): English writer and wit (1854–1900). Oscar Wilde was himself as much of a paradox as any of those triumphs of contradiction that have become a hallmark of his wit. On the one hand there is the *poseur*, the "aesthete" in knee breeches—lily in hand, sunflower in lapel—so easily caricatured by *Punch* and by Gilbert and Sullivan in *Patience*; but on the other hand there is the literary artist of importance both as an author and an influence, especially in the development of modern English drama.

Born in Dublin (and thus another in the group of Irish men of letters prominent in the nineties) and sent to Trinity College, Wilde continued a very successful academic career by going, in 1874, to Oxford, where he became a leader in the "aesthetic movement." There the influence of Matthew *Arnold, with his crusade against philistinism, of John *Ruskin, with his revolt against ugliness, and of Walter Pater, with his defense of hedonism, was to be superficially reflected in Wilde's extravagant costumes and posturings, and more seriously mirrored in his writings. He attempted many literary forms: poetry—largely derivative and suggestive of the Romantics and the Pre-Raphaelites; short stories (*The Canterville Ghost*, 1887); fairy tales (*The Happy Prince and Other Tales*, 1888); Platonic dialogues (*Intentions*, 1891); a novel (*The Picture of Dorian Gray*, 1890); and plays. It is in this last medium, especially in comedy, that he has had his greatest success and significance.

Wilde's contribution to English drama was to restore to it a spirit of comedy; to the dull, moralistic Victorian stage he brought a wit reminiscent of the Restoration *comedy of manners and a genuine sense of the dramatic. *Lady Windermere's Fan* (1892), his first success, catered to a middle-class taste with a plot centering on a woman "with a past," Lady Windermere's unrevealed mother, who sacrificed her honor to save the reputation of her daughter; but it goes beyond the typical claptrap melodrama of the 19th century by giving a rather complex picture of contemporary society and the dilemma of an individual in it. Moreover, its paradoxical epigrams—"I can resist everything except temptation"—"a cynic is a man who knows the price of everything and the value of nothing"—"life is far too important a thing ever to talk seriously about it"—provide a unique, Wildean flavor and anticipate that almost perfect farce, *The Importance of Being Earnest* (1895). In this play, undoubtedly his best, Wilde has abandoned everything to the trivial and witty; the situation is completely ridiculous—Jack Worthington has created a fictitious brother, Ernest, to keep his rakish activities from his ward, Cecily. Just when he has decided to do away with Ernest, his foppish friend Algernon (who has his own creation for avoiding obligations, his sick friend Bunbury) appears in the guise of the infamous Ernest so that he may meet the sheltered Cecily. The confusion in identities continues until all ends happily when Jack is revealed as a genuine Ernest, a long-lost infant who had been misplaced by his nurse, when she absent-mindedly confused him with the manuscript of her novel. If it is, as George Bernard *Shaw has said, a heartless play, it is also a masterpiece of the worldly and cynical blended with laughter, and it demonstrates conclusively what can be achieved with dialogue.

It has often been said that Wilde is most sincere artistically when he is depicting insincere characters and that there is always a note of artistic falseness and insincerity in the declarations of his few sincere characters. Both *A Woman of No Importance* (1894) and *An Ideal Husband* (1895) lend some support to this criticism. In *A Woman of No Importance*, the superficial situations of the frivolous dinner party—whose purpose is "to mirror the manners, not to reform the morals, of its day," as Wilde described the aim of all social comedy—far overshadow the more serious struggles of the fallen woman Mrs. Arbuthnot, her son Gerald, and the puritanical young American girl with her experiences in sophisticated English society. The first three acts display fast-moving and ingenious dialogue; in the last act, however, the interaction of the three "good" characters becomes highly artificial. *An Ideal Husband* is another attempt at social satire, broader in scope, but suffering from too many contrived situations which culminate in incredible confusion and end with happy reconciliations. The focus of the comedy is on the exposure of a Cabinet member's past and on the deflation of his wife's smug morality. But in spite of its faults, *An Ideal Husband* has some of the marks of a comedy of ideas.

Wilde's checkered career, with its flamboyant tour of America, his notorious trial for sexual perversion and imprisonment (movingly reflected in *De Profundis* and *The Ballad of Reading Gaol*), and, finally, his death in poverty in France, has made him one of the most colorful figures in English literature; but his literary position was honestly won by a considerable, if limited, talent.

Wilder, Thornton Niven: American novelist and dramatist whose central themes exalt human beings who accept life and are resigned to its vicissitudes (1897–1975). Most popular of his plays were *Our Town* (1938) and his experiment in Joycean-Viconian cyclical philosophy, *The Skin of Our Teeth* (1942), with its recall of some of the themes of *Finnegans Wake.* He was originally an archaeologist, and his writings contain a strong historical strain. His most famous novel, *The Bridge of San Luis Rey* (1927), which won the Pulitzer Prize in 1928, sought to inquire whether there was indeed a destiny in the fall of a sparrow; the book was a series of fictional biographies of several persons who died in the same accident, and Wilder showed that they did so at the time when their lives had actually run their course. Wilder successfully adapted *The Matchmaker* (1954), a revision of his earlier *The Merchant of Yonkers*, from *Einen Jux will er sich machen* by Johann Nestroy, in turn adapted from John Oxenham. Other novels include *Heaven's My Destination* (1934) and *The Ides of March* (1948). One of his last works was a large-scale novel, *The Eighth Day*, published in 1968.

Typical of Wilder's dramatic writing is the renunciation of the linear course of the action; the ironic destruction of illusion; the cleaned-up stage almost devoid of props which calls on the spectator's imagination and forces the actor to practice mimic accuracy—all these are stylistic devices which Wilder did not of course discover but which he rescued from the distant past and made useful again for the theater.

Williams, Tennessee: pen-name of Thomas Lanier Williams, American dramatist (1914–83). Born in Columbus, Mississippi, Williams moved at the age of 12 to St. Louis, where his family lived in conditions similar to those of the Wingfields in *The Glass Menagerie* (1944), his first decisive success. When his early one-act plays, *American Blues*, appeared in 1939, he was admitted to Ervin Piscator's courses for young dramatists in New York.

Williams likes to create women figures, such as the vivacious Serafina in *The Rose Tattoo* (1951), but also such delicate creatures as Laura Wingfield, the crippled daughter in *The Glass Menagerie*, Blanche Dubois of *A Streetcar Named Desire* (1947), and Alma Winemiller of *Summer and Smoke* (1948)—women who break down when confronted with sober reality or who flee into illusion. The plays abound with themes of sickness, failure, and human inadequacy. Mendacity, hypocrisy, hatred, homosexuality, and greed are combined in a play such as *Cat on a Hot Tin Roof* (1955). In *The Night of the Iguana* (1961) an assortment of life's victims work out their destiny in a run-down tourist hotel in Mexico. It is Williams' technique to employ a realism permeated with symbols, to combine lyric tenderness with shocking brutality.

Wolfram von Eschenbach: Middle High German poet (*fl. c.* 1210). Wolfram wrote some fragmentary works and a series of love-lyrics which finally abandon the conventions of *courtly love in favor of marriage, but he is remembered primarily as the author of the great narrative poem *Parzival*. This poem, based on but going far beyond *Chrétien de Troyes, gave the story of the *Holy Grail its greatest impetus and possibly its definitive form. Various later writers undertook to compose sequels to it, and the fact that some 80 manuscripts of the poem exist is ample evidence of its popularity. It is sometimes considered the outstanding work of Middle High German literature, and in recent times it served as the primary source (though considerably modified) of Wagner's music-drama *Parsifal*.

Woolf, Virginia: English novelist and essayist (1882–1941). One of the most gifted and innovative of the *stream-of-consciousness novelists, Virginia Woolf's early fiction showed her moving from the first toward subjective exploration. *Joyce's *Ulysses* provided her, very much as it did William *Faulkner, with the technical modes she needed and could apply in her own way. In *Mrs. Dalloway* (1925) she showed a thorough grasp of Joyce's devices, imitating some of them but working for high condensation and glimpses of moments of experience rather than attempting the illusion of a total picture. Joyce's day in Dublin occupies more than 800 closely printed pages; Mrs. Woolf's day in London in *Mrs. Dalloway* is less than 300 pages printed in large type. The most striking difference between the two is Mrs. Woolf's use of her own poetic medium to portray the inner world of each character rather than allowing these minds to express themselves in their particular idiom, as in Joyce. *To the Lighthouse* (1927), *The Waves* (1931), and her posthumous *Between the Acts* (1941) are her most original works, blending the subjective modes of Joyce with those of *Proust. A brilliant stylist, Mrs. Woolf filled four volumes of criticism. In her seminal essay on fiction, "Mr. Bennett and Mrs. Brown" (1924), she advocated freedom for the novelist to capture the "shower of atoms" and the discontinuity of experience, and pictured men and women as enclosed in their "envelope" of consciousness from birth to death. A friend of Lytton Strachey, and one of the original members of the *Bloomsbury group, Mrs. Woolf was fascinated by Strachey's biographical methods. She wrote *Orlando* at his suggestion, a work which carries the hero-heroine from Elizabethan days to the 20th century and satirizes traditional biography. She also wrote a biography of the painter Roger Fry and in a *jeu d'esprit* demonstrated her command of stream-of-*senses* by writing a biography of Elizabeth Barrett's dog Flush. In *A Room of One's Own* (1929) she spoke out for women's liberation. She committed suicide after the first bombings of England during the Second World War. A portion of her diaries was published by Leonard Woolf, her husband, who also edited a number of her works and described the years of his marriage to her in the third and fourth volumes of his five-volume autobiography.

Virginia Woolf, with her husband, founded a small personal press, the Hogarth Press, which quickly became a flourishing institution. In addition to publishing the early writings of T. S. *Eliot, *Forster, and Mrs. Woolf's own works, the press ultimately brought out in England the bulk of Sigmund *Freud's writings in admirable translations.

Wordsworth, William: English poet (1770–1850). The many hours that the boy Wordsworth spent wandering about the hills and woods prepared him (or perhaps reflected his preparation) for the two principal achievements of his life—the production of some of the finest poetry on nature in any language and the leadership of the early part of the English *Romantic Movement. Left an orphan by the age of 13, he was educated by an uncle. Before graduating from Cambridge he took a walking tour on the Continent (1790), and he returned to France for over a year in 1791–92. Here he sired an illegitimate daughter and became involved in the early enthusiasm of the French Revolution. Fortunately, his money ran out and he returned to England before his associates began to be guillotined. Various legacies and a sinecure as Distributor of Stamps enabled him to devote himself to literature for the rest of his life, which was passed in the "Lake Country" of northern England except for such occasional travel as his significant trip to Germany with his sister Dorothy and *Coleridge in 1798–99. As he grew older his revolutionary ardor and liberalism cooled, and when Southey died in 1843 Wordsworth was sufficiently staid and conservative to succeed him as Poet

Laureate. Dorothy, his lifelong companion and adviser, outlived him by five years.

Wordsworth began his literary career in 1793 with the publication of two immature poems, *An Evening Walk* and *Descriptive Sketches.* His meeting with Coleridge two years later had a profound effect on both men. Their joint publication of *Lyrical Ballads* (1798) is normally considered as the beginning of the English Romantic Movement proper, and Wordsworth's *Preface* to the second edition (1800) was the literary manifesto of the movement. It formally announced the revolution against *Neo-Classicism and explained the intent of the collaborators. Wordsworth had selected subjects from nature (*Lines Composed a Few Miles Above Tintern Abbey*) and rustic life (*Michael*) and had sought to show their dignity and artistic validity by presenting them with the strangeness and freshness of a new vision. Coleridge, conversely, had sought to present the strange and the supernatural with the simple convincingness of everyday occurrences (*The Ancient Mariner*). Poetry was defined as "the spontaneous overflow of powerful feelings," arising from "emotion recollected in tranquillity." The language of poetry was to be no artificial poetic diction, but a "selection of the real language of men in a state of vivid sensation." It is a matter of frequent comment (first pointed out by Coleridge) that Wordsworth is not consistent in the application of his principles and that some of his best poetry violates his theories in its elevation of poetic diction, whereas some of his worst seems to result from a too-conscious following of his own rules.

This is typical of Wordsworth, for his poetry is very uneven. At its best it ranks with any poetry in the language, and at its worst it is simply flat, trivial, and silly. Wordsworth wrote large quantities of both sorts, and a great deal that falls between them. Strangely enough, he seems to have lacked any real power of self-criticism and to have been entirely unable to distinguish his best from his worst. Some feeble stanzas in otherwise good poems were suppressed or modified at Coleridge's suggestion.

A large part of Wordsworth's poetry, both good and bad, was written in the period between 1797 and 1808 but was not published until much later. The works of this period include *Poems, in Two Volumes* (1807), *The White Doe of Rylstone* (1815), *The Waggoner* and *Peter Bell* (both 1819), *The Borderers* (Wordsworth's only play, published in 1842, nearly half a century after it was written), and *The Prelude*. This last work (written 1799–1805; published 1850) is the first part of a sort of spiritual autobiography in *blank verse which was planned to appear in three parts under the collective title *The Recluse*. The second part, *The Excursion*, had been published shortly after its completion, in 1814, and the third part was planned, but never written. The list of Wordsworth's important publications is completed by *The River Duddon* (1820) and *Ecclesiastical Sonnets* (1822), both of which show his mastery of the *sonnet form.

In general, Wordsworth is more famous—and deservedly so—for his poems of short to moderate length than for his most ambitious undertakings. Only a few of the best known can be mentioned here. *Tintern Abbey* (1798) traces the development of the poet's love of nature, which has been first a sensuous animal passion, then a moral influence, and finally a mystical communion. *Michael*, a study in simple sturdiness of character and the healing power of nature, is a moving poem in spite of its oversimplified and tractish contrast between the innocent country and the wicked city. The five "Lucy Poems," written in Germany to an imaginary (or, at least, unidentified) woman in 1799, are among his best lyrics. *Lucy Gray* (*not* one of the "Lucy Poems," 1800) is a good specimen of the successful use of everyday language in a simple ballad. The *Ode on Intimations of Immortality from Recollections of Early Childhood* (1807) is a magnificent *ode in free form developing the poet's idea that an unconscious memory of a previous existence is the source of the unthinking wisdom and the sense of the glory of the world which he attributes to childhood: "Not in entire forgetfulness, / And not in utter nakedness, / But trailing clouds of glory do we come / From God, who is our home." But the light grows dim as we grow up until "At length the man perceives it die away, / And fade into the light of common day." Other famous and highly successful poems are *The Solitary Reaper*,

Ode to Duty, Resolution and Independence, the sonnets *London, 1802* (on *Milton), and *The World Is Too Much with Us*, and *I Wandered Lonely as a Cloud* (often called "The Daffodils").

Wordsworth is not only one of England's greatest lyric poets; he has profoundly influenced modern attitudes and sensibilities. Many of his points of view had already been advanced by *Rousseau (who seems to have had little direct influence on Wordsworth), but it is Wordsworth more directly than anyone else who has conditioned our belief in the natural goodness of childhood, the moral value of the simple life, and the inspiring and healing powers of nature.

Wyclif, John: English religious reformer and Bible translator (*c.* 1320–84). Wyclif was an Oxford don and a churchman in various positions. He stood firmly for both political and religious liberty and led a movement attacking several branches of papal doctrine. He wrote many controversial works in both Latin and English, but his importance in literature comes from the fact that he instigated the first complete translation of the Bible (from the Latin *Vulgate) into English. Wyclif certainly translated some of the Gospels himself; how much of the rest is his personal work cannot be clearly established. The first version of this translation appeared about the year of Wyclif's death. A later version edited out some of its harshness and infelicity of style. This work made the Bible, for the first time, available to the common people of England and began the tradition which culminated in the King James version (see *Bible). (Wyclif's name is also spelled *Wycliffe*, *Wiclif*, Wicklif, and in almost every conceivable way.)

Xenophon: Greek historian (*c.* 430–*c.* 354 B.C.). Xenophon was born in the country near Athens soon after the start of the Peloponnesian War. Like many young men of his generation, he was a friend and admirer of the philosopher *Socrates. Against Socrates' advice, however, in 401 B.C., he joined some 10,000 Greek mercenaries in the service of Cyrus the Younger, who was attempting to snatch the throne of Persia from his brother. As a member of this force, Xenophon marched from Sardis in Asia Minor to Cunaxa, some 50 miles northwest of Babylon, where the Greek troops easily routed the Persians drawn up against them. But Cyrus was killed in the battle, and the Greek generals were murdered a few days later at a conference called by the Persians, supposedly to consider an armistice. In the midst of the danger and confusion that followed this act, the Greeks chose Xenophon as their commander, and by his skill and courage he succeeded in leading them up the Tigris River valley and across the mountains of Armenia, first to the Greek colonies on the Black Sea coast and then to Thrace. The *Anabasis (March Up Country)*, his account of the expedition, is one of the great adventure stories of literature and, because of its influence, an extremely important book. It exposed the weakness concealed behind the imposing façade of the Persian Empire and paved the way for the invasion of Alexander the Great.

Xenophon is a voluminous writer, numbering among his important works the *Hellenica (History of Greece)*, a continuation of *Thucydides' work on the Peloponnesian War; the *Memorabilia (Recollections of Socrates)*, written in the philosopher's defense; the *Oeconomicus (Household Management)*, interesting for the light it throws on Greek marriage customs; and the *Cyropaedia (Education of Cyrus)*, based on the life of Cyrus the Elder, the founder of the Persian Empire. This last is a book difficult to classify; it is cast in the form of a historical novel but is strictly didactic in purpose, being intended to set forth Xenophon's ideas concerning good government.

After Xenophon returned from Persia, he took service with Agesilaus, King of Sparta, and was consequently banished from Athens, although the decree was rescinded before his death. His works show that he was an aristocrat with strong Spartan sympathies; an active, capable man, though not a profound thinker; and the master of an easy, pleasant prose style.

Yeats, William Butler: English poet (1865–1939). Yeats is one of the greatest English poets of the first half of the 20th century. Like his slightly older contemporaries, Oscar *Wilde and George Bernard *Shaw, he was born in Dublin of Protestant parents and went to London as a young man to pursue a literary career; unlike Wilde and Shaw, however, he used Celtic literary subjects and he soon returned to Ireland. There he founded the famous Abbey Theatre (1894) and became the leader of the *Irish Literary Revival.

By 1908, Yeats had already completed a successful career; at the age of 43 he was Ireland's best-known poet and dramatist (having published more than a hundred volumes, including about six volumes each of his own poems, plays, and prose works, besides numerous editions and anthologies of the works of others) and had just brought out his own *Collected Works* in eight volumes. His career, however, was far from over. His best works were still unwritten, and he was entering a new phase. Whereas he had been a late "romantic" poet, writing of love and Irish fairy tales and Celtic myths, he became, to the surprise of many and to the dissatisfaction of some, a "modern" poet. This change may be attributed in part to the influence of the American Ezra *Pound, the dean of "modern" poets (Pound's later influence on T. S. *Eliot, the associate dean, has been widely acknowledged). In 1908, Pound, then 23 years old, came to London to learn how to write poetry from Yeats. Whatever the influence and counterinfluences may have been, the poems in Yeats' next two collections, *The Green Helmet* (1910) and *Responsibilities* (1914), exhibit many of the characteristics of the new poetry as formulated by Pound and his friends, the *Imagists, in their manifestoes (*e.g.*, that of 1912): direct treatment of the poetic object, complete freedom of subject matter, verbal economy and concentration (each word doing a full-time job), and the refusal to let poetry sink below the level of good prose, by recourse, for example, to poeticism or padding for the sake of rhythm or rime alone.

Yeats was fully conscious of his new direction, as the

quatrain "The Coming of Wisdom with Time" (published in *The Green Helmet*) shows. "Romantic Ireland's dead and gone," he wrote in *September 1913 (Responsibilities)*, and in the final poem of the collection, *A Coat*, he indicated that his vogue was in part responsible for the change. He condemned the imitators of his early style and discarded his old, successful mythologies. In his next collection, *The Wild Swans at Coole* (1917), there is a poem called *The Fisherman* in which Yeats announced his hope that "Before I am old / I shall have written him one / Poem maybe as cold / And passionate as the dawn." He fulfilled this hope, but not until he had passed through another mythology far more elaborate than the Celtic. Meanwhile he continued writing plays occasionally, but, stimulated by Pound's interest in Japanese classical drama, he turned from the stage of the Abbey Thêatre to write private salon plays for dancers.

In 1917, the year of his marriage, Yeats again changed direction as a poet. During the first few years of his marriage, he received a new, universal mythology through the medium of his wife. This mythology is embodied in a book called *A Vision* (1925, revised edition 1937). In the preface Yeats tells us that he regards his second mythology as a set of stylistic arrangements of experience, from which to draw metaphors for his poetry. The mythology—far more complex, private, and systematized than the Irish myths behind his earlier poetry—is easily confused with popular astrology on the one hand and Oswald Spengler's *Decline of the West* on the other. It concerns the 28 phases of the moon, relating them to types of human personality, and the history of civilization, seen as huge complementary cycles. The famous sonnet, *Leda and the Swan* (1924), takes on added meaning when we realize that for Yeats each of the great cycles of Western history, the classical and the Christian, began with a conception, by a mortal woman, of the child of a god disguised as a bird. The analogues are Leda and the Virgin Mary, Zeus and God, Swan and Dove, and Helen of Troy and Jesus Christ. Another poem, *The Second Coming* (1920), gains in power when we realize that it envisions the dissolution of the Christian cycle and foresees the beginning of another cycle:

"what rough beast, its hour come round at last, /
Slouches towards Bethlehem to be born?"

Two of Yeats' finest poems of this period, *Sailing to
Byzantium* (from *The Tower*, 1928) and *Byzantium*
(from *Words for Music, Perhaps*, 1932), are closely related to the mythology of *A Vision*. Yeats viewed the
Byzantine culture of the 11th century as the zenith of
the Christian cycle, *i.e.*, the turning point in the cycle
that is now almost completed. He paralleled it with the
age of Phidias (Periclean Athens, 5th century B.C.) in the
classical cycle. Yeats "discovered" his mythology, because the mythologies currently available did not have
enough vitality for his purposes. While T. S. Eliot was
shoring fragments against ruins *(The *Waste Land)*,
Yeats was constructing a startling edifice from fragments;
the two Byzantium poems and *A Dialogue of Self and
Soul* (from *The Winding Stair*, 1929) more than justify
his system, and there are many more poems of which
the same must be said.

By 1928, Yeats was beginning to move toward yet an-
other poetic style, his fourth, in the present analysis, and
his last. The second generation of modern English poets
(W. H. *Auden, Stephen Spender, C. Day Lewis, and
Louis MacNeice) were university students, soon to begin
publishing their poetry. Of the first-generation figures,
T. S. Eliot had just become a British subject, and Ezra
Pound was writing his *Cantos* in Italy, where Yeats, visiting him, was convalescing from a serious illness. Now
Yeats seemed to be abandoning, although never completely, his second mythology. He continued to write
full-cadenced, richly textured, complex poems of the sort
made possible by *A Vision*, but he had a resurgence of
interest in "walking naked," as he had begun to do in
the period 1908–17. This time, however, he really did
"wither into the truth," writing poems "as cold and passionate as the dawn" in a bare, colloquial style and in
simple stanzaic forms based on the ballad and folk song.
Among the most powerful of these are the eight *Crazy
Jane* poems (1930 *ff*). In them poetry is pared down to
the bone. Crazy Jane is an old, crazed woman who sings
about the central experience of her life—her youthful
love affair with Jack, a journeyman tinker, and their ex-

communication by the Bishop; she is Yeats' *King Lear and Fool in one. The meanings of "life" that are worked with in the series are similar to those in the Byzantium poems (as Yeats had said, "Though leaves are many, the root is one"), but the expression is far simpler; Yeats is now speaking "to the multitude and the few alike."

Two of Yeats' latest poems, *Lapis Lazuli* (1936) and *Long-legged Fly* (1938), well represent his ripest poetic manner. Both link with the *Crazy Jane* series in their affirmation of life and their expression of the sense of glory that makes tragedy meaningful and orders the transitory world: "All things fall and are built again, / And those that bind them again are gay." In three short stanzas, *Long-legged Fly* juxtaposes the generative vitality of Caesar, at the end of the classical cycle, of Helen, at the beginning, and of Michelangelo, painting "the first Adam." A moment of significant choice occurs for each while the mind moves upon silence "Like a long-legged fly upon the stream." Like Yeats himself, each of these great generators of creative and destructive forces practices an art, in his own medium, in order "that civilisation may not sink." Creation and destruction are inseparable, and they are simultaneously necessary to keep civilization afloat, as Yeats clearly perceived. Yeats' poetic legacy is at once a richly varied expression and a far-reaching exploration of this perception. Yeats anticipated the disillusionment and dissolution of values of our era: 'Things fall apart; the center cannot hold; / Mere anarchy is loosed upon the world / . . . The best lack all conviction, while the worst / Are full of passionate intensity." He was awarded the Nobel prize in 1923.

Yevtushenko, Yevgeny Alexandrovich: Russian poet (1933–   ). His position as the unchallenged spokesman for the younger generation of Soviet poets rests on a half dozen volumes of original poetry (he has also done some verse translations from the Georgian language, some criticism, some film scripts). The autobiographical "Zima Junction" ("Stantsiya Zima," 1953), published in 1956, made him instantly famous and popular. It reveals those qualities which, deepened and matured in later poems, are the hallmarks of his style—a lyric tone (many of his poems have been set to music), compassion, integrity. "Zima Junction" (the name of Yevtushenko's native village) weaves together, effortlessly, social and intimately personal themes—the cataclysmic political events of 1953 (death of Stalin, arrest of Beria, etc.), and the remembrance of things past as they affect the sensibilities of a youth returned to his childhood home in Siberia. The "right phrase," the mark of poetic genius, is difficult to illustrate in translation: *Hemingway's beard "like the white foam of the sea brimming. . . ." ("Encounter": "Vstrecha v Kopengagene"); "some crumbs of gentleness" ("Gentleness": "Nezhnost," 1960); "not people die but worlds die in them" ("People": "Lyudi," 1961); "Over Babiy Yar . . . I feel myself slowly growing grey. And I am one silent cry over the many thousands of the buried" ("Babiy Yar," 1961). Yevtushenko's honesty, his sense of moral justice, his refusal to be silenced or stifled by political dogmatism, his love and hopes for his country—these are the essence of his passionate commitment to his art and to humanity.

Zarathustra: see *Zoroaster.

Zen: a blend of Indian mysticism with the naturalism of China, influenced by both *Confucianism and *Taoism. In recent years, as a form of Japanese Buddhism, Zen has had an enormous attraction for the West. It is believed to have originated in India, then was absorbed by China in the sixth century A.D. It was actually carried to Japan as late as the 12th and 13th centuries and is today a religion of great vitality there. It eschews the common verbalizations and insists upon a focusing upon immediate reality. It has no dialectic, but in form often uses questions and answers while at the same time reminding the practitioners that they must arrive at the answers for themselves and in their own formulations.

Zen is difficult to explain since it relies on intuition; it refuses to rely on scriptures for these necessitate verbalization. "No dependence on words," suggests a dependence on unverbalized feeling. But much emphasis is placed on seeing into one's own nature. In this aspect certain Westerners have seen relationships between Zen and *psychoanalytic thought. A highly spiritual religion, of great refinement and subtlety, it warns against mistaking things for ideas. There is great emphasis on everyday feeling and thought. As one historian has put it, the whole of Zen points in the direction of "the importance of humanness."

Zend Avesta: see *Zoroaster.

Zeno: Greek philosopher (*fl. c.* 300 B.C.). The philosopher Zeno, the founder of Stoicism, was born on the island of Cyprus but migrated to Athens, where, after studying with Crates the Cynic and others, he began to teach in the Painted Porch, or *Stoa*, that gave his school its name. Zeno was interested chiefly in ethics, which he based on the belief that the Universe is One, that it is rational, and that man, as a part of it, must guide his life by reason if he is to attain to virtue, which is the only good. Except for fragments, Zeno's works have perished, as have those of his immediate successors, and we must turn to writers living in the Roman period for any connected account of his philosophy. When we use these sources, however, we must remember that they are late and therefore present a modified form of Stoicism, not necessarily reflecting Zeno's views in all particulars. (See *Stoicism, *Seneca, *Epictetus, Marcus *Aurelius.)

Zeus: the supreme god of the Greeks, identified by the Romans with Jupiter.

Zola, Emile: French novelist (1840–1902). Zola, the author most often associated with *naturalism in literature, was born in Paris of a Greek-Italian father and a French mother. Much of his boyhood was spent at Aix near Marseilles, the "Plassans" of his stories. After failing his examinations at a *lycée* in Paris and enduring about two years of penniliess misery in the Latin Quarter, he was rescued by a friend who secured him a job with a publisher—the job of wrapping books for shipment (1862).

His literary taste had previously run to romantics such as *Rousseau, *Hugo, *Musset, *Lamartine, and de *Vigny, and his first early and unimportant writing had been sentimentally romantic poetry giving no hint of the realistic attitude of his maturity. Then Zola discovered *Balzac and *Flaubert. When his *Tales for Ninon* (*Contes à Ninon*, 1864) received some critical attention, his literary career was under way. As he turned out a stream of articles and reviews, Zola's convictions about realism crystallized and deepened. He determined to go beyond the *realism* of his friend Flaubert to *naturalism.*

Zola's theories of naturalism are to be found in the Preface to *The Fortune of the Rougons* (1871) and in *The Experimental Novel* (1880), his faith in the gospel of science in *Paris* (1898). The novel, according to Zola, should reflect the process of research and observation, as in a laboratory. Characters were to be conceived in accordance with psychology, sociology, and laws of heredity. They were to be placed in an accurately constructed environment, representing a segment of time and space, and their conduct was to evolve naturally from the interaction of their personalities and environment. The novel thus is a study of the source and development of physical and psychological traits, and at the same time a study of the society of contemporary France. Instead of being artistically selective, as Flaubert had been, the writer includes every phenomenon that would arise in a real situation. Essentially the world of the *naturalistic* novel was mechanistic and materialistic. Fancy, subjectivity, the personal eccentricity of the writer were to be excluded from the creative process.

The idea of a scientific experiment in a novel is, of course, a fallacy. Nevertheless, it can pose an interesting problem and serve as a stimulus to a writer by giving him a person of known heredity and background, putting him in a known environment, and trying to work out the probable results. Similarly, though no writer can be utterly objective, the effort to be so can make him far more impersonal than he might otherwise have been. The theories of naturalism, like those of any other literary school, are aids and suggestions rather than absolutes.

In keeping with his theories, Zola began work on a series of novels tracing the "natural and social history of a family under the Second Empire" (1852–70), to supplement, in a sense, the picture which Balzac had given of the early decades of the century. Each volume was to center upon one or a few members of the family. In addition to the influence of heredity on these characters, the psycho-socio-biological history of a whole era would be revealed. This project was the famous Rougon-Macquart series, which ran to twenty volumes and covered the histories of many occupations—farmer, miner, city-worker, scholar, prostitute, artist, statesman, laundress, etc.—and every social level both in Paris and in the provinces.

The reader can obtain a fairly comprehensive grasp of the psycho-hereditary element in the series by reading its first and last volumes—*The Fortune of the Rougons* (*La Fortune des Rougon*, 1871), and *Dr. Pascal* (*Le Docteur Pascal*, 1893). *The Fortune of the Rougons* lays the basis for all the succeeding volumes; Dr. Pascal, scientist and central character of the last work, presents to the reader clinical case histories of individuals in the famous family. To understand charges of pornography and "gutter-sweeping" against Zola the reader may select *The Dram-Shop* (*L'Assommoir*, 1877) and *Nana* (1880). *The Dram-Shop*, Zola's first great success, was a powerful study of the effects of alcoholism. *Nana* is the story of a prostitute, beautiful, stupid, and unscrupulous. *Germinal* (1885) deals with the social problems of a mining community. *The Earth* (*La Terre*, 1887) presents such a sordid picture of the avaricious French peasantry that it lost Zola some of his original followers. *The Debacle* (1892) is an exposure of the disintegration of the people and of corruption of the government during the Franco-Prussian War.

In 1880 Zola had also collaborated with *Maupassant and other naturalists in *Evenings at Médan (Les Soirées de Médan)*, a collection of short stories. In addition to the Rougon-Macquart series, Zola composed two others: the series of the cities *(Les Trois Villes): Lourdes* (1894), *Rome* (1896), *Paris* (1898), and the series of the four gospels *(Les Quatre Evangiles): Fécondité* (1899), *Travail* (1901), *Vérité* (1903); the fourth volume was interrupted by Zola's death. These contain some fine characters and powerful scenes, but in them Zola ceases to be the disinterested observer and becomes the preacher of various social gospels. As a result, these novels have the faults—repetitiousness, oversimplifications, dogmatism—which usually result when a piece of social propaganda tries to disguise itself as a work of art.

During his last years Zola played an essential part in the Dreyfus Affair by calling public attention to it with a ringing open letter to the President *(J'Accuse)*, by battling in court, and even by his necessary flight and period of hiding in England. Fighting for Dreyfus and justice, Zola was (as Anatole *France said) "a moment in the conscience of mankind." After Dreyfus was "pardoned" in 1900, Zola was something of a national hero, but he was accidentally asphyxiated by fumes from a clogged flue before Dreyfus was officially declared innocent of the treason for which he had been sentenced.

The power of Zola's novels is often independent of the author's theories and derives from his personal characteristics. It was a part of naturalistic theory that an author should study his settings carefully and accurately; and Zola amassed huge notebooks full of information of such subjects as railroading and the stock market before he began to write the novels using these settings. At heart, however, Zola was a poet, and all the dead information is brought to life by the energy and passion he was able to infuse into it. What he communicated in *L'Argent* (1891) is not so much the workings of the market—they are merely background—as the lyrical passion of the speculator, and no amount of documentation can communicate that. It is true that he is not a stylist in the manner of Flaubert, but his "journalistic style" has often been misunderstood. *L'Assommoir*, for example, is deliberately written in the idiom of the Parisian working classes, and in this idiom Zola succeeds in being not only flippant and brutal but, on occasion, poetic and sublime.

As the fashion shifted from naturalism to the psychological novel, Zola's reputation naturally declined. A successful author's reputation usually declines in the generation immediately after his death. But he exerted a strong international influence on fiction (the American naturalism of *Dreiser and Frank Norris was primarily a belated discovery of Zola and his followers), and in recent years, with the controversy over his novels largely forgotten, they are coming to be valued for their own merits.

Zoroaster (or Zarathustra): founder of the religion of ancient Persia (7th century B.C., or earlier). Zoroastrianism was prominent in western Asia for a thousand years, until it was largely superseded by Islam. Much of the creed continues to live, however, in the Old and New Testaments. The religion sees the world as a duality, a continuous struggle between two *independent* cosmic forces: Ahura Mazda, "Lord of Wisdom," maker of the material world, who is righteousness; and Angra Mainyu (Ahriman), "All Death," who is the spirit of evil. Man is a free agent and has the duty of aiding the ultimate triumph of Ahura Mazda. Zoroaster preached the healing power of constructive work and advanced an ethical code in which righteousness consists of justice, truthfulness, good deeds. Fire and the sun are symbols of Ahura Mazda; hence the Zoroastrians are sometimes thought of as fire or sun worshipers. When the final struggle ends with the triumph of Ahura Mazda, there will be a last judgment, and the worthy, resurrected, will go to Paradise (the word is Persian) and the unworthy to hell.

The *Avesta* (or *Zend Avesta*) is a miscellaneous body of the surviving scriptures of Zoroastrianism, written in Avestan, a language closely related to Old Persian and Vedic Sanskrit. It was compiled long after Zoroaster's death and has suffered various losses since its original compilation. It contains five archaic poems, the *Gathas*, which are ascribed to the prophet himself, apparently with good reason. Other parts include prayers, rules, and traditional stories.

READ THE TOP 20
SIGNET CLASSICS

1984 BY GEORGE ORWELL

ANIMAL FARM BY GEORGE ORWELL

NARRATIVE OF THE LIFE OF FREDERICK DOUGLASS
    BY FREDERICK DOUGLASS

THE INFERNO BY DANTE

ROMEO AND JULIET BY WILLIAM SHAKESPEARE

WHY WE CAN'T WAIT BY DR. MARTIN LUTHER KING, JR.

NECTAR IN A SIEVE BY KAMALA MARKANDAYA

FRANKENSTEIN BY MARY SHELLEY

BEOWULF TRANSLATED BY BURTON RAFFEL

HAMLET BY WILLIAM SHAKESPEARE

THE FEDERALIST PAPERS BY ALEXANDER HAMILTON

THE ODYSSEY BY HOMER

MACBETH BY WILLIAM SHAKESPEARE

CRIME AND PUNISHMENT BY FYODOR DOSTOYEVSKY

THE HOUND OF THE BASKERVILLES
    BY SIR ARTHUR CONAN DOYLE

THE SCARLET LETTER BY NATHANIEL HAWTHORNE

DR. JEKYLL AND MR. HYDE BY ROBERT L. STEVENSON

A MIDSUMMER NIGHT'S DREAM BY WILLIAM SHAKESPEARE

THE CLASSIC SLAVE NARRATIVES BY HENRY L. GATES

A TALE OF TWO CITIES BY CHARLES DICKENS

PENGUIN.COM
FACEBOOK.COM/SIGNETCLASSIC

S0154